Cesar was proconsul of

Dorothy Alt

Eng III 214

Cum causal — verb in subj., any tense according to sequence
(since)

Cum adversative — verb in subj. any tense according to sequence
(although)

ibi = there (in that place)
eō = " (to that place)

The acc. supine has the same
form as the acc. s. n. of the
perf. pass. part.
Use acc. supine only after verbs
of motion.

64 - "
11. 5
11

grátiam habēre — to have gratitude
  "   referre   be thankful
grátiās agere — to return thanks
                 to express thanks

58 - Helvetions - Germans
57 - Belgians
56 - Deneti
55 - Germans - Britain

AVE ROMA IMMORTALIS

From an engraving by Rossini

LATIN - SECOND YEAR

BY

LILLIAN GAY BERRY

PROFESSOR OF LATIN, INDIANA UNIVERSITY

AND

JOSEPHINE L. LEE

TEACHER OF LATIN, SHORTRIDGE HIGH SCHOOL
INDIANAPOLIS, INDIANA

bellum gerere cum + abl. - wage
inferre + dat. = make war on war
impetum facere in + acc. - an attack with
upon.

SILVER, BURDETT AND COMPANY

NEW YORK   NEWARK   BOSTON   CHICAGO   SAN FRANCISCO

THE CLIMAX SERIES

RALPH VAN DEMAN MAGOFFIN

PROFESSOR AND HEAD, DEPARTMENT OF CLASSICS
NEW YORK UNIVERSITY

EDITOR

EDITOR'S PREFACE

The Climax Series of Latin textbooks for the secondary school, of which this volume is the second, embodies the spirit of the recommendations made in the General Report of the Classical Investigation.

The Series contains the material that has been sanctioned by experience and also other material that may have a stronger appeal to teachers and pupils of today. Latin, from the point of view of linguistics, receives due emphasis and at the same time its ethical, cultural, and literary values receive the attention they deserve. From the outset, the material and method are designed to cultivate interest in the study of Latin. By awakening and developing an interest in Latin for its human significance, it is believed that this Series will give the work in Latin renewed effectiveness.

LATIN–SECOND YEAR is the product of many years' experience both in teaching Latin to pupils in the second year of high school and in conducting courses for teachers who were teaching or were to teach Latin in the second year. LATIN–SECOND YEAR and LATIN–FIRST YEAR meet every requirement for the first two years of Latin.

The illustrations and the descriptions of them provide many opportunities to deepen and widen the knowledge and interest of pupils in the life, language, and literature of the Romans; and the Latin subject matter emphasizes the Roman characteristics of **virtus, fortitūdō,** and **disciplīna.**

RALPH VAN DEMAN MAGOFFIN

NEW YORK UNIVERSITY

idem, eadem, idem – same
quidam, quaedam, quiddam – certain
quisque, quaeque, quidque – each one
aliquis, aliquid – some

VIRGINIBUS PUERĪSQUE

— HORACE

AUTHORS' PREFACE

LATIN–SECOND YEAR is the result of the conviction of the authors that Latin may be so selected and taught that the pupil will find pleasure in reading it for its content, satisfaction in acquiring power to read it with some ease and rapidity, and an abiding interest in language and literature.

READING CONTENT. The reading content of LATIN–SECOND YEAR serves to give a cultural background by affording a knowledge of Roman life, institutions, ideals, literature, and men of letters, and of the influence of these on civilization. The selections chosen are varied, attractive, adapted to the interest and capacity of high school pupils, and of a character to develop progressive power to read Latin. The wealth of subject matter affords the teacher much freedom in the selection of material suitable for different classes and for the varying ability of pupils. The content is divided into four parts.

Part I, Myths, consists of twelve stories from classical mythology selected for their appeal to human interest and their significance in relation to present-day life.

Part II, The Argonauts, has as its subject matter the story of the Argonautic expedition as told by Ritchie in "Fābulae Facilēs," which is a conscious imitation of the style, language, and syntax of Caesar's "Gallic War." Thus, through an interesting and ancient tale of adventure with an appeal to the imagination of youth, the pupil is prepared to read Caesar with greater facility. Part II is to be used by the teacher as best fits the needs of the class. Some teachers may wish to use it for intensive study of syntax, while others may prefer to use it for rapid reading.

Part III, Readings from Roman Literature, consists of simple and interesting readings selected after careful study and experiment from a wide range of Latin authors. They include *Glimpses of Roman History*, which embraces important episodes in the history of Rome; *Rome Day by Day*, which contains selections touching almost every phase of daily life; *The Story-Teller*, which gives versions of many folk tales, fables, and legends as found in Latin authors. Part III is taken directly from Latin authors. The selections have been simplified only by the omission of the more difficult passages and the elimination of certain unusual words that the pupil does not need to know for subsequent reading. Points of unusual difficulty are carefully annotated or translated. Part III is especially adapted for meeting the individual differences of pupils. For some pupils parts of it may be used as sight reading.

Part IV, Caesar's **Commentāriī dē Bellō Gallicō,** includes selections from the seven books of the Gallic War. All chapters omitted are briefly summarized that the pupil may see, as in a moving picture, the continuous story of the seven dramatic years which were destined to have a profound effect upon the history of civilization.

The chapters included in the text are those which have been found to be most valuable from the point of view of historical background; which give an idea of typical methods of Roman warfare, such as a land battle, a sea fight, and a great siege; which give information concerning the life of the ancient Gauls, Germans, and Britons; and which throw light on the character of Caesar.

In order that too many difficulties may not at once confront the pupil and that he may gain confidence in himself and interest in the story through being able to read it with some speed, some of the rather long and involved passages in Liber I are omitted, or if in indirect discourse, they are changed to the direct form.

REQUIRED VOCABULARY. The lack of a *vocabulary* of permanently retained words constitutes the pupil's greatest handicap in reading and understanding Latin. Special attention has been given to this vexing problem. The words listed under *Required Vocabulary* are those specified for the second year of Latin (and some first year words not generally found in first books) by the

College Entrance Examination Board and the New York State Revised Syllabus. Each of these words is set down to be learned in the lesson in which it *first* occurs. As a rule, it is to be used in an English-Latin sentence of a lesson or in a review, and later is recalled through an English derivative. All first and second year required words are starred in the *Latin-English Vocabulary*. A thorough mastery of this limited number of words often used, or important from the point of view of English derivative, as an integral part of each lesson will result in increased ability to read Latin with ease and understanding.

WORD STUDY. The *word studies* are designed not merely to afford knowledge of the derivation and formation of specified Latin words, but to develop the ability to determine the meaning of new words through a knowledge of the significance of roots, prefixes, and suffixes. English derivatives are taken up in the lessons in which their Latin ancestors occur and are confined to words in general use. The majority of these are to be found in Thorndike's "Teacher's Word Book." Occasional little stories are included which give the ancestry and life histories of interesting words.

Underlying all the suggested vocabulary work is the thought that the study of words is not dry and dull but that in a single word often lies a hidden world in which one may travel with profit and pleasure.

FORMS AND SYNTAX. *Forms* and *syntax* are not taught as an end but as a very necessary means to an end which cannot be realized without a thorough understanding of each. New points are taken up under the heading *Rēs Grammaticae* and points to be reviewed under the heading *Iterātiō*.

Part I takes up for intensive study the forms and constructions necessary for second year reading which are not now usually studied in the first year. Each new point is first met functionally in the Latin narrative of the lesson in which it is explained, compared with similar expressions in English, and illustrated by Latin examples.

Part II continues the study of additional new constructions and by reviewing several special points in each lesson systematically covers all forms and syntax that have been studied in first year Latin and in second year up to this point. Part II is to be used by the teacher as best fits the needs of the class. The review may not be necessary with all classes, as all important points of syntax are again taken up in Part IV.

Part III is not intended as an exercise ground for the study of syntax, but the abundance and variety of its subject matter afford ample practice for applying in adequate translation the principles of syntax previously studied.

Part IV takes up for systematic study, largely review, all important points of syntax necessary for second year reading. One point is taken up for special study in each lesson. It is presented in four ways: an example in the context of the lesson and in *Syntax for Reference*, a Latin quotation, a Latin question, and an English-Latin sentence. The use of any or all of this material is optional. Each important point of syntax has, if possible, three references to it in the notes of the lessons.

The examples used as illustrations in *Syntax for Reference* are taken from Caesar's "Gallic War."

EXERCISE. The *Exercises* (**Exercitātiō** in Part IV) afford oral and written practice on the required vocabulary and the forms or points of syntax taught or reviewed in the lesson. The sentences under *Respondē Latīnē* and *Scrībe Latīnē* may be used at the discretion of the teacher. Some teachers may choose to take them up at stated intervals, dealing with a number of sentences in one composition lesson.

COMPREHENSION. The *Comprehension* questions are not meant to be exhaustive, but merely suggestive of questions that deal with the story or thought of the lesson unit.

ORAL LATIN. The *oral side* of Latin is provided for in an abundance of short, easy, Latin questions which may be asked and answered orally in Latin.

In order that the pupil may get the aid in the interpretation of the thought that should come from fluent and intelligent oral reading of the Latin, the quantity of the vowels is marked in the poetry as well as in the prose. It is not intended or even advisable to make a study of the meter of the poems, or to attempt to read them metrically. But since the proper reading of Latin poetry depends upon the correct pronunciation of the vowels and syllables and a knowledge of the simple principle of elision, some pupils with a little help from the teacher may be able to read it as poetry.

LITERARY BACKGROUND. The *literary background* of LATIN–SECOND YEAR includes suggested collateral readings in English, pertinent quotations from many ancient and modern sources, and brief sketches of the lives of Roman writers from whose works selections are included in the text. These have been selected with a view to giving a deeper understanding of the subject matter in its broader implications, and a wider acquaintance with and appreciation of literature in general.

ILLUSTRATIONS. Each *illustration* is an integral part of the lesson in which it occurs. The illustrations represent various types of art and include examples of Roman architecture, coins, mosaics, sculptured reliefs, and statuary; Greek vase paintings; medieval drawings, engravings, and tapestries; photographs of places referred to in the text; and reproductions of illustrated Latin manuscripts. Thanks are due to the museums and libraries which have graciously granted the privilege of photographing antiquities which they cherish among their treasures. Grateful acknowledgment is made to the many friends of the classics who have contributed to this effort to visualize effectively and artistically the daily life of the ancient Romans and to add to the pupils' knowledge and appreciation of art.

The authors wish to express their indebtedness to the many teachers of Latin from whom they have received valuable suggestions and assistance. It is not possible to name all to whom most grateful acknowledgment is due.

LILLIAN GAY BERRY
JOSEPHINE L. LEE

CONTENTS

PART I. MYTHS

xiii

* Part II includes a comprehensive review, *Iterātiō*, of the forms and syntax of LATIN–FIRST YEAR and Part I of LATIN–SECOND YEAR. Two or more of these review points are taken up in each lesson in connection with their occurrence in the Latin reading, and practice in their use is given in the exercises.

PART III. READINGS FROM ROMAN LITERATURE

PART IV. CAESAR'S COMMENTĀRIĪ DĒ BELLŌ GALLICŌ

MAPS

PART I

MYTHS

They wove bright fables in the days of old,
When Reason borrowed Fancy's painted wings;
When Truth's clear river flowed o'er sands of gold
And told in song its high and mystic things.

THOMAS K. HERVEY, Cupid and Psyche

THE FALL OF ICARUS

This illustration of the flight of Daedalus and Icarus is found in a seventeenth-century text of this story in Ovid's *Metamorphoses*.

I

OPUSCULUM PRĪMUM

Nīl mortālibus arduī est ;
Caelum ipsum petimus stultitiā.

Nothing is hard for mortals;
In our folly we try the sky itself.

HORACE

1. THE FIRST AVIATORS

Daedalus erat artifex perītissimus. Is cum fīliō Īcarō
Crētam vēnit, ubi multīs officiīs [1] Mīnōī rēgī fūnctus est.
Rēx locum tūtum Mīnōtaurō,[2] quod mōnstrum [3] hominibus
vēscēbātur, cupiēbat. Huic bēstiae saevae, quae corpus hominis habuit sed caput taurī, Daedalus labyrinthum aedificā- 5
vit, in quō erant multae ambāgēs. In labyrinthum Mīnōs
tandem īrātus Daedalum et Īcarum in custōdiam coniēcit.
Daedalus cupidus lībertātis sibi et fīliō suō ālās fēcit.
Pinnīs et cērā ūsus est. Hīs ad umerōs affīxīs, ut avēs, tum
volāre cōnātī sunt. Īcarus cōnārī nōn verēbātur. Hic, quī 10
ālīs suīs fruēbātur, patre invītō,[4] altius volāre incipiēbat.
Volāvit prope sōlem, quī cēram liquidam fēcit. Ālae ex
umerīs dēcidērunt et ipse igitur in mare, quod ex eō Īcarium
Mare [5] appellātum est, dēcidit. Daedalus autem ad Graeciam
patriam tūtus pervēnit. Ibi multōs annōs vītā frūctus est. 15
Poēta Horātius scrīpsit :
Expertus vacuum Daedalus āera [6] pinnīs nōn hominī datīs.[7]

This story and others of a mythological character are found in:
Classical Myths That Live Today, FRANCES E. SABIN, Silver, Burdett and Company.
Classic Myths in English Literature and in Art; CHARLES MILLS GAYLEY, Ginn and Company.
Greek and Roman Mythology, JESSIE M. TATLOCK, The Century Company.
Myths of Greece and Rome, H. A. GUERBER, American Book Company.
Myths and Their Meaning, MAX J. HERZBERG, Allyn and Bacon.

2.   REQUIRED VOCABULARY

Ēdiscenda, nōn modo in manibus cotīdiē habenda, *To be learned thoroughly, not merely to be held in the hand each day.* PLINY. This advice of a Roman writer should be followed in the study of the required vocabulary.

In your first year of Latin you have learned about five hundred Latin words. If you will learn the words included in each required vocabulary of this book, you will have at the end of the year a working vocabulary that will increase your ability to read Latin. Moreover, you will then have learned all the words required for the first two years of Latin.

cōnor, -ārī, -ātus sum try
experior, -īrī, -pertus sum make trial of, attempt
incipiō, -ere, -cēpī, -ceptus begin
vacuus, -a, -um empty

perītus, -a, -um skillful
sōl, sōlis, *m.* sun
ut as
ūtor, ūtī, ūsus sum use

3.   NOTES ON THE STORY

1. **multīs officiīs:** translate as if direct object of **fūnctus est.**
2. **Mīnōtaurō:** dative of **Mīnōtaurus.**
3. **quod mōnstrum:** *a monster which;* the antecedent is within the relative clause and agrees in case with the relative **quod** (**560,** *a*).
4. **patre invītō:** *against his father's will;* ablative absolute.
5. **Īcarium Mare:** predicate nominative with **appellātum est.**
6. **āera:** direct object of **expertus (est);** the Greek form of the accusative; the Latin form, if used, would be **āerem.**
7. **pinnīs . . . datīs:** translate *on wings not given to man.*

4.   COMPREHENSION

1. What did Daedalus do for King Minos? **2.** How was he at a later time treated by the angry king? **3.** In what way did he escape? With what result?

5.   RĒS GRAMMATICAE

Deponent verbs. In the sentence, **pater et fīlius volāre cōnātī sunt, cōnātī sunt** is active in meaning, but passive in form. Such a verb is called a *deponent* (from **dēpōnere,** *lay aside*) because it has laid aside or lost its active forms and its passive meaning. The forms of the deponent verbs in each of the four conjugations are the same as those of the passive voice of regular verbs.

First Conj.:	**cōnor,** *I attempt*	**cōnārī,** *to attempt*	**cōnātus sum,** *I have attempted*
Second Conj.:	**vereor,** *I fear*	**verērī,** *to fear*	**veritus sum,** *I have feared*
Third Conj.:	**ūtor,** *I use*	**ūtī,** *to use*	**ūsus sum,** *I have used*
Fourth Conj.:	**experior,** *I attempt*	**experīrī,** *to attempt*	**expertus sum,** *I have attempted*

Point out in the story five deponent verbs. For the conjugation of deponent verbs see **493**.

The ablative with special deponents (547). In the sentence, **Daedalus cērā ūsus est,** *Daedalus used wax,* **cērā** is in the ablative case instead of the accusative of direct object, the case required in the English sentence. With the five verbs, **ūtor, fruor, fungor, potior,** and **vēscor,** the ablative case is thus used.

Point out four examples of the ablative so used with special deponent verbs.

6.   EXERCISE

Write the synopsis of: **cōnor** in the third person plural; **experior** in the first person plural; **ūtor** in the third person singular.

Respondē Latīnē: **1.** Quis erat Daedalus? **2.** Quem ad locum Daedalus vēnit? **3.** Quis cum Daedalō erat? **4.** Cūr altius Īcarus volāvit? **5.** Quid sōl fēcit?

Scrībe Latīnē: **1.** King Minos uses the labyrinth. **2.** Daedalus and his son as birds will use wings. **3.** The son was attempting to fly with his skillful father. **4.** Icarus makes trial of the empty air. **5.** He did not enjoy the sun.

7.   WORD STUDY

To what word in the story is each of these words related by derivation: *aviator, experiment, fruition, function, liquefy, solarium, useful, utility?*

Roger Bacon, a thirteenth century scholar who was interested in scientific discoveries, foretold the invention of the airplane, which would be propelled " in the manner of a flying bird."

The birds can fly, an' why can't I?

J. T. Trowbridge, *Darius Green and His Flying Machine*

And lest his wings should melt apace old Daedalus flies low,
But Icarus beats up, beats up, he goes where lightnings go.
He cares no more for warnings, he rushes through the sky,
Braving the crags of ether, daring the gods on high,
Black against the crimson sunset, gold over cloudy snows,
With all Adventure in his heart the first winged man arose.

Stephen Vincent Benét, *The Winged Man* *

The Langley Medal   Courtesy of Smithsonian Institution

The Air Is Also Man's Dominion
The Langley Medal was given for a non-stop flight across the Atlantic Ocean.

* From *Young Adventure*, by Stephen Vincent Benét, published by Doubleday, Doran and Company.

THISBE HIDES FROM THE LION

This illustration is from a 1563 edition of Ovid's *Metamorphoses*, in which the story of Pyramus and Thisbe is told.

II

OPUSCULUM SECUNDUM

> In such a night
> Did Thisbe fearfully o'ertrip the dew,
> And saw the lion's shadow ere himself,
> And ran dismayed away.
>
> SHAKESPEARE, *The Merchant of Venice*

8. AN OLD LOVE STORY, I *

Urbem Babylōniam, Pӯramus, adulēscēns fortis, incolēbat. Thisbē, puella pulcherrima, domum adiūnctam habitābat. Quod inter sē [1] amābant, Pӯramus eam in mātrimōnium dūcere statuit. Hoc tamen parentēs crūdēlēs vetuērunt. Alterum alteram vidēre nōn patiēbantur. Amantēs autem signīs inter 5 sē loquēbantur.

* A burlesque on this story is found in Shakespeare, *A Midsummer Night's Dream*, V, 1.

7

DUAE DOMŪS

Venus, dea amōris, adulēscentibus [2] favēbat. " Brevī tempore," inquit, " eīs auxilium mīserō.[3] " Auxiliō eius amantēs rīmam parvam in pariete commūnī quī domum alterīus ā
10 domō [4] alterīus dīvidēbat vīdērunt. Multās epistulās, quās per rīmam trādēbant, scrībēbant. Ā deā inductī,[5] parentibus invītīs, ē domibus [6] excēdere dēcrēvērunt. Singulās rēs [7] tōtīus fugae sīc cōnstituērunt : " Ante mediam noctem ē domō excesserō," Pȳramus scrīpsit.
15 Thisbē respondit, " Ante illud tempus urbem relīquerō et ad vetustum tumulum Nīnī rēgis pervēnerō."

Post haec adulēscēns, " Sī prīma ad illum locum pervēneris, sub mōrum tē cēlā.[8] " In epistulā puella respondit, " Pallam albam meam mēcum portābō et, cum tē venientem au-
20 dīverō, eam induam. Facile eam in umbrā vidēbis."

Thisbē autem, quae sōla ad locum cōnstitūtum vēnerat, cōnspectū leōnis perterrita est. Abiectā pallā, quae nōn erat ūtilis, in cavernam fūgit.

9.   REQUIRED VOCABULARY

adulēscēns, -entis, *m.* young man
dēcernō,-ere,-crēvī,-crētus decide
dīvidō, -ere, -vīsī, -vīsus separate
excēdō, -ere, -cessī, -cessus depart
incolō, -ere, -uī, — live in
indūcō, -ere, -dūxī, -ductus influence

loquor, -ī, locūtus sum talk, speak
patior, -ī, passus sum permit
tōtus, -a, -um all, the whole
tumulus, -ī, *m.* tomb, mound
ūtilis, -e useful
vetustus, -a, -um ancient

10. NOTES ON THE STORY

This story is told for the first time in the *Metamorphoses*, a poem by Ovid, a great Roman story teller.

1. inter sē: *among themselves;* translate *each other.*
2. adulēscentibus: dative used with the intransitive verb **favēbat.**
3. mīserō: *I shall have sent;* future perfect indicative.
4. ā domō: *from the house.*
5. inductī: perfect passive participle, modifying the subject understood of dēcrēvērunt.
6. domibus: When **domus** means *house,* a preposition is used with it to express *place from which* and *to which.*
7. Singulās rēs: *the single things;* translate *the details.*
8. cēlā: *conceal;* imperative.

11. COMPREHENSION

1. How did Pyramus and Thisbe talk to each other? **2.** What did they plan to do? **3.** Why did Thisbe fail to carry out their plan?

12. RĒS GRAMMATICAE

Future perfect tense (492). The future perfect tense denotes an action that will be completed before a definite time in the future. Observe that in the active the future perfect tense is formed by adding to the perfect stem the tense sign **-eri-** and to this the personal endings. In the first person singular, **i** drops out before **ō: portāv-er-ō.**

In the passive, the future perfect tense is formed by using the perfect passive participle with the future tense forms of **sum: portātus erō.**

Point out in the story all verbs in the future perfect indicative and tell whether they are active or passive.

Adjectives in -*īus* and -*ī* (478). There are nine irregular adjectives which have the ending **-īus** in the genitive singular and **-ī** in the dative singular. Otherwise they are declined as adjectives of the first and second declension. **Alius,** however, has the form **aliud** in both the neuter nominative and accusative singular.

Point out the irregular adjectives in the story and give the case of each.

13.   EXERCISE

Write or give the future perfect indicative of : amō, indūcō, loquor.

Give the Latin for : to the whole city, of another night, of neither city, for one thing.

Decline : nūlla puella, aliud auxilium.

Respondē Latīnē : **1.** Quam urbem incolēbant Pȳramus et Thisbē? **2.** Quid dē eīs Venus dīxit? **3.** Cūr fuga erat difficillima? **4.** Quem ad tumulum Thisbē fūgit? **5.** Quid puellae nōn ūtile erat?

Scrībe Latīnē : **1.** The home of the one is separated from the home of the other by an ancient wall. **2.** Before that time I shall have decided the whole matter. **3.** The one was not influenced by the other. **4.** Before night they will have permitted them to talk with each other. **5.** Before midnight the young man will have departed from the house.

14.   WORD STUDY

Many English words derived from Latin are spelled almost like their Latin ancestors. Find five such ancestors and give an English descendant of each : mātrimōnium, *matrimony.*

PYRAMUS AND THISBE

How does this picture illustrate the story?

III

OPUSCULUM TERTIUM

Ut amēris, amābilis estō, *That you may be loved, be lovable.* OVID

15.   AN OLD LOVE STORY, II

Thisbē, leōne vīsō, arbitrāta est, " Leō ad flūmen ut aquam capiat [1] aggreditur. Ab aquā sē nōn āvertit ut mē sequātur. Revertitur! Longius in cavernam ingrediar [2] nē bēstia mē videat."

Animal albam pallam puellae vīdit. Pallam arripiēns, eam 5 sanguine ex ōre crūdēlī maculātam relīquit.

Post bēstiae discessum Pȳramus ad eundem locum vēnit. Pallā inventā, arbitrātus est, " Thisbē ā leōne interfecta est. Sine Thisbē vīvere nōn iam possum. Ut cum eā sim, mē interficiam. Pallam eius in hōc locō pōnam ut sanguinem meum 10 etiam recipiat. Nunc veniō ut iterum verba eius audiam."

Hīs dictīs, in gladium suum sē iēcit et sub arbore cecidit.

Intereā Thisbē in cavernā remanēbat. Tandem putāvit.
" Hīc diū exspectō ut Pȳramus leōnem caedat."
15 Fortiter, timōre victō, prōgressa est et oculī arborem, quae
inūsitāta vidēbātur, statim petīvērunt. Mōra nōn iam alba
erant sed purpurā maculāta erant. Mox corpus Pȳramī humī
vīdit. Iterum et iterum eum vocābat. Eum complexa est.
Dēnique is ³ oculōs suōs aperuit et eam vīdit. Tum adulēscēns
20 dē vītā dēcessit.

Deinde Thisbē arbitrāta est, " Pȳramus, pallā inventā,
putāvit mē mortuam esse et sē mē secutūrum esse.⁴ Nunc
eum sequar." Gladiō amantis sē interfēcit.

Duo corpora mortua humī inventa parentēs in eōdem tumulō
25 condidērunt. Posthāc mōra, quod mortem Pȳramī et Thisbēs
dolēbant, nōn iam erant alba.

16.   REQUIRED VOCABULARY

arbitror, -ārī, -ātus sum think
avertō, -ere, -vertī, -versus turn away
caedō, -ere, cecīdī, caesus cut down, kill
condō, -ere, -didī, -ditus bury
ingredior, -ī, -gressus sum go into
inveniō, -īre, -vēnī, -ventus come upon, find

nē that not, lest (*conj.*)
oculus, -ī, *m.* eye
prōgredior, -ī, -gressus sum advance, proceed
revertor, -tī, -versus sum * go back, return
sequor, -ī, secūtus sum follow
ut that, in order that (*conj.*)
verbum, -ī, *n.* word
vīvō, -ere, vīxī, vīctus live

17.   NOTES ON THE STORY

1. **ut . . . capiat:** *that he may get water;* translate *to get water.*
2. **ingrediar:** future indicative.
3. **is:** *i.e.,* Pyramus.
4. **et . . . esse:** *and that he would follow me.*

18.   COMPREHENSION

1. Why did Pyramus think that Thisbe had been killed? 2. What did
he do then? 3. What did Thisbe do when she found Pyramus?

* Regularly **revertī**, the perfect of **revertō**, the active form, is used in the perfect tense.

19. RĒS GRAMMATICAE

The subjunctive mood. In English, a distinction between
the indicative mood and the subjunctive is rarely made. It is
occasionally found in such expressions as: if this *be* true; God
bless you. It is more common in conditions with the verb
were : if he *were* rich; if I *were* strong. An auxiliary verb is used
in English to convey the idea that is expressed in Latin by the
subjunctive: *let there be light*, **fīat lūx.**

In Latin, the subjunctive mood is used to represent an act
as willed, purposed, wished, possible, or doubtful, whereas
the indicative mood is used to state a fact or ask a question.
The subjunctive is most frequently used in subordinate clauses.
Its different uses will be taken up as they occur in opuscula
following.

The subjunctive mood has four tenses: present, imperfect,
perfect, and past perfect (pluperfect).

PRESENT SUBJUNCTIVE, ACTIVE, SINGULAR

First	*Second*	*Third*	*Fourth*	*Sum*	*Possum*
portem	videam	mittam	audiam	sim	possim
portēs	videās	mittās	audiās	sīs	possīs
portet, etc.	videat, etc.	mittat	audiat	sit	possit

Present subjunctive. Observe that in the first conjugation
the sign of the present subjunctive is **ē**; in each of the other
three conjugations, it is **ā.** In the first and third conjugations,
the final vowel of the present stem is dropped before the **e** or the
a. In the second and fourth conjugations, the **a** is added to the
present stem. The regular active and passive personal endings
are used.

Observe that, before **nt** and final **m** and **t,** (long) **ē** or **ā** of the
present tense is replaced by (short) **e** or **a : portēs, portet.**
The same principle holds true before final **r** and **ntur** of the
passive.

For the entire conjugation of the present subjunctive of the model verbs, see (**492**).

Purpose clauses (586). *The lion goes to the river to get water,* **leō ad flūmen aggreditur ut aquam capiat.** In the English sentence the purpose of the act denoted by the verb *goes* is expressed by the infinitive phrase *to get water*. This is the usual way of expressing purpose in English.

In the Latin sentence purpose is expressed in a clause introduced by **ut** with its verb **capiat** in the subjunctive. If the purpose clause is negative, **nē** is used as the introductory word: **nē bēstia mē videat,** *in order that the beast may not see me.* Point out in the story five other purpose clauses. Note that in Latin prose an infinitive phrase is never used to express purpose.

20.   EXERCISE

Give the present subjunctive of: **arbitror, remaneō, ingredior, inveniō.**

Respondē Latīnē: **1.** Quō cōnsiliō leō ad flūmen aggreditur? **2.** Quae erant verba Thisbēs ubi leōnem vīdit? **3.** Cūr puella in cavernā remanēbat? **4.** Quid facit Thisbē ut cum Pȳramō sit? **5.** Ubi parentēs duo corpora condidērunt?

Scrībe Latīnē: **1.** Thisbe turns away in order that the lion may not follow her. **2.** Thisbe thought, "I shall proceed farther into the cave." **3.** Thisbe returns to find Pyramus. **4.** Pyramus did not live long.

21.   WORD STUDY

To what word in the story is each of these related by derivation: *immaculate, ingredient, invent, oculist, progress,* and *verbatim?* Define each.

Give and define one or more English words derived from either the present or the participial stem of **sequor** combined with each of the following prefixes: **con, ē** or **ex, ob, per, prō,** and **sub.** For example, *execute, to finish,* is derived from **ex + secūtus** (perfect passive participle of **sequor**), and means *follow out (to the end).*

What is the *sequel* to a story? What is a *sequence* of events?

APOLLO DRIVES THE SUN-CHARIOT

This lovely cameo represents Apollo, the sun-god, driving his fiery steeds.

IV

OPUSCULUM QUĀRTUM

Mediō tūtissimus ībis, *You will go safest in the middle course.* OVID

22.   A RECKLESS DRIVER, I*

Phaethōn, quī erat fīlius Apollinis, deī sōlis, curruī[1] patris ūnum diem praeesse cupiēbat. Puer, ut hanc veniam petat,[2] ad patrem iterum atque iterum sē cōnfert. "Hunc ūnum diem," inquit, "Ō pater, currum tuum dīrigere cupiō. Is[3] tē multōs diēs tulit; mē ūnum diem facile ferre potest."   5

Apollō postulātum fīlī nōn probāvit. Eī nōn cessit. "Phaethontī nōn cēdam," arbitrātus est. "Hominibus orbis terrārum[4] exitium īnferet."

Tandem postulātīs fīlī victus est, quod ōlim eī postulātum aliquod pollicitus erat. Magnā cum cūrā puerum monēbat. 10 "Via," inquit, "difficilis est. Currus bonus est et onus

*The story of Phaëthon is found in Sabin, *Classical Myths That Live Today*, pp. 21-23.

15

maius quam tē saepe fert, sed timeō. Fīdūcia tua omnibus exitium īnferre potest. Mediō tūtissimus ībis.⁵ "

Phaethōn audāx ob adulēscentiam suam sine cūrā hoc audīvit, 15 et in currum ascendēns per iter ignōtum equōs laetus et fortis⁶ dīrēxit. Currus altius et altius in caelum lātus est.

23.   REQUIRED VOCABULARY

audāx, audācis bold

cōnferō, -ferre, contulī, collātus bring together; sē cōnferre go

dīrigō, -ere, -rēxī, -rēctus guide

ferō, ferre, tulī, lātus bear, carry

fīdūcia, -ae, *f.* self-confidence

ignōtus, -a, -um unknown, strange

īnferō, -ferre, intulī, illātus carry in, bring to

onus, -eris, *n.* load

polliceor, -ērī, -itus sum promise, offer

praesum, -esse, -fuī, — be in command of

probō, -āre, -āvī, -ātus approve

24.   NOTES ON THE STORY

1. **curruī**: dative with the compound verb **praeesse**.
2. **petat**: what mood? Why?
3. **Is**: the antecedent is **currum** in the preceding sentence.
4. **orbis terrārum**: translate *of the whole world;* an idiom. What is it literally?
5. **ībis**: *you will go;* future of **eō**.
6. **fortis**: *fearlessly;* an adjective, but translated as if it were an adverb.

25.   COMPREHENSION

1. Why did Apollo at first refuse to let Phaëthon drive his chariot?
2. Why did he at last grant his son's request? 3. What warning did he give his son? 4. How was it received?

26. Present indicative of *ferō* (497).

Active		*Passive*	
ferō	ferimus	feror	ferimur
fers	fertis	ferris	feriminī
fert	ferunt	fertur	feruntur

Learn the conjugation of **ferō**.

27.

Transitive and intransitive verbs. In Latin, as in English, verbs are transitive or intransitive. Some verbs, however, are used in both a transitive and an intransitive sense. Thus in the sentence, **hoc postulātum fīliō concessit,** *he granted this request to his son,* **concessit,** which denotes an action that goes over to an object, is a transitive (**trānsīre,** *go over*) verb. This same verb **concēdō** may have the meaning of *yield* or *give in,* as in the sentence, **fīliō concessit,** *he yielded to his son.* Here **concessit,** which shows no action going over to an object, is an intransitive (**in,** *not* + **trānsīre**) verb.

Point out in the story the transitive or intransitive verbs.

Dative with a compound verb (518). The dative is used with many verbs which are compounds of a verb and a preposition : **fīdūcia puerō exitium īnfert,** *self-confidence brings destruction to the boy.* If such verbs are transitive, both the accusative case and the dative are used with them ; if they are intransitive, the dative only is used : **Phaethōn curruī patris praeesse cupiēbat,** *Phaëthon wished to be in charge of the chariot of his father;* **pater fīliō nōn oberat,** *the father did not oppose his son.*

28. EXERCISE

Compare the forms of the present indicative of **ferō** with those of **mittō,** and point out the forms of **ferō** that are irregular (**497, 492**). What forms of **ferō** are used in the story?

Respondē Latīnē : **1.** Cuius fīlius erat Phaethōn? **2.** Quō audāx puer sē contulit? **3.** Cūr pater nōn probāvit? **4.** Ubi Phaethōn lātus est?

Scrībe Latīnē : **1.** The horses will carry the strange load easily. **2.** They have carried many loads. **3.** Self-confidence brings destruction on all. **4.** Formerly Apollo was in command of the chariot of the sun. **5.** What did Apollo promise Phaëthon?

29. WORD STUDY

Give an English word derived from : **arbitrātus, audāx, cōnferō, fīlius, onus, orbis, pater, Phaethōn, probāre, sine** + **cūra.**

A REMINDER OF PHAËTHON

This is the picture of the tomb of Q. Sulpicius Maximus. When the Porta Salaria was destroyed in 1870, this tomb was found in the Aurelian Wall, which surrounds Rome. An inscription beneath the statue of Sulpicius says that at the age of eleven he won a prize for the best Greek poem on the rebuke administered by Jupiter to Apollo for allowing Phaëthon to drive the chariot of the sun.

V

OPUSCULUM QUĪNTUM

30.   **A RECKLESS DRIVER, II**

Equī agitātōrem esse ignōtum et dominum suum sē nōn dīrigere [1] brevī tempore cognōvērunt. Pondus etiam currūs tam parvum erat ut perterrērentur.[2] Nunc Phaethontī erat [3] summa cūra. Dum [4] puer perterritus manibus curruī adhaeret 5 nē caderet, equōs dīrigere nōn poterat.

Interim equī solitam viam nōn sequēbantur. Prīmō ad stellās altissimās currēbant, deinde praecipitēs īnfrā ad terram. Currus sōlis tam prope īnferiōrem mundī partem lātus est ut

maria omnia et flūmina incenderet atque frūmentum in agrīs
et arborēs in silvīs combūreret. In Āfricā sōl tam prope terram 10
vēnit ut ignis colōrem hominum converteret et herbae iterum
crēscere nōn possent. Omnēs mortālēs [5] ob sōlis aestum tam
miserī erant ut ab Iove auxilium implōrārent. Pater deōrum
hominumque tam īrātus erat ut puerum fulmine occīsum [6]
dē currū dēiceret. Equī ad stabula sua revertī coāctī sunt. 15
Corpus Phaethontis in flūmen, quod in Italiā est, cecidit.
Sorōrēs eius adeō lacrimāvērunt ut ā deīs in pōpulōs stantēs
prope hoc flūmen converterentur.

31.   REQUIRED VOCABULARY

adeō so (adv.)   **incendō, -ere, -cendī, -cēnsus**
aestus, -ūs, m. heat   set on fire, burn
convertō, -ere, -vertī, -versus   **interim** in the meantime (adv.)
              change   **prīmō** at first (adv.)
dum while (conj.)   **soror, -ōris,** f. sister

32.   NOTES ON THE STORY

1. **dominum . . . dīrigere:** *that their master was not driving them;* an
indirect statement used with **cognōvērunt.**

2. **perterrērentur:** see **587.**

3. **Phaethontī erat:** *to Phaëthon was;* translate *Phaëthon had.* The
dative as used here denotes possession.

4. **Dum:** the present indicative is regularly used with **dum** meaning
while (**600**), but it may be translated as if it were past time.

5. **mortālēs:** *liable to die, mortal;* translate *people.*

6. **occīsum:** a perfect passive participle modifying **puerum.**

33.   COMPREHENSION

1. Where did the horses carry the sun-chariot? **2.** What happened to
Phaëthon? **3.** What did the gods do to the sisters of Phaëthon? **4.** What
explanation did the ancients have for the deserts of Africa?

34.   RĒS GRAMMATICAE

Imperfect subjunctive (492). The imperfect subjunctive, both
active and passive, is formed by adding to the present stem

the imperfect tense sign -rē-* and to this the personal endings. An easy rule to follow in forming the imperfect subjunctive is: add the personal endings to the present infinitive: **portā-re-m, vidē-re-m, mitte-re-m, audī-re-m, esse-m.**

Point out in the story five verbs in the imperfect subjunctive.

Result clauses (587). In the sentence, **pondus tam parvum erat ut perterrērentur,** *the weight was so little that they were frightened,* **ut perterrērentur** expresses result.

Apollō currum sōlis sīc dīrēxit ut herbās nōn incenderet, *Apollo drove the chariot of the sun so that he did not set fire to the green plants.* Observe that a negative result clause is introduced by **ut ... nōn.** What word introduces a negative purpose clause?

Result is regularly expressed by a subordinate clause introduced by **ut** or **ut ... nōn.** The main clause often contains a word such as **ita, sīc, tam,** meaning *so,* or **tantus,** *so great,* which anticipates the result clause.

35. **EXERCISE**

Give the imperfect subjunctive of: **lacrimō, adhaereō, convertō, veniō.**

Point out the words in main clauses which anticipate result clauses.

Respondē Latīnē: **1.** Quid equī cognōvērunt? **2.** Cūr Phaethōn eōs dīrigere nōn poterat? **3.** Dum puer curruī adhaeret, ubi equī concurrērunt? **4.** Quam īrātus erat Iuppiter?

Scrībē Latīnē: **1.** Phaëthon was so frightened at first that he clung to the chariot. **2.** In the meantime the horses were so frightened that they did not follow the usual path. **3.** His sister was so wretched that the gods changed her into a poplar tree. **4.** The heat of the sun has been so great (**tantus**) that it set fire to the fields.

36. **WORD STUDY**

Find in the story the Latin ancestor of each of the following words and give its English equivalent: *crescent, mundane, ponderous, prime, silvan, stellar.*

* Remember that a long vowel is always shortened before **nt,** and final **m, r,** and **t.**

From a painting by John Singer Sargent   *Courtesy of Museum of Fine Arts, Boston*

THE FALL OF PHAËTHON

**Hīc situs est Phaethōn, currūs aurīga paternī,
Quem sī nōn tenuit magnīs tamen excidit ausīs.**

Here lies Phaëthon, driver of his father's chariot;
If he did not control it, still he fell in a great enterprise.

OVID, *Metamorphoses*

The shining way still dares the driver's skill,
And all the azure vault
    Dares the assault
Of wings.   They can who will!
And I —
Icarus am I, and Phaëthon!

O. R. HOWARD THOMSON, *Quaesitor Aeternus* *

* Reprinted by permission of the NEW YORK TIMES and the author.

MIDAS

King Midas finds that even his food turns to gold at his touch.

VI

OPUSCULUM SEXTUM

By this mythologic story we are very plainly told,
That, though gold may have its uses, there are better things than gold;
That a man may sell his freedom to procure the shining pelf;
And that Avarice, though it prosper, still contrives to cheat itself.

JOHN G. SAXE, *The Choice of King Midas*

 37.   THE TOUCH OF GOLD

Erat quīdam rēx Phrygiae, nōmine Midās, quī ōlim Bacchum
deum vīnī iūverat. Deus praemiō [1] eī dēlēctum dōnī dedit.
Rēx quandam rem petere nōn haesitāvit. "Omnia," inquit,
"quae tangam aurum fīant." [2]

5 Bacchus postulātum nōn laetus concessit. Midās fortūnam
statim explōrāre coepit. Quaedam in rēgiā quae digitīs tan-
gēbat omnia aurum facta sunt. Prīmum hōc dōnō fruēbātur.

22

"Lectī, librī, mēnsae, gladiī, sellae, mūrī, tāctū meō [3] aurum
fīunt," sēcum dīxit.

In hortum ingressus est. "Arborēs et flōrēs manū meā [10]
tāctī aurum etiam fīent," arbitrātus est rēx. Mox rosae
decōrae albae et quaedam ex herbīs pulchrīs dūrae et aureae
erant.

Tandem ad cēnam vēnit. Neque cibum edere neque aquam
bibere poterat. Nam cibus ōre rēgis tāctus aurum dūrum [15]
fīēbat. Aqua et vīnum flūmina aurea fīēbant. Rēx sē citissimē
famē moritūrum esse [4] intellēxit. "Cibus meus aurum fit.
Moriar," [5] magnā cum vōce conclāmāvit.

Fīlia parva hoc audiēns ad patrem cucurrit ut eum cōnsō-
lārētur. Midās fīliae ōsculum dedit, et statim puella aurum [20]
facta est. Pater miser dīxit, "Et tū aurum fīs!"

Rēx perīculum suum cognōvit. Iterum et iterum Bacchum
ōrāvit ut tāctum aureum sibi ēriperet.[6] Conclāmābat, "Dā
mihi veniam, pater, peccāvī." Tandem deus bonus hominem
famē et sitī cōnfectum atque fātō crūdēlī perterritum audīvit et [25]
dīxit, "Tāctum aureum tibi ēripiam. Omnia aurea fīent ut
quondam erant."

Bacchus rēgem caput sub aquās cuiusdam flūminis, quī [7]
nōminātus est Pactōlus, ter submergere tum iussit. Hoc imperātum Midās facere statim mātūrāvit. Arēnās Pactōlī [30]
aureās fierī laetus vīdit. Tāctum aureum sē relīquisse intellēxit. Aquā ex flūmine Midās omnia ut quondam erant fēcit.
Posteā aurum eī ingrātum erat.

38. REQUIRED VOCABULARY

concēdō, -ere, -cessī, -cessus
    grant
digitus, -ī, *m.* finger
explōrō, -āre, -āvī, -ātus try out
famēs, -is, *f.* hunger
fīō, fierī, factus sum (*pass. of*
    faciō) be made, become

imperātum, -ī, *n.* command;
    with facere obey
mēnsa, -ae, *f.* table
quīdam, quaedam, quiddam a
    certain one
tangō, -ere, tetigī, tāctus touch

39.   NOTES ON THE STORY

1. **praemiō:** *for a reward.*

2. **Omnia, fīant:** *let all things become;* **aurum,** a predicate nominative, is used with **fīant.**

3. **tāctū meō:** *at my touch;* **tāctus** is a noun. How do you know that it is not the participle of **tangō?**

4. **sē . . . moritūrum esse:** *that he would very quickly perish from hunger;* an indirect statement used with **intellēxit.**

5. **Moriar:** future indicative.

6. **ut . . . ēriperet:** *that he take away the golden touch from him.*

7. **quī:** agrees in gender with **Pactōlus,** the predicate nominative, instead of with its antecedent, **flūminis** (560, *d*). The Pactolus was famous for the gold found in its bed.

40.   COMPREHENSION

1. Why did Bacchus give the golden touch to Midas?   **2.** How did the king use this gift?   **3.** How did he free himself from it?

41.   RĒS GRAMMATICAE

The irregular verb *fīō* **(498).** Learn the conjugation of **fīō,** observing very carefully the quantity of the stem vowel **i.** All forms of **fīō** which are built upon the present stem are used as the passive of **faciō: omnia aurum fīēbant,** *all things became (were made) gold.*

Point out five forms of **fīō** in the story.

The indefinite pronoun *quīdam* **(491). Quīdam** may be used either as pronoun or adjective. Learn its declension. Observe that in the neuter, **quiddam** is the form used for the pronoun and **quoddam** the one used for the adjective.

In the story identify forms of **quīdam.**

With forms of **quīdam,** the ablative with **ex** or **dē** is used in place of the genitive which might be expected: **quaedam ex herbīs:** *certain of the plants* (510, *a*).

42.   EXERCISE

Give the synopsis of: **fīō** in the third person singular; in the first person plural.

Give the Latin for : on a certain table, to a certain dinner, a certain girl, for a certain king, certain gifts.

Respondē Latīnē : **1.** Cui praemium Bacchus dedit? **2.** Quid Midās petīvit? **3.** Quid Bacchus rēgī concessit? **4.** Quem in locum Midās ingressus est? **5.** Quid in hortō rēx fēcit? **6.** Cūr aurum rēgī ingrātum fīēbat?

Scrībe Latīnē : **1.** A reward was given to a certain king by Bacchus. **2.** He immediately tried out this gift. **3.** The king said, " The tables touched by my fingers are becoming gold." **4.** A certain one of his daughters had become gold. **5.** Worn out with hunger, Midas carried out (**faciō**) the command of Bacchus.

43.   **WORD STUDY**

Give and define five English words derived from **tangō.**

THE REWARD OF AVARICE

Mulier quaedam habēbat gallīnam quae eī cotīdiē ōvum pariēbat aureum. Mulier ita exīstimābat, " Mea gallīna sine dubiō pondus aurī intus habet; sī gallīnam occīdam, omne aurum statim habēbō." Itaque eam occīdit. Sed nihil in eā repperit nisi quod in aliīs gallīnīs reperīrī solet. Itaque dum ₅ maiōrēs rēs cupit, minōrēs etiam perdidit.

THE TEMPLE OF NEPTUNE

This beautiful temple, dedicated to the god of the sea, was built in the fifth century B.C. by Greek colonists at Paestum, a town originally named Poseidonia from Poseidon, the Greek word for Neptune. It is of the Doric type of architecture and perfectly proportioned. Facing the sea, it stands in simple grandeur — the finest temple in Italy.

VII

OPUSCULUM SEPTIMUM

Cūra piī deīs sunt, *The good are a care to the gods.* OVID

44. THE FLOOD *

Ōlim omnēs hominēs maximē impiī erant. Iuppiter ubīque nefās et scelus vidēbat. Tandem deus sēcum dīxit, " Genus hūmānum omne dēlēbō. Nihil aliud facere possum." Neptūnum, frātrem suum, ad sē vocāvit et quaesīvit quōmodo is 5 iuvāre sē posset. Auxiliō Neptūnī aquās ōceanī et omnium flūminum super terram mīsit. Poena erat maxima.

Ubīque hominēs dīcēbant, " Neque scīmus quid fēcerīmus neque vidēmus cūr deī dē nōbīs supplicium sūmant." Iuppiter autem precibus eōrum nōn mōtus est. Ubīque terram dīluviō

---

* The story of *The Flood* is told in Ovid, *Metamorphoses, I,* 125-437. The story of *The Flood,* as found in the *Bible,* is in *Genesis,* 6: 11–8: 22.

inundāvit. Summī montēs ipsī tegēbantur. Aquae erant super 10
omnem terram praeter ēditum caput Parnāsī montis.
Tandem duo mortālēs sōlī vīvēbant. Deucaliōn et Pyrrha
piissimī semper fuerant. Itaque dē dīluviō monitī,[1] salūtem
sibi prōvidēre potuerant. Arcam magnam, in quā per tempus
dīluvī habitārent,[2] aedificāverant. Haec in marī īnfīnītō vecta[3] 15
dēnique in monte Parnāsō stetit. Neptūnō nūbēs dispersās
revocante, aquae recēdere coepērunt, et terra paulātim ēminēbat.

Deucaliōn et Pyrrha sōlī et trīstēs erant. Ā deīs quaesīvērunt cūr servātī essent et quōmodo sine aliīs mortālibus vīvere
possent. Iuppiter imperāvit ut ossa parentis[4] magnae post 20
tergum iacerent.[5] Quaesīvērunt ubi ossa essent et num respōnsum eius rēctē audīvissent.

Tandem arbitrātī sunt terram esse parentem magnam
omnium. Quārē lapidēs, quī ossa Terrae Mātris * sunt, post
tergum iaciēbant. Lapidēs quī ā Deucaliōne iaciēbantur virī 25
factī sunt, illī ā Pyrrhā iactī, fēminae, quī omnēs Deucaliōnem
et Pyrrham secūtī sunt.

Ita Iuppiter, omnibus impiīs hominibus dēlētīs, terrae hūmānum genus melius restituit.

45. REQUIRED VOCABULARY

dispergō, -ere, -spersī, -spersus scatter

respōnsum, -ī, *n.* response
restituō, -ere, -uī, -ūtus restore
ēditus, -a, -um lofty
sūmō, -ere, sūmpsī, sūmptus take
lapis, -idis, *m.* stone
supplicium sūmere dē inflict
modus, -ī, *m.* manner, way
punishment upon
paulātim gradually (*adv.*)
supplicium, -ī, *n.* punishment
prex, precis, *f.* prayer
tegō, -ere, tēxī, tēctus cover
tergum, -ī, *n.* back

46. NOTES ON THE STORY

1. monitī: *warned;* modifies the subject understood of **potuerant.**
2. in . . . habitārent: *in which to live during the time of the flood.*

* The Romans thought of the earth as the mother of all. A story embodying this thought is found
on page 119.

3. **vecta:** *borne;* from **vehō.**
4. **parentis:** what is its gender? why?
5. **imperāvit ut, iacerent:** *ordered (them) to throw.*

47. COMPREHENSION

1. Why and how did Jupiter punish men? **2.** For what reason did Deucalion and Pyrrha escape punishment? How? **3.** How was the earth repeopled?

48. RĒS GRAMMATICAE

Perfect subjunctive (492). Observe that in the active the perfect subjunctive is formed by adding to the perfect stem the tense sign **-erī-** and to this the personal endings: **portāv-eri-m, vīd-eri-m, mīs-eri-m, audīv-eri-m, fu-eri-m.** In the passive, the perfect subjunctive is formed by using the perfect passive participle together with the forms of the present subjunctive of the verb **sum: portātus sim.**

Past perfect subjunctive (492). Observe that in the active the past perfect (pluperfect) subjunctive is formed by adding to the perfect stem the tense sign **-issē-** and to this the personal endings: **portāv-isse-m, vīd-isse-m, mīs-isse-m, audīv-isse-m, fu-isse-m.** In the passive, the past perfect subjunctive is formed by using the perfect passive participle together with the forms of the imperfect subjunctive of the verb **sum: portātus essem.**

Learn the conjugation of the perfect and past perfect subjunctive of the model verbs.

Sequence of tenses (577–8). In the sentence, *I know who you are,* if the tense of the main verb *know* is changed to the past, *knew,* the tense of the verb in the subordinate clause is made to harmonize with it: *I knew who you were.* This principle of English speech is the rule in Latin if the verb of the subordinate clause is in the subjunctive: **sciō quis sīs; scīvī quis essēs.** This is a very important principle in Latin because of the extensive use of the subjunctive. This relationship between the tense of the verb in the principal clause and the tense of the verb in the subordinate clause in a complex sentence is called *sequence of tenses*.

Tenses expressing present or future time are called *primary* or *principal* tenses; those expressing past time are called either *secondary* or *historical* tenses. Primary tenses are regularly followed by primary tenses and secondary by secondary, as shown in the following table.

TENSE	VERB IN PRINCIPAL CLAUSE	VERB IN SUBORDINATE CLAUSE SUBJUNCTIVE
PRIMARY	*Present* *Future* *Future Perfect* } followed by	*Present* (action incomplete at the time of the action of the verb in the principal clause) *Perfect* (action completed at the time of the action of the verb in the principal clause)
	Quaerunt quid faciāmus, *they ask what we are doing.* **Quaerunt quid fēcerīmus,** *they ask what we did.*	
SECONDARY	*Imperfect* *Perfect* *Past Perfect* } followed by	{ *Imperfect* (action incomplete etc.) *Past perfect* (action completed etc.)
	Quaesīvērunt quid facerēmus, *they asked what we were doing.* **Quaesīvērunt quid fēcissēmus,** *they asked what we had done.*	

Indirect questions (595). **Scīmus quid fēcerīmus,** *we know what we have done.* **Quaesīvērunt cūr servātī essent,** *they asked why they had been saved.* An indirect question is a subordinate clause, introduced by an interrogative word, depending on a verb meaning to *ask, inquire, tell, know,* or *perceive.* The verb of the indirect question is in the subjunctive mood. Its tense follows the rule of sequence of tenses.

Point out the indirect questions in the story, give the tense of the verb in each, and explain the sequence.

49. EXERCISE

Give the perfect and past perfect subjunctive of : **aedificō, audiō, quaerō, moneō.**

Courtesy of Museum of Fine Arts, Boston

DEUCALION AND PYRRHA

A new race is springing up from the stones thrown by Deucalion and Pyrrha.
This illustration is found in a 1767 edition of Ovid's *Metamorphoses*.

Give the use of: **impiī,** l. 1, **dīluviō,** l. 9, **essent,** l. 19, **virī,** l. 25,
Pyrrhā, l. 26.

Respondē Latīnē: **1.** Quid Iuppiter ubīque vīdit? **2.** Quōmodo deus
omnēs dēlēvit? **3.** Quis deum iūvit? **4.** Quam alta (*deep*) erat aqua?
5. Ubi dēnique arca stetit?

Scrībe Latīnē: **1.** Gradually the waters covered the land. **2.** The father
of the gods hears their prayers. **3.** Jupiter sees how he can restore the race
of men. **4.** They asked why he had inflicted this punishment on them.
5. They knew what the response was. **6.** Do you know who scattered stones
behind their backs?

Read the Labors of Hercules

VIII

OPUSCULUM OCTĀVUM

> Nīl sine magnō vīta labōre dedit mortālibus,
> *Life has given nothing to mankind without great labor.*
>
> HORACE

50. THE LABORS OF HERCULES, I *

In antīquā Graeciā Herculēs erat vir [1] praeclārus. Īnfāns [2] in cūnābulīs duās serpentēs magnās dextrā suā strangulāvit. Multīs post annīs [3] Apollō eum ob quoddam scelus ulcīscī voluit. Deus Eurystheō rēgī poenam virī commīsit. Rēx Herculem poenae causā duodecim labōribus fungī volēbat. 5 Dē hīs labōribus plūrima ā poētīs scrīpta sunt.

Prīmum manibus suīs leōnem ingentem, quī vallem Nemeae incolēbat et animālibus [4] hominibusque nocēbat, interfēcit. Tum mortuum leōnem ad rēgem umerīs tulit.

Post haec iussus est ab Eurystheō Hydram necāre. Hoc 10 mōnstrum, quod novem capita, quōrum ūnum immortāle erat, habēbat, vīcit. Sagittās sanguine mōnstrī tīnxit et eās mortiferās fēcit.

Haec rēs rēgī nōn placuit, quī tum dīxit, " Tē aprum Erymanthium capere volō." Tandem Herculēs summā difficultāte 15 aprum laqueō implicātum ad rēgem dūxit.

Eurystheus deinde cervō, quī numquam dēfessus in campīs Arcadiae vagābātur, potīrī voluit. Huic cervō erant [5] cornua ex aurō et pedēs ex aere. Vir, rēgī pārēre coāctus, tōtum annum cervum sequēbātur, et dēnique eum cēpit.   20

Post haec Herculēs, avēs Stymphālidēs, quae carne hominum vēscēbantur, necāre iussus, ad Minervam iit. " Avēs in lacū Stymphālicō," inquit, " interficere volō." Dea virō fāvit et

---

* The story of Hercules is found in Sabin, *Classical Myths That Live Today*, pp. 211–229.

THE TEMPLE OF HERCULES AT CORI

This ancient temple, standing in a garden of roses at the highest point of an ancient hill town on the Appian Way, commands a wide view of the Roman campagna.   It is not definitely known to what god this temple was dedicated.   It is usually attributed to Hercules.

eum iūvit. Hās avēs, quae pinnīs suīs prō sagittīs ūtēbantur,
tēlīs mortiferīs dēlēvit.   25

Deinde Eurystheus Herculī hunc labōrem gravissimum
imposuit. Augēae [6] stabula, quae trīgintā annōs nōn lauta [7]
erant, fuērunt. Vir dīxit, " Sī volēs, ūnō diē stabula tua lavābō.
Vīsne [8] mē id facere? " Herculēs, ubi Augēas annuerat, flūmen
per stabula convertit et ea facillimē lāvit.   30

51.   REQUIRED VOCABULARY

aes, aeris, *n.* bronze
campus, -ī, *m.* field
labor, -ōris, *m.* labor
noceō, -ēre, -uī, -itus be harmful
pāreō -ēre, -uī, — obey
placeō, -ēre, -uī, -itus please
    volō, velle, voluī, — wish

potior, -īrī, -ītus sum get posses-
    sion of
sagitta, -ae, *f.* arrow
tēlum, -ī, *n.* weapon
vagor, -ārī, -ātus sum roam about
vallēs, vallis, *f.* valley

52.   NOTES ON THE STORY

1. **vir:** *hero;* contrast this meaning with that of **homō.**
2. **Īnfāns:** translate *when an infant.*
3. **Multīs post annīs:** *after many years.*
4. **animālibus:** dative used with **nocēbat.**
5. **huic . . . erant:** translate *this stag had;* **cervō** is a dative denoting possession.
6. **Augēae:** *to (King) Augeas.*
7. **lauta:** *washed.*
8. **Vīsne:** second singular of the present tense of **volō** with the enclitic, **-ne,** a sign of a question.

53.   COMPREHENSION

1. Why were labors imposed on Hercules?   **2.** Describe the first six labors.

54.   RĒS GRAMMATICAE

The irregular verb *volō* (499). Learn the conjugation of **volō.**
Point out in the story and identify the forms of **volō.**

Dative with special intransitive verbs (517). **Herculēs rēgī placuit,** *Hercules pleased the king.* **Dea virō fāvit,** *the goddess favored the man.* The dative is used with certain verbs, such as **faveō,** *favor;* **placeō,** *please;* **parcō,** *spare;* and **persuādeō,** *persuade.* This dative is usually translated into English as if it were an accusative of direct object.

Point out in the story the verbs with which this dative is used.

55.   *Tuesday*   EXERCISE

Identify these forms: **quoddam,** l. 3; **fungī,** l. 5; **umerīs,** l. 9; **iussus,** l. 10.

Respondē Latīnē: **1.** Quis erat Herculēs? **2.** Cūr eum ulcīscī Apollō vult? **3.** Cui poenam virī deus commīsit? **4.** Quōmodo leōnem Herculēs interfēcit? **5.** Cuius stabula vir lāvit?

Scrībe Latīnē: **1.** The labors of Hercules pleased the god. **2.** The hero said, "I am forced to obey you." **3.** The weapons of Hercules were arrows. **4.** They wish to favor the hero and will not injure him. **5.** The stag, which had feet of bronze, wandered in the fields and valleys.

56.   WORD STUDY

The diphthongs **oe** and **ae,** found in certain Latin words, become *e* in their English derivatives: **poena,** *penal.* Give other derivatives of **poena.**

To what word in the story is each of these related by derivation: *agency, infantile, lavatory, placate, studious, vagrant, volition?*

Marble relief, Borghese Gallery, Rome   *Courtesy of Newark Public Library*

FIVE LABORS OF HERCULES

A HEAVY BURDEN

One of the feats of strength performed by Hercules was that of holding the earth for Atlas.

IX

OPUSCULUM NŌNUM

Fīnis ecce labōrum, *Lo, the end of labors.*

MOTTO OF THE EARL OF SELKIRK

57.   THE LABORS OF HERCULES, II

Eurystheus Herculī septimum labōrem imposuit. Eum ad sē ex īnsulā Crētā bovem quendam vīvum referre iussit. Herculēs igitur sē ad īnsulam contulit. Hoc erat opus difficillimum, sed Herculēs ad Eurystheum magnō labōre captum hunc vīvum tandem rettulit. 5

Cum Herculēs bovem ad rēgem portāvisset, Eurystheus dīxit, " Nisi equōs Diomēdis vīceris, nōlī revertī." [1]

Herculēs cum equōs vīcisset, Diomēdem, quī eōs carne hominum aluerat, interfēcit et eīs corpus eius dedit.

Hōc labōre cōnfectō, fīlia Eurystheī zōnā pulcherrimā rēgīnae 10 Amāzonum potīrī cupiēbat. Vir, rēgīnā occīsā, zōnā potītus est.

From a Greek vase painting
An Amazon on Horseback

The Amazons were warlike women, who won much fame by fighting with men on equal terms. Hercules overcame the Queen of the Amazons.

Herculēs deinde multōs bovēs Gēryonis, gigantis triplicī corpore,[2] capere iussus est. Bovēs ā pāstōre magnō corpore et ā cane bicipite [3] custōdiēbantur. Custōdibus interfectīs, vir 15 cum bōbus [4] revertitur.

Eurystheus cum bovēs Gēryonis accēpisset, graviōrem labōrem Herculī imposuit. Iussit enim eum aurea māla ex hortō Hesperidum auferre. Māla aurea Hesperidum ā fīliābus Atlantis et ā dracōne ingentī, quī oculōs suōs numquam clau- 20 dēbat, custōdiēbantur. Herculēs ad Atlantem,[5] custōdem mālōrum, vēnit. Atlās,* quī caelum umerīs sustinēbat, virō dīcere ubi essent māla nōluit. Ipse māla referre māluit. " Mihi," inquit, " sustinē caelum. Tum iterum sustinēbō, cum revertar." Itaque Herculēs, illō absente, caelum sus- 25 tinuit. Atlās cum māla retulisset, Herculī dīxit, " Nōlī mihi caelum iterum dare. Nunc id semper sustinē ! " Sed Herculēs per dolum [6] Atlantem caelum recipere coēgit et cum mālīs revertit.

---

* In *The Three Golden Apples* in The Wonder Book Nathaniel Hawthorne gives in detail the story of Hercules' experience with Atlas.

Herculēs alacer, aureīs mālīs relātīs, extrēmum labōrem, quī erat difficillimus, suscēpit. Cerberum, canem trīcipitem, 30 ex Tartarō in terram tulit. Herculēs cum hīs labōribus fūnctus esset, servitūte ab Eurystheō līberātus est.

58.   REQUIRED VOCABULARY

alacer, -cris, -cre eager
alō, -ere, -uī, -itus feed
claudō, -ere, clausī, clausus close
cum when (conj.)
extrēmus, -a, -um last
mālō, mālle, māluī, — prefer
nōlō, nōlle, nōluī, — not wish, be unwilling

referō, -ferre, rettulī, relātus bring back
rēgīna, -ae, f. queen
servitūs, -tūtis, f. slavery
suscipiō, -ere, -cēpī, -ceptus undertake
vīvus, -a, -um alive

59.   NOTES ON THE STORY

1. **revertī:** present infinitive of the deponent verb **revertor.**
2. **triplicī corpore:** *with triple body;* an ablative of description.
3. **bicipite:** Why does this mean *two-headed?*
4. **bōbus:** *bulls;* from **bōs.**
5. **Atlantem:** accusative of **Atlās.**
6. **per dolum:** *by a trick;* i.e., Hercules asked Atlas to hold the heavens a moment while he fixed a pad on his shoulder.

60.   COMPREHENSION

1. What were the last six labors of Hercules? **2.** Which was the most difficult? **3.** Why did Atlas take back the sky?

61.   RĒS GRAMMATICAE

The irregular verbs *nōlō* and *mālō* (499). The verb **nōlō** is formed from the words **nōn** and **volō.** The verb **mālō** is formed from **magis** and **volō.** Learn the conjugation of each.

Point out in the story and identify the forms of **nōlō** and **mālō.**

Negative commands (611, a). Nōlī mihi caelum dare, *be unwilling to give the sky to me,* translate, *do not give the sky to me;*

nōlīte eī māla dare, *do not give the apples to him.* A negative command is regularly expressed by the imperative of **nōlō** (**nōlī,** singular ; **nōlīte,** plural) and a complementary infinitive. In **nōlīte eī māla dare** what is the complementary infinitive?

Point out in the story two negative commands. What complementary infinitive is used in each?

Cum **temporal with the subjunctive (circumstantial) (597).** **Herculēs cum equōs vīcisset, Diomēdem interfēcit,** *when Hercules had conquered the horses, he killed Diomedes.* In this sentence **cum,** *when,* introduces the clause, **Herculēs equōs vīcisset,** which gives the circumstance or situation connected with the action expressed by the verb, **interfēcit,** in the main clause.

The verb in a **cum** circumstantial clause is in the past perfect subjunctive if the action expressed by it has occurred before the action expressed by the verb in the principal clause. The verb is in the imperfect subjunctive if the two actions occur at the same time.

Cum **temporal with the indicative (596).** In the sentence, **tum iterum sustinēbō, cum revertar,** *when I (shall) return, then I will hold it again,* the verb in the **cum** clause, **revertar,** is in the indicative because it defines or dates the time at which the action of the verb in the principal clause, **sustinēbō,** is to occur.

The verb in a **cum** clause is in the indicative if the clause merely indicates time and not circumstance.

Point out in the story three examples of **cum** circumstantial clauses and give the reason for the tense of the verb in each.

62.   EXERCISE

Give the present indicative of : **nōlō** and **mālō.**

Explain the use of : **portāvisset,** l. 6 ; **zōnā,** l. 10 ; **essent,** l. 22 ; **revertar,** l. 25 ; **absente,** l. 25 ; **sustinē,** l. 27 ; **labōribus,** l. 32.

Respondē Latīnē : **1.** Cūr Herculēs alacer erat? **2.** Cuius zōnā fīlia rēgis potīrī volēbat? **3.** Ā quibus bovēs Gēryonis custōdiēbantur? **4.** Quis caelum umerīs sustinēbat? **5.** Quālis (*what sort of*) canis Cerberus erat?

Scrībe Latīnē: **1.** Hercules prefers to be freed from servitude. **2.** The man said, " Do not feed the animal flesh." **3.** The queen does not wish to close her eyes. **4.** Atlas did not eagerly (use adj.) undertake the task. **5.** When the hero had brought back the dog alive, his last task was finished.

63.

WORD STUDY

The word *canary* is derived from **canis,** *dog.* The *Canary Islands* were so called because of the *dogs* found there by the Romans. Later the name *canary* was applied to the birds found on these islands.

To what word in the story is each of these related by derivation: *alimentary, Atlantic, fury, revive, triple, zone?*

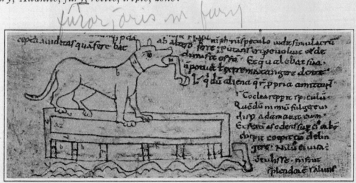

Library, University of Leiden, Holland

THE DOG THAT SAW HIS SHADOW

This crude illustration is from an eleventh-century manuscript of *Aesop's Fables.*

Canis Cum Carne

Canis trāns flūmen carnem in ōre ferēbat. Mox in aquā imāginem suam vīdit. Crēdēns hanc esse alteram canem cum carne, hanc praedam ab alterō cane ēripere voluit. Itaque cibum quem tenēbat ōre dīmīsit. Neque cibum quem petēbat attingere potuit. Is enim meritō suum āmittit quī aliēnum petit.

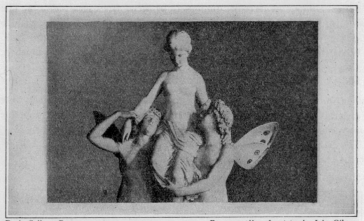

PSYCHE CARRIED BY THE ZEPHYRS

Psyche is carried to the palace of Cupid from the lonely mountain where she
had been left in accordance with the decree of the oracle.

X

OPUSCULUM DECIMUM

Amāre et sapere vix deō concēditur. LABERIUS

The proverb holds that to be wise and love
Is hardly granted to the gods above. DRYDEN

64.   CUPID AND PSYCHE, I

Erant in quādam cīvitāte rēx et rēgīna. Psȳchē erat fīlia
minima nātū [1] huius rēgis et rēgīnae. Eīs erant [2] trēs fīliae
pulchrae, quārum Psȳchē erat pulcherrima. Cum [3] puella tam
pulchra esset, omnēs eam mīrātī sunt. Multīs in terrīs fābulae
5 dē eius pulchritūdine audiēbantur. Multī dīcēbant, " Psȳchē
pulchrior quam Venus est." Genus hūmānum omne deam ob
puellam pulchram neglegere coepit. Tandem Venus maximē
īrāta fīlium suum Cupīdinem vocāvit ut sē iuvāret. Statim
Cupīdō ad domum Psȳchēs [4] īre mātūrāvit ut mātrem suam

40

ulcīscerētur. Cum autem pulchritūdinem puellae vidēret, deus [10] amōris sagittīs suīs vulnerātus est.

Cum [5] omnēs eam mīrārentur, nēmō virginem pulchram in mātrimōnium dūcere voluerat. Rēx et rēgīna, cum fīlia sua neque ā rēge neque prīncipe in mātrimōnium ducta esset, ad ōrāculum Apollinis iērunt et cūr Psȳchē deīs ingrāta esset [15] quaesīvērunt. Deinde interrogāvērunt cūr deī puellae nūllum marītum dedissent. Ōrāculum respondit, " Fīliae vestrae erit nūllus marītus mortālis, sed mōnstrum [6] quod in summō monte puella vidēbit eam in mātrimōnium dūcet."

Mox Psȳchē cum parentibus dolentibus et amīcīs miserīs ad [20] montem cōnstitūtum iit. Virgō, cum sociī eam sōlam relīquissent, lacrimāre coepit. Brevī tempore ventus eam ad rēgiam magnificam in valle pulchrā portāvit. Psȳchē arbitrāta est, " Cum omnia pulchra sint, ego fortior erō." In rēgiam ingressa est. Vōcēs eī dīxērunt, " Cum nōs vidēre nōn [25] possīs, tamen tibi serviēmus."

Ad eam cibum et vīnum ferēbant atque eī cantābant. Cum Psȳchē corpora nūlla vidēret, vōcēs saepe audiēbat. Cum nox vēnisset, dominus rēgiae revertit. Puella cum eum vidēre nōn posset, vōcem dulcem eius audiēbat. Semper prīmā nocte [7] [30] veniēbat et ante lūcem proficīscēbātur.

Tandem Cupīdō, quī erat dominus huius rēgiae, Psȳchēn [8] uxōrem suam fēcit. Uxor autem nescīvit quis marītus esset. Deus dīxit, " Nōlī mē vidēre cōnārī aut mihi gravissimum dolōrem et tibi summum exitium ferēs."

35

Cum Psȳchē omnia pulchra habēret, tamen sorōrēs suās vidēre cupiēbat. Cum [5] Cupīdō esset invītus, cum [3] uxōrem amāret, ventum mīsit ut duās sorōrēs ad eam ferret. Sorōrēs, cum Psȳchē anteā misera nunc tam laeta esset et rēs tam magnificās habēret, invidae erant. Persuādent eī [9] ut vultum marītī intueātur. [10]

40

Psȳchē, cum sorōrēs profectae essent, sēcum dīxit, " Cum marītum meum amem, eius vultum numquam vīdī. Cum requiēscet, [11] tum lucernam capiam et ad eum ībō."

65.   REQUIRED VOCABULARY

anteā before, formerly (*adv.*)

aut or (*conj.*)

eō, īre, iī, -itus go

interrogō, -āre, -āvī, -ātus ask

mīror, -ārī, -ātus sum admire

neglegō, -ere, -lēxī, -lēctus neg-
    lect, disregard

numquam never (*adv.*)

persuādeō, -ēre, -suāsī, -suāsus
    persuade

proficīscor, -ī, -fectus sum depart

uxor, -ōris, *f.* wife

ventus, -ī, *m.* wind

66.   NOTES ON THE STORY

1. minima nātū : *least by birth;* translate *the youngest.*
2. Eīs erant : translate *they had.* See **521.**
3. Cum : *since.*
4. ad domum Psȳchēs : *to the house of Psyche.*
5. Cum : *although.*
6. mōnstrum : *monster;* nominative, subject of dūcet.
7. prīmā nocte : *at first night;* translate *at nightfall.*
8. Psȳchēn : a Greek form of the accusative.
9. eī : why is this case used?
10. ut . . . intueātur : a substantive clause used as object of **persuādē-bimus** and expressing an act as willed. In what mood is **intueātur** ?
11. Cum requiēscet : the indicative is used in this **cum** clause because it fixes the time and does not emphasize the circumstance.

67.   RĒS GRAMMATICAE

Cum causal clauses (604). Cum puella tam pulchra esset, omnēs eam mīrātī sunt, *because the girl was so beautiful, all admired her.* When the conjunction **cum** means *because* or *since,* it introduces a clause with its verb in the subjunctive.

Cum adversative (concessive) clauses (606). Psȳchē cum corpora nūlla vidēret, tamen vōcēs saepe audiēbat, *although Psyche saw nobody (no bodies), she often heard (their) voices.* When the conjunction **cum** means *although,* it introduces a clause with its verb in the subjunctive.

Dative of possession (521). In English, possession is usually expressed by the verb *have: they had three daughters.* The Romans used the verb **habeō** in the same way : **trēs fīliās habu-**

ērunt, but they also expressed this same idea of possession by using a dative with the verb **sum** : **eīs erant trēs fīliae,** *to them were three daughters;* translate *they had three daughters.* This use of the dative is very common in Latin and is called the *dative of possession.* Observe that the *thing possessed* is in the nominative case.

The irregular verb *eō* (**500**). Learn the conjugation of **eō.**

68.   EXERCISE

Identify the **cum** clauses in the story. What is the mood and tense of the verb in each?

Identify the forms of the verb **eō.** Identify as to person, voice, tense, and number : **it, īstis, ierat, eat, īssētis, itūrus, euntem.**

Identify as to case and use : **sē,** l. 8; **fīliae,** l. 17; **tibi,** l. 26; **mihi,** l. 34.

Respondē Latīnē : **1.** Quālis puella erat Psȳchē? **2.** Quem ad locum iit Cupīdō? **3.** Cuius sagittīs Cupīdō vulnerātus est? **4.** Quandō (*when*) ad ōrāculum rēx et rēgīna iērunt? **5.** Quōmodo Psȳchē ad rēgiam portāta est?

Scrībe Latīnē : **1.** Although Psyche was formerly neglected, she was now very happy. **2.** Because Cupid admired the girl, he asked who she was. **3.** Cupid (dative of possession) now had a wife, Psyche. **4.** Did Psyche see or hear her husband? **5.** Although the wind carried the sisters to the royal palace, they never saw its master. **6.** When they had persuaded the girl, they departed. **7.** Are you (sing.) going?

69.   WORD STUDY

To what word in the story is each of these related by derivation : *admirable, interrogative, negligent, response, reversal, serve, translate?*

Fresco, House of the Vettii, Pompeii   *Courtesy of Newark Public Library*

CUPIDS AS FLORISTS

MERCURY CONDUCTS PSYCHE TO JUPITER

This is part of the border of the painted ceiling in the Cupid and Psyche room of the Villa Farnesina.

XI

OPUSCULUM ŪNDECIMUM

Nīl dēspērandum, *Nothing should be despaired of.* HORACE
Superanda omnis fortūna ferendō est, *Every blow of fortune must be overcome by enduring.* VERGIL

70. CUPID AND PSYCHE, II

Posterā nocte igitur Psȳchē in cubiculum lucernam portāvit ut vultum marītī intuērētur. Prō [1] mōnstrō virum pulcherrimum vultū dīvīnō vīdit. Dum puella marītum amantibus oculīs intuētur, gutta oleī ferventis dē lucernā in eius cervīcem 5 cecidit. Ille, ē somnō excitātus, ē lectō subsiluit. Cum uxōrem suam hoc fēcisse intellegeret, dīxit, " Tū mihi dēserenda es,[2] cum mihi crēdere nōn possīs. Māter mea Venus mē ut dē tē supplicium sūmerem mīsit. Ego autem ā tē vulnerātus sum."

Cupīdō maestus rēgiam relīquit. Mox rēgia et vallēs flō- 10 rentēs ē cōnspectū Psȳchēs abiērunt. Psȳchē ipsa ad urbem in quā sorōrēs habitābant ventō portāta est. Duae sorōrēs, verbīs eius audītīs, ad rēgiam Cupīdinis iterum īre voluērunt. Ā summō monte dēsilientēs sine auxiliō ventī, periērunt.

Psȳchē misera multōs diēs per orbem terrārum marītī petendī

causā [3] errābat. "Mihi," inquit, "marītus meus videndus [15] est."

Interim Cupīdō domī [4] mātris suae custōdiēbātur. Cum alba avis facta [5] Cupīdinis et Psўchēs ad Venerem rettulisset, dea amōris īrāscēbātur. "Dē illā puellā," inquit, "deīs supplicium gravissimum sūmendum est." [20]

Psўchē maesta ad Cererem sē contulit ut auxilium peteret. Dea respondit, "Venus tibi plācanda est. Hōc factō, marītum tuum recipere poteris."

Tandem Psўchē ad rēgiam Veneris vēnit. Haec īrātissima miserae puellae gravissimum labōrem imperāvit. "Prīmō," [25] inquit, "haec sēmina tibi ante noctem sēparanda sunt." Sīc locūta abiit. Puella labōrāre coepit. Mox formīcae dīligentēs iuvandī [6] causā vēnērunt, et prīmum opus ante noctem ad fīnem perductum est. Prīmā nocte Venus rediit. "Hoc," inquit, "factum nōn est ā tē." [30]

Deīnde Venus secundum opus imperat, "Vellus aureum ovium saevārum, quae prope flūmen sunt, tibi ad templum meum portandum est." Psўchē ad flūmen īre mātūrāvit.

Vōcēs dulcēs dīxērunt, "Tibi nōs audiendae sumus, tibi serviēmus. Ovēs saevae merīdiē dormient." Psўchē, cum [35] merīdiē sōl ovēs in umbram ad dormiendum [7] īre coēgerat, vellus aureum dē rubīs et sentibus lēgit. Eō ad Venerem portātō, secundum opus ad fīnem perductum est.

Tum dea etiam īrāta dīxit, "Aqua in hāc urnā ex fonte Stygis flūminis tibi ferenda est." Avis Iovis ad eam auxilī ferendī [40] causā volāvit. Urnam capiēns avis ad fontem Stygis volāvit et eam complēvit. Puella urnam plēnam portāns ad mātrem marītī laeta revertit. Itaque tertium opus ad fīnem perductum est. Etiam tunc saevam deam plācāre nōn potuit.

Dēmum Venus sēcum dīxit, "Mihi paulum dē pulchritūdine [45] Prōserpinae, deae Orcī, habendum est. Psўchae [8] ea pulchritūdō capienda est et in hāc arcā ad terram superam referenda est. Illa puella ultrā Stygem ad Orcum mihi mittenda est."

Psȳchē alacris ad imperāta facienda ad Orcum dēscendit.
50 Puellae miserae trāns Stygem flūmen eundum est et canis Cerberus plācandus est. Tamen potentiā dīvīnā iūta,[9] pulchritūdine Prōserpinae captā, portāns arcam ad terram superam iterum
venīre potuit. Dēfessa et misera autem arcae aperiendae causā
cōnsēdit. Somnus gravis ex arcā veniēns statim eam pervāsit.
55 Hīc Cupīdō, quī ē cubiculō in quō custōdiēbātur ēvāserat,
eam invēnit. Ad Iovem celeriter iit. Mox Iuppiter Mercurium, nūntium deōrum, mīsit ut Psȳchēn ad sē dūceret.
Puellae nectar dedit, " Immortālis," inquit, " semper eris."
Venus Cupīdinī [10] et eius uxōrī ignōvit.
60 Deī nūptiās celebrāvērunt. Vulcānus cēnam coxit, Apollō
ad citharam cantāvit, et Venus saltāvit. Hōrae item saltāvē-
runt atque omnia rosīs et cēterīs flōribus ōrnāvērunt. Omnēs
laetissimī fuērunt et eīs grātulātiōnēs magnās fēcērunt.

71. REQUIRED VOCABULARY

cōnsequor, -ī, -secūtus sum obtain
cōnsīdō, -ere, -sēdī, -sessus take
a seat
dēscendō, -ere, -dī, -scēnsus
descend
dēserō, -ere, -uī, -sertus desert,
leave
dīligēns, -entis industrious

grātulātiō, -ōnis, f. congratulation
hōra, -ae, f. hour
legō, -ere, lēgī, lēctus pick
perdūcō, -ere, -dūxī, -ductus
lead through, bring
pereō, -īre, -iī, -itus perish
posterus, -a, -um next, following
superus, -a, -um upper
ultrā beyond (prep. with acc.)

72. NOTES ON THE STORY

1. **Prō**: *instead of.*
2. **mihi dēserenda es**: translate *I must desert you.* See **501.**
3. **marītī petendī causā**: *for the sake of seeking her husband;* genitive of
the gerundive **petendī**, agreeing with **marītī**; used with **causā** to express
purpose.
4. **domī**: *at home;* locative case (**555**).
5. **facta**: *acts, affairs;* accusative plural, object of **rettulisset**.

From the Vassar College Tapestry   *Courtesy of The Library, Vassar College*

PSYCHE ARRIVES AT MOUNT OLYMPUS

Venus stands in the center with Cupid at her side. Psyche in the lower left-hand corner raises an appealing hand toward her. Minerva may be recognized by her helmet, Jupiter by his crown, Neptune by his trident, Apollo by his laurel wreath, and Hercules by his club.

6. **iuvandī:** genitive of the gerund used with **causā** to express purpose. Read Chapter 15 in Owen Johnson's *The Varmint*, which gives the story of the experience of Stover and his schoolmates with gerunds and gerundives.

7. **dormiendum:** *sleeping;* accusative of the gerund used with **ad** to express purpose.

8. **Psȳchae:** translate *by Psyche;* dative of agent.

9. **iūta:** *aided;* perfect passive participle of **iuvō.**

10. **Cupīdinī:** why dative (**517**)?

73.   COMPREHENSION

1. What did Cupid do when he discovered Psyche's lack of trust in him? 2. How were the sisters punished? 3. What four labors did Psyche perform?

74.   RĒS GRAMMATICAE

The gerund (629). In the phrase, *the art of writing*, the verb form, *writing*, is a verbal noun. Such a form, since it is a noun, may be used in all cases and, since it has a verbal idea, may have an object : *the art of writing books*. Such a verbal noun is called a *gerund*.

Latin has a gerund corresponding to the English gerund except that it has no nominative form : **ars scrībendī librōs,** *the art of writing books;* **ūtilis legendō,** *useful for reading;* **idōneum tempus ad legendum,** *a suitable time for reading;* **iuvandī causā vēnērunt,** *they came for the sake of aiding.*

Learn the forms of the gerunds (**492**). Observe that a gerund is a neuter noun of the second declension, used only in the singular, and has the distinctive letters **-nd-** : ——, **iuva*nd*ī, iuva*nd*ō, iuva*nd*um, iuva*nd*ō.**

The gerundive (**630**). In Latin there is a verbal adjective form, the *future passive participle* or *gerundive*, for which in English there is no corresponding form : **iuvandus, -a, -um,** *to be aided*. Because it is an adjective, it agrees with its noun in number, gender, and case : **ars librōrum scrībendōrum,** *the art of books to be written*, translate *the art of writing books;* **eius iuvandae causā,** *for the sake of her to be aided*, translate *for the sake of aiding her.*

The gerundive is generally used instead of a gerund with an object and should be used instead of a gerund with an object if it is (1) dependent upon a preposition, (2) in the dative case : **in librīs legendīs,** *in reading books;* **Psȳchē alacris ad imperāta facienda** (l. 49), *Psyche eager to carry out the demands.*

Note that the gerund or gerundive may be used with **ad** or **causā** to express purpose. For examples, see NOTES ON THE STORY, 3, 6, and 7.

Learn the forms of the gerundives (**492**).

Passive periphrastic conjugation (**501**). In the sentence, **Psȳchē mihi mittenda est,** *Psyche must be sent by me*, or *I must send Psyche*, **mittenda est,** which is made up of the future passive participle (gerundive) and a form of the auxiliary verb **sum,** expresses necessity. The future passive participle (gerundive)

From a Greek vase painting
THE TOILETTE OF VENUS

is used with all tenses of the indicative and subjunctive of the verb **sum,** and with the present infinitive of **sum,** to form a special conjugation, called the *passive periphrastic conjugation.* *Periphrastic* is from a Greek word meaning a *round about way of speaking.* The passive periphrastic conjugation expresses *necessity* or *obligation.*

Dative of agent (522). Mihi in the Latin sentence in the preceding paragraph is in the dative case and denotes the person *by whom* the sending, **mittenda est,** must be done. This dative used with the passive periphrastic conjugation is called the *dative of agent.* It is preferably translated as if it were the subject or as an ablative of agent.

Translate: **Tibi hoc faciendum erit; eī Venus plācanda est.**

75. EXERCISE

Point out: the gerunds and gerundives in the story and give the case and use of each; examples of the passive periphrastic conjugation and of the dative of agent; examples of different ways of expressing purpose.

Respondē Latīnē: **1.** Cūr Psȳchē Cupīdinī dēserenda erat? **2.** Quot diēs Psȳchē errābat? **3.** Cuius recipiendī causā labōrābat Psȳchē?

Scrībe Latīnē: **1.** How did the sisters perish? **2.** The girl descended beyond the Styx to the Lower Regions for the sake of obtaining aid. **3.** On the following day the diligent girl must pick the fleece. **4.** The work must be brought to an end by the girl.

76. WORD STUDY

Define: *agenda, Amanda, legend, memorandum, Miranda, referendum.*

TWO ROMAN BEAUTIES

The problem of permanent waves must have been an engrossing one with Roman women! The illustration at the left is of an unknown Roman girl; the one at the right is of Julia, daughter of the Emperor Titus.

XII

OPUSCULUM DUODECIMUM

Was this the face that launched a thousand ships
And burnt the topless towers of Ilium? MARLOWE

77.   **THE FIRST BEAUTY CONTEST**

Nēreō [1] multae fīliae erant, quae Nēreidēs appellātae sunt. Pulcherrimae erant Nēreidēs, quārum Thetis erat pulchrior quam sorōrēs. Eam Nēreus Pēleō in mātrimōnium dedit. Iuppiter ad nūptiās Pēleī et Thetidis deōs deāsque omnēs, 5 Discordiā exceptā, convocāvit. Discordia īrāta iniūriam ulcīscī dēcrēvit. Ea, cum omnēs ad cēnam nūptiālem essent, mediōs in deōs et deās [2] aureum mālum iēcit.

"Pulcherrimae," inquit, "hoc sit praemium."

Statim, cum omnēs deae mālum sibi cuperent, summum erat 10 certāmen dē praemiō maximē inter Iūnōnem, Venerem, Mi-

nervam. Clāmitābant, " Eāmus [3] ad Iovem, ut pulcherrimam
ēligat." Sed Iuppiter, nē eārum animōs in perpetuum in sē
incitāret, respondit, " Nē deus iūdicet."

Paridem, fīlium Priamī, rēgis Trōiae, ad rem iūdicandam
ēlēgit. Mercuriō imperāvit ut deās cupidās praemī in Īdam 15
montem dūceret, ut Paris, quī ibi ovēs custōdiēbat, iūdicāret.

Magnum erat opus iūdicandī quae dea esset pulcherrima.
Trēs deae Paridī clam dīxērunt quod praemium eī darent.

Iūnō, " Sī," inquit, " mē pulcherrimam iūdicāveris, magnum
tibi imperium dabō." Minerva prōmīsit eum omnium sapien- 20
tissimum virum futūrum esse. Venus sē eī pulcherrimam
fēminam orbis terrārum uxōrem datūram esse prōmīsit. Paris,
quibus audītīs, Venerem pulcherrimam iūdicāvit, " Venus habeat [4] aureum mālum."

Hōc tempore pulcherrima fēmina erat Helena, uxor Menelāī, 25
rēgis Lacedaemonis, quam multī nōbilissimī in mātrimōnium
dūcere cupīverant. Tandem Paris omnēs fōrmam Helenae
ēgregiam laudāre audīvit. Ad Venerem īre mātūrāvit. " Volō,"
inquit, " ut mihi uxōrem prōmissam dēs."

Venus Paridī imperāvit ut Lacedaemonem īret [5] et Helenam 30
victam amōre Trōiam dūceret. Paris laetus Venerī pāruit.
Nāve celeriter parātā, in Graeciam profectus est. Cum mare
trānsīsset et Lacedaemonem advēnisset, in amīcitiam ā Menelāō
rēge receptus est. Paris, auxiliō Veneris ūsus, Helenae facile
persuādet ut ūnā sēcum Trōiam eat.[6]   35

Ob hanc perfidiam īrātus Menelāus cum Graecīs [7] multīs et
nōbilissimīs eum Trōiam secūtus est. Haec erat causa bellī [8]
quod Graecī decem annōs ad Trōiam gessērunt.

78.   REQUIRED VOCABULARY

clam secretly (*adv.*)   perfidia, -ae, *f.* treachery
ēgregius, -a, -um remarkable   perpetuus, -a, -um continuous
fōrma, -ae, *f.* beauty   in perpetuum (*tempus*) forever
incitō, -āre, -āvī, -ātus incite   trānseō, -īre, -iī, -itus go across
laudō, -āre, -āvī, -ātus praise   ūnā along with (*adv.*)

79.　　　　　NOTES ON THE STORY

1. Nereus with his fifty daughters dwelt in the depths of the sea.
2. **mediōs . . . deās:** *into the midst of the gods and goddesses.*
3. **Eāmus:** *let us go.*
4. **Venus habeat:** *let Venus have.*
5. **ut, īret:** *that he go;* translate *to go.*
6. **eat:** present subjunctive of **eō.**
7. **cum Graecīs:** Helen's former suitors had taken an oath to avenge any wrong done to her or her husband.
8. **bellī:** Helen of Troy and the Trojan war which followed her abduction have been the inspiration of many writers. The greatest Greek poet, Homer, in the *Iliad* narrates the story of the last year of the siege of Troy, and in the *Odyssey* describes the wanderings and adventures of Odysseus (Ulysses) on his journey back home to Ithaca after the fall of Troy. Vergil, Rome's greatest poet, in the *Aeneid* follows the fortunes of another of the heroes who survived this war, Aeneas, the founder of the Roman race.

80.　　　　　COMPREHENSION

1. How did the contest arise? **2.** What return did each contestant for the prize offer the judge for a favorable decision? **3.** What connection had this contest with the Trojan war?

81.　　　　　RĒS GRAMMATICAE

Independent volitive subjunctive (580). The subjunctives used in preceding opuscula have all been in subordinate clauses. They were used in indirect questions, and in purpose, **cum,** and result clauses. In this opusculum the subjunctive is used in principal clauses to express an act as willed : **Hoc sit praemium,** *let this be the prize ;* **nē deus iūdicet,** *let not a god decide.* This independent subjunctive, called the volitive, usually occurs in the first and third persons and is generally translated by *let.* The negative is **nē** instead of **nōn.** For the second person the imperative is regularly used : **Dā mihi praemium,** *give me the prize ;* **nōlī mihi praemium dare,** *do not (be unwilling) give me the prize.*

Substantive volitive subjunctive (589). A volitive subjunctive is often used in a subordinate clause which is the object of a

From a Greek vase painting

GETTING READY FOR THE CONTEST

verb meaning *to will* or *command*. Such a clause is called a *substantive (noun) clause*: **Imperat ut hoc sit praemium,** *he orders that this be the prize;* **imperāvit nē hoc esset praemium,** *he ordered that this should not be the prize.*

Accusative of place to which (529). Limit of motion, or place to which, is expressed by the accusative with a preposition: **in Graeciam profectus est,** *he set out for Greece.* With names of towns and with **domus,** *home,* the accusative is used without a preposition: **Paris Trōiam vēnit,** *Paris came to Troy.*

82.   EXERCISE

Point out at least one example of: substantive volitive clause, independent volitive, **cum** circumstantial clause, **cum** adversative clause, clause of purpose, deponent verb, indirect question, ablative absolute, gerund, gerundive, dative with a special verb, future perfect indicative, future infinitive, primary sequence of tenses, accusative of place to which, dative of possession.

Respondē Latīnē: **1.** Quid Discordia deābus dīxit? **2.** Quid dīxit Iuppiter? **3.** Cūr Venus imperāvit ut Paris Lacedaemonem īret?

Scrībe Latīnē: **1.** Let the gods praise the remarkable beauty of that girl. **2.** Let Discord not go to the banquet. **3.** The god ordered Discord not to go. **4.** The case (**rēs**) must be judged by the son of Priam. **5.** Venus commands Paris to cross the sea.

83.   WORD STUDY

To what word in the story is each of these related: *convocation, elect, imperious, irate, laudatory, nuptial, perfidy, perpetuity, pulchritude?*

It is interesting to recognize the descendants of Latin words in different modern languages: descendants of **soror** are **sœur,** French; **sorella,** Italian; **sor,** Spanish; and **sorosis,** English.

Courtesy of The Classical Center, Los Angeles

ANCIENT LIFE IN VASE PAINTINGS

The beautiful black-figured cup and red-figured vase and mixing bowl here shown are Greek originals in the collection of antiquities, illustrative of the life of the ancient Greeks, Romans, and Etruscans, which has been assembled by the Classical Center of the Los Angeles Schools.

XIII

OPUSCULUM TERTIUM DECIMUM

REITERANDUM EST

Forsan et haec ōlim meminisse iuvābit.
Perchance sometime it will please you to remember these things.

VERGIL

84. EXERCISE

1. *Decline:* **aliud onus, quīdam campus. 2.** Write the synopsis in the third person plural of: **arbitror** in the indicative; **sequor** in the subjunctive. **3.** Identify as to mood, voice, tense, person, and number: **lātus est, eam, vīs, nōlēmus, tulissētis, mālēbant, ieram, voluerīs, secūtus erit, arbitrārētur. 4.** Give the forms for the gerund and gerundive of: **incitō, persuādeō, sūmō, prōgredior. 5.** Give the synopsis in the indicative and subjunctive: active and passive of **ferō,** first person singular; **nōlō,** second person plural.

1. *Give the synopsis in the indicative and subjunctive of:* **volō** and **eō** in the first person plural; **fīō** and **mālō** in the third person plural. **2.** Give

54

the synopsis of **laudō** in the passive periphrastic conjugation, indicative and subjunctive, second person singular. **3.** Write the subjunctive of **sum**.

1. *Name:* three compound verbs with which the dative case is used; three ways of expressing purpose; five deponent verbs with which the ablative case is used; five special verbs with which the dative case is used; the nine irregular adjectives; the primary tenses, the secondary tenses. **2.** Give the rule for sequence of tenses.

How is each of the following expressed in Latin: result; negative command; place to which; indirect question; a clause of circumstance; a command in the third person; a command in a substantive clause; the agent with the passive periphrastic conjugation? Write an English sentence illustrating the use of each.

Write the Latin for the italicized words: A. **1.** Daedalus *went* (*betook himself*) to Crete *for the purpose of aiding his father.* **2.** He said, " *I must make wings.*" **3.** *Since Thisbe had sent the letter,* her lover followed her. **4.** *She prefers to remain* in the cave. **5.** The parents said, " *Do not go home.*"

B. **1.** *Although the lion did not see her,* the girl was thoroughly frightened. **2.** *When Pyramus opened his eyes,* he saw her. **3.** The queen *attempts to kill herself.* **4.** The god of the sun asks *why Phaëthon wishes* to drive his horses. **5.** At last Apollo *will favor his son.*

C. **1.** Midas was so unhappy *that he cried aloud,* " I shall die." **2.** Deucalion and Pyrrha *are borne* to a lofty mountain. **3.** Neptune *was in charge of the sea.* **4.** Hercules undertook his labors *that he might be freed from servitude.* **5.** Venus orders Psyche *to depart from her sight.*

D. **1.** *Menelaus* (use dative) *had* a wife praised for her beauty. **2.** He was sent *to undertake the work* (express in three ways). **3.** Pyramus and Thisbe *had wished to be buried* in the same tomb. **4.** *One sister* said *to the other,* " In a short time *we shall have persuaded her.*"

Scrībe Latīnē: **1.** Do you approve of the young man's plan of flying? **2.** Let that diligent girl be praised. **3.** The most beautiful goddess was to be selected by the king's son. **4.** The tables became gold. **5.** Have you enjoyed the gods and heroes of these stories?

85.   REVIEW OF REQUIRED VOCABULARY

Each of the following words is derived from, or connected in derivation with, a word in the required vocabularies of *Opuscula* I–XII.   Give the

Latin word suggested by each and its meaning. Define the English word on the basis of its Latin derivation: *e.g., abuse* is derived from **ūsus,** perfect participle of **ūtor,** *use,* combined with **ab,** *away from.* It means *away from use, misuse.* *Adolescence* is derived from **adulēscēns, -entis,** *young man,* and means the *period of young manhood.*

Abscond, adverb, alacrity, arbitrate, audacity, avalanche, aversion, benevolent, camp, clause, collaborator, concession, conference, congratulation, consecutive, convert, decree, desert, detect, digit, diligent, dirigible, disperse, divisor, egregious, elegant, era, estuary, excess, exit, exonerate, expert, exploration, extravagant, famine, fiat, fiduciary, hour.

Incense, incipient, inductive, inference, inoculate, intangible, interim, interrogative, invention, involuntary, lapidary, laud, loquacious, mode, patient, perfidious, perish, perpetual, persuasive, posterior, precarious, present, presumption, probation, progression, referee, relation, restitution, reversible, sagittarius, servitude, solar, sorority, susceptible, tangent, teetotaler, transient, ulterior, utilitarian, vacuum, verbose, vivacious.

From a Greek vase

ANCIENT LIFE IN VASE PAINTINGS

IMPERIUM ROMANUM

Scale of Miles

0   100   200   300   400   500

Roman territory at time of Caesar's death, 44 B.C.

Additions made to Roman territory by the end of
Hadrian's reign. 138 A.D.

ROMA

CAMPUS
MARTIUS

IANICULUM

MONS
CAPITOLINUS

PONS
SUBLICIUS

Tiberis Fl.

FORUM
VIA SACRA

MONS
PALATINUS

CIRCUS
MAXIMUS

MONS
AVENTINUS

MONS ESQUILINUS

MONS
CAELIUS

VIA FLAMINIA

COLLIS QUIRINALIS

COLLIS VIMINALIS

Agger Servi Tulli

VIA APPIA

MARE CASPIUM

ACFA

(Danube)

Tomi

PONTUS EUXINUS
(BLACK SEA)

CAUCASUS MONS

Phasis Fl.
Phasis

COLCHIS

THRACIA
Salmydessus

Byzantium
(Constantinople)
Bosporus

ARMENIA

S
I
A

Hellespont
Troja
(Troy)
MYSIA

Cyzicum

BITHYNIA

Ancyra

GALATIA

PONTUS

ASIA

CAPPADOCIA

CILICIA

MESOPOTAMIA

ASSYRIA

Tigris

PARTHIA

MARE
AEU

Pactolus
Fl.

Ephesus

Antiochia

Euphrates

Babylon

Fl.

athenae
aemon MARE
arta ICARIUM

RHODUS

CYPRUS

PHOENICIA

SYRIA

Ida
ons CRETA

Sidon

R U M

Hierosolyma
(Jerusalem)

PALESTINA

Alexandria

ARABIA

AEGYPTUS

Nilus Fl.
(Nile)

GENERAL DRAFTING CO., INC., N.Y.

PART II

THE ARGONAUTS

An Ancient Greek Story of Adventure

And mistily, as through a veil,
I catch the glances of a sea
Of sapphire dimpled with a gale
Toward Colch's blowing, where the sail
Of Jason's Argo beckons me.

JAMES WHITCOMB RILEY

Pretium labōris nōn vīle, *The reward of toil not cheap.*
MOTTO OF THE ORDER OF THE GOLDEN FLEECE

The story of Jason and the Argonauts in their search for the Golden Fleece is an ancient Greek tale full of wonderful adventure. Jason, the hero and leader of the expedition, was the son of Aeson, King of Thessaly. The story tells why Jason decided to go on the expedition for which Argus built the good ship Argo; what perilous experiences Jason and his fifty heroic companions had on their journey to Colchis, where the Golden Fleece was hidden; how they finally succeeded in their quest with the help of Medea, the daughter of the king of Colchis, who was an enchantress; and how the love story of Jason and Medea ended in tragedy.

The story was originally told in the third century B.C. by a Greek writer, Apollonius of Rhodes. *The Argonauts,* a prose translation of this poem by R. C. Seaton, is in the Loeb Classical Library. A poetic translation has been made by A. S. Way. Other interesting versions of the story are: *The Argonauts,* by Gaius Valerius Flaccus, a Latin writer, translated by Thomas Noble; *The Life and Death of Jason,* a poem by William Morris; and *The Golden Fleece* in *Tanglewood Tales* by Nathaniel Hawthorne.

> May Colchis curse the dawn of day when first she thundered free
> And our golden captain, Jason, in glory put to sea!
> WILLIAM ROSE BENÉT, *The Argo's Chantey* *

---

* From *Merchants from Cathay,* by William Rose Benét, published by Yale University Press.

58

From an engraving by Bernard Picart   *Courtesy of Newark Public Library*

THE ARGO PASSES THROUGH THE CLASHING ROCKS

JASON RELATES THE STORY OF HIS ADVENTURES

XIV

OPUSCULUM QUĀRTUM DECIMUM

This Pelias, being covetous and strong
And full of wiles, and deeming naught was wrong
That wrought him good, thrust Aeson from his throne,
And over all the Minyae reigned alone.*

86.   SAVED FROM A WICKED UNCLE

Erant ōlim in Thessaliā [1] duo frātrēs, quōrum alter Aesōn,[2] alter Peliās appellābātur. Ex hīs Aesōn prīmum rēgnum obtinuerat; at post paucōs annōs Peliās, rēgnī cupiditāte adductus,[3] nōn modo frātrem suum expulit, sed etiam in animō
5 habēbat Iāsonem, Aesonis fīlium, interficere. Quīdam tamen ex amīcīs [4] Aesonis, ubi sententiam Peliae intellēxērunt, puerum ē tantō perīculō ēripere cōnstituērunt. Noctū igitur Iāsonem ex urbe abstulērunt, et cum posterō diē ad rēgem

*This quotation and all those used as headings in Part II, unless otherwise specified, are from *The Life and Death of Jason* by William Morris.

government

rediissent, eī renūntiāvērunt puerum mortuum esse. Peliās
cum haec audīvisset, etsī rē vērā [5] magnum gaudium per-
cipiēbat, speciem tamen dolōris praebuit, et quae causa essēt
mortis [6] quaesīvit. Illī tamen cum intellegerent [7] dolōrem
eius falsum esse,[8] fābulam dē morte puerī fīnxērunt.

make imagine

87.   NOTES ON THE STORY

1. **Thessaliā:** follow on a map the course of the voyage of the Argonauts.
2. **Aesōn:** predicate nominative with **appellābātur.**
3. **rēgnī . . . adductus:** *influenced by a desire for (of) royal power.*
4. **Quīdam, ex amīcīs:** *certain (of the) friends.*
5. **rē vērā:** translate *in fact.*
6. **quae . . . mortis:** *what was the cause of his death;* an indirect question.
7. **cum intellegerent:** a causal clause.
8. **dolōrem . . . esse:** translate *that his grief was assumed.*

88.   COMPREHENSION

1. Why was a false report of Jason's death made to Pelias? **2.** How
did Pelias act when he heard the report of Jason's death?

89.   RĒS GRAMMATICAE

Objective genitive (512). You have learned that the genitive
case in Latin corresponds to the possessive case in English:
Aesonis fīlius, *Aeson's son.* In Latin, in such phrases as **amor
patriae,** *love of country,* and **spēs lībertātis,** *hope of liberty,* the
genitive case is also used to denote the object of the feeling expressed by a noun or adjective containing a verbal idea. In
the phrase, **rēgnī cupiditāte,** *by a desire of power,* l. 3, **rēgnī**
indicates the object of the feeling expressed by **cupiditāte** and
the phrase is equivalent to a verb and its object, **rēgnum cupit,** *he
desires power.* A genitive so used is called an *objective genitive.*

90.   EXERCISE

*Iterātiō:** *A.* **1.** Point out in the story: nouns of the *first declension* (**468**);
of the *second declension* (**469**). **2.** Decline: **causa, fābula, annus, rēgnum.**

     Iterātiō, review, is derived from the Latin verb **iterō,** meaning *do a second time.*

3. Conjugate in the indicative active, present, imperfect, and future tenses (**492**) : **appellō, habeō, intellegō, audiō. 4.** Identify as to person, number, and tense : **habēs, appellābat, habēbit, intellegēmus, audītis, interficiam, habēbunt.**

B. **1.** Point out in the story : two different uses of the *nominative case* (**507–8**) ;· two examples of the *possessive genitive* (**509**) ; one example of the *ablative of time when* (**553**).

Respondē Latīnē : **1.** Cuius cupiditāte Peliās addūcēbātur? **2.** Quis erat Iāsōn? **3.** Quid amīcī Aesonis faciēbant?

Scrībe Latīnē : **1.** The son of Aeson is called Jason. **2.** Desire for the kingdom was not the cause of his death. **3.** Although friends report the opinion of Pelias, still Jason shows no appearance of grief. **4.** The king's son will not only return in the following year, but will also obtain the kingdom.

91.   VERBA

Master each word in the required vocabulary by learning its meaning; the genitive and gender of each noun; the principal parts of each verb; and the nominative forms of each adjective.

Required Vocabulary : **at, causa, cupiditās, etsī, modo, noctū, obtineō, praebeō, redeō, renūntiō, sententia, speciēs.**

Word Study. The suffix -tās (in English -*ty*), denoting *a state of*, added to adjective or noun stems, forms feminine nouns of the third declension. For example, **cupiditās** is formed from **cupidus,** *eager,* and the suffix -tās (**cupidi-** + -tās), and means *state of being eager* or *eagerness, desire.* What nouns are formed with the suffix -tās from : **vērus, posterus,** and **paucus?**

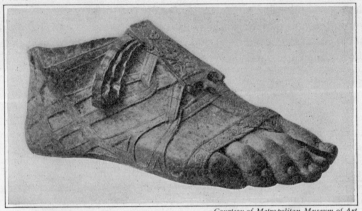

AN ANCIENT SHOE

The shoe, **calceus,** worn by Jason was similar to the sandal, **solea,** shown here, which consists of a heavy leather sole held in place by straps.

XV

OPUSCULUM QUĪNTUM DECIMUM

Now Jason, by Anaurus left alone,
Found that, indeed, his right-foot shoe was gone,
But, as the Goddess bade him, went his way
Halfshod, and by an hour before mid-day
He reached the city gates, and entered there,
Whom the folk mocked, beholding his foot bare.

92.   THE RETURN OF JASON

Post breve tempus Peliās, veritus nē rēgnum suum tantā vī et fraude occupātum āmitteret,[1] amīcum quendam Delphōs [2] mīsit, quī ōrāculum cōnsuleret.[3] Ille igitur quam celerrimē [4] Delphōs sē contulit et quam ob causam vēnisset dēmōnstrāvit. Respondit ōrāculum nūllum esse in praesentiā perīculum; [5] 5 monuit tamen Peliam ut aliquem calceum ūnum gerentem cavēret.[6] Post paucōs annōs accidit ut Peliās magnum sacrificium factūrus esset; [7] nūntiōs in omnēs partēs dīmīserat et

63

diem conveniendī [8] dīxerat. Diē cōnstitūtō magnus numerus
10 hominum undique ex agrīs convēnit; inter aliōs autem vēnit
etiam Iāsōn, quī ā puerō [9] apud centaurum quendam habitāverat.
Dum tamen iter facit, calceum alterum in trānseundō flūmine [10]
āmīsit.

93.   NOTES ON THE STORY

1. **veritus nē . . . āmitteret:** after a verb of fearing, **nē** is translated
that and is used to introduce a substantive clause whose verb is in the
subjunctive. **Ut** in a similar clause is translated *that not.* (**592**)
2. **Delphōs:** *to Delphi;* what accusative is this? (**529**) Apollo's shrine
was at Delphi, and many came there to consult the oracle.
3. **quī . . . cōnsuleret:** *to consult the oracle;* a relative clause expressing
purpose.
4. **quam celerrimē:** translate *as quickly as possible.*
5. **nūllum . . . perīculum:** *that there was no danger for the present.*
6. **ut . . . cavēret:** *to beware of anyone wearing one shoe.*
7. **ut . . . esset:** *that Pelias was going to make a great sacrifice.*
8. **conveniendī:** *for assembling;* the genitive of the gerund.
9. **ā puerō:** *from a boy;* translate *from boyhood.*
10. **in . . . flūmine:** *in crossing a river;* **trānseundō,** what form of the
gerundive?

94.   COMPREHENSION

1. On what occasion did Jason return to the kingdom of his uncle?
2. What misfortune befell him on the way? 3. What connection did this
have with the response sent to Pelias by the oracle?

95.   RĒS GRAMMATICAE

Active periphrastic conjugation (501). The Romans had a
special form to convey the idea of the expression *about to* or *going
to,* meaning *intend : he is going to speak,* **dictūrus est;** *that which
they were going to carry with them,* **id quod sēcum portātūrī erant.**
For this purpose they used the future active participle and a
form of the verb **sum.** This special form is called the *active
periphrastic conjugation.*

Point out one form of the active periphrastic conjugation.

Translate: **ventūrus erat; calceum gestūra est; amīcum missūrī sunt; ōrāculum respōnsūrum est.**

96. EXERCISE

Iterātiō: ‍*A.* **1.** Point out in the story two *adjectives of the first and second declension* (**475**). **2.** Decline **magnus** in all genders. **3.** Conjugate in the *indicative active, perfect, past perfect,* and *future perfect tenses* (**492**): **habitō, moneō, mittō, veniō. 4.** Identify as to person, number, and tense: **monuerāmus, mīsistī, fēcerit, habitāvistis, vēnērunt, monuerō, mīsī, vēnerint.**

B. **1.** Find in the story two adjectives of the first and second declension and show the *agreement of the adjective* with the noun it modifies (**562**). **2.** Point out in the story: five examples of the *accusative of direct object* (**525**); one example of the *accusative of limit of motion* (**529**). **3.** With what *prepositions* in the story is the accusative case used (**533**)?

‍*Respondē Latīnē:* **1.** Quem Delphōs Peliās mīsit? **2.** Cūr Peliās ōrāculum cōnsuluit? **3.** Dē quō perīculō ōrāculum Peliam monuit? **4.** Ubi Iāsōn ā puerō habitāverat?

Scrībe Latīnē: **1.** A few friends went (betook themselves) to Delphi and consulted the oracle. **2.** They are going to send messengers to other kingdoms. **3.** On the appointed day a great number will have assembled from all quarters.

97. VERBA

Required Vocabulary: **accidō, aliquis, cōnsulō, conveniō, undique, vereor.**
Word Study. The suffixes **-ulum, -bulum, -culum** (in English **-le, -ble, -cle**), added to verb stems, form nouns denoting *means, instrument,* or *place:* **ōrāculum** (ōrā- + -culum), the *place* where the responses of the oracle were given. Show how *vehicle* and *stable* are derived from **vehō** and **stō.**

> Contingit use of things we like,
> But **accidit** when evils strike.

> Vereor nē, I fear he will;
> Vereor ut, I fear he won't.

These couplets are from a Latin book published in 1846. Jingles used to be learned to help remember Latin words and rules.

"THE RAM THAT BORE UNSAFELY THE BURDEN OF HELLE." LONGFELLOW

This life-size marble figure of a ram is the work of a Roman artist of the first century A.D. It is one of the finest original specimens of ancient sculpture in this country.

XVI

OPUSCULUM SEXTUM DECIMUM

> Then, if but ten lay hold upon the oar,
> And I, the eleventh, steer them toward the east,
> To seek the hidden fleece of that gold beast,
> I swear to Jove that only in my hand
> The fleece shall be, when I again take land
> To see my father's hall.

98. JASON PROMISES TO OBTAIN THE GOLDEN FLEECE

Iāsōn igitur, cum calceum āmissum nūllō modō recipere posset, ūnō pede nūdō,[1] in rēgiam pervēnit. Illum cum vīdisset Peliās, subitō timōre affectus est; intellēxit enim hunc esse hominem quem ōrāculum dēmōnstrāvisset.[2] Hoc igitur iniit
5 cōnsilium. Rēx erat quīdam Aeētēs, quī rēgnum Colchidis illō tempore obtinēbat. Huic commissum erat vellus illud aureum[3] quod Phrixus ōlim ibi relīquerat. Cōnstituit igitur Peliās Iāsonī negōtium dare, ut hōc vellere potīrētur;[4] cum enim

rēs esset magnī perīculī,[5] spērābat eum in itinere peritūrum
esse.[6] Iāsonem igitur ad sē arcessīvit et quid fierī vellet dēmōn- 10
strāvit. Iāsōn autem, etsī bene intellegēbat rem [7] esse dif-
ficillimam, negōtium libenter suscēpit.

99.   NOTES ON THE STORY

1. **ūnō . . . nūdō:** translate _with one foot bare;_ an ablative absolute.

2. **dēmōnstrāvisset:** the verb in a subordinate clause of indirect discourse
is in the subjunctive.

3. **vellus . . . aureum:** the reference is to the famous Golden Fleece
of the ram which had carried Phrixus and his sister Helle away from their
cruel stepmother. On the way Helle fell off into the sea, which was thereafter called Hellespont from this incident. Phrixus was borne to Colchis,
where he sacrificed the ram. Its fleece was kept in a sacred grove and
guarded by a dragon who never slept.

4. **ut . . . potīrētur:** translate _of obtaining this fleece;_ a substantive
clause in apposition with **negōtium.**   What case is used with **potior?**

5. **magnī perīculī:** translate _very dangerous;_ a genitive of quality or
description used in the predicate.

6. **eum . . . peritūrum esse:** _that he (Jason) would die on the journey;_
an indirect statement depending upon **spērābat.**

7. **rem:** translate _the undertaking._   **Rēs** may be translated by any English word that satisfies the context.

100.   COMPREHENSION

1. Why did Jason's misfortune make Pelias fear him? **2.** How did Pelias
plan to destroy Jason? **3.** Give examples from history or literature of
other quests, for example, the search for the Holy Grail.

101.   EXERCISE

Iterātiō: A. **1.** Decline **hic** and **ille**, all genders (**487**). **2.** Give the Latin
for: _to that kingdom, of this fear, to that man, with this plan._ **3.** Decline:
hic calceus, illud perīculum, haec rēgia. **4.** Conjugate in the _indicative
passive, present, imperfect,_ and _future tenses_ (**492**): **dēmōnstrō, videō, intellegō, recipiō, potior.** **5.** Identify as to person, number, tense, and
voice: **āmittēbar, obtinēs, āmittam, afficientur, datur, obtinēmur, daminī.**

B. **1.** Point out in the story an example of: _ablative of place where_ (**552**);
ablative of means (**546**).

Respondē Latīnē: **1.** Quōmodo Iāsōn in rēgiam pervēnit? **2.** Quō in locō erat illud vellus aureum? **3.** Quis erat rēx Colchidis illō tempore?

Scrībe Latīnē: **1.** Jason was not affected by this great danger. **2.** That man will be summoned by the king. **3.** Since he hoped to recover the golden fleece, he formed this plan. **4.** Was there a king in that great palace?

102.   VERBA

Required Vocabulary: **afficiō, arcessō, ineō, recipiō, spērō.**

Word Study. Find words in the story which contain these prefixes: ā- or ab-, ad-, cum-, dē-, dis-, in-, ob-, per-, sub-. Give the literal meaning of each word. What assimilations of final consonants of prefixes do you find?

Bassanio says of Portia:

> "And her sunny locks
> Hang on her temples like a golden fleece;
> Which makes her seat of Belmont Colchos' strand
> And many Jasons come in quest of her."
>
>   SHAKESPEARE, *Merchant of Venice*, Act I, Scene 1.

Rome, Italy

CAPITAL DECORATED WITH RAMS' HEADS

This ornate capital, fashioned in Corinthian style, is from a column of the Temple of Concordia, which once stood in the Roman Forum.

THE GODS AID ARGUS

XVII

OPUSCULUM SEPTIMUM DECIMUM

So Argus[1] laboured, and the work was sped
Moreover, by a man with hoary head,
Whose dwelling and whose name no man could know,
Who many a secret of the craft did show.

103.   THE BUILDING OF THE ARGO

Cum tamen Colchis multōrum diērum iter ab eō locō abesset,
sōlus Iāsōn proficīscī nōluit. Dīmīsit igitur nūntiōs in omnēs
partēs, quī causam itineris docērent[2] et diem conveniendī
dīcerent. Intereā, postquam omnia quae sunt ūsuī[3] ad armandās nāvēs[4] comportārī iussit, negōtium[5] dedit Argō cuidam, 5
quī summam scientiam rērum nauticārum habēbat, ut nāvem
aedificāret.[5] In hīs rēbus circiter decem diēs cōnsūmptī sunt;
Argus enim, quī operī[6] praeerat, tantam dīligentiam adhibēbat
ut nē nocturnum[7] quidem tempus ad labōrem intermitteret.[8]
Ad multitūdinem hominum multa mīlia passuum[9] trānsportan- 10

69

dam nāvis paulō erat lātior quam quibus [10] in nostrō marī [11]
ūtī cōnsuēvimus, et ad vim tempestātum perferendam tōta [12]
ē rōbore facta est.

104.   NOTES ON THE STORY

1. **Argus:** the gods aided him in his task.

2. **quī, docērent:** translate *to make known*, or *to show*.

3. **ūsuī:** *for a use;* translate *useful.* What form is this?

4. **ad . . . nāvēs:** *for equipping the ships;* **armandās** is the accusative
of the gerundive with **ad** and a noun to express purpose. Point out two
other examples in the story.

5. **negōtium, ut . . . aedificāret:** *the business of building the ship.*

6. **operī:** dative with **praeerat.**

7. **nocturnum:** this word is made emphatic by its position between
nē and **quidem.**

8. **ut . . . intermitteret:** translate *that he did not cease work even at
night.*

9. **multa . . . passuum:** translate *many miles.*

10. **quibus:** (*the ships*) *which;* ablative with **ūtī.**

11. **nostrō marī:** the Mediterranean. To whom does **nostrō** refer?

12. **tōta:** *wholly;* an adjective, but translate as if it were an adverb.

105.   COMPREHENSION

1. How did Jason prepare for his journey? **2.** Why were his preparations
completed so quickly?

106.   RĒS GRAMMATICAE

Relative clause of purpose (585). Section **19** gives examples
of purpose clauses introduced by **ut** or **nē** with their verbs in
the subjunctive. In the sentences, **dīmīsit nūntiōs quī causam
itineris docērent,** *he sent out messengers to (who should) show the
cause of the journey,* l. 2, and **Peliās amīcum quendam Delphōs
mīsit, quī ōrāculum cōnsuleret,** *Pelias sent a certain friend to
Delphi to (who should) consult the oracle* (**92**), what is the introductory word of each purpose clause? What is its antecedent?

If a definite antecedent is expressed or implied in the main clause, a relative pronoun may be used to introduce the clause of purpose.

Dative of purpose (523). In the sentence, *he gives a book as a present*, the phrase, *as a present*, states the purpose of the action indicated by the verb *gives*. In Latin, *as a present* is expressed by the dative **dōnō: librum dōnō dat**; *he selected a place for a camp*, **locum castrīs dēlēgit. Ūsuī**, *for a use*, l. 4, expresses purpose. This dative, naming that *for which* a thing serves, is called the *dative of purpose*.

107.   EXERCISE

Iterātiō: A. **1.** Point out in the story five *nouns of the third declension* (**470–1**). **2.** Decline: **iter nocturnum, nāvis lāta, summum opus. 3.** Review the *conjugation of* **sum** in the indicative (**495**). **4.** Identify as to person, number, tense, and voice: **estis, erant, erimus, fuistī, fueram, fuerit.**

B. **1.** Find in the story one example of: *accusative of extent of space* (**530**); *dative with a compound verb* (**518**).

Respondē Latīnē: **1.** Cūr Iāsōn sōlus nōn proficīscitur? **2.** Quis operī praeest? **3.** Quālem nāvem Argus aedificāvit? **4.** Cūr erat paulō lātior nāvis?

Scrībe Latīnē: **1.** The ship endured a very great storm for about ten miles. **2.** The multitude will collect all things (**omnia**) which will be of use (for a use) for equipping ships. **3.** He sends men to build the ship. **4.** The men who are in charge of the work are not accustomed to interrupt their labor even at night time.

108.   VERBA

Required Vocabulary: **armō, circiter, cōnsuēscō, cōnsūmō, intermittō, nocturnus, paulō, perferō, postquam, quidem, tempestās, ūsus.**

Word Study. Give the formation and meaning of **dīligentia** and **scientia**. What is the English equivalent of the Latin suffix **-ia** or **-tia**?

With the suffix **-tūdō** what nouns are formed from the adjectives: **lātus, multus, sōlus?** Give the English equivalent of each.

THE ARGO

Courtesy of Museum of Fine Arts, Boston

Orpheus hath harped her,
Her prow hath drunk the sea. WILLIAM ROSE BENÉT *

XVIII

OPUSCULUM DUODĒVĪCĒSIMUM

And now behold within the haven rides
Our good ship, swinging in the changing tides.

109. THE ARGO SAILS WITH MANY HEROES ABOARD

Intereā is diēs appetēbat quem Iāsōn per nūntiōs ēnūn-
tiāverat, et ex omnibus regiōnibus Graeciae multī, quōs aut reī
novitās aut spēs glōriae movēbat, undique conveniēbant. Trāditum est autem in hōc numerō fuisse Herculem, dē quō suprā
5 multa perscrīpsimus, Orpheum,[1] citharoedum praeclārissimum,
Thēseum,[2] Castorem,[3] multōsque aliōs quōrum nōmina sunt
nōtissima. Ex hīs Iāsōn, quōs[4] arbitrātus est ad omnia perīcula
subeunda[5] parātissimōs esse, eōs ad numerum quīnquāgintā
dēlēgit et sociōs sibi adiūnxit; tum paucōs diēs commorātus, ut
10 ad omnēs cāsūs subsidia comparāret, nāvem dēdūxit, et tempestātem ad nāvigandum[6] idōneam nactus, magnō cum gaudiō
omnium solvit.[7]

110.   NOTES ON THE STORY

1. **Orpheum:** by his music he could charm wild beasts and move rocks
and trees.

* From *The Argo's Chantey* in MERCHANTS FROM CATHAY, published by Yale University Press

2. **Thēseum:** the national hero of Athens; his most famous act was the killing of the Minotaur.

3. **Castorem:** the half brother of Pollux. They were so devoted to each other that when Castor was killed, Pollux, though immortal, took Castor's place in Hades every other day.

4. **quōs:** its antecedent is eōs, object of dēlēgit.

5. **ad . . . subeunda:** *to undergo all dangers.*

6. **ad nāvigandum:** *for sailing.*

7. **solvit:** nāvem is understood.

111.   COMPREHENSION

1. Why did so many heroes wish to go with Jason? **2.** On what basis did Jason choose his companions? **3.** Why did he not set sail at once?

112.   RĒS GRAMMATICAE

Impersonal use of verbs (502). In Latin, as in English, some verbs do not have a personal subject: **pluit,** *it rains;* **accidit,** *it happens.* Such verbs are called *impersonal verbs.* Impersonal verbs often have an infinitive phrase or a substantive clause as subject: **licet īre,** *it is permitted to go;* **multa oportet discat,** *it is necessary to learn many things.*

Verbs are used impersonally in Latin more often than in English, especially in the passive of intransitive verbs: **pugnātum est,** *it was fought,* instead of **pugnāvērunt** for *they fought;* **ventum est,** instead of **vēnērunt,** *they came.* **Trāditum est,** l. 3, *it has been handed down,* is used impersonally with the infinitive phrase, **fuisse Herculem,** as its subject.

113.   EXERCISE

Iterātiō: A. **1.** Point out in the story: a noun of the *fourth declension* (**473**); the demonstrative is (**487**). **2.** Decline: ea regiō, id subsidium, is cāsus. **3.** Give the *comparison of the adjectives:* nōtus, magnus, praeclārus, multus. **4.** Conjugate in the *indicative passive, perfect, past perfect,* and *future perfect tenses* (**492**): moveō, conveniō, comparō, dēdūcō. **5.** Give the synopsis of dēligō in all tenses of the indicative, active and passive, third person, singular number. **6.** Identify as to person, number, and tense: dēductus est, comparātī erunt, mōtī erāmus, dēlēctī sunt.

B. **1.** Point out in the story: an *ablative of manner* (**542**); an *accusative of extent or duration of time* (**530**).

Respondē Latīnē: **1.** Cūr paucōs diēs commorātī sunt? **2.** Quid dē sociīs Iāsonis trāditum est? **3.** Quōmodo Iāsōn nāvem solvit?

Scrībe Latīnē: **1.** This most famous ship had been launched with great danger. **2.** Jason's comrades were influenced either by the hope of glory or the danger of the enterprise (**rēs**). **3.** Aid from this region will have been obtained for the emergencies. **4.** It was reported that Jason had sailed.

114.   VERBA

Required Vocabulary: cāsus, commoror, dēdūcō, ēnūntiō, glōria, nancīscor, regiō, solvō, subsidium, suprā.

Word Study. Give and define ten English words derived from solvō.

From a Greek vase painting

AN ANCIENT SHIP

XIX

OPUSCULUM ŪNDĒVĪCĒSIMUM

So when they had done this thing,
They saw the face of Cyzicus the king.
But Jason, when he saw him, wept and said:
" Ill hast thou fared, O friend, that I was led
To take thy gifts and slay thee."

115. THE FATAL RESULT OF MISTAKEN IDENTITY

Nōn multō post[1] Argonautae, ita enim appellātī sunt quī in istā nāvī vehēbantur, īnsulam quandam, nōmine[2] Cyzicum, attigērunt et, ē nāvī ēgressī, ā rēge illīus regiōnis magnō hospitiō[3] exceptī sunt. Paucīs post hōrīs ad sōlis occāsum rūrsus solvērunt. At, postquam pauca mīlia passuum[4] prōgressī sunt, tanta tempestās subitō coorta est ut cursum tenēre nōn possent, et in eandem partem īnsulae unde nūper profectī erant magnō cum perīculō dēicerentur. Incolae tamen, cum nox esset, Argonautās nōn agnōscēbant et, nāvem inimīcam vēnisse arbitrātī, arma rapuērunt et eōs ēgredī prohibēbant.[5] Ācriter in lītore pugnātum est,[6] et rēx ipse, quī cum aliīs dēcucurrerat, ab Argonautīs[7] occīsus est. Mox tamen, cum iam lūx esset, sēnsērunt incolae sē errāre et arma abiēcērunt; Argonautae autem, cum vidērent rēgem occīsum esse, magnum dolōrem percēpērunt. 5 10 15

116. NOTES ON THE STORY

1. **Nōn . . . post:** translate *a little later*. What is the literal translation?

2. **nōmine:** *by name;* an ablative of specification (**551**).

3. **hospitiō:** what use of the ablative? Find another example.

4. **passuum:** what case?

5. **eōs . . . prohibēbant:** translate *tried to keep them from going ashore.*

6. **pugnātum est**: *they fought;* what use of the verb?

7. **Argonautīs**: what use of the ablative (**538**)? From what two nouns is this word formed?

117.   COMPREHENSION

1. What misfortune overtook the Argonauts soon after they set sail?
2. What mistake was made? With what fatal outcome?

118.   RĒS GRAMMATICAE

Ablative of measure of difference (550). In the phrase, **paucīs post hōrīs**, *a few hours later*, l. 4, the ablative **hōrīs** is used with the adverb **post** to show *how much* later it was; *i.e., by a few hours.* It is called the *ablative of measure of difference* and is used generally with adverbs and comparatives.

Translate the following phrases literally: **multīs ante diēbus; paulō longius.**

Genitive of the whole (510). Latin corresponds to English in the use of a genitive to express the *whole* with a word denoting a part; **multī incolārum**, *many of the inhabitants;* **pars urbis**, *part of the city.* But Latin differs from English in using the *genitive of the whole* with neuter pronouns and adjectives used substantively: **nihil novī**, *nothing (of) new;* **satis causae**, *sufficient (of) cause;* **minus dolōris**, *less (of) sorrow.* Give the literal translation of **mīlia passuum**, l. 5.

119.   EXERCISE

Iterātiō: A. **1.** Point out in the story two of the *nine irregular adjectives* (**478**). **2.** Decline the intensive pronoun **ipse** (**488**). **3.** Decline **ipsa nāvis, alius cursus.** **4.** Give the Latin for: *of the whole ship, to the other inhabitants, of one island, of grief alone.* **5.** Conjugate in the *subjunctive, active* and *passive, present* and *imperfect* (**492**): **appellō, videō, attingō, sentiō.** **6.** Identify as to mood, voice, tense, person, and number: **dēicerentur, esset, appellet, vehant, agnōscēbant, vidērent.**

B. **1.** Point out in the story: two examples of the *ablative of agent* (**538**); two **cum** *causal clauses* (**604**).

Respondē Latīnē: **1.** Cūr Argonautae ita appellātī sunt? **2.** Quot mīlia passuum Argonautae prōgressī erant? **3.** Vēnēruntne Argonautae in lītus alīus īnsulae?

Scrībe Latīnē: **1.** Since the storm was so great, they again held their course toward the west whence they themselves had set out. **2.** A few hours later they were received with great hospitality by the king of the island. **3.** When the ship had reached the shore, a part of the inhabitants suddenly seized their arms.

120. **VERBA**

Required Vocabulary: **attingō, cursus, ēgredior, excipiō, iste, ita, lītus, occāsus, rūrsus, subitō, unde, vehō.**

Word Study. From what verbs in the story are the following nouns derived: **raptor, arbitrātor, pugnātor?** Define each.

The word *Argonauts* (**Argo + nauta**), originally applied to Jason and the band of heroes who sailed with him on the Argo, later was used to characterize persons beginning a hazardous enterprise, particularly a long and dangerous journey in quest of something. The name has frequently been applied to the gold seekers who crossed the continent to California in '49. Bret Harte says, "I regard the story of the Argonauts of '49 as an episode in American life as quaint as that of the Greek adventurers."

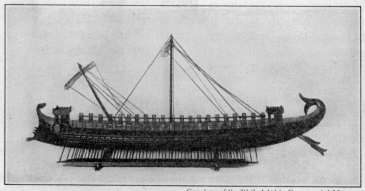

Courtesy of the Philadelphia Commercial Museum

A GREEK TRIREME

XX

OPUSCULUM VĪCĒSIMUM

And bore him, sleeping still, as by some spell,
Unto the depths where they were wont to dwell.

121.   HYLAS IS KIDNAPPED BY THE NYMPHS

Postrīdiē eius diēī [1] Iāsōn, tempestātem satis idōneam esse arbitrātus, summa enim tranquillitās iam cōnsecūta erat, ancorās sustulit et, pauca mīlia passuum prōgressus, ante noctem Mȳsiam attigit. Ibi paucās hōrās in ancorīs [2] exspectāvit; 5 ā nautīs enim cognōverat aquae cōpiam quam sēcum [3] habērent [4] iam dēficere; quam ob causam quīdam ex Argonautīs, in terram ēgressī, aquam quaerēbant. Hōrum in numerō erat Hylās quīdam, puer fōrmā maximā; [5] quī, dum fontem quaerit, ā comitibus paulum sēcesserat. Nymphae autem quae fontem 10 colēbant, cum iuvenem vīdissent, eī persuādēre cōnātae sunt ut sēcum manēret; [6] et cum ille negāret sē hoc factūrum esse, [7] puerum vī abstulērunt.

Comitēs eius, postquam Hylam āmissum esse sēnsērunt, magnō dolōre affectī, diū frūstrā quaerēbant. Herculēs autem 15 et Polyphēmus, quī vēstīgia puerī longius secūtī erant, ubi tandem ad lītus rediērunt, Iāsonem solvisse [8] cognōvērunt.

122.   NOTES ON THE STORY

1. **Postrīdiē eius diēī:** translate *on the following day;* an idiom.

2. **in ancorīs:** translate *at anchor.*

3. **sēcum:** = **cum sē**; the preposition **cum** is used regularly as an enclitic following a personal, reflexive, or relative pronoun which is its object.

4. **habērent:** the subjunctive in a subordinate clause of indirect statement.

5. **fōrmā maximā:** translate *of extraordinary beauty;* an ablative of description.

diū, diūtius, diūtissimē

6. **ut . . . manēret:** *that he remain with them;* object of **persuādēre.**

7. **cum . . . esse:** *when he said that he would not do this;* the verb **negō** is translated regularly, *say . . . not,* with the negative idea transferred to the clause which is dependent on **negō.**

8. **solvisse: nāvem** is the object understood; an indirect statement. Hercules returned to Greece after the expedition had sailed away without him.

123. COMPREHENSION

1. What adventure did the Argonauts have at Mysia? 2. Who was lost here? How?

124. EXERCISE

Iterātiō: A. 1. Decline: **diēs; magna rēs (474)**. 2. Point out a *reflexive pronoun of the third person* (**486**). 3. Give the Latin for: *he saw himself, they had this with them, she persuades herself.* 4. Conjugate in the *subjunctive, active* and *passive, perfect* and *past perfect* (**492**): **exspectō, videō, tollō, dēficiō, sentiō.** 5. Give the synopsis of **sum** in the subjunctive, third person, singular number. 6. Identify as to mood, voice, tense, person, and number: **habērent, vīdissent, fuissem, exspectātus sit, quaerit, vīderint, sēnsī essent, faciam, fuerītis.**

B. 1. Point out in the story: an example of the *dative with special verbs* (**517**); a *substantive volitive clause* (**589**).

Respondē Latīnē: 1. Sēnsēruntne quam ob causam quīdam ex Argonautīs cum Nymphīs mānsisset? 2. Quālis puer erat Hylās? 3. Quid Nymphae Hylae persuādēre cōnātae sunt ut faceret?

Scrībe Latīnē: 1. Since supplies were lacking, they weighed anchor on the following day. 2. They persuaded their comrades to seek the boy with them. 3. For a long time the sailors sought Hylas in vain.

125. VERBA

Required Vocabulary: **ancora, dēficiō, diū, frūstrā, nauta, negō, postrīdiē, quaerō, satis, tollō.**

Word Study. Define the following words derived from **quaerō,** showing that each contains the idea of *seeking: acquire, acquisition, exquisite, inquest, inquisitive, prerequisite, quest, requisition.*

Define **sēcēdō, redeō,** and **prōgredior,** showing the force of the prefix in each.

From a Greek vase painting

THE HARPIES

XXI

OPUSCULUM VĪCĒSIMUM PRĪMUM

These through the hall unheard-of shrieking sent,
And rushed at Phineus, just as to his mouth
He raised the golden cup to quench his drouth,
And scattered the red wine, and buffeted
The wretched king.

126. PHINEUS SAVED FROM THE HARPIES

Post haec Argonautae ad Thrāciam cursum tenuērunt, et,
postquam ad oppidum Salmydēssum nāvem appulerant, in
terram ēgressī sunt. Ibi cum ab incolīs quaesīssent quis rēgnum
eius regiōnis obtinēret, certiōrēs factī sunt [1] Phīneum quendam
5 tum rēgem esse. Cognōvērunt etiam hunc caecum esse et dīrō
quōdam suppliciō afficī, quod ōlim sē crūdēlissimum in fīliōs
suōs praebuisset.[2] Cuius suplicī hoc erat genus. Missa erant
ā Iove mōnstra quaedam speciē horribilī, quae capita virgi-
num, corpora avium habēbant. Hae avēs, quae Harpȳiae
10 appellābantur, Phīneō summam molestiam afferēbant; quotiēns enim ille accubuerat,[3] veniēbant et cibum statim auferēbant.
Rēs igitur male sē habēbat cum Argonautae nāvem appu-
lērunt. Phīneus autem, simul atque audīvit eōs in suōs fīnīs

ēgressōs esse, magnopere gāvīsus est.[4] Sciēbat enim quantam opīniōnem virtūtis [5] Argonautae habērent, nec dubitābat quīn sibi 15 auxilium ferrent.[6] Nūntium igitur ad nāvem mīsit, quī Iāsonem sociōsque ad rēgiam vocāret. Eō cum vēnissent, Phīneus dēmōnstrāvit quantō in perīculō suae rēs essent, et prōmīsit sē magna praemia datūrum esse, sī illī remedium repperissent.[7]

Argonautae negōtium libenter suscēpērunt et, ubi hōra vēnit, 20 cum rēge accubuērunt; at, simul ac cēna apposita est, Harpȳiae domum intrāvērunt et cibum auferre cōnābantur. Argonautae prīmum gladiīs avēs petiērunt; cum tamen vidērent hoc nihil prōdesse,[8] Zētēs et Calais, quī ālīs erant īnstrūctī, in āera sē sublevāvērunt ut dēsuper impetum facerent. Quod [9] cum sēn- 25 sissent Harpȳiae, reī novitāte perterritae, statim aufūgērunt, neque posteā umquam rediērunt.

127.   NOTES ON THE STORY

1. **certiōrēs factī sunt**: translate *they were informed.* This idiom is used to introduce an indirect statement, **Phīneum . . . esse.**

2. **sē . . . praebuisset**: translate *had acted cruelly toward his sons.* What is the literal translation?

3. **accubuerat**: Roman men reclined on couches at their meals. This custom is here ascribed to Phineus.

4. **gāvīsus est**: perfect of **gaudeō**, a semi-deponent verb (**494**).

5. **opīniōnem virtūtis**: translate *reputation for bravery.*

6. **nec . . . ferrent**: *and he did not doubt that they would bring aid to him* (**591**).

7. **sī . . . repperissent**: *if they should find a remedy.* This past perfect tense represents a future perfect indicative of the direct statement (**623, a,** *Note*).

8. **nihil prōdesse**: translate *was of no advantage.*

9. **Quod**: translate *this;* a connecting relative referring to the thought of the preceding sentence.

128.   COMPREHENSION

1. What three things did the Argonauts learn from the inhabitants? **2.** By whom, for what, and how was Phineus punished? **3.** How did the Argonauts finally frighten the Harpies away?

129. RĒS GRAMMATICAE

Subjunctive in subordinate clause of indirect discourse (623).
Praebuisset, l. 7 : the verb in a subordinate clause that is part
of an indirect statement is in the subjunctive. Although in
the subjunctive, it should be translated as if it were in the indicative, *had acted.* Find another example in the story of this
use of the subjunctive. Write two English sentences which, if
translated into Latin, will illustrate this use of the subjunctive.

130. EXERCISE

Iterātiō: A. **1.** Point out in the story five *infinitives* (**492**). **2.** Form and
translate the infinitives of : **dubitō, habeō, petō, reperiō, sum.**

B. **1.** Point out in the story the *infinitives in indirect statements* (**620**).
On what does each depend? What is the tense of each? **2.** Explain what
is meant by *sequence of tenses* in indirect discourse (**623**). **3.** Find in the
story an *ablative of accompaniment* (**541**) ; a *purpose clause* (**586**). **4.** Point
out the *reflexive pronouns* and *adjectives* and explain the use of each.

Respondē Latīnē: **1.** Ā (*from*) quibus cognōvērunt hunc, quī esset rēx,
caecum esse? **2.** Cūr Phīneus nūntium ad nāvem mittit? **3.** Quanta
praemia sē datūrum esse prōmīsit? **4.** Quōcum Argonautae accubuērunt?

Scrībe Latīnē: **1.** They are informed that nothing has been done. **2.** The
king discovers that the Argonauts who came there first will give him aid.
3. Phineus with his comrades heard that the Argonauts, who had a great
reputation, were coming. **4.** The Argonauts bring aid to Phineus in order
that the Harpies may not make an attack upon him. **5.** The Harpies had
wings that they might rise (lift themselves) into the air.

131. VERBA

Required Vocabulary: ac, afferō, certus, dubitō, eō (*adv.*), impetus, nec,
nihil, opīniō, prīmum, quantus, reperiō, simul, sublevō, umquam.

Word Study. The suffixes -iō, -siō, -tiō (in English *-tion*), are added to
verb roots or stems to form nouns expressing *action* or *a state of.* From
what verb in the story and with what suffix is each of the following
formed : **affectiō, appositiō, dēmōnstrātiō, missiō, petītiō, vīsiō,** and **vocātiō?**
What is the English equivalent of each?

XXII

OPUSCULUM VĪCĒSIMUM SECUNDUM

Then with a mighty shout,
They rose rejoicing, and poured many a cup
Of red wine to the gods, and hoisting up
The weather-beaten sail, with mirth and song,
Having good wind at will, they sped along.

132. THE ARGO PASSES BETWEEN THE CLASHING ROCKS

Hōc factō, Phīneus, ut prō tantō beneficiō meritās grātiās referret, Iāsonī dēmōnstrāvit quā ratiōne Symplēgades vītāre posset. Symplēgades autem duae erant rūpēs ingentī magnitūdine,[1] quae ā Iove positae erant eō cōnsiliō, nē quis ad Colchida pervenīret.[2] Hae parvō intervāllō [3] in marī natābant 5 et, sī quid in medium spatium vēnerat, incrēdibilī celeritāte concurrēbant. Postquam igitur ā Phīneō doctus est quid faciendum esset,[4] Iāsōn, sublātīs ancorīs, nāvem solvit et, lēnī ventō prōvectus, mox ad Symplēgades appropinquāvit; tum in prōrā stāns,[5] columbam quam in manū tenēbat ēmīsit. Illa 10 rēctā viā [6] per medium spatium volāvit et, priusquam rūpēs cōnflīxērunt, incolumis pervāsit, caudā tantum āmissā. Tum rūpēs utrimque discessērunt; antequam tamen rūrsus concurrerent, Argonautae, bene intellegentēs omnem spem salūtis in celeritāte positam esse, summā vī rēmīs contendērunt et nāvem 15 incolumem perdūxērunt. Hōc factō, deīs grātiās libenter ēgērunt, quōrum auxiliō ē tantō perīculō ēreptī erant; bene enim sciēbant nōn sine auxiliō deōrum rem ita fēlīciter ēvēnisse.

133. NOTES ON THE STORY

1. **ingentī magnitūdine:** *of great size;* an ablative of description.
2. **eō ... pervenīret:** *with this purpose, that no one might come to Colchis;* **Colchida** is the accusative case.

3. **parvō intervāllō** : translate *with a narrow space between them.*
4. **faciendum esset**: *must be done.* What form of the verb is this? **(501)**
5. **stāns**: *standing;* present participle of **stō.** Why is it in the nominative case?
6. **rēctā viā** : translate *in a straight line.*

134.　　　COMPREHENSION

1. How did Phineus show gratitude for his deliverance? **2.** By what plan did the Argonauts escape from danger?

135. ╱ ᶭⁱᵉˢ.　　　RĒS GRAMMATICAE

Subjunctive of anticipation (599, 601). In English, the verb in a clause introduced by *until* (*till*) or *before* is usually in the indicative mood: *he waits until Caesar passes along.* It is rarely found in the subjunctive: *There will I stand till Caesar pass along.**

In Latin, if **dum,** *until,* **antequam,** *before,* or **priusquam,** *before,* introduces a clause that states a fact, its verb is in the indicative mood. On the other hand, the verb is in the subjunctive mood if it expresses an action as expected or anticipated.

The verb in the dependent clause in the sentence, **dum conveniunt, morātur,** *he waits while they are assembling,* states a fact and is in the indicative. The verb in the dependent clause in the sentence, **dum convenīrent, morātus est,** *he waited until they could assemble,* expresses an action as *looked forward to* or *anticipated* and is in the subjunctive. This use is called the *subjunctive of anticipation.*

Translate the following sentences and explain the use of the verb in the dependent clause of each: **priusquam rūpēs cōnflīxērunt, pervāsit,** l. 11 ; **antequam rūrsus concurrerent, Argonautae nāvem incolumem perdūxērunt; dum dīcis, tempus fugit; exspectō dum dīcās.**

136.　 ╱ᶭⁱᵉˢ.　　　EXERCISE

Iterātiō: A. **1.** Point out in the story five *adjectives of the third declension* **(476). 2.** Decline: **nāvis incolumis, ventus lēnis, omnis spēs. 3.** Give the

---

* From Shakespeare, *Julius Caesar.*

synopsis of **possum** (**496**) in the third person, plural, all tenses, indicative and subjunctive. **4.** Give the Latin for: *I can avoid, you could approach, we have been able to stand, you had been able to learn.*

B. **1.** Point out in the story four examples of the *ablative absolute* (**545**); translate each in two ways. **2.** Find one *complementary infinitive* (**614**). **3.** Explain the case of: **celeritāte**, l. 6; **salūtis**, l. 14; **rēmīs**, l. 15; **deīs**, l. 16.

Respondē Latīnē: **1.** Quae erant Symplēgadēs? **2.** Quōmodo Iāsōn Symplēgadēs vītāre potuit? **3.** Columbā ēmissā, quid Argonautae facere poterant?

Scrībe Latīnē: **1.** The Argonauts approached two huge rocks standing in the middle (of the) sea. **2.** Before the rocks could come together, the Argonauts by the help of the gods passed through unharmed. **3.** Since the danger has been avoided (the danger having been avoided), they will give deserved thanks to the gods. **4.** Since hope of safety had been lost, they were not able to avoid the danger.

137. VERBA

Required Vocabulary: **appropinquō, grātia, incolumis, intervāllum, medius, mereō, priusquam, rēmus, salūs, stō, vītō.**

Word Study. Account for the meaning of *intelligent* derived from **intellegō** (**inter,** *between* + **legō** *gather, select*). **Intervāllum** (**inter** + **vāllum,** *a wall*), which originally meant the *space between two walls,* in time came to be a word used in general for space between, *an interval.*

THE CLASHING ROCKS

High o'er the main two rocks exalt their brow,
The boiling billows thundering roll below;
Through the vast waves the dreadful wonders move,
Hence named Erratic by the gods above.
Scarce the famed Argo passed these raging floods,
The sacred Argo filled with demigods!

HOMER, *Odyssey,* TRANSLATED BY POPE

THE ARRIVAL AT COLCHIS

Jason demands the golden fleece from King Aeëtes.

XXIII

OPUSCULUM VĪCĒSIMUM TERTIUM

Take thou the sack that holds the serpent's teeth
Our fathers slew upon the sunless heath;
There sow those evil seeds, and bide thou there
Till they send forth a strange crop, nothing fair,
Which garner thou, if thou canst 'scape from death.

138.   THE PRICE TO BE PAID FOR THE GOLDEN FLEECE

Brevī intermissō spatiō, Argonautae ad flūmen Phāsim vēnērunt, quod in fīnibus Colchōrum erat. Ibi cum nāvem appu-
lissent et in terram ēgressī essent, statim ad rēgem Aeētem sē
contulērunt et ab eō postulāvērunt ut vellus aureum sibi trā-
5 derētur. Ille cum audīvisset quam ob causam Argonautae
vēnissent, īrā commōtus est et diū negābat sē vellus hominibus
trāditūrum esse.[1] Tandem tamen, quod sciēbat Iāsonem nōn
sine auxiliō deōrum hoc negōtium suscēpisse, mūtātā sententiā,
prōmīsit sē vellus trāditūrum, sī Iāsōn labōrēs duōs magnae

86

difficultātis prius perfēcisset; [2] et, cum Iāsōn dīxisset sē ad omnia 10
perīcula subeunda parātum esse, quid fierī vellet ostendit.
Prīmum iungendī erant duo taurī [3] speciē horribilī, quī flammās
ex ōre ēdēbant; tum, hīs iūnctīs, ager quīdam arandus erat et
dentēs dracōnis serendī. Hīs audītīs, Iāsōn, etsī rem esse
summī perīculī [4] intellegēbat, tamen, nē hanc occāsiōnem reī 15
bene gerendae [5] āmitteret, negōtium suscēpit.

139.   NOTES ON THE STORY

1. **negābat . . . esse:** *he said he would not give up the fleece to mortals.*
2. **sī . . . perfēcisset:** *if Jason should first have completed two very
difficult labors* (**623**).
3. **iungendī . . . taurī:** *two oxen had to be yoked.* Find two other
examples of the passive periphrastic conjugation.
4. **summī perīculī:** what is the literal translation?
5. **reī . . . gerendae:** *of performing the task well.*

140.   COMPREHENSION

1. On what condition did the king of Colchis promise to hand over the
Golden Fleece? **2.** How did Jason treat the king's offer? Why?
3. What were the tasks which he was required to perform?

141.   RĒS GRAMMATICAE

Genitive and ablative of description (**511, 544**). The English
expression, *man of courage*, translated into Latin is **vir fortis.**
But if an adjective modifies the noun in a descriptive phrase, *e.g.,*
of great courage, the phrase is expressed in Latin either by the
genitive or the ablative: **vir magnae virtūtis** or **vir magnā
virtūte.** The ablative is used generally to describe a *physical
quality.* The genitive often indicates *measure* or *number:* **mūrus
sex pedum,** *a six-foot wall.* Such phrases are often used in the
predicate: **opus summae difficultātis erat,** *the work was very
difficult.*

Point out in the story an example of the ablative of description
and two of the genitive of description. Write an English sentence illustrative of this usage.

142. *learn*   **EXERCISE**

Iterātiō: *A.* **1.** Give in Latin the *cardinal numerals* from one to twenty (**484**). **2.** Count in Latin by tens to one hundred. **3.** Decline: **duo, trēs, mīlia.**

B. **1.** Point out in the story: two examples of the *dative of indirect object* (**516**); three **cum** *circumstantial clauses* (**597**).

Respondē Latīnē: **1.** Cum Iāsōn in fīnēs Colchōrum vēnisset, ad quem sē contulit? **2.** Cui sē vellus aureum trāditūrum esse rēx pollicitus est? **3.** Quot labōrēs Iāsōn perficiet?

Scrībe Latīnē: **1.** The king demands two tasks of the greatest difficulty. **2.** When the king had shown him what the opportunity was, Jason yoked the two oxen. **3.** What will the dragon's teeth produce? **4.** The oxen were of horrible appearance.

143. *well 2 ways*   **VERBA**

Required Vocabulary: **dēns, difficultās, ēdō, iungō, mūtō, occāsiō, ostendō, perficiō, postulō.**

Word Study. The suffixes **-bilis** and **-ilis** (in English *-ble* and *-ile*), added to verb stems, form adjectives meaning *able* or *capable of:* **horribilis,** *horrible,* is so derived from **horreō,** *shudder at.* From words in the story explain the derivation of: *arable, audible, facile, intelligible, mutable, ostensible, susceptible.*

Define the following words derived from **iungō,** showing by your definition that the idea of *joining* appears in each: *adjoin, adjunct, disjunctive, enjoin, injunction, junction, subjunctive.*

MEDEA AND JASON

Medea gives Jason the magic ointment.

XXIV

OPUSCULUM VĪCĒSIMUM QUĀRTUM

But soon he rose to fit him for the strife
And ere the sun his orb began to lift
O'er the dark hills, with fair Medea's gift
His arms and body he anointed well.

144. THE KING'S DAUGHTER FALLS IN LOVE WITH JASON

At Mēdēa, rēgis fīlia, Iāsonem amāvit et, ubi audīvit eum
tantum perīculum subitūrum esse, rem aegrē ferēbat.[1] Intellegēbat enim patrem suum hunc labōrem prōposuisse eō ipsō
cōnsiliō, ut Iāsōn morerētur.[2] Quae cum ita essent,[3] Mēdēa,
quae summam scientiam[4] medicīnae habēbat, hoc cōnsilium[5]
iniit. Mediā nocte, īnsciente patre,[5] ex urbe ēvāsit et, postquam
in montēs fīnitimōs vēnit, herbās quāsdam carpsit; tum, sūcō
expressō, oleum parāvit quod vī suā corpus aleret[6] nervōsque
cōnfirmāret. Hōc factō, Iāsonī oleum dedit; praecēpit autem

89

10 ut eō diē quō istī labōrēs cōnficiendī essent⁷ corpus suum et arma māne oblineret.⁸ Iāsōn, etsī paene omnēs magnitūdine et vīribus corporis antecēdēbat (vīta enim omnis in vēnātiōnibus atque in studiīs reī mīlitāris cōnstiterat⁹), tamen hoc cōnsilium nōn neglegendum esse cēnsēbat.

145.   NOTES ON THE STORY

1. **rem . . . ferēbat:** translate *she was greatly annoyed.*
2. **eō . . . morerētur:** *with this very plan, that Jason should die.*
3. **Quae . . . essent:** translate *since these things were so.* What use of the relative pronoun (**560,** *e*)?
4. **scientiam:** Medea's art suggests that of the witches in *Macbeth* IV, 1.
5. **Mediā . . . patre:** translate *in the middle of the night, without the knowledge of her father.*
6. **quod . . . aleret:** translate *which with its essence should nourish his body;* a relative clause of purpose.
7. **quō . . . essent:** *on which these labors were to be performed.*
8. **oblineret:** subjunctive in a substantive volitive clause depending on **praecēpit,** a verb of commanding.
9. **cōnstiterat:** translate *had been spent.*

146.   COMPREHENSION

1. For what purpose does Medea think that the king has imposed the labors on Jason? **2.** How does she help Jason? Why?

147.   RĒS GRAMMATICAE

Ablative of specification (551). Iāsōn omnēs magnitūdine et vīribus antecēdēbat, *Jason surpassed all in size and strength.* The ablatives **magnitūdine** and **vīribus** tell *in what respect* Jason surpassed all others.

Translate literally: **pār numerō; linguā differunt; rēx nōmine; maiōrēs nātū.**

The ablative of specification answers the question *in what respect.*

148.   EXERCISE

Iterātiō: A. **1.** Point out in the story the *relative pronouns* (**489**). **2.** Give the Latin for: *to whom, by whom, of whom, whose.* **3.** Give the synopsis of

ferō (**497**) in the indicative active, all tenses, second person, singular.
4. Identify as to voice, tense, and mood: **fertis, ferēbam, tulit, feram, lātus sim, ferāmur, tulerit, lātī essēmus, tulerat, lātus erō.**

B. **1.** On what verb in the story does each of the following verbs depend: **morerētur, essent, aleret, cōnfirmāret, oblineret?** Explain the tense of each by telling why it is primary or secondary (**577–8**). **2.** Point out the antecedent of each relative pronoun in the story and show how the relative agrees with it (**560**).

Respondē Latīnē: **1.** Quis erat Mēdēa? **2.** Quid Mēdēa mediā nocte fēcit? **3.** Cui Mēdēa oleum ferēbat?

Scrībe Latīnē: **1.** Medea was angry (bore it ill) because her father had proposed this work. **2.** The king's daughter surpassed almost all in strength. **3.** Medea, who loved Jason, advised him to do this. **4.** Since these things (**quae**) were so, Jason formed this plan.

149. **VERBA**

Required Vocabulary: **aegrē, antecēdō, cēnseō, cōnsistō, paene, praecipiō, prōpōnō.**

Word Study. What is the literal meaning of *antecedent?* Of *penult?*

From what verb stem and with what suffix is **initium** formed? Give and define five nouns that are formed with this suffix.

MEDEA

The enchantress Medea and her love for Jason has always been a favorite theme in literature, art, and music. Euripides made her the heroine of his famous tragedy MEDEA, a rôle which has been played by great actresses. Many operas are based on the story of Medea's love and hate. Scenes from her life are portrayed in ancient vase paintings and in frescoes on the walls of Pompeii and Herculaneum.

MEDEA'S LETTER TO JASON

Ovid, a Roman poet of the first century, in his book on Heroines writes an imaginary letter from Medea to Jason, in which she says: "Then I saw you, then I began to know you. That was the beginning of my downfall. I saw you and I was lost. You were handsome, and the fates were dragging me on to my doom. Your eyes had taken away my power to see. Traitor, you saw it — for can any one hide love?"

XXV

OPUSCULUM VĪCĒSIMUM QUĪNTUM

Then he saw the mounds
Bursten asunder, and the muttered sounds
Changed into loud strange shouts and warlike clang,
As with the freed feet at last the earth-born sprang
On to the tumbling earth, and the sunlight
Shone on bright arms, clean, ready for the fight.

150. THE HARVEST OF THE DRAGON'S TEETH

Ubi is diēs vēnit quem rēx ad arandum agrum dīxerat, Iāsōn,
ortā lūce,[1] cum sociīs ad locum cōnstitūtum sē contulit. Ibi
stabulum ingēns repperit in quō taurī inclūsī erant; tum,
portīs apertīs, taurōs in lūcem trāxit et summā cum difficultāte
5 iugum imposuit. At Aeētēs cum vidēret taurōs nihil[2] contrā
Iāsonem valēre,[2] magnopere mīrātus est; nesciēbat enim fīliam
suam auxilium eī dedisse.

Tum Iāsōn, omnibus aspicientibus, agrum arāre coepit; quā
in rē tantā dīligentiā ūsus est ut ante merīdiem tōtum opus
10 cōnfēcerit.[3] Hōc factō, ad locum ubi rēx sedēbat adiit et dentēs
dracōnis postulāvit; quōs ubi accēpit, in agrum quem arāverat
magnā cum dīligentiā sparsit. Hōrum autem dentium nātūra
erat tālis ut, in eō locō ubi sparsī essent,[4] virī armātī mīrō quōdam
modō gignerentur.

15 Nōndum tamen Iāsōn tōtum opus cōnfēcerat; imperāverat
enim eī Aeētēs ut armātōs virōs quī ē dentibus gignerentur[5]
sōlus interficeret. Postquam igitur omnēs dentēs in agrum
sparsit, Iāsōn, lassitūdine exanimātus, quiētī sē trādidit, dum
virī istī gignerentur. Paucās hōrās dormiēbat; sub vesperum
20 tamen, ē somnō subitō excitātus, rem ita ēvēnisse ut praedictum
erat cognōvit; nam in omnibus agrī partibus virī ingentī mag-

nitūdine corporis, gladiīs galeīsque armātī, mīrum in modum [6]
ē terrā oriēbantur.

Hōc cognitō, Iāsōn cōnsilium quod dedisset Mēdēa nōn omittendum esse putābat; saxum igitur ingēns, ita enim prae- [25] cēperat Mēdēa, in mediōs virōs [7] coniēcit. Illī undique ad locum concurrērunt et, cum quisque sibi id saxum habēre vellet, magna contrōversia orta est. Mox, strictīs gladiīs, inter sē pugnāre coepērunt et, cum hōc modō plūrimī occīsī essent, reliquī vulneribus cōnfectī ā Iāsone nūllō negōtiō [8] interfectī [30] sunt.

151. NOTES ON THE STORY

1. **ortā lūce:** translate *at daybreak*. What is the literal translation?
2. **nihil, valēre:** translate *had no strength*.
3. **cōnfēcerit:** for the tense see **578**, *a*.
4. **sparsī essent:** the subjunctive by attraction, dependent on **gignerentur (610)**.
5. **quī . . . gignerentur:** *who should spring up from the teeth*.
6. **mīrum in modum:** *in a marvelous manner*.
7. **in mediōs virōs:** translate *in the midst of the men*.
8. **nūllō negōtiō:** translate *with no difficulty*.

152. COMPREHENSION

1. What happened when the dragon's teeth were planted? **2.** What additional task did the king impose on Jason? **3.** How did Jason accomplish this task?

153. EXERCISE

Iterātiō: **A.** **1.** Give the synopsis of eō (**500**), third person, plural, indicative and subjunctive. **2.** Identify as to tense and mood: **ībam, ierim, eat, ībitis, īstī, ierāmus, ierit, īrēmus. 3.** Decline the indefinite pronoun and adjective **quisque (491).**

B. 1. Point out in the story: one example of the *ablative of cause* (**540**); two *clauses of result* (**587**). **2.** Explain the use of each of the subjunctives: **vidēret,** l. 5; **gignerentur,** l. 16; **interficeret,** l. 17; **dedisset,** l. 24; **vellet,** l. 27; **occīsī essent,** l. 29.

Respondē Latīnē : **1.** Quantā dīligentiā Iāsōn ūsus est? **2.** Quā rē Iāsōn exanimātus est? **3.** Dum virī istī orīrentur, quid fēcit Iāsōn? **4.** Cūr magna contrōversia orta est?

Scrībe Latīnē : **1.** When the yoke was put on (abl. abs.), Jason opens the gate and drags the oxen into the field. **2.** Each one used such great diligence that nothing availed against him. **3.** Toward evening the king ordered each one to approach. **4.** Because of a quarrel he had not yet finished before noon the work begun at daybreak.

154. VERBA

Required Vocabulary : **adeō** (verb), **aperiō, aspiciō, contrā, contrōversia, exanimō, impōnō, iugum, merīdiēs, nōndum, orior, quiēs, quisque, saxum, trahō, valeō, vesper.**

Word Study. To what word in the story is each of the following related : *confection, impostor, magnitude, tractor?* Define and give the formation of the Latin word to which each is related.

Define on the basis of Latin derivation : *sparse, retaliate.*

THE MEDEA OF EURIPIDES

Jason's appreciation of Medea's advice and help, through which he was enabled to perform superhuman tasks and thereby save his life, is portrayed by the Greek poet Euripides in his tragedy *Medea :*

"Since you exaggerate so proudly your services, I deem that to Venus alone of gods or men is due the safety of my voyage.

"Since you did aid me, it was kindly done. Yet by saving me you received more than you gave, as I shall prove : first, you live in Grecian lands instead of on barbarian shores. You have learned the meaning of justice and to live by law and not by the dictates of brute force, and all the Greeks recognize your wisdom, and you have gained fame; but had you still dwelt in that distant land, no tongue would have named you."

XXVI

OPUSCULUM VĪCĒSIMUM SEXTUM

All seemed asleep, but now Medea went
With beating heart to work out her intent.

155. MEDEA PREPARES TO FLEE WITH JASON

Rēx Aeētēs, ubi Iāsonem labōrem prōpositum [1] cōnfēcisse cognōvit, īrā graviter commōtus est; id enim per dolum factum esse intellegēbat, nec dubitābat quīn Mēdēa eī auxilium tulisset. Mēdēa autem, cum intellegeret sē in magnō fore [2] perīculō, sī in rēgiā manēret, fugā salūtem petere cōnstituit. Omnibus 5 rēbus igitur ad fugam parātīs, mediā nocte, īnsciente patre, cum frātre Absyrtō ēvāsit, et quam celerrimē [3] ad locum ubi Argō subducta erat sē contulit. Eō cum vēnisset, ad pedēs Iāsonis sē prōiēcit, et multīs cum lacrimīs eum obsecrāvit nē in tantō discrīmine mulierem dēsereret quae eī tantum prōfuisset.[4] 10 Ille, memoriā tenēns sē per eius auxilium ē magnō perīculō ēvāsisse, libenter eam excēpit et, postquam causam veniendī audīvit, hortātus est nē patris īram timēret. Prōmīsit autem sē quam prīmum eam in nāvī suā āvectūrum.[5]

156. NOTES ON THE STORY

1. **prōpositum**: *which had been set (for him)*. The participle is often best translated by a clause.

2. **fore**: *would be;* **fore** is often used for **futūrum esse,** the future infinitive of sum.

3. **quam celerrimē**: *as quickly as possible.*

4. **quae ... prōfuisset**: *who had been of such great assistance to him.*

5. **sē ... āvectūrum (esse)**: *that he would bear her away in his ship as soon as possible.*

157. COMPREHENSION

1. Why did Medea flee from her father's kingdom? **2.** What did Jason promise her? Why?

158. RĒS GRAMMATICAE

Substantive clauses with words of doubting (591). Nec dubitābat quīn Mēdēa eī auxilium tulisset, l. *3, and he did not doubt that Medea had brought aid to him (Jason).* **Nōn dubium est quīn illa patrem timeat,** *there is no doubt that she fears her father.* These sentences illustrate the use of **quīn** and the subjunctive in substantive clauses that follow negative expressions of *doubting* or *ignorance.*

159. EXERCISE

Iterātiō: **A. 1.** Give and translate the *participles* (**492, 495**) of: **dubitō, maneō, subdūcō, audiō, sum. 2.** Complete: **rēx īrā** (*moved*), **mulier perī-culum** (*fearing*), **pater** (*about to come*).

B. **1.** Point out the participles in the story and give the form and use of each.

Respondē Latīnē: **1.** Cūr rēx īrā commōtus est? **2.** Quōcum Mēdēa, fugā salūtem petītūra, ēvāsit? **3.** Quem ad locum Mēdēa auxilium obsecrāns sē contulit?

Scrībe Latīnē: **1.** When the task was finished (abl. abs.), the woman goes (betakes herself) to the ship which has been beached. **2.** She was about to throw herself at Jason's feet. **3.** Aeētes did not doubt that Medea had encouraged Jason. **4.** Jason brings aid to Medea escaping from her father.

160. VERBA

Required Vocabulary: **hortor, mulier, prōiciō, quīn, subdūcō.**

Word Study. To what word in the story is each of these related by derivation: *celerity, dole, evasive, exhortation, fratricide, fugue, pare, projectile, timidity, salutary?* Define each.

Define the following words derived from **petō,** showing by your definition that the idea of *seeking* appears in each: *appetite, competitive, impetus, repeat.*

From an engraving by Gunst   *Courtesy of Indiana University Library*

JASON PUTS THE DRAGON TO SLEEP

This illustration is from the story of Medea and Jason in a 1732 edition of
Ovid's poems.

XXVII

OPUSCULUM VĪCĒSIMUM SEPTIMUM

> Nor longer now the heroes silence kept
> So joyously their hearts within them leapt,
> But loud they shouted, seeing the gold fell
> Laid heaped before them, and longed sore to tell
> Their fair adventure to the maids of Greece.

161.   THE GOLDEN FLEECE AT LAST

Postrīdiē eius diēī Iāsōn cum sociīs suīs, ortā lūce, nāvem
dēdūxit, et, tempestātem idōneam nactī, ad eum locum rēmīs contendērunt quō in locō [1] Mēdēa vellus cēlātum esse dēmōnstrābat.
Eō cum vēnissent, Iāsōn in terram ēgressus est, et, sociīs ad mare
relictīs quī praesidiō [2] nāvī essent, ipse cum Mēdēā in silvās sē 5
contulit. Pauca mīlia passuum per silvam prōgressus, vellus
quod quaerēbat ex arbore suspēnsum vīdit. Id tamen auferre

97

erat summae difficultātis,[3] nōn modo enim locus ipse ēgregiē et
nātūrā et arte mūnītus erat, sed etiam dracō quīdam speciē
10 terribilī arborem custōdiēbat.

Tum Mēdēa, quae, ut suprā dēmōnstrāvimus, medicīnae
summam scientiam habuit, rāmum quem dē arbore proximā
dēripuerat venēnō īnfēcit. Hōc factō, ad locum appropinquāvit,
et dracōnem, quī faucibus apertīs eius adventum exspectābat,
15 venēnō sparsit; deinde dum dracō somnō oppressus dormit,
Iāsōn vellus aureum ex arbore dēripuit, et cum Mēdēā quam
celerrimē pedem rettulit.

Dum[4] autem ea geruntur, Argonautae, quī ad mare relictī
erant, animō ānxiō reditum Iāsonis exspectābant; id enim
20 negōtium summī esse perīculī intellegēbant. Postquam igitur
ad occāsum sōlis frūstrā exspectāvērunt, dē eius salūte dēspē-
rāre coepērunt, nec dubitābant quīn aliquī[5] cāsus accidisset.[6]
Quae cum ita essent,[7] mātūrandum sibi[8] cēnsuērunt ut auxilium
ducī ferrent; sed, dum proficīscī parant, lūmen quoddam subitō
25 cōnspiciunt, mīrum in modum intrā silvās refulgēns, et, magnopere mīrātī quae causa esset eius reī, ad locum concurrunt.
Quō cum vēnissent, Iāsonī[9] et Mēdēae advenientibus occurrērunt, et vellus aureum lūminis eius causam esse cognōvērunt.
Omnī timōre sublātō, magnō cum gaudiō ducem suum excēpē-
30 runt et deīs grātiās ēgērunt, quod vellere potītī essent et rēs
tam fēlīciter ēvēnisset.[10]

162.   NOTES ON THE STORY

1. quō in locō: *in which;* the antecedent is here repeated in the relative
clause (**560,** *a*).

2. praesidiō: *for a protection.*

3. Id . . . difficultātis: translate *however, to carry it away was very
difficult.* The infinitive is here used as the subject of the verb, as in English:
to err is human (**613**).

4. Dum: what is the meaning of this word as used in two other clauses
in the story? What is the mood of the verb in these clauses? Why?

5. aliquī: adjective form of the indefinite pronoun aliquis (**491**).

6. accidisset: account for the mood.

THE GOLDEN FLEECE

7. **Quae . . . essent:** translate *and so.* What is it literally?

8. **mātūrandum sibi :** translate *they must hurry;* **sibi** is dative of agent used with a verb in the passive periphrastic conjugation.

9. **Iāsonī:** with the compound **occurrērunt.**

10. **quod . . . ēvēnisset:** (**603,** *a*).

163.   COMPREHENSION

1. Where did Jason find the Golden Fleece? **2.** How was it guarded? **3.** How did Medea help Jason to obtain it? **4.** What was the attitude of his companions?

164.   RĒS GRAMMATICAE

Dative of reference (519). **Sociī praesidiō nāvī sunt,** *the comrades are a protection to (for) the ship.* The dative of purpose, **praesidiō,** is used with the dative, **nāvī,** which names the thing *to which* the companions are (for) a protection. This dative, which indicates the *person or thing concerned* or *to whom* or *to which* a statement refers, is called the *dative of reference.* It is used commonly with the dative of purpose, especially with **auxiliō, cūrae, impedīmentō, praesidiō,** and **subsidiō : cūrae mihi est,** *it is (for) a care to me;* **Mēdēa Iāsonī auxiliō vēnit,** *Medea came (for) as an aid to Jason.*

These two datives, when used together, are sometimes called the " double dative."

165.   EXERCISE

Iterātiō: **A. 1.** Give the synopsis of the following *deponent verbs* in the indicative and subjunctive, third person singular (**493**): **mīror, nancīscor, ēgredior, orior.** **2.** Translate: **mīrātī eritis, nactus sum, ēgrederis, nancīscar, oriēbātur, mīrāminī, prōgrediēns, ēgressūrus.** **3.** Point out five deponent verbs in the story. **4.** Give the Latin for: *suitable weather arising, his companions having proceeded, Medea having obtained the poison, Jason having disembarked.*

B. **1.** Point out an example of the *ablative with special deponents* (**547**). **2.** Explain the case of: **lūce,** l. 1 ; **rēmīs,** l. 2 ; **locō,** l. 3 ; **sociīs,** l. 4 ; **arbore,** l. 7 ; **arte,** l. 9 ; **factō,** l. 13 ; **faucibus,** l. 14 ; **venēnō,** l. 15 ; **somnō,** l. 15 ; **animō,** l. 19 ; **salūte,** l. 21 ; **timōre,** l. 29 ; **gaudiō,** l. 29.

Respondē Latīnē: **1.** Cui praesidiō sociī Iāsonis relictī sunt? **2.** Cūr vellus auferre erat summae difficultātis? **3.** Quid Argonautae cōnspēxērunt?

Scrībe Latīnē: **1.** To see the fleece is (a matter) of very great difficulty. **2.** This was (for) a protection to the tree. **3.** Having obtained the fleece, he then met his comrades. **4.** Jason's comrades, overcome by the fear of some accident, despaired of his safety.

166. VERBA

Required Vocabulary: **cōnspiciō, deinde, dēspērō, intrā, occurrō, opprimō, praesidium.**

Word Study. The endings of present participles of Latin verbs appear also in English derivatives as the suffixes *-ant, -ent,* and *-ient.* To what word in the story is each of the following related: *accident, cognizant, concurrent, expectant, refulgent?*

From the Harleian Manuscript

Courtesy of the British Museum

JASON AND THE DRAGON

This sixteenth century illustration of Jason putting to sleep the dragon that guarded the Golden Fleece is from an illustrated manuscript of an old French poem "The Romance of the Rose." This manuscript is a very splendid one, written on vellum and illustrated by woodcuts so overlaid with gold and colors that they really are miniature paintings.

XXVIII

OPUSCULUM DUODĒTRĪCĒSIMUM

A little more, a little more,
O carriers of the Golden Fleece!
A little labor with the oar,
Before we reach the land of Greece.

167. **FLIGHT AND PURSUIT**

Hīs rēbus gestīs, omnēs sine morā nāvem rūrsus cōnscen-
dērunt et, sublātīs ancorīs, prīmā vigiliā [1] solvērunt; neque
enim satis tūtum esse arbitrātī sunt in eō locō manēre. At rēx
Aeētēs, quī iam ante inimīcō in eōs fuerat animō,[2] ubi cognōvit
5 fīliam suam nōn modo ad Argonautās sē recēpisse sed etiam ad
vellus auferendum auxilium tulisse, hōc dolōre gravius exārsit.
Nāvem longam [3] quam celerrimē dēdūcī iussit [4] et, mīlitibus im-
positīs, fugientēs [5] īnsecūtus est.

Argonautae, quī bene sciēbant rem in discrīmine esse,[6] sum-
10 mīs vīribus rēmīs contendēbant; cum tamen nāvis quā vehēbantur ingentī esset magnitūdine, nōn eādem celeritāte quā
Colchī [7] prōgredī poterant; neque longius intererat quam quō
tēlum adicī posset.[8] At Mēdēa, cum vīdisset quō in locō rēs
essent, paene omnī spē dēpositā, īnfandum hoc cōnsilium cēpit.

15 Erat in nāvī Argonautārum fīlius quīdam rēgis Aeētae, nōmine
Absyrtus, quem, ut suprā dēmōnstrāvimus, Mēdēa ex urbe
fugiēns sēcum abdūxerat. Hunc puerum Mēdēa interficere
cōnstituit eō cōnsiliō, ut, membrīs eius in mare coniectīs, cursum
Colchōrum impedīret; certō enim sciēbat Aeētem, cum membra
20 fīlī vīdisset, nōn longius prōsecūtūrum esse. Neque opīniō
Mēdēam fefellit,[9] omnia enim ita ēvēnērunt ut spērāverat.
Aeētēs, ubi prīmum membra vīdit, ad ea colligenda nāvem
tenērī iussit.

Dum tamen ea geruntur, Argonautae, nōn intermissō rēmigandī labōre, mox ē cōnspectū hostium auferēbantur; neque 25 prius [10] fugere dēstitērunt quam [10] ad flūmen Ēridanum pervēnērunt. At Aeētēs, nihil sibi prōfutūrum esse arbitrātus [11] sī longius prōgressus esset, domum revertit ut fīlī corpus ad sepultūram daret.

168. NOTES ON THE STORY

1. **prīmā vigiliā:** ablative of time when; the first watch was early in the evening, just after sunset.

2. **inimīcō . . . animō:** translate *had been unfriendly toward them.* What kind of ablative is **animō**?

3. **Nāvem longam:** *warship.*

4. **iussit:** an infinitive with subject accusative is always used as the object of **iubeō** instead of a substantive volitive clause (**589,** *Note*).

5. **fugientēs:** *the fugitives;* a participle used as a substantive.

6. **rem . . . esse:** translate *that the situation was critical.*

7. **eādem . . . Colchī:** *with the same swiftness as (with which) the Colchians.*

8. **neque . . . posset:** translate *and the distance between them was no more than a javelin's throw.*

9. **Neque . . . fefellit:** translate *nor was Medea deceived in her expectation;* **fefellit** is from **fallō.**

10. **prius, quam:** *before.* **Prius** is often separated from **quam** by one or more words. It introduces a verb in what mood here? Why?

11. **nihil . . . arbitrātus:** translate *thinking it would do him no good.*

169. COMPREHENSION

1. Why were the Argonauts at a disadvantage in their flight from the king? **2.** What was Medea's plan for delaying her father? **3.** How did it succeed?

170. EXERCISE

Iterātiō: *A.* **1.** Give in Latin: the *ordinal numerals* from one to ten (**484**); the even ordinal numerals from ten to twenty. **2.** Give the *gerunds* and *gerundives* of (**492**): **spērō, valeō, trahō, aperiō, orior.**

B. **1.** Point out in the story: two gerundives and give the case and use of each (**630**); one gerund, and its case and use (**629**).

Respondē Latīnē: **1.** Quandō Argonautae solvērunt? **2.** Quis erat auxiliō ad vellus auferendum? **3.** Cūr Aeētēs nāvem tenērī iubet? **4.** Quod cōnsilium fugiendī Mēdēa cēpit?

Scrībe Latīnē: **1.** In the first watch they desisted from flight (to flee). **2.** Was Medea's plan of fleeing safe? **3.** He laid aside his plan of pursuing the ship. **4.** Certain ones in the sight of all pursued the fugitives (fleeing) without delay. **5.** Medea did this for the purpose of (**causā**) impeding the course of the Colchians.

171.   **VERBA**

Required Vocabulary: adiciō, colligō (3rd conj.), cōnspectus, dēpōnō, dēsistō, fugiō, impediō, īnsequor, intersum, mora, prōsequor, tūtus, vigilia.

Word Study. The suffix -**ūra** (in English -*ure*), attached to participial stems, forms nouns meaning *an act* or *the result of an act.* **Sepultūra** in this lesson is so formed from **sepeliō.** Give three English words derived from Latin words having this suffix.

Give the literal meaning of **īnfandum** (**in** + **for,** *speak*); of *infant.*

Queen Mathilda Bayeux Tapestry

ELEVENTH CENTURY ARGONAUTS

The Bayeux Tapestry is a very famous piece of colored embroidery two hundred and thirty feet long. It pictures the story of the Norman Conquest and the events that led up to it. The subject of each scene is given in Latin. The inscription on this one says: "With (sails) full of wind he (Harold of England) came into the land of Count Guy (of France)."

XXIX

OPUSCULUM ŪNDĒTRĪCĒSIMUM

With that they came into the royal house
Where Pelias dwelt, grown old and timorous,
Oppressed with blood of those that he had slain,
Desiring wealth and longer life in vain.

172. *Nvel* JASON'S DEMAND AND THE PROMISE OF PELIAS

Tandem post multa perīcula Iāsōn in eundem locum per-vēnit unde profectus erat. Tum ē nāvī ēgressus, ad rēgem Peliam, quī rēgnum adhūc obtinēbat, statim sē contulit et, vellere aureō mōnstrātō, ab eō postulāvit ut rēgnum sibi trā-derētur; Peliās enim pollicitus erat, sī Iāsōn vellus rettulisset, 5 sē rēgnum eī trāditūrum.[1] Postquam Iāsōn quid fierī vellet ostendit, Peliās prīmō nihil respondit, sed diū in eādem trīstitiā tacitus permānsit; tandem ita locūtus est, " Vidēs mē aetāte iam esse cōnfectum, neque dubium est quīn diēs suprēmus mihi appropinquet. Liceat igitur mihi, dum vīvam,[2] hoc 10 rēgnum obtinēre; cum autem tandem dēcesserō, tū mihi suc-cēdēs." Hāc ōrātiōne adductus Iāsōn respondit sē id factūrum quod ille rogāvisset.

173. NOTES ON THE STORY

1. sī . . . trāditūrum: *if Jason should bring back the fleece, he would hand over the kingdom to him.*

2. Liceat . . . vīvam: translate *therefore, permit me as long as I shall live.*

174. COMPREHENSION

1. After he brought back the Golden Fleece, what demand did Jason make of Pelias? **2.** What request did Pelias make? **3.** How did Jason treat this request?

175.   EXERCISE

Iterātiō: A. **1.** Give the synopsis, indicative and subjunctive of: **fīō,** third person singular (**498**); **volō,** second person plural (**499**).

B. **1.** Point out: two examples of the *ablative of place from which* (**535**); one example of an *independent volitive subjunctive* (**580**). **2.** Explain the mood and tense of the following: **trāderētur,** l. 4; **rettulisset,** l. 5; **vellet,** l. 6; **appropinquet,** l. 10; **rogāvisset,** l. 13.

Respondē Latīnē: **1.** Quem in locum tandem pervēnit Iāsōn? **2.** Quid Iāsōn voluit? **3.** Quid Peliās pollicitus erat? **4.** Quandō Iāsōn rēx fīet?

Scrībe Latīnē: **1.** They set out from the same place. **2.** Let Jason become king. **3.** Let his kingdom continue for a long time. **4.** The king wished to depart from this life. **5.** At first Jason asks that he succeed the king.

176.   VERBA

Required Vocabulary: **permaneō, prīmō, rogō, succēdō.**

Word Study. Give five English derivatives of **loquor.** Define these derivatives of **rogō:** *abrogate, arrogance, interrogation, prerogative, surrogate.*

Pompeii, Italy   *Courtesy of Philadelphia Commercial Museum*

THE END OF THE VOYAGE

This relief on a tomb shows a ship in still water. It symbolizes the end of the voyage of life. The sailors furl the sails, and the helmsman sits idly at the stern.

THE MAGIC BREW

Medea demonstrates to the daughters of Peleus the efficacy of her magic brew in restoring the strength and youth of the aged ram.

XXX

OPUSCULUM TRĪCĒSIMUM

> And let king Pelias rise if now he can,
> And stop the coming of the half-shod man.

177.   **MEDEA'S MAGIC FAILS TO RESTORE PELIAS**

Hīs rēbus cognitīs, Mēdēa rem aegrē tulit et, rēgnī cupiditāte adducta, mortem rēgī per dolum īnferre cōnstituit. Hōc cōnstitūtō, ad fīliās rēgis vēnit atque ita locūta est:

"Vidētis patrem vestrum aetāte iam esse cōnfectum, neque ad labōrem rēgnandī perferendum [1] satis valēre. Vultisne eum 5 rūrsus iuvenem fierī?"

Tum fīliae rēgis, hīs audītīs, ita respondērunt, "Num [2] hoc fierī potest? Quis enim umquam ē sene iuvenis [3] factus est?"

At Mēdēa respondit, "Nōnne scītis mē medicīnae summam 10

habēre scientiam? Nunc igitur vōbīs dēmōnstrābō quōmodo haec rēs fierī possit."

Hīs dictīs, cum arietem aetāte iam cōnfectum interfēcisset, membra eius in vās aēneum posuit et, igne suppositō, in aquam
15 herbās quāsdam īnfūdit. Tum, dum aqua effervēsceret, carmen magicum cantābat. Post breve tempus ariēs ē vāse exsiluit et, vīribus [4] refectīs, per agrōs currēbat. Dum fīliae rēgis hoc mīrāculum stupentēs intuentur, Mēdēa ita locūta est:
"Vidētisne quantum valeat medicīna? [5] Vōs [6] igitur, sī
20 vultis patrem vestrum in adulēscentiam redūcere, id quod fēcī ipsae [6] faciētis. Vōs patris membra in vās conicite; [7] ego herbās magicās praebēbō."

Quod ubi audītum est, fīliae rēgis cōnsilium quod dedisset Mēdēa sibi nōn omittendum esse putāvērunt. Patrem igitur
25 Peliam necāvērunt et membra eius in vās aēneum coniēcērunt; nihil enim dubitābant quīn hoc maximē eī prōfutūrum esset.[8] At rēs omnīnō aliter ēvēnit ac [9] spērāverant; Mēdēa enim nōn eāsdem herbās dedit quibus ipsa ūsa erat. Itaque, postquam diū frūstrā exspectāvērunt, patrem suum rē vērā mortuum esse
30 intellēxērunt. Hīs rēbus gestīs, Mēdēa sē cum coniuge suō rēgnum acceptūram esse spērābat; sed cīvēs cum intellegerent quō modō Peliās periisset, tantum scelus aegrē tulērunt. Itaque, Iāsone et Mēdēā ē rēgnō expulsīs, Acastum rēgem creāvērunt.

178. NOTES ON THE STORY

1. **ad . . . perferendum:** *to endure the labor of ruling.*

2. **Num:** implies that the answer " no " is expected. What does **nōnne** imply?

3. **iuvenis:** predicate nominative.

4. **vīribus:** what is the nominative singular?

5. **quantum . . . medicīna:** *how strong the medicine is.*

6. **Vōs, ipsae:** *you, yourselves.* **Vōs** is used for emphasis and contrast (**556**).

7. **conicite:** *place;* an imperative.

8. **quīn . . . esset:** translate *that this would be very beneficial to him.*

9. **aliter . . . ac:** *otherwise . . . than.*

179. COMPREHENSION

1. What proposal did Medea make to the king's daughters? **2.** What magic feat did she perform? **3.** What did Medea hope to gain by the death of the king? **4.** How did her plan succeed?

180. EXERCISE

Iterātiō: **A. 1.** Decline: the *interrogative pronoun* **quis** (**490**); the *interrogative adjective* **quī** (**490**). **2.** Decline the *personal pronouns of the first and second persons* (**485**). **3.** Give the synopsis in the *passive periphrastic conjugation,* third person, singular, neuter, indicative and subjunctive (**501**) of **dēmōnstrō.**

B. **1.** Point out in the story: an interrogative pronoun; an interrogative adjective. **2.** Point out an example of: *dative of agent* (**522**); *emphatic use of personal pronouns* (**485**); *possessive adjective* (**564**); *passive periphrastic conjugation; indirect question* (**595**).

Respondē Latīnē: **1.** Scīsne cui Mēdēa mortem īnferre velit? **2.** Quam scientiam fīliābus rēgis dēmōnstrāvit? **3.** Num vīs patrem tuum ē sene fierī iuvenem? **4.** Quid fīliae rēgis sibi nōn omittendum esse putant?

Scrībe Latīnē: **1.** You (tibi) must make a fire. **2.** Medea did not wish him to become young, did she? **3.** You ought to hear the plan. **4.** They will show us what they wish (to be) done, will they not? **5.** Who wishes to do this? **6.** We must select a king. **7.** I must do this.

181. VERBA

Required Vocabulary: **aetās, aliter, currō, ignis, itaque, omnīnō.**

MEDEA

A relief on the side of a marble sarcophagus showing Medea, after having given the fatal robe to Creusa, escaping in the chariot drawn by dragons.

XXXI

OPUSCULUM TRĪCĒSIMUM PRĪMUM

And now is all that ancient story told
Of him who won the guarded Fleece of Gold.

182. THE FATE OF MEDEA AND JASON

Iāsōn et Mēdēa, ē Thessaliā expulsī, ad urbem Corinthum vēnērunt, cuius urbis Creōn quīdam rēgnum tum obtinēbat. Erat autem Creontī fīlia ūna, nōmine Glaucē. Quam cum vīdisset, Iāsōn cōnstituit Mēdēam uxōrem suam repudiāre, eō 5 cōnsiliō, ut Glaucēn in mātrimōnium dūceret.

At Mēdēa, ubi intellēxit quae ille in animō habēret, īrā graviter commōta, iūre iūrandō cōnfirmāvit sē tantam iniūriam ultūram.[1] Hoc igitur cōnsilium cēpit. Vestem parāvit summā arte contextam et variīs colōribus tīnctam; hanc mortiferō quōdam 10 venēnō īnfēcit, cuius vīs tālis erat ut, sī quis eam vestem induisset,[2] corpus eius quasi ignī ūrerētur. Hōc factō, vestem ad Glaucēn mīsit; illa autem, nihil malī[3] suspicāns, dōnum libenter accēpit et vestem novam, mōre fēminārum, statim induit.

Vix vestem induerat Glaucē, cum dolōrem gravem per omnia 15 membra sēnsit, et post paulum, crūdēlī cruciātū affecta, ē vītā excessit. Hīs rēbus gestīs, Mēdēa, furōre atque āmentiā impulsa, fīliōs suōs necāvit. Tum magnum sibi[4] fore[5] perīculum arbitrāta sī diūtius ibi manēret, ex eā regiōne fugere cōnstituit. Hōc cōnstitūtō, Sōlem ōrāvit ut in tantō perīculō auxilium sibi praebēret. Sōl autem, hīs precibus commōtus, currum mīsit, 20 cui dracōnēs, ālīs īnstrūctī, iūnctī erant. Mēdēa, nōn omittendam tantam occāsiōnem arbitrāta, currum cōnscendit, itaque per āera vecta incolumis ad urbem Athēnās pervēnit.

Iāsōn autem post breve tempus mīrō modō occīsus est. Ille enim, sīve cāsū sīve cōnsiliō deōrum, sub umbrā nāvis suae, quae 25 in lītus subducta erat, ōlim dormiēbat. Nāvis, quae adhūc ērēcta steterat, in eam partem ubi Iāsōn iacēbat subitō dēlāpsa, virum īnfēlīcem oppressit.

183.   NOTES ON THE STORY

1. ultūram (esse): *would avenge;* from ulcīscor.
2. sī . . . induisset: *if anyone put on this dress.*
3. malī: *wrong;* genitive of the whole with nihil.
4. sibi: *to herself.*
5. fore: = futūrum esse; depends on arbitrāta.

184.   COMPREHENSION

1. Where did Jason and Medea go? 2. How did Jason wrong Medea? 3. How did Medea avenge the wrong done to her? 4. Do Jason and Medea receive their just deserts in this story?

185.   RĒS GRAMMATICAE

Ablative of accordance (537). The ablative without a preposition is used to express the idea *in accordance with :* **mōre fēminārum,** *in accordance with the custom of women,* l. 13.

Translate: Iāsōn eō cōnsiliō ēgit; Colchī ea suīs mōribus fēcērunt; suō cōnsiliō Glaucē vestem induit.

186.   EXERCISE

Iterātiō : A. 1. Compare the adjectives: **magnus, brevis, īnfēlīx, superus** (479) (480). 2. From what adjectives in the story are these adverbs formed: **crūdēliter, mīrē, breviter?** 3. Compare: **graviter, libenter** (482).

B. **1.** Point out in the story an example of *dative of possession* (**521**). **2.** Explain the use of nōmine, l. 3; quam, l. 3; vīdisset, l. 4; dūceret, l. 5; habēret, l. 6; quōdam, l. 9; ūrerētur, l. 11; arbitrāta, l. 18; hōc, l. 19; praebēret, l. 20; omittendam, l. 21; modō, l. 24.

Respondē Latīnē: **1.** Cui erat fīlia ūna Glaucē? **2.** Quārum mōre vestem novam statim Glaucē induit? **3.** Cūr Mēdēa in Thessaliā manēre nōluit? **4.** Quam ad urbem Mēdēa vecta est?

Scrībe Latīnē: **1.** Creon had (to Creon was) a kingdom. **2.** Jason had scarcely seen the king's daughter when he begged to marry her. **3.** Medea, impelled by great anger, with an oath vowed to do this. **4.** Jason was expelled in accordance with the customs of the city.

187.   **VERBA**

Required Vocabulary: **cruciātus, impellō, iūs iūrandum, mōs, ōrō, sīve, vestis, vix.**

MEDEA'S LETTER TO JASON *

"Why did I take too great a joy in your golden locks, your beauty, and the false charm of your speech?

"There is some pleasure in reproaching an ingrate with favors done. This shall be my pleasure; this the only delight I shall bear from you.

"But for you, I remember, I the queen of Colchis could find time, when you asked that my art should bring you aid. You were the first to speak with faithless lips: 'Fortune has handed over to you the right to decide my safety, and in your hand is life and death.' Thus was I, a mere girl, quickly beguiled by your words.

"I wish that the Symplegades had caught and crushed our lives out together! Yet safe and a victor you return to your city, and the golden fleece is placed before your father's gods.

"I am abandoned, I have lost my throne, my native land, my home, my husband — who for me alone took the place of everything."

OVID

* Continued from page 91.

XXXII

OPUSCULUM TRĪCĒSIMUM SECUNDUM

REITERANDUM EST

Repetītiō est māter studiōrum,
Repetition is the mother of learning.

188. EXERCISE

Give the name of the construction that would be used in translating each of the italicized expressions into Latin : **1.** They surpass all others *in strength.* **2.** *They fought* long and hard. **3.** Aeson knew that Jason would return *if he obtained the fleece.* **4.** Medea waited *until the caldron should boil.* **5.** To pass the clashing rocks was *very difficult.* **6.** A certain king, Pelias *by name,* did not doubt *that Jason would perish.* **7.** Medea's love *for Jason* was *an aid to him in accomplishing his task.* **8.** Suspecting *no danger* she sings *while she waits.* **9.** *In accordance with the advice* of certain *of his friends,* he selects men *to appoint* a day *of assembling.* **10.** *A little* later *he is going to go to his home.*

Write the Latin for the italicized words : **1.** *Desire of obtaining the kingdom* led Pelias on. **2.** *How long did they fight?* **3.** To kill the monster *of great size* was a task *of very great danger.* **4.** Jason's comrades waited *until he should bring back the fleece.* **5.** Pelias sends Jason *to obtain the golden fleece.*

Scrībe Latīnē: A. **1.** A few days later he decided the time was suitable for changing their course. **2.** There was a space of two miles between. **3.** That friend of yours has to finish two difficult labors. **4.** He says (**negō**) he will not stay with them after his comrades have returned to the ship. **5.** Did Jason's ship surpass that of the Colchians? **6.** In accordance with their custom they rowed (contended with the oars) with greatest strength.

B. **1.** Medea does not doubt that she will bring aid to Jason. **2.** He leaves his comrades as a protection to the ships. **3.** Worn out with these tortures, she does not doubt that her last day is approaching. **4.** She was borne through the air to Athens. **5.** When all were looking on, he ordered him to open the gates. **6.** The nature of the garment was such that, as soon

113

as she had put it on, she was overcome with torture. **7.** Either by chance or by the will (plan) of the gods, Jason got possession of the fleece. **8.** Is there ever any rest for that man who seeks glory?

189.   REVIEW OF REQUIRED VOCABULARY

Each of the words in the following paragraphs is derived from, or related in derivation to, a word in the required vocabularies of *Opuscula* XIV–XXXI. Give the Latin word to which each is related and its meaning. Then define each English word on the basis of its Latin derivation:

Accidental, adorable, affect, afferent, ancestor, anchor, armature, arrogant, aspect, attract, casual, causal, censure, centrifugal, collect, conjugate, conspectus, conspicuously, consultation, consumption, contradict, controversy, convene, cruciate, current, cursory, custom.

Deduction, deficit, depose, desist, desperation, difficulty, editor, egress, equivalent, except, expostulate, extol, extract, glorify, hortatory, igneous, immutable, impede, impel, imposition, impulse, indent, indubitable, inevitable, ingratiate, initiation, interest, intermittent, interval, intramural, invest.

Juncture, juror, littoral, mediator, meridian, meritorious, morale, moratorium, nihilist, nautical, negative, nocturne, obstacle, obtain, occasional, occur, opinion, oppress, oriental, peninsula, perfect, permanent, precept, primer, projector, proposition, prosecutor, quantity.

Reception, regional, repertory, requiem, salubrious, satisfactory, sentence, simultaneous, solution, specious, subsidy, substance, successor, tempestuous, usual, valentine, vehicular, vespers.

190.   REVIEW OF WORD STUDY

Explain the formation of each word in the following paragraph, the meaning of the word from which each is derived, the force of prefix or suffix (**637–9**), and the meaning of the word as a whole: **īnscientia**, in- (*not*) + -sciēns (sciō, *know*) + -tia (*condition of*), = *the condition of not knowing, ignorance.*

Aspiciō, auferō, comportō, contrōversia, dīmittō, ēveniō, impediō, incrēdibilis, magnitūdō, mīrāculum, nātūra, novitās, occurrō, ōrātiō, perferō, præedīcō, prōpōnō, renūntiō, sacrificium, subeō, trānspōrtō, trīstitia.

Tues – review suffixes
irregular
Wed – Vocab – test review verbs
review pages 60 – 85
Fri – review pages 60 – 111

PART III

READINGS FROM ROMAN LITERATURE

Teach him on these as stairs to climb
And live on even terms with time.   EMERSON
MOTTO OF ART AND ARCHAEOLOGY

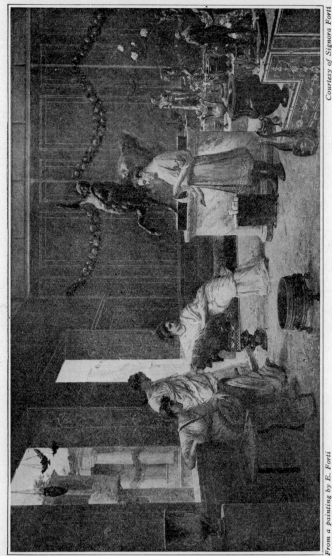

From a painting by E. Forti

Courtesy of Signora Forti

A LITERARY READING

A Roman author reads from a roll or book, **volūmen,** of his new work to a rapt audience.   The rest of the rolls can be seen in their circular case, **capsa.**   A Roman book was written on papyrus sheets which were glued together at the sides forming one long strip.   This was rolled up when not in use.   Since it had to be *unrolled* as it was read, the word for *reading a book* was **ēvolvō.**

THE ROMAN FORUM IN 1929

The monument of Victor Emmanuel, where the body of the Unknown Soldier lies, towers in the background beyond the Capitoline Hill over the Arch of Septimius Severus. The newly excavated Forum of Augustus is behind the houses on the right.

GLIMPSES OF ROMAN HISTORY

191.   THE KINGS OF ROME

The following selection is taken from a brief history of Rome written by Eutropius in the fourth century A.D.

Rōmānum imperium ā Rōmulō initium habet. Is, decem et octō annōs nātus,[1] urbem exiguam in Palātīnō monte cōnstituit. Conditā cīvitāte, quam ex nōmine suō Rōmam vocāvit, multitūdinem fīnitimōrum in cīvitātem recēpit, centum ex seniōribus lēgit, quōs senātōrēs nōmināvit propter senectūtem. Tum, cum 5 uxōrēs ipse et populus nōn habērent, invītāvit ad spectāculum lūdōrum vīcīnās Rōmae nātiōnēs atque eārum virginēs rapuit. Annō rēgnī trīcēsimō septimō ad deōs trānsīsse crēditus est [2] et cōnsecrātus.

Posteā Numa Pompilius rēx creātus est, quī bellum quidem 10

117

nūllum gessit, sed lēgēs Rōmānīs mōrēsque cōnstituit et Rōmae
sacra ac templa cōnstituit. Dēcessit [3] quadrāgēsimō et tertiō
imperī annō.

Huic successit Tullus Hostīlius. Hic bella gessit, Albānōs
15 vīcit, urbī Caelium montem [4] adiēcit.

Post hunc Ancus Mārcius, Numae ex fīliā nepōs, suscēpit
imperium. Contrā Latīnōs dīmicāvit, Aventīnum montem
cīvitātī adiēcit et Iāniculum. Vīcēsimō et quārtō annō imperī
morbō periit.

20 Deinde rēgnum Prīscus Tarquinius accēpit. Hic Rōmae
Circum [5] aedificāvit, lūdōs Rōmānōs [6] īnstituit, mūrōs fēcit et
cloācās,[7] Capitōlium incohāvit.

Post hunc Servius Tullius suscēpit imperium, nātus ex nōbilī
fēminā, captīvā tamen et ancillā. Hic quoque Sabīnōs subēgit;
25 montēs trēs, Quirīnālem, Vīminālem, Ēsquilīnum, urbī adiūnxit;
mūrum [8] et fossās circum urbem dūxit.

L. Tarquinius Superbus, septimus atque ultimus rēx, templum Iovī in Capitōliō aedificāvit. Posteā imperium perdidit.
Brūtus [9] populum concitāvit et imperium adēmit Tarquiniō,[10]
30 quī cum uxōre et līberīs suīs fūgit. Ita Rōmae rēgnātum est
per septem rēgēs annōs ducentōs quadrāgintā trēs.

Hinc cōnsulēs coepērunt, prō ūnō rēge duo, hāc causā creātī ut,
sī ūnus malus esse voluisset, alter habēns potestātem similem eum
coercēret. Et placuit nē imperium longius quam annum habērent.

1. nātus: translate *at the age of;* perfect participle of nāscor. 2. ad . . . est:
Romulus disappeared during a storm which came up while he was holding a review
of the army. The Romans cherished the idea that he had been translated to the
gods, but some secretly thought that he had been torn to pieces by the senators.
3. Dēcessit: *died.* 4. Caelium montem: one of the seven hills of Rome; the
Janiculum was not included in " the seven hills." 5. Circum: the Circus Maximus,
in the valley between the Palatine and Aventine. 6. lūdōs Rōmānōs: yearly
games in honor of the gods. They were also called the Lūdī Magnī. 7. cloācās:
sewers; the greatest of these, the Cloāca Maxima, is still to be seen in Rome.
8. mūrum: parts of the Servian wall are still standing. 9. Brūtus: this is the Brutus
who feigned stupidity while waiting a chance to free Rome from the tyrant.
See 193. 10. Tarquiniō: *from Tarquin.*

192. THE PROPHECY OF AN IMPERIAL ROME

Titus Livius (Livy, 59 B.C.–17 A.D.), one of the greatest writers of Latin prose, relates the story of this prophecy. He was the author of a history of Rome, containing one hundred and forty-two books, many of which have been lost. In those that remain he has told with eloquence the story of the glory that was Rome's.

Bōs in Sabīnīs [1] nāta est mīrandā magnitūdine ac speciē. Haruspicēs cecinērunt,[2] " Cuius cīvitātis eam cīvis Diānae immolāverit,[3] ibi imperium erit; " idque [4] pervēnerat ad sacerdōtem templī Diānae. Sabīnus, ut prīma apta diēs sacrificiō vīsa est,[5] bovem Rōmam āctam [6] dēdūcit ad templum Diānae et 5 ante āram statuit. Ibi sacerdōs Rōmānus, cum eum magnitūdō victimae mōvisset, memor respōnsī, " Quid [7] tū, hospes, parās," inquit, " impium sacrificium Diānae facere? Quīn [8] tū vīvō [9] flūmine lavāris. Īnfimā valle fluit Tiberis." Hospes, quī omnia cuperet rīte facta, dēscendit ad Tiberim. Intereā Rō- 10 mānus immolat Diānae bovem. Id grātum rēgī cīvitātīque fuit.

1. **Sabīnīs**: the Sabines, although defeated in many battles, still hoped to gain supremacy over the Romans. 2. **cecinērunt**: translate *predicted;* from **canō**. 3. **Cuius . . . immolāverit**: *of whatever state a citizen shall have sacrificed this heifer to Diana.* 4. **id**: the prophecy. 5. **ut . . . est**: translate *as soon as a day seemed suitable for the sacrifice.* 6. **āctam**: *driven.* 7. **Quid**: = **cūr.** 8. **Quīn**: *why not.* 9. **vīvō**: translate *flowing.*

193. LŪCIUS IŪNIUS BRŪTUS *

Livy, in one of the many interesting stories found in his history of Rome, relates how Tarquin, the last king of Rome, sent his two sons to Delphi to consult the oracle as to the meaning of a terrifying portent. In sport the sons took along a relative whom they called **Brūtus,** *the dullard.* Brutus, however, had been feigning stupidity while awaiting an opportunity to save Rome from the tyrant king Tarquin. A little later he was instrumental in driving the Tarquins from Rome and in establishing a republic of which he became one of the first consuls.

Quō [1] postquam ventum est,[2] perfectīs patris mandātīs, cupīdō incessit animōs iuvenum quaerendī ad quem eōrum rēgnum esset ventūrum. Ex īnfimā [3] cavernā vōx reddita est,

* For Roman names see JOHNSTON, *Private Life of the Romans,* pp. 35–48.

Courtesy of Prescott W. Townsend

THE TEMPLE OF APOLLO AT DELPHI

On the right are the foundations of the temple; on the left, the ruins of an ancient Greek theater. The road at the foot of the mountain is a modern highway following the route traveled by Brutus and the Tarquins when they came to consult the oracle.

" Imperium summum Rōmae habēbit quī vestrum prīmus, Ō
5 iuvenēs, ōsculum mātrī tulerit." Uter prior, cum Rōmam
redīsset, mātrī ōsculum daret, sortī [4] permittunt.

Brūtus aliō ratus spectāre vōcem,[5] velut sī dēlāpsus cecidisset,[6]
terram ōsculō contigit, quod ea [7] commūnis māter omnium mor-
tālium est.

1. Quō: *i.e.* Delphi, a city in Greece famous for its shrine of Apollo to which the young Tarquins went to get the response of the oracle. **2. ventum est:** translate *had come;* impersonal use of the verb. **3. īnfimā:** *the depths of* (567). **4. sortī:** *to chance; i.e.,* they cast lots. **5. aliō . . . vōcem:** *thinking the response pointed to another thing.* **6. velut . . . cecidisset:** translate *just as if he had slipped and fallen.* **7. ea:** *i.e.,* the earth.

194.   THE PEOPLE GAIN THEIR RIGHTS

In his account of the long and bitter struggle between the patricians and plebeians, Livy tells the following story of the effort of the plebeians to secure such rights as marriage with the patricians and a share in the public affairs.

The plebeians, oppressed by debt, were promised relief if they would help to defeat the Volscians (494 B.C.). Although the Volscians were defeated, the patricians did not keep their promise. The plebeians marched out of Rome to the Sacred Mount, and there they stayed until they were granted officials, **tribūnī plēbis,** to guard their rights.

Plēbs in Sacrum montem sēcessit trāns Aniēnem, tria ab urbe mīlia passuum. Ibi sine ūllō duce vāllō fossāque quiētī per aliquot diēs, neque lacessītī neque lacessentēs, sēsē tenuērunt. Timor ingēns erat in urbe. Timet relicta ab suīs plēbs [1] patrēs; timent patrēs relictam in urbe plēbem. 5

Sīc placuit igitur ad plēbem mittī ōrātōrem,[2] fācundum virum et, quod inde [3] oriundus erat, plēbī cārum. Agī deinde dē concordiā coeptum [4] concessumque est ut plēbis magistrātūs essent sacrōsānctī,[5] quibus auxilī lātiō adversus cōnsulēs esset,[6] nēve cui patrum eum magistrātum capere licēret.[7] Ita duo 10 tribūnī plēbis creātī sunt.

1. relicta . . . plēbs: *the plebeians left (in the city) by their own people.* **2. ōrā-tōrem:** this envoy, Agrippa, told the story of the strike declared against the stomach by other members of the body, and showed them how all parts of the body must do their work for the good of the whole. The plebeians saw the point. **3. inde:** translate *from them.* **4. Agī . . . coeptum (esse):** translate *then they began to discuss peace.* **5. sacrōsānctī:** the persons of the tribunes of the plebs were inviolate. Their duty was to safeguard the rights of the common people. They could *veto* any proposal that they felt harmful to the interest of the plebeians. This office gave the common people a powerful weapon. **6. quibus . . . esset:** *through whom there might be the right of bringing aid against the consuls.* **7. nēve . . . licēret:** translate *and that no one of the senators be permitted to hold this office.*

195.   HANNIBAL, THE ENEMY OF ROME

The historian, Cornelius Nepos, born about 100 B.C., interested himself chiefly in the manners, characters, and customs of people. He wrote biographies of the men who were exemplars of the virtues of earlier Greece and Rome. *Hannibal, The Enemy of Rome,* and *Hannibal Hides His Money* are both taken from his biography of Hannibal.

Hannibal, who had vowed eternal enmity to Rome, was the greatest Carthaginian leader in the long struggle between Rome and Carthage, 264–241; 218–201; and 149–146 B.C. Hannibal was in command in 218–201.

Hannibal erat Hamilcaris [1] fīlius Carthāginiēnsis. Hic velut hērēditāte relictum [2] odium in Rōmānōs cōnservāvit. Dē fidē

suā et odiō in Rōmānōs hoc commemorat, " Pater Hamilcar,
puerō mē nōn amplius novem annōs nātō, imperātor proficīscēns
5 Carthāgine Iovī optimō maximō ³ victimās immolāvit. Quae ⁴
dīvīna rēs dum cōnficiēbātur,⁵ quaesīvit ā mē vellemne ⁶ sēcum
in castra proficīscī. Id cum libenter accēpissem atque ab eō
petere coepissem nē dubitāret ⁷ dūcere, tum ille, ' Faciam,'
inquit, ' sī mihi fidem ⁸ quam postulō dederis.' Simul mē ad
10 āram addūxit, apud quam sacrificium facere īnstituerat, eamque
tenentem ⁹ fidem dare iussit numquam mē in amīcitiā cum
Rōmānīs fore.¹⁰ Id ego iūs iūrandum patrī datum usque ad
hanc aetātem cōnservāvī."

1. Hamilcaris: a general in the first Punic War. **2. velut . . . relictum:**
left just as if by an inheritance. **3. Iovī . . . maximō:** *to Jupiter, all good and all
powerful.* According to the Roman author, a Carthaginian is here sacrificing to a
Roman god. **4. Quae:** modifies **rēs;** translate as if **haec (560,** *e*). **5. dum cōnficiēbātur:** the use of the imperfect with **dum** is an exception to the rule (**600,**
Note). **6. vellemne:** *whether I wished.* **7. nē dubitāret:** *that he should not hesitate.*
8. fidem: *pledge.* **9. eamque tenentem:** translate *and laying my hand on the
altar;* modifies **mē.** **10. fore:** the other form for **futūrum esse,** future infinitive.

196.   HANNIBAL HIDES HIS MONEY

Hannibal Crētam vēnit. Vīdit autem vir omnium calli-
dissimus in magnō sē fore perīculō, nisi quid prōvīdisset,¹ propter
avāritiam Crētēnsium ; magnam enim sēcum pecūniam portābat,
dē quā sciēbat exīsse fāmam.² Itaque capit tāle cōnsilium.
5 Amphorās complūrēs complet plumbō, summās ³ operit aurō
et argentō. Hās, praesentibus prīncipibus, dēpōnit in templō
Diānae, simulāns sē suās fortūnās illōrum fideī crēdere. Hīs
dēceptīs, statuās quās sēcum portābat omnī suā pecūniā complet
eāsque in vēstibulō domī abicit.⁴ Crētēnsēs templum magnā
10 cūrā custōdiunt, nōn tam ā cēterīs quam ab Hannibale, nē ille,
īnscientibus eīs,⁵ tolleret sua sēcumque dūceret.

1. nisi . . . prōvīdisset: *if he did not make some provision;* the past perfect subjunctive for the future perfect indicative of the direct discourse (**623,** *a, Note*).
2. exīsse fāmam: *a report had gone out.* **3. summās (amphorās):** *the tops of the wine-
jars.* **4. abicit:** *throws;* as if of no value. **5. īnscientibus eīs:** *without their knowledge.*

From a painting by E. Forti   *Courtesy of Signora Forti*

ROMAN WOMEN HOLD THE REINS

The painter represents these women as riding in a chariot within the city, a privilege which was denied them by the Oppian law. Cato would have called them very bold, for they even do the driving.

197.   **AN EARLY CHAMPION OF WOMAN'S RIGHTS**

After the defeat of the Romans at Cannae in 216 B.C., Rome turned all of her resources toward the defeat of Hannibal. In order to discourage luxurious living, the Oppian Law was passed, which forbade women to wear parti-colored garments, to have more than a half ounce of gold, and to ride in a chariot within or near the city.

In 195 B.C. the war was over, and the women wanted this war-time measure rescinded. They found a champion in Lucius Valerius, a tribune of the plebs. He and a colleague proposed the repeal of the Oppian Law. Its repeal was violently opposed by Cato, who, seeing the women gathering in numbers to urge the restoration of their rights, made a speech in the Senate severely criticizing the bold methods of these " new " women and warning the senators to be on their guard against such feminist movements. Valerius answers Cato's speech and urges that the women, too, be permitted to enjoy the fruits of peace.

Livy in his history quotes the speeches made in the Senate for and against the women, the former of which is given here in a somewhat simplified and abridged form.

L. Valerius prō rogātiōne [1] ita dīxit: " Cum [2] cōnsul M.
Porcius [3] ōrātiōne longā contrā rogātiōnem nostram dīxerit,
necesse est paucīs verbīs respondēre. Sēditiōnem et sēcessiōnem
fēminārum appellāvit, quod mātrōnae in pūblicō vōs rogāvissent
5 ut lēgem in sē lātam [4] per bellum, temporibus dūrīs, in pāce et
flōrentī ac beātā rē pūblicā abrogārētis. Nam quid tandem
novī [5] mātrōnae fēcērunt? Numquam ante hoc tempus in
pūblicō vīsae sunt? Tuās adversus tē *Orīginēs* recitābō. [6]

" ' Accipe quotiēns id fēcerint et quidem semper bonō pūb-
10 licō. Cum, Capitōliō ab Sabīnīs captō, mediō in forō dīmicā-
rētur, nōnne mātrōnae, inter aciēs duās sē īnferentēs, [7] dīmicandī
fīnem fēcērunt; cum, Coriolānō [8] duce, legiōnēs Volscōrum
castra ad quīntum lapidem [9] posuissent, nōnne id agmen mātrōnae āvertērunt? Iam, urbe captā [10] ā Gallīs, aurum quō
15 redēmpta urbs est nōnne mātrōnae in pūblicum contulērunt? '

" Veniō nunc ad id dē quō agitur. [11] Cōnsul est indignātus
eam praecipuē lēgem abrogārī [12] quae lūxuriae fēminārum
coercendae causā lāta esset. Cūr lēx sit autem lāta, ipsum
indicābit tempus. [13] Hannibal in Italiā erat, victor ad Cannās;
20 ad urbem Rōmam admōtūrus [14] exercitus vidēbātur; nōn
mīlitēs, nōn sociōs, nōn pecūniam habēbāmus. Tālī tempore
in lūxuriā et ōrnātū mātrōnae occupātae erant ut ad ea coer-
cenda Oppia lēx necesse esset.

" Ad coniugēs tantum [15] nostrās pācis frūctus nōn perveniet?
25 Purpurā [16] virī ūtimur, praetextātī [17] in magistrātibus, in sacer-
dōtiīs; līberī nostrī praetextātīs togīs ūtuntur; magistrātibus
in colōniīs togae praetextātae habendae iūs permittimus.
Fēminīs purpurae ūsū interdīcēmus? [18]

" Dolor et īra est cum sociōrum uxōribus vident ea concessa
30 ōrnāmenta quae sibi adēmpta sunt, [19] cum īnsignīs [20] eās esse
aurō et purpurā vident, cum illās vehī per urbem, sē [21] pedibus
sequī. Virōrum hoc animōs vulnerāre posset; quid mulierculārum [22] cēnsētis, quās etiam parva movent? Nōn magistrātūs
nec sacerdōtia nec triumphī nec īnsignia [23] nec dōna aut spolia

DANCING SUFFRAGETTES

These figures are painted on the side of a die made of bone.

bellica eīs contingere possunt; [24] ōrnātus et cultus,[25] haec fēmi- 35
nārum īnsignia sunt, hīs gaudent et glōriantur. Inīquīs nōminibus ūtēbātur modo cōnsul [26] sēditiōnem fēminārum et
sēcessiōnem appellandō.''

Haec cum prō lēge [27] dicta essent, maior multitūdō mulierum
posterō diē sēsē in pūblicum effūdit, ūnōque agmine omnēs 40
Brūtōrum [28] iānuās obsēdērunt, nec ante abstitērunt quam [29]
abrogāta lēx Oppia [30] est.

1. rogātiōne: *proposal; i.e.,* to annul the law. **2. Cum:** *since.* **3. M. Porcius:**
this was Marcus Porcius Cato. **4. lēgem . . . lātam:** *a law passed against them-*
selves. **5. novī:** genitive of the whole with **quid (510). 6. Tuās . . . recitābō:**
translate *to answer you I will read your Orīginēs;* Valerius quotes Cato's own book
in which the services of women to the state are enumerated. **7. sē īnferentēs:**
translate *rushing.* **8. Coriolānō:** for the story of Veturia and Coriolanus see
SHAKESPEARE, *Coriolanus,* Act V, Scenes 3–5. **9. lapidem:** for milestones on
Roman roads see JOHNSTON, *Private Life of the Romans,* p. 283. **10. urbe captā:**
in 390 B.C. **11. id . . . agitur:** *the point which is being discussed.* **12. indignātus**
. . . abrogārī: *he is incensed especially that this law is being annulled.* **13. tempus:**
translate *state of affairs.* **14. admōtūrus:** *about to move on.* **15. tantum:** *only.*
16. Purpurā: Roman purple was not the purple of today; it was more nearly

scarlet. **17. praetextātī**: *clothed in the toga praetexta;* this had a scarlet border. It was worn by boys, magistrates, and priestly officials. **18. Fēminīs . . . inter-dīcēmus**: *shall we prohibit women only the use of purple?* **19. cum . . . sunt**: *when they see granted to wives of allies those ornaments of which they have been deprived.* Valerius appeals to the pride of the Roman men. They would not want the wives of provincials to be better dressed than their own. **20. insignīs**: *resplendent with;* modifies **eās**, which refers to the wives of the allies of Rome. **21. sē**: the women of Rome; subject of **sequī**. **22. mulierculārum**: *mere women;* modifies **animōs**, *feelings.* **23. insignia**: *decorations;* granted to public officials as badges of their office, or to soldiers for bravery, like the Congressional Medal or Croix de Guerre. **24. eīs . . . possunt**: *can be their (the women's) good fortune.* **25. ōrnātus et cultus**: *adornment and dress.* **26. cōnsul**: Cato. **27. prō lēge**: *i.e.*, the new bill restoring rights to the women. **28. Brūtōrum**: Marcus and Publius Brutus, tribunes of the plebeians, had opposed the repeal of the Oppian Law. **29. ante, quam**: translate as one word, *before.* **30. lēx Oppia**: the bill was passed by a unanimous vote. Dio Cassius, a historian in the second century A.D., in telling this tale says that the women put on some of their ornaments right there in the senate and went out dancing.

198.   AN HONEST GOVERNOR

Gaius Gracchus and his brother, Tiberius, belonged to the famous Sempronian family. Their father had held important public offices and their mother, Cornelia, the daughter of Cornelius Scipio, was a woman of great ability. She encouraged her two sons to carry out a program involving the division of the public lands as a means of relieving the poor.

This account of a speech made by Gaius Gracchus, told by Aulus Gellius (125–175 A.D.) in **Noctēs Atticae**, *Attic Nights*, reveals the high integrity for which the Gracchi were famous.

C. Gracchus, cum ex Sardiniā Rōmam rediit, ōrātiōnem ad populum habuit. Eius verba sunt haec: "Versātus sum," [1] inquit, "in prōvinciā quōmodo ex ūsū vestrō [2] exīstimābam esse, non quōmodo mihi condūcere [3] arbitrābar. Nulla apud
5 mē fuit popīna.[4] Ita versātus sum in prōvinciā uti nēmō posset dīcere assem [5] aut eō [6] plūs in mūneribus mē accēpisse aut meā operā quemquam sūmptum fēcisse.[7] Biennium fuī in prōvinciā; cum Rōmam profectus sum, zōnās,[8] quās plēnās argentī extulī, eās ex prōvinciā inānēs retulī; aliī vīnī amphorās, quās plēnās
10 tulērunt, eās argentī plēnās domum reportāvērunt."

1. Versātus sum: *lived.* **2. ex ūsū vestrō:** *to your advantage.* **3. mihi con-dūcere:** *was of advantage to me.* **4. popīna:** *tavern.* The public eating places and inns were little frequented by the better classes. Gracchus means that his house was not a rendezvous for low characters. **5. assem:** *a penny.* **6. eō:** an ablative with the comparative **plūs.** **7. meā . . . fēcisse:** *on my own account had incurred any expense.* **8. zōnās:** *belts;* often used to carry money. The provinces were regarded by Roman officials as sources of legitimate graft. Verres robbed the Sicilians of their most valued possessions. The poet Catullus complained that he came home from his province with his pocket full of cobwebs. Gellius, discussing in another passage the subject of honesty, quotes Cato the Censor to the effect that thieves who steal private property spend their lives in prison, while public grafters flourish in gold and purple.

199. CICERO WRITES TO A FRIEND ON CAESAR'S STAFF

Marcus Tullius Cicero was born in 106 B.C. Of equestrian rank, a **novus homō,** without famous ancestry, he rose through all the ranks of public office to the highest, that of consul. In his consulship he rendered most patriotic service to his country by crushing Catiline's conspiracy against the state. He was not only Rome's most eloquent orator but also her most gifted writer of Latin prose. Many of his orations are extant, as well as his works on rhetoric, oratory, and philosophy, and many of his letters.

CICERŌ TREBĀTIŌ [1]

Ego tē commendāre nōn dēsistō; sed, quid prōficiam,[2] ex tē scīre cupiō. Spem maximam habeō in Balbō, ad quem dē tē dīligentissimē et saepissimē scrībō. Illud [3] soleō mīrārī, nōn mē totiēns [4] accipere tuās litterās quotiēns [4] ā Quīntō mihi frātre afferuntur.   5

In Britanniā nihil esse audiō neque aurī neque argentī. Id sī ita est, essedum aliquod capiās [5] persuādeō et ad nōs quam prīmum redeās. Perfice [6] ut sīs in familiāribus Caesaris.[6] Multum tē in eō frāter adiuvābit meus, sed, mihi crēde, tuus pudor et labor plūrimum.[7] Imperātōrem [8] līberālissimum, aetātem [9] 10 opportūnissimam, commendātiōnem [10] certē singulārem habēs, ut [11] tibi ūnum timendum sit, nē ipse tibi dēfuisse videāris.[11]

1. Trebātiō: *to Trebatius.* A common form of salutation in Roman letters* was the use of the nominative, giving the name of the writer, followed by the

---

* For a description of a Roman letter read JOHNSTON, *Private Life of the Romans,* pp. 287–290.

ROMAN WRITING MATERIALS

A writing tablet, which looked like an old-fashioned slate, had a waxed surface on which the letters were traced with a sharp-pointed instrument, **stilus.**

dative of the person addressed. Trebatius was a young man on Caesar's staff in Gaul. Cicero, who was very fond of him, sought every opportunity to advance him in favor with Caesar. He strongly urged him, however, to do his part. **2. quid prōficiam:** translate *what success I am having.* **3. illud:** *this;* explained by the words **nōn . . . litterās.** Cicero may suspect Trebatius of neglecting to answer his letters. **4. totiēns . . . quotiēns:** *so often . . . as.* **5. (ut) capiās:** *to seize.* **6. Perfice . . . Caesaris:** *bring it about that you are one of Caesar's intimate friends.* **7. plūrimum** (530, *a*). **8. Imperātōrem:** *i.e.,* Caesar. **9. aetātem:** of Trebatius, who was thirty-five. **10. commendātiōnem:** of Cicero. **11. ut . . . videāris:** translate *so you have but one thing to fear, that you yourself may seem to be wanting.* In another letter Cicero says that men in Gaul say Trebatius is conceited. Notwithstanding Cicero's advice to Trebatius and his persistence in recommending him to Caesar, Trebatius evidently did not distinguish himself, for his name is nowhere mentioned in Caesar's Gallic War. However, he became a devoted admirer of Caesar and served under him in the Civil War. He was a trained jurist, and Caesar doubtless found his advice valuable in settling administrative problems of the newly conquered country. Horace and Cicero each dedicated a book to him.

200.   CAESAR REWARDS AN EX-SERVICE MAN

L. Annaeus Seneca, a Spaniard by birth, became one of Emperor Nero's advisers, but finally fell into disfavor and was forced to take his own life.

In **Dē Beneficiīs,** the most famous of his moral and philosophical essays, Seneca tells the following story of Caesar's gratitude to one of his veterans for a service which the latter had once rendered to him.

Causam dīcēbat [1] apud Iūlium ex veterānīs quīdam paulō violentior [2] adversus vīcīnōs suōs et causa premēbātur. [3] " Meministī," inquit, " imperātor, tē in Hispāniā vulnerātum esse? " Cum Caesar sē meminisse dīxisset, " Meministī quidem," [4] inquit, " sub quādam arbore minimum umbrae spar- 5 gente [5] cum vellēs requiēscere, ferventissimō sōle, [6] et esset asperrimus locus, quendam ex mīlitibus sagulum suum tibi supposuisse? " Cum dīxisset Caesar, " Cūr nōn meminerim? [7] Et quidem sitī cōnfectus, [8] quia impedītus [9] īre ad fontem proximum nōn poteram, īre manibus volēbam, [10] nisi homō fortis 10 aquam mihi in galeā suā attulisset." " Potes ergō," inquit, " imperātor, agnōscere illum hominem aut illam galeam? " Caesar ait sē nōn posse galeam cognōscere, hominem posse et adiēcit, " Tū ille nōn es." " Meritō," inquit, " Caesar, mē nōn agnōscis; nam cum hoc factum est, integer eram. Posteā 15 ad Mundam [11] in aciē oculus mihi effossus est. Nec galeam illam, sī vīderis, agnōscēs. Gladiō enim Hispānō dīvīsa est."

Caesar mīlitī suō dedit agrōs dē quibus cum vīcīnīs līs [12] fuerat.

1. **Causam dīcēbat:** *pleading his case;* quīdam is the subject. 2. **paulō violentior:** translate *somewhat vehemently.* 3. **premēbātur:** *was being hard pressed.* 4. **quidem:** *surely.* 5. **arbore . . . spargente:** *a tree casting very little shade.* 6. **ferventissimō sōle:** *when the sun was very hot.* 7. **Cūr . . . meminerim:** *why should I not remember?* 8. **sitī cōnfectus:** *worn out with thirst.* 9. **impedītus:** *i.e.,* by his injured ankle. 10. **īre . . . volēbam:** *I wished to crawl on my hands (and would have done so).* 11. **Mundam:** this battle in Spain established Caesar's supremacy in the Roman world. 12. **līs:** the controversy concerned some land. Caesar's biographers say that he did not permit his veterans, when their service was over, to spend their last days in poverty, but always provided them with grants of land and gifts of money.

Rome   *Courtesy of Grace A. Emery*

TRIBUTE OF ONE ROMAN DICTATOR TO ANOTHER

This illustration shows the wreath placed by Mussolini on the steps of the Temple of Julius Caesar in the Roman Forum. The letters S. P. Q. R. on the ribbon are the abbreviations for SENĀTUS POPULUSQUE RŌMĀNUS. The columns in the background are those of the Temple of Antoninus and Faustina.

201.   THE IDES OF MARCH

This account of the murder of Caesar was written by Gaius Tranquillus Suetonius, who lived in the second century of our era. His chief work is Dē Vītā Caesarum. These biographies contain many personal details and gossipy stories, but as history they are not valued highly.

Caesar was murdered on March 15, 44 B.C. He had had many warnings of disaster impending on the Ides of March. These warnings, together with illness, almost made him stay at home that day, but he was finally induced to go to the Senate.*

Caesar introiit cūriam, Spūrinnam irrīdēns, quod sine ūllā suā [1] noxiā Īdūs Mārtiae adessent. Is respondit, " Vēnērunt

---

* See SHAKESPEARE, *Julius Caesar*, Act III, Scene 2.

quidem eae, sed nōn transiērunt." Sedentem [2] cōnspīrātī speciē officī [3] circumstetērunt; Cimber, quī prīmās partēs suscēperat, quasi aliquid rogātūrus, propius accessit; manū 5 in aliud tempus differentīque [4] ab utrōque umerō togam arripuit; deinde clāmantem, "Ista quidem vīs est," alter [5] ē Cascīs āversum vulnerat paulum īnfrā iugulum. [6] Caesar Cascae bracchium arreptum graphiō trāiēcit; [7] cōnātusque [8] prōsilīre, aliō vulnere tardātus est. Ubi animadvertit undique sē petī, [9] togā caput 10 obvolvit. Atque ita tribus et vīgintī vulneribus trāiectus est, ūnō [10] modo ad prīmum ictum gemitū sine vōce ēditō. [10] Effugientibus cūnctīs, aliquamdiū iacuit dōnec lectīcae impositum, [11] dēpendente bracchiō, [12] trēs servolī domum retulērunt.

1. suā: *his;* translate *to him* (557, *a*). 2. Sedentem: *as he sat;* modifies **Caesarem** understood. 3. speciē officī: *with a show of respect.* 4. in . . . differentī: *putting him off to another time;* **differentī** modifies **Caesarī** understood, and is a dative of reference (519). Cimber took hold of Caesar's toga at the shoulders. 5. alter: there were two brothers of the Casca family among the conspirators. 6. āversum . . . iugulum: *wounds him a little below the neck as he turned,* i.e., in the breast. 7. arreptum . . . trāiēcit: *seized and stabbed with his writing-stylus.* 8. cōnātusque: *and attempting.* 9. petī: *was being attacked.* 10. ūnō . . . ēditō: *without a word, uttering one moan only at the first blow.* Suetonius says that Caesar recognized Marcus Brutus and said in Greek, "Thou, too, my son." 11. impositum: modifies **Caesarem,** the understood object of **retulērunt.** 12. dēpendente bracchiō: these words and the diminutive **servolī,** *poor slaves,* suggest the contrast now with his power when in life. "The paths of glory lead but to the grave."

BRUTUS GLORIES IN CAESAR'S DEATH

Coins commemorating the death of Caesar. The one on the right shows Brutus with attendants; a head of **Lībertās** is on the reverse side. The one on the left bears the head of Brutus. The reverse shows two daggers and the liberty cap worn by freed slaves. **EID**(ibus) **MART**(iis) gives the date, *on the Ides of March.*

Uffizi Gallery, Florence

ĀRA PĀCIS AUGUSTAE

Rōmānōs, rērum dominōs, gentemque togātam, *The Romans, the masters of the world, the toga-clad race.* VERGIL. This fragment from the beautiful marble Altar of Peace, built by Augustus, portrays a religious procession, showing Augustus in the dress of a high priest and others in typical Roman costumes.

202.   THE DEEDS OF AUGUSTUS

The Emperor Augustus wrote a summary of his offices and of his services to the state. After his death this account was inscribed on two bronze tablets and placed at the entrance of his tomb. The original at Rome disappeared, but most of the text has been found in a copy at Ancyra in Asia Minor. The following passage is taken from this inscription, called **Rēs Gestae Dīvī Augustī,** *Deeds of the Deified Augustus.*

Bella terrā et marī [1] tōtō in orbe terrārum suscēpī victorque omnibus cīvibus pepercī. Omnium prōvinciārum [2] populī Rō-mānī, quibus fīnitimae fuērunt gentēs, quae nōn pārērent im-periō nostrō, fīnēs auxī. Galliās et Hispāniās prōvinciās et
5 Germāniam pācāvī. Iānum Quirīnum, [3] quem clausum esse maiōrēs nostrī voluērunt, cum per tōtum imperium populī Rōmānī terrā marīque esset parta victōriīs pāx, cum [4] prius-quam nāscerer, ā conditā urbe [5] bis omnīnō clausum esset, ter, mē prīncipe, senātus claudendum esse cēnsuit.

A COIN OF AUGUSTUS

The senate deified Julius Caesar after his death. This is indicated by the
word **DIVOS** (**DIVUS**) as shown on the coin at the right. The coin at the left
shows the head of Augustus, who was the adopted son of Julius (**DIVI F.**).

Nōn recūsāvī in summā frūmentī inopiā cūram annōnae,[6] 10
quam ita administrāvī ut paucīs diēbus metū et perīculō populum
ūniversum meīs impēnsīs līberārem. Plēbī Rōmānae sēstertiōs [7]
trecēnōs dedī ex testāmentō patris meī. Ter mūnus gladiā-
tōrium [8] dedī meō nōmine et quīnquiēns fīliōrum meōrum aut
nepōtum nōmine; quibus in mūneribus pugnāvērunt hominum 15
circiter decem mīlia. Nāvālis proelī spectāculum [9] populō
dedī trāns Tiberim.

Rīvōs [10] aquārum complūribus locīs refēcī, et aquam quae
Mārcia[11] appellātur duplicāvī, fonte [12] novō in rīvum eius im-
missō. Forum Iūlium et basilicam, quae est inter aedem Cas- 20
toris [13] et aedem Sāturnī,[14] incohāvī et, sī vīvus nōn perfēcerō,
perficī ab hērēdibus iussī. Duo et octōgintā templa [15] deum [16]
in urbe ex dēcrētō senātūs refēcī, nūllō praetermissō quod eō
tempore reficī dēbēbat. Viam Flāminiam [17] ab urbe Arīminum
fēcī et pontēs omnēs praeter Mulvium et Minucium. In prīvātō 25
solō Mārtis [18] Ultōris templum forumque Augustum fēcī, theātrum [19] in solō magnā ex parte ā prīvātīs ēmptō [20] fēcī sub nōmine
M. Mārcellī.

Cum scrīpsī haec, annum agēbam septuāgēnsimum sex-
tum. 30

1. terrā et marī: *on land and sea.* This expression is used regularly without a preposition to express place. **2. prōvinciārum:** modifies **fīnēs**, l. 4; **quibus . . . gentēs:** translate *which had as neighbors tribes.* **3. Iānum Quirīnum:** an ancient temple, the gates of which were closed when Rome was at peace. Before the time of Augustus it had been closed only twice. **4. cum:** *although.* **5. ā conditā urbe:** *from the foundation of the city.* The traditional date is 753 B.C. **6. cūram annō-nae:** this was the office of food administrator. The problem of an adequate food supply at Rome was a serious matter. **7. sēstertiōs:** a sesterce was a small silver coin worth a little less than our five-cent piece. "Here is the will, and under Caesar's seal, To every Roman citizen he gives, To every several man, seventy-five drachmas." Antony's speech, in Shakespeare's *Julius Caesar*, III, 2. **8.** An account of gladiatorial combats may be found in *A Day in Old Rome*, by Davis, Sections 330–344. **9.** A lake was built across the Tiber for this purpose. The exhibition given was a magnificent one representing a great sea-fight. **10. Rīvōs:** *channels.* **11. Mārcia:** the Marcian Aqueduct still brings water to Rome. **12. fonte:** *spring.* **13. Castoris:** the three remaining columns of this temple are among the finest architectural remains in Rome. **14. Sāturnī:** eight columns of this temple are still standing. **15. templa:** Augustus said that he found Rome made of brick and left it made of marble. **16. deum:** = **deōrum. 17. Flāminiam:** this road ran north-east from Rome to **Arīminum,** *Rimini.* **18. Mārtis:** this was one of the most splendid temples in Rome. Several beautiful columns are now standing. **19. theātrum:** this building is still standing. The Orsini Palace occupies its upper stories. **20. in . . . ēmptō:** *on ground in great part bought from private individuals.*

Courtesy of The Detroit Institute of Arts

Augustus

This portrait head represents Augustus as a young man.

REMAINS OF THE FORUM AT POMPEII

203. THE LAST DAY OF POMPEII

C. Plinius Caecilius Secundus (Pliny the Younger) was born at Comum in Italy about 62 A.D. He was one of the most learned men of his age and had a distinguished career as a lawyer and as a public official. Ten books of his letters are extant. They are of great interest and value for the light they throw upon the life of a Roman gentleman of refinement and culture.

The following selection is taken from a letter which Pliny wrote to the Roman historian Tacitus. Tacitus wished to include in his history an account of the eruption of Vesuvius in 79 A.D. and asked Pliny to write him concerning the death of his uncle, Pliny the Elder, who perished in the eruption. That part of Tacitus' history has been lost, but two long letters of Pliny to Tacitus describing the eruption are in existence today.

Nōnum Kal. Septembrēs hōrā ferē [1] septimā māter mea indicat eī [2] appārēre nūbem inūsitātā et magnitūdine et speciē. Nūbēs, incertum erat ex quō monte (Vesuvium fuisse posteā cognitum est), oriēbātur. Longissimō truncō ēlāta in altum, rāmīs diffundēbātur.[3] 5

Cinis incidēbat, calidior et dēnsior, iam pūmicēs [4] etiam nigrīque et combustī et frāctī igne lapidēs. Interim ē Vesuviō monte plūribus locīs lātissimae flammae altaque incendia oriēbantur, quōrum fulgor tenebrīs noctis excitābātur.[5] Iam diēs

THE FLIGHT OF THE POMPEIANS
An artist's conception of the people fleeing from flaming Vesuvius.

10 alibī, illīc nox omnibus noctibus nigrior dēnsiorque; iam quas-
sātīs tēctīs, magnus erat metus.

Tum dēmum excēdere oppidō vīsum;[6] sequitur vulgus.
Multa ibi mīranda, multōs metūs patimur. Nec multō post illa
nūbēs dēscendit in terrās, operuit maria. Audīrēs[7] fēminārum
15 ululātūs, clāmōrēs virōrum; aliī parentēs, aliī līberōs, aliī coniugēs appellābant; hī suum cāsum, illī suōrum[8] miserābantur;
erant quī metū mortis mortem precārentur; multī ad deōs
manūs tollēbant, plūrēs nusquam iam deōs ūllōs aeternamque
illam et novissimam noctem mundō[9] interpretābantur.

1. Nōnum . . . ferē: *about noon, August 24, 79* A.D. The date usually would
have been written **a.d. IX Kal. Sept.** **Ante diem** is understood with **nōnum;** for
dates see **632–5**.   2. eī: *to him, i.e.,* to Pliny the Elder.   3. Longissimō . . .
diffundēbātur: *(the cloud) lifted on high by a very long trunk was spread out in
branches.* Pliny compared it to the umbrella pine tree which is still typical of an
Italian landscape.   4. pūmicēs: *pieces of pumice stones;* the **lapidēs** were solid
rock; **incidēbant** is to be understood with these two nouns.   5. excitābātur: *was*

made brighter. **6. vīsum (est):** *it seemed best.* **7. Audīrēs:** *one might hear;* second person indefinite, potential subjunctive (**582,** *a*). **8. illī suōrum:** *others (lamented the fate) of their friends.* **9. aeternamque . . . mundō:** *that last and final night for the world.*

204.   THE EARLY CHRISTIANS

One of the first Romans to write in defense of Christianity was Q. Septimius Florens Tertullianus (Tertullian), who was born at Carthage about 160 A.D. In the passage quoted here Tertullian gives the substance of a letter still extant, written by Pliny the Younger about 112 A.D., when he was governor of Bithynia, to the Emperor Trajan in regard to the proper treatment of the Christians.

Plīnius enim Secundus cum prōvinciam regeret, damnātīs quibusdam Christiānīs, quibusdam pulsīs, ipsā tamen multitūdine perturbātus est. Quid ageret [1] cōnsuluit tunc Trāiānum imperātōrem, dīcēns praeter pertināciam nōn immolandī nihil aliud sē dē sacrāmentīs eōrum comperisse quam [2] coetūs [3] ante 5 lūcem ad canendum Christō ut deō, homicīdium, adulterium, fraudem, perfidiam, et cētera scelera prohibentēs.[4] Tunc Trāiānus Plīniō scrīpsit eōs inquīrendōs quidem nōn esse, oblātōs vērō pūnīrī oportēre.[5]

1. ageret: *he should do.* **2. quam:** *than.* **3. coetūs:** *meetings,* on the Sabbath. **4. prohibentēs:** modifies **coetūs.** **5. oblātōs . . . oportēre:** *but if brought before him, it was fitting for them to be punished.*

THE CONVERSION OF A ROMAN EMPEROR

Eusebius, the biographer of Constantine (emperor 306–337 A.D.), relates the story of the adoption of Christianity by Constantine. Constantine himself told Eusebius that on the day before the great battle at the Mulvian Bridge (312 A.D.), he saw with his own eyes the symbol of the cross shining in the sky with the inscription, "by this conquer." The troops carried this emblem the following day in the battle in which they defeated Maxentius. As a memorial of this victory, the Senate later erected the triumphal arch shown on page 162.

A HOUSEHOLD GOD

One of the Lares carved on the side of the marble altar of Gaius Manlius.
The Lar holds a **patera,** *libation plate*, in his hand.   On either side are branches
of laurel.

205.   THE HOUSEHOLD GOD

The Household God, **Lār Familiāris,** is an extract from the prologue of a play, **Aululāria,** *The Pot of Gold*, by Titus Maccius Plautus. Plautus, born about 254 B.C., wrote comedies which, although based upon Greek originals, were very Roman in spirit. Twenty of these comedies are still in existence. They are excellent examples of early Roman drama and of the everyday speech of that period.

The **Lār Familiāris,** who watched over the safety of the household, is represented as telling the story of the pot of gold which had been buried by his old master, the grandfather of his present master, Euclio, an old miser. Because Euclio's good daughter makes due sacrifices to the **Lār,** the latter makes known to Euclio the hiding place of the gold, in order that the daughter may have a suitable marriage dowry.

LĀR FAMILIĀRIS.   Nē quis mīrētur quī sim,[1] paucīs [2] ēloquar.
ego Lār sum familiāris ex hāc familiā
unde exeuntem mē aspexistis.[3]   Hanc domum
iam multōs annōs est cum possideō [4] et colō
patrī avōque [5] iam huius quī nunc hīc habet,[6]   5
sed mihi avus huius obsecrāns concrēdidit
aurī thēsaurum clam [7] omnīs : in mediō focō
dēfōdit, venerāns mē ut id servārem sibi.
Is quoniam moritur (ita avidō ingeniō [8] fuit),
numquam indicāre id fīliō voluit suō.   10
Is [9] ex sē hunc [10] relīquit quī hīc nunc habitat fīlium
pariter mōrātum ut [11] pater avusque huius fuit.
Huic fīlia ūna est.   Ea mihi cotīdiē
aut tūre [12] aut vīnō aut aliquī [13] semper supplicat,
dat mihi corōnās.   Eius honōris grātiā [14]   15
fēcī thēsaurum ut hīc reperīret Eucliō [15]
quō illam facilius nūptum, sī vellet, daret.[16]

1. Nē . . . sim: *that no one may wonder who I am.* **2. paucīs:** *in a few words.* **3. unde . . . aspexistis:** *from which you saw me coming out.* **4. iam . . . possideō:** translate *now for many years I have possessed.* **5. avōque:** *and for the grandfather.* **6. habet:** *i.e.* vīvit. **7. clam:** *unknown to;* followed by the accusative **omnīs.** **8. ita . . . ingeniō:** *of such a greedy disposition.* **9. Is:** the son of the first owner of the house did not pay due honor to the household god, so he too died. He left a son whose character was like his own. **10. hunc:** with fīlium. This is Euclio, the grandson of the one who buried the gold. **11. pariter . . . ut:** translate *of similar character to.* **12. tūre:** *with incense.* **13. aliquī:** *with something.* **14. Eius . . . grātiā:** translate *for the sake of honor to her.* **15. fēcī . . . Ecliō:** translate *I saw to it that Euclio found the treasure here.* **16. quō . . . daret:** *in order that he might more easily give her in marriage, if he wished.*

Pompeii, Italy   *Courtesy of Roy C. Flickinger*

SHRINE OF HOUSEHOLD GOD

The figures on either side of the niche are of household gods. Such shrines usually have two snakes painted on them. This snake is about to partake of the offering to the god.

COURT OF A ROMAN HOUSE

A lovely vista met the eyes of the bride as she was carried over the threshold of her new home. Through a formal reception room, **ātrium,** decorated with marble pillars, mosaic floor with fountain in the center, and beautiful frescoed walls, she looked into the master's room, **tablīnum,** and beyond that into a lovely court surrounded by a colonnade, adorned with fountains, flowers, and statuary. There is a reproduction of such an open-air court in the Metropolitan Museum. Its walls are painted in colors copied from Pompeian houses. Roman works of art placed here and there create an atmosphere of reality.

206.   HERE COMES THE BRIDE

The poet, Gaius Valerius Catullus, whose lyric poems are among the finest in literature, was born at Verona about 87 B.C.

These five stanzas are from a marriage hymn written in honor of the wedding * of two of his friends. They refer to the ceremony of conducting the bride to her husband's home after the wedding. The bride comes forth from her home and the procession led by boys carrying torches moves to the home of the groom. Here the bride is carefully lifted over the threshold, as it would be a bad omen for her to stumble on entering her new home.

---

* For interesting accounts of a Roman wedding read: JOHNSTON, *Private Life of the Romans,* pp. 53–64; PAXSON, *Two Latin Plays,* A Roman Wedding.

Prōdeās,[1] nova nūpta, sī
Iam vidētur,[2] et audiās
Nostra verba.   Vidē ut facēs
Aureās quatiunt comās:[3]
5   Prōdeās, nova nūpta.

Tollite, Ō puerī, facēs.
Flammeum videō venīre.
Īte, concinite in modum,[4]
" Ō Hymēn Hymenaee iō,
10   Ō Hymēn Hymenaee."

Vōsque item simul, integrae
Virginēs, quibus advenit
Pār diēs, agite in modum
Dīcite, " Ō Hymenaee Hymēn,
15   Ō Hymēn Hymenaee."

En tibī * domus ut potēns[5]
Et beāta virī tuī;
Quae tibī[6] sine serviat.[7]
Ō Hymēn Hymenaee iō,
20   Ō Hymēn Hymenaee.

Trānsfer ōmine cum bonō
Līmen aureolōs pedēs,
Rāsilemque subī forem.[8]
Ō Hymēn Hymenaee iō,
25   Ō Hymēn Hymenaee.

1. Prōdeās: *come forth;* volitive subjunctive.   **2. vidētur:** *seems best.*   **3. ut . . . comās:** *how the torches scatter their golden rays.*   **4. concinite . . . modum:** translate *sing in unison.*   **5. En . . . potēns:** *Lo, how fine and splendid is the home of your husband.*   **6. tibī:** dative, pointing out the person interested (519).   **7. Quae . . . serviat:** *allow it to serve you.*   **8. Rāsilemque subī forem:** *enter the polished doorway.*

*Note that for metrical reasons the second i of tibī must be read long. In Latin poetry the quantity of a vowel is sometimes changed to meet the requirements of the meter.

207.   A COURAGEOUS WIFE

This story of a Roman wife and mother is found in a letter written by Pliny the Younger to a friend.

Aegrōtābat Caecīna Paetus, marītus eius,[1] aegrōtābat et fīlius. Fīlius dēcessit.   Huic illa ita fūnus parāvit ut ignōrāret marītus; quīn immō,[2] quotiēns cubiculum eius intrāret, vīvere fīlium atque etiam commodiōrem [3] esse simulābat ac saepe quaerentī quid [4] ageret puer, respondēbat, " Bene dormīvit, libenter cibum 5 sūmpsit."   Deinde, cum lacrimae vincerent, ēgrediēbātur; [5] tum sē dolōrī dabat; siccīs oculīs, quiētō vultū redībat.   Prae-clārum erat quidem illud eiusdem [6] perfodere pectus, extrahere ferrum, dare marītō, addere vōcem paene dīvīnam, " Paete, nōn dolet."   Sed quō [7] maius est sine praemiō gloriae abdere 10 lacrimās, āmissōque fīliō, mātrem adhūc agere.[8]

Scrībōniānus arma in Īllyricō contrā Claudium mōverat; fuerat Paetus in partibus,[9] occīsō Scrībōniānō, Rōmam trahē-bātur.   Erat ascēnsūrus nāvem.   Arria mīlitēs ōrābat ut simul impōnerētur.[10] " Virō enim datūrī estis," inquit, " servōs 15 aliquōs quōrum ē manū cibum capiat, ā quibus vestiātur; omnia sōla praestābō." [11]   Nōn impetrāvit; condūxit nāviculam ingēnsque nāvigium minimō [12] secūta est.

1. eius: refers to Arria, the heroine of this story, wife of Caecina Paetus, an ex-consul.   2. quīn immō: *why even.*   3. vīvere . . . commodiōrem: *that the son was alive and even more comfortable.*   4. quaerentī quid: *to her (husband) asking how.*   5. ēgrediēbātur: *kept going out;* translate *would leave the room.*   6. illud eiusdem: *that (act) of hers;* explained by the infinitives.   Paetus was condemned to die because he had joined the conspiracy of Scribonianus against the Emperor Claudius.   When he was about to commit suicide, his courage failed him, but Arria, stabbing herself, handed him the dagger with these words, " It does not hurt, Paetus."   7. quō: *than this.*   8. āmissōque . . . agere: *and though her son was dead, still act the part of a mother.*   9. in partibus: *on his side.*   10. ut . . . impō-nerētur: translate *to be taken aboard with him.*   11. omnia . . . praestābō: *I alone will perform all these services.*   12. minimō: translate *in a tiny boat.*   Arria's heroism sometimes borders on rashness, but the Romans regarded her as a typical example of fortitūdō.

From a Greek vase painting

THE RETURNED TRAVELER

208.   WELCOME HOME

Catullus expresses his joy at the return of his friend Veranius from Spain.

> Vērānī,[1] omnibus ē meīs amīcīs
> Antistāns mihi mīlibus trecentīs,[2]
> Vēnistīne domum ad tuōs Penātēs [3]
> Frātrēsque ūnanimōs anumque [4] mātrem?
> 5   Vēnistī! Ō mihi nūntiī beātī!
> Vīsam [5] tē incolumem audiamque Hibērum [6]
> Nārrantem [7] loca, facta, nātiōnēs.
> Quid mē [8] laetius [9] est beātiusve?

    1. Vērānī: *Veranius;* vocative case, modified by **antistāns. 2. Antistāns . . .
trecentīs:** *preferred by me to three hundred thousand.* **3. Penātēs:** these were
ancient deities who were guardians of the household. They were also regarded as
guardians of the state, which is a union of households. **4. anum:** *old;* the fourth
declension noun **anus** used as an adjective. **5. Vīsam:** *I shall behold.* **6. Hibērum:**
of the Iberians (Spaniards); modifies the nouns in the following line. **7. Nārran-
tem:** *telling of;* modifies **tē,** the understood object of **audiam. 8. mē:** ablative of
comparison (**539**). **9. laetius:** neuter gender to agree with the subject **quid,** *what.*
The English idiom for this is *who.* In Latin, the neuter form is sometimes used
when reference is made to a person.

Pompeii, Italy

A POMPEIAN KITCHEN

This illustration shows a corner of the kitchen in a house at Pompeii. On the stove, built up of masonry, are the pots and pans as they were in 79 A.D. when Pompeii was covered by the eruption of Vesuvius. Note the cooking utensils hanging on the wall.

209. CATO'S IDEA OF A HOUSEKEEPER

Marcus Porcius Cato was a Roman of the old school. He felt that the salvation of Rome rested upon two things, the destruction of Carthage and the maintenance of the simple virtues of early days. Born at Tusculum near Rome in 234 B.C., the son of a farmer, Cato always kept his interest in agriculture even after he had attained fame as a soldier, statesman, orator, and author. His **Dē Agricultūrā,** from which this selection is taken, is a practical work containing random notes on housekeeping and farm management. An interesting account of Cato's life is found in *Plutarch's "Lives."*

Nē vīlica [1] pigra sit. [2] Vīcīnīs aliīsque mulieribus quam minimum ūtātur. [3] Ad cēnam nē quō eat, nēve ambulātrīx sit. Rem dīvīnam nē faciat iniussū dominī aut dominae. Sciat dominum prō tōtā familiā rem dīvīnam facere. Munda sit. Vīllam mundam habeat. Focum mundum cotīdiē, priusquam dormiat, [5] faciat. Kalendīs, [4] Īdibus, Nōnīs, fēstus diēs cum erit, corōnam in focum impōnat. Per eōsdemque diēs Larī familiārī prō cōpiā supplicet. Cibum dominō et familiae cūret et coctum [5] habeat. Gallīnās multās et ōva habeat.

1. **vīlica:** the housekeeper was usually the wife of the **vīlicus,** *farm manager.*
2. **Nē, sit:** *shall not be;* a volitive subjunctive. All subjunctives in principal clauses in this passage are volitive and should be translated by *let* or *shall.* Observe also the English usage, " Thou shalt honor thy father and mother." 3. **ūtātur:** *let her associate.* 4. **Kalendīs:** ablative of time. For dates see (**634**). 5. **coctum:** modifies **cibum.** She is to see to it that she has food cooked for the household.

210.   CATO'S RECIPE FOR CHEESE-CAKE

Bray well two pounds of cheese in a mortar, and when this is done, pour in a pound of corn-meal (or if you want to be more dainty, a half pound of flour) and mix it thoroughly with the cheese. Add one egg and beat well. Pat into a cake, place on
5 leaves, and bake slowly on a hot hearth stone under a dish.

FAIRFAX HARRISON, *Roman Farm Management.**

211.   THE GODS OF THE FARMER

A learned man of the first century B.C., who wrote many books about language, antiquities, law, medicine, architecture, and agriculture, was Marcus Terentius Varro. The passage given here is from his work, **Dē Agricultūrā,** written when he was eighty-one years of age.

Invocābō deōs:[1] nec, ut Homērus[2] et Ennius,[3] Mūsās,[4] sed XII deōs neque tamen deōs urbānōs, quōrum imāginēs[5] ad forum stant, sex marēs[6] et fēminae totidem, sed illōs XII deōs quī maximē agricolārum ducēs sunt. Prīmum, quī omnīs frūctūs
5 agricultūrae continent, Iovem[7] et Tellūrem.[8] Itaque, quod eī parentēs magnī dīcuntur, Iuppiter pater appellātur, Tellus terra māter. Sōlem et Lūnam, quōrum tempora observantur cum quaedam seruntur et conduntur. Cererem et Līberum, quod hōrum frūctūs maximē necessāriī sunt. Ab hīs enim cibus
10 et pōtiō venit. Rōbīgum et Flōram, quibus faventibus, neque rōbīgō frūmenta atque arborēs corrumpit, neque nōn tempes- tīvē[9] flōrent. Item invocābō Minervam et Venerem, quārum ūnīus cūra olīvētī, alterīus hortōrum.[10] Precor etiam Lym- pham[11] ac Bonum Ēventum,[12] quoniam sine aquā omnis
15 ārida ac misera agricultūra et sine bonō ēventū frūstrā est.

*This is a delightful book on farming, based upon the writings of Cato and of Varro, written " for those who love the country."

From a painting by E. Forti   Courtesy of Signora Forti

SCENE AT A ROMAN VILLA

The **vīlicus** and his **familia** are at work during the vintage season.

1. deōs: as Varro is going to write a book on farming, he invokes the gods of agriculture, all of whom are not Great Gods.* **2. Homērus:** the greatest Greek poet, author of the *Iliad* and *Odyssey.* **3. Ennius:** (239 B.C.) wrote a poem of eighteen books, **Annālēs,** recounting the history of Rome. He is often called the father of Roman poetry. **4. Mūsās:** the nine goddesses of music, poetry, and other liberal arts. **5. imāginēs:** a part of the portico in which these statues stood can still be seen in the Roman Forum. **6. marēs:** *male;* from **mās.** **7. Iovem:** this and the following names of gods in the accusative are in apposition with **deōs,** l. 2. **8. Tellūrem:** Tellus was Earth personified as a productive, nourishing divinity. **9. nōn tempestīvē:** *out of season.* **10. quārum . . . hortōrum:** *the care of the one of whom is (of) the olive, of the other, gardens.* **11. Lympham:** goddess of water and fountains. **12. Bonum Ēventum:** the god of good fortune or success.

212.   FAMOUS ROMAN FARMERS

This passage is from Cicero's essay, **Dē Senectūte,** *On Old Age,* in which he represents Cato as the chief speaker, setting forth the charms of farm life to those who have retired from active public life.

---

* For an account of the gods of the Romans see SABIN, *Classical Myths That Live Today.*

MANIUS CURIUS SCORNS THE GOLD OF THE SAMNITES

Veniō ad agricolās. In hāc vītā M'. Curius,[1] cum dē Sam-
nītibus, dē Sabīnīs, dē Pyrrhō triumphum dēportāverat, cōn-
sūmpsit extrēmum tempus aetātis. Cuius quidem ego vīllam
vidēns (abest enim nōn longē ā mē) admīrārī satis nōn possum
5 vel hominis ipsīus continentiam[2] vel temporum disciplīnam.
Curiō ad focum sedentī[3] magnum aurī pondus[4] Samnītēs cum
attulissent, dīmissī sunt; nōn[5] enim aurum habēre praeclārum
sibi vidērī dīxit, sed eīs quī habērent aurum imperāre.[5] Arantī
L. Quīnctiō Cincinnātō[6] nūntiātum est eum dictātōrem esse fac-
10 tum. Poteratne tantus animus nōn efficere beātam senectūtem?

1. M'. Curius: an example of old-time Roman simplicity and virtue. After
defeating Pyrrhus he returned to his farm. The favorite story connected with his
mode of life was that the Samnites found him preparing a dinner of turnips.
2. continentiam: *self-control.* 3. sedentī: modifies Curiō, which is dative with the
compound, attulissent. 4. pondus: this was not a bribe, but a present from the
Samnites, whose patron Curius became after their subjugation by Rome under
his generalship. 5. nōn . . . imperāre: *he said that to have gold did not seem to him
so splendid as to rule over those* (eīs) *who had it.* 6. Cincinnātō: Cincinnatus was
another hero of the Romans. Called from the plow to be dictator in 458 B.C.,
he defeated the enemy and then returned to his farm.

213. THE FARM MANAGER

Cato outlines the duties of a farm manager in the following extract from his **Dē Agricultūrā.**

Haec erunt vīlicī officia.[1] Disciplīnā bonā ūtātur.[2] Diēs fēstī serventur.[3] Sua servet dīligenter. Nē[4] sit ambulātor,[5] nē quō ad cēnam eat.[6] Familiam exerceat; faciat ea quae dominus imperāvit. Nē cēnseat plūs sē scīre quam dominum. Iniussū dominī crēdat nēminī. Sēmen, cibāria, vīnum, oleum 5 mūtuum det nēminī. Duās aut trēs familiās habeat unde roget[7] et quibus det. Nē quid ēmisse velit, īnsciente dominō, nē quid dominum cēlāvisse[8] velit. Opus rūsticum omne cūret ut sciat facere,[9] et id faciat saepe. Sī hoc faciet, minus libēbit ambulāre et valēbit rēctius et dormiet libentius.[10] Prīmus 10 māne surgat, postrēmus dormiat.

1. **vīlicī officia:** *duties of an overseer.* 2. **ūtātur:** *let him use,* or *he shall use.* This subjunctive is a volitive of command. Translate the other volitives in this lesson by *let* or *shall.* 3. **serventur:** *shall (let) be observed.* 4. **Nē:** introduces here, as elsewhere in the reading, a negative command in the volitive. Translate *let not* or *shall not.* This is usually expressed by the imperative of **nōlō** with the present infinitive (**611,** *a*). 5. **ambulātor:** *a gad-about,* or *idler.* 6. **quō, eat:** *go anywhere.* 7. **unde roget:** *from whom he may borrow.* 8. **quid . . . cēlāvisse:** translate *to conceal anything from the master.* 9. **cūret . . . facere:** *let him see to it that he knows how to do.* 10. **minus . . . libentius:** translate *he will not want to run around and will have better health and enjoy his sleep.* What is the literal translation?

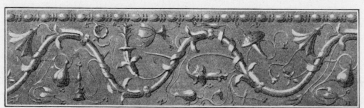

Pompeii, Italy   *Courtesy of Newark Public Library*
FLOWERS AND FRUITS IN TERRA COTTA

STREET SCENE

214.   A ROMAN'S DAY

This poem and the eight which follow are by Gaius Valerius Martialis (Martial), who lived in Rome in the last half of the first century A.D. In his poems, called epigrams, he gives a picture of the daily life of a man-about-town in the capital city.*

The epigram is a literary form consisting of two parts. The first part arouses one's curiosity or interest, the second gives the real point of the poem, often with a clever or unexpected turn. An illustration of this may be seen in the following translation of one of Martial's epigrams by Paul Nixon in *A Roman Wit:*

" I hear that Lycoris has buried every friend she's had in her life;
    I sincerely regret, Fabianus, that she's not introduced to my wife."

Prīma [1] salūtantēs [2] atque altera conterit [3] hōra,
    Exercet raucōs tertia [4] causidicōs.[5]
In quīntam [6] variōs extendit Rōma labōrēs,
    Sexta [7] quiēs lassīs, septima fīnis erit :
5   Sufficit in nōnam nitidīs [8] octāva [9] palaestrīs
    Imperat extrūctōs frangere nōna [10] torōs.[11]

* For the daily life of a Roman see : FOWLER, *Social Life at Rome*, pp. 263–284; JOHNSTON, *Private Life of the Romans*, pp. 308–9.

1. Prīma: for the division of a Roman day see **636.** **2. salūtantēs:** the first thing in the morning a Roman of position held a **salūtātiō** to which his followers and clients came in order to salute or greet him. **3. altera conterit:** *the second hour uses up,* that is *tires out;* the object is **salūtantēs.** **4. tertia:** modifies **hōra.** **5. causidicōs:** what two words enter into the formation of this word? **6. quīntam:** this would be about noon. **7. Sexta:** then the Roman rested and had lunch. **8. nitidīs:** *shining;* because of the oil used on the bodies of the bathers. **9. octāva:** at the eighth hour he went to one of Rome's many bathing establishments where he had his exercise and bath. **10. nōna:** subject of **imperat;** this was the usual dinner hour. The time varied, according to the season of the year, from one to three in the afternoon. **11. torōs:** Roman men reclined at meals, and when they took their places on the couches, they disturbed (**frangere**) the couches piled high (**extrūctōs**) with cushions.

This poem outlines the daily routine of a Roman gentleman. Pliny in a letter tells how his day is spent, " I was present at the ceremony of a youth assuming the toga of manhood; I attended an engagement party and went to a wedding. One man asked me to witness his will, another asked me to represent him in court, and a third asked me for a private consultation."

215. A POET'S PRESCRIPTION

Martial often satirizes Zoilus as typical of Rome's new-rich, fond of vulgar display. He here accuses him of pretending to be sick in order to display his expensive coverlets.

> Zōilus aegrōtat; faciunt hanc strāgula febrem.
>   Sī fuerit sānus,[1] coccina[2] quid facient?
> Quid torus[3] ā Nīlō, quid Sīdone tīnctus olentī[4]
>   Ostendit stultās quid nisi morbus opēs?[5]
> Quid tibi cum medicīs? Dīmitte Machāonăs[6] omnēs.   5
>   Vīs fierī sānus, strāgula sūme mea.

1. sānus: *well.* **2. coccina:** *scarlet bed-coverings;* **coccina** was a dye. **3. torus:** his mattresses and pillows were imported from Egypt. **4. quid . . . olentī:** *what good will be his couch dipped in odorous Sidon (purple)?* Sidon was famous for its purple dye. **5. Ostendit . . . opēs:** *what, except sickness, will show off his foolish wealth?* **6. Machāonăs:** a general word for doctors. Machaon was the son of Aesculapius, god of medicine. Note that the meter requires that the last **a** be short.

216. NŌN AMŌ TĒ

> Nōn amŏ tē, Sabidī, nec possum dīcere quārē:
> Hoc tantum possum dīcere, nōn amŏ tē.

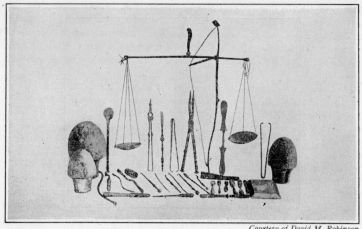

Courtesy of David M. Robinson

ROMAN SURGICAL INSTRUMENTS

This collection was found in the grave of a Roman surgeon. Some are similar to those used today. They are now in the Archaeological Museum of The Johns Hopkins University.

217.   AN OLD-TIME CLINIC

A prospective doctor at Rome received his training by associating himself with an experienced doctor such as the Symmachus of this poem seems to be. When he visits his patient he takes his students with him.

> Languēbam,[1] sed tū comitātus [2] prōtinus ad mē
>   Vēnistī centum, Symmache, discipulīs.
> Centum mē tetigēre manūs aquilōne gelātae.[3]
>   Nōn habuī febrem, Symmache, nunc habeō.

1. Languēbam: *I was a trifle ill.* **2. comitātus:** *accompanied;* modified by **centum discipulīs. 3. gelātae:** modifies **manūs.**

218.   AN OLD EXCUSE

Gellius refuses all requests for money with the excuse, "I am building."

> Gellius aedificat semper. Modo līmina [1] pōnit,
>   Nunc foribus clāvēs aptat emitque serās,

Nunc hās, nunc illās reficit mūtatque fenestrās;
    Dum tantum [2] aedificet, quidlibet [3] ille facit —
Ōrantī nummōs ut dīcere possit amīcō   5
    Ūnum illud verbum Gellius, " Aedificō."

1. līmina: līmen, *the lintel of a door,* is here used for *door.* **2. Dum tantum:** *provided only.* **3. quidlibet:** *anything at all.*

219.   A SNOWSTORM AT ROME

Snowstorms are rare at Rome. Martial hints that this one was sent to garb Horatius in white instead of the dark color which he alone wore at a show where the Emperor was present.

    Spectābat modo [1] sōlus inter omnēs
      Nigrīs mūnus Horātius lacernīs,
    Cum plēbs et minor ōrdō maximusque
      Sānctō cum duce candidus sedēret. [2]
    Tōtō nix cecidit repente caelō: 5
      Albīs spectat Horātius lacernīs.

1. modo: *recently.* **2. Cum . . . sedēret:** *when the plebs, the knights, and the senators, dressed in white, were seated with the sacred leader.* **Plēbs,** *plebians,* **minor ōrdō,** *knights,* and **maximus** (ōrdō), *senators,* were the three classes of Roman citizens. The emperor is called **sānctus.** The people of Rome had reached such a point of abject flattery that they often referred to their emperor as a god.

220.   THE LESSER OF TWO EVILS

After Caecilianus has been refused the loan of a thousand pieces of money, he asks for the loan of a dish, **lānx,** and a few utensils, **vāsa,** worth about five thousand sesterces, giving as an excuse, **causātus,** the arrival of a friend. Martial hints that these would never be returned.

    Mīlle tibī [1] nummōs hesternā lūce rogantī
      In sex aut septem, Caeciliāne, diēs,
    " Nōn habeō," dīxī; sed tū causātus amīcī
      Adventum lancem paucaque vāsa rogās.
    Stultus es? an stultum mē crēdis, amīce? negāvī   5
      Mīlle tibī [1] nummōs, mīlia quīnque dabō?

1. tibī: note that because of the meter final i is long.

221.   REQUIĒSCANT IN PĀCE

Septima iam, Philerōs, tibi conditur uxor in agrō ;
Plūs nūllī,[1] Philerōs, quam tibi reddit ager.

1. **nūllī:** dative of **nūllus.**

222.   HOPE DEFERRED

Nīl mihi dās vīvus ;[1] dīcis post fāta[2] datūrum :[3]
Sī nōn es stultus, scīs, Marŏ, quid cupiam.

1. **vīvus:** *while alive.*   2. **post fāta:** *after death.*   3. **datūrum (esse):** tē is the subject understood.

223.   THE MISER'S LAMENT

This passage is from Plautus' comedy **Aululāria,** *The Pot of Gold.* The miser, Euclio, discovers that his treasure has been stolen. His grief over the loss is not unlike that of Shylock's lament for his lost ducats and his daughter, in Shakespeare's *Merchant of Venice.*

EUCLIO. Periī,[1] interiī, occīdī. Quō curram? Quō nōn
     curram? Tenē, tenē. Quem? Quis?
Nesciō, nīl videō, caecus eō[2] atque equidem quō eam[3] aut ubi
     sim aut quī sim
5 nequeō animō certum invēstīgāre.[4] Obsecrō[5] ego vōs, mī
     auxiliō[6]
ōrō, obtestor,[5] sītis et hominem dēmōnstrētis quis eam abstulerit.
Quid ais tū? tibi crēdere certum est,[7] nam esse[8] bonum ex
     vultū cognōscō.
10 Quid est? Quid rīdētis? Nōvī omnīs, sciō fūrēs esse hīc
     complūrīs,
quī vestītū et crētā[9] occultant sēsē atque sedent[10] quasi sint
     frūgī.[11]
Hem, nēmō habet hōrum? Occīdistī. Dīc igitur, quis habet?
15   nescīs?
     heu mē miserum,[12] miserē periī.

1. **Periī:** the past tense of the verb suggests Euclio's utter despair. The rapid change of mood and tense shows his excitement.   2. **caecus eō:** *I go blindly.*

A ROMAN THEATER

Courtesy of Prescott W. Townsend

Roman and Greek plays were presented in theaters similar to this well-preserved one at Timgad, in northern Africa, where many interesting Roman ruins have been excavated.

3. quō eam: *where I am going;* an indirect question. **4. nequeō . . . invēstīgāre:** *I cannot tell for certain.* **5. Obsecrō, ōrō, obtestor:** *I beg, I pray, I implore;* followed by the two subjunctives, **sītis,** *that you be,* and **dēmōnstrētis,** *that you point out.* Euclio here turns to the audience and asks for aid. **6. mī auxiliō:** *(for) an aid to me;* translate with **sītis; mī** is a short form of **mihi. 7. certum est:** *I am determined.* **8. esse:** the subject is **tē** understood. **9. vestītū et crētā:** translate by *clothes whitened with chalk.* **10. sedent:** the reference is to the seated audience. **11. frūgī:** an indeclinable adjective. **12. mē miserum:** *wretch that I am* **(532).**

224.   **ECHO ANSWERS**

> Of sweet companions, mine, for choice,
> Is Echo of the dulcet voice
> Who carols rounds and glees with me
> And thoroughly agrees with me.
>
> ARTHUR GUITERMAN, Echo *

The following lines are taken from one of the poems of Publius Ovidius Naso (Ovid), the Roman story-teller. In fifteen books, called **Metamor-**

*From *The Light Guitar*, by Arthur Guiterman, published by Harper & Brothers.

phōsēs, he tells fascinating stories based upon Greek and Roman mythology. Ovid is typical of the cultivated, gay, and witty society man of his day at Rome. The Emperor Augustus sent him in exile to Tomi on the Black Sea, where he died about 17 A.D.

> Forte puer,[1] comitum sēductus ab agmine fīdō,[2]
> Dīxerat, " Ecquis adest? " [3] et " Adest," respōnderat Ēchō.
> Hic stupet, atque aciem partēs dīmittit [4] in omnēs;
> Vōce, " Venī! " magnā clāmat. Vocat illa vocantem.[5]
> 5 Respicit, et rūrsus nūllō veniente, " Quid," [6] inquit,
> " Mē fugis? " et totidem quot dīxit, verba recēpit.
> Perstat, et alternae dēceptus imāgine vōcis,[7]
> " Hūc coeāmus," [8] ait, nūllīque libentius umquam
> Respōnsūra sonō,[9] " Coeāmus," rettulit Ēchō.

1. **puer:** Narcissus, a beautiful youth, with whom the nymph Echo had fallen in love. 2. **comitum . . . fīdō:** *separated from the band of his faithful companions.* 3. **Ecquis adest?:** *is there anyone here?* 4. **aciem, dīmittit:** *directs his gaze.* 5. **vocantem:** modifies **eum** understood. 6. **Quid:** *why.* 7. **alternae . . . vōcis:** *deceived by the echo of an answering voice.* 8. **Hūc coeāmus:** *let us meet here.* 9. **nūllīque . . . sonō:** *destined to answer no sound more gladly.*

Other and much later writers of Latin verse have exercised their ingenuity in writing echo poems similar to this, in which the echo repeats the last syllables of the final word of the question and is itself an answer to the question. A sixteenth century poet has this line: " **Diū miserum mē fore rēris?** " " **Eris.** " *Do you think that I will be wretched long? You will be.* Capellanus in **Sprechen Sie Lateinisch,** *Do You Speak Latin,* has imitated this kind of a poem in the following dialogue: (*Read these in Latin before translating.*)

> " Fuerōne beātus sī perservābō in bonīs litter*īs?* "   " *Eris.* "
> " Quid, sī uxōrem dū*xerō?* "   " *Sērō.* "
> " Nōn mē dēlectant sermōnēs tuī disyll*abī.* "   " *Abī.* " [1]
> " Fācundior essēs,[2] opīnor, sī longius ab*essem?* "   " *Essem.* "
> 5 " Coepī prior, sed videō nōn posse vītārī, quīn posterior dē*sinās.* "
>   " *Sinās.* "
> " Sī mē volēs abīre, dīc*itō.* "   " *Ītō!* [3] "

1. **Abī:** the imperative. 2. **essēs:** *you would be.* 3. **Itō:** *go;* future imperative of **eō.** Observe that the Echo does not always repeat the quantity of a vowel correctly.

From a painting by E. Forti   *Courtesy of Signora Forti*

THE LADY'S FAVORITE

225.   **AT THE RACES**

This monologue of a gallant, seated beside his sweetheart at the circus, is a translation from one of Ovid's poems, the **Amōrēs,** *Loves.* It gives a picture of a Roman chariot race.*

I am not sitting here because I am a fancier of blooded horses, yet I hope that the one you favor may win. I came to talk with you and to sit with you, that you might know the love you inspire. You look at the races. I look at you. Let us both look at that which pleases, each feast our eyes.

O happy driver, who has your support! So it is his good fortune to arouse your interest!

You there on the right, whoever you are, have a care, for the lady is annoyed by your pressing on her side!

Would you like in the meantime to summon the ready breezes, the fan moved by my hand will start them. While I have been speaking your white dress has been sprinkled with light dust. Away, vile dust, from this fair form!

---

* For a full account of the races see: JOHNSTON, *Private Life of the Romans,* Sections 328–343; LEW WALLACE, *Ben Hur,* Book Five, Chapter XIV.

But your feet do not touch the floor. If you like, you can stick
the tips of your toes through the grating. The circus is now
clear for the big show and the praetor has sent the four-horse
chariots from the starting place. I see the one whom you favor.
Whoever has your favor will win. The very horses seem to know
what you desire. Wretch, he has gone around the post in a wide
curve! What are you doing? The next one with wheel close
gains on you. What are you doing? Pull, I beg, the left rein
with all your might! We are favoring a ne'er-do-well. But
call them back, Romans, and as a signal toss your togas from
every side! Good! they call them back!

And now the barriers are unbarred again and the gates are
open wide; the many-colored line flies forth at full speed.
Pass them, push forward, see that the prayers of my sweetheart are fulfilled!

Realized are my lady's prayers, but mine are not. Your
driver has won his palm, my prize is yet to be won.

She smiled and with sparkling eyes promised — something.
That is enough for this time.

226.   LOVERS' QUARRELS

This epigram expresses the feeling of Catullus for a young woman whom
he calls Lesbia, who is the inspiration of many of his poems.

> Ōdī [1] et amō; quārē id faciam fortasse requīris.
> Nesciŏ,[2] sed fierī sentiō [3] et excrucior.

1. Ōdī: translate as a present tense (**503**).   **2.** Note that final **o** is marked
short because of the meter.   **3. fierī sentiō:** *I know it is* (*true*).

227.   A CONFIRMED BACHELOR

This story is told by Gellius in **Noctēs Atticae.**

Multīs et doctīs audientibus, legēbātur ōrātiō Metellī, gravis
ac fācundī virī, quam habuit ad populum dē dūcendīs uxōribus,[1]
cum eum ut in mātrimōnium mulierem dūceret hortārētur.[2]
In eā ōrātiōne ita scrīptum fuit: " Sī sine uxōre vīvere possēmus,

omnī eā molestiā carērēmus; [3] sed quoniam ita nātūra fēcit ut [5] nec cum illīs satis commodē, nec sine illīs ūllō modō vīvī [4] possit, salūtī perpetuae potius quam brevī voluptātī cōnsulendum est." [5]

1. dē . . . uxōribus: *concerning marriage.* **2. cum . . . hortārētur:** *when the people were urging him to marry.* **3. omnī . . . carērēmus:** *we would do without all that nuisance;* the conclusion of the contrary to fact condition, **sī . . . possēmus. 4. vīvī:** passive infinitive; complementary with **possit. 5. salūtī . . . est:** *(we) ought to consult for our permanent good rather than passing pleasures.*

228.   A ROMAN JOKE

Quintilian in **Īnstitūtiōnēs Ōrātōriae,** *Education of an Orator,* tells this story, first told by Cicero, as an example of wit in which the point is not stated in so many words, but implied from the context.

M. Fabius Quintilianus (35–95 A.D.), born in Spain, became Rome's most celebrated teacher of rhetoric.

Quāle illud [1] apud Cicerōnem [2] querentī,[3] quod uxor sua ex fīcō sē suspendisset, " Rogō dēs [4] mihi surculum ex illā arbore ut īnseram; " intelligitur enim, nōn dīcitur.

1. illud: *that (answer);* supply **erat. 2. apud Cicerōnem:** *in Cicero; i.e.,* in his book, *The Orator.* **3. querentī:** *to one complaining.* **4. (ut) dēs:** *that you give.*

229.   THE BORE

The following selection is taken from one of the best known satires of Quintus Horatius Flaccus (Horace), who was one of Rome's greatest poets. Perhaps no other poet has been studied, read, and quoted more than Horace.

Ībam forte viā Sacrā,[1] sīcut meus est mōs,
accurrit quīdam nōtus mihi nōmine tantum,[2]
arreptāque manū, " Quid agis, dulcissime rērum? " [3]
" Suāviter, ut nunc est," inquam, " et cupiō omnia quae vīs."
Cum assectārētur, " Numquid vīs? " [4] occupō.[5] At ille   [5]
" Nōrīs nōs," [6] inquit, " doctī sumus ! " Hīc ego, " Plūris
hōc," [7] inquam, " mihi eris." Miserē discēdere quaerēns,[8]
īre [9] modo ōcius, interdum cōnsistere, in aurem
dīcere nesciŏ * quid puerō,[10] cum quidlibet [11] ille
garrīret, vīcōs, urbem laudāret. Ut illī   [10]

* **nesciŏ:** the **o** is shortened for metrical purposes.

Rome   *Courtesy of Grace A. Emery*

SACRA VIA

It was down this ancient street through the Roman Forum that Horace was walking when he was pursued by the bore.

nīl respondēbam, " Miserē cupis," inquit, " abīre;
iam dūdum videō; sed nīl agis; [12] usque tenēbō; [13]
persequar; hinc quō nunc iter est tibi?" [14] " Nīl opus est tē
circumagī; [15] quendam volō vīsere nōn tibi nōtum;
15 trāns Tiberim longē cubat is, prope Caesaris hortōs."
" Nīl habeō quod agam, et nōn sum piger; usque sequar tē."

1. viā Sacrā: a famous street through the Roman Forum. **2. tantum:** *only.*
3. Quid . . . rērum: *how do you do, my dear fellow?* What is it literally? **4. Numquid vīs:** *you don't want anything, do you?* **5. occupō:** *I anticipate him with.*
6. Nōrīs nōs: translate *make my acquaintance;* **nōrīs = nōverīs,** perfect subjunctive; **nōs,** note the editorial first person in this and the following expression. **7. Plūris hōc:** *of more worth for this reason;* the genitive used in the predicate (**511,** *c*). **8. Miserē . . . quaerēns:** *desperately trying to get away.* **9. īre:** this and the following infinitives are to be translated as verbs, *I go,* etc. **10. in aurem . . . puerō:** *say something or other into the ear of my slave.* **11. quidlibet:** translate *at random;* object of **garrīret,** *chattered about.* **12. iam dūdum . . . agis:** *I saw (that) long ago; but it is of no use.* **13. usque tenēbō:** *I shall hold on to you to the end.* **14. hinc . . . tibi:** *from this place where does your way now lead?* **15. Nīl . . . circumagī:** *there is no need for you to be taken out of your way.*

230.   FRIENDSHIP

This discussion of friendship is from one of Cicero's best known and charming essays, **Dē Amīcitiā.** The principal speaker is Gaius Laelius, whose friendship with Scipio the Younger was famous.

Quid dulcius quam habēre quīcum [1] omnia audeās sīc loquī ut tēcum? Quī esset tantus frūctus,[2] beātīs rēbus, nisi habērēs quī illīs magis quam tū ipse gaudēret? [3]   Adversās [4] vērō ferre difficile esset [5] sine eō quī illās [6] gravius etiam quam tū ferret. Amīcitia rēs plūrimās continet; quōquō tē verterīs,[7] praestō 5 est, nūllō locō exclūditur, numquam gravis est; itaque nōn aquā, nōn ignī,[8] ut aiunt, locīs plūribus ūtimur quam amīcitiā.

1. **quīcum:** *(one) with whom.*   The antecedent is omitted, **(560,** *b*). 2. **Quī . . . frūctus:** *what sort of enjoyment would there be?* 3. **nisi . . . gaudēret:** *if you did not have (one) who in these would rejoice more than you yourself.* This same sentiment is found in Bacon's essay on *Friendship.* 4. **Adversās (rēs):** *adversity.* 5. **esset:** *would be.* 6. **illās:** refers to **adversās.** 7. **quōquō . . . verterīs:** translate *wherever one turns;* perfect subjunctive **(582,** *a*). 8. **aquā, ignī:** ablatives with **ūtimur.** Water and fire were symbols of prime necessities. To deprive a Roman citizen of fire and water was to sentence him to exile.

231.   IMMORTALITY

This extract is from Cicero's **Dē Senectūte.** The author has just finished his discussion to the effect that a happy old age must rest on a good foundation laid in youth.

Vīxī ita ut nōn frūstrā mē nātum [1] exīstimem, et ex vītā ita discēdō ut ex hospitiō, nōn ē domō.   Ō praeclārum diem,[2] cum in illud dīvīnum animōrum concilium coetumque proficīscar cumque ex hāc turbā discēdam! Proficīscar enim nōn ad eōs sōlum virōs dē quibus ante dīxī, vērum etiam ad fīlium meum 5 quō nēmō vir melior nātus est, cuius [3] ā mē corpus est cremātum, animus vērō nōn mē dēserēns, in ea loca discessit quō mihi ipsī cernēbat esse veniendum.[4]

1. **nātum:** supply **esse;** an indirect statement with **exīstimem; mē** is the subject. 2. **diem:** an accusative of exclamation. 3. **cuius:** *his.* 4. **quō . . . veniendum:** *where it saw that I too must come;* **mihi** is a dative of agent with the periphrastic form, **esse veniendum.**

232.   THE HEAVENS DECLARE THE GLORY OF GOD

This passage is from one of Cicero's philosophical works.

Cum vidēmus speciem prīmum candōremque caelī;[1] deinde
conversiōnis celeritātem tantam quantam cōgitāre nōn possumus; tum vicissitūdinēs[2] diērum atque noctium; sōlem
lūnamque; tum in eōdem orbe,[3] in XII partīs distribūtō, quīn-
5 que[4] stellās ferrī; nocturnamque caelī fōrmam[5] undique
sīderibus ōrnātam; hominemque ipsum; haec igitur et alia
plūrima cum cernimus, possumus dubitāre quīn iīs praesit
aliquis vel effector,[6] sī haec nāta sunt, ut Platōnī[7] vidētur, vel,
sī semper fuērunt, moderātor tantī operis et mūneris?[8]

1. speciem . . . caelī: *the beauty and splendor of the heavens.* A thought similar
to this is found in *Psalm XIX.* **2. vicissitūdinēs:** *changes.* **3. orbe:** the Zodiac.
4. quīnque: Mercury, Venus, Mars, Jupiter, and Saturn. **5. fōrmam:** *beauty.*
6. quīn . . . effector: *that there is over these someone, either a maker.* **7. Platōnī:**
Plato was a famous Greek philosopher. **8. mūneris:** *display;* this word, which is
used very often to designate a show given to the people by an official, suggests the
beautiful spectacle the Maker of the Universe has provided for man's enjoyment.

Rome, Italy

THE TRIUMPHAL ARCH OF CONSTANTINE

233. AN HONORABLE MAN

A **vir bonus** is thus characterized by Seneca in **Dē Beneficiīs.**

Vir bonus, quod honestē sē factūrum putāverit, faciet, etiam sī labōriōsum erit; faciet, etiam sī damnōsum erit; faciet, etiam sī perīculōsum erit. Rūrsus, quod turpe erit nōn faciet, etiam sī pecū-niam afferet, etiam sī voluptātem, etiam sī potentiam. Ab honestō nūllā rē dēterrēbitur; ad turpia nūllā spē invītābitur.

CĪVIS RŌMĀNUS

This portrait statue represents a Roman citizen. He appears to be a man of great dignity. His face is strong and sensitive with a trace of humor. He wears a toga, the distinctive garb of a Roman citi-zen. Note the grace and dignity of the toga. This garment was usually made of heavy white wool and was about five yards long and four yards wide. It was doubled lengthwise and thrown over the left shoulder in such a way that a short end almost reached the ground in front. The long end was brought from the back under the right arm and carried across the chest to the left shoulder over which it was thrown in folds which hung to the ground in the back.

Courtesy of Cleveland Museum of Art

234.   FOOTPATH TO PEACE

Junius Juvenalis (Juvenal) lived in the last half of the first century A.D. and the first half of the second.

He wrote sixteen satires in which he bitterly assailed the vices and folly of his time. He said, "Indignation makes verses" and "It is difficult not to write satire." The verses quoted here are from a famous satire which has been imitated, quoted, and referred to by many writers. The best imitation is by Dr. Samuel Johnson in his *Vanity of Human Wishes.*

Ōrandum est [1] ut sit mēns sāna in corpore sānō.
Fortem posce animum, mortis terrōre carentem,[2]
quī [3] spatium vītae extrēmum inter mūnera [4] pōnat
nātūrae, quī [3] ferre queat quōscumque [5] labōrēs,
5   nesciat īrāscī,[6] cupiat nihil et potiōrēs [7]
Herculis aerumnās crēdat saevōsque labōrēs
et Venere [8] et cēnīs et plūmā [9] Sardanapallī.[10]
Mōnstrŏ [11] quod ipse tibī possīs dare. Sēmita certē
tranquillae per virtūtem patet ūnica vītae.[12]

1. Ōrandum est: *one should pray.* 2. carentem: *free from.* 3. quī: its ante-cedent is animum; it is the subject of the five verbs in this clause. 4. spatium . . . mūnera: *the end of life among the blessings.* 5. quōscumque: *any what-soever.* 6. nesciat īrāscī: *knows not anger.* 7. potiōrēs: *better than;* modifies aerumnās and labōrēs. 8. Venere: translate *than love.* 9. plūmā: *downy couch.* 10. Sardanapallī: king of Assyria, noted for his love of luxury. 11. Mōnstrŏ: the second o is marked short because of the meter. 12. Sēmita . . . vītae: This sentiment is found in Pope's *Essay on Man:* "Know then this truth enough for man to know, virtue alone is happiness below."

235.   TO SEE OURSELVES AS OTHERS SEE US

The following lines are by Phaedrus, who lived in the first century A.D. He is the author of nearly a hundred fables and stories.

Pērās imposuit Iuppiter nōbīs duās:
Propriīs replētam vitiīs [1] post tergum dedit,
Aliēnīs ante pectus suspendit gravem; [2]
Hāc rē [3] vidēre nostra mala nōn possumus.

1. Propriīs . . . vitiīs: *one filled with our own defects.* 2. Aliēnīs, gravem: *one heavy with (those of) others.* 3. Hāc rē: *for this reason.*

236.   IGNŌRANTIA LĒGIS NĒMINEM EXCŪSAT

The language of the law is full of Latin expressions. Some of these are in the form of words and phrases, such as *mandamus, venire, habeas corpus*, which are used so commonly that they are no longer thought of as Latin. Many important principles of law are to be found also in Latin, summarized in brief statements called maxims.

Accūsāre nēmō sē dēbet.

Bona fidēs exigit ut quod convēnit fīat.

Cōnsentīre vidētur quī tacet.

Diēs dominicus nōn est iūridicus.

Ex nihilō nihil fit.   5

Facta sunt potentiōra verbīs.

Generāle nihil certī implicat.

Hērēditās est successiō in ūniversum iūs quod dēfūnctus habuerat.

Id possumus quod dē iūre possumus.   10

Iūris praecepta sunt haec, honestē vīvere, alterum nōn laedere, suum cuique tribuere.

Lēx prōspicit, nōn respicit.

Minātur innocentibus quī parcit nocentibus.

Nēmō est suprā lēgēs.   15

Omnia praesūmuntur rīte et solemniter esse ācta dōnec probētūr in contrārium.

Plūs peccat auctor quam āctor.

Quod dubitās, nē fēcerīs.

Rēs ipsa loquitur.   20

Salūs populī est suprēma lēx.

Testis oculātus ūnus plūs valet quam aurītī decem.

Ubi iūs, ibi remedium.

Vēritās habenda est in iūrātōre; iūstitia et iūdicium in iūdice.

"There is no better way for the student to train himself in the choice of the very word that will fit his thought than by translation from Latin and Greek. Such habits are worth more to the lawyer than all training which a modern school may impart."

ROSCOE POUND, Dean of Law School, Harvard University.

Museum at Trier, Germany

A TARDY SCHOLAR

This ancient relief depicts a school scene which is typically Roman. The teacher occupies the middle chair between two pupils, who hold book rolls.

237. THE FIRST LATIN PRIMER

In Roman days there were no texts especially prepared for young people. The education of children began with the reading of Horace, Vergil, and other authors, very difficult for beginners. In order to provide easier material for reading, a schoolmaster of the fourth century made a collection of Latin couplets to serve as a first reader and a textbook in morals. This book, called the *Distichs of Cato*, was much used in the schools of the middle ages and continued to be a very popular text until the beginning of the nineteenth century. The quaint translations of the couplets included here are from an old English translation made in 1663, and from one published in Philadelphia in 1735 by Benjamin Franklin.

Cum tibi vel socium vel fīdum quaeris amīcum,
Nōn tibi fortūna est hominis sed vīta petenda.

When-e'er a trusty friend thou dost desire,
Not of his wealth but of his life inquire.

Disce ā doctīs, indoctōs ipse docētō;
Prōpāganda etenim est rērum doctrīna bonārum.

Learn only of the learned, teach the untaught;
Knowledge of truth must to all men be brought.

Contrā verbōsōs nōlī contendere verbīs;
Sermŏ datur cūnctīs, animī sapientia paucīs.

Try not with words the talker to outdo;
On all is speech bestowed; good sense on few.

Sī tibi prō meritīs nēmō succurrit amīcus,
Incūsāre deōs nōlī, sed tē ipse coercē.

When in thy time of need friends fail to come,
Blame not the gods, because the fault's at home.

Coniugis īrātae nōlī tū verba timēre;
Nam lacrimīs struit īnsidiās, cum fēmina plōrat.

Thy wroth wife's speech fear not. But have a care;
A woman by her weeping can ensnare.

Verbera cum tuleris discēns aliquandŏ magistrī,
Fer patris imperium, cum verbīs exit in īram.

Since thou at school thy teacher's blows hast known,
Thou'lt better bear thy father's angry tone.

Mīrāris versūs nūdīs mē scrībere verbīs?
Hoc brevitās fēcit, sēnsū ūnō iungere bīnōs.

Dost ask why I this form of verses choose?
Know brevity did bid me couplets choose.

LABORA ASELLE
QVOMODO
EGO LABORAVI
FIPRODERIITIBI

THE REWARD OF TOIL

This caricature of a donkey turning a mill, found on the walls of one of the palaces on the Palatine Hill, was probably scratched by a page or a schoolboy. The translation of the inscription is: " Labor, little donkey, as I have labored, and it will be of advantage to you." Find the Latin for each of these words.

Thus thou hast seen in	Ita vidisti summatim
short, all things	res omnes
that can be shewed,	quæ poterunt ostendi,
and hast learned	& didicisti
the *chief Words*	*Voces primarias*
of the *English* and *Latin*	*Anglicæ* & *Latinæ*
Tongue.	*Linguæ.*
Go on now	Perge nunc
and read other good *Books*	& lege diligenter alias
diligently,	bonos *Libros,*
and thou shalt become	ut fias
learned, wise, and *godly.*	*doctus, sapiens,* & *pius.*
Remember these things;	Memento horum ;
fear God, and call upon	Deum time, & invoca
him, that he may bestow	eum, ut largiatur
upon thee	tibi
the *Spirit of Wisdom.*	*Spiritum Sapientiæ.*
Farewell.	Vale.

238.   THE FIRST ILLUSTRATED LATIN TEXTBOOK

This is page 194 from the first illustrated text for the use of students of Latin. This book, called **Orbis Pictus,** *The Pictured World*, was written by a seventeenth century educator named Comenius, who thought that pupils would learn Latin more easily if the word and the object were associated. **Orbis Pictus** soon became the most popular textbook in Europe. The English translation here given is from one made in 1727.

239.   GAUDEĀMUS IGITUR

Gaudeāmus Igitur is a student song, the second and third stanzas of which
appeared in the thirteenth century as a religious song.   Other stanzas were
added from time to time.   The author is unknown.

Gaudeāmus igitur,
Iuvenēs dum sumus;
Post iūcundam iuventūtem,
Post molestam senectūtem
Nōs habēbit humus,   5
Nōs habēbit humus.

Ubi sunt, quī ante nōs
In mundō fuēre?
Vādite ad superōs
Trānsīte ad īnferōs,   10
Ubi iam fuēre,
Ubi iam fuēre.

Vīta nostra brevis est,
Brevī fīniētur;
Venit mors vēlōciter,   15
Rapit nōs atrōciter,
Nēminī parcētur,
Nēminī parcētur.

Vīvat acadēmia,
Vīvant professōrēs,   20
Vīvat membrum quodlibet,
Vīvant membra quaelibet;
Semper sint in flōre,
Semper sint in flōre.

The Story-Teller

Quid rīdēs? Mūtātō nōmine, dē tē fābula nārrātur. *Why do you laugh? If the name is changed, the story is told about yourself.* Horace

240. THE PRICE OF LUXURY

This fable is from a collection of fables which have been handed down under the name of Aesop, who was a Greek slave of the fifth century B.C.

Lupus, quī canem bene nūtrītum vidēbat, dīxit, " Quanta est tua fēlīcitās ! Tū, ut vidētur, bene vīvis, at ego famē pereō ! " Respondit canis, " Venī mēcum in urbem, ibi eandem fēlīcitātem habēbis." Lupus condiciōnem accēpit. Dum ūnā iter faciunt, 5 animadvertit lupus cervīcem canis attrītam. " Quid," inquit, " hoc est? Num iugum sustinēs? " " Nihil est," respondit canis, " sed interdiū mē alligant ut noctū sim custōs melior. Haec sunt vēstīgia vinculī quod in cervīcem meam pōnitur." Tum lupus dīxit, " Valē, amīce. Fēlīcitās servitūte ēmpta mihi 10 nōn placet."

A Chained Dog

A FELINE ENEMY

This sculptured relief was lately found on a slab in the old wall of Themistocles at Athens, Greece.

241. WHO WILL BELL THE CAT?

This fable and the two following are from a group of fables collected by Odo, an English monk of the twelfth century, for use in the pulpit and classroom.

Mūrēs iniērunt cōnsilium quōmodo ā fēle sē praecavēre possent, et ait quaedam sapientior cēterīs, " Alligētur tintinnābulum in fēle, tunc poterimus praecavēre fēlem ipsum et audīre quōcumque perrēxerit, et sīc eius īnsidiās vītāre." Placuit omnibus cōnsilium hoc, et dīxit ūna, " Quae mūs igitur 5 est inter nōs tantā armāta audāciā ut in fēle alliget tintinnābulum? " Respondit ūna mūs, " Certē nōn ego ! " Respondit alia, " Certē nōn ego audeō prō tōtō mundō ad fēlem appropinquāre."

242. THE FOX IN THE WELL

Vulpēs cāsū cecidit in puteum. Vēnit lupus et quaesīvit quid faceret ibi vulpēs; quae ait, " Bone frāter, hīc habeō multōs piscēs et magnōs. Volō ut mēcum partem habeās ! " Et ait lupus, " Quōmodo possum ibi dēscendere? " Ait vulpēs, " Superest ūna situla, pōne tē intus, et veniēs deorsum." Et 5 erant ibi duae situlae; quandō ūna dēscenderat, alia ascenderat.

Lupus posuit sē in situlam quae erat suprā et dēscendit; vulpēs in aliā situlā ascendit. Ubi alter alterī occurrit, ait lupus, "Bone frāter, quō vādis?" Et ait vulpēs, "Satis comēdī
10 et ascendō; tū dēscendēns inveniēs incrēdibilia." Dēscendit miser lupus, nec invenit aliquid nisi aquam. Vēnērunt māne rūsticī et extrāxērunt lupum et interfēcērunt.

243.   A SACK OF TRICKS

Vulpēs, sīve Reynardus, occurrit fēlī et ait Reynardus, "Quot fraudēs vel artificia nōvistī?" Ait fēlis, "Certē, sciō ūnum." Et ait Reynardus, "Quod est illud?" Respondit fēlis, "Ubi canēs mē īnsequuntur, sciō ascendere in arborēs et
5 ēvādere. Et tū, quot scīs?" Respondit Reynardus, "Sciō xvii, et adhūc habeō sacculum plēnum. Venī mēcum et docēbō tē artificia mea nē canēs tē capiant." Annuit fēlis et ūnā cum vulpe ībat. Canēs īnsequēbantur eōs. Ait fēlis, "Audiō canēs, iam timeō!" Et ait Reynardus, "Nōlī timēre. Bene
10 tē īnstruam. Ēvādēs." Appropinquāvērunt canēs. "Certē," dīxit fēlis, "longius nōn tēcum ībō; volō ūtī artificiō meō." Et ascendit in arborem. Canēs eum dīmīsērunt, et Reynardum īnsecūtī sunt et tandem cēpērunt, quīdam per tībiās, quīdam per dorsum, quīdam per caput. Fēlis in altā arbore sedēns
15 clāmitābat, "Reynarde, Reynarde! Aperī sacculum tuum! Certē omnēs fraudēs tuae nōn valent ōvum."

244.   HARD TO PLEASE

This story and the three following are by Jacques de Vitry, a Roman bishop of the thirteenth century, whose sermons are famous for the "Exempla" or stories which they contain. These four stories are typical of the illustrations which he used to make his discourses interesting.

Servī virī potentis, cum dūcerent quendam hominem ut eum suspenderent, venientēs ad silvam illī dīxērunt, "Oportet ut suspendāmus tē, sīcut iniūnctum est nōbīs, sed hanc grātiam facimus, ut ex omnibus arboribus huius silvae ēligās tibi aliquam

in quā māvīs suspendī; multās et pulchrās et altās inveniēs 5
quae tē bene sustentābunt et poteris honestē suspendī." Cum
autem dūcerent illum per multās arborēs, dīcēbant, "Tibi
placet haec arbor?" At ille, "Nōn placet mihi, in istā suspendī
nōlō." Cum per omnēs trānsīssent, numquam arborem in-
venīre quae illī placuit poterant. 10

245.   A HORSEBACK RIDE

Mulier cum in amphorā ad forum lac portāret, coepit
cōgitāre in viā quōmodo posset fierī dīves. Cum dē suō lacte
trēs nummōs habēret, coepit cōgitāre quid dē illīs tribus nummīs emeret. "Emam," inquit, "gallīnam et ex ōvīs multōs
pullōs habēbō. Quibus vēnditīs, emam porcum, quem 5
nūtrītum vēndam, et inde emam equum aptum ad equi-
tandum." Tum coepit dīcere, "Equitābō equum illum et
dīcam eī, 'Iō, iō.'" Cum autem haec cōgitāret, coepit movēre
pedēs, quasi calcāria in pedibus habēret, et manūs; ita mōtū
pedum et manuum amphoram frēgit, et, lacte in terrā effūsō, 10
in manibus suīs nihil invēnit; et sīcut anteā pauper fuerat, ita
posteā pauperior fuit. Multī enim multa prōpōnunt et nihil
faciunt.

From a Greek vase painting

MY KINGDOM FOR A HORSE!

246.   THE POWER OF SUGGESTION

Cum rūsticus agnum portāret ad forum, quīdam ait sociīs
suīs, " Facite id quod dīcam vōbīs et grātīs illum agnum habē-
bimus." Eōs in dīversīs locīs posuit, sēparātim, ūnum post
ūnum. Trānseunte autem rūsticō, prīmus ait, " Homō, vīs
5 vēndere illum canem? " At ille nihil respondit et prōcessit.
Cum autem venīret ubi alius stābat, dīxit ille, " Frāter, vīs
mihi vēndere illum canem? " " Domine, nōn ferō canem sed
agnum." Rūsticus, cum autem idem tertius dīxisset, coepit
admīrārī et īrāscī. Quartō autem et quīntō idem dīcentibus,
10 rūsticus, quod totiēns dictum esset eum esse canem, sextō ait,
" Nōlō vēndere, sed grātīs accipe, et nōlī mihi irrīdēre." Et
illī abstulērunt agnum et comēdērunt.

247.   HAVING THE LAST WORD

This folk tale with many variations is found in several different languages.

Dē fēminā audīvī hoc : cum trānsīret per campum cum virō
suō, dīxit vir, " Hic campus falcātus." At illa, " Immō
est tōnsus." " Immō falce," ait marītus, " falcātus est."
Respondit uxor, " Nōn est, sed forcipe tōnsus ; " et coepērunt
5 lītigāre. Tandem marītus īrātus abscīdit linguam uxōris.
Illa vērō cum digitīs forcipēs exprimēns signō significābat
campum tōnsum esse et, cum nōn posset ōre, digitīs lītigāre
coepit. Sīc faciunt quīdam sī quandō eīs silentium imperātur.

248.   THE LAZY SLAVE

This story and the one that follows are from a collection of tales, chiefly
Oriental, which was made in the twelfth century by Petrus Alfonsus while at
the court of Alfonso of Aragon.

Dominus Maymundō praecēpit quādam nocte ut domūs
iānuam clauderet. Ille piger surgere nōluit et dīxit, " Clausa
est." Māne dominus servō dīxit, " Maymunde, aperī iānuam."
Cui servus, " Domine, quod volēbās eam māne esse apertam,

eam sērō claudere nōluī." Tunc prīmum comperit dominus 5
eum esse pigrum et illī, " Surge," inquit, " fac opus tuum,
diēs est, et sōl iam altus est." Cui servus,
" Sī sōl iam altus est, dā mihi cibum."
Cui dominus, " Serve male, vīs nocte
comedere? " Cui servus, " Sī nox est, 10
permitte ut dormiam."

Item dominus noctū, " Maymunde, surge
et vidē utrum pluat annōn." Ipse vērō
advocāvit canem, quī iacēbat extrā iānuam,
et cum vēnisset canis, pedibus inventīs 15
siccīs, " Domine," inquit, " nōn pluit."

Item ab eō dominus nocte quaesīvit num
ignis esset in domō. Ipse vērō, vocātā fēle,
temptāvit sī calida esset annōn; et cum
invēnisset frīgidam, dīxit, " Nōn est." 20

WORK DOES NOT
WORRY HIM

249. BREAKING THE NEWS

Different English versions of this medieval story in dialogue form are
to be found in old school readers.

Dominus dē forō laetus veniēbat. Servus, Maymundus,
contrā dominum exiit. Quem cum vidēret, dominus timuit
nē aliquōs malōs rūmōrēs, ut mōs eius erat, dīceret.

DOMINUS: " Cavē nē dīcās rūmōrēs malōs."

SERVUS: " Domine, nōn dīcam rūmōrēs malōs. Canis nostra 5
parvula mortua est."

DOMINUS: " Quōmodo mortua est? "

SERVUS: " Mūlus noster perterritus est, et dum fugit sub
pedibus suīs canem oppressit."

DOMINUS: " Quid āctum est dē mūlō? " 10

SERVUS: " In puteum cecidit et mortuus est."

DOMINUS: " Quōmodo perterritus est mūlus? "

SERVUS: " Fīlius tuus cecidit dē tēctō et mortuus est, et
inde territus est mūlus."

15 Dominus: "Quid agit puerī māter?"
Servus: "Magnō dolōre mortua est."
Dominus: "Quis custōdit domum?"
Servus: "Nēmō, quoniam in cinerem versa
est, et omnia quae in eā erant."
20 Dominus: "Quōmodo combusta est?"
Servus: "Eādem nocte quā domina mortua
est, ancilla oblīta est lucernae in cubiculō, et ita
combusta est domus tōta."
Dominus: "Ubi est ancilla?"
25 Servus: "Cecidit trabs super eius caput, et
mortua est."
Dominus: "Tū vērō quōmodo ēvāsistī, cum
tam piger sīs?"
Servus: "Cum vidērem ancillam dēfūnctam,
30 effūgī."

Ancient Lantern

250. PLEASE EVERYBODY, PLEASE NOBODY

This story is told by Petrarch, an Italian scholar of the
seventeenth century.

Ūnam tibi ē fābulīs vulgō nōtīs referam.
Senex cum adulēscente fīliō agēbat iter. Hīs
erat ūnus parvus asellus. Mox occurrunt
duābus virginibus. Maxima nātū ex hīs dīxit,
5 "Num quid potest esse stultius illīs quī pedibus iter faciunt,
nec asellō vehuntur?" Hoc ubi audīvit senex, fīlium asellum
ascendere iussit, et ipse cum alacritāte iter pergēbat. Nōn
procul ab eō locō aliquī senēs sermōnem inter sē habēbant.
Tum ūnus, "Quantum tempora mūtantur! Ubi nunc est ille
10 senectūtis proprius honor?" Pudōre fīlius victus patrem
ascendere coēgit.

Via secundum flūmen dūcēbat in quō duae fēminae vestēs
lavābant. Hae ūnā vōce dūrum fīlī labōrem questae sunt.
Senex igitur, quī omnibus placēre vult, puerum post sē sedēre

This lantern,
from a villa near
Boscoreale at the
foot of Mt. Vesu-
vius, is one of the
treasures which
belong to the Field
Museum of Nat-
ural History.

iubet. Nec tamen ea rēs bene ēvenit quod alius viātor eīs 15
occurrit. "Facilius potestis," inquit, "asellum vehere quam vōs
miserum animal." Tum pater respondit : "Nihil quod ab omnibus probētur fierī potest ; repetēmus prīstinum mōrem nostrum."

Nihil amplius dīcam, nec necesse est ; rudis fābula, sed bona.
Valē.   20

251.   THE HEAVY LOAF
This story is found in **Gesta Rōmānōrum.**

Duo caecī erant in cīvitāte Rōmānā. Ūnus ex eīs cotīdiē
clāmitābat per vīcos cīvitātis, " Bene iuvātur quem Dominus
vult iuvāre." Alter vērō clāmitābat, " Bene iuvātur quem
imperātor vult iuvāre." Cum imperātor hoc cotīdiē audīret,
praecēpit ut pānis fieret, et in pāne impōnerentur talenta multa 5
et alterī caecō pānis darētur. Quō acceptō, alter propter
pondus pānis alterī caecō pānem vēndidit. Caecus quī pānem
ēmerat domum vēnit et, frāctō pāne, invēnit plēnum talentōrum
et Deō grātiās ēgit, et posteā permānsit sine labōre. Alter
vērō, cum adhūc pānem quaereret per cīvitātem, vocātus est ab 10
imperātōre, quī eī dīxit, " Ubi est pānis quem ego tibi praecēpī
darī? " Ille respondit, " Vēndidī sociō meō, quia gravis mihi
vidēbātur." " Vērē," ait imperātor, " bene iuvātur quem Deus
iuvat ! " et caecum ā sē reppulit.

A LOAF FROM POMPEII
This loaf of bread, baked more
than eighteen hundred years ago,
was found intact in the ruins of
Pompeii.

252.   THE DAUGHTERS OF KING LEAR

Shakespeare probably took the plot of *King Lear* from this story, found in **Gesta Rōmānōrum,** a thirteenth century collection of stories, which has been used by many writers as a source for plots of stories and plays.

Imperātor potēns in cīvitāte Rōmānā erat quī trēs fīliās pulchrās habēbat. Dīxitque fīliae maximae nātū, " Quantum dīligis mē? " Illa, " Certē," inquit, " plūs quam mē ipsam." Ait eī pater, "Et tē ad magnam dignitātem prōmovēbō."
5 Statim ipsam dedit rēgī dīvitī et potentī in uxōrem. Post haec vēnit ad secundam fīliam et ait eī, " Quantum dīligis mē? " Illa, " Tantum sīcut mē ipsam." Post haec vēnit ad tertiam fīliam et ait eī, " Quantum mē dīligis? " Illa, " Tantum sīcut valēs, et nōn plūs neque minus."
10 Post haec imperātor bellum contrā vīcīnum rēgem gessit. Rēx vērō imperātōrem ex imperiō expulit. Pater scrīpsit litterās prīmae fīliae suae quae, ut dīxit, patrem suum plūs quam sē ipsam dīlēxit, ut sibi succurreret in suā necessitāte, quod ex imperiō expulsus erat. Fīlia cum hās litterās eius
15 lēgisset, virō suō rēgī cāsum patris nārrābat. Marītus, " Eī," inquit, " succurram. Colligam exercitum et adiuvābō eum." Ait illa, " Istud nōn potest fierī sine magnīs impēnsīs. Concēde, quamdiū est extrā imperium suum, quīnque mīlitēs." Et sīc factum est. Fīlia patrī scrīpsit aliud auxilium habēre
20 eum nōn posse, nisi quīnque mīlitēs. Imperātor cum hoc audīvisset, " Heu mihi," inquit, " tōta spēs mea erat in maximā nātū fīliā meā quod, ut dīxit, plūs mē dīlēxit quam sē ipsam, et propter hoc ad magnam dignitātem ipsam prōmōvī."
Scrīpsit statim secundae fīliae, quae dīxerat, " Tantum tē
25 dīligō quantum mē ipsam," ut succurreret sibi in tantā necessitāte. At illa cum audīvisset, virō suō hoc cōnsilium dedit, ut nihil aliud patrī concēderet nisi vīctum et vestītum quamdiū vīveret, et hoc patrī suō scrīpsit. Imperātor cum hoc audīsset, dīxit, " Dēceptus sum per duās fīliās. Iam temptābō tertiam,
30 quae mihi dīxit, ' Tantum tē dīligō quantum valēs.' "

Tertiae fīliae litterās scrīpsit. Ea cum vīdisset inopiam patris, virō suō, " Domine mī," inquit, " mihi succurre. Iam pater meus expulsus est ab hērēditāte suā." Eī vir eius, " Quid vīs tū ut eī faciam? " Illa, " Exercitum collige, perge cum patre meō." Statim collēgit magnum exercitum, impēnsīs 35 propriīs suīs, et ūnā cum imperātōre perrēxit ad bellum. Victōriam obtinuit et imperātōrem in imperiō suō posuit. Tunc ait imperātor : " Fīliam meam minimam nātū minus aliīs fīliābus dīlēxī. Sed illa mihi in magnā necessitāte succurrit, et aliae fīliae meae dēfēcērunt. Eī tōtum imperium relinquam." 40

Post dēcessum patris fīlia minima nātū rēgnāvit et in pāce vītam fīnīvit.

253.   TWO AFTER DINNER STORIES, I

These two stories are taken from a story-telling contest in a **Colloquium** of Erasmus which contains anecdotes to be related at a banquet.

Erasmus was born at Rotterdam in 1466. He loved learning, associated with the great men of his day, and became a great scholar and leader. Among his many writings are **Colloquia,** which consist of seventy-nine Latin conversations intended to give valuable information on various subjects, and also to serve as models of conversational Latin. He always wrote and spoke in Latin.

Lūdovīcus Galliārum rēx occāsiōne vēnātiōnis nactus est amīcitiam cum Conōne, homine rūsticō. Ad eum saepe dēverterat rēx ex vēnātiōne et magnā cum voluptāte vēscēbātur rāpīs.

Uxor monuit Conōnem ut rāpās aliquot īnsignēs rēgī dōnō afferret. Conōn nōluit sed uxor vīcit. Conōn rāpās aliquot 5 īnsignēs dēlēgit. Vērum ipse per viam paulātim omnēs comēdit, ūnā magnā exceptā. Ubi ad rēgiam pervēnit statim agnitus est ā rēge. Ille magnā cum alacritāte mūnus dētulit. Rēx maiōre alacritāte accēpit, mandāns ut dīligenter pōnerētur inter ea quae habēret cārissima. Conōnem iubet sēcum 10 accumbere. Post cēnam Conōnī grātiās ēgit et prō rāpā mīlle nummōs aureōs darī iussit.

Cum huius reī fāma, ut fit, per rēgiam perlāta esset, quīdam

rēgī dōnō dedit equum pulchrum. Rēx intellegēns illum,
15 propter mūnus quod Cononī dedisset, praedae cupidum esse,
vultū laetō mūnus accēpit, et, convocātīs prīncipibus, cōn-
sultāre coepit quid prō pulchrō equō daret. Interim is quī
equum dederat spēs magnās habēre coepit, sīc cōgitāns, " Sī
tantōs nummōs prō rāpā dedit, quantōs prō equō pulchrō
20 datūrus est? " Cum rēgī alius aliud respondēret, tandem
rēx, " Venit," inquit, " in mentem quod illī dem." Quōdam
ē prīncipibus accersītō, dīxit in aurem ut afferret id quod in
cubiculō reperīret (simulque locum dēmōnstrat) dīligenter
obvolūtum. Affertur. Eam rem obvolūtam rēx suā manū
25 illī dat, dīcēns eam sibi mīlle nummīs aureīs cōnstitisse. Iste
avidus linteum tollit, prō thēsaurō reperit rāpam iam āridam.

254.   TWO AFTER DINNER STORIES, II

Quīdam astābat ad iānuam fēminae quae frūctūs vēndēbat,
oculīs intentīs in aliquōs fīcōs. Illa cum vidēret hominem, ex
mōre quaesīvit sī quid vellet. " Vīs," ait, " fīcōs? Sunt
optimī." Cum ille annuisset, rogat quot librās vellet. " Vīs,"
5 inquit, " quīnque librās? " Ille annuit. Fīcōs effūdit in
manum ēmptōris. Dum illa pōnit lancēs, ille cum fīcīs sē
subdūcit. Cum acceptūra pecūniam prōdīsset, vīdit ēmptōrem
abīre. Magnā vōce īnsequitur. Ille pergit quō coepit īre ;
tandem, multīs ad fēminae vōcem concurrentibus, restitit.
10 Ibi in populī corōnā agitur causa ; ēmptor negābat sē ēmisse,
sed sē quod ultrō datum esset accēpisse. Omnēs rīsērunt.

255.   THE MAGIC RING

Cicero in his essay on *Moral Duties* tells this story. Plato had previously
used it in illustration of the point that wrong should not be committed,
though gods and men do not see it.

Gȳges, cum terra discessisset magnīs imbribus, dēscendit in
cavernam, aēneumque equum, ut ferunt fābulae, animadvertit,
cuius in lateribus forēs erant ; quibus apertīs, hominis mortuī

vīdit corpus magnitūdine inūsitātā ānulumque aureum in
digitō; quem ut dētrāxit, ipse induit, (erat autem rēgis pāstor), 5
tum in concilium sē pāstōrum recēpit. Ibi cum pālam eius
ānulī ad palmam converterat, ā nūllō vidēbātur, ipse autem
omnia vidēbat; īdem rūrsus vidēbātur cum in locum ānulum
inverterat. Itaque hāc opportūnitāte ānulī ūsus rēgem
dominum interfēcit sustulitque quōs inimīcōs arbitrābātur; 10
nec in hīs eum facinoribus quisquam potuit vidēre. Sīc
repente ānulī beneficiō rēx factus est.

Hunc igitur ipsum ānulum sī habeat sapiēns, nihilō plūs
sibi licēre putet peccāre quam sī nōn habēret. Honesta enim
ā bonīs virīs, nōn occulta, quaeruntur.   15

256. THE DREAM THAT CAME TRUE

From a work of Cicero in which he discusses dreams and omens.

Cum duo familiārēs iter ūnā facerent et in oppidum vēnissent,
alter ad caupōnem dēvertit, ad hospitem alter. Cum requiēs-
cerent, ille vīsus est ōrāre in somniīs alterum, quī erat in hos
pitiō, ut subvenīret, quod sibi ā caupōne interitus parārētur;
is prīmō perterritus somniō surrēxit; deinde cum sē collēgisset 5
idque vīsum prō nihilō habendum esse dūxisset, recubuit. Tum
eī dormientī īdem ille vīsus est rogāre, quoniam sibi vīvō nōn
subvēnisset, ut mortem suam ulcīscerētur; dīxit sē interfectum
in carrum ā caupōne esse coniectum; petīvit ut māne ad portam
adesset, pruisquam currus ex oppidō exīret. Is hōc somniō 10
commōtus māne ad portam erat, quaesīvit ex agitātōre carrī
quid esset in carrō; ille perterritus fūgit, mortuus inventus est,
caupō poenās dedit.

257. THE CASKET STORY OF THE MERCHANT OF VENICE

This story is found in **Gesta Rōmānōrum** with a moral attached to
it which makes it applicable to the life of a Christian. It was used as
a text for sermons by preachers of the late Middle Ages. This story
was used by Shakespeare in the casket episode of *The Merchant of
Venice.*

Imperātor ūnicum fīlium habuit, quem multum dīlēxit.
Fāma eius imperātōris per mundum volābat quod erat iūstus.
Tamen contrā vīcīnum rēgem bellum gerēbat. Hic rēx tandem
cōgitābat, " Ūnicam fīliam habeō et adversārius meus ūnicum
5 fīlium. Sī per aliquam viam fīliam meam dare possum fīliō
eius in mātrimōnium, pācem perpetuam obtinēbō." Post hoc
puellam cum mūneribus ad imperātōrem mīsit. Imperātor
cum eam vīdisset, dīxit, " Cārissima fīlia, bene tibi sit nunc et
in perpetuum. Sed, fīlia, antequam fīlium meum habueris in
10 marītum, tē probābō."

Statim fēcit trēs cophinōs. Prīmus erat ex aurō pūrissimō
et lapidibus pretiōsīs et erat tālis superscrīptiō super hunc
cophinum, " Quī mē aperiet, in mē invēnerit quod meruit."
Et tōtus cophinus erat plēnus ossibus mortuōrum. Secundus
15 erat ex argentō pūrissimō, plēnus gemmīs, quī tālem superscrīptiōnem habēbat, " Quī mē ēlēgerit in mē invēnerit quod
nātūra dedit." Is cophinus terrā plēnus erat. Tertius
cophinus erat ē plumbō habēns superscrīptiōnem, " Potius
ēligō hīc esse et requiēscere quam in thēsaurīs rēgis permanēre."
20 In hōc cophinō erant trēs ānulī pretiōsī.

Tunc imperātor puellae dīxit, " Cārissima, hīc sunt trēs
cophinī; ēlige quemcumque volueris; et, sī bene ēlēgeris, fīlium
meum in marītum obtinēbis." Illa vērō trēs cophinōs respexit
et ait in corde suō, " Deus, quī omnia videt, det mihi grātiam
25 sīc ēligendī ut nōn dēficiam." Prīmum cophinum tetigit et
superscrīptiōnem lēgit. Illa cōgitābat, " Cophinus est pretiōsus, sed quid intus lateat ignōrō, ideō eum ēligere nōlō."
Deinde secundam lēgit et dīxit, " Numquam nātūra dedit ut
fīlia patris meī darētur fīliō imperātōris." Tertiam lēgit et
30 altā vōce dīxit, " Cophinum tertium ēligō."

Imperātor cum hoc audīsset, dīxit, " Ō bona puella, magnā
cum prūdentiā ēlēgistī. In istō cophinō sunt trēs ānulī pretiōsī;
ūnum prō mē, ūnum prō fīliō, tertium prō tē." Statim nūptiās
celebrāvit et trādidit eī fīlium suum, et sīc in pāce vītam fīniērunt.

258.   THE BOY WHO WENT TO THE SENATE

The story of the boy who went to the Senate was a favorite of Roman writers and is found in collections of stories as late as the Middle Ages. This version is by Aulus Gellius and is the source of many medieval variations of the story.

Mōs anteā senātōribus Rōmae fuit in cūriam cum prae-textātīs fīliīs introīre. Tum, cum in senātū rēs maior cōn-sultāta eaque in diem posterum prōlāta est placuitque nē quis eam rem ēnūntiāret pruisquam dē-crēta esset, māter Papīrī puerī, quī 5 cum parente suō in cūriā fuerat, rogābat fīlium quidnam in senātū patrēs ēgissent. Puer respondit id dīcī nōn licēre. Mulier fit audiendī cupidior; silentium puerī animum eius 10 excitat; quaerit igitur vehementer.

Tum puer, mātre urgente, magnī mendācī cōnsilium capit. Āctum esse in senātū dīxit, utrum vidērētur ūtilius exque rē pūblicā esse ūnus 15 vir ut duās uxōrēs habēret, an ut ūna duōbus nūpta esset. Hoc illa ubi audīvit, domō trepidāns ēgreditur ad cēterās mātrōnās. Pervēnit ad senātum postrīdiē mātrōnārum multi- 20 tūdō. Lacrimantēs ōrant ūna potius ut duōbus nūpta fieret quam ut ūnī virō duae.

Courtesy of Metropolitan Museum of Art

A ROMAN BOY

This well preserved statue of an unknown Roman boy has a charm rarely equaled in ancient sculpture. It is one of the finest specimens of bronze sculpture to be found in America.

Senātōrēs ingredientēs in cūriam postulātum mulierum mīrātī sunt. Puer Papīrius in mediam cūriam prōgressus, 25 quid ipse mātrī dīxisset, nārrat. Senātus cōnsultum facit, nē posthāc puerī cum patribus in cūriam introeant, praeter Papīrium.

Courtesy of S. E. Stout

THE GREAT DISCOVERER

One of the Latin editions of Columbus' letter contains eight woodcuts depicting the ships of Columbus and his voyage. The one shown here pictures his journey to the West Indies. Note the king of Spain on the one side of the water and the Aborigines on the other.

259.   COLUMBUS DISCOVERS AMERICA

A Latin translation was made in 1493 of the letter written by Columbus telling of his discovery of the West Indies. The following excerpt, taken from this letter, is of historic interest, although the Latin is far from classical. Since the number of days occupied by the voyage was written originally in Roman numerals, the number thirty-three in the letter may be due to an error made by a copyist who wrote XXXIII instead of LXXIII.

Trīcēsimō tertiō diē postquam Gādibus discessī, in mare Indicum pervēnī, ubi plūrimās īnsulās ab multīs habitātās hominibus repperī, quārum omnium prō fēlīcissimō rēge nostrō possessiōnem accēpī. Prīmaeque eārum Dīvī Salvātōris nōmen
5 imposuī, cuius frētus auxiliō ad hanc īnsulam pervēnimus.

Quippe vīdī eās īnsulās ita flōrentēs atque decōrās ut mēnse Maiō in Hispāniā solent esse. Sunt in īnsulā Iōhanā septem vel octō palmārum genera, quae pulchritūdine, quem ad modum cēterae omnēs arborēs, herbae frūctūsque, nostrās facile praestant. Sunt et altae pīnūs, agrī vāstissimī, variae āvēs, varia 10 mella, varia metalla, ferrō exceptō.

Incolae ubi nostrōs appropinquāre vidēbant, celeriter fūgērunt. Ubi sē cernunt tūtōs, omnī metū repulsō, sunt admodum amīcī ac bonae fideī, et in omnibus quae habent, līberālissimī; dant magna prō parvīs, minimō et nihilō contentī. 15

260. **VERBA**

Rīdent stolidī verba Latīna, *The stupid laugh at Latin words.* OVID

Required vocabulary*: advertō, auctor, cōgitō, colloquium, commodus, contemnō, dīversus, familiāris, grātīs, integer, magister, pābulor, perdō, rapiō, repleō, simulō, supportō, tot, todidem, trabs, vīcīnus.

NŌSCE TĒ IPSUM

Sunt bona, sunt quaedam mediocria, sunt mala plūra
Quae legis hīc. Aliter nōn fit, Avīte, liber.
MARTIAL

* As PART III is not intended for drill, the required vocabulary has not been entered under each selection. The list of words given above comprises only those required first and second year words that are not found elsewhere in this book.

Queen Mathilda Bayeux Tapestry

TRAJAN'S COLUMN

This tall column, erected by the Emperor Trajan, on which is sculptured the history of the wars which he waged, is still standing in Rome.

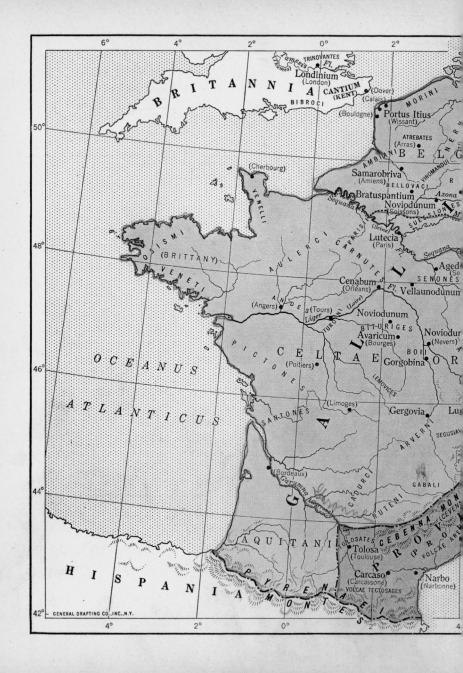

BRITANNIA

6° 4° 2° 0° 2°

Tamesis Fl. TRINOVANTES
Thames
Londinium
(London)
CANTIUM
(KENT) (Dover)
BIBROCI (Calais)
MORINI
(Boulogne) Portus Itius
(Wissant)
ATREBATES
(Arras)
AMBIANI BELG
VIROMANDUI
Samarobriva NERV
(Cherbourg) (Amiens) BELLOVACI R
Sequana Bratuspantium Axona
Noviodunum
VENELLI (Soissons) M
OSISMI (Seine) SUESSIONES
(BRITTANY) AULERCI Lutecia
VENETI PARISII (Paris) Sequana
CARNUTE Aged
Cenabum (Se
ANDES (Orléans) Loire Fl. Vellaunodun SENONES
(Angers) (Tours) L
Liger TURONI Noviodunum
BIT-URIGES
PICTONES Avaricum Noviodur
(Bourges) (Nevers)
(Poitiers) CELTAE BOII OR
OCEANUS Gorgobina
LEMOVICES
ATLANTICUS SANTONES (Limoges) Gergovia Lu
G A SEGUSIA
Corumna (Bordeaux) ARVERNI
(Lot-Garonne) CADURCI GABALI
RUTENI CEBENNA MON
(CEVEN
AQUITANI OSATES PRO
Tolosa VOLCAE ARE
(Toulouse)
PYRENAEI Carcaso
HISPANIA MONTES (Carcassonne) Narbo
VOLCAE TECTOSAGES (Narbonne)

50°

48°

46°

44°

42° GENERAL DRAFTING CO., INC., N.Y.

6° 4° 2° 0° 2° 4

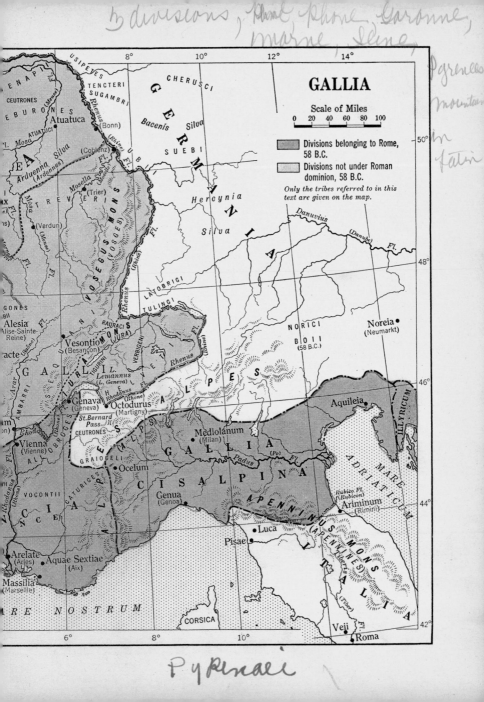

3 divisions, Rhine, Rhone, Garonne,
Marne, Seine,

Pyrenees
mountains
in
Latin

GALLIA

Scale of Miles

0 20 40 60 80 100

Divisions belonging to Rome,
58 B.C.

Divisions not under Roman
dominion, 58 B.C.

*Only the tribes referred to in this
text are given on the map.*

USIPETES

MENAPII

CEUTRONES

EBURONES

Atuatuca

ATUATUCI

(I. Mosa (Meuse)

EA

Arduenna Silva
(Ardennes)

(Verdun)
(Meuse)

TENCTERI

SUGAMBRI

Rhenus Fl.

(Bonn)

(Rhine) Fl.

UBII

CHERUSCI

Bacenis Silva

SUEBI

GERMANIA

Hercynia

Silva

Danuvius

(Danube) Fl.

50°

48°

46°

44°

42°

TREVERI

Mosella Fl.

(Trier)

(Coblenz)

VOSEGUS MONS
(VOSGES)

Rhenus Fl. (Rhine)

LATOBRIGI

TULINGI

Rhenus (Rhine)

NORICI

BOII
(58 B.C.)

Noreia
(Neumarkt)

GONES

Alesia
(Alise-Sainte-
Reine)

Vesontio
(Besançon)

RAURACI

SEQUANI MONS
JURA

TIGURINI

VERBIGENI

HELVETII

ALPES

Aquileia

ILLYRICUM

GALLIA

Genava
(Geneva)

Lemannus
(L. Geneva)

Rhodanus
(Rhone)

St. Bernard
Pass

CEUTRONES

Octodurus
(Martigny)

ALPES

Mediolanum
(Milan)

GALLIA

Padus (Po) Fl.

MARE ADRIATICUM

Vienna
(Vienne)

Ocelum

CISALPINA

GRAIOCELI

VOCONTII

CATURIGES

Genua
(Genoa)

Rubico Fl.
(Rubicon)

Ariminum
(Rimini)

ALLOBROGES

ALPES

APENNINUS MONS
(APENNINES)

Arelate
(Arles)

Aquae Sextiae
(Aix)

Massilia
(Marseille)

Luca

Pisae

ITALIA

CORSICA

(Tiber) Fl.

Veii

Roma

MARE NOSTRUM

Pyrenaei

PART IV

C. IŪLĪ CAESARIS

COMMENTĀRIĪ DĒ BELLŌ GALLICŌ

GAIUS JULIUS CAESAR

This statue represents Caesar in the dress of a commander.

INTRODUCTION

261.   GAIUS JULIUS CAESAR

Gaius Julius Caesar was born in the year 100 B.C. His family name, Julius, shows that he belonged to the Julian gens, which traced its descent back through Iulus and Aeneas, the Trojan founders of the Roman State, to the goddess Venus. July, the name of the month in which Caesar was born, still perpetuates his family name.

The young Caesar had the usual education of an aristocratic Roman youth of his day. He studied grammar, rhetoric, philosophy, and oratory. One of his teachers was from Gaul, the land destined to play such an important part in his life. Later he continued his studies abroad under a celebrated teacher in Rhodes.

Many stories are told of Caesar's youth. These, like the story of George Washington and his hatchet, may not be literally true, but they correspond to his character as it has been handed down in history. The pirate story, a favorite one, tells how Caesar, en route to Rhodes, was captured by pirates and held for a ransom of $20,000. He urged his captors to ask for $50,000 and then sent his companions away to collect the ransom money while he stayed with the pirates. He joined in their games and exercises, telling them often that after he was ransomed he would return and crucify them. And he did. He is said to have wept when he read the life of Alexander the Great because, at the age when Alexander had conquered so many nations, he himself had done nothing memorable.

He was by nature somewhat frail, but by constant athletic

exercise he developed great powers of endurance. He covered long distances with incredible speed, swimming rivers which barred his path or crossing on inflated bags, often arriving ahead of his messengers. One of his biographers, Suetonius, says that he was highly skilled in arms and horsemanship; that, an expert rider from childhood, he would sit with his hands joined together behind his back and ride at full speed; also, that while he was riding horseback he could give dictation to two secretaries at the same time.

There were two political parties in Rome when Caesar began his public career. The aristocratic party (**Optimātēs**) wished to keep all the power in the hands of the Senate. The democratic party (**Populārēs**) had as its ideal the safeguarding of the rights of the people. With this party Caesar cast his lot. Its leaders were Marius, his uncle by marriage, and Cinna, his father-in-law. This relationship and his own forceful personality were responsible for Caesar's being put on the list of those proscribed by Sulla when the **Optimātēs** gained the upper hand. When offered his life if he would divorce the daughter of Cinna, the former democratic leader, Caesar refused to comply and was forced to flee from Italy. He was allowed to return only through the intercession of friends and under the protest of Sulla that " in Caesar there was many a Marius." After his return, realizing that he had no chance of a career under Sulla, he went to Asia Minor and fought against Mithridates. There he won a civic crown for saving in battle the life of a citizen. He was not yet twenty years of age.

Sulla died in 78 B.C. Caesar then returned to Rome and gradually assumed the leadership of the popular party, **Populārēs**. After he was elected military tribune, he helped to overthrow the aristocratic constitution established by Sulla. He was next elected quaestor (68 B.C.), then aedile (65 B.C.), an office which gave him the opportunity to win popular favor through the magnificence of the shows which he gave the people. These left him, as he said, in need of 2,000,000 sesterces to be worth nothing. He held the office of praetor in 62 B.C. In 61 B.C. he went to Spain as propraetor. Here his military ability was tested in successful battles with the native tribes.

Caesar returned to Rome in 60 B.C. to stand for the consul-ship, the highest political office. He felt the need of strong friends to support him against the opposition of the Senate. He found this support already prepared. Pompey, the popular hero, who had just returned victorious from his campaign in the East, was having trouble in persuading the Senate to give a bonus to his veterans. Crassus was the richest man in Rome. Caesar joined these two and in 60 B.C. formed the First Tri-umvirate, a powerful alliance, because it embraced the wealth of Crassus, the popularity and prestige of Pompey, and the brains and energy of Caesar.

Caesar was elected consul for the year 59 B.C. His first act was to secure the passage of a bill giving lands to Pompey's soldiers, while he himself, as proconsul for five years, was granted the governorship of the province of Illyricum, Cisalpine and Transalpine Gaul. At the age of forty-two he deliberately chose to leave Rome behind him and to bury himself as a soldier for five years (later this was extended another five years) in a province itself turbulent and menaced by restless Teutons.

The story of Caesar's nine years in Gaul has come down to us in the words of Caesar himself in **Commentāriī dē Bellō Gallicō,** *Notes about the Gallic War.* This was really a political document written that the Romans might know of his great achievements in Gaul in contrast to Pompey's victories in the East; a promise of what he would do in the future. It is a truthful record. Although twenty centuries have elapsed since the writing of the **Commentāriī,** critical investigation of Caesar's account of his great adventure in Gaul has found it a singularly truthful narrative.

The Gallic War is a great story, simply told by the famous Roman who checked by force of arms a vast Helvetian migration through the Roman province; put to rout a haughty German king and his followers, who never stopped until they reached the Rhine; suppressed a widespread uprising of the Belgians; defeated the coast tribes of western Gaul in the first great sea battle on the Atlantic Ocean; twice invaded Germany; opened up Britain to the civilized world; quelled disturbances in every part of Gaul; and crowned these successes by the famous siege of Alesia when Gaul made its last stand for freedom under the dauntless leader, Vercingetorix.

While Caesar was protecting civilization from the hordes of invaders from the north, and while he was Romanizing Gaul, Crassus had died, and Pompey had gone over to the aristocratic party, thus joining Caesar's enemies in the Senate. Now that Caesar's work in Gaul was finished, he wished to run again for the consulship. But the Senate, jealous of his success and fearful of his growing power, refused to allow him to return to Italy unless he laid down the command of his army.

Caesar with his army set out for Rome. When he reached the boundary he is said to have turned to his staff and nearby soldiers and said, " Even now we may turn back, but once cross yon little bridge and the whole issue is with the sword." After a moment's hesitation, with the famous phrase, **" Alea iacta est,"** " The die is cast," he crossed the Rubicon River and marched on Rome. Pompey fled. Caesar gained control of Rome, defeated the followers of Pompey in Spain, followed Pompey to Greece, defeated him in the Battle of Pharsalia in 48 B.C., set Egypt in order, and in a series of successes ending at Munda,

Spain, in 45 B.C., became complete master of the Roman world. He returned to Rome to celebrate a magnificent triumph in which he mounted the Capitol by the light of torches carried by forty elephants. The story of his achievements was briefly told on a banner borne in the triumphal procession, "**Vēnī, vīdī, vīcī.**"

The personal qualities of a man who played such an important part in the history of the world constitute an interesting study. He is said to have been tall of stature, with a fair complexion, shapely limbs, a somewhat full face, and keen black eyes. He was very particular in the care of his person, being always carefully trimmed and shaved. His baldness troubled him greatly. His biographer, Suetonius, says that, because of it, of all the honors voted him by the senate and the people, there was none which he received or made use of more gladly than the privilege of wearing a laurel wreath at all times.

Caesar's preëminent success in four different fields, war, oratory, literature, and statesmanship, was due to natural brilliancy, the wisdom which consists in knowing what to do next, indefatigable energy, an indomitable will, courage, sympathy, appreciation of others' achievements, and a willingness to forgive and forget.

As a general he set an example of bravery to his soldiers. When all was confusion in the battle of the Nervii, by his personal bravery he restored order and won a great victory. He kept his men on the alert by leading them out sometimes at a moment's notice. He attacked the enemy when least expected. He was a master at moving large bodies of troops rapidly. Within two weeks after he had heard in Rome of the plan of the Helvetians to march through the province, he had collected his forces and stood on the banks of the Rhone ready to dispute their passage. When in the dead of winter Quintus Cicero's camp was besieged, in a few hours Caesar's forces and those of two divisions of the army from different places were rushing to the rescue. His appreciation of his soldiers is seen in his citing, with painstaking care for details, every act unusually brave. This sympathy was a great factor in developing loyalty among his men.

Some idea of Caesar's oratory may be gained from his speeches as given in the story of the Gallic War. A critic of his own time says that he would have rivaled Cicero had he had time for the practice of oratory. Cicero himself writes of him to Nepos, " What orator would you rank above him of those who have devoted themselves to nothing else? Who has more clever or more numerous epigrams? Who is purer or more picturesque in his style? "

Caesar was always keenly interested in literature. Even in the midst of his hottest campaigns in Gaul he wrote to Cicero his criticism of the latter's new Greek poem. Caesar's writings included poetry, works on grammar, astronomy, and history. All but the last, namely the Gallic and Civil Wars, have been lost. Even in his own day Roman critics regarded his language and style as most elegant. One of his generals writes, " All know how splendidly, how faultlessly, but we know also how easily and rapidly he completed his commentaries." Cicero compares these to beautiful and unadorned statues.

Caesar was great as a general, but he was even greater as a statesman. When he became supreme master at Rome, his task was to give an efficient government to a widespread nation that, rapidly losing religious, moral, economic, and industrial standards, was beginning to crave free food and free fun, or as the Romans put it, **pānem ac circēnsēs,** *bread and circuses.* The times called for a one-man government that had in view the highest welfare of all.

The few remaining years of Caesar's rule were filled with great reforms. Soldiers were settled on farms, some of the Gauls were granted citizenship, the calendar was made over, the Senate was reorganized, the administration of government in the provinces was improved, and beautiful public buildings were begun.

Caesar was busily engaged with many projects when a conspiracy against him was formed by a handful of Roman citizens who, actuated by love of the republic, the old-time Roman hatred of a king, and jealousy of Caesar, feared the assumption of too much power on the part of an individual. On the Ides of March (March 15), 44 B.C., despite sickness, omens, prophecies, and a note warning him of impending disaster on that day, he entered the Senate, jokingly reminding the soothsayer who had foretold his death that the Ides of March had come. To this he received the reply, " Yes, but not passed." Struck down by the daggers of men whom he had favored, he fell at the base of Pompey's statue, " the noblest Roman of them all."

MARK ANTONY DELIVERS CAESAR'S FUNERAL ORATION

262.   ROMAN WARFARE

The Roman legion, **legiō,** was a body of infantry the full strength of which was 6,000 men. In Caesar's time, however, there were approximately 3,600 men in a legion. Theoretically these were Roman citizens, but in Caesar's army many provincials were enrolled. The legion consisted of ten cohorts, **cohortēs,** each cohort of three maniples, **manipulī,** and each maniple of two centuries, **centuriae.** A century, as the word itself shows, originally contained 100 men but, since the places of those who fell were not filled, the number probably was much less. In Caesar's day the legions were designated by numbers.

The auxiliary forces, **auxilia,** were not citizens. As their name indicates they served as " aids " and were not depended upon for heavy fighting. They included the slingers, **funditōrēs,** and archers, **sagitāriī.**

Caesar's cavalry, **equitēs,** were Gauls or Germans. They were divided into squadrons, **ālae,** troops, **turmae,** and squads, **decuriae.** They did not play an important part, as their chief duties were to skirmish, to begin the engagement, and to pursue the enemy.

OFFICERS

The commander-in-chief, **dux,** was the highest officer of the army. After he had won an important victory, he was called an **imperātor.**

The staff officers, **lēgātī,** had no definite commands as they have today but performed whatever duty the commander saw fit to assign, such as commanding a legion in battle, building a fleet, or taking charge of winter quarters. They also acted as an advisory body.

The quartermaster, **quaestor,** was second in rank. He had charge of supplies and was paymaster.

Each legion had six military tribunes, **tribūnī mīlitum,** usually ambitious young men who were getting their first military experience, although some of the tribunes were experienced soldiers. They were often put in command of the line of march and of the camp and performed various services.

There were sixty centurions, **centuriōnēs,** to a legion. They were promoted from the ranks because of merit. The highest centurion, **prīmipīlus,** led the first maniple of the first cohort.

The engineers, **fabrī,** standard bearers, **aquiliferī** and **signiferī,** scouts, **explōrātōrēs,** and spies, **speculātōrēs,** were of minor rank.

The prefects, **praefectī,** were in charge of the **ālae** of the cavalry and auxiliary forces, and decurions, **decuriōnēs,** in charge of the squads, **decuriae.**

DRESS AND EQUIPMENT

The legionary soldier wore a woolen sleeveless tunic reaching about to the knees, hobnailed shoes held on by leather thongs, and a heavy woolen cloak.

British Museum, London
BRONZE HELMET
This helmet with neck-guard and visor-mask was found in England.

His armor consisted of a helmet, **galea,** of leather or metal surmounted by a crest; a coat of mail, **lōrīca,** made of leather with metal bands; a shield, **scūtum,** which was curved, covered with leather, and measured about four by two and a half feet.

His weapons were a javelin, **pīlum,** and a sword, **gladius.** The shaft of the javelin was about four feet long, made of wood with a head of soft iron about two and a half feet long, and tipped with a hard point. The sword, about two feet

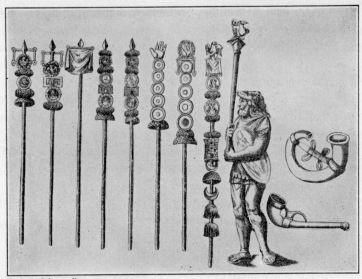

Trajan's Column, Rome

STANDARDS AND MUSICAL INSTRUMENTS

long, straight, pointed, and two-edged, was used largely for thrusting. It hung on the right side from a belt, **balteus,** suspended from the left shoulder.

STANDARDS

The standard, **signum,** of the legion was an eagle of bronze or silver. Each cohort had a standard of its own ornamented with symbolic figures and decorations which it had won. The auxiliaries carried a crimson flag on a staff.

MUSICAL INSTRUMENTS

The trumpet, **tuba,** a straight instrument with a shrill sound, was used to give signals in battle. A curved horn, **cornū,** was also used.

Trajan's Column, Rome   ARMY MUSICIANS

Each of the three men at the left carries a curved horn with a crosspiece, **cornū.**   The one leading blows his trumpet, **tuba.**

Trajan's Column, Rome *   LEGIONNAIRES

The general is addressing a group of soldiers.   Note their dress and equipment.

* The sculptures on this column, see page 186, give valuable information concerning the Roman army, its dress, its equipment, and modes of warfare.   Although Trajan lived more than a hundred years after Caesar's time, warfare had changed so little that a general idea of Caesar's army may be gained from the scenes depicted on Trajan's Column.   These and other illustrations from Trajan's Column were obtained through the courtesy of the Library of the University of Pennsylvania.

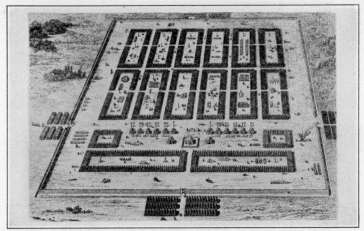

From a drawing by Leveil

A Two-Legion Camp

This drawing is not quite accurate, because it was drawn before the late excavations of actual Roman camps. However, it shows correctly the shape of the camp, the position of the two main roads and the four gates. Note the position of the headquarter's tent of the commander-in-chief just athwart one main road, and adjacent to the other.

THE CAMP

The army, when on the march, went into a regular camp each night. The camp, which had been laid out by an advance party, even if temporary, was made with greatest care. It was rectangular, laid out in streets, **viae,** fortified with a trench, **fossa,** a rampart, **agger,** and breast works, **vāllī.**

THE MARCH

The average day's march was about fifteen miles. Each soldier carried his weapons, food, clothing, cooking utensils, and tools for building the camp. This baggage, **sarcina,** was carried on a forked stick over the shoulder. The cavalry and light-armed auxiliaries usually went in advance. Each legion was usually followed by its own baggage train, **impedīmentum.**

SIEGE WORKS AT ALESIA
This model shows Caesar's elaborate siege works at Alesia.

THE BATTLE LINE

The triple line, **triplex aciēs,** was the regular battle formation. In front there were four cohorts of experienced soldiers; in the second and third lines there were three cohorts each. The cavalry was usually on the wings. When the battle began the first line of cohorts advanced, threw a volley of javelins, and then used their swords in a hand to hand conflict until they were relieved by the second line.

OPERATIONS AGAINST WALLED TOWNS

Walled towns were taken by storm, **oppugnātiō,** or by a siege, **obsidiō.** In taking a town by storm, hurling engines, **tormenta,** throwing great stones or beams, drove the defenders from the walls, the ditches were then filled in, and Roman soldiers, locking their shields together in a **testūdō,** advanced to the walls and broke down the gates with battering rams or scaled the walls with ladders.

In a regular siege a huge mound, **agger,** was built up to the top of the enemy's wall. The besiegers were protected by heavy shields, **pluteī,** or movable sheds, **vīneae,** placed end to end. Sometimes they gained access to the town by huge towers, **turrēs ambulātōriae,** brought up on rollers to the wall.

The artillery used in storming and besieging were the **ballista,** which hurled heavy stones, and the **catapulta,** which threw great javelins.

Sometimes a besieging army blockaded a town and starved it out. Caesar's siege of Alesia was of this character. The historian Froude called it " the most daring feat in the military annals of mankind."

A MANUSCRIPT OF "THE GALLIC WAR"

The illustration on page 204 is from a well-preserved and beautiful manuscript of the fifteenth century, made in Italy. The title of the book is in red capitals, the initial *G* at the beginning is blue and green on a gold background, inclosing a warrior in silver armor on a white horse. The handsome border of white and violet vine tendrils has a blue, green, and crimson background with two narrow bands of gold in the center interlaced with cupids, peacocks, hares, helmets, and winged horses.

The page shown here gives Chapters I, II, and part of III of Liber Prīmus.

BOOKS FOR REFERENCE

ABBOTT, FRANK FROST, *A Short History of Rome*. Scott, Foresman and Company

CLARKE, MICHAEL, *The Story of Caesar*. American Book Company

DODGE, THEODORE A., *Caesar* (A History of the Origin and Growth of War from the Earliest Times to the Wars of Napoleon). Houghton, Mifflin Company

FOWLER, W. WARDE, *Julius Caesar*. G. P. Putnam's Sons

FROUDE, JAMES A., *Caesar, A Sketch*. Harper and Brothers

HAAREN, JOHN H., and POLAND, A. B., *Famous Men of Rome*. American Book Company

HAMILTON, MARY AGNES, *Ancient Rome: The Lives of Great Men*. Oxford University Press

HOLMES, T. RICE, *Caesar's Conquest of Gaul*. Oxford University Press

HOLMES, T. RICE, *Ancient Britain and Julius Caesar*. Oxford University Press

JONES, H. STUART, *A Companion to Roman History*. Oxford University Press

JUDSON, HARRY PRATT, *Caesar's Army*. Ginn and Company

McCARTNEY, E. S., *Warfare by Land and Sea*. Marshall Jones Company

OMAN, CHARLES, *Seven Roman Statesmen of the Later Republic*. Longmans, Green and Company

PELHAM, HARRY FRANCIS, *Outlines of Roman History*. G. P. Putnam's Sons

SIHLER, E. G., *Annals of Caesar*. G. E. Stechert & Company

WHITE, JOHN S., *Plutarch's "Lives."* G. P. Putnam's Sons

STORIES FOR COLLATERAL READING

ANDERSON, PAUL L., *With the Eagles*. D. Appleton and Company

DAVIS, WILLIAM STEARNS, *A Friend of Caesar*. The Macmillan Company

HANNAH, IAN C., *Voadica*. Longmans, Green and Company

MITCHISON, NAOMI M., *The Conquered*. Harcourt, Brace and Company

WELLS, R. F., *With Caesar's Legions*. Lothrop, Lee & Shepard Company

WHITEHEAD, A. C., *The Standard Bearer*. American Book Company

LATIN PLAYS BASED ON CAESAR

HORNER, BRITA L., *The Conspiracy of Orgetorix*. Classical Journal XIII, 61.

LAWLER, LILLIAN B., *Rex Helvetiorum*. Classical Journal, XV, 365.

RADIN, MAX, *Dumnorix*. Classical Journal, XIII, 314.

SCHLICHER, JOHN J., *Latin Plays: Exitus Helvetiorum*. Ginn and Company.

SMITH, M. D., *Exitium Caesaris*. Classical Journal, XVI, 156.

SUTHERLAND, OLIVE R., *The Schoolboy's Dream*. Classical Journal, VII, 181.

A Caesar Manuscript

"Surely you have splendid material for a book! What situations, what kinds of things and places, what customs, what races, what battles, and indeed what a general you have!"

From a letter of Cicero to his brother Quintus, who was on Caesar's staff

LIBER PRĪMUS

The Campaign Against the Helvetians. The War With Ariovistus

58 B.C.

The geography and the inhabitants of Gaul

" There is probably no production of the ancient world that has such an emphatic modern ring as Caesar's description of his Gallic wars. . . . The very first page of the ' Gallic Wars ' might almost have been written by a correspondent in the present war." WORLD'S WORK, October, 1917.

1. GALLIA est omnis [1] dīvīsa in partēs trēs; ūnam [2] incolunt Belgae, aliam [3] Aquītānī, tertiam Gallī. Hī omnēs linguā,[4] īnstitūtīs, lēgibus differunt. Gallōs [5] ab Aquītānīs Garumna flūmen,[6] ā Belgīs Matrona [7] et Sēquana dīvidit.[8]

Hōrum omnium fortissimī sunt Belgae,[9] quod ā cultū atque 5 hūmānitāte Prōvinciae [10] longissimē absunt, minimēque ad eōs mercātōrēs saepe [11] commeant atque ea [12] quae effēminant animōs important; proximīque sunt Germānīs,[13] quī trāns Rhēnum incolunt, quibuscum continenter bellum gerunt.

Quā dē causā [14] Helvētiī [15] quoque reliquōs Gallōs virtūte 10 praecēdunt, quod ferē cotīdiānīs proeliīs [16] cum Germānīs contendunt.

Eōrum ūna pars, quam Gallī obtinent, initium capit ā flūmine Rhodanō; continētur Garumnā flūmine, Ōceanō, fīnibus Belgārum; attingit etiam ab [17] Sēquanīs et Helvētiīs flūmen 15 Rhēnum; vergit ad septentriōnēs. Belgae ab extrēmīs Galliae fīnibus oriuntur; pertinent ad īnferiōrem partem flūminis Rhēnī; spectant in septentriōnēs et orientem sōlem. Aquītānia ā Garumnā flūmine ad Pȳrēnaeōs montēs et eam partem Ōceanī quae est ad [18] Hispāniam pertinet; spectat inter occāsum 20 sōlis et septentriōnēs.

1. Gallia, omnis: *Gaul as a whole;* including **Belgium, Gallia Celtica,** and **Aquītānia.** The people of central Gaul called themselves **Celtae,** *Celts,* but the Romans called them **Gallī,** *Gauls.* Study the map of Gaul and locate all places referred to in the text. Modern France, together with southern Holland, Belgium, western Germany, and Switzerland, now embraces the territory occupied by Gaul as a whole. **2. ūnam:** *one* (*part*). **3. aliam:** *the second* (*part*); object of **incolunt** understood. **4. linguā:** *in respect to language* (**147**). **5. Gallōs:** *the Gauls,* living in central or Celtic Gaul. **6. Garumna flūmen:** *the Garonne river;* subject of **dīvidit** understood. **7. Matrona:** *the Marne;* of special interest since the famous battle of the World War. In translating names of places, use the modern names: *Seine* for **Sēquana. 8. dīvidit:** for the use of the singular number see **568,** *a.* **9. Belgae:** were the modern Belgians in the World War true to their ancestral inheritance? **10. Prōvinciae:** *i.e.,* the strip of southern Gaul which had been conquered by Rome and which was Caesar's *province.* A part of the district included in the **Prōvincia** is today called *Provence.* **11. minimē, saepe:** *least often;* translate *very seldom.* **12. ea:** *those things, i.e.,* wares for sale. **13. Germānīs:** (**524**). **14. Quā dē causā:** *for this reason.* **15. Helvētiī:** the Helvetians occupied part of what is modern Switzerland. **16. ferē . . . proeliīs:** *in almost daily battles.* **17. ab:** *on the side of.* Latin prepositions have many shades of meaning. Learn to select with care the meaning that best fits the context. **18. ad:** *near.*

263.   COMPREHENSION

1. Locate and point out the boundaries of the three divisions of Gaul; of the Roman Province. **2.** What countries now comprise what was ancient Gaul? **3.** What three reasons does Caesar give to account for the bravery of the Belgians? **4.** What does Caesar say about the effect of civilization on the Gauls? **5.** What reasons does he give for the bravery of the Helvetians?

264.   EXERCITĀTIŌ

Iterātiō: **Ablative of specification** (**551**).

Memoriae mandā: **Mīrābile dictū,** *Wonderful to say.* VERGIL

The Latin motto found under the *Memoriae mandā* of each chapter contains a construction which illustrates the point of syntax to be given special attention in that chapter. If you will commit each one to memory, you will have at the close of the year examples of many constructions that you wish to fix in mind, and you will at the same time have stored away a collection of quotations and mottoes which are often used.

Respondē Latīnē: Quā rē Helvētiī reliquōs Gallōs praecēdēbant? (Always answer in a complete sentence.)

Scrībe Latīnē: The Romans differed from the Gauls in institutions, language, and refinement.

265. VERBA

Required Vocabulary: alius, cotīdiānus, differō, ferē, hūmānitās, initium, īnstitūtum, lingua, mercātor, quoque, saepe.

Word Study. To what word in the chapter is each of these related by derivation: *belligerent, caption, humanity, indivisible, Occident, Orient, pertinent, quorum, rebel, spectator?* Explain the meaning of each.

Determine the meaning of each, if possible, without consulting the dictionary, by applying your knowledge of (1) the meaning of the Latin word to which it is related by derivation and (2) the force of any prefix or suffix.

Orgetorix persuades the war-loving Helvetians to invade Gaul

" Roman agents in the Province were alarmed by the appearance of bands of marauders on the right bank of the Rhone. They had been sent by the Helvetii. A generation before . . . they had spread desolation along the valley of the Rhone, defeated a consular army, and compelled the survivors to pass under the yoke. Now, in their turn, they were hard pressed by the Germans; and they had formed the resolution of abandoning their country and seeking a new home." T. RICE HOLMES, *Caesar's Conquest of Gaul*

2. Apud Helvētiōs longē nōbilissimus fuit et dītissimus Orgetorīx.[1] Is, M. Messālā, M. Pīsōne cōnsulibus,[2] rēgnī cupiditāte [3] inductus coniūrātiōnem nōbilitātis fēcit, et cīvitātī [4] persuāsit ut dē fīnibus suīs cum omnibus cōpiīs exīrent,[5] " Perfacile [6] est," inquit, " tōtīus Galliae imperiō potīrī." 5

Id facilius eīs persuāsit,[7] quod undique locī nātūrā [8] Helvētiī continentur: ūnā ex parte [9] flūmine Rhēnō lātissimō atque altissimō,[10] quī agrum Helvētium ā Germānīs dīvidit; alterā ex parte monte Iūrā altissimō, quī est inter Sēquanōs et Helvētiōs; tertiā, lacū Lemannō [11] et flūmine Rhodanō, quī prō- 10 vinciam nostram [12] ab Helvētiīs dīvidit.

Hīs rēbus [13] minus lātē vagābantur et minus facile fīnitimīs [14] bellum īnferēbant; quā ex parte [15] hominēs bellandī cupidī [16]

Lake Geneva, Switzerland   *Courtesy of Official Information Bureau of Switzerland*

THE ROMAN-HELVETIAN BOUNDARY

magnō dolōre afficiēbantur. Prō [17] multitūdine autem hominum et prō glōriā bellī atque fortitūdinis angustōs sē fīnēs [15]
habēre [18] arbitrābantur, quī in longitūdinem mīlia [19] passuum
CCXL,[20] in lātitūdinem CLXXX patēbant.

1. Apud . . . Orgetorīx: the normal order of words in a Latin sentence is
reversed here for the sake of emphasis. **2. M. . . . cōnsulibus:** translate *in the
consulship of Marcus Messala and Marcus Piso;* 61 B.C. (**632**). **3. rēgnī cupiditāte:**
by a desire of royal power. **4. cīvitātī:** why dative (**54**)? **5. ut, exīrent:**
that they should emigrate; translate *to emigrate.* **6. Perfacile:** neuter; predicate
adjective; **imperiō potīrī** is the subject. **7. Id . . . persuāsit:** *he more easily persuaded them* (*of*) *this.* **8. locī nātūrā:** translate *by natural barriers.* See map of
Gaul. **9. ūnā ex parte:** *on one side.* Which? **10. lātissimō atque altissimō:** *very
wide and very deep* (**566**). **11. lacū Lemannō:** *Lake Geneva.* **12. prōvinciam nostram:** whose? Why is the possessive adjective expressed? **13. Hīs rēbus:** ablative
of cause. **14. fīnitimīs:** dative with the compound **īnferēbant. 15. quā ex parte:**
translate (*and*) *for this reason.* **16. bellandī cupidī:** *desirous of fighting;* **cupidī**
modifies **hominēs. 17. Prō:** *in proportion to.* **18. sē, habēre:** *that they had.*
19. mīlia: why accusative? The Roman mile was equivalent to 4,584 feet.
20. CCXL: ducenta quadrāgintā. In reading Latin orally always express the
Roman numbers in Latin words. Learn to count by hundreds from one hundred
to a thousand (**484**).

266.   COMPREHENSION

1. What position did Orgetorix hold among the Helvetians? **2.** What
was his chief ambition? **3.** What was his plan? **4.** Why were the Helvetians easily persuaded to emigrate?

267.   EXERCITĀTIŌ

Iterātiō: **Dative with special verbs (517).**

Memoriae mandā: **Nimium nē crēde colōrī,** *Do not trust too much to
appearances.* VERGIL.

Respondē Latīnē: Quibus Orgetorīx persuādet?

Scrībe Latīnē: Orgetorix easily persuaded the nobility, because they
thought their territories were narrow.

268.   VERBA

Required Vocabulary: **alter, angustus, lātitūdō, nōbilitās, pateō.**

Word Study. The suffix **-idus** (in English *-id*), meaning in a *state* or *condition of*, is attached to verb stems to form adjectives: **cupidus** (**cup-** + **-idus**), *state of desiring.* Give the adjective formed from the stem of each of the following verbs combined with the suffix **-idus**: **placeō, valeō, vīvō.** Give the English derivative of each adjective.

Give five English derivatives of **pars** and show how its meaning enters into the meaning of each word: *participate* (**pars** + **capiō**), *take part in.*

The Helvetians prepare for a great migration

" An ambitious chieftain, Orgetorix, found no difficulty in inspiring them with the desire to seek elsewhere a more fertile territory and a milder climate. They resolved to go and establish themselves in the country of the Santones."

NAPOLEON BONAPARTE III, *History of Julius Caesar*

3. Hīs rēbus adductī et auctōritāte Orgetorīgis permōtī[1] cōnstituērunt ea quae ad proficīscendum[2] pertinērent comparāre. Iūmentōrum et carrōrum quam maximum[3] numerum emunt; sēmentēs quam maximās faciunt ut in itinere cōpia 5 frūmentī suppeteret; cum proximīs cīvitātibus pācem et amīcitiam cōnfirmant. Ad eās rēs cōnficiendās biennium sibi satis esse dūxērunt[4]; in[5] tertium annum profectiōnem lēge cōnfirmant.[6]

Ad eās rēs cōnficiendās[4] Orgetorīx dēligitur. Is sibi lēgā-10 tiōnem ad cīvitātēs suscēpit. In eō itinere persuādet Casticō[7] Sēquanō, cuius pater rēgnum in Sēquanīs multōs annōs obtinuerat et ā senātū populī Rōmānī amīcus[8] appellātus erat, ut rēgnum in cīvitāte suā occupāret,[9] quod pater ante habuerat; itemque[10] Dumnorīgī[11] Aeduō, frātrī Dīviciācī, quī[12] eō tem-15 pore prīncipātum in cīvitāte obtinēbat, idem[13] persuādet, eīque fīliam suam in mātrimōnium[14] dat.

Perfacile esse illīs probat cōnāta perficere: " Ipse meae cīvitātis imperium obtentūrus sum;[15] tōtīus Galliae plūrimum Helvētiī possunt;[16] meīs cōpiīs meōque exercitū vōbīs[17] rēgna 20 conciliābō."

Hāc ōrātiōne adductī tōtīus Galliae sēsē potīrī posse[18] spērant.

1. adductī, permōtī: agree with **Helvētiī**, the subject understood of **cōnstituērunt. 2. ad proficīscendum:** *for a departing*, translate *to an emigration* (**629,** *a*). **3. quam maximum:** translate *the greatest possible.* **4. Ad . . . dūxērunt:** translate *for completing these preparations they considered that two years would be time enough for them;* **cōnficiendās:** (**630,** *a*). **5. in:** *for.* **6. cōnfirmant:** *they fixed;* for the tense see **570,** *a.* Give other examples in this chapter of this use of the present tense. What sequence follows each? **7. Casticō:** why dative? **8. amīcus:** predicate nominative; this title was given by the Roman senate in recognition of a service rendered or expected. **9. ut . . . occupāret:** *to seize the royal power in his own state;* substantive volitive clause with **persuādet. 10. itemque:** *and also.* **11. Dumnorīgī:** dative with **persuādet. 12. quī:** Dumnorix. **13. idem:** object of **persuādet. 14. in mātrimōnium:** among the royalty the strengthening of alliances through marriage has been a common practice from early times. **15. obtentūrus sum:** *I am going to seize* (**95**). **16. plūrimum . . . possunt:** translate *the Helvetians are the most powerful (people).* **17. vōbīs:** *for you.* **18. tōtīus . . . posse:** translate *that they could get control of all Gaul;* **Galliae, 515.**

269.   COMPREHENSION

1. What three special preparations for emigration did the Helvetians make? **2.** On what mission did Orgetorix go? **3.** With what success? **4.** How did Orgetorix strengthen his alliance with Dumnorix?

270.   EXERCITĀTIŌ

Iterātiō: Gerund and gerundive (**74**) (**629-30**).

Memoriae mandā: Aliquod crāstinus diēs ad cōgitandum dabit, *Tomorrow will give something (as food) for thought.* CICERO.

Respondē Latīnē: Quod tempus proficīscendī dēlēctum est?

Scrībe Latīnē: Influenced by the authority of the embassy, the Helvetians decide to prepare for departing, and for the purpose of accomplishing this thing, they buy wagons.

271.   VERBA

Required Vocabulary: **auctōritās, carrus, cōnstituō, emō, item, lēgātiō, permoveō, prīncipātus, profectiō.**

Word Study. The word *senate,* from the Latin word **senātus** (**senex,** *old*), originally meant *a council of elders.* The name **senātor** was given by Romulus to the members of his advisory council, composed of *older* men.

To what word in the chapter is each of these related by derivation: *compare, confirmation, constitutional, fraternity, incomparable, satiate?*

The conspiracy, trial, and death of Orgetorix

4. Ea rēs [1] est Helvētiīs per indicium [2] ēnūntiāta. Mōribus suīs [3] Orgetorīgem ex [4] vinculīs causam dīcere [5] coēgērunt.

Diē cōnstitūtā Orgetorīx ad iūdicium omnem suam familiam,[6] ad [7] hominum mīlia decem, undique coēgit, et omnēs clientēs 5 suōs, quōrum magnum numerum habēbat, eōdem condūxit; per eōs sē ēripuit.[8]

Cum cīvitās ob eam rem incitāta armīs iūs suum exsequī cōnārētur,[9] multitūdinemque hominum ex agrīs magistrātūs cōgerent, Orgetorīx mortuus est; Helvētiī arbitrantur ipsum 10 sibi mortem cōnscīvisse.[10]

1. Ea rēs: *this plot.* The noun **rēs** has various meanings, according to the context. **2. per indicium:** translate *through spies;* what is the literal translation? **3. Mōribus suīs:** (537). **4. ex:** translate *in;* the Latin expression is more literal than the English idiom. **5. causam dīcere:** translate *to plead his case.* **6. familiam:** *household,* including slaves. **7. ad:** *about;* with a numeral **ad** is an adverb. **8. sē ēripuit:** translate *he saved himself.* **9. cōnārētur:** see **61.** What other verb is in the same construction? **10. ipsum . . . cōnscīvisse:** translate *that he committed suicide.*

272.   COMPREHENSION

1. What did Orgetorix do in preparation for his trial? **2.** What action did the state take? **3.** Why did the Helvetians object to the conduct of Orgetorix? **4.** Tell in full the story of Orgetorix. **5.** What charge could the Helvetians rightfully bring against him?

273.   EXERCITĀTIŌ

Iterātiō: **Cum** with the subjunctive (*Cum*-circumstantial) (**597**).

Respondē Latīnē: Quandō Orgetorīx mortuus est?

Scrībe Latīnē: When the magistrates forced Orgetorix to plead his cause in chains, he led his household and clients to the same place.

274.   VERBA

Required Vocabulary: **cliēns, eōdem, ēripiō, familia, magistrātus, vinculum.**

Word Study. The English word *client* comes from **cliēns, clientis** (from **clueō**, *to hear* or *to obey*). A Roman **cliēns** was dependent on some influential man to whom he gave his services and in return received support and protection. What does the word *client* mean today?

Give English derivatives of: **cōgō, condūcō, ēnūntiō, iūs, mors.**

Vatican Museum, Rome

A ROMAN FLOUR MILL

The Helvetians took along with them ground grain sufficient for three months. Their mills for grinding were very primitive compared with those of the Romans. Remains of Roman mills have been found at Pompeii.

The cap, **catillus,** of a stone mill, **mola,** for grinding grain was the solid piece shaped like an hour glass. The base, **mēta,** was conical at the top. The cap turned round on it, and the grain, poured in at the top, came out as meal at the lower edge of the cap.

The Helvetians and allies burn their homes before migrating

" The resolution to burn all dwellings reveals the decisive character of a movement long entertained."

E. G. SIHLER, *Annals of Caesar*

5. Post eius [1] mortem nihilō minus [2] Helvētiī cōnantur ē fīnibus suīs proficīscī.

Oppida sua omnia, numerō ad duodecim, vīcōs ad quadringentōs, 5 reliqua prīvāta aedificia incendunt; frūmentum omne, praeter quod [3] sēcum portātūrī erant,[4] combūrunt,[5] ut, domum reditiōnis spē sublātā,[6] parātiōrēs ad omnia 10 perīcula subeunda essent; [7] trium mēnsium [8] molita cibāria [9] sibi [10] quemque domō efferre iubent.

Persuādent Rauracīs et Tulingīs et Latobrīgīs fīnitimīs utī eōdem 15 cōnsiliō ūtantur; Boiōsque [11] sociōs sibi ascīscunt.

1. eius: *i.e.,* Orgetorix. **2. nihilō minus:** *nevertheless;* nihilō (**550**). **3. quod:** *that which;* the antecedent of a relative pronoun is often omitted. **4. portātūrī erant:** translate *they intended to carry* (**95**). **5. combūrunt:** *burn up;* contrast the meaning with that of **incendunt** in the preceding clause. **6. spē sublātā**: translate *if hope were taken away;* ablative absolute (**545**). **7. ut, parātiōrēs** . . . **essent**: translate *that they might be better prepared to meet all dangers.* **8. trium mēnsium**: translate *for three months;* modifies **cibāria**; what kind of genitive (**511**)? This company of nearly four hundred thousand would require a great baggage train. **9. molita cibāria**: *grain ground in a mill;* translate *meal.* **10. sibi**: *for himself.* Why dative? Explain the case of: **domum**, l. 9; **domō**, l. 13; **quemque**, l. 13; **Rauracīs**, l. 14; **cōnsiliō**, l. 16; **sociōs**, l. 16. **11. Boiōsque**: the Boii were ancestors of the Bohemians.

275.   COMPREHENSION

1. Did the death of Orgetorix have any effect upon the Helvetian migration? **2.** What does this show? **3.** What did the Helvetians do before they started from home? Why? **4.** How long did they think the journey would take?

276.   EXERCITĀTIŌ

Iterātiō: Ablative absolute (**545**). Active Periphrastic Conjugation (**501**).

Memoriae mandā: **Fidē abrogātā, omnis hūmāna societās tollitur,** *When good faith is abolished, all human society is destroyed.* LIVY

Respondē Latīnē: Quibus, omnibus rēbus parātīs, persuāsūrī sunt Helvētiī ut sēcum proficīscantur?

Scrībe Latīnē: After their private houses and all the grain, except what they were going to carry away, had been set on fire, the Helvetians set out from their villages.

277.   VERBA

Required Vocabulary: **aedificium, efferō, mēns, prīvātus, vīcus.**

Word Study. Define the following words showing that each contains the idea expressed by **parō**: *apparatus, irreparable, parade, parasol, preparation, repair, reparation, separate.*

Find in the story the Latin word to which each of the following is related by derivation: *combustion, counsellor, demented, deportment, desperation, duo-decimal, incendiary, molar, mortality, numerator, post-mortem, mortuary.* Give the meaning of each word on the basis of its derivation.

Pas de l'Écluse   *Courtesy of George R. Swain*

THE ROUTE THROUGH THE TERRITORY OF THE SEQUANIANS

This narrow pass was one of the two ways open to the migrating Helvetians.

They choose the route through the Roman Province

" As the mountain chain of the Jura, stretching from the Rhine to the Rhone, almost completely closed in the Helvetic country on the west, and its narrow defiles were as ill adapted for defense, the leaders had resolved to go round in a southerly direction and to open up for themselves a way to the west at the point where the Rhone had broken through the mountain chain between the southwestern and highest part of the Jura and the Savoy mountains." THEODOR MOMMSEN, *History of Rome*

6. Erant omnīnō itinera duo quibus [1] itineribus domō exīre possent : [2] ūnum per Sēquanōs,[3] angustum et difficile, inter montem Iūram et flūmen Rhodanum, vix quā [4] singulī [5] carrī dūcerentur ; [6] mōns autem altissimus impendēbat ut facile perpaucī prohibēre possent ; [7] alterum [8] per prōvinciam nostram, 5 multō [9] facilius atque expedītius,[10] proptereā quod inter fīnēs Helvētiōrum et Allobrogum, quī nūper pācātī erant,[11] Rhodanus fluit, isque [12] nōn nūllīs [13] locīs [14] vadō trānsītur.

Extrēmum oppidum Allobrogum est proximumque Helvētiō-
10 rum fīnibus Genava. Ex eō oppidō pōns ad Helvētiōs pertinet. Allobrogibus sēsē vel persuāsūrōs,[15] quod nōndum bonō
animō [16] in [17] populum Rōmānum vidērentur, exīstimābant, vel
vī [18] coāctūrōs ut per suōs fīnēs eōs īre paterentur.

Omnibus rēbus ad profectiōnem comparātīs, diem dīcunt
15 quā diē ad rīpam Rhodanī omnēs conveniant.[19] Is diēs erat
a. d. v. Kal. Apr.,[20] L. Pīsōne, A. Gabīniō cōnsulibus.

1. quibus: *by which.* The repeated antecedent (**itineribus**) is not to be translated (**560,** *a*). **2. possent:** the subjunctive is used here in a relative clause which
describes (**584**). **3. per Sēquanōs:** translate *through the territory of the Sequanians.*
The name of the people is often given instead of the territory inhabited by them.
4. quā: *by which way;* adverb. **5. singulī:** *one by one.* **6. dūcerentur:** *could be
drawn* (**582**). **7. possent:** (**587**). **8. alterum** (**iter**): *the other* (*route*). **9. multō:**
(**550**). **10. facilius atque expedītius:** *easier and more convenient.* **11. quī . . .
erant:** the Allobroges, who were first conquered in 121 B.C., had revolted and were
again subdued in 61 B.C. **12. isque:** *and it;* the Rhone. **13. nōn nūllīs:** *several;*
what is it literally? Double negatives are used frequently in Latin. **14. locīs:**
the ablative of **locus** without a preposition is used to express *place where* (**552,** *a*).
15. sēsē vel persuāsūrōs (**esse**): *that they would either persuade;* a principal statement in indirect discourse depending on **exīstimābant.** **16. bonō animō:** *well
disposed;* what is it literally (**141**)? **17. in:** *toward.* **18. vī:** *by force.* **19. omnēs
conveniant:** *all were to assemble;* in a relative clause of purpose. **20. a. d. v. Kal.
Apr.:** ante diem quīntum Kalendās Aprīlēs; (**635**).

278.   COMPREHENSION

1. Which of the two ways possible to the Helvetians was the more difficult? Why? **2.** Why did the Helvetians think the Allobroges might be
willing to help them?

279.   EXERCITĀTIŌ

Iterātiō: **Ablative of description** (**544**).

Memoriae mandā: **Fac animō magnō fortīque sīs,** *See to it that you are of
a great and courageous soul.*

Respondē Latīnē: **Quō animō in Caesarem erant Allobrogēs?**

Scrībe Latīnē: The Rhone, a river of great depth (**altitūdō**), where it
flows between these territories, is crossed by several fords.

280. VERBA

Required Vocabulary: fluō, nōn nūllus, pācō, proptereā, quā, singulī, vadum, vel.

Word Study. To what word in the chapter is each of these related by derivation: *convention, dome, impending, null, riparian, superfluous, unanimous?* What is a *bonus?*

Caesar hurries to Geneva and prepares to stop the Helvetians

" Caesar, learning that the Helvetii intended to pass through the Roman province, left Rome hastily in the month of March, hurried by forced marches into Transalpine Gaul, and according to Plutarch, reached Geneva in eight days. As he had in the province only a single legion, he ordered a levy of as many men as possible and then destroyed the bridge of Geneva."

NAPOLEON BONAPARTE III, *History of Julius Caesar*

7. Caesarī [1] cum id [2] nūntiātum esset eōs per prōvinciam nostram iter facere cōnārī, mātūrat ab urbe [3] proficīscī et quam maximīs potest itineribus [4] in Galliam ulteriōrem [5] contendit et ad Genavam pervenit. Prōvinciae tōtī quam maximum potest mīlitum numerum imperat [6] (erat omnīnō in Galliā ulteriōre legiō ūna [7]); pontem quī erat ad Genavam iubet rescindī.

Ubi dē eius adventū Helvētiī certiōrēs factī sunt, [8] lēgātōs ad eum mittunt nōbilissimōs cīvitātis, quī rogārent [9] ut iter per Prōvinciam facere eius voluntāte sibi licēret. [10]

Caesar, quod memoriā tenēbat L. Cassium cōnsulem occīsum [11] exercitumque eius ab Helvētiīs pulsum [11] et sub iugum missum, [11] concēdendum [12] nōn putābat. Tamen, ut spatium intercēdere posset dum [13] mīlitēs quōs imperāverat convenīrent lēgātīs respondit, " Diem [14] ad dēlīberandum sūmam; sī quid vultis, [15] ad Īd. Apr. revertiminī."

1. **Caesarī:** this word is given an emphatic position because it introduces the hero of the story, Gaius Julius Caesar. The preceding chapters have set forth the situation which confronts him. 2. **id:** *it;* explained by the infinitive clause, eōs . . . cōnārī, which is used in apposition. 3. **urbe:** *i.e.,* Rome, *the city,* as distinguished from other cities in Italy. 4. **quam . . . itineribus:** *by marches as long*

as possible. It is said that Caesar on this journey marched ninety miles a day.
5. Galliam ulteriōrem: see Map. **6. Prōvinciae tōtī, imperat:** *he levied upon the whole Province* (517). **7. legiō ūna:** the famous Tenth Legion. **8. Ubi, Helvētiī certiōrēs factī sunt:** translate *when the Helvetians were informed;* **certiōrem faciō** is one of Caesar's favorite idioms; what is the literal translation? **ubi:** (602). **9. quī rogārent:** *to ask.* Why subjunctive? **10. ut . . . licēret:** translate *that, with his consent, permission be granted to them to journey through the Province;* a substantive volitive clause, the object of rogārent. **11. occīsum, pulsum, missum:** **esse** is understood. **12. concēdendum (esse):** translate *he should grant the request;* passive periphrastic conjugation in indirect statement with **putābat.** **13. dum:** *until* (601). **14. diem:** note the meaning here, *time.*

281.   COMPREHENSION

1. Where was Caesar when he learned of the plan of the Helvetians? **2.** What did he do? **3.** What did Helvetian envoys ask Caesar? **4.** Why did Caesar take so much time to consider the request of the Helvetians?

282.   EXERCITĀTIŌ

Iterātiō: **Temporal clauses with *ubi* and the indicative (602).**

Memoriae mandā: **Ubi sōlitūdinem faciunt, pācem appellant,** *When they make a solitude, they call it peace.* Tacitus, a great Roman historian, thus characterized the Roman method of making peace.

Respondē Latīnē: Ubi Caesar certior dē hōc cōnsiliō factus est, quid Prōvinciae imperāvit? Quot legiōnēs erant in ulteriōre Galliā?

Scrībe Latīnē: When time (a day) for deliberating has intervened, the ambassadors return.

283.   VERBA

Required Vocabulary: **imperō, intercēdō, lēgātus, legiō, licet, pellō, tamen, ulterior, voluntās.**

Word Study. The word *subjugate* is derived from two Latin words, **sub** and **iugum,** *under the yoke.* This yoke consisted of three spears, two placed upright and a third placed horizontally across so low that those passing under had to bow their heads. The ceremony of sending a conquered people *under the yoke* was indicative of complete submission and *subjugation.*

Define the following words derived from **pellō,** showing that each contains the idea of *driving: compulsory, dispel, expulsion, impulsive, propel, repellent, repulsive.*

Trajan's Column, Rome

SOLDIERS BUILDING A WALL

A wall was often built of trunks of trees and then covered with earth.

Caesar refuses a right of way to the Helvetians

" The Helvetii were kept back by evasive answers to their request for a passage; and, after a vain attempt to break through the rampart, they went into the territory of the Sequani." E. S. SHUCKBURGH, *History of Rome*

8. Intereā [1] eā legiōne quam sēcum habēbat mīlitibusque quī ex Prōvinciā convēnerant, ā lacū Lemannō ad montem Iūram, quī fīnēs Sēquanōrum ab Helvētiīs dīvidit, mīlia passuum XVIIII mūrum in altitūdinem pedum sēdecim fossamque per- dūcit. Eō opere perfectō, praesidia dispōnit,[2] castella com- 5 mūnit, quō [3] facilius, sī trānsīre cōnārentur, prohibēre posset.

Ubi lēgātī ad eum revertērunt, negat [4] sē mōre et exemplō [5] populī Rōmānī posse [4] iter ūllī.[6] per Prōvinciam dare.

Helvētiī eā spē dēiectī, nāvibus iūnctīs ratibusque com- plūribus factīs,[7] aliī [8] vadīs Rhodanī, quā minima altitūdō 10 flūminis erat, perrumpere cōnātī,[8] operis mūnītiōne [9] et mīlitum concursū et tēlīs repulsī, hōc cōnātū dēstitērunt.

1. **Intereā**: the time during which the soldiers whom Caesar had levied were assembling and while Caesar was considering his answer to the Helvetians. 2. **dis- pōnit**: translate *he posted at intervals;* what is the force of the prefix? 3. **quō**: introduces a purpose clause (585, *a*). 4. **negat sē, posse**: *he said he could not.* The word **negō** is usually translated, *I say*, with *not* in the subordinate clause. 5. **mōre**

et exemplō: *in accordance with the custom and precedent* (**537**). **6. ūllī:** why dative (**516**)? **7. nāvibus . . . factīs:** (*some*) *fastened their boats together and made several rafts;* translate an ablative absolute by a clause. **8. aliī, cōnātī:** *others attempting;* contrasted with those who tried to cross on the joined boats and rafts. **9. operis mūnītiōne:** translate *by the strength of the work;* i.e., the fortifications made by Caesar. Caesar's statement that this wall was nineteen miles long is not to be understood literally. In his *History of Julius Caesar,* Napoleon Bonaparte III points out the fact that the left bank of the Rhone in this region is so steep that it would be unnecessary to build extensive fortifications except in a few places. It is probable that Caesar cut down the face of the bank from the top for sixteen feet, making a steep front difficult to surmount. A row of palisades may have been driven along the top of this wall.

284.   COMPREHENSION

1. What reason for refusing their request did Caesar give to the Helvetian envoys? **2.** In what ways did the Helvetians try to cross the Rhone? **3.** How were they kept back? **4.** What was Caesar's real reason for not giving the Helvetians permission to go through the Roman province?

285.   EXERCITĀTIŌ

Iterātiō: **Purpose clauses introduced by *quō* (585, *a*).**

Memoriae mandā: **Lēgem brevem esse oportet, quō facilius ab imperītīs teneātur,** *It is fitting that a law should be brief in order that it may be the more easily grasped by the unlearned.* SENECA

Respondē Latīnē: Quō cōnsiliō mūrum et fossam ā lacū ad montem fēcit?

Scrībe Latīnē: In the meantime Caesar made many fortresses by which he might more easily repulse the Helvetians.

286.   VERBA

Required Vocabulary: altitūdō, castellum, complūrēs, fossa, intereā, mūnītiō, mūrus, opus, ūllus.

Word Study. From the Latin word **dīvidere,** the English word *dividend,* the thing to be *divided,* is derived. Give five other terms used in mathematics derived from **dīvidere.**

To what word in the chapter is each of the following related by derivation: *dejection, flume, minimize, mural, prohibition, operate?* Define each English word on the basis of its derivation.

They gain permission to go through the Sequanian territory

9. Relinquēbātur ūna per Sēquanōs via,[1] quā, Sēquanīs invītīs,[2] propter angustiās īre nōn poterant. Hīs[3] cum[4] suā sponte[5] persuādēre nōn possent, lēgātōs ad Dumnorīgem Aeduum mittunt ut, eō dēprecātōre,[6] ā Sēquanīs impetrārent.[7]

Dumnorīx grātiā et largitiōne apud Sēquanōs plūrimum poterat[8] 5 et Helvētiīs erat amīcus, quod ex eā cīvitāte Orgetorīgis fīliam in mātrimōnium dūxerat, et cupiditāte rēgnī[9] adductus novīs rēbus[10] studēbat et quam plūrimās cīvitātēs suō beneficiō habēre obstrictās[11] volēbat. Itaque rem suscipit et ā Sēquanīs impetrat ut per fīnēs suōs Helvētiōs īre patiantur, obsidēsque[12] utī inter 10 sēsē dent[13] perficit: Sēquanī, nē itinere Helvētiōs prohibeant;[14] Helvētiī, ut sine maleficiō et iniūriā trānseant.

1. **Relinquēbātur ūna, via:** what is the effect of the unusual position of the verb? 2. **Sēquanīs invītīs:** ablative absolute; translate by a clause expressing condition. 3. **Hīs:** *i.e.*, the Sequanians; dative with **persuādēre.** 4. **cum:** *since.* 5. **suā sponte:** translate *by their own influence.* 6. **eō dēprecātōre:** translate *through his intercession;* an ablative absolute, consisting of two substantives (540). 7. **ut, impetrārent:** purpose clause. 8. **plūrimum poterat:** translate *was very influential.* 9. **rēgnī:** (89). 10. **novīs rēbus:** *for a revolution* (517). 11. **suō . . . obstrictās:** *to have bound through his favor;* translate *under obligation because of his kindness.* 12. **obsidēs:** *hostages;* as a pledge of good faith, a state would give to another some of its citizens, usually children of influential men. 13. **utī, dent:** *that they give;* depends upon **perficit,** *he brings (it) about.* 14. **Sēquanī, nē . . . prohibeant:** *the Sequanians (promising) that they will not stop the Helvetians from their march (through their territory).*

287. COMPREHENSION

1. Why did the Helvetians ask permission to go through the territory of the Sequanians? 2. What was the controlling motive of Dumnorix in interceding for the Helvetians? 3. In the exchange of hostages, what did each side promise?

288. EXERCITĀTIŌ

Iterātiō: **Objective genitive (512).**

Memoriae mandā: **Crēscit amor nummī quantum ipsa pecūnia crēvit,** *The love of money increases as fast as the money has increased.* JUVENAL

Respondē Latīnē: Quā cupiditāte adductus Orgetorīx novīs rēbus studēbat?

Scrībe Latīnē: Dumnorix, influenced by the desire for power, of his own accord obtained his request that the Helvetians (though) unwilling give hostages.

289.   **VERBA**

Required Vocabulary: angustiae, impetrō, invītus, maleficium, obses, sponte, studeō.

Word Study. The word *trivial* is derived from the Latin words **trēs,** *three,* and **via,** *road.* Since crowds would gather at a crossroad to gossip, the word *trivial* was applied to unimportant or trifling affairs.

Give English words related by derivation to the following: **beneficium, fīlia, grātia, mātrimōnium, perficiō, sponte, via.**

Caesar prepares to check the invaders and protect the Province

" He (Caesar) showed no hesitation. He had immediately proceeded from Geneva in person to Italy, and with characteristic speed brought up the three legions cantoned there as well as two newly formed legions of recruits." THEODOR MOMMSEN, *History of Rome*

10. Caesarī renūntiātur Helvētiīs esse in animō [1] per agrum Sēquanōrum [2] et Aeduōrum iter in Santonum fīnēs facere, quī nōn longē ā Tolōsātium fīnibus absunt, quae cīvitās est in Prōvinciā. Intellegēbat magnō cum perīculō Prōvinciae
5 futūrum [3] ut hominēs bellicōsōs, populī Rōmānī inimīcōs, locīs [4] patentibus maximēque frūmentāriīs fīnitimōs habēret.

Ob eās causās eī mūnītiōnī [5] quam fēcerat T.[6] Labiēnum lēgātum praefēcit; ipse in Italiam [7] magnīs itineribus [8] contendit duāsque ibi legiōnēs cōnscrībit, et trēs,[9] quae circum
10 Aquileiam hiemābant, ex hībernīs ēdūcit; et, quā [10] proximum [11] iter in ulteriōrem Galliam per Alpēs erat, cum hīs quīnque legiōnibus īre contendit.

Ibi Ceutronēs et Graiocelī et Caturīgēs, locīs superiōribus occupātīs, itinere exercitum prohibēre cōnantur. Com-
15 plūribus hīs proeliīs [12] pulsīs, ab Ocelō, quod est oppidum citeriōris [13] Prōvinciae extrēmum,[14] in fīnēs Vocontiōrum ul-

ROMAN MONUMENTS IN THE PROVINCE   © *Ewing Galloway*
This Roman arch and mausoleum are near Saint-Rémy, France, in Provence.

teriōris Prōvinciae diē septimō pervenit; inde in Allobrogum
fīnēs, ab Allobrogibus in Segusiāvōs exercitum dūcit. Hī
sunt extrā Prōvinciam trāns Rhodanum prīmī.

1. Helvētiīs . . . animō: translate *that the Helvetians had it in mind;* **Helvētiīs**
is dative (**521**). What is the literal translation? **2. agrum Sēquanōrum:** locate
on the map the territories of the four peoples named. **3. futūrum (esse):** *it would
be;* an infinitive in indirect statement; the substantive clause, **ut, habēret,**
to have, is its subject. **4. locīs:** dative with the adjective **fīnitimōs. 5. eī mūnītiōnī: (27). 6. T.: Titum. 7. Italiam:** northern Italy, Cisalpine Gaul, which
was included in Caesar's province. **8. magnīs itineribus:** an idiomatic expression
for *by forced marches.* **9. trēs:** the Seventh, Eighth, and Ninth Legions; the
other two legions mentioned were the Eleventh and Twelfth. About how many
legionaries did Caesar now have? **10. quā:** *where;* the adverb. **11. proximum:**
nearest; translate *shortest.* Follow on the map the route taken by Caesar.
12. Complūribus, proeliīs: ablative of means modifying the ablative absolute, **hīs
pulsīs. 13. citeriōris:** nearer to Rome. **14. extrēmum:** farthest west.

290.   COMPREHENSION

1. What was the plan of the Helvetians as reported to Caesar? **2.** How
did this concern the Romans? **3.** What characteristics of Caesar are dis-
played by the activities recorded in this chapter?

291.　　　　　　　　EXERCITĀTIŌ

Iterātiō: Dative with a compound verb (**518**).

Memoriae mandā: **Nōn ignāra malī miserīs succurrere discō,** *Not un-acquainted with misfortune myself, I know how to aid others in trouble.*

VERGIL

Respondē Latīnē: Quem lēgātum Caesar hībernīs praefēcit?

Scrībe Latīnē: Caesar placed a lieutenant in command of the legions which had wintered in hither Gaul.

292.　　　　　　　　VERBA

Required Vocabulary: **circum, citerior, cōnscrībō, extrā, frūmentārius, hīberna, hiemō, inde, intellegō, praeficiō, superior.**

Word Study. The suffix -ōsus (in English *-ose, -ous*) meaning *full of,* attached usually to noun stems, forms adjectives: **bellicus, bellicōsus,** *bellicose.* Give such derivatives from: **perīculum, cōpia, verbum.**

Three Gallic tribes complain of outrages of invaders

11. Helvētiī iam per angustiās [1] et fīnēs Sēquanōrum suās cōpiās trādūxerant, et in Aeduōrum fīnēs pervēnerant eōrum-que [2] agrōs populābantur.[3] Aeduī lēgātōs ad Caesarem mittunt rogātum [4] auxilium, "Paene in cōnspectū exercitūs tuī agrī 5 nostrī vāstantur, līberī in servitūtem abdūcuntur, oppida ex-pugnantur."

Eōdem tempore Ambarrī, necessāriī et cōnsanguineī [5] Aedu-ōrum, Caesarem certiōrem faciunt sēsē,[6] dēpopulātīs [7] agrīs, nōn facile ab oppidīs vim hostium prohibēre. Item Allobrogēs, 10 quī trāns Rhodanum vīcōs possessiōnēsque habēbant, fugā sē ad Caesarem recipiunt [8] et dēmōnstrant sibi praeter agrī solum nihil esse reliquī.[9]

Quibus rēbus adductus Caesar nōn exspectandum sibi [10] statuit dum in Santonōs Helvētiī pervenīrent.[11]

1. **angustiās:** what did you learn in Chapters 6 and 9 about the character of this road at the Pas de l'Écluse? 2. **eōrumque:** the friendship of Dumnorix with the Helvetians did not save his people from the ravages of the migrating Helvetians. 3. **populābantur:** *were laying waste.* 4. **rogātum:** *to ask* (**294**). 5. **necessāriī et**

Vienne, France

THE LAND OF THE ALLOBROGES

These ruins are of a fort on the Rhone River at Vienne, **Vienna,** the ancient capital of the Allobroges, one of the tribes who complained that the Helvetians were devastating their lands.

cōnsanguineī: the former include connections by marriage, the latter blood relations only. **6. sēsē:** accusative, subject of prohibēre. **7. dēpopulātīs:** sometimes the perfect participle of a deponent verb has a passive meaning. **8. fugā sē, recipiunt:** one of Caesar's idioms for *flee*. **9. dēmōnstrant . . . reliquī:** *they say that they have nothing left except the bare ground;* sibi: (**521**); reliquī (**510**). **10. nōn . . . sibi:** translate *that he ought not to wait;* sibi (**522**). **11. pervenīrent:** *should come*, anticipatory subjunctive with **dum** (**601**).

293.   COMPREHENSION

1. What had the Helvetians done while Caesar was mobilizing his army?
2. Follow their course on the map. **3.** Was Caesar justified in proceeding against the Helvetians? Why?

294.   RĒS GRAMMATICAE

Purpose expressed by the supine in -*um* (631, *a*). In the sentence, **lēgātōs mittunt rogātum auxilium,** *they send ambassadors* *to ask aid*, **rogātum** is a verbal noun used with **mittunt,** a verb of motion, to express purpose. Such a verbal noun, which is used only in the accusative and ablative cases, is called a *supine*. Learn the supines of the model verbs (**492**).

There are also other ways of expressing purpose which you have already learned. How is it expressed in each of the following sentences?

1. **Lēgātōs mittunt ut auxilium rogent.**
2. **Lēgātōs mittunt quī auxilium rogent.**
3. **Lēgātōs mittunt rogandī auxilī causā.**
4. **Lēgātōs mittunt parātōs ad cōpiās rogandās.**
5. **Lēgātōs mittunt rogandī causā.**
6. **Mīlitēs mittunt parātōs ad pugnandum.**

295.   EXERCITĀTIŌ

Memoriae mandā: **Spectātum veniunt, veniunt spectentur ut ipsae,** *They come to see, they come that they themselves may be seen.* OVID

Respondē Latīnē: Quī lēgātōs ad Caesarem mīsērunt rogātum auxilium?

Scrībe Latīnē: The Helvetians send armies to lay waste and devastate the fields and storm the towns. Nothing is left to the Aeduans except their children.

296.   VERBA

Required Vocabulary: **expugnō, līberī, necessārius, populor, praeter, statuō, vāstō.**

Word Study. To what word in the chapter is each of these related: *tradition, annihilation, sanguinary, recipe?* Explain the meaning of each.

Define the following words derived from **finis,** showing that each contains the idea of *end: confine, define, fine* (noun), *finally, finish, infinite, infinitive, refine.*

Caesar almost annihilates the Tigurini

" The Helvetii had moved very slowly and had occupied twenty days in bridging the Saône, which was the first considerable obstacle they met with in their progress westwards." W. WARDE FOWLER, *Julius Caesar*

12. Flūmen est Arar,[1] quod per fīnēs Aeduōrum et Sēquanōrum in Rhodanum īnfluit incrēdibilī lēnitāte.[2] Oculīs in utram partem fluat iūdicārī nōn potest. Id Helvētiī ratibus ac lintribus iūnctīs trānsībant.

Ubi per explōrātōrēs Caesar certior factus est trēs iam partēs 5 cōpiārum Helvētiōs id flūmen trādūxisse,[3] quārtam ferē partem citrā flūmen Ararim reliquam esse, dē tertiā vigiliā [4] cum legiōnibus tribus ē castrīs profectus [5] ad eam partem pervēnit quae nōndum flūmen trānsierat. Eōs impedītōs et inopīnantēs aggressus [6] magnam partem eōrum concīdit; reliquī sēsē fugae 10 mandārunt [7] atque in proximās silvās abdidērunt. Is pāgus appellābātur Tigurīnus; [8] nam omnis cīvitās Helvētia in quattuor pāgōs dīvīsa est.

Hic pāgus ūnus, cum domō exīsset, patrum nostrōrum memoriā [9] L. Cassium cōnsulem interfēcerat et eius exercitum 15 sub iugum mīserat.[10] Ita sīve cāsū sīve cōnsiliō deōrum immortālium, quae pars [11] cīvitātis Helvētiae īnsignem calamitātem populō Rōmānō intulerat, ea [11] prīnceps poenās persolvit.[12]

Quā in rē Caesar nōn sōlum pūblicās sed etiam prīvātās iniūriās ultus est, quod eius socerī L. Pīsōnis avum, L. Pīsōnem 20 lēgātum, Tigurīnī eōdem proeliō quō Cassium interfēcerant.[13]

1. Arar: the modern name of this river is the Saône. It empties into the Rhone at Lyons. Locate on map. **2. incrēdibilī lēnitāte:** *of smoothness past belief.* **3. trādūxisse:** has two objects, **partēs** and **flūmen** (**528**). **4. dē tertiā vigiliā:** between midnight and three A.M. The night was divided into four watches of three hours each, the first beginning at sunset. **5. profectus:** *having set out,* agreeing with the subject **Caesar. 6. aggressus:** *attacking;* perfect participles of deponent verbs are often best translated in English by present participles (**626**). **7. sēsē . . . mandārunt:** *they fled;* **mandārunt = mandāvērunt. 8. Tigurīnus:** (**508**). **9. memoriā:** *within the memory.* **10. L. Cassium . . . mīserat:** in Chap. 7 this is given as the reason for Caesar's refusing permission to the Helvetian forces to pass through the Roman province. **11. quae pars, ea:** *that part which* (**560**, *a*). **12. prīnceps . . . persolvit:** *was the first to pay the penalty in full;* the prefix **per** has the force of *thoroughly.* **13. quod . . . interfēcerant:** *because the Tigurini, in the same battle in which they had killed Cassius, had killed Lucius Piso, the lieutenant-general, grandfather of his (Caesar's) father-in-law, Lucius Piso.*

A ROMAN AQUEDUCT NEAR LYONS

The remains of several great aqueducts built during the Roman era are among the interesting and beautiful Roman monuments in France.

297.   COMPREHENSION

1. How many of the Helvetians did Caesar attack? **2.** What was the outcome? **3.** What had the Tigurini done which seemed to justify their punishment?

298.   EXERCITĀTIŌ

Iterātiō: **Predicate nouns and adjectives (508).**

Respondē Latīnē: Caesarne certior factus est uter pāgus Rōmānōs aggressus reī publicae calamitātem īnsignem intulisset?

Scrībe Latīnē: Caesar was informed that this was the canton which had inflicted a noteworthy disaster on the Roman people.

299.   VERBA

Required Vocabulary: abdō, aggredior, calamitās, īnsignis, mandō, nōn sōlum . . . sed etiam, pāgus, pūblicus, sōlum, uter.

Word Study. To what word in the chapter is each of the following related: *insignia, lenient, mandamus, mandate, republic, subpoena, vigil?* Give the meaning of each so as to show its relation to its Latin ancestor.

Trajan's Column, Rome
ARMY CROSSING A RIVER

Caesar may have made a pontoon bridge such as is shown in the illustration, when he pursued the Helvetians across the **Arar,** *Saône.*

A delegation of Helvetians comes to Caesar with promises and threats

13. Hōc proeliō factō, reliquās cōpiās Helvētiōrum ut cōnsequī posset, pontem in Ararī fēcit atque ita exercitum trādūxit.

Helvētiī repentīnō eius adventū commōtī, cum id quod ipsī diēbus xx aegerrimē cōnfēcerant, ut flūmen trānsīrent, illum ūnō diē fēcisse intellegerent,[1] lēgātōs ad eum mittunt; 5 cuius lēgātiōnis Dīvicō [2] prīnceps fuit, quī bellō Cassiānō [3] dux Helvētiōrum fuerat.   Is ita cum Caesare ēgit :

" Sī pācem populus Rōmānus cum Helvētiīs faciet, in eam partem ībunt atque ibi erunt Helvētiī ubi cōnstitueris ; sīn bellō persequī [4] persevērābis, reminīscere [5] et veteris incommodī [6] 10 populī Rōmānī et prīstinae virtūtis Helvētiōrum.   Quod [7] imprōvīsō ūnum pāgum adortus es, cum eī quī flūmen trānsierant suīs auxilium ferre nōn possent, nōlī [8] ob eam rem aut tuae magnopere virtūtī tribuere [8] aut nōs dēspicere ; nōs ita ā patribus maiōribusque nostrīs didicimus [9] ut magis virtūte contendāmus 15 quam dolō aut īnsidiīs nītāmur." [10]

1. **cum . . . intellegerent:** *when they perceived that he (Caesar) in one day had done that which they themselves had accomplished in twenty days with great difficulty, namely the crossing of the river.*   **2. Dīvicō:** in 107 B.C., he had been at the head of the Tigurini in the great migration of the Cimbri and Teutons.   About how old

was he now? **3. bellō Cassiānō**: *the war with Cassius;* in Latin a proper adjective is often used instead of the possessive genitive of a proper noun. **4. persequī**: *to continue in.* **5. reminīscere**: *bear in mind;* imperative. What case is used with this verb (**514**)? **6. incommodī**: *defeat.* **7. Quod**: *as to the fact that;* Divico's attitude is one of defiance. **8. nōlī, tribuere**: *do not attribute* (**611**, *a*). **9. didicimus**: from **discō**. **10. quam . . . nītāmur**: *rather than rely upon deceit and ambuscade.*

300. COMPREHENSION

1. How is Caesar's efficiency demonstrated in this chapter? **2.** Was Divico successful as a diplomat? Why? **3.** What points did he make in his speech?

301. EXERCITĀTIŌ

Ablative of source (**536**).

Memoriae mandā: **Disce sed ā doctīs,** *Learn but from the learned.* CATO

Respondē Latīnē: Quid ā maiōribus didicerant?

Scrībe Latīnē: They had learned from former wars to despise ambushes. With their old-time bravery they attack and follow up the Romans.

302. VERBA

Required Vocabulary: **adorior, dēspiciō, īnsidiae, magis, maior, persequor, prīstinus, repentīnus, tribuō, vetus.**

Caesar's demand for satisfaction is rejected

14. Hīs Caesar ita respondit, " Eō [1] mihi minus dubitātiōnis datur, quod eās rēs quās vōs commemorāvistis memoriā teneō, atque eō gravius ferō quō minus meritō [2] populī Rōmānī accidērunt. Quod sī veteris contumēliae oblīvīscī [3] vellem, [4] num [5]
5 etiam recentium iniūriārum, quod, [6] mē invītō, iter per prōvinciam per vim temptāvistis, quod Aeduōs, quod Ambarrōs quod Allobrogēs vexāvistis, memoriam dēpōnere possum? Quod vestrā victōriā tam īnsolenter glōriāminī, quodque tam diū vōs impūne iniūriās intulisse admīrāminī, eōdem pertinent. [7]
10 Cōnsuēvērunt enim dī immortālēs, quō gravius hominēs ex commūtātiōne rērum doleant, quōs prō scelere eōrum ulcīscī

volunt, hīs secundiōrēs interdum rēs et diūturniōrem impūni-
tātem concēdere.⁸ Cum haec ita sint, tamen, sī obsidēs ā
vōbīs mihi dabuntur, et sī Aeduīs, item sī Allobrogibus satis-
faciētis, vōbīscum pācem faciam."   15

Dīvicō respondit, " Helvētiī ā maiōribus suīs īnstitūtī sunt
utī obsidēs accipere, nōn dare, cōnsuēverint; eius reī populus
Rōmānus est testis."

Hōc respōnsō datō, discessit.

1. Eō: *on this account;* the quod clause states the reason. **2. eō . . . meritō:**
translate *I am the more indignant, the less in accordance with the deserts;* **eō, quō,**
ablatives of measure of difference. **3. contumēliae oblīvīscī:** *to forget the disgrace*
(514). 4. vellem: what does the imperfect subjunctive indicate as to Caesar's
wish **(609)**? **5. num:** indicates that the answer *no* is expected; **num iniūriārum,
memoriam . . . possum:** *I cannot lay aside the memory of recent wrongs, too,
can I?* **6. quod:** *the fact that;* introduces substantive clauses explaining
iniūriārum. **7. Quod . . . pertinent:** *that you boast so insolently concerning
your victory, and that you wonder that you have committed wrongs so long without
punishment, point in the same direction.* **8. Cōnsuēvērunt . . . concēdere:** *for
the immortal gods are accustomed, in order that men may grieve more bitterly in consequence of changes of conditions, to grant for a time more prosperous affairs and a rather
long escape from punishment to those whom they wish to punish for their wickedness.*
Point out in the text the Latin for each expression in this English sentence. Caesar's
idea of the gods' method of punishment, the result of his study of Greek dramas,
does not seem to have impressed the barbarian Divico.

303.   COMPREHENSION

1. What terms of peace did Caesar propose? **2.** What reply did Divico
make? **3.** What characterizes this reply?

304.   EXERCITĀTIŌ

Iterātiō: **Ablative of measure of difference (550).**

Memoriae mandā: **Quantō plūra parāstī, tantō plūra cupis,** *The more you
have, the more you desire.* HORACE

Respondē Latīnē: Tulitne Caesar recentem contumēliam eō gravius quō
minus meritō acciderat?

Scrībe Latīnē: The Roman people are a witness of that which was
recounted. The Helvetians were not trained to make restitution.

305.   VERBA

Required Vocabulary: **admīror, commemorō, contumēlia, īnstituō, recēns, satisfaciō, tam, testis.**

Word Study. The Latin adverb **item,** *also,* was formerly used before the name of each article, except the first, on a bill or account. It gradually lost its original significance and became the English noun, *item,* which is in common use today.

To what word in the chapter is each of the following related: *ad-miration, date, deposit, impunity, indolent, oblivion, tempt, testimony, vex?* Define each.

The Helvetians advance, and Caesar follows

(15.) Posterō diē castra ex eō locō movent. Idem facit Caesar equitātumque omnem, ad numerum quattuor mīlium, quem ex omnī prōvinciā et Aeduīs atque eōrum sociīs coāctum habēbat, praemittit, quī videant quās in partēs [1] hostēs iter faciant.[2]
5 Quī [3] cupidius novissimum agmen īnsecūtī [4] aliēnō [5] locō cum equitātū Helvētiōrum proelium committunt; et paucī dē nostrīs cadunt.

Quō proeliō sublātī Helvētiī, quod quīngentīs equitibus tantam multitūdinem equitum prōpulerant, audācius subsistere nōn 10 numquam et novissimō agmine [6] proeliō nostrōs lacessere coepē-runt. Caesar suōs ā proeliō continēbat ac satis habēbat in praesentiā [7] hostem rapīnīs,[8] pābulātiōnibus populātiōnibusque prohibēre.

Ita diēs circiter quīndecim iter fēcērunt utī inter novissimum 15 hostium agmen et nostrum prīmum nōn amplius quīnīs aut sēnīs mīlibus [9] passuum interesset.

1. quās in partēs: *in what direction.* **2. faciant:** why subjunctive (**48**)? **3. quī:** *they.* **4. cupidius . . . īnsecūtī:** *following the rear line too eagerly.* **5. aliēnō:** *unfavorable.* **6. novissimō agmine:** *with their rear line* (they attacked our men who were following them). Why does **novissimum agmen** mean *rear line?* **7. ac . . . praesentiā:** *and he considered it enough for the time being.* **8. rapīnīs:** *from plundering* (**534**). **9. quīnīs . . . mīlibus:** an ablative of comparison. Point out in the chapter and name four different uses of the ablative.

devasting devastating

Trajan's Column, Rome

CAVALRY

The chief duty of the cavalry was to start an engagement and to pursue the enemy.

306.   COMPREHENSION

1. Why did the Helvetians become more bold?   **2.** How was this shown?
3. What plan did Caesar follow for the time being?   Why?

307.   EXERCITĀTIŌ

Iterātiō: **Indirect question (595).**

Memoriae mandā: **Nōn rēfert quam multōs sed quam bonōs librōs habeās,** *It is not a question of how many but how good books you have.*   SENECA

Respondē Latīnē: Vidēbantne quās in partēs hostēs iter audācter facerent?

Scrībe Latīnē: Did the Helvetians see why our cavalry was sent ahead into an unfavorable place?

308.   VERBA

Required Vocabulary: **agmen, aliēnus, amplius, audācter, cadō, eques, equitātus, praemittō, tantus.**

Word Study. How has the Latin word **nostrum** come to be applied to a quack medicine?

To what word in the chapter is each of the following related: *alienate, amplifier, cadaver, deciduous, rapine?* Define each English word on the basis of its derivation.

Trajan's Column, Rome
TRANSPORTING SUPPLIES BY BOAT

Caesar was in need of the grain promised by the Aeduans, for when he turned from the Arar to follow the Helvetians, he could no longer use the supplies that he was bringing down the river by boat.

The Story of Chapters 16-20

Caesar learns that the Aeduans are not furnishing the grain promised, because they are being influenced by anti-Roman propaganda. The brother of Diviciacus, Dumnorix, who is rich, ambitious, unprincipled, and powerful, is the leader of the anti-Roman movement. He favors the Helvetians, through whose influence he hopes to become king. It was he who, as head of the Aeduan cavalry, had treacherously started the retreat that led to the recent Roman defeat. Caesar thinks that Dumnorix should be punished but hesitates to offend his brother Diviciacus, a loyal friend of the Roman people. Accordingly, he summons Diviciacus, relates to him all the facts, and asks him to pass judgment on his brother. Diviciacus acknowledges the truth of the accusations but makes a strong appeal for his brother's life. This Caesar grants but keeps Dumnorix under surveillance.

"In a private conference with Liscus, Caesar learns more exactly the actual domestic situation among the Aedui, particularly of the feud between the brothers, the Druid Diviciacus, and the aspirant for monarchy, Dumnorix. One learns how ambitious noblemen rose, or planned to rise among the Kelts." E. G. SIHLER, *Annals of Caesar*

" It was, indeed, good policy not to alienate the Aeduan people by any excessive severity against a man of power among them." NAPOLEON BONAPARTE III, *History of Julius Caesar*

In writing to one of Caesar's staff, Cicero jokingly refers to the Aeduans as " our brothers."

Caesar plans an attack from two sides

21. Eōdem diē ab explōrātōribus certior factus [1] hostēs sub monte cōnsēdisse mīlia passuum ab ipsīus castrīs octō, quālis esset nātūra montis et quālis in circuitū [2] ascēnsus, quī cognōscerent,[3] mīsit. Renūntiātum est facilem esse.

Dē tertiā vigiliā [4] Titum Labiēnum,[5] lēgātum prō praetōre, 5 cum duābus legiōnibus et eīs ducibus quī iter cognōverant summum iugum montis ascendere iubet; quid suī cōnsilī sit ostendit.[6] Ipse dē quārtā vigiliā eōdem itinere quō hostēs ierant ad eōs contendit equitātumque omnem ante sē mittit.

P. Cōnsidius, quī reī mīlitāris [7] perītissimus habēbātur et in 10 exercitū L. Sullae et posteā in M. Crassī fuerat, cum explōrātōribus praemittitur.

1. certior factus: *informed;* modifies **Caesar** understood, the subject of **mīsit**. **2. in circuitū:** translate *on all sides;* circuitus is a compound of what two words? Caesar planned a double attack: one division was to attack the Helvetians in front; the other was to follow a circuitous route, ascend the mountain unseen, and charge down upon them from above. **3. (explōrātōrēs) quī cognōscerent:** *scouts to find out.* **4. tertiā vigiliā:** about what time was this? **5. Labiēnum:** an interesting character to follow through the Gallic War because he plays an important part. Caesar placed him in a class by himself and seemed to have great faith in his ability. It is surprising to find that he fought against Caesar in the Civil War that followed. **6. quid . . . ostendit:** *he shows what his plan is.* **7. reī mīlitāris:** (**310**). It is strange that one " so highly skilled in military affairs " would make the mistake that Caesar tells of in the next chapter. Explain the mood of: **esset**, l. 3; **cognōscerent**, l. 3; **sit**, l. 7; the case of: **passuum**, l. 2; **cōnsilī**, l. 7.

309. COMPREHENSION

1. What was the reputation of Considius and how had he gained it? 2. Why does Caesar emphasize this reputation?

310.   RĒS GRAMMATICAE

Genitive with adjectives. In the phrase, **reī mīlitāris perītissi-mus,** *skillful in military science,* l. 10, **reī mīlitāris** in the genitive case is used with **perītissimus** to specify *that in which* Considius is skillful. For the other adjectives with which the genitive is used, see **513.**

Translate: **integer vītae, nostrae cōnsuētūdinis imperītī, plēna cōnsiliōrum.**

311.   EXERCITĀTIŌ

Memoriae mandā: **Vir bonus dīcendī perītus,** *A good man skilled in speaking.* This definition of an orator, attributed to Cato, is often quoted by Roman writers.

Respondē Latīnē: Cuius reī erat P. Cōnsidius perītissimus?

Scrībe Latīnē: Caesar sent a scout who was skilled in military science.

312.   VERBA

Required Vocabulary: **explōrātor, mīlitāris.**

Word Study. The suffixes **-āris** and **-ārius** (in English *-ar, -ary*), meaning *pertaining to,* added to stems, usually of nouns and adjectives, form adjectives: **mīles, mīlit- + -āris, mīlitāris,** *military.* Give the derivation of: *January, legionary, popular, singular.*

To what word in the chapter is each of the following related: *conjugation, October, quality, renounce?* Define each on the basis of its derivation.

The mistake of Considius causes the failure of Caesar's plan

" Caesar planned to strike the migratory post in front and rear; but this design was defeated by an elderly sub-officer, who blundered through nervousness and poor eyesight. There were no field glasses then." E. G. SIHLER, *Annals of Caesar*

22. Prīmā lūce,[1] cum [2] summus mōns [3] ā Labiēnō tenērētur, ipse ab hostium castrīs nōn longius mīlle et quīngentīs passibus abesset, neque,[5] ut [4] posteā ex captīvīs comperit, aut [5] ipsīus adventus aut [5] Labiēnī cognitus esset, Cōnsidius, equō admissō,[6] 5 ad eum accurrit, dīcit montem quem ā Labiēnō occupārī voluerit

ab hostibus tenērī; id sē ā Gallicīs armīs atque īnsignibus cog-
nōvisse. Caesar suās cōpiās in proximum collem subdūcit,
aciem īnstruit.

Labiēnus, ut erat eī praeceptum [7] ā Caesare nē proelium
committeret, nisi ipsīus cōpiae prope hostium castra vīsae 10
essent, monte occupātō, nostrōs exspectābat proeliōque ab-
stinēbat.

Multō dēnique diē [8] per explōrātōrēs Caesar cognōvit et
montem ā suīs tenērī et Helvētiōs castra mōvisse et Cōnsidium
timōre perterritum quod nōn vīdisset prō vīsō [9] sibi renūntiā- 15
visse.

Eō diē, quō cōnsuērat intervāllō,[10] hostēs sequitur et mīlia
passuum tria ab eōrum castrīs castra pōnit.

1. Prīmā lūce: translate *at daybreak;* at this time of the year in this locality,
daybreak comes at about four o'clock.   **2. cum:** what verbs are introduced by
this conjunction?   **3. summus mōns:** translate *the top of the mountain.*   **4. ut:**
as, is followed by the indicative mood.   **5. neque, aut, aut:** *and, neither, nor.*
6. equō admissō: translate *with his horse at full speed.*   **7. ut . . . praeceptum:**
translate *as he had been instructed.*   What is it literally?   **8. Multō, diē:**
translate *late in the day.*   **9. quod . . . vīsō:** *as seen, what he had not seen.*   Caesar
does not record what he then said to Considius.   **10. quō . . . intervāllō:** translate *at the usual distance;* about five miles; **intervāllō,** the antecedent of **quō** is
in the relative clause; **cōnsuērat:** = **cōnsuēverat.**

313.   COMPREHENSION

1. What report did Considius make to Caesar?   **2.** What did Caesar do?
3. What mistake did Considius make?   Why?

314.   EXERCITĀTIŌ

Iterātiō: Idiomatic use of adjectives to denote a part (**567,** *a*).

Memoriae mandā: **Feriunt summōs fulgura montēs,** *The lightning strikes
the tops of the mountains.*   HORACE

Respondē Latīnē: Quandō Labiēnus summum collem occupābat?   Quid
Caesar multō diē ex captīvīs cognōvit?

Scrībe Latīnē: At daybreak Labienus was on the top of the mountain, as
Caesar found out late in the day.

315.   **VERBA**

Required Vocabulary: **admittō, captīvus, collis, comperiō, prope.**

Word Study. The suffixes **-icus, -ius, -nus,** and **-ēnsis,** denoting *pertaining to* or *connected with,* added to noun stems, form adjectives. **Gallicus** is an example of this formation. Give the formation and meaning of the following words, derived from words that you have already studied: **rēgius, frāternus, Athēniēnsis, Italicus, forēnsis.** Show how **ēgregius** (**grex, gregis,** *herd*) means *remarkable.*

To what word in the chapter is each of these related: *admissible, captivate, consequence, elucidate, instruction, itinerant, proximity?* Define each.

Autun, France   *Courtesy of Railways of France*

ROMAN GATE NEAR BIBRACTE

This is a restoration of a Roman gate at Autun, a city situated a few miles from the site of ancient Bibracte, the capital of the Aeduans.

Caesar turns to Bibracte for supplies. The Helvetians pursue

23. Postrīdiē eius diēī,[1] quod omnīnō bīduum supererat[2] cum exercituī frūmentum mētīrī oportēret, et quod ā Bibracte,[3] oppidō Aeduōrum longē maximō et cōpiōsissimō, nōn amplius mīlibus[4] passuum XVIII aberat, reī frūmentāriae prōspiciendum[5] exīstimāvit; iter ab Helvētiīs āvertit ac Bibracte īre contendit.

Ea rēs per fugitīvōs L. Aemilī, decuriōnis [6] equitum Gallōrum, hostibus nūntiātur. Helvētiī, seu quod timōre perterritōs Rōmānōs discēdere ā sē exīstimārent,[7] sīve quod rē [8] frūmentāriā interclūdī posse cōnfīderent, itinere conversō,[9] nostrōs ā novissimō agmine īnsequī ac lacessere coepērunt.   10

1. Postrīdiē eius diēī: *on the day after this day;* translate *the next day.* **Postrīdiē** is an adverb formed from **posterō** + **diē**. **2. quod . . . supererat:** *because only two days remained.* **3. Bibracte:** the site of the Aeduan capital, now called Mont Beuvray. Recent excavations show that there was once a city on this site. **4. mīlibus:** an ablative of comparison. **5. prōspiciendum:** supply **sibi** and **esse**; translate *that he should look out for* (**74**), passive periphrastic conjugation in indirect discourse. **6. decuriōnis:** a **decuriō** was a petty cavalry officer in charge of a **decuria**. The word **decuria** suggests how many men? **7. exīstimārent:** what does the subjunctive in the **quod** causal clause indicate (**603,** *a*)? What other verb in this sentence is used in the same way? **8. rē:** ablative of separation with **interclūdī**. **9. itinere conversō:** point out on the map the course followed by the Helvetians and by Caesar, as given from Chap. 15 to this point.

316.   COMPREHENSION

1. Why did Caesar change his course and go toward Bibracte? **2.** How did the Helvetians interpret his movement? **3.** What change did this make in the plans of the Helvetians?

317.   RĒS GRAMMATICAE

Ablative of comparison (539). *He is braver than you,* **ille fortior est quam tū.** In this Latin sentence comparison is expressed just as in the English sentence, by a comparative **fortior** (*braver*) + **quam** (*than*) + **tū** (*you*) in the same case as **ille** (*he*). Comparison may also be expressed in Latin by the ablative case without **quam** (but only as a substitute for the nominative or the accusative case) : **ille fortior tē est.**

Translate : **Haec via lātior illā erat; mōns altior colle est.**

318.   EXERCITĀTIŌ

Memoriae mandā: **Nihil est virtūte amābilius,** *Nothing is more attractive than virtue.* CICERO

Respondē Latīnē: Quod oppidum nōn amplius mīlibus passuum XVIII aberat?

Scrībe Latīnē: Only two days remain, and he is more than eighteen miles away.

319.   **VERBA**

Required Vocabulary: **bīduum, cōnfīdō, interclūdō, mētior, prōspiciō, supersum.**

Word Study. The suffix **-īvus** (in English *-ive*), denoting *pertaining to*, usually added to the stems of perfect passive participles, forms adjectives: from **fugiō, fugitīvus** (fugit- + -īvus), *fugitive.* From words thus formed are derived the names for moods and cases: *indicative* from **indicātīvus**; *nominative* from **nominātīvus**; *dative* from **datīvus.** Give other examples.

Romans and Helvetians prepare for an engagement

24. Postquam [1] id animadvertit, cōpiās suās Caesar in proximum collem [2] subdūcit equitātumque quī sustinēret [3] hostium impetum mīsit.

Ipse interim in colle mediō triplicem aciem īnstrūxit legiōnum
5 quattuor veterānārum; atque suprā sē in summō iugō duās legiōnēs quās in Galliā citeriōre proximē cōnscrīpserat et omnia auxilia [4] collocārī ac tōtum montem hominibus complērī, et intereā sarcinās [5] in ūnum locum cōnferrī et eum [6] ab hīs quī in superiōre aciē cōnstiterant mūnīrī iussit.

10 Helvētiī cum omnibus suīs carrīs secūtī impedīmenta in ūnum locum contulērunt; ipsī cōnfertissmā [7] aciē, reiectō nostrō equitātū, phalange factā,[8] sub prīmam nostram aciem successērunt.

1. Postquam: *after;* used with a verb in what mood?   **2. collem:** near Armecy, about eighteen miles south of Bibracte.   **3. quī sustinēret:** *to check.*   **4. auxilia:** not Romans, but from states allied to Rome (**262**); **auxilia collocārī** depends on **iussit.** **5. sarcinās:** *packs,* containing personal belongings, weapons, and tools carried by the soldiers.   **6. eum:** the place just mentioned. It was fortified by a trench and rampart of earth. Traces of the trench have been found by excavators.   **7. cōnfertissmā:** *very compact.*   **8. phalange factā:** a phalanx was formed by lapping shields together in front and overhead.

320.   **COMPREHENSION**

1. Describe the arrangement of Caesar's forces.   **2.** Which side had the more advantageous position?

321.   EXERCITĀTIŌ

Iterātiō: Postquam and the indicative **(602)**.

Respondē Latīnē: Quandō Caesar equitātum quī impetum faceret mīsit?

Scrībē Latīnē: After Caesar placed the baggage, he noticed that the mountain was filled with men in a compact line

322.   VERBA

Required Vocabulary: **animadvertō, cōnfertus, collocō, compleō, impedīmentum.**

Word Study. The suffixes **-men** and **-mentum** (in English *-ment*), denoting *means of*, added to verb stems, form nouns: **flūmen (flū- + -men)**, *a river*, is derived from the stem of **fluō**, *flow*. Give nouns formed with this suffix from: **īnstruō, impediō, compleō.** Give the literal meaning of each word thus formed.

To what word in the chapter is each of the following related: *completion, inadvertent, phalanges, square, sustenance?* Define each English word on the basis of its derivation.

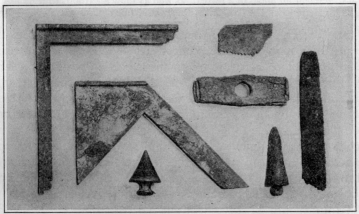

British Museum, London

CARPENTERS' TOOLS
Can you identify each tool shown in the illustration?

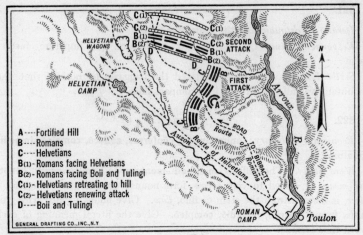

THE BATTLE WITH THE HELVETIANS

The Romans charge. The Helvetians fall back, then rally

" He sent back his horse, and the rest followed his example. This he did to prevent all hopes of a retreat, as well as show his troops that he would take his share in all the danger." PLUTARCH, *Life of Caesar*

25. Caesar, prīmum suō,[1] deinde omnium ex cōnspectū remōtīs equīs, ut spem fugae tolleret, cohortātus[2] suōs proelium commīsit.

Mīlitēs, ē locō superiōre pīlīs[3] missīs, facile[4] hostium phalangem perfrēgērunt et gladiīs dēstrictīs in eōs impetum fēcērunt.

5 Gallīs[5] magnō ad pugnam erat impedīmentō[6] quod, plūribus eōrum scūtīs ūnō ictū pīlōrum trānsfīxīs et colligātīs, cum ferrum sē īnflexisset, neque ēvellere neque, sinistrā impedītā, satis commodē pugnāre poterant.[5] Multī, diū iactātō[7] bracchiō, praeoptāvērunt scūtum manū ēmittere et nūdō[8] corpore pugnāre.

10 Tandem vulneribus dēfessī et pedem referre[9] et, quod mōns suberat circiter mīlle passuum spatiō, eō[10] sē recipere coepērunt.

Captō monte et succēdentibus nostrīs, Boiī et Tulingī,[11] quī hominum mīlibus circiter xv agmen hostium claudēbant et novissimīs praesidiō erant, ex itinere nostrōs ab latere apertō

Trajan's Column, Rome

DISMOUNTED

wanted in 2 divisions

Caesar sent away his own horse and those of the other officers because he wished to set his soldiers an example and at the same time to remove from his timid tribunes the temptation of running away from the fight.

aggressī circumvēnērunt; id cōnspicātī Helvētiī, quī in montem 15 sēsē recēperant, rūrsus īnstāre et proelium redintegrāre coepērunt.

Rōmānī conversa signa [12] bipertītō intulērunt: prīma et secunda aciēs, ut victīs [13] ac summōtīs [14] resisteret; tertia, ut venientēs [15] sustinēret.

1. prīmum suō (equō remōtō): *first (Caesar) sent away his own horse.* **2. cohortātus:** Caesar is eager for the success of his first battle in Gaul. **3. pīlīs:** many Roman javelins have been found on Caesar's battlefields. **4. facile:** it was easy to break up the phalanx because of the weight and force of the weapons thrown from above. **5. Gallīs . . . poterant:** translate *it was a great disadvantage to the Gauls in fighting that many of their shields were pierced and held together by one stroke of the (Roman) javelins, and when the iron (head) had bent, they (the Gauls) were not able to pull the javelins out, nor to fight very conveniently with their left hands hampered.* **6. Gallīs, impedīmentō:** (164) (106). **7. iactātō:** they threw their arms about in an effort to pull the bent javelins from their shields. **8. nūdō:** *i.e.,* without a shield. **9. pedem referre:** translate *to fall back;* an idiomatic expression. What is it literally? **10. eō:** *to that place; i.e.,* the hill. **11. Boiī et Tulingī:** they arrived when the Romans were pursuing the retreating Helvetians and, without reforming, attacked the Romans on the exposed flank and began to surround them. The Helvetians, seeing this, began to fight again, and the Romans now had to divide their forces, holding two lines against the Helvetians and the third against the advancing Boii and Tulingi.   **12. conversa signa:** translate *faced about.*   **13. victīs:** Explain the case of this and the following words: **fugae,** l. 2; **gladiīs,** l. 4; **ictū,** l. 6; **monte,** l. 12; **novissimīs,** l. 14; **praesidiō,** l. 14.   **14. summōtīs:** *dislodged (Helvetians).*   **15. venientēs:** *those who were coming up;* a participle used substantively.

323.   COMPREHENSION

1. What did Caesar do before beginning battle? Why? **2.** What effect did the arrival of reinforcements have upon the Helvetians? **3.** Why did many of the Helvetians throw down their shields?

324.   *Study*   EXERCITĀTIŌ

Iterātiō: **Dative of purpose (523). Dative of reference (519).**

Memoriae mandā: **Cui bonō,** *What's the use?* CICERO

Respondē Latīnē: **Cui agminī erant praesidiō Boii et Tulingī?**

Scrībe Latīnē: Their shields and javelins were an impediment to the weary Gauls. They press forward to the open side and surround our men.

325. *Wed*   VERBA

Required Vocabulary: **apertus, circumveniō, cōnspicor, dēfessus, īnstō, latus, pīlum, removeō, resistō, scūtum, sinister.**

Word Study. The Latin word **sinister** comes down unchanged in English in its form. What is its meaning?

To what word in the chapter is each of the following related: *assignment, circumvent, emissary, gladiatorial, instant, integer, lateral, reference?*

The Helvetians are defeated and put to rout

26. Ita ancipitī [1] proeliō diū atque ācriter pugnātum est. [2] Diūtius cum sustinēre nostrōrum impetūs nōn possent, alterī [3] sē, ut coeperant, in montem recēpērunt, alterī [3] ad impedīmenta et carrōs suōs sē contulērunt. Nam hōc tōtō proeliō, cum [4]
5 ab hōrā septimā ad vesperum pugnātum sit, āversum [5] hostem vidēre nēmō potuit.

Ad multam noctem etiam ad impedīmenta pugnātum est,

proptereā quod prō vāllō carrōs obiēcerant et ē locō superiōre [6]
in nostrōs venientēs tēla coniciēbant,[7] et nōn nūllī inter carrōs
rotāsque matarās ac trāgulās subiciēbant nostrōsque vulnerābant. 10
Diū cum esset pugnātum, impedīmentīs castrīsque nostrī potītī
sunt. Ibi Orgetorīgis fīlia atque ūnus ē fīliīs [8] captus est.

Ex eō proeliō circiter hominum mīlia cxxx superfuērunt eāque
tōtā nocte [9] continenter iērunt; in fīnēs Lingonum diē quārtō
pervēnērunt. Propter vulnera mīlitum et propter sepultūram 15
occīsōrum nostrī eōs sequī nōn potuērunt.

Caesar ad Lingonēs litterās nūntiōsque mīsit nē eōs frūmentō nēve [10] aliā rē iuvārent; quī sī iūvissent, sē eōdem locō
quō Helvētiōs habitūrum.[11] Ipse, trīduō intermissō, cum
omnibus cōpiīs [12] eōs sequī coepit. 20

1. ancipitī: translate *on two fronts*. **2. pugnātum est**: impersonal use (**502**);
translate using *they* or *the battle* as the subject. **3. alterī, alterī**: the Helvetians,
the Boii and Tulingi. **4. cum**: *although;* adversative (**67**). **5. āversum**: *turned;*
i.e., their backs. **6. ē locō superiōre**: *i.e.*, from the rampart made of carts. **7. coniciēbant**: *kept throwing;* note the force of the imperfect. **8. ē fīliīs**: *of the sons;*
instead of the genitive of the whole (**510**, *a*). Ē plūribus ūnum is also an example
of this use. **9. eāque tōtā nocte**: *during that whole night;* extent of time is sometimes expressed by the ablative (**553**, *a*). **10. nēve**: *nor.* **11. nē . . . habitūrum**:
indirect discourse; nē . . . iuvārent: the subjunctive represents a negative command of the direct discourse (**622**); iūvissent: represents the future perfect
indicative iūveritis (**623**, *a*, Note); habitūrum, the future habēbō (**619**). **12. cōpiīs**:
explain the use of this word and the following: possent, l. 2; coeperant, l. 3;
venientēs, l. 9; esset pugnātum, l. 11; impedīmentīs, l. 11; fīnēs, l. 14; diē, l. 14.

326.   COMPREHENSION

1. What praise does Caesar bestow upon the enemy? **2.** What message
did he send the Lingones? **3.** Why did he not follow at once?

327.   EXERCITĀTIŌ

Iterātiō: **Adversative clauses with *cum* (606).**

Respondē Latīnē: Quid Helvētiī prō vāllō obiēcērunt?

Scrībe Latīnē: Although three days had intervened, the messengers with
letters had not gone.

328.   VERBA

Required Vocabulary: littera, nēve, nūntius, obiciō, trīduum, vāllum.

Word Study. To what word in the chapter is each of these words related:
dial, objector, obliterate, diurnal, journal, recipient, sepulchral?

The Helvetians beg for peace.   One division attempts to escape

27. Helvētiī omnium rērum inopiā adductī lēgātōs dē
dēditiōne ad eum mīsērunt. Quī [1] cum eum in itinere con-
vēnissent suppliciterque [2] locūtī flentēs [3] pācem petīssent,[2] eōs
in eō locō quō tum essent [4] suum adventum exspectāre iussit.

5 Eō postquam Caesar pervēnit, obsidēs, arma, servōs quī
ad eōs perfūgissent [5] poposcit. Dum [6] ea conquīruntur et
cōnferuntur, circiter hominum mīlia sex eius pāgī quī Verbigenus
appellātur, sīve timōre perterritī, sīve spē salūtis inductī,[7] quod
in tantā multitūdine suam fugam aut occultārī aut omnīnō
10 ignōrārī posse exīstimārent, prīmā nocte [8] ē castrīs Helvētiōrum
ēgressī ad Rhēnum fīnēsque Germānōrum contendērunt.

1. Quī: *they* (**560**, *e*).   2. suppliciterque . . . petīssent: *and speaking in suppliant
manner with tears had begged for peace.*   3. flentēs: present participle, modifies **quī**
(**625**).   4. essent: in direct discourse this would be **erant**.   5. perfūgissent: *had
taken refuge;* represents **perfūgerant** of direct discourse.   6. dum: *while* (**600**).
7. inductī: modifies **mīlia** but agrees in sense with **hominēs** understood.   Point
out in the chapter: three perfect passive participles; two objective genitives;
two **cum** circumstantial clauses.   8. prīmā nocte : *in the first (part of the) night;*
translate *at nightfall.*   Give the Latin for: *late at night; early in the morning.*

329.   COMPREHENSION

1. Compare the attitude of the Helvetians with that described in Chapters
13 and 14.   2. What terms of peace did Caesar impose?   3. Why did one
division flee from the camp of the Helvetians?

330.   EXERCITĀTIŌ

Iterātiō: **Use of participles (625–8).**

Memoriae mandā: **Timeō Danaōs et dōna ferentēs,** *I fear the Greeks
even (when) bringing gifts.* VERGIL

Respondē Latīnē: Quōmodo Helvētiī pācem petīvērunt?

Scrībe Latīnē: Caesar seeks out the deserters (fleeing ones) whose flight had been concealed or not known.

331. VERBA

Required Vocabulary: conquīrō, dēditiō, fleō, ignōrō, occultō, perfugiō, poscō.

Word Study. From the word **pāgus** comes the word *pagan,* one who lived in a **pāgus,** *village* or district away from the city. Since the **pāgānī,** people who lived in the villages, were Christianized much later than city dwellers, the term *pagan* came to have the meaning of *non-Christian.*

To what word in the chapter is each of these related: *adventure, appellation, circumlocution, convenient, feeble, ignoramus, jussive, salute?* Give the meaning of each on the basis of its derivation.

Trajan's Column, Rome THE RETURN HOME

The Helvetians, sent back home with their wives, children, and flocks, must have presented a scene similar to the one shown in this illustration.

The fugitives are captured; the rest sent back home

28. Quod ubi Caesar resciit, quōrum per fīnēs ierant, hīs utī conquīrerent et redūcerent, sī sibi pūrgātī esse vellent, imperāvit;[1] reductōs in hostium numerō[2] habuit; reliquōs omnēs, obsidibus, armīs, perfugīs trāditīs, in dēditiōnem accēpit.

Helvētiōs, Tulingōs, Latobrīgōs in fīnēs suōs, unde erant 5

profectī, revertī iussit; et, quod, omnibus frūgibus āmissīs,
domī [3] nihil erat quō famem tolerārent,[4] Allobrogibus imperāvit ut eīs frūmentī cōpiam facerent; [5] ipsōs [6] oppida vīcōsque,
quōs incenderant, restituere iussit.

10 Id eā maximē ratiōne fēcit, quod nōluit eum locum unde
Helvētiī discesserant vacāre,[7] nē [8] propter bonitātem agrōrum
Germānī,[8] quī trāns Rhēnum incolunt, ē suīs fīnibus in Helvētiōrum fīnēs trānsīrent [8] et fīnitimī Galliae Prōvinciae Allobro-
gibusque essent.   Petentibus Aeduīs, quod ēgregiā virtūte erant
15 cognitī,[9] ut in fīnibus suīs Boiōs collocārent, concessit.

1. Quod . . . imperāvit: *when Caesar found this out, he ordered those through
whose territories they (the Verbigeni) had gone to hunt them up and bring them back
if they wished to be guiltless in his sight;* **sibi (519).**   Can you explain the subjunctives?   **2. in . . . numerō:** Caesar does not say what punishment he inflicted
on these, but he probably sold them into slavery or had them put to death.
3. domī: locative case **(555). 4. tolerārent:** *could satisfy;* a descriptive clause
(584). 5. ut, facerent: *to furnish;* dependent on **imperāvit (81).** Compare with
the construction used with **iussit,** l. 6 **(589,** *Note*). **6. ipsōs:** Helvetians.   The
destruction of their villages was described in Chap. 5. **7. vacāre:** *to be unoccupied.*
8. nē, Germānī, trānsīrent: *for fear that the Germans might cross.*   Caesar here
gives an additional reason for his opposition to the Helvetian migration.   He was
protecting the Province and Italy from the Germans.   **9. quod . . . cognitī:** *i.e.,* Boiī.

332.   COMPREHENSION

1. When Caesar discovered the flight of the Verbigeni, what command did
he give?   2. Compare his treatment of the Verbigeni with that given to the
rest.   3. Why were the Helvetians permitted to reëstablish their homes?

333.   EXERCITĀTIŌ

Iterātiō: Substantive volitive clause **(589). Infinitive with** *iubeō* **(589,**
Note).

Memoriae mandā: **Cūrā ut valeās,** *See to it that you are well.* CICERO
This expression was often used by Romans at the end of a letter.   Its
English equivalent would be: *Take care of yourself.*

Respondē Latīnē: Quid facere Allobrogēs Caesar iussit?   Quid Caesar,
bellō cōnfectō, Helvētiīs imperāvit ut facerent?

Scrībe Latīnē: Caesar commands the Helvetians to restore their (own)
villages and orders them to give hostages.

The number of the Helvetians and their allies

29. In castrīs Helvētiōrum tabulae [1] repertae sunt, litterīs Graecīs [2] cōnfectae, et ad Caesarem relātae, quibus in tabulīs nōminātim [3] ratiō [4] cōnfecta erat, quī [5] numerus domō [6] exīsset eōrum quī arma ferre possent,[7] et item sēparātim puerī, senēs mulierēsque. Quārum omnium rērum summa erat capitum 5 Helvētiōrum mīlia CCLXIII,[8] Tulingōrum mīlia XXXVI, Latobrīgōrum XIIII, Rauracōrum XXIII, Boiōrum XXXII; ex hīs, quī arma ferre possent, ad [9] mīlia nōnāgintā duo.

Summa omnium fuērunt [10] ad mīlia CCCLXVIII.

Eōrum quī domum rediērunt, cēnsū habitō, ut Caesar im- 10 perāverat, repertus est numerus mīlium Ç et X.

1. tabulae: *lists.* **2. Graecīs:** it is probable that the Gauls had learned the Greek alphabet from traders coming from **Massilia** (*Marseilles*), a Greek colony. **3. nōminātim:** translate *in detail.* **4. ratiō:** *record.* **5. quī:** interrogative adjective. **6. domō:** compare with ē suīs fīnibus, Chap. 28, l. 12. **7. quī . . . possent:** a descriptive clause. **8. Quārum . . . CCLXIII:** *of all these there was a total of* 263,000 *Helvetians;* **capitum** need not be translated. **9. ad:** *about.* **10. fuērunt:** Why plural **(568,** *b*)?

334.   COMPREHENSION

1. What per cent of the Helvetians and their allies failed to return home?

335.   EXERCITĀTIŌ

Iterātiō: **Ablative of place from which (535).**

Respondē Latīnē: Quae summa erat Helvētiōrum sociōrumque quī domō exierant? Quot domum rediērunt?

Scrībe Latīnē: All who go forth from their territories do not return home.

336.   VERBA

Required Vocabulary: **summa.**

Word Study.   The suffix -tus or -sus, denoting *action* or the *result of an action,* added to verb stems, forms nouns of the fourth declension: from **cēnseō,** *estimate,* **cēnsus** (**cēn-** + -sus), *census,* an *estimation* of the number of people.   What noun is formed with this suffix from: **exeō, redeō**?

Give English derivatives from: **Caesar, caput, domus, exeō, ratiō, redeō, senex, summa, tabula.**

Vatican Museum, Rome

A ROLL OF ROMAN SOLDIERS

A list of the names of certain soldiers of a Roman legion is shown in this illustration. The centurions' names appear in the genitive case, the consuls' in the ablative. The letter in front of each soldier's name is the abbreviation for his praenomen, that at the end is the last letter of his nomen, after which follows the name of his native town. The letters **EVOC** here and there indicate that the soldier is a reënlisted veteran, ēvocātus.

The story of Chapters 30–34

" The news of this brilliant victory produced its natural effect. The success of the Helvetians would have been a calamity to all, except Dumnorix and his following; and this calamity Caesar had averted. He appeared as a conqueror, not of Gaul, but of the invaders of Gaul." T. RICE HOLMES, *Caesar's Conquest of Gaul*

Gallic tribes, who had encouraged the Helvetians and given no aid to Caesar, now applaud his victory. They send chieftains to congratulate him on his defeat of the Helvetians. Diviciacus, as spokesman for the Gauls, asks for aid against the encroachment of the Germans under Ariovistus, who was imposing taxes on the Gauls, demanding hostages, and pushing them out of their lands. Caesar promises aid against Ariovistus for the sake of the Aeduans, who have been called brothers and kinsmen by the Roman Senate, and to insure the safety of the Province and of Italy. There was danger that, like the Teutons and Cimbri, the Germans after invading the Province would push on into Italy. This possibility, together with the haughty and arrogant speech and conduct of Ariovistus, urges Caesar to take immediate action.

Caesar sends his demands to Ariovistus

35. Hīs respōnsīs ad Caesarem relātīs, iterum ad eum Caesar lēgātōs cum hīs mandātīs mittit:

" Quoniam meō populīque Rōmānī beneficiō affectus, cum in cōnsulātū meō rēx atque amīcus ā senātū appellātus es, hanc mihi populōque Rōmānō grātiam refers, ut in colloquium venīre 5 invītātus gravēris neque dē commūnī rē dīcendum tibi et cognōscendum putēs, haec sunt quae ā tē postulō: prīmum, nōlī multitūdinem hominum amplius trāns Rhēnum in Galliam trādūcere; deinde, obsidēs quōs habēs ab Aeduīs redde Sēquanīsque permitte ut quōs ipsī habent voluntāte tuā reddere illīs 10 liceat; nōlī Aeduōs iniūriā lacessere, aut hīs sociīsque eōrum bellum īnferre. Sī ita fēceris, mihi populōque Rōmānō perpetua grātia atque amīcitia tēcum erit; sī nōn impetrābō, quoniam, M. Messālā M. Pīsōne cōnsulibus, senātus cēnsuit utī quīcumque Galliam prōvinciam obtinēret Aeduōs cēterōsque amīcōs populī 15 Rōmānī dēfenderet, Aeduōrum iniūriās nōn neglegam."

337. COMPREHENSION

1. What criticism of Ariovistus did Caesar make? **2.** What five things did he demand? **3.** Why did he protect the Aeduans?

Ariovistus sends a defiant reply

36. Ad haec Ariovistus respondit: " It is the law of war that those who have conquered shall rule over the conquered in any way they wish; in like manner, the Roman people have not been accustomed to rule the ones whom they have conquered according to the dictates of another but in accordance with their own judgment. If I do not dictate to the Roman people how they shall exercise their rights, it is not fitting that I should be interfered with in my rights by the Roman people.

" The Aeduans became subject to payment of tribute to me, since they tried the fortune of war, contended in arms, and were overcome. Caesar is doing a great wrong since, by his arrival, he makes the tribute less for me. I will not return the hostages to the Aeduans, nor shall I, without a reason, make war upon them and their allies, if they stand by that which has been agreed upon and pay their yearly taxes; if they do not do this, the name ' brothers of the Roman people ' will be far from benefiting them.

" As to Caesar's threatening me that he will not disregard wrongs done to the Aeduans, no one has ever contended with me without his own destruction. Whenever he wants to fight let him come on; he will find out how brave are the invincible Germans, well-trained in fighting, who have not been under a roof for fourteen years."

The Story of Chapters 37-54

The Aeduans and Treveri report to Caesar that German tribes are devastating their lands, and that a horde of them is preparing to cross the Rhine. Caesar decides to meet Ariovistus before the latter can be reinforced by these German tribes.

He advances at full speed. On the third day he learns that Ariovistus plans to seize the chief town of the Sequanians, Vesontio, well-fortified and well-supplied with provisions. Caesar arrives first and seizes the town.

While awaiting supplies here, the Roman soldiers are panic-stricken because of wild stories they hear of the Germans, their great size and courage. They could kill, it was said, with a glance of their eyes. Many of the soldiers with tears and excuses beseech Caesar to allow them to go home. They even threaten mutiny. Caesar dryly remarks, " There was a general making of wills."

Chapter 39 is of especial interest in setting forth how danger was met by the young men on Caesar's staff who, appointed through friendship or politics, had gone to Gaul to gain experience of various kinds. Letters from Cicero to his friend Trebatius, who was with Caesar, throw much light on this practice, common among young Romans, of serving an apprenticeship under some great leader. In writing to Trebatius, Cicero constantly admonishes him not to be faint hearted. He twits him with avoiding danger, " I see you are a safe campaigner since you did not cross the channel to Britain and look at the British war-chariots when you never miss a two-cent show at home." Trebatius and others of his type must have been very trying to Caesar.

40-53. Caesar calls his officers together and makes a spirited speech.

He reminds them that he is still in command, and that the Germans are not invincible, having been defeated more than once by the Romans and even by the Helvetians.   He rebukes their cowardice, calms their fears, and asserts that, if they will not follow, he will advance with the Tenth Legion only.   Caesar's speech quells the threatened mutiny of his army. The Tenth Legion thanks him, and the others apologize.

Caesar now continues his pursuit of Ariovistus, who asks for a conference. He grants this request.   At the parley he diplomatically reminds Ariovistus of the favors shown the latter, but reiterates his demands.   He defends the claims of the Roman people to Gaul because of (1) their allies there, (2) the right of the Romans to Gaul by priority of time of conquest, and (3) the decision of the Senate that Gaul should observe its own laws.   Ariovistus, on the other hand, lays claim to his part of Gaul and warns Caesar to withdraw.

The conference is abruptly ended by a treacherous attack by the Germans.   When two days later Ariovistus asks for another conference, Caesar sends to him two trusted envoys, whom Ariovistus casts into chains.   Ariovistus encamps two miles beyond Caesar to cut off his grain supplies.   Each day, for five days, Caesar gives him an opportunity for battle but it is ignored. When Caesar learns from

National Museum, Rome

TROPHIES OF WAR

Trophies composed of the arms of the conquered enemy were erected to celebrate victories. What equipment is found in this?

prisoners that German matrons have prophesied that the battle would be unsuccessful if fought before the new moon, he advances on the camp of the enemy and compels them to fight.   The Germans, routed, flee and do not stop until they reach the Rhine River.   Caesar rescues the two envoys who had been thrown into chains.   Ariovistus escapes.

54. Caesar establishes his army in winter quarters at Vesontio and goes to Cisalpine Gaul to preside over the provincial courts.   In this chapter Caesar tersely summarizes the achievements of the summer in these words, **" duōbus maximīs bellīs cōnfectīs "**

Orange, France

A THEATER IN THE PROVINCE

In this Roman theater at Orange, plays are still occasionally presented. Several Latin plays have been given here.

REITERANDUM EST

Numquam nimis dīcitur quod numquam satis discitur, *That is never too often repeated which is not sufficiently learned.* SENECA

338. EXERCITĀTIŌ

Scrībe Latīnē: Caesar's province, one part of which was next to Italy, the other next to Gaul, extended many miles in width. The Gauls were surpassed by the Belgians in bravery, because the latter did not use the things imported by Roman merchants.

The Helvetians, likewise, surpassed the rest of the Gauls in bravery, because they fought (contended in) almost daily battles with the Germans. Orgetorix persuaded the Helvetians to prepare for departure from their narrow territories. He, likewise, formed a plan of obtaining the leadership for himself. When this plan was reported to the state, Orgetorix killed himself.

When the Helvetians, having set fire to their villages, are about to set out, they send ambassadors to ask Caesar that they be permitted (that it be permitted to them) with his consent to (that they) go (make a way) through the Roman Province. Either because the Romans never give this right of way to anyone, or because people not subdued are of an unfriendly mind toward the Romans, Caesar says (**negō**) he cannot do this. He makes

Nîmes, France   © *Publishers Photo Service*

ROMAN TEMPLE IN THE PROVINCE

This temple of Diana is at Nîmes, a town which is very rich in important Roman monuments, among which is a beautiful temple, the Maison Carrée, and also a well-preserved amphitheater.

a fortification in order that he may more easily stop them, if they begin to cross (if a beginning of crossing is made by them). The Helvetians understand that, if the Sequanians are unwilling, they cannot do this because wagons can scarcely go through the narrow pass one at a time, and there is no other way.

The Helvetians, nevertheless, led on by desire for greater territories, decide to go through the territory of the Sequanians. When they wish to cross with their children and food supply, they obtain this request from the Sequanians. But they do not cross without wrongdoing.

Caesar enrolls new legions outside of Gaul and leads them from there to make war on the Helvetians. The Aeduans and their relatives send ambassadors to Caesar to say that their fields are being devastated and to ask for aid. Caesar is informed that one canton is crossing the river. He attacks this and many of them fall. The rest not only flee (betake themselves to flight) but also hide. They attribute their adversity to the treachery of the Romans rather than to their bravery. Caesar demands hostages for the Romans. The Helvetians say (**negō**) they will not make restitution

Courtesy of City Art Museum of St. Louis

A GALLO-ROMAN PLATE

This plate, dating from the third century A.D., was found near Arles, France, a city which was in the Roman Province. It is bronze with a silver lining and has a delicately modelled pattern of honeysuckle on the rim.

to the Romans or to the Aeduans. When the Helvetians move their camp, between their line and that of the Romans there is not more than five miles.

Caesar orders a lieutenant skilled in military science to learn who is on the top of the mountain.

Caesar turns away from the river. After the Helvetians see this, they believe they can cut off his food supply. Caesar, by his sudden arrival, repulses the Helvetians, although they resist for a long time. Their left line is not an aid to them. A few days later the Helvetians weeping come to beg (for) peace. Caesar orders that they shall not be cut off from food supplies nor from other things. Not many of so great a multitude who had set out from home return to their territories.

339.   **REVIEW OF REQUIRED VOCABULARY**

Each of the following words is derived from, or connected in derivation with, a word in the required vocabularies of **Liber I.** Give the Latin word to which each is related and its meaning. Define the English word on the basis of its Latin derivation.

Admire, admittance, aggressor, alias, alien, alter, amplify, announcement, annul, authority, bilateral, calamity, captivate, carriage, circumvention, client, collocate, colloquy, commemoration, compliment, confidential, conquest, conscript, constitute, contumely, coöperative, decadent, dementia, depopulate, despicable.

Escutcheon, explorer, extraordinary, familiar, fosse, hibernation, humanitarian, ignorant, illicit, illiterate, immure, impediment, initial, insidious, institution, instance, intellect, intercede, irresistible, itemize, legation, legate, legion, linguist, magistrate, major, mandatory, militarism, munition.

Necessary, nobility, nullify, objection, Pacific, paganism, patent, persecute, premise, principate, pristine, privacy, prospectus, publication, pulse, recently, redeem, remove, spontaneity, satisfaction, singularly, sinistrous, solitary, statute, student, summary, tantamount, tribute, vicinity, voluntary, wall.

340.   REVIEW OF LATIN WORD FORMATION

Explain the formation of each of the following words, the meaning of the word from which each is derived, the force of the prefix or suffix (**637–9**), and the meaning of the word as a whole: **agmen, captīvus, concursus, cōpiōsus, difficilis, explōrātor, fortitūdō, frūmentārius, hūmānitās, indicium, nūntius, prīncipātus, profectiō, veterānus, victōria, vinculum, voluntās.**

*Museum of Saint Jean,
at Angers, France*

A GALLO-ROMAN BUCKET

A GATE OF A ROMAN CAMP

The **Porta Sinistra** of the restored Roman camp, Saalburg, in Germany is here shown. There is an illustration of this camp on page 270.

LIBER SECUNDUS

THE CAMPAIGN AGAINST THE BELGIANS
57 B.C.

The Belgians unite against Caesar

1. CUM esset Caesar in citeriōre Galliā,[1] ita utī suprā dēmōn-strāvimus,[2] crēbrī ad eum rūmōrēs afferēbantur,[3] litterīsque item Labiēnī certior fīēbat[4] omnēs[5] Belgās, quam[6] tertiam esse Galliae partem dīxerāmus, contrā populum Rōmānum coniūrāre

5 obsidēsque inter sē dare.[5]

Coniūrandī hās esse causās: prīmum, quod verērentur nē,[7] omnī pācātā Galliā, ad eōs exercitus noster addūcerētur; deinde, quod ab nōn nūllīs Gallīs sollicitārentur, partim quī,[8] ut[9] Ger-mānōs diūtius in Galliā versārī nōluerant, ita[9] populī Rōmānī

10 exercitum hiemāre atque inveterāscere in Galliā molestē ferē-bant,[10] partim quī[11] mōbilitāte et levitāte animī novīs imperiīs studēbant;[12] ab nōn nūllīs[13] etiam, quod in Galliā ā potentiōribus atque eīs quī ad condūcendōs hominēs facultātēs habēbant

258

vulgō rēgna occupābantur,[14] quī minus facile eam rem imperiō
nostrō [15] cōnsequī poterant.   15

1. in . . . Galliā: Cisalpine Gaul, now northern Italy, one of Caesar's three
provinces. **2. ita . . . dēmōnstrāvimus:** *just as we have shown above;* at the
end of Liber I. Note Caesar's use of the editorial *we* when he speaks of himself
as a writer. **3. afferēbantur:** the imperfect tense shows that the reports were
frequently brought. **4. certior fīēbat:** note the skill with which Caesar summarizes the reports, and the letters of Labienus. **5. omnēs . . . dare:** *that all
the Belgians, who, as we had said, are a third part of Gaul, were forming a league
against the Roman people and were exchanging hostages;* an indirect statement (**620**).
6. quam: agrees with **partem** and not with its antecedent **Belgās. 7. nē:** for
translation see (**342**). **8. partim quī:** translate *by some who.* **9. ut, ita:** *as, so*
(**602**). **10. molestē ferēbant:** *were greatly annoyed.* **11. partim quī:** *by others
who.* **12. novīs . . . studēbant:** translate *were eager for new government.* **13. ab
nōn nūllīs:** *by some;* modifies **sollicitārentur,** l. 8. **14. eīs . . . occupābantur:**
kingships were commonly seized by those who had means for employing mercenaries.
15. imperiō nostrō: *under our rule.*

341.   COMPREHENSION

1. What two reasons does Caesar give for the forming of the league of
the Belgians against the Romans? **2.** What three classes of Gauls were
urging the Belgians to revolt?

342.   RĒS GRAMMATICAE

**Substantive clauses with verbs of fearing. Verēbantur nē
ad eōs exercitus noster addūcerētur,** *they feared that our army
would be led against them.* In this sentence, **verēbantur,** a verb
of fearing, has as its object a substantive clause introduced by
nē with its verb in the subjunctive, **nē . . . addūcerētur.**
Used with a verb of fearing, **nē** introduces a clause expressing
what is *not* wanted: they hope that the army *will not* be led
against them, but they *fear* that it will be. Hence **nē** is translated *that (lest).* **Ut** used with a verb of fearing is translated
that not: **verēbantur ut . . . addūcerētur** means that they
hope that the army *will* be led to them, but they fear that it will
not be.

Translate: Let the army not winter in Gaul, I fear this;

I fear that the army will winter in Gaul; they feared that they did not have resources.

What is the meaning of **nē** in a purpose clause and in a substantive volitive clause? What does **ut** mean in such a clause?

343.   EXERCITĀTIŌ

Memoriae mandā: **Vereor nē neglegentius vīvam,** *I fear that I shall live too carelessly.* PLINY THE YOUNGER

Respondē Latīnē: Verēbanturne Belgae, omnī pācātā Galliā, ut Rōmānī in Galliā versārentur?

Scrībe Latīnē: Caesar fears that the Belgians, excited by frequent rumors, are conspiring against the Romans.

344.   VERBA

Required Vocabulary: **coniūrō, crēber, facultās, partim, rūmor, sollicitō, versor.**

Word Study. To what word in the chapter is each of these related by derivation: *adduce, counter, faculty, molest, mobility, rumor, solicitous, vulgar?* Define each on the basis of its derivation.

Trajan's Column, Rome   MOVING THE ARTILLERY

On the march each legion was followed by its baggage wagons. This relief shows a two-wheeled cart carrying a catapult.

Caesar enlists two new legions and advances toward the territory of the Belgians

2. Hīs nūntiīs litterīsque commōtus Caesar duās legiōnēs in citeriōre Galliā novās cōnscrīpsit et, initā aestāte,[1] in ulteriōrem Galliam quī dēdūceret,[2] Q. Pedium [3] lēgātum mīsit. Ipse, cum prīmum pābulī cōpia esse inciperet,[4] ad exercitum vēnit. Dat negōtium Senonibus [5] reliquīsque Gallīs, quī fīnitimī Belgīs 5 erant, utī ea quae apud eōs gerantur [6] cognōscant sēque dē hīs rēbus certiōrem faciant.

Hī cōnstanter omnēs nūntiāvērunt manūs cōgī,[7] exercitum in ūnum locum condūcī. Tum vērō dubitandum nōn exīstimāvit quīn ad eōs proficīscerētur.[8] Rē frūmentāriā comparātā, castra 10 movet diēbusque [9] circiter quīndecim ad fīnēs Belgārum pervenit.

Caesar rejoined his legions in person, probably at **Vesontiō**, *Besançon*, where they had been in winter quarters. See I, 54. **1. initā aestāte:** an ablative absolute expressing time (**545**). **2. dēdūceret:** (**585**). **3. Q. Pedium:** Caesar's nephew; he became consul in 43 B.C. **4. cum prīmum . . . inciperet:** *as soon as there began to be a supply of fodder* (**597**). **5. Dat . . . Senonibus:** *he instructed the Senones;* followed by the substantive volitive clauses, **utī . . . cognōscant . . . faciant. 6. gerantur:** (**610**). **7. manūs cōgī:** *that forces were being mobilized;* what is the construction? **8. Tum . . . proficīscerētur:** *then, indeed, he thought he ought not to hesitate to set out against them.* **Dubitō**, meaning *hesitate*, although usually followed by the infinitive, is here followed by a substantive clause. **9. diēbusque:** time within which.

345.   COMPREHENSION

1. Why did Caesar send Quintus Pedius into Transalpine (Farther) Gaul? 2. What did the Senones report to Caesar? 3. What did Caesar decide to do? 4. About how many miles did the army march each day?

346.   EXERCITĀTIŌ

Iterātiō: Ablative of time (**553**).

Respondē Latīnē: Quot diēbus ad fīnēs Belgārum pervēnit?

Scrībe Latīnē: In the middle of the summer there was a supply of fodder.

347.   VERBA

Required Vocabulary: aestās, pābulum.

Word Study. Define the following words derived from **movēre,** showing that each contains the idea of *moving: emotion, immovable, locomotion, mobile, mobilize, motorist, promoter, remote.*

Mob is an abbreviated form of the two Latin words, **mōbile vulgus,** *the movable common people.* What is its present meaning?

Automobile is derived from the Greek word **autos,** *self,* and the Latin word **mōbilis (movēre),** *movable,* and means *capable of moving itself.*

The Remi pledge allegiance and give information to Caesar

" A single canton alone, that of the powerful Remi (about Rheims), discerned in this invasion of the foreigners an opportunity to shake off the rule which their neighbors, the Suessiones, exercised over them, and prepared to take up in the north the part which the Aedui had played in Central Gaul." THEODOR MOMMSEN, *History of Rome*

3. Eō[1] cum dē imprōvīsō[2] celeriusque omnī opīniōne[3] vēnisset, Rēmī,[4] quī proximī Galliae ex Belgīs sunt, ad eum lēgātōs Iccium et Andebrogium, prīmōs cīvitātis,[5] mīsērunt, quī dīcerent:[6]

5 Sē suaque omnia in fidem atque potestātem populī Rōmānī permittere, neque sē cum reliquīs Belgīs cōnsēnsisse, neque contrā populum Rōmānum coniūrāsse, parātōsque esse et obsidēs dare et imperāta facere et oppidīs recipere[7] et frūmentō cēterīsque rēbus iuvāre.

10 Reliquōs[8] omnēs Belgās in armīs esse, Germānōsque quī cis Rhēnum incolant sēsē cum hīs coniūnxisse, tantumque esse eōrum omnium furōrem ut nē Suessiōnēs[9] quidem, frātrēs cōnsanguineōsque suōs, quī eōdem iūre et īsdem lēgibus ūtantur, ūnum imperium ūnumque magistrātum cum ipsīs habeant, 15 dēterrēre potuerint[10] quīn cum hīs cōnsentīrent.[11]

---

1. Eō: *there;* where? **2. dē imprōvīsō:** translate *unexpectedly.* **3. opīniōne:** *than opinion,* translate *than anyone expected;* ablative of comparison. **4. Rēmī:** what famous city of modern France derives its name from this people? **5. prīmōs cīvitātis:** *leaders of the state.* **6. quī dīcerent:** *to say;* a relative purpose clause; the message carried by the envoys is given in the following indirect statements.

In translating Latin, indirect discourse should be turned into the direct form, which is more effective in English than indirect discourse. **sē:** represents **nōs** of the direct statement; **suaque, nostraque**; **permittere, permittimus**; **cōnsēnsisse, cōnsēnsimus**; **coniūrāsse, coniūrāvimus**; **parātōsque esse, parātīque sumus (620)**. **7. recipere:** supply **Caesarem** as the object. **8. reliquōs:** the direct form is **reliquī.** What are the direct forms for **Belgās, esse, Germānōsque, incolant, coniūnxisse, tantumque esse, furōrem, suōs, ūtantur, cum ipsīs, habeant (616–23)? 9. Suessiōnēs:** object of **dēterrēre. 10. potuerint:** perfect subjunctive in a result clause introduced by **ut**, l. 12 **(578, *a*)**; it will still be subjunctive in the direct form, **potuerīmus. 11. quīn . . . cōnsentīrent:** *from combining with these;* a substantive clause dependent on a verb of hindering **(590).**

348.   COMPREHENSION

1. Give the substance of the message of the envoys of the Remi. **2.** What was the connection between the Remi and the Suessiones?

349.   EXERCITĀTIŌ

Iterātiō: **Ablative of comparison (539).**

Memoriae mandā: **Nihil est vēritātis lūce dulcius,** *Nothing is sweeter than the light of truth.* CICERO

Senlis, France
TOWER IN ROMAN WALL

Senlis, a charming town near Paris, preserves evidence of Roman times in an arena and the remains of Roman walls.

Respondē Latīnē: Quam celeriter Caesar ad fīnēs Belgārum pervēnit?

Scrībe Latīnē: The Remi were better (more) prepared than the rest of the (remaining) Belgians.

350.   VERBA

Required Vocabulary: **cēterī, coniungō, cōnsentiō, fidēs, permittō.**

Word Study. The suffix **-ātus,** attached to noun stems, forms nouns denoting *office* or an *official body.* From **magister** is formed **magistrātus,** *the office of magistrate.* Give the word formed with this suffix from: **cōnsul, senex.**

The report of the Remi on the history of the Belgians

4. Cum ab eīs quaereret quae[1] cīvitātēs quantaeque[1] in armīs essent et quid[1] in bellō possent,[2] sīc reperiēbat:

Plērōsque Belgās esse ortōs[3] ā Germānīs Rhēnumque antī-quitus trāductōs propter locī fertilitātem ibi cōnsēdisse, Gal-
5 lōsque quī ea loca incolerent expulisse, sōlōsque esse quī patrum nostrōrum memoriā, omnī Galliā vexātā, Teutonōs Cimbrōsque intrā suōs fīnēs ingredī prohibuerint;[4] quā ex rē fierī utī eārum rērum memoriā magnam sibi auctōritātem magnōsque spīritūs in rē mīlitārī sūmerent.[5]

10 Dē numerō eōrum omnia sē habēre explōrāta[6] Rēmī dīcē-bant, proptereā quod, propinquitātibus affīnitātibusque con-iūnctī, quantam quisque multitūdinem in commūnī Belgārum conciliō ad id bellum pollicitus sit[7] cognōverint.

1. quae, quantaeque, quid: introduce indirect questions; **essent** represents *sunt* of the direct form; **possent, possunt. 2. quid, possent:** *how much strength they had;* the neuter pronoun **quid** is used to express degree (530, *a*). **3. plērōsque . . . ortōs:** represents **plērīque Belgae sunt ortī** of the direct statement; **trāductōs, trāductī; ibi cōnsēdisse, hīc cōnsēdērunt; expulisse, expulērunt; sōlōsque esse, sōlīque sunt; fierī, fit.** Explain the use of each infinitive (616–20). Point out and explain the mood and tense of each verb in the subordinate clauses. **4. Teutonōs . . . prohibuerint:** *kept the Teutons and Cimbri from entering their territories.* These terrible hordes sweeping toward Italy through Gaul were defeated by Marius in 102 B.C. **5. utī . . . sūmerent:** a substantive clause of result, the subject of the impersonal verb **fierī** (593). **6. omnia sē habēre explōrāta:** *they had found out everything;* **habeō** used with the perfect passive participle, agreeing with the object of **habeō**, has the force of a past perfect tense. **7. quantam . . . sit:** *how large a number each had promised in the general council of the Gauls.* The various Belgian tribes promised in all 296,000 men for the war. (This is told in lines 12–28, which are not included in this text.)

351.   COMPREHENSION

1. What was the ground for the Belgians' confidence in themselves?
2. How did the Remi learn of the numbers promised by the various tribes?

352.   EXERCITĀTIŌ

Iterātiō: Indirect discourse (616–23).

Memoriae mandā: **Solōn sē cotīdiē aliquid addiscentem dīcit senem fierī,** *Solon says he is growing old learning something new daily.* CICERO

Respondē Latīnē: Quid Caesar dē plērīsque Belgīs repperit?

Scrībe Latīnē: He asks from whom the Belgians are descended. He found out this (sīc): that the Belgians were the only ones who were descended from the Germans.

353.   **VERBA**

Required Vocabulary: **concilium, plērīque, sīc, sōlus.**

Word Study. Define the following words, showing that each is a derivative of **dīcere :** *addict, benediction, dictation, edict, indite, interdict, prediction.*

Trajan's Column, Rome   FORTIFYING A CAMP

Caesar always fortified his camp with a wall and a ditch.

Caesar encamps across the Aisne River

" Caesar did not venture to give battle to the brave enemy six times as strong." THEODOR MOMMSEN, *History of Rome*

5. Caesar, Rēmōs cohortātus līberāliterque ōrātiōne prōsecūtus, omnem senātum ad sē convenīre prīncipumque līberōs obsidēs ad sē addūcī iussit. Quae omnia ab hīs dīligenter ad diem [1] facta sunt.

5　Ipse Dīviciācum Aeduum magnopere cohortātus docet quantō
opere reī pūblicae commūnisque salūtis intersit manūs hostium
distinērī,[2] nē [3] cum tantā multitūdine ūnō tempore cōnflīgendum
sit : [3] id fierī posse,[4] sī suās cōpiās Aeduī in fīnēs Bellovacōrum
intrōdūxerint [5] et eōrum agrōs populārī coeperint. Hīs man-
10 dātīs, eum ab sē dīmittit.

Postquam omnēs Belgārum cōpiās in ūnum locum coāctās
ad sē venīre [6] vīdit, neque iam longē abesse, ab eīs quōs
mīserat explōrātōribus et ab Rēmīs cognōvit, flūmen [7] Axonam, quod est in extrēmīs Rēmōrum fīnibus, exercitum [7] trā-
15 dūcere mātūrāvit atque ibi castra posuit. Quae rēs et latus
ūnum castrōrum rīpīs flūminis mūniēbat et post eum quae
erant tūta ab hostibus reddēbat [8] et commeātūs ab Rēmīs reliquīsque cīvitātibus ut sine perīculō ad eum portārī possent
efficiēbat.[9]

20　In eō flūmine pōns erat. Ibi praesidium pōnit et in alterā
parte flūminis Q. Titūrium Sabīnum lēgātum cum sex cohortibus
relinquit ; castra in altitūdinem pedum duodecim vāllō fossāque
duodēvīgintī pedum mūnīrī iubet.

1. ad diem: *on time.* 2. quantō . . . distinērī: *how important it was to the
state and the general welfare for the forces of the enemy to be kept apart.* 3. nē, cōnflīgendum sit: translate *that he might not have to fight.* 4. id . . . posse: an
indirect statement with docet; id refers to the plan of dividing the forces of the
enemy. 5. intrōdūxerint: the perfect subjunctive here represents the future
perfect indicative of the direct statement. 6. coāctās . . . venīre: translate
had assembled and were coming toward him. 7. flūmen, exercitum: used with
trādūcere, which may have two accusatives (528); Axonam: the Aisne ; near the
present village of Berry-au-Bac. In the World War the German line crossed the
Aisne in this region. 8. Quae . . . reddēbat: *this movement fortified one side of
the camp by the banks of the river and made the rear safe from the enemy.* Give the
literal translation. 9. Quae rēs, ut, possent, efficiēbat: (355).

354.　　　　COMPREHENSION

1. Whom did Caesar demand as hostages from the Remi? Why?
2. What was the object in attacking the Bellovaci? 3. What three advantages did Caesar's position afford?

355. RĒS GRAMMATICAE

Substantive clause of result (593). The result clauses that you have studied thus far have been adverbial clauses. In the sentence, **quae rēs . . . commeātus . . . ut ad eum portārī possent efficiēbat,** *this movement brought it about that supplies could be carried to him,* l. 15, result is expressed by the substantive clause **ut . . . possent,** which is the object of **efficiēbat.** A substantive clause of result is used as the *object* of a verb of *doing* or *accomplishing,* or as the *subject* of an *impersonal verb:* **faciam ut intellegās,** *I will see to it that you understand;* **fit ut adsint,** *it happens that they are present;* **accidit ut esset lūna plēna,** *it happened that the moon was full.* Often the idea of result has almost disappeared, and the clause expresses a fact.

356. EXERCITĀTIŌ

Memoriae mandā: **Ex quō efficitur ut voluptās nōn sit summum bonum,** *From this it results that pleasure is not the greatest blessing.* CICERO

Respondē Latīnē: **Quō mandātō factum est ut cum multitūdine nōn cōnflīgendum esset?**

Scrībe Latīnē: This command brought it about that the cohorts and their supplies were safe.

357. VERBA

Required Vocabulary: **cohors, commeātus, cōnflīgō, efficiō, mandātum.**

The Belgians try to storm Bibrax

6. Ab hīs castrīs oppidum Rēmōrum, nōmine Bibrax, aberat mīlia passuum octō. Id ex itinere [1] magnō impetū Belgae oppugnāre coepērunt. Aegrē eō diē sustentātum est.

Gallōrum eadem atque Belgārum oppugnātiō est haec.[2] Ubi, circumiectā multitūdine hominum tōtīs moenibus,[3] undique 5 in mūrum lapidēs iacī [4] coeptī sunt, mūrusque dēfēnsōribus nūdātus est,[5] testūdine [6] factā, portās succendunt mūrumque subruunt. Quod tum facile fīēbat. Nam cum tanta multitūdō lapidēs ac tēla conicerent,[7] in mūrō cōnsistendī potestās erat nūllī.[8]

10 Cum fīnem oppugnandī nox fēcisset, Iccius Rēmus, summā nōbilitāte et grātiā inter suōs, quī tum oppidō praeerat, ūnus ex eīs quī lēgātī dē pāce ad Caesarem vēnerant, nūntium ad eum mittit : nisi subsidium sibi summittātur, sēsē diūtius sustinēre nōn posse.[9]

1. **ex itinere :** the Belgians, turning aside from the line of march, made an attack on the town without encamping. 2. **Gallōrum . . . haec :** *the (method of) attack of the Gauls, the same as that of the Belgians, is as follows.* 3. **moenibus :** dative with **circumiectā.** 4. **iacī :** present passive infinitive. 5. **nūdātus est :** *was stripped of.* 6. **testūdine :** a **testūdō** (*turtle*) was formed by shields held close together above the heads of the soldiers. Protected thus, the soldiers could advance close to the walls. 7. **conicerent :** why is a plural verb used here with **multitūdō (568,** *b*)? 8. **nūllī :** what kind of dative? 9. **posse :** why is an infinitive used? Explain the use of : **passuum,** l. 2 ; **sustentātum est,** l. 3 ; **conicerent,** l. 9 ; **oppugnandī,** l. 10 ; **oppidō,** l. 11 ; **sibi, summittātur,** and **sēsē,** l. 13. Point out in the chapter an example of each of these uses of the ablative case : description, manner, time when, absolute, separation, specification.

Trajan's Column, Rome

A ROOF OF SHIELDS

The Belgians adopted the Roman method of storming a town, advancing to the wall protected by shields held over their heads in a formation, **testūdō,** named from its likeness to a turtle shell.

358.   COMPREHENSION

1. Describe the Belgians' method of attack.
2. What message did Iccius send to Caesar?

359.   EXERCITĀTIŌ

Iterātiō : **Dative of possession (521).**

Memoriae mandā : **Nūllī est hominī perpetuum bonum,** *No man has a continuous blessing.* PLAUTUS

Respondē Latīnē : Cui erat summa grātia inter Rēmōs?

Scrībe Latīnē : The Remi say, " Unless we have aid, the Belgians will attack our walls, stripped of defenders."

360.   VERBA

Required Vocabulary : **dēfēnsor, nisi, nūdō, oppugnātiō, oppugnō.**

Caesar sends aid to Bribax.   The Belgians advance toward Caesar

7. Eō dē [1] mediā nocte Caesar, īsdem ducibus ūsus quī nūntiī ab Icciō vēnerant, Numidās et Crētās sagittāriōs et funditōrēs Baleārēs subsidiō oppidānīs [2] mittit; quōrum adventū et [3] Rēmīs cum spē dēfēnsiōnis studium prōpugnandī [4] accessit, et [3] hostibus [5] eādem dē causā spēs potiundī oppidī discessit.   5

Itaque paulisper apud oppidum morātī [6] agrōsque Rēmōrum dēpopulātī, omnibus vīcīs aedificiīsque quō adīre potuerant [7] incēnsīs, ad castra Caesaris omnibus cōpiīs [8] contendērunt et ā [9] mīlibus [10] passuum minus duōbus castra posuērunt; quae castra, ut fūmō atque ignibus significābātur, amplius mīlibus 10 passuum octō in lātitūdinem patēbant.

1. dē: translate *just after.*   **2.** subsidiō oppidānīs: *as an aid to the townspeople* (519).   **3.** et, et: *not only, but also.*   **4.** studium prōpugnandī: *enthusiasm for fighting.*   **5.** hostibus: *from the enemy;* dative of separation.   **6.** morātī: *having delayed;* modifies the subject of contendērunt.   **7.** quō . . . potuerant: (*to*) *which they could approach.*   **8.** omnibus cōpiīs: why is no preposition used (541, Note)?   **9.** ā: *away;* an adverb.   **10.** mīlibus: why ablative (550)?

361.   COMPREHENSION

1. What effect did the reinforcements from Caesar have on the Remi? Upon their enemies?   **2.** What was the size of the enemy's camp?

362.   EXERCITĀTIŌ

Iterātiō: Ablative of accompaniment (541).

Memoriae mandā: Parēs cum paribus facillimē congregantur, *Equals most easily gather with equals,* i.e., *Birds of a feather flock together.*   PROVERB

Respondē Latīnē: Quibuscum Caesar accessit? Quibuscum Belgae?

Scrībe Latīnē: Having delayed a little while, the archers and slingers indicate their desire of fighting.

363.   VERBA

Required Vocabulary: accēdō, funditor, moror, oppidānus, paulisper, sagittārius, significō, studium.

Word Study.   To what word in the chapter is each of these related: *fumigate, insignificant, perfume, student?*

A REAL ROMAN CAMP

To hold the frontier against Germany, a number of camps were built by the Romans from the headwaters of the Rhine to those of the Danube. The former German Emperor had this particular camp, the Saalburg, restored at his personal expense, on the exact lines of the ruins. A model of this camp and of many objects found there is on exhibition at Washington University.

Caesar fortifies his position and prepares for battle

8. Caesar prīmō et propter multitūdinem hostium et propter eximiam opīniōnem virtūtis proeliō supersedēre statuit; cotīdiē tamen equestribus proeliīs quid hostis virtūte posset [1] et quid nostrī audērent [2] perīclitābātur.[3]

5 Ubi nostrōs nōn esse īnferiōrēs intellēxit, locō [4] prō castrīs ad aciem īnstruendam nātūrā opportūnō [4] atque idōneō, quod is collis ubi castra posita erant paululum [5] ex plānitiē ēditus, tantum adversus in lātitūdinem patēbat quantum locī aciēs īnstrūcta occupāre poterat,[5] atque ex utrāque parte lateris 10 dēiectūs [6] habēbat et in frontem lēniter fastīgātus paulātim ad plānitiem redībat, ab utrōque latere eius collis trānsversam fossam obdūxit [7] circiter passuum quadringentōrum et ad extrēmās fossās [8] castella cōnstituit ibique tormenta [9] collocāvit, nē, cum aciem īnstrūxisset, hostēs, quod tantum multi-

tūdine poterant,[10] ab lateribus pugnantēs suōs [11] circumvenīre 15 possent.

Hōc factō, duābus legiōnibus quās proximē cōnscrīpserat in castrīs relictīs, ut, sī quō opus esset, subsidiō dūcī possent,[12] reliquās sex legiōnēs prō castrīs in aciē cōnstituit. Hostēs item suās cōpiās ex castrīs ēductās [13] īnstrūxerant.   20

1. **quid . . . posset:** *what the enemy were able in courage;* translate *the courage of the enemy.* 2. **quid . . . audērent:** translate *the daring of our men.* "He wished nevertheless to ascertain what he could expect from the cavalry, which was composed of Gauls." NAPOLEON BONAPARTE III, *History of Julius Caesar.* 3. **perīclitābātur:** *kept making trial of;* for the tense, see **571.** To what Latin noun is this verb related? 4. **locō, opportūnō:** *as the place was suitable;* ablative absolute. Point out three examples of the ablative of specification; one of the genitive of the whole. 5. **paululum . . . poterat:** *rising a little from the plain, facing the enemy, extended in width over just as much (of) space as a battle line, when drawn up, would occupy.* 6. **ex . . . dēiectūs:** *i.e.,* steep slopes on each side. 7. **ab . . . obdūxit:** *i.e.,* he made an intrenchment at right angles to the ridge of the hill. 8. **ad . . . fossās:** *i.e.,* at the end of the ditches (**567,** *a*). 9. **tormenta:** translate *hurling engines.* See p. 201. 10. **quod . . . poterant:** translate *because they were so numerous.* 11. **pugnantēs suōs:** *his men (while) fighting.* 12. **ut . . . possent:** *so that, if there should be need at any point, they could be brought up as a reserve;* **subsidiō (523).** 13. **ēductās:** translate *led out (and)* (**627**).

364.   EXERCITĀTIŌ

Iterātiō: **Ablative of means (546).**

Memoriae mandā: **Crēscit eundō,** *It increases as it goes.* VERGIL

Respondē Latīnē: **Quōmodo Caesar proelium facere cotīdiē audet?**

Scrībe Latīnē: In front the plain opposite was suitable for an equestrian battle. On either side he placed hurling engines.

365.   VERBA

Required Vocabulary: **adversus, audeō, cotīdiē, equester, frōns, opportūnus, plānitiēs, tormentum, uterque.**

Word Study. Define each of the following words derived from **frōns**: *affront, confront, frontier, frontispiece.*

Flounce, originally *frounce,* is derived from the verb **frontiāre (frōns),** *to wrinkle the forehead.* It is now applied to a ruffle.

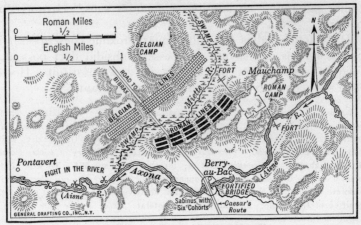

THE BATTLE ON THE AXONA (AISNE)

The Belgians attempt to ford the river and storm the fort

" He pitched his camp on a plateau rendered almost unassailable on all sides, partly by the river and by morasses, partly by fosses and redoubts."
THEODOR MOMMSEN, *History of Rome*

9. Palūs erat nōn magna inter nostrum atque hostium exercitum. Hanc[1] sī nostrī trānsīrent[2] hostēs exspectābant; nostrī autem, sī ab illīs initium trānseundī fieret, ut impedītōs aggrederentur parātī in armīs erant.[3] Interim proeliō equestrī 5 inter duās aciēs contendēbātur. Ubi neutrī trānseundī initium faciunt, secundiōre equitum proeliō nostrīs,[4] Caesar suōs in castra redūxit.

Hostēs prōtinus ex eō locō ad flūmen Axonam contendērunt, quod esse post nostra castra dēmōnstrātum est. Ibi, vadīs 10 repertīs, partem suārum cōpiārum trādūcere cōnātī sunt, eō cōnsiliō,[5] ut, sī possent,[6] castellum cui praeerat Q. Titūrius lēgātus expugnārent pontemque interscinderent; sī minus potuissent, agrōs Rēmōrum populārentur, quī magnō nōbīs ūsuī[7] ad bellum gerendum erant, commeātūque[8] nostrōs prohibērent.

1. Hanc: what is the antecedent? **2. trānsīrent:** why is this tense used (**577–8**)? **3. nostrī . . . erant:** *our men, moreover, were ready in arms to attack them at a disadvantage, if they should begin to cross.* **4. secundiōre . . . nostrīs:** *though the cavalry battle was favorable to our men.* **5. eō cōnsiliō:** *with this plan;* explained by the four substantive clauses, the verbs of which are **expugnārent, interscinderent, populārentur, prohibērent.** **6. sī possent:** *if they could;* this represents a subordinate clause of implied indirect discourse, giving the thought of the enemy; so also does **sī . . . potuissent (624). 7. magnō . . . ūsuī:** translate *very useful to us* (**519**). **8. commeātūque:** what use of the ablative?

366.   COMPREHENSION

1. What was the Belgians' purpose in crossing the river? **2.** How did the river Aisne figure in the World War?

367.   EXERCITĀTIŌ

Iterātiō: **Ablative of separation (534).**

Memoriae mandā: **Bonōrum vīta vacua est metū,** *The life of the good is free from fear.*

Respondē Latīnē: Quōmodo Belgae Rōmānōs fīnibus Rēmōrum prohibēre cōnātī sunt?

Scrībe Latīnē: The swamp keeps neither line from its supplies.

368.   VERBA

Required Vocabulary: **neuter, palūs, prōtinus.**

Word Study. The suffixes **-lus, -olus, -ulus, -culus, -ellus** (in English *-le, -cle, -cule*), attached to noun stems, form diminutives. **Castellum** is so formed from **castrum,** *a fortified place,* with the diminutive suffix **-ellum** and means *a little fort.* Its English equivalent is *castle.* Explain the derivation of the following: *animalcule, corpuscle, gladiolus, muscle, particle,* and *umbrella.*

To what word in the chapter is each of these related: *agrarian, dual, gesture, neutrality?* Define each on the basis of its derivation.

The Belgians are defeated with great losses

10. Caesar certior factus ab Titūriō omnem equitātum et levis armātūrae [1] Numidās, funditōrēs sagittāriōsque pontem [2] trādūcit atque ad eōs contendit. Ācriter in eō locō pug-

A SLINGER

The figure in the center is a slinger, who carries in the fold of his cloak a full supply of stones.   In his right hand he has one ready to throw.

nātum est.   Hostēs impedītōs nostrī in flūmine aggressī magnum
5 eōrum numerum occīdērunt; per eōrum corpora reliquōs audācis-
simē trānsīre cōnantēs multitūdine tēlōrum reppulērunt; [3]
prīmōs, quī trānsierant, equitātū circumventōs interfēcērunt. [4]

Hostēs, ubi et dē expugnandō oppidō et dē flūmine trānseundō spem sē fefellisse [5] intellēxērunt neque [6] nostrōs in locum
10 inīquiōrem prōgredī pugnandī causā vīdērunt, atque ipsōs rēs
frūmentāria dēficere coepit, cōnsiliō convocātō, cōnstituērunt
optimum esse domum suam quemque revertī, [7] et, quōrum [8]
in fīnēs prīmum Rōmānī exercitum intrōdūxissent, ad eōs dēfen-
dendōs undique convenīrent ut potius in suīs quam in aliēnīs [9]
15 fīnibus dēcertārent et domesticīs [10] cōpiīs reī frūmentāriae
ūterentur.

Ad eam sententiam cum reliquīs causīs haec quoque ratiō [11]
eōs dēdūxit, quod Dīviciācum [12] atque Aeduōs fīnibus Bellovacōrum appropinquāre cognōverant.   Hīs persuādērī [13] ut diū-
20 tius morārentur neque suīs auxilium ferrent nōn poterat.

1. levis armātūrae: translate *light-armed;* why genitive? **2. pontem:** what other accusatives are used with **trādūcit (528)**? **3. per . . . reppulērunt:** translate *they drove back with a storm of weapons the rest, who were attempting very boldly to cross over the bodies of these.* **4. circumventōs interfēcērunt:** *they surrounded and killed.* The perfect participle is often equivalent to a coördinate clause **(627).** Point out the participles in the chapter and give the use of each. **5. spem . . . fefellisse:** *that their hope had failed them.* **6. neque:** = **et nōn;** translate with **prōgredī. 7. optimum . . . revertī:** *that it was best for each to return to his own home.* **8. quōrum:** the antecedent is **eōs. 9. aliēnīs:** translate *of others* **(509,** *Note 2).* **10. domesticīs:** *home.* **11. haec, ratiō:** *this consideration;* explained by the **quod** clause. **12. Dīviciācum:** he was advancing to the territories of the Bellovaci in order to carry out Caesar's plan of keeping the forces of the enemy separated. **13. Hīs persuādērī, nōn poterat:** *these (the Bellovaci) could not be persuaded;* the impersonal use of **persuādērī** in the passive **(569).**

369.   COMPREHENSION

1. Give two reasons why the Belgians decided to return home. **2.** What did they plan to do when they reached home?

370.   EXERCITĀTIŌ

Iterātiō: Uses of the participle **(625–8).**

Memoriae mandā: **Avē, Caesar, moritūrī tē salūtant,** *Hail, Caesar, those about to die salute thee.* This salutation was addressed to the emperor by gladiators about to enter the combat.

Audentēs deus ipse iuvat, *The god himself helps those who dare.*   OVID

Respondē Latīnē: Quōs repulsōs nostrī aggressī interfēcērunt?

Scrībe Latīnē: The light-armed soldiers, using a multitude of weapons, attacked the enemy as they advanced (*use participle*) into an unfavorable place.

371.   VERBA

Required Vocabulary: **dēcertō, inīquus, levis, potius.**

Word Study. The suffixes **-ānus, -ēnus, -īnus** (in English *-an, -ane, -ain, -ine*), meaning *pertaining to,* added to the stems of nouns, adjectives or adverbs, form adjectives: thus from **Rōma, Rōmānus (Rōm- + -ānus),** *pertaining* or *belonging to Rome,* is derived. Give the formation and meaning of: **aliēnus, cotīdiānus, oppidānus.**

To what word in the chapter is each of these related: *ablative, elevator, false, infallible, iniquity, levity, optimist?* Define each.

Caesar routs and pursues the Belgians

11. Eā rē cōnstitūtā, secundā vigiliā [1] magnō cum strepitū [2] ac tumultū castrīs ēgressī nūllō certō ōrdine neque imperiō, cum sibi quisque prīmum itineris locum peteret et domum pervenīre properāret, fēcērunt ut cōnsimilis fugae profectiō vidērētur. [3]

5 Hāc rē statim Caesar per speculātōrēs cognitā īnsidiās veritus, quod quā dē causā discēderent nōndum perspexerat, exercitum equitātumque castrīs continuit. Prīmā lūce cōnfirmātā rē ab explōrātōribus, omnem equitātum quī novissimum agmen morārētur praemīsit. Hīs Q. Pedium et L. Aurunculeium
10 Cottam lēgātōs praefēcit; T. Labiēnum lēgātum cum legiōnibus tribus subsequī iussit.

Hī, novissimōs adortī et multa mīlia passuum prōsecūtī, magnam multitūdinem eōrum fugientium [4] concīdērunt, cum ab extrēmō agmine, ad quōs ventum erat, [5] cōnsisterent fortiterque
15 impetum nostrōrum mīlitum sustinērent, [6] priōrēs, [7] quod abesse ā perīculō vidērentur [8] neque ūllā necessitāte neque imperiō continērentur, exaudītō clāmōre, perturbātīs ōrdinibus, [9] omnēs in fugā sibi praesidium pōnerent.

Ita sine ūllō perīculō tantam eōrum multitūdinem nostrī
20 interfēcērunt quantum fuit diēī spatium; [10] sub occāsum sōlis dēstitērunt sēque in castra, ut erat imperātum, recēpērunt.

1. secundā vigiliā: about what time was this? **2. magnō . . . strepitū:** *with great uproar;* what ablative? **3. vidērētur:** why subjunctive? **4. fugientium:** translate *as they fled.* **5. ventum erat:** impersonal use (**502**). Point out another example of this use. **6. cum . . . sustinērent:** translate *since those (of the enemy) on the rear, to whom (our men) had come, would take a stand and bravely sustain the attack of our soldiers.* **7. priōrēs:** *(while) those in front;* subject of **pōnerent. 8. vidērentur:** (**610**). **9. exaudītō . . . ōrdinibus:** translate *when they heard the shouting, they broke ranks.* **10. quantum . . . spatium:** *as was the length of the day;* i.e., while daylight lasted.

372.   COMPREHENSION

1. Describe the departure of the Belgians. **2.** Why did Caesar fear an ambush? **3.** What plan of pursuit did he follow?

373.   EXERCITĀTIŌ

Iterātiō: **Ablative of manner (542).**

Memoriae mandā: **Quid fors feret, ferēmus aequō animō,** *Whatever fortune shall bring, we will bear with equanimity.* TERENCE

Respondē Latīnē: Quōmodo omnēs Belgae ēgressī sunt?

Scrībe Latīnē: With great clamor and tumult they follow. Those in front, seeing this, are immediately thrown into confusion.

374.   VERBA

Required Vocabulary: **clāmor, concīdō, perspiciō, perturbō, prior, statim, subsequor, tumultus.**

Word Study. **Perspicere,** *see through,* is formed from **per-** and **-spicere** (which appears only in compounds). Define each of the following words derived from **-spicere,** showing that each contains the idea of *seeing* or *looking: circumspect, despise, inspector, introspective, perspective, prospect, respectable, specimen, spectacle, specter, suspicious.*

Explain why **exaudiō** means *hear from a distance.*

Caesar besieges and takes a town of the Suessiones

" Before the cantons could concentrate their strength a second time, their untiring enemy bore down upon them one by one. He swooped upon Noviodunum, the fortress of the Suessiones; though its entrenchments were too strong to be carried at a first assault, the appearance of his artillery effected an immediate surrender." W. WARDE FOWLER, *Julius Caesar*

12. Postrīdiē eius diēī Caesar, priusquam sē hostēs ex terrōre ac fugā reciperent,[1] in fīnēs Suessiōnum, quī proximī Rēmīs erant, exercitum dūxit et magnō itinere ad oppidum Noviodūnum[2] contendit. Id ex itinere oppugnāre cōnātus, quod vacuum[3] ab dēfēnsōribus esse audiēbat, propter lātitūdinem 5 fossae mūrīque altitūdinem, paucīs dēfendentibus, expugnāre nōn potuit. Castrīs mūnītīs, vīneās[4] agere[5] quaeque ad oppugnandum ūsuī erant comparāre[6] coepit.

Interim omnis ex fugā Suessiōnum multitūdō in oppidum proximā nocte convēnit. Celeriter vīneīs ad oppidum āctīs, 10 aggere iactō turribusque[7] cōnstitūtīs, magnitūdine operum, quae neque vīderant ante Gallī neque audierant, et celeritāte

Trajan's Column, Rome

ON THE MARCH

The soldiers are not expecting an attack, for they do not wear their helmets, which are suspended from their right shoulders. Note the rest of their equipment, shields, swords, coats of mail, and baggage carried on long sticks.

Rōmānōrum permōtī [8] lēgātōs ad Caesarem dē dēditiōne mittunt et, petentibus Rēmīs ut cōnservārentur,[9] impetrant.

1. reciperent: *could recover* (**135**).   **2. Noviodūnum:** near the modern city of Soissons.   **3. vacuum:** *destitute of.*   **4. vīneās:** *sheds;* made of timber or thick wickerwork with rawhides stretched over them to protect them against fire. These sheds were moved forward before an attack. A row of them formed a passageway to the front.   **5. agere:** *to move up.*   **6. quaeque . . . comparāre:** this was a great mound sloping gradually from the rear up toward the top of the wall of the town which was being attacked.   **7. turribusque:** these movable towers were filled with soldiers and rolled up near the walls. Sometimes they consisted of several stories.   **8. permōtī:** modifies **Gallī.**   **9. petentibus . . . cōnservārentur:** *as the Remi urged that they be spared.*

375.   COMPREHENSION

1. Why did the Remi intercede for the Suessiones?   **2.** Follow on the map Caesar's route from the Axona (*Aisne*) to Noviodunum.   **3.** What was the last war fought over this ground?

376.   EXERCITĀTIŌ

Iterātiō: Subjunctive of anticipation (**599, 601**).

Respondē Latīnē: Quid fēcit Caesar priusquam hostēs in oppidum convenīrent?

Scrībe Latīnē: Before they can recover from their terror, he makes a rampart and moves the towers.

377. *F ri.* VERBA

Required Vocabulary: **agger, terror, turris.**

Word Study. To what word in the chapter is each of these related: *auditory, comparison, conservatory, exaggerate, potency, turret?* Define each on the basis of its derivation.

Define the following words derived from **agere,** showing that each contains the idea of *doing* or *acting: actress, counteract, enact, exact, mitigate, reaction, transaction, variegated.*

The Suessiones surrender. The Bellovaci sue for peace

13. Caesar, obsidibus acceptīs prīmīs cīvitātis atque ipsīus Galbae rēgis duōbus fīliīs, armīsque omnibus ex oppidō trāditīs, in dēditiōnem Suessiōnēs accipit exercitumque in Bellovacōs dūcit.

Quī cum sē suaque omnia in oppidum Bratuspantium contulissent, atque ab eō oppidō Caesar cum exercitū circiter mīlia 5 passuum quīnque abesset, omnēs maiōrēs nātū ex oppidō ēgressī manūs ad Caesarem tendere et vōce significāre coepērunt sēsē in eius fidem ac potestātem venīre neque contrā populum Rōmānum armīs contendere. Item, cum ad oppidum accessisset castraque ibi pōneret, puerī mulierēsque ex mūrō passīs manibus 10 suō mōre pācem ab Rōmānīs petiērunt.

Diviciacus pleads the cause of the Bellovaci

14. Prō hīs Dīviciācus (nam post discessum Belgārum, dīmissīs Aeduōrum cōpiīs, ad eum reverterat) facit verba:[1]

Bellovacōs omnī tempore in fidē atque amīcitiā cīvitātis Aeduae fuisse; impulsōs ab suīs prīncipibus, quī dīcerent Aeduōs ā Caesare in servitūtem redāctōs omnēs indignitātēs 5 contumēliāsque perferre, et ab Aeduīs dēfēcisse et populō Rōmānō bellum intulisse. Quī[2] eius cōnsilī prīncipēs fuissent, quod intellegerent quantam calamitātem cīvitātī intulissent, in Britanniam profūgisse.

Petere nōn sōlum Bellovacōs, sed etiam prō hīs Aeduōs, ut 10 suā clēmentiā ac mānsuētūdine in eōs ūtātur.[3] Quod sī fēcerit,[4]

Aeduōrum auctōritātem apud omnēs Belgās amplificātūrum, quōrum auxiliīs atque opibus, sī qua [5] bella inciderint, sustentāre cōnsuērint.

1. facit verba: translate *spoke.* Give the form that would be used in a direct statement for each of the following: **Bellovacōs**, l. 3; **fuisse**, l. 4; **impulsōs**, l. 4; **dīcerent**, l. 4; **redāctōs**, l. 5; **dēfēcisse**, l. 6; **intulisse**, l. 7; **fuissent**, l. 7; **intellegerent**, l. 8; **profūgisse**, l. 9; **amplificātūrum (esse)**, l. 12; **inciderint**, l. 13; **cōnsuērint**, l. 14. **2. Quī:** its antecedent is **eōs** understood, the subject of **profūgisse**. **3. ut . . . utātur:** translate *that he exercise his usual kindness and compassion;* object of **petere**, *they ask.* **4. fēcerit:** perfect subjunctive; represents the future perfect, **fēceris**, of the direct statement. Account for the primary sequence of tenses. **5. sī qua:** *if any;* the indefinite pronoun (**559**).

378.   COMPREHENSION

1. What excuses did Diviciacus offer for the conduct of the Bellovaci?
2. What reason did he give for his request? **3.** What statement best shows the diplomacy of Diviciacus?

379.   EXERCITĀTIŌ

Iterātiō: **Ablative with special deponents (547).**

Memoriae mandā: **Suō cuique ūtendum est iūdiciō,** *Each man must use his own judgment.*

Respondē Latīnē: Caesarne clēmentiā in omnēs ūsus est?

Scrībe Latīnē: If a war occurs, he will return and use their resources.

380.   VERBA

Required Vocabulary: **incidō, ops, redigō, revertō.**

Caesar spares the Bellovaci.   The Ambiani surrender.   The Nervii

15. Caesar honōris [1] Dīviciācī atque Aeduōrum causā sēsē eōs in fidem receptūrum et cōnservātūrum dīxit; et, quod erat cīvitās magnā inter Belgās auctōritāte [2] atque hominum multitūdine praestābat, DC obsidēs poposcit. Hīs trāditīs omnibusque 5 armīs ex oppidō collātīs, ab eō locō in fīnēs Ambiānōrum pervēnit; quī sē suaque omnia sine morā dēdidērunt.

Eōrum fīnēs Nerviī attingēbant; quōrum dē nātūrā mōribusque Caesar cum quaereret, sīc reperiēbat:

Nūllum [3] aditum esse ad eōs mercātōribus; [4] nihil patī vīnī [5] reliquārumque rērum ad lūxuriam pertinentium īnferrī, quod 10 hīs rēbus relanguēscere animōs eōrum et remittī virtūtem exīstimārent; esse hominēs ferōs magnaeque virtūtis; [6] increpitāre atque incūsāre reliquōs Belgās, quī [7] sē populō Rōmānō dēdidissent patriamque virtūtem prōiēcissent; cōnfirmāre sēsē neque lēgātōs missūrōs neque ūllam condiciōnem pācis acceptūrōs.[3] 15

1. honōris: with **causā;** translate *as a mark of respect to.* **2. auctōritāte:** ablative of description. What other case might have been used? **3. Nūllum . . . acceptūrōs:** indicate all changes necessary to make this a direct statement. **4. mercātōribus:** dative of possession (**521**). **5. vīnī:** modifies nihil (**510**). **6. virtūtis:** what other case could have been used? **7. quī:** translate *since they;* a relative clause may express cause.

381. COMPREHENSION

1. Why did Caesar spare the Bellovaci? **2.** To what does Caesar attribute the strength and courage of the Nervii? **3.** What was their attitude toward the Romans? Toward the other Belgians who had surrendered?

382. EXERCITĀTIŌ

Iterātiō: **Genitive of description (511).**

Memoriae mandā: **Homō ūnīus librī,** *A man of one book.* Thomas Aquinas thus characterized a man who had thoroughly mastered one book.

Respondē Latīnē: Quis erat summī honōris inter Belgās?

Scrībe Latīnē: There is no approach to the territory of those fierce men who surpass all in bravery. They are men of great bravery.

383. VERBA

Required Vocabulary: **aditus, dēdō, ferus, honor, praestō.**

The story of Chapters 16–19

Caesar finds the Nervii encamped across the river **Sabis,** *Sambre,* awaiting his army. Since the Romans have been advancing with a baggage train between each two legions, the Nervii plan to attack the legions separately and destroy them one by one as they advance with difficulty through the impenetrable hedges.

Caesar selects a place for his camp on a hill across the river from the

Courtesy of George R. Swain

THE COUNTRY OF THE NERVII

This illustration shows fields and hedges in modern Belgium. Caesar's soldiers found it almost impossible to make their way through the hedges of this country because at that time they were practically impenetrable.

Nervii. A surprise awaits the Nervii, for as Caesar approaches he changes the formation of his line so that six legions precede the baggage. These legions begin to fortify the camp, while the cavalry engages with that of the Nervii. Suddenly the host of the Nervii come out from the woods, rush across the river, and dash up the hill to the Roman camp.

Caesar's soldiers are equal to the emergency *

" Caesar, calm in the midst of the storm, recalled by bugle the fatigue parties gone in search of wood, got his men into some sort of order, and gave the signal for battle. Even so, if the men had not been veterans, capable of independent action in an emergency, there must have been a disaster."
E. S. SHUCKBURGH, *History of Rome*

20. Caesarī [1] omnia ūnō tempore erant agenda : [2] vexillum [3] prōpōnendum, quod erat īnsigne cum ad arma concurrī oportēret ; [4] signum tubā [5] dandum ; ab opere revocandī mīlitēs ; quī paulō longius aggeris [6] petendī causā prōcesserant arcessendī ;
5 aciēs īnstruenda, mīlitēs cohortandī, signum dandum.[7] Quārum rērum magnam partem temporis brevitās et incursus hostium impediēbat.

Hīs difficultātibus duae rēs erant subsidiō, scientia atque ūsus

---

* Read in Longfellow's *Courtship of Miles Standish* the story of the battle of the Nervii; also in A. C. Whitehead's *The Standard Bearer*.

mīlitum, quod, superiōribus proeliīs exercitātī,[8] quid fierī oportēret nōn minus commodē ipsī sibi praescrībere quam ab aliīs 10 docērī poterant,[9] et quod ab opere singulīsque [10] legiōnibus singulōs lēgātōs Caesar discēdere nisi mūnītīs castrīs vetuerat. Hī propter propinquitātem et celeritātem hostium nihil [11] iam Caesaris imperium exspectābant, sed per sē [12] quae vidēbantur [13] administrābant. 15

1. Caesarī: explain the case and position. **2. erant agenda:** *had to be done;* passive periphrastic conjugation (74). How many times is this construction used in this chapter? What must be supplied each time? **3. vexillum:** *banner;* put up at the tent of the general as a sign of battle. **4. cum . . . oportēret:** *when it was necessary to rush to arms.* **5. signum tubā:** this was the signal to form in line. **6. aggeris:** *(material) for the rampart.* **7. signum dandum:** this was the signal to begin the attack. **8. exercitātī:** *well trained.* **9. quid . . . poterant:** translate *they could direct themselves (as to) what should be done just as easily as they could be shown by others.* **10. singulīs:** *respective.* **11. nihil:** translate *not.* **12. per sē:** translate *on their own initiative.* **13. vidēbantur:** *seemed best.*

384. COMPREHENSION

1. What impression does Caesar here give by the frequent use of the periphrastic conjugation? **2.** What does this chapter tell about the training of his soldiers and of his appreciation of them? **3.** How many things did Caesar have to do at one time? **4.** What were they? **5.** Why was he caught off his guard by the Nervii?

385. EXERCITĀTIŌ

Iterātiō: Dative of agent (**522**). Passive periphrastic conjugation (**501**).

Memoriae mandā: Dēlenda est Carthāgō, *Carthage must be destroyed.* Cato is said to have ended every speech he made in the Senate with this sentence.

Respondē Latīnē: Quae rēs Caesarī administrandae erant?

Scrībe Latīnē: When it was necessary to advance, the signal had to be given on the trumpet by a soldier.

386. VERBA

Required Vocabulary: administrō, oportet, prōcēdō, tuba.

Word Study. To what word in the chapter is each of these related: *administrator, document, prescription, propinquity, revoke, veto?* Explain the meaning of each on the basis of derivation.

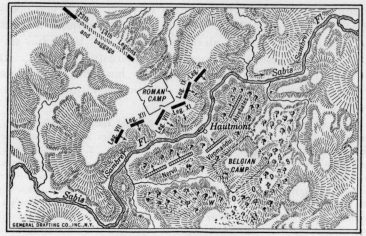

THE BATTLE WITH THE NERVII

A word of encouragement from Caesar, and the ranks form hurriedly

21. Caesar, necessāriīs rēbus imperātīs, ad cohortandōs mīlitēs, quam in partem fors obtulit,[1] dēcucurrit et ad legiōnem decimam dēvēnit. Mīlitēs nōn longiōre ōrātiōne cohortātus quam utī suae prīstinae virtūtis memoriam retinērent[2] neu[3]
5 perturbārentur animō hostiumque impetum fortiter sustinērent, quod nōn longius hostēs aberant quam quō tēlum adigī posset,[4] proelī committendī signum dedit. Atque in alteram partem item cohortandī causā profectus pugnantibus occurrit.[5]

Temporis tanta fuit exiguitās hostiumque tam parātus ad
10 dīmicandum animus ut nōn modo ad īnsignia[6] accommodanda, sed etiam ad galeās[7] induendās scūtīsque tegimenta dētrahenda,[8] tempus dēfuerit. Quam quisque ab opere in partem cāsū dēvēnit quaeque prīma signa cōnspexit, ad haec cōnstitit,[9] nē in quaerendīs suīs pugnandī tempus dīmitteret.[10]

---

1. quam . . . obtulit: *into whatever part (of the field) chance led.* **2. retinērent:** represents a command of the direct discourse (**622**). Point out other examples of this use. **3. neu:** = et nē. **4. quam . . . posset:** *than (the distance) to which*

a weapon could be thrown. **5. pugnantibus occurrit:** *he ran up to* (*his men*) *fighting.*
6. īnsignia: especially the crests on their helmets. **7. galeās:** these, when not
needed, were usually suspended by a cord from the neck. **8. scūtīsque . . .
dētrahenda:** *and for taking the coverings from their shields;* **scūtīs:** dative of separation (**520**). **9. Quam . . . cōnstitit:** *to whatever place each one by chance came
from the work and whatever standards he first saw, by these he took his stand.*
10. nē . . . dīmitteret: (19).

387. COMPREHENSION

1. What three things did Caesar enjoin upon the Tenth Legion? **2.** How
did he regard this legion? **3.** What did he himself do?

388. EXERCITĀTIŌ

Iterātiō: **Adverbial purpose clauses (586).**

Respondē Latīnē: Cūr quisque ad signa sua nōn cōnstitit?

Scrībe Latīnē: When chance offers, they hurl their weapons that time
may not be lacking for fighting.

389. VERBA

Required Vocabulary: **adigō, decimus, dēsum, dīmicō, fors, offerō.**

Word Study. Define the following words derived from **currere,** showing
that each contains the idea of *running: concourse, courier, discourse, excur-
sion, incur, occurrence, precursor, recourse, recurrent, succor.*

The story of Chapters 22–24

The Romans are at a great disadvantage, because the legions are scattered,
and the hedges hide them from each other.

The Ninth and Tenth Legions drive the Atrebatians across the river;
the Eighth and Eleventh rout the Viromandui. The Nervii advance in
mass formation. Part of them surround the Seventh and Twelfth Legions
on their unprotected side, and part storm the Roman camp. Here panic
prevails, and the auxiliaries flee. The situation seems hopeless.

The Roman situation critical. Caesar leads the attack

25. Caesar ab decimae legiōnis cohortātiōne ad dextrum
cornū profectus,[1] ubi suōs urgērī, signīsque in ūnum locum
collātīs,[2] XII legiōnis cōnfertōs mīlitēs sibi ipsōs ad pugnam esse
impedīmentō vīdit, quārtae cohortis omnibus centuriōnibus

5 occīsīs signiferōque interfectō, signō āmissō, reliquārum cohortium omnibus ferē centuriōnibus aut vulnerātīs aut occīsīs, in hīs prīmipīlō P. Sextiō Baculō, fortissimō virō, multīs gravibusque vulneribus cōnfectō [3] ut iam sē sustinēre nōn posset, reliquōs esse tardiōrēs [4] et nōn nūllōs ab novissimīs, dēsertō locō, proeliō
10 excēdere ac tēla vītāre,[5] hostēs [6] neque ā fronte ex īnferiōre locō subeuntēs intermittere et ab utrōque latere īnstāre et rem esse in angustō [7] vīdit,[8] neque ūllum esse subsidium quod summittī posset; scūtō ab novissimīs ūnī mīlitī [9] dētractō, quod ipse eō sine scūtō vēnerat, in prīmam aciem prōcessit, centuriōnibusque
15 nōminātim [10] appellātīs, reliquōs cohortātus mīlitēs signa īnferre [11] et manipulōs laxāre iussit, quō [12] facilius gladiīs ūtī possent.

Cuius adventū spē illātā mīlitibus ac redintegrātō animō, cum prō sē quisque in cōnspectū imperātōris etiam in extrēmīs suīs rēbus operam nāvāre cuperet,[13] paulum hostium impetus
20 tardātus est.

1. profectus: *setting out.* Caesar here takes up the thread of the story which he dropped in Chap. 21. **2. signīsque, collātīs:** the first of the many ablative absolutes in this chapter; point out the others; translate by short sentences. **3. multīs . . . cōnfectō:** *weakened by many severe wounds.* Baculus recovered from these wounds. Read the story of his heroic action as told in VI, 38. **4. tardiōrēs:** *somewhat slow.* **5. nōn nūllōs . . . vītāre:** translate *that some in the rear, having deserted their positions, were withdrawing from battle and avoiding the weapons.* **6. hostēs:** subject of intermittere and īnstāre. **7. rem . . . angustō:** translate *the situation was critical.* **8. vīdit:** repeated from l. 4 because of the length of the sentence. **9. ūnī mīlitī:** *from a soldier* (**520**). **10. nōminātim:** the fact that Caesar knew all his non-commissioned officers by name is one of many reasons for his success as a leader. **11. signa īnferre:** *to advance;* an idiom; military movements depended largely on movements of the standards. **12. quō:** introduces a purpose clause

Vatican Museum, Rome
JULIUS CAESAR

(**585**, *a*). **13. cum . . . cuperet:** translate *since each one desired to do his best in the sight of his commander, even at extreme peril to himself.*

390.   COMPREHENSION

1. Give a word picture of the situation that confronted Caesar. **2.** Why does he use one long and involved sentence in describing the condition of affairs? **3.** What inspired the soldiers to do their best?

391.   EXERCITĀTIŌ

Iterātiō: **Dative of separation (520).**

Respondē Latīnē: Cui Caesar scūtum dētrāxit?

Scrībe Latīnē: Through the work of Caesar, who seized a shield from a centurion, the attack was retarded a little.

392.   VERBA

Required Vocabulary: **centuriō, opera, paulum, tardō, tardus.**

Word Study. To what word in the chapter is each of these related: *detractor, dexterous, emperor, onion, relax, tardy, urge, virtue?* Define each on the basis of its derivation.

Labienus sends the Tenth Legion to the rescue

" The dread of being cut off, which often paralyses even the best soldiers, gradually left them, and they began to fight with greater freedom and pluck."
W. WARDE FOWLER, *Julius Caesar*

26. Caesar cum septimam legiōnem, quae iūxtā cōnstiterat, item urgērī ab hoste vīdisset, tribūnōs mīlitum monuit ut paulātim sēsē legiōnēs coniungerent et conversa signa[1] in hostēs īnferrent. Quō factō, cum aliīs[2] aliī subsidium ferrent neque timērent nē āversī ab hoste circumvenīrentur,[3] audācius resistere 5 ac fortius pugnāre coepērunt.

Interim mīlitēs legiōnum duārum quae in novissimō agmine praesidiō impedīmentīs fuerant, proeliō nūntiātō, cursū incitātō, in summō colle ab hostibus cōnspiciēbantur, et T. Labiēnus,[4] castrīs hostium potītus et ex locō superiōre quae rēs in nostrīs 10 castrīs gererentur cōnspicātus, decimam legiōnem subsidiō nostrīs mīsit. Quī cum ex equitum et cālōnum fugā quō in locō rēs esset[5] quantōque in perīculō et castra et legiōnēs et imperātor versārētur cognōvissent, nihil[6] ad celeritātem sibi reliquī[7] fēcērunt.[6]   15

1. conversa . . . īnferrent: translate *"about face"* and *advance against the enemy.* **2. aliīs:** *to the others.* **3. nē . . . circumvenīrentur:** *that they would be surrounded in the rear* (**āversī**) *by the enemy* (**342**). **4. Labiēnus:** he had driven the Atrebatians back to their camp and, having gained possession of it, could look across to the Roman camp on the opposite hill. **5. quō . . . esset:** translate *at what a crisis the battle stood.* **6. nihil . . . fēcērunt:** translate *they hurried as fast as they could.* **7. reliquī:** give the form and use of this word and the following: **vīdisset,** l. 2; **īnferrent,** l. 4; **praesidiō,** l. 8; **castrīs,** l. 10; **gererentur,** l. 11; **nostrīs,** l. 12; **esset,** l. 13.

393.   COMPREHENSION

1. What did Caesar instruct the Seventh Legion to do? **2.** What encouraged the soldiers? **3.** What legions came to the rescue?

394.   EXERCITĀTIŌ

Iterātiō: **Substantive clauses with verbs of fearing** (**592**).

Respondē Latīnē: Signīs conversīs, quid mīlitēs Rōmānī nōn iam timēbant?

Scrībe Latīnē: The tribune fears that his legion will be seen by the enemy.

395.   VERBA

Required Vocabulary: **tribūnus.**

Caesar, the victor, praises the courage of the Nervii

> You all do know this mantle; I remember
> The first time ever Caesar put it on;
> 'Twas on a summer's evening, in his tent,
> That day he overcame the Nervii.
>
> SHAKESPEARE, *Julius Caesar*

27. Hōrum adventū tanta rērum commūtātiō est facta ut [1] nostrī, etiam quī vulneribus cōnfectī prōcubuissent,[2] scūtīs innīxī [3] proelium redintegrārent; cālōnēs, perterritōs hostēs cōnspicātī, etiam inermēs [4] armātīs occurrerent; equitēs vērō, 5 ut [5] turpitūdinem fugae virtūte dēlērent, omnibus in locīs pugnandō sē legiōnāriīs mīlitibus praeferrent.[6]

At hostēs etiam in extrēmā spē salūtis tantam virtūtem praestitērunt ut,[7] cum prīmī eōrum cecidissent, proximī iacentibus

īnsisterent [7] atque ex eōrum corporibus pugnārent; hīs dēiectīs
et coacervātīs cadāveribus, quī superessent, ut ex tumulō,[8] tēla 10
in nostrōs conicerent et pīla intercepta remitterent;[9] ut nōn
nēquīquam tantae virtūtis hominēs iūdicārī dēbēret ausōs
esse [10] trānsīre lātissimum flūmen, ascendere altissimās rīpās,
subīre inīquissimum locum; quae facilia ex difficillimīs animī
magnitūdō redēgerat.[11]   15

1. ut: introduces what three clauses of result? **2. prōcubuissent:** *had fallen;*
attracted to the subjunctive by **redintegrārent (610). 3. scūtīs innīxī:** *leaning
upon their shields.* **4. inermēs:** *(though) unarmed;* modifies **cālōnēs;** it is emphasized by its position next to **armātīs. 5. ut:** *in order to.* **6. sē . . . praeferrent:** *tried to surpass the legionaries,* or " *regulars.*" The strength of the Roman
army was in its legionary soldiers. **7. ut, proximī . . . īnsisterent:** *that the nearest
took their stand on those who had fallen.* **8. ut ex tumulō:** *as from a mound.*
9. (ut) conicerent, remitterent: coördinate with **īnsisterent.** Why subjunctive?
10. ut . . . ausōs esse: *so that it ought not to be judged that men of such courage
dared in vain.* **11. quae . . . redēgerat:** translate *deeds which, although most
difficult, their tremendous courage had made easy.*

396.   COMPREHENSION

1. Give a description of the battle with the Nervii. **2.** What evidence
is here given of Caesar's appreciation of bravery even in an enemy?

397.   EXERCITĀTIŌ

Iterātiō: **Result clauses (587).**

Memoria mandā: **Bellum autem ita suscipiātur ut nihil aliud nisi pāx
quaesīta videātur,** *Let war be so carried on that nothing else but peace seems
to be sought.* CICERO

Respondē Latīnē: Quantam commūtātiōnem adventus decimae legiōnis
fēcit?

Scrībe Latīnē: The unarmed (men) were so very brave that they ran to
meet the armed.

398.   VERBA

Required Vocabulary: **inermis.**

Word Study. To what word in the chapter is each of these related:
adjacent, cadaverous, cadence, commutation, debt, preference, turpitude?
Define each.

The story of Chapters 28–35

The Nervii lose 60,000 men; Caesar mercifully spares the survivors.
Caesar now advances against the Atuatuci, who have taken refuge in a
stronghold fortified by steep cliffs and a high wall. From this wall they
jeer at Caesar's men and ridicule his moving towers, but when they see a
tower actually approaching, terrified, they offer to surrender.

"The approach of a moving tower, surmounting the topmost walls, was
as terrifying as the attack of an aeroplane, and defense was almost as hopeless." EUGENE S. McCARTNEY, *Warfare* in *Our Debt to Greece and Rome.*

The Atuatuci beg to keep their arms, but Caesar demands an uncon-
ditional surrender. They agree to this but conceal a part of their arms
with which they attempt a treacherous attack upon the Romans. They
meet with defeat and are sold into slavery.

In the meantime, Crassus brings the states on the northwestern coast
under Roman dominion, and German tribes offer their submission; the
army goes into winter quarters and the victory is celebrated at Rome by a
fifteen days' thanksgiving, " **quod ante id tempus accidit nūllī.** "

Nîmes, France   *From Oroc*

IN THE PROVINCE

It is thought that this canal at Nîmes was originally built by the Romans.

Arles, France © *Publishers Photo Service*

AN AMPHITHEATER IN THE PROVINCE

Many important Roman monuments are found at Arles. One of the most interesting is this amphitheater, which accommodated twenty-six thousand spectators. It was built of great blocks of stone. The tower seen above the entrance is a part of a twelfth-century building constructed in the arena. Bullfights and plays are given here each summer.

REITERANDUM EST

Multa rogā; retinē docta, *Ask many questions; hold fast to what you have learned.* COMENIUS

399. EXERCITĀTIŌ

Scrībe Latīnē: Caesar was informed that all the Belgians were conspiring. Immediately enlisting two new legions, he set out with these. By forced marches he came to the territory of the Remi. They had not agreed with nor joined with the rest of the Belgians, and they entrusted themselves to the protection of the Romans. From the Remi Caesar found out what states were in arms and how great a number of men each one had.

The Belgians attacked a town of the Remi, which was less than eight miles away. These sent messengers to Caesar to ask for aid. When this had been sent, the Belgians turned away from the siege and with all their forces set out toward Caesar. Caesar attacked them as they attempted to cross a river. The Belgians, after many of their men had been killed, decided, rather than fight to a finish, to return home. Other states surrendered immediately.

The Nervii, who were men of great bravery, suddenly made an attack before Caesar could do all the things which he had to do. This brought it about that the Romans were thrown into confusion. Caesar, calling the centurions by name, seized a shield from a soldier and advanced to the front line. Urged on by his arrival, the soldiers showed so great bravery that the enemy was repulsed. Fearing that they would be reduced to servitude, they surrendered themselves and all their possessions. Caesar ordered the other states to permit (that they permit) the Nervii to use their towns and supplies.

400. REVIEW OF REQUIRED VOCABULARY

Each of the following words is derived from, or connected in derivation with, a word in the required vocabularies of **Liber II.** Give the Latin word to which each is related and its meaning. Define the English word on the basis of its Latin derivation.

Accession, acquisitive, administration, adversary, alleviate, centurion, clamorous, cohort, concise, conflict, conjure, conversation, councilor, defensive, diversity, equestrian, fierce, frontal, honorable, incidental, infidel, iniquitous, neutral, oblation, opportunist, oppugn, opulence, paludine, permission, perturb, priority, procedure, query, retard, reverse, sagittate, signify, solicitude, solo, subsequent, tower, tribunal.

401. REVIEW OF LATIN WORD FORMATION

Explain the formation of each of the following words, the meaning of the word from which each is derived, the force of the prefix or suffix (**637–9**), and the meaning of the word as a whole.

Armātūra, cohortātiō, dēditiō, domesticus, incursus, līberālis, levitās, maleficium, necessārius, patrius, paululum, speculātor, tegimentum, turpitūdō.

A MILITARY DIPLOMA

An honorable discharge issued in duplicate by direction of the Roman emperor Trajan to the cavalry and infantry of the squadrons and cohorts mentioned on the right leaf. These were foreign auxiliaries. The diploma granted to them and to their descendants the rights of citizens and made legal their marriages to foreign women. The names of the seven witnesses appear on the left.

MARTIGNY, THE STARTING POINT OF THE GREAT ST. BERNARD PASS

This modern town is near the site of Octodurus, where Galba was stationed to guard the pass through the Alps. Because the surrounding heights were held by mountaineers, Galba thought it best to retire to a less exposed position.

LIBER TERTIUS

THE CAMPAIGN AGAINST THE VENETI

57–56 B.C.

The story of Chapters 1–6

In the fall of 57 B.C., Caesar sends Servius Galba with the Twelfth Legion to make safe for Roman traders the road through the Alps across what is now the Great Saint Bernard Pass. Galba establishes winter quarters at Octodurus, a village surrounded by high mountains.

The Alpine tribes, thinking that the Romans are preparing to gain a permanent foothold, secretly take possession of the heights. Surprised by the action of the mountaineers, Galba calls a council. The majority decide to defend the camp. The enemy in great numbers attack the Romans, who fight gallantly for six hours. Finally they decide that their one hope of safety is in a sally. T. Rice Holmes describes this as follows: " Suddenly, at a given signal, four compact little columns dashed out from all four gates, and cut their way through the loose ranks of the astounded mountaineers. There was no time to rally. Discipline prevailed over numbers; and the mountaineers were driven with heavy loss out of the plain, and chased over the hills."

Successful, Galba decides not to tempt fortune further, but to spend the winter among the Allobroges.

The story of Chapters 7–13

Assuming quiet for the rest of the winter, Caesar has gone to Illyricum. Here he is informed of a rebellion on the Atlantic coast led by the Veneti. Resenting foreign ascendency and repenting their recent tame submission, they detain Roman officers sent to them to arrange for a supply of grain and to demand the return of their hostages. This action of the strongest state inspires other tribes to revolt. When Caesar hears of this, he orders a fleet to be built at the mouth of the **Liger,** *Loire,* and sailors and oarsmen to be assembled. The Veneti, likewise, make great preparations. They have the advantage in position, ships, and knowledge of the coast and of the art of sailing.

Caesar feels justified in proceeding against the Veneti because of their retention of Roman envoys and their rebellion after they had surrendered and had given hostages. In order to prevent a general uprising, he distributes the legions more widely over Gaul. He places Brutus in command of the fleet, and in the spring leads the land forces in person to the land of the Veneti.

The location of the towns of the Veneti on almost inaccessible promontories makes it practically impossible for Caesar to capture them. The Veneti also have an advantage over the Romans because of the form and construction of their ships. Made of oak, with flat keels, high prows and sterns, and leather sails, they ride the storms; they are not stranded at low tide; and are not easily rammed by the bronze beaks of the low lying Roman galleys.

Caesar witnesses the first naval battle on the Atlantic Ocean

14. Complūribus expugnātīs oppidīs,[1] Caesar, ubi intellēxit frūstrā tantum labōrem sūmī, neque hostium fugam, captīs oppidīs, reprimī neque eīs nocērī posse,[2] statuit exspectandam classem.

Quae ubi convēnit ac prīmum ab hostibus vīsa est, circiter CCXX nāvēs eōrum, parātissimae atque omnī genere armōrum 5 ōrnātissimae, profectae ex portū nostrīs adversae cōnstitērunt; neque satis Brūtō, quī classī praeerat, vel tribūnīs mīlitum cen-

turiōnibusque, quibus singulae nāvēs erant attribūtae, cōnstābat ³ quid agerent aut quam ratiōnem pugnae īnsisterent.⁴
10 Rōstrō ⁵ enim nocērī nōn posse cognōverant; turribus autem
excitātīs,⁶ tamen hās altitūdō puppium ex barbarīs nāvibus ⁷
superābat ut neque ex īnferiōre locō satis commodē tēla adigī
possent et missa ⁸ ā Gallīs gravius acciderent.

Ūna erat magnō ūsuī ⁹ rēs praeparāta ā nostrīs, falcēs ¹⁰ prae-
15 acūtae īnsertae affīxaeque longuriīs, nōn absimilī fōrmā mūrālium falcium.¹¹ Hīs ¹² cum fūnēs quī antemnās ad mālōs
dēstinābant comprehēnsī adductīque erant,¹³ nāvigiō rēmīs
incitātō, praerumpēbantur. Quibus abscīsīs, antemnae necessāriō concidēbant; ut, cum omnis Gallicīs nāvibus ¹⁴ spēs in
20 vēlīs armāmentīsque cōnsisteret, hīs ēreptīs, omnis ūsus nāvium
ūnō tempore ēriperētur.¹⁵

Reliquum erat certāmen positum in virtūte, quā nostrī mīlitēs
facile superābant, atque eō magis, quod in cōnspectū Caesaris
atque omnis exercitūs rēs gerēbātur ut nūllum paulō fortius
25 factum ¹⁶ latēre posset; omnēs enim collēs ac loca superiōra
unde erat propinquus dēspectus in mare ab exercitū tenēbantur.

1. **Complūribus . . . oppidīs:** note the different ideas expressed by the various
ablative absolutes in this chapter. **2. neque . . . posse:** *and that it was not
possible to injure these.* **3. neque satis Brūtō, cōnstābat:** *and it was not sufficiently
evident to Brutus.* Later Brutus commemorated this victory on a Roman coin.
4. quid . . . īnsisterent: *what they should do, or what method of fighting they should
adopt;* questions in indirect discourse **(621). 5. Rōstrō: (546). 6. turribus,
excitātīs:** ablative absolute with concessive force. Towers were raised on the front
parts of the ships, and from these towers weapons were hurled over into ships close
at hand. **7. ex . . . nāvibus:** *on the foreign ships.* **8. missa: tēla** is understood. **9. magnō ūsuī:** dative of purpose. **10. falcēs:** in apposition with **rēs;**
these sickle-shaped hooks, which were sharpened at the ends, were inserted into
and fastened to long poles. These were somewhat like wall hooks used to pry
stones out of walls, and not unlike modern boat hooks. **11. falcium:** genitive
with **absimilī (513). 12. Hīs:** *by these (hooks).* **13. comprehēnsī . . . erant:**
had been caught and drawn tight. **14. Gallicīs nāvibus:** *(for) of the Gallic ships;*
dative of reference. **15. hīs . . . ēriperētur:** *when these were cut away, all control
of the ships was taken away at the same time.* Why? **16. nūllum . . . factum:**
translate *no act extraordinarily brave;* what is it literally?

THE COAST OF BRITTANY   © *Ewing Galloway*

The country of the Veneti is today called Brittany. The towns of this region in Caesar's time were located on promontories such as the one here pictured. How does this illustration help prove the truth of Caesar's statement of the difficulties which confronted him here?

402.   COMPREHENSION

1. Describe the manner in which the Romans attacked and boarded the ships of the Veneti. **2.** Why would weapons thrown by the Gauls have the greater effect? **3.** What incentive did the Romans have for showing unusual bravery?

403.   EXERCITĀTIŌ

Respondē Latīnē: Cuius in cōnspectū rēs gerēbātur?

Scrībe Latīnē: The fleet of the Veneti was unlike the fleet of the Romans. This was not clear to those in the near-by port to whom the ships had been assigned.

404.   VERBA

Required Vocabulary: **classis, comprehendō, concidō, cōnstō, portus, propinquus.**

Word Study. The English word *rostrum*, a speaker's platform, is the Latin word **rōstrum,** the *beak* of a ship. The speaker's platform in the Roman Forum was decorated with the beaks of ships taken as trophies in the first great naval victory won by the Romans. The name **rōstra** (*beaks*) in time came to be used to mean the platform itself.

Trajan's Column, Rome   ROMAN GALLEYS

How does this representation of Roman ships fit the description in the text?
Note the size of the soldiers in proportion to the size of the ships.

To what word in the chapter is each of these related: *abrupt, attribute,
class, comprehension, degenerate, derivation, funicular, innocent, latent?*
Define each on the basis of its derivation.

A great victory for the Romans

15. Dēiectīs, ut dīximus, antemnīs, cum[1] singulās bīnae ac
ternae nāvēs[2] circumsteterant, mīlitēs summā vī trānscendere in
hostium nāvēs contendēbant. Quod[3] postquam barbarī fierī
animadvertērunt, expugnātīs complūribus nāvibus, cum eī reī[4]
5 nūllum reperīrētur auxilium, fugā salūtem petere contendērunt.

Ac iam conversīs in eam partem nāvibus quō ventus ferēbat,[5]
tanta subitō malacia ac tranquillitās exstitit ut sē ex locō movēre
nōn possent.[6] Quae quidem rēs ad negōtium cōnficiendum
maximē fuit opportūna; nam singulās nostrī cōnsectātī expug-
10 nāvērunt ut perpaucae ex omnī numerō noctis interventū[7] ad
terram pervēnerint,[8] cum ab hōrā ferē quārtā usque ad sōlis
occāsum[9] pugnārētur.

1. **cum:** *whenever.* 2. **singulās . . . nāvēs:** the fact that two or three of the
Roman ships would surround one ship of the Veneti does not mean that the Romans

had more ships, but that several attacked one enemy ship at a time. **3. Quod:** *this;* a relative used as a demonstrative; subject of **fierī. 4. eī reī:** *for this thing;* refers to the same action as **quod. 5.** quō . . . **ferēbat:** translate *toward which the wind was blowing.* **6. tanta . . . possent:** *i.e.,* during a calm the Veneti, who relied on sails alone, were at the mercy of the Romans. **7. noctis interventū:** *when night came on.* **8. pervēnerint:** perfect tense (**578,** *a*). **9. ad . . . occāsum:** the battle lasted from about ten o'clock until sunset.

405. COMPREHENSION

1. What aided the Romans in their naval battle? **2.** How long did the battle last? **3.** What was the outcome?

406. EXERCITĀTIŌ

Cum temporal with the indicative — repeated action (**596,** *a*).

Respondē Latīnē: Cum (*whenever*) bīnae nāvēs singulās hostium circumsteterant, quid hostēs faciēbant?

Scrībe Latīnē: The soldiers kept climbing upon the ships of the enemy until (up to) sunset.

407. VERBA

Required Vocabulary: **bīnī, circumsistō, trānscendō, usque.**

Word Study. In what way are the following forms related to **ferō: afferō, anteferō, cōnferre, distulī, efferō, illātum, offerre, praetulī, prōferre, sustulī?** Give the English equivalent of the first person, singular, indicative of each and at least one English derivative of each verb: **afferō = ad** (*to*)+ **ferō** (*bring*), *I bring to,* AFFERENT.

To what word in the chapter is each of these related: *combination, opportune, salutation, transcendentalism, ventilate?* Define each on the basis of its derivation.

The Veneti surrender and are sold into slavery

16. Quō proeliō bellum Venetōrum tōtīusque ōrae maritimae cōnfectum est. Nam cum [1] omnis iuventūs, omnēs etiam graviōris [2] aetātis, in quibus aliquid cōnsilī [3] aut dignitātis fuit,[2] eō convēnerant, tum [1] nāvium quod ubīque fuerat [4] in ūnum locum coēgerant; quibus āmissīs, reliquī neque quō [5] sē recipe- 5

rent, neque quem ad modum [6] oppida dēfenderent, habēbant. Itaque sē suaque omnia Caesarī dēdidērunt.

In quōs eō gravius Caesar vindicandum statuit, quō [7] dīligentius in reliquum tempus ā barbarīs iūs lēgātōrum [8] cōnservā-
10 rētur. Itaque, omnī senātū necātō, reliquōs sub corōnā [9] vēndidit.

1. cum . . . tum: translate *not only . . . but also* (596). 2. graviōris . . . fuit: *of more advanced age, in whom there was any wisdom or dignity.* 3. cōnsilī: why genitive? 4. nāvium . . . fuerat: translate *what ships they had had anywhere.* 5. quō: (*any place*) *where.* 6. quem ad modum: *any means by which.* 7. In quōs . . . quō: *Caesar decided that he should inflict more severe punishment on these for this reason, in order that.* 8. iūs lēgātōrum: the protection of which was the real cause of the war. 9. sub corōnā: as a wreath was placed on the head of a captive sold at auction, this expression came to refer to the sale of a captive into slavery.

408.   COMPREHENSION

1. Why did the naval battle with the Veneti end the war along the sea-coast? 2. Why did Caesar punish these people more severely than others?

409.   EXERCITĀTIŌ

Cum temporal clauses with the indicative — cum . . . tum (596).

Respondē Latīnē: Cum oppida maritima sē dēdidērunt, tum omnia sua āmīsērunt?

Scrībe Latīnē: When the rest had surrendered, then he killed all (men) of (in whom there was any) dignity.

410.   VERBA

Required Vocabulary: dignitās, maritimus.

Word Study. The word *coroner* is derived from **corōna.** In England it originally meant an officer of the *crown.* In *Hamlet,* Act V, Scene 1, Shakespeare refers to him as the " *crowner."*

To what Latin word in this chapter is each of these related: *coronet, internecine, vendor, vindication, ubiquitous?* Define each.

The story of Chapters 17–29

While Caesar is engaging in war with the Veneti, Quintus Titurius Sabinus carries on a war in the north with the Venelli. Sabinus, pretending fear, brings himself into contempt by refusing to fight. He sends a spy, a crafty Gaul, into the camp of the enemy to report that Sabinus intends to slip out of camp secretly that night and go to Caesar. The enemy is thus influenced to make a surprise attack on the Roman camp. Sabinus, however, surprises them and wins a decisive victory.

Meanwhile, Publius Crassus is engaged in a campaign in the south. In a hard fought battle he defeats the Sotiates, the strongest state in Aquitania. Several other states of Aquitania, alarmed by this defeat, unite against Crassus, who defeats their combined forces, after which the majority of the remaining states voluntarily surrender.

After the conquest of the Veneti, Caesar himself advances against two Belgian tribes, the Morini and Menapii. They withdraw into their marshes and forests. Caesar follows, but violent storms cause him to give up the attempt and to retire into winter quarters.

REITERANDUM EST

Prīma virtus est vitiō carēre, *The beginning of excellence is to be free from error.* QUINTILIAN

411.　EXERCITĀTIŌ

Scrībe Latīnē: The first great battle on the sea was fought in the sight of Caesar. Two of our ships would surround a ship of the enemy. Whenever the ropes had been seized and cut, the sail-yards fell. Then the Romans would climb on the ship. When Caesar had finished the war against the maritime states, then he advanced against two states of the Belgians.

412.　REVIEW OF REQUIRED VOCABULARY

Each of the following words is derived from, or connected in derivation with, a word in the required vocabulary of **Liber III.** Give the Latin word to which each is related and its meaning. Define the English word on the basis of its Latin derivation: *attributive, binate, classical, comprehensive, constant, dignitary, incomprehensible, maritime, port, transcendent.*

413.　REVIEW OF WORD FORMATION

Explain the formation of each of the following words, the meaning of the word from which each is derived, the force of the prefix or suffix (**637–9**), and the meaning of the word as a whole.

Altitūdō, armāmenta, attribuō, certāmen, cōgō, concidō, dēiciō, dignitās, expugnō, maritimus, mūrālis, negōtium, perpaucī.

GUARDING THE FRONTIER

A watchtower, stockade, and two thatched huts at a Roman outpost in the
time of Trajan are here shown. After the conquest of Gaul, Rome found it
necessary to protect her new dominions from further invasions of the Germans
by a line of fortifications from the Rhine to the Danube.

LIBER QUĀRTUS

THE FIRST INVASION OF GERMANY. THE FIRST INVASION OF BRITAIN

55 B.C.

German tribes invade Gaul. Customs of the Suebi

" On the right bank, the Suebi were all-powerful, a veritable hive, from
which ever new swarms of warriors issued forth, pressing to the westward.
The Usipetes and Tencteri sought an asylum from this pressure." E. G.
SIHLER, *Annals of Caesar*

1. Eā quae secūta est hieme, quī [1] fuit annus Cn. Pompeiō,
M. Crassō cōnsulibus,[2] Usipetēs Germānī et item Tēncterī
magnā cum multitūdine hominum flūmen Rhēnum trānsiērunt,
nōn longē ā marī quō Rhēnus īnfluit. Causa trānseundī fuit

302

quod, ab Suēbīs complūrēs annōs exagitātī, bellō premēbantur 5
et agricultūrā prohibēbantur.

Suēbōrum gēns est longē maxima et bellicōsissima Germānōrum omnium. Hī centum pāgōs habēre dīcuntur, ex quibus
quotannīs singula mīlia [3] armātōrum bellandī causā ex fīnibus
ēdūcunt. Reliquī, quī domī mānsērunt, sē atque illōs alunt; 10
hī rūrsus in vicem annō post [4] in armīs sunt, illī domī remanent.
Sīc neque agricultūra nec ratiō atque ūsus bellī intermittitur.[5]
Sed prīvātī ac sēparātī agrī [6] apud eōs nihil est, neque longius
annō [7] remanēre ūnō in locō colendī causā licet.

Neque multum frūmentō, sed maximam partem [8] lacte atque 15
pecore vīvunt, multumque sunt [9] in vēnātiōnibus; quae rēs,
et cibī genere et cotīdiānā exercitātiōne et lībertāte vītae, quod,
ā puerīs nūllō officiō aut disciplīnā assuēfactī, nihil omnīnō
contrā voluntātem faciunt, et vīrēs alit [10] et immānī corporum
magnitūdine hominēs efficit. Atque in eam sē cōnsuētūdinem 20
addūxērunt, ut locīs frīgidissimīs neque vestītūs [11] praeter pellēs
habeant quicquam, quārum propter exiguitātem magna est
corporis pars aperta, et laventur in flūminibus.[12]

1. **quī**: attracted to the gender of the predicate noun **annus**; refers to **hieme**
(**560**, *d*). This was 55 B.C.   2. **cōnsulibus**: at the conference at Luca in the spring
of 56 B.C., it was arranged that Pompey and Crassus were to be the next consuls
and Caesar was to have a five years' extension of his proconsulship in Gaul.   3. **singula mīlia**: *a thousand each.*   4. **annō post**: translate *the following year* (**550**).
Point out and give the use of five different kinds of ablatives in this chapter.   5. **neque . . . intermittitur**: *neither tilling of the soil nor their system of military training
is interrupted.*   6. **agrī**: genitive of the whole with **nihil**, *no land* (**118**).   7. **annō**:
(*than*) *a year* (**539**).   8. **partem**: (**530**, *a*).   9. **multumque sunt**: translate *they are
much engaged.*   10. **alit**: both this verb and **efficit** have as their subject **quae rēs**.
11. **vestītūs**: what kind of genitive?   12. **laventur in flūminibus**: a decided
contrast to the elaborate and luxurious baths of the Romans. This chapter and
the two following are valuable sources of information on the life and customs of the
early Germans.

414.   COMPREHENSION

1. According to Caesar, what was the full fighting force of the Suebi?
2. What do you think of the reasons given for the size and strength of the

Germans? **3.** Why were they not permitted to remain in one place more than a year?

415.   EXERCITĀTIŌ

Iterātiō: **Genitive of the whole (510).**

Memoriae mandā: **Satis ēloquentiae, sapientiae parum,** *Enough eloquence, too little wisdom.* SALLUST

Respondē Latīnē: Num habent quicquam cibī praeter lac domī?

Scrībe Latīnē: A part of the strength of this tribe is brought about by exercise and training.

416.   VERBA

Required Vocabulary: **cibus, disciplīna, exercitātiō, gēns, quisquam.**

Word Study. To what word in the chapter is each of these related by derivation: *alimony, cent, corporation, frigid, influx, lacteal, pelt, vest, vicarious, vitamines?* Explain the meaning of each.

Additional facts concerning the customs of the Suebi

2. Mercātōribus [1] est aditus magis eō,[2] ut quae bellō cēperint [3] quibus vēndant habeant, quam quō [4] ūllam rem ad sē importārī dēsīderent. Quīn etiam iūmentīs, quibus maximē Gallī dēlectantur quaeque impēnsō parant pretiō,[5] Germānī importātīs [6] 5 nōn ūtuntur, sed quae sunt apud eōs nāta, parva atque dēfōrmia, haec cotīdiānā exercitātiōne summī ut sint labōris efficiunt.[7]

Equestribus proeliīs saepe ex equīs dēsiliunt ac pedibus [8] proeliantur, equōsque eōdem [9] remanēre vēstīgiō [9] assuēfēcērunt, ad quōs sē celeriter, cum ūsus [10] est, recipiunt; neque eōrum 10 mōribus [11] turpius quicquam aut inertius habētur quam ephippiīs ūtī. Itaque ad quemvīs numerum ephippiātōrum equitum quamvīs [12] paucī adīre audent.

Vīnum [13] omnīnō ad sē importārī nōn patiuntur, quod eā rē ad labōrem ferendum remollēscere hominēs atque effēminārī 15 arbitrantur.

1. Mercātōribus: Caesar has several times referred to the demoralizing effect upon primitive people of the introduction by traders of the customs and habits of civilized nations (I, 1; II, 15). **2. magis eō:** *more on this account.* **3. cēperint:**

what use of the subjunctive (**610**)? **4. quam quō**: *than because;* a rejected reason
(**603,** *b*). **5. pretiō**: ablative of price (**548**). **6. importātīs**: modifies **iūmentīs**, which
is in the ablative with **ūtuntur**. **7. summī . . . efficiunt**: *they render them capable
of enduring the greatest labor.* **8. pedibus**: (**542**). **9. eōdem, vēstīgiō**: *in the same
spot* (**552,** *a*). **10. ūsus**: *need.* **11. mōribus**: (**185**). **12. quamvīs**: *however;* modifies **paucī**. **13. Vīnum**: in telling of the strength and courage of the Nervii, Caesar
comments on their avoidance of wine. As to Caesar himself, his biographer Suetonius
says, "Even his enemies did not deny that he was sparing in his use of wine."

417.   COMPREHENSION

1. Why did the Suebi permit traders to come to their country? **2.** How
did their cavalry compare with that of the Romans? **3.** What was their
attitude toward the use of wine?

418.   EXERCITĀTIŌ

Iterātiō: **Ablative of accordance (537).**

Memoriae mandā: **Lībertās est potestās faciendī id quod iūre licet,** *Liberty
is the privilege of doing that which the law permits.* LEGAL MAXIM

Respondē Latīnē: Quid mōribus Suēbōrum turpe habēbātur?

Scrībe Latīnē: According to their custom, it is disgraceful to desire wine.

419.   VERBA

Required Vocabulary: **dēsīderō, nāscor, turpis.**

Word Study. Define each of these words on the basis of its derivation
from a word in the chapter: *delight, desideratum, effeminate, paucity, precious,
situation, vend, vestige, vinegar.*

Define each of the following words derived from **nāscor**: *cognate, innate,
international, naïve, nascent, natal, nation, nativity, natural, renaissance.*

The story of Chapters 3–12

Two German tribes, the Usipetes and Tencteri, are driven out of their
homes by the powerful Suebi. In their wanderings they come to the Rhine.
In spite of the resistance of the Menapii, a Gallic tribe with possessions on
both sides of the river, they cross the Rhine into Gaul and settle there.
Caesar, informed of this, fears the fickleness of the Gauls. His fears are
confirmed when he learns that the Germans are being summoned by the
Gauls. Distrusting such an alliance, he decides to begin war on the latter.

German envoys come to him pretending friendship and with arrogant
boasts demand lands in Gaul. Caesar says that he cannot be a friend of

the Germans if they remain in Gaul, but that he will permit them to settle among the Ubii. The envoys ask three days' time for deliberation, which he refuses, because he thinks they are waiting for the arrival of their cavalry. In response to another request for a three days' delay, Caesar sets the following day for a conference. The Germans violate the truce by a treacherous attack upon the Roman cavalry, in which eight hundred Germans put to flight five thousand Roman horsemen.

The brave Piso brothers *

12. In eō proeliō ex equitibus nostrīs interficiuntur IIII et LXX, in hīs vir fortissimus, Pīsō Aquītānus, amplissimō genere nātus, cuius avus in cīvitāte suā rēgnum obtinuerat, amīcus ā senātū nostrō appellātus. Hic cum frātrī interclūsō ab hostibus auxi-
5 lium ferret, illum ex perīculō ēripuit, ipse, equō vulnerātō, dēiectus quoad potuit fortissimē restitit; cum circumventus, multīs vulneribus acceptīs, cecidisset, atque id frāter, quī iam proeliō excesserat, procul animadvertisset, incitātō equō, sē hostibus obtulit atque interfectus est.

420.   **VERBA**

Required Vocabulary: **procul.**

The story of Chapters 13–16

Caesar, thinking the Germans should now be given no concession, holds the envoys who come to make apologies. (This act in violation of the law of nations was later attacked in the senate by Caesar's enemy, Cato, who demanded that in return for this Caesar be handed over to the Germans for punishment.) Caesar makes a swift march against the German camp, surprises it, throws it into confusion, and, with little loss of his own forces but with heavy slaughter of the enemy, drives them in headlong flight to the river where great numbers perish. After this battle he decides to cross the Rhine in order to inspire fear in the Germans and to protect suppliant nations who are hard pressed by the Suebi.

Caesar's bridge across the Rhine

17. Despite the width, the rapidity, and the depth of the river, Caesar decided to build a bridge across. He regarded this means of crossing as the only

* The first paragraph of this chapter is included in the *Story of Chapters 3–12.*

CAESAR'S BRIDGE ACROSS THE RHINE

safe one and the only one becoming the dignity of the Roman people.   The
plan and construction of the bridge is described as follows:

He joined together, with a space of two feet between, a pair of beams a
foot and a half thick, sharpened a little at the lower end.   When he had
lowered these into the river by machinery and had fixed them firmly, and
had driven them in with pile-drivers, not, like a pile, straight up and down,
but leaning forward with a slant, so as to slope in the direction of the
current, in a like manner he placed opposite these, two beams, joined in
the same manner, at a distance of forty feet downstream, slanted against
the violent force of the current.   Both pairs of posts, after there had been
let in from above a crossbeam two feet thick, the distance between the
posts, were kept apart by a pair of braces on each side at the end; since
these were held apart and braced in opposite directions, so great was the
strength of the structure and such was the nature of the arrangement,
that the greater the force with which the water rushed against it, the more
closely were the beams held and bound together.

The trestles were bound together by timbers laid in the direction of the
bridge and were covered by long poles and wicker-work; nevertheless, piles
were driven in a slant on the downstream side, which, placed below like a
buttress and joined with the entire structure, were to withstand the force
of the current; and other piles likewise were put down at a short distance

above the bridge, so that, if trunks of trees or boats were sent by the barbarians for the purpose of destroying the work, by these defenses the force of such things would be lessened and they would not damage the bridge.

The story of Chapters 18–19

The bridge is completed within ten days. Over it the Roman army crosses into Germany and advances against the Sugambri, who flee. Caesar devastates their lands, receives hostages, and at the end of eighteen days recrosses the Rhine and destroys the bridge.

Caesar feels the lack of definite knowledge of Britain *

Caesar, the soldier, went to Britain to punish the people who had given aid to Rome's enemies in Gaul; Caesar, the man, was led on by the desire of adventure in a strange land. The story he tells of his expeditions is the first definite information concerning ancient Britain.

20. Exiguā parte aestātis reliquā,[1] Caesar, etsī in hīs locīs, quod omnis Gallia ad septentriōnēs vergit, mātūrae sunt hiemēs, tamen in Britanniam proficīscī contendit, quod omnibus ferē Gallicīs bellīs hostibus nostrīs inde sumministrāta auxilia[2]
5 intellegēbat et, sī tempus annī ad bellum gerendum dēficeret, tamen magnō sibi ūsuī fore[3] arbitrābātur, sī modo īnsulam adīsset,[4] genus hominum perspexisset, loca, portūs, aditūs cognōvisset; quae omnia ferē Gallīs erant incognita. Neque enim temerē praeter mercātōrēs illō[5] adit quisquam, neque eīs
10 ipsīs quicquam praeter ōram maritimam atque eās regiōnēs quae sunt contrā Galliās nōtum est.

Itaque vocātīs ad sē undique mercātōribus, neque quanta esset īnsulae magnitūdō, neque quae aut quantae nātiōnēs incolerent, neque quem ūsum bellī habērent aut quibus īnstitūtīs
15 ūterentur, neque quī essent ad maiōrem nāvium multitūdinem idōneī portūs[6] reperīre poterat.

* Interesting books in connection with Roman occupation of Britain are:
  COLLINGWOOD, ROBIN G., *Roman Britain*
  HANNAH, IAN C., *Voadica*
  HAVERFIELD, FRANCIS J., *Romanization of Roman Britain*
  HOLMES, T. RICE, *Ancient Britain*
  WHITEHEAD, A. C., *The Standard Bearer*

ROMAN MILESTONE IN ENGLAND

From Oroc

Milestones, **mīliāria**, were set up on Roman roads at intervals of a mile. They usually were inscribed with the name of the emperor in whose administration the road was built, the name of the builder of the road, and the distance from the place from which the measurement was made.

The milestone shown in the illustration stands in its original position, near Vindolana, England, along an old Roman wall built during the Roman occupation of Britain, probably in the second century A.D.

1. Exiguā . . . reliquā: *although a small part of the summer was left.* **2. inde . . . auxilia:** In III, 9 (omitted in this text) Caesar makes a brief statement to the effect that the Veneti had received aid from Britain. What reference is made to Britain in II, 14? **3. magnō . . . fore:** *that it would be very useful to him.* **4. adīsset:** represents what tense of the direct statement? What other verbs are in the same construction? **5. illō:** *there;* adverb. **6. portūs:** subject of **essent;** modified by the interrogative **quī.**

421.   COMPREHENSION

1. What was Caesar's purpose in going to Britain? **2.** What questions did Caesar ask the traders? **3.** Why did he not get the desired information? **4.** Do you think he was planning the conquest of Britain?

422.   EXERCITĀTIŌ

Tense in subordinate clauses of indirect discourse (623).

Respondē Latīnē: Arbitrāturne, sī nōverit īnstitūta illīus nātiōnis, magnō sibi ūsuī fore?

Scrībe Latīnē: Time will be lacking for making war if he rashly goes (shall have gone) to Britain in early winter. Rewrite this sentence making it dependent on **arbitrābātur.**

423.   VERBA

Required Vocabulary: exiguus, mātūrus, nātiō, nōscō, temerē.

Word Study. Define each of these words on the basis of its derivation from a word in the chapter: *deficient, insulator, opportunity, possible, vocabulary.*

Volusenus and Commius are sent to Britain

21. Ad haec cognōscenda, pruisquam perīculum faceret, idōneum esse arbitrātus C. Volusēnum cum nāvī longā praemittit. Huic mandat ut, explōrātīs omnibus rēbus, ad sē quam prīmum revertātur.

5   Ipse cum omnibus cōpiīs in Morinōs proficīscitur, quod inde erat brevissimus in Britanniam trāiectus.[1] Hūc nāvēs undique ex fīnitimīs regiōnibus et quam [2] superiōre aestāte ad Veneticum bellum effēcerat classem iubet convenīre.

Interim, cōnsiliō eius cognitō et per mercātōrēs perlātō ad 10 Britannōs, ā complūribus īnsulae cīvitātibus ad eum lēgātī veniunt, quī polliceantur obsidēs dare atque imperiō populī Rōmānī obtemperāre. Quibus audītīs, līberāliter pollicitus hortātusque ut in eā sententiā permanērent, eōs domum remittit; et cum eīs ūnā Commium, quem ipse, Atrebātibus supe-15 rātīs, rēgem ibi cōnstituerat, cuius et virtūtem et cōnsilium probābat et quem sibi fidēlem esse arbitrābātur, cuiusque auctōritās in hīs regiōnibus magnī [3] habēbātur, mittit. Huic imperat quās possit adeat cīvitātēs, hortēturque ut populī Rōmānī fidem sequantur, sēque celeriter eō ventūrum nūntiet.

20   Volusēnus, perspectīs regiōnibus omnibus quantum eī facultātis darī potuit,[4] quī nāvī ēgredī ac sē barbarīs committere nōn audēret, quīntō diē ad Caesarem revertitur quaeque ibi perspexisset renūntiat.

1. **trāiectus:** this is in the neighborhood of modern Boulogne. 2. **quam:** its antecedent is **classem.** 3. **magnī:** translate *in high esteem* (**511,** *c*). 4. **quantum**

. . . **potuit:** *to the best of his ability;* explained in the following **quī** clause, which expresses cause.

424.   COMPREHENSION

1. On what mission was Volusenus sent? **2.** Was he successful? **3.** Why was the seacoast of the Morini selected as a starting point? **4.** How did the Britons learn of Caesar's plans? **5.** Why was Commius sent to Britain with the envoys?

425.   VERBA

Required Vocabulary: **brevis, fidēlis.**

Caesar prepares to sail with eighty transports

22. Dum in hīs locīs Caesar nāvium parandārum causā morātur,[1] ex magnā parte Morinōrum ad eum lēgātī vēnērunt quī sē dē
superiōris temporis cōnsiliō excūsārent,[2] quod hominēs barbarī [3]
et nostrae cōnsuētūdinis imperītī [3] bellum populō Rōmānō fēcissent,[4] sēque ea quae imperāsset factūrōs pollicērentur.   5

Hoc sibi Caesar satis opportūnē accidisse arbitrātus, quod
neque post tergum hostem relinquere volēbat neque bellī gerendī
propter annī tempus facultātem habēbat neque hās tantulārum
rērum occupātiōnēs [5] Britanniae antepōnendās iūdicābat, magnum eīs numerum obsidum imperat. Quibus adductīs, eōs 10
in fidem recēpit.

Nāvibus circiter LXXX onerāriīs coāctīs contractīsque, quot
satis esse ad duās trānsportandās legiōnēs exīstimābat, quod
praetereā nāvium longārum habēbat, quaestōrī, lēgātīs prae-
fectīsque distribuit. Hūc accēdēbant [6] XVIII onerāriae nāvēs, 15
quae ex eō locō ā mīlibus passuum octō ventō tenēbantur quōminus [7] in eundem portum venīre possent;[7] hās equitibus
distribuit.

Reliquum exercitum Q. Titūriō Sabīnō et L. Aurunculeiō
Cottae lēgātīs in Menapiōs atque in eōs pāgōs Morinōrum, ā 20
quibus ad eum lēgātī nōn vēnerant, dūcendum dedit; P. Sul-
picium Rūfum lēgātum cum eō praesidiō quod satis esse arbitrābātur portum tenēre iussit.

Trajan's Column, Rome

TRANSPORTING TROOPS AND HORSES

The arrival of a great fleet of ships must have caused much excitement among the barbarian Britons.

1. Dum . . . morātur: explain the use of the indicative (**135**). **2. sē . . . excūsārent:** translate *to excuse their action of the preceding year.* See III, *The Story of Chaps. 17–29.* **3. hominēs barbarī, imperītī:** *being uncivilized and unacquainted with.* **4. quod . . . fēcissent (624). 5. hās . . . occupātiōnēs:** *this attention to trifling affairs.* Caesar had not found the subjugation of these people a " *trifling matter* " the year before. **6. Hūc accēdēbant:** *in addition to this number there were.* **7. quōminus, possent:** *so that they could not* (**590**).

426.   COMPREHENSION

1. Compare the number carried on one of Caesar's transports with that carried on one of our transports during the World War. **2.** Did Caesar think he had conquered the Morini?

427.   EXERCITĀTIŌ

Iterātiō: **Dum** with the indicative (**600**).

Memoriae mandā: **Dum recitās incipit esse tuus,** *While you recite it begins to be your own.* MARTIAL

Respondē Latīnē: **Dum legātī veniunt quid fēcit Caesar?**

Scrībe Latīnē: While Caesar was assigning the warships to the prefects and quaestors, the transports were held back by the wind.

428.   VERBA

Required Vocabulary: **distribuō, onerārius, praefectus, praetereā, quaestor, quōminus.**

decline ictus, mare

Caesar crosses the channel and seeks a safe landing place

That the people at Rome were interested in Caesar's expedition to Britain is attested by a sentence in a letter written at this time by Marcus Cicero, " The result of the war is looked forward to with anxiety, the approach to the island is guarded by great masses of rock." He ends with a joke at the expense of the barbarian Britons, " I do not fancy that you will find any musical or literary talent among them."

23. Hīs cōnstitūtīs rēbus, nactus [1] idōneam ad nāvigandum tempestātem tertiā ferē vigiliā solvit, equitēsque in ulteriōrem portum [2] prōgredī et nāvēs cōnscendere et sē sequī iussit. Ā quibus cum paulō tardius esset administrātum,[3] ipse hōrā diēī circiter quārtā cum prīmīs nāvibus Britanniam attigit, atque ibi 5 in omnibus collibus expositās hostium cōpiās armātās cōnspexit.

Cuius locī [4] haec erat nātūra atque ita montibus angustīs mare continēbātur utī ex locīs superiōribus in lītus tēlum adigī posset. Hunc ad ēgrediendum nēquāquam idōneum locum arbitrātus, dum reliquae nāvēs eō convenīrent,[5] ad hōram 10 nōnam in ancorīs exspectāvit.

Interim lēgātīs tribūnīsque mīlitum convocātīs, et quae ex Volusēnō cognōvisset et quae fierī vellet ostendit, monuitque, ut [6] reī mīlitāris ratiō, maximē ut [6] maritimae rēs postulārent, ut,[7] cum celerem atque īnstabilem mōtum habērent, ad nūtum 15 et ad tempus [8] omnēs rēs ab eīs administrārentur.[7] Hīs dīmissīs, et ventum et aestum ūnō tempore nactus secundum, datō signō et sublātīs ancorīs, circiter mīlia passuum septem ab eō locō prōgressus apertō ac plānō lītore [9] nāvēs cōnstituit.

1. **nactus:** from **nancīscor;** modifies **Caesar,** the subject understood of **iussit.**
2. **ulteriōrem portum:** Ambleteuse, the harbor eight miles away; the cavalry transports were held by unfavorable winds. 3. **Ā . . . administrātum:** translate _while the orders were carried out with a little too much delay by these (the cavalry)._
4. **Cuius locī:** Dover, with its high chalk cliffs. Edgar in _King Lear_ says of this place: " How dizzy 'tis to cast one's eyes so low! The fishermen that walk upon the beach appear like mice." 5. **dum . . . convenīrent** (135). 6. **ut:** _as;_ its verb, **postulārent,** is attracted into the subjunctive by the subjunctives that follow.
7. **ut . . . administrārentur:** substantive clause, object of **monuit.** 8. **ad . . . tempus:** translate _instantly at the word of bidding._ 9. **lītore:** the vicinity of Deal.

429.   COMPREHENSION

1. At what hour of the day did the Romans sail? **2.** Compare the time taken in crossing today with the time required by Caesar. **3.** Why did he not land at Dover?

430.   EXERCITĀTIŌ

Iterātiō: **Clauses of anticipation (601).**

Respondē Latīnē: Exspectābatne Caesar dum tempus esset secundum?

Scrībe Latīnē: Caesar did not wait until the forces of the enemy should be drawn up.

431.   VERBA

Required Vocabulary: **expōnō.**

Word Study. **Secundus (sequor),** which originally meant *following,* has developed several other meanings. When used to indicate place in a series, it means *second.* When a wind was *following* (**secundus**) a ship, it helped it on its way and thus **secundus** came to mean *favorable.*

Define each of these words on the basis of its derivation from a word in the chapter: *explanation, quart, quarter, solve, unstable.*

Under great difficulties the Romans attempt to land

24. At barbarī, cōnsiliō Rōmānōrum cognitō, praemissō equitātū et essedāriīs, quō [1] plērumque genere [1] in proeliīs ūtī cōnsuērunt, reliquīs cōpiīs subsecūtī nostrōs nāvibus ēgredī [2] prohibēbant.

5   Erat ob hās causās summa difficultās, quod nāvēs propter magnitūdinem nisi in altō cōnstituī nōn poterant; mīlitibus [3] autem, ignōtīs locīs, impedītīs manibus, magnō et gravī onere armōrum oppressīs,[4] simul et dē nāvibus dēsiliendum et in flūctibus cōnsistendum et cum hostibus erat pugnandum, cum 10 illī, aut ex āridō aut paulum in aquam prōgressī, omnibus membrīs expedītīs, nōtissimīs locīs, audācter tēla conicerent et equōs īnsuēfactōs incitārent. Quibus rēbus nostrī perterritī atque huius omnīnō generis pugnae imperītī [5] nōn eādem alacritāte ac studiō quō [6] in pedestribus ūtī proeliīs cōnsuērant ūtēbantur.

© *Ewing Galloway*

THE CHALK CLIFFS OF DOVER
Why did Caesar think this was not a suitable place for landing?

1. quō, genere: *a kind of fighting which.* **2. ēgredī:** *from disembarking* (**590,** *Note*). **3. mīlitibus:** dative of agent with **dēsiliendum** (**erat**) and the two following passive periphrastic forms; an emphatic contrast to the nominative **illī,** referring to the Britons. **4. mīlitibus . . . oppressīs:** *the* (*Roman*) *soldiers, however, in an unfamiliar place, with hands hampered, weighed down by a great and heavy burden of armor, had to.* **5. huius . . . imperītī:** *wholly inexperienced in this kind of fighting* (**513**). **6. quō:** explain the case of this word and the following: **genere,** l. 2; **cōpiīs,** l. 3; **nāvibus,** l. 3; **manibus,** l. 7; **onere,** l. 7; **generis,** l. 13.

432. COMPREHENSION

1. What was the plan of the Britons? **2.** At what disadvantage were the Romans? **3.** In what ways did the Britons have the advantage? **4.** How does Caesar indirectly praise the bravery of his men?

433. EXERCITĀTIŌ

Respondē Latīnē: Quae nostrīs facienda erant?
Scrībe Latīnē: Their infantry were unencumbered by armor.

434. VERBA

Required Vocabulary: **expediō, pedester.**
Word Study: The word **barbarus** is connected in derivation with a word meaning *to stammer.* It was probably first used in an attempt to imitate the speech of peoples who did not use the Greek or Latin language.

Roman artillery drives back the Britons. A brave Roman standard bearer

25. Quod ubi Caesar animadvertit, nāvēs longās,[1] quārum et speciēs erat barbarīs inūsitātior [2] et mōtus ad ūsum expedītior [3] paulum removērī ab onerāriīs nāvibus et rēmīs incitārī et ad latus apertum hostium cōnstituī, atque inde fundīs, sagittīs,
5 tormentīs hostēs prōpellī ac summovērī iussit; quae rēs magnō ūsuī nostrīs fuit. Nam et nāvium figūrā et rēmōrum mōtū et inūsitātō genere tormentōrum permōtī barbarī cōnstitērunt ac paulum modo [4] pedem rettulērunt.

Atque nostrīs mīlitibus cūnctantibus, maximē propter alti-
10 tūdinem maris, quī [5] decimae legiōnis aquilam ferēbat, obtes-
tātus deōs ut ea rēs legiōnī fēlīciter ēvenīret, " Dēsilīte," inquit,
" commīlitōnēs,[6] nisi vultis aquilam hostibus prōdere; ego [7]
certē meum reī pūblicae atque imperātōrī officium praestiterō." [8]

Hoc cum vōce magnā dīxisset, sē ex nāvī prōiēcit atque in
15 hostēs aquilam ferre coepit. Tum nostrī, cohortātī inter sē
nē tantum dēdecus admitterētur,[9] ūniversī ex nāvī dēsiluērunt.
Hōs item ex proximīs prīmī nāvibus [10] cum cōnspexissent, subsecūtī hostibus appropinquārunt.

1. **nāvēs longās:** *war vessels*, propelled chiefly by oars; subject of what three infinitives? 2. **quārum . . . inūsitātior:** *the appearance of which was quite strange to the barbarians.* They were more accustomed to sailing vessels. 3. **ad . . . expedītior:** translate *easier to handle.* 4. **paulum modo:** *just a little.* 5. **quī:** = is quī. 6. **commīlitōnēs:** why was this word more effective than the word mīlitēs would have been? 7. **ego:** why is the personal pronoun expressed (**556**)? 8. **praestiterō:** (**575**). Explain the tense of: iussit, l. 5; ferēbat, l. 10; ēvenīret, l. 11; dīxisset, l. 14. 9. **cohortātī . . . admitterētur:** *urging one another not to allow so great a disgrace.* 10. **ex . . . nāvibus:** modifies eī, the subject understood of the verbs that follow.

435.　　　　　COMPREHENSION

1. What on the Roman vessels corresponded to the guns on a modern battleship? 2. To what modern symbol does the eagle of the Roman legion correspond? 3. What made the speech of the standard bearer so effective? 4. Why does Caesar quote this speech?

Trajan's Column, Rome   UNDAUNTED BY DIFFICULTIES

The scene shown here from Trajan's Column, of soldiers crossing a river, is not unlike that described in this chapter where soldiers, following their standard bearer, jump into the sea.   Note that one carries his possessions on his shield.

436.   EXERCITĀTIŌ

Respondē Latīnē: Sī mīles aquilam Britannīs prōdiderit, dēdecus admittet?

Scrībe Latīnē: Our men all say, "We at least shall have followed the eagle."

437.   VERBA

Required Vocabulary: **aquila, ūniversus.**

Word Study.   Define each of these words on the basis of its derivation from a word in the chapter: *decimate, decorum, expeditious, felicity, officious.*

The Romans land and rout the Britons

26. Pugnātum est ab utrīsque ācriter. Nostrī tamen, quod neque ōrdinēs servāre neque firmiter īnsistere neque signa subsequī poterant, atque alius aliā ex nāvī [1] quibuscumque signīs occurrerat sē aggregābat,[2] magnopere perturbābantur;
5 hostēs vērō, nōtīs omnibus vadīs, ubi ex lītore aliquōs singulārēs [3] ex nāvī ēgredientēs cōnspexerant, incitātīs equīs, impedītōs adoriēbantur, plūrēs paucōs circumsistēbant, aliī ab latere apertō in ūniversōs tēla coniciēbant.

Quod cum animadvertisset Caesar, scaphās longārum nāvium,
10 item speculātōria nāvigia, mīlitibus complērī iussit et, quōs labōrantēs cōnspexerat, hīs subsidia summittēbat. Nostrī simul [4] in āridō cōnstitērunt, suīs omnibus cōnsecūtīs, in hostēs impetum fēcērunt atque eōs in fugam dedērunt; neque longius [5] prōsequī potuērunt, quod equitēs cursum tenēre atque īnsulam
15 capere [6] nōn potuerant. Hoc ūnum ad prīstinam fortūnam Caesarī dēfuit.

1. alius . . . nāvī: *one from one ship, another from another.* 2. quibuscumque . . . aggregābat: *joined whatever standard they met.* 3. aliquōs singulārēs: *any by themselves;* contrasted with plūrēs, *a large number.* 4. simul (atque): *as soon as.* 5. neque longius: *but not very far.* 6. capere: *to reach.*

438. COMPREHENSION

1. Why did the Romans not follow the Britons farther? 2. Where was the Roman cavalry? 3. Did Caesar believe in luck (fortūna)?

439. EXERCITĀTIŌ

Idiomatic use of *alius* (561, *e*).

Memoriae mandā: Aliud aliīs placet, *One thing pleases some, another others.*

Respondē Latīnē: Quibus signīs alius aliā ex nāvī sē aggregābat?

Scrībe Latīnē: The enemy surround one at a time whatever men they see.

440. VERBA

Required Vocabulary: quīcumque, singulāris.

Word Study. Distinguish between the meanings of the compounds of **sequor** found in this chapter. What does **assequor** mean? **Īnsequor**?

The Britons submit

27. Hostēs proeliō superātī, simul atque sē ex fugā recēpērunt, statim ad Caesarem lēgātōs dē pāce mīsērunt; obsidēs sēsē datūrōs quaeque imperāsset factūrōs pollicitī sunt. Ūnā cum hīs lēgātīs Commius Atrebās vēnit, quem suprā [1] dēmōnstrāveram ā Caesare in Britanniam praemissum. Hunc illī [2] ē nāvī ēgressum, cum ad eōs ōrātōris modō [3] Caesaris mandāta dēferret, comprehenderant atque in vincula coniēcerant; tum, proeliō factō, remīsērunt. In petendā pāce eius reī culpam in multitūdinem contulērunt et propter imprūdentiam ut ignōscerētur [4] petīvērunt. 10

Caesar questus quod, cum ultrō,[5] in continentem lēgātīs missīs, pācem ab sē petīssent, bellum sine causā intulissent, ignōscere sē imprūdentiae [6] dīxit obsidēsque imperāvit; quōrum illī partem statim dedērunt, partem ex longinquiōribus locīs arcessītam paucīs diēbus sēsē datūrōs dīxērunt. Intereā suōs 15 remigrāre in agrōs iussērunt, prīncipēsque undique convenīre et sē cīvitātēsque suās Caesarī commendāre coepērunt.

1. suprā: see Chap. 21. **2. Hunc illī:** to whom does each of these pronouns refer? **3. ōrātōris modō:** *in the capacity of envoy.* **4. ut ignōscerētur:** translate *that they be pardoned;* impersonal use of the verb. **5. ultrō:** see Chap. 21. **6. imprūdentiae:** dative with ignōscō (**517**).

441. COMPREHENSION

1. What principle of international law had the Britons violated? **2.** Why was Caesar lenient with them? **3.** How had Caesar treated the Veneti when they were guilty of throwing his envoys into chains?

442. EXERCITĀTIŌ

Respondē Latīnē: Cūr Caesar queritur?

Scrībe Latīnē: The ambassadors, who are bringing commands, of their own accord entrust themselves to Caesar.

443. VERBA

Required Vocabulary: **commendō, dēferō, queror, ultrō.**

From Corstopitum   Corbridge, Northumberland

A ROMAN SQUADRON IN BRITAIN

This inscription was found in 1906. It reads: **VEXILLATIO,** *squadron,*
LEG(ionis) **VI,** *of the Sixth Legion,* **VIC**(tricis), *victorious,* **P**(iae), *loyal,* **F**(elicis), *lucky,*
F(idelis), *faithful,* **SUB CURA,** *under the command,* **SEX**(ti) **CALPURN**(i) **AGRICOLAE,**
of Sextus Calpurnius Agricola, **LEG**(ati) **AUG**(usti) **PR**(o) **PR**(aetore), *imperial legate
with the power of praetor.* There was an earlier inscription on the stone, which
was chipped out partially before its later use.

A storm prevents the cavalry transports from landing

28. Hīs rēbus pāce cōnfirmātā, post diem quārtum quam [1] est
in Britanniam ventum,[2] nāvēs XVIII, dē quibus suprā dēmōnstrātum est, quae equitēs sustulerant, ex superiōre portū [3] lēnī
ventō solvērunt.

5   Quae cum appropinquārent Britanniae et ex castrīs vidērentur, tanta tempestās subitō coorta est ut nūlla eārum cursum
tenēre posset, sed aliae eōdem unde erant profectae referrentur,[4]
aliae ad īnferiōrem partem īnsulae, quae est propius sōlis occāsum,
magnō suō cum perīculō [5] dēicerentur; quae, tamen ancorīs
10 iactīs, cum flūctibus complērentur, necessāriō adversā nocte in
altum prōvectae continentem petiērunt.

1. post ... quam : *on the fourth day after.* **2.** est, ventum : *they came;* impersonal
use. **3.** superiōre portū : see Chap. 23, Note 2. **4.** referrentur : why subjunctive?
5. suō cum perīculō : *with danger to themselves.*

funicular

Thur

The fleet is wrecked by a storm

29. Eādem nocte accidit ut esset lūna plēna,[1] quī diēs mari-
timōs aestūs maximōs in Ōceanō efficere cōnsuēvit, nostrīsque
id erat incognitum.[2]   Ita ūnō tempore et longās nāvēs, quibus
Caesar exercitum trānsportandum[3] cūrāverat, quāsque in
āridum subdūxerat, aestus complēbat, et onerāriās, quae ad 5
ancorās erant dēligātae, tempestās afflīctābat, neque ūlla nostrīs
facultās aut administrandī aut auxiliandī dabātur.

Complūribus nāvibus frāctīs, reliquae cum essent (fūnibus,
ancorīs, reliquīsque armāmentīs āmissīs) ad nāvigandum
inūtilēs, magna, id quod necesse erat accidere, tōtīus exercitūs 10
perturbātiō facta est.   Neque enim nāvēs erant aliae quibus
reportārī possent,[4] et omnia deerant quae ad reficiendās nāvēs
erant ūsuī; et, quod omnibus cōnstābat hiemārī in Galliā oportēre, frūmentum in hīs locīs in hiemem prōvīsum nōn erat.

Finish Fri

1. **lūna plēna:** astronomical calculations show that this date was August 30.
2. **incognitum:** the Romans were accustomed to the Mediterranean, where the
tide is scarcely perceptible.   3. **trānsportandum:** used with **cūrō (630, b).   4. possent:** (584).

444.   COMPREHENSION

1. From statements in this and the preceding chapter, work out the
date of Caesar's arrival in Britain.   **2.** Why had Caesar not foreseen the
danger from high tide?   **3.** Why were the Romans so alarmed because of
the disaster to the ships?

445.   EXERCITĀTIŌ

Respondē Latīnē: Quid erat necesse hāc nocte accidere?

Scrībe Latīnē: Caesar sees to it that the shattered ships are repaired.   *Fri*

446.   *Thur*   VERBA

Required Vocabulary: **cūrō, frangō, lūna, necesse, reficiō.**

Word Study.   Lunatic, a derivative of **lūna,** originally meant *moonstruck*
and was applied to a form of mental derangement that was supposed to be
influenced by the changes of the moon.

Define *incognito* by relating it to a word in the chapter.   *Fri*

The Britons plan to renew hostilities

30. Quibus rēbus cognitīs, prīncipēs Britanniae, quī post proelium ad Caesarem convēnerant, inter sē collocūtī, cum et equitēs et nāvēs et frūmentum Rōmānīs deesse intellegerent, et paucitātem mīlitum ex castrōrum exiguitāte cognōscerent, quae 5 hōc erant etiam angustiōra, quod sine impedīmentīs Caesar legiōnēs trānsportāverat, optimum factū esse dūxērunt, rebelliōne factā, frūmentō commeātūque nostrōs prohibēre et rem in hiemem prōdūcere; quod, hīs superātīs aut reditū interclūsīs, nēminem posteā bellī īnferendī causā in Britanniam trānsitūrum 10 cōnfīdēbant.

Itaque, rūrsus coniūrātiōne factā, paulātim ex castrīs discēdere ac suōs clam ex agrīs dēdūcere coepērunt.

447.   COMPREHENSION

1. What additional trouble threatened the Romans? **2.** What two things did the Britons hope to accomplish?

448.   VERBA

Required Vocabulary: **colloquor, nēmō, prōdūcō.**

IIQVAESTORIVSTII·COL·SECVNDVS
PREF · FABR · II · SIBI · ET
CLAVDIAEANTHEMIDI·CONTVBERNALI
OPTIMAE ·VIX · ANN · XX

AN ARMY ENGINEER

This inscription to the chief engineer, who superintended repairs on bridges and roads and was chief officer over the corps of mechanics in a Roman army, is: *Tiberius Quaestorius Secundus, son of Tiberius, of the Colline tribe, prefect of the engineer corps for the second time (puts up this monument), for himself and for Claudia Anthemis, his excellent wife, aged twenty.* The first two letters of the inscription are **TI**, the abbreviation for **Tiberius. TI F** stands for **Tiberi filius; COL, Collina; VIX, vixit.**

Caesar hastens to gather supplies and to repair the fleet

31. At Caesar, etsī nōndum eōrum cōnsilia cognōverat, tamen et ex ēventū nāvium suārum et ex eō, quod obsidēs dare inter-mīserant, fore id quod accidit suspicābātur.

Itaque ad omnēs cāsūs subsidia cōmparābat. Nam et frū-mentum ex agrīs cotīdiē in castra cōnferēbat et, quae gravissimē 5 afflīctae erant nāvēs, eārum māteriā atque aere ad reliquās reficiendās ūtēbātur et, quae ad eās rēs erant ūsuī, ex continentī comportārī iubēbat. Itaque, cum summō studiō ā mīlitibus administrārētur, XII nāvibus āmissīs, reliquīs ut nāvigārī com-modē posset effēcit.   10

449.   COMPREHENSION

1. What ground did Caesar have for suspecting the Britons? **2.** How did he meet the emergency? **3.** To whom does he give the credit?

450.   VERBA

Required Vocabulary: ēventus, māteria, suspicor.

The Britons attack a Roman legion which is foraging

32. Dum ea geruntur, legiōne ex cōnsuētūdine ūnā frūmen-tātum[1] missā, quae appellābātur septima, neque ūllā ad id tempus bellī suspīciōne interpositā, cum pars hominum in agrīs rema-nēret, pars etiam in castra ventitāret, eī quī prō portīs castrōrum in statiōne erant Caesarī nūntiāvērunt pulverem maiōrem 5 quam cōnsuētūdō ferret[2] in eā parte vidērī quam in partem legiō iter fēcisset. Caesar id quod erat suspicātus, aliquid novī ā barbarīs initum cōnsilī,[3] cohortēs quae in statiōnibus erant sēcum in eam partem proficīscī, ex reliquīs duās in stati-ōnem cohortēs succēdere, reliquās armārī et cōnfestim sēsē 10 subsequī iussit.

Cum paulō longius ā castrīs prōcessisset, suōs ab hostibus premī atque aegrē sustinēre et, cōnfertā legiōne, ex omnibus partibus tēla conicī animadvertit. Nam quod, omnī ex reliquīs partibus dēmessō frūmentō, pars ūna erat reliqua, suspicātī 15

Trajan's Column, Rome

SOLDIERS HARVESTING GRAIN

These soldiers are probably foraging in the enemy's territory.   Some cut the grain, and others carry it away.

hostēs hūc nostrōs esse ventūrōs noctū in silvīs dēlituerant; tum dispersōs,[4] dēpositīs armīs, in metendō occupātōs subitō adortī, paucīs interfectīs, reliquōs, incertīs ōrdinibus, perturbāverant, simul equitātū atque essedīs circumdederant.

1. frūmentātum: (**631,** *a*). **2. quam** . . . **ferret:** translate *than usual.* What is the literal translation? **3. id** . . . **cōnsilī:** translate *suspecting the truth, that some new plan had been inaugurated by the barbarians.* **4. dispersōs:** modifies **nostrōs** understood, the object of **adortī.**

451.   EXERCITĀTIŌ

Respondē Latīnē: Quibus Rōmānī cōnfestim circumdātī sunt?

Scrībe Latīnē: When they saw the dust, those on guard reported their suspicions to Caesar.

452.   VERBA

Required Vocabulary: **circumdō, cōnfestim, pulvis, statiō, suspiciō.**

The chariot fighting of the Britons

33. Genus hoc est ex essedīs [1] pugnae. Prīmō per omnēs partēs perequitant et tēla coniciunt atque ipsō terrōre equōrum [2]

et strepitū rotārum ōrdinēs plērumque perturbant; et cum sē
inter equitum turmās īnsinuāvērunt, ex essedīs dēsiliunt et
pedibus proeliantur.   5

Aurīgae interim paulātim ex proeliō excēdunt atque ita
currūs collocant ut, sī illī ā multitūdine hostium premantur,
expedītum ad suōs receptum habeant.[3]

Ita mōbilitātem equitum, stabilitātem peditum in proeliīs
praestant; ac tantum ūsū cotīdiānō et exercitātiōne efficiunt 10
utī in dēclīvī ac praecipitī locō incitātōs[4] equōs sustinēre[5]
et brevī moderārī ac flectere, et per tēmōnem percurrere et in
iugō īnsistere et sē inde in currūs citissimē recipere cōnsuērint.

1. **essedīs**: Cicero jokingly writes to his friend Trebatius, "I hear there is no
gold and silver in Britain. If this is so, I advise you to seize a war chariot and
hurry home as soon as possible." Read *Cicero Writes to a Friend on Caesar's
Staff*, p. 127. **2. terrōre equōrum**: *terror caused by the horses* (**512**, *Note*). **3. expedītum . . . habeant**: *they may have an easy retreat to their (chariots)*. **4. incitātōs**:
translate *at full speed*. **5. sustinēre**: translate *control*. This infinitive and the
following ones are complementary, dependent upon **cōnsuērint**.

453.   COMPREHENSION

1. Describe the chariot fighting of the Britons.   **2.** How effective was it?
3. Do you think Caesar was impressed by it?

454.   VERBA

Required Vocabulary: **dēclīvis, pedes.**

Word Study. Define each of these words on the basis of its derivation
from a word in the chapter: *expedite, immoderate, insinuate, insistent,
precipice, reflect, rotary.*

Caesar comes to the rescue. The Britons plan an attack

"The Britons then watched their chance and fell upon the men of a legion
sent out to cut grain; that was the last considerable tract left uncut; it
was probably so left for a bait." E. G. SIHLER, *Annals of Caesar*

34. Quibus rēbus perturbātīs nostrīs[1] novitāte pugnae
tempore opportūnissimō Caesar auxilium tulit; namque eius
adventū hostēs cōnstitērunt, nostrī sē ex timōre recēpērunt.

Quō factō, ad lacessendum hostem et ad committendum proe-
5 lium aliēnum esse tempus arbitrātus, suō sē locō continuit et,
brevī tempore intermissō, in castra legiōnēs redūxit.

Dum haec geruntur, nostrīs omnibus occupātīs, quī [2] erant in
agrīs reliquī discessērunt. Secūtae sunt continuōs complūrēs
diēs tempestātēs, quae et nostrōs in castrīs continērent [3] et
10 hostem ā pugnā prohibērent.

Interim barbarī nūntiōs in omnēs partēs dīmīsērunt pauci-
tātemque nostrōrum mīlitum suīs praedicāvērunt et, quanta
praedae faciendae atque in perpetuum suī [4] līberandī facultās
darētur, sī Rōmānōs castrīs expulissent,[5] dēmōnstrāvērunt.
15 Hīs rēbus celeriter magnā multitūdine peditātūs equitātūsque
coāctā, ad castra vēnērunt.

1. Quibus . . . nostrīs: *to our men, thrown into confusion by these things.* **2. quī:**
i.e., the Britons (**560,** *b*); they too joined the revolt. **3. continērent:** (**587**).
4. suī: plural (**486**). **5. expulissent:** represents the future perfect tense of the
direct discourse.

455.   EXERCITĀTIŌ

Respondē Latīnē: Quid barbarī dē Rōmānīs praedicant?

Scrībe Latīnē: For several days in succession they had an opportunity
of getting booty.

456.   VERBA

Required Vocabulary: **continuus, namque, praeda, praedicō.**

Caesar puts the Britons to flight

35. Caesar, etsī idem quod superiōribus diēbus acciderat
fore vidēbat, ut, sī essent hostēs pulsī, celeritāte perīculum
effugerent, tamen nactus equitēs circiter XXX, quōs Commius
Atrebās, dē quō ante dictum est, sēcum trānsportāverat, legi-
5 ōnēs in aciē prō castrīs cōnstituit. Commissō proeliō, diūtius
nostrōrum mīlitum impetum hostēs ferre nōn potuērunt ac terga
vertērunt. Quōs tantō spatiō secūtī quantum cursū et vīribus
efficere potuērunt, complūrēs ex eīs occīdērunt; deinde, omnibus
longē lātēque aedificiīs incēnsīs, sē in castra recēpērunt.

The Britons sue for peace. Caesar returns to Gaul

36. Eōdem diē lēgātī ab hostibus missī ad Caesarem dē pāce vēnērunt. Hīs Caesar numerum obsidum quem ante imperāverat duplicāvit eōsque in continentem addūcī iussit, quod, propinquō diē aequinoctī, īnfirmīs nāvibus, hiemī nāvigātiōnem subiciendam nōn ex-5 istimābat.

Ipse idōneam tempestātem nactus paulō post mediam noctem nāvēs solvit; quae omnēs incolumēs ad continentem per- 10 vēnērunt, sed ex eīs onerāriae duae eōsdem portūs quōs reliquae capere nōn potuērunt et paulō īnfrā dēlātae sunt.

*From an old print　Courtesy of the Philadelphia
Commercial Museum*

A ROMAN GALLEY

This print is of a marble carving found at the old harbor of Ostia, the port of Rome. The carving represents a ship described by an ancient writer.

The Morini attack the Romans as they are landing

37. Quibus ex nāvibus cum essent expositī mīlitēs circiter CCC atque in castra contenderent, Morinī, quōs Caesar in Britanniam proficīscēns pācā-5 tōs relīquerat, spē praedae adductī prīmō nōn ita magnō suōrum numerō circumstetērunt ac, sī sēsē interficī nōllent, arma pōnere iussērunt. Cum illī, orbe factō, sēsē dēfenderent, celeriter ad clāmōrem hominum circiter mīlia sex convēnērunt. Quā rē nūntiātā, Caesar omnem ex castrīs equitātum suīs auxiliō mīsit. 10

Interim nostrī mīlitēs impetum hostium sustinuērunt atque amplius hōrīs quattuor fortissimē pugnāvērunt; et, paucīs vulneribus acceptīs, complūrēs ex hīs occīdērunt. Posteā vērō quam equitātus noster in cōnspectum vēnit, hostēs, abiectīs armīs, terga vertērunt magnusque eōrum numerus est occīsus. 15

Finish Thur.

Trajan's Column, Rome

VICTORY

The winged Victory is writing on the shield a record of Roman successes. The two trophies on either side are the helmets, shields, and arms taken from the enemy.

Rome celebrates Caesar's victories with a thanksgiving

38. Caesar posterō diē T. Labiēnum lēgātum cum eīs legiōnibus quās ex Britanniā redūxerat in Morinōs, quī rebelliōnem fēcerant, mīsit. Quī cum propter siccitātēs palūdum quō sē reciperent nōn habērent, quō perfugiō superiōre annō erant 5 ūsī, omnēs ferē in potestātem Labiēnī pervēnērunt.

At Q. Titūrius et L. Cotta lēgātī, quī in Menapiōrum fīnēs legiōnēs dūxerant, omnibus eōrum agrīs vāstātīs, frūmentīs succīsīs, aedificiīs incēnsīs, quod Menapiī sē omnēs in dēnsissimās silvās abdiderant, sē ad Caesarem recēpērunt.

10 Caesar in Belgīs omnium legiōnum hīberna cōnstituit. Eō duae omnīnō cīvitātēs ex Britanniā obsidēs mīsērunt, reliquae neglēxērunt.

Hīs rēbus gestīs, ex litterīs Caesaris diērum xx supplicātiō ā senātū dēcrēta est.

457.   COMPREHENSION, CHAPTERS 35–38

1. Who was Commius? **2.** What does the word **aequinoctium** tell as to the approximate date of Caesar's sailing from Britain? **3.** What did Caesar accomplish in Britain? **4.** How were Caesar's suspicions concerning the Morini (*Chap. 22*) confirmed? **5.** Why were the Morini so quickly defeated at this time? **6.** Why did Caesar select Belgium for his winter quarters? **7.** Why did Rome declare a longer thanksgiving this year than in 57 B.C.?

458. Tues   VERBA, CHAPTERS 35–38

Required Vocabulary: **effugiō, īnfrā, posteāquam, vertō.**

Word Study. Define the following words derived from **vertō**, showing that each contains the idea of *turning: advertise, anniversary, avert, converse, divorce, inverse, perverse, revert, traverse, universe, vertical.*

Thur,

A FLAG BEARER'S TOMB

This stone is cut to represent the **vexillum**, *flag*, carried in the Second Roman Legion. It was found at Corstopitum, England.

"When we dig a Roman inscription out of some misty fastness in our northern moors and read of some forgotten captain who died for Rome as he made a road across the rocks, we are driving against a truth." THE MANCHESTER GUARDIAN

Photograph of a model in the Philadelphia Commercial Museum

MODEL OF A GALLEY

This ship was modeled after the one shown on page 327.

REITERANDUM EST

Memoria est thēsaurus omnium rērum custōs, *Memory is the treasure-house and guard of all things.* CICERO

459.   EXERCITĀTIŌ

Scrībe Latīnē: Although (only) a small part of the summer was left, Caesar decided to set out for Britain. He sends a faithful lieutenant to learn everything about the Britons. While he waits until this ambassador shall return, Caesar prepares a fleet. With two legions and many transports, he sets out by the shortest way.

Before our men could reach the shore, the Britons, seeing them from a distance, attacked them. Our infantry, impeded by a great load of armor, had to fight with an unencumbered enemy. When all were thrown in confusion, the one who was bearing the eagle said in a loud voice that if they did their duty, they would not surrender the eagle to the enemy. He threw himself from the ship, and the rest followed, one from one ship and one from another. In a little while they overcame the enemy.

The transports which were bearing the cavalry could not reach Britain

on account of a storm.   On the same night it happened that the warships
were shattered by the storm.   Caesar lacked all materials for repairing
these.   All were thrown into confusion for no one wished to prolong the
war.   The Britons, encouraged by this disaster, secretly talked together
(conferred) and decided to attack our men.

460.   **REVIEW OF REQUIRED VOCABULARY**

Each of the following words is derived from, or connected in derivation
with, a word in the required vocabulary of **Liber IV**.   Give the Latin word
to which each is related and its meaning.   Define each English word.

*Abbreviate, accuracy, aquiline, colloquial, commendation, continuity,
declivity, deference, depreciate, disciplinarian, distribution, eventually,
exiguous, expedite, exponent, fidelity, gentle, lunar, matter, native, notice,
onerous, pedestrian, predacious, prefect, product, pulverize, querulous,
refectory, station, suspect, university, version.*

461.   **REVIEW OF WORD FORMATION**

Explain the formation of each of the following words, the meaning of the
word from which each is derived, the force of the prefix or suffix (**637–9**),
and the meaning of the word as a whole.

**Aequinoctium, animadvertō, āridus, cultūra, essedārius, frīgidus, frūmentum,
īnstabilis, nāvigium, nāvigō, onerārius, rebelliō, speculātōrius, stabilitās, tantulus.**

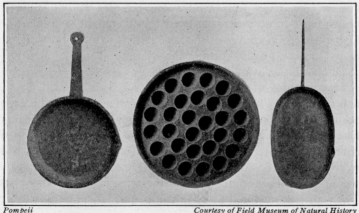

Pompeii   *Courtesy of Field Museum of Natural History*

COOKING UTENSILS

This is a photograph of the first lines of Liber V as they appear in a medieval manuscript of Caesar's "Gallic War," in the Vatican Library at Rome.

This manuscript is of parchment and is in the form of a book similar to those in use today. It is not so difficult to read as some ancient ones which do not have the words separated from each other.

The first line is not a part of the text of Caesar but was added by the copyist. It reads: "The fifth book begins. Read with joy." The writer's religious training is seen in the next phrase *in dno*, which is an abbreviation for **in Dōminō.**

The translation of the four lines from Caesar is as follows: "In the consulship of Lucius Domitius and Appius Claudius, Caesar, departing from winter quarters for Italy, as he was accustomed to do yearly, ordered the lieutenant generals whom he had placed in charge of the legions to see to the building of as many ships as possible during the winter and to the repairing of others. The style and form of these . . ."

The writings of Roman authors have been handed down in manuscripts. The original manuscripts were written on papyrus. Some papyrus book rolls have been brought to light by excavations, but no originals of great Roman writers have been discovered. The manuscripts of these authors exist in copies which were made in the Middle Ages in the monasteries by monks to whom the task of copying manuscripts was given as "busy work." The copies were stored away in vaults and later brought to light in the Revival of Learning.

From a medieval drawing

CAESAR EMBARKS FOR BRITAIN

Caesar is here represented as a knight. Medieval drawings illustrating ancient authors are valuable because they picture contemporary arms and armor.

LIBER QUĪNTUS

THE SECOND INVASION OF BRITAIN. THE REVOLT OF NORTHERN GAUL

54 B.C.

The story of Chapters 1–11

Before going into winter quarters, Caesar orders a new fleet built in preparation for a second invasion of Britain. He then goes to Illyricum and exacts punishment of the Pirustae, who menace the Province. In the course of the winter he holds courts both in Cisalpine Gaul and Illyricum.

Returning to Gaul, Caesar visits winter quarters, inspects the fleet, praises the troops and the officers in charge of the work, and then leads a force against the Treveri, a powerful state, whom he binds through hostages to keep the peace. He now repairs to Port Itius, where he finds the fleet ready to sail. In order to avoid uprisings in his absence, he decides to take to Britain with him some of the leading Gallic chieftains of whose loyalty he is not convinced. Among these is Dumnorix, a powerful and ambitious Aeduan, hostile to Roman influence, who protests vigorously against being taken.

Seeing that his protests and excuses are of no avail, Dumnorix tries to influence other chieftains to refuse to accompany Caesar to Britain. This is reported to Caesar. While the latter is occupied with the embarkation of the fleet, Dumnorix tries to escape, but he is captured and killed. His last words are, " I am a free man and of a free state." They justify Caesar's characterization of him as a man of high spirit, **magnī animī.**

Caesar sails for Britain a second time, leaving Labienus in charge of his army in Gaul. When the Britons see a fleet of eight hundred ships, they flee, and the Romans land without opposition.

Caesar leaves his fleet at anchor, moves inland, seizes a stronghold, and on the following day advances against the enemy. He is in sight of the latter when he learns that his fleet has been wrecked by a storm. Returning to the shore, he finds forty ships shattered and others seriously damaged. He sends to the continent for help. Soldiers labor day and night for ten days repairing the fleet, which they beach and surround with a wall. Caesar continues his pursuit of the Britons, who in great numbers are mobilizing under the leadership of a capable chieftain, Cassivellaunus.

Inhabitants and products of ancient Britain

12. Britanniae pars interior ab eīs incolitur quōs nātōs in īnsulā ipsā[1] memoriā prōditum dīcunt; maritima pars ab eīs quī praedae ac bellī īnferendī causā ex Belgiō trānsiērunt (quī omnēs ferē eīs nōminibus cīvitātum appellantur quibus
5 ortī ex cīvitātibus eō pervēnērunt),[2] et, bellō illātō, ibi permānsērunt atque agrōs colere coepērunt. Hominum est īnfīnīta multitūdō crēberrimaque aedificia ferē Gallicīs cōnsimilia, pecorum[3] magnus numerus. Ūtuntur aut aere aut nummō aureō aut tāleīs ferreīs[4] ad certum pondus exāminātīs prō
10 nummō.

Nāscitur ibi plumbum album[5] in mediterrāneīs regiōnibus, in maritimīs ferrum, sed eius exigua est cōpia; aere ūtuntur importātō. Māteria cuiusque generis ut in Galliā est praeter fāgum atque abietem.

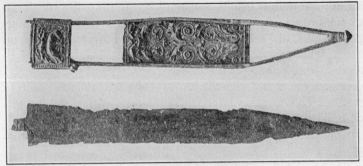

British Museum, London

ROMAN SWORD AND SCABBARD

These were found in the Thames River.

Leporem et gallīnam et ānserem gustāre fās nōn putant; 15
haec tamen alunt animī voluptātisque [6] causā. Loca sunt
temperātiōra quam in Galliā, remissiōribus frīgoribus.

1. nātōs . . . ipsā: *born on the island itself;* they claimed that they were
aborigines. Many ancient nations claimed to be sprung from the soil. **2. quibus
. . . pervēnērunt:** *from which states having sprung they have come to this place.*
3. pecorum: two English derivatives of this word are *pecuniary* and *peculiar.*
4. tāleīs ferreīs: some of these iron bars have been found in Sussex. **5. plumbum
album:** tin mines are found in Cornwall, while iron is found in Sussex. **6. animī
voluptātisque:** translate *of entertainment.* What is it literally?

Caesar's idea of the geography of Britain

13. Īnsula nātūrā triquetra, cuius ūnum latus est contrā
Galliam. Huius lateris alter angulus, quī est ad Cantium,
quō ferē omnēs ex Galliā nāvēs appelluntur, ad orientem sōlem,
īnferior ad merīdiem spectat. Hoc latus pertinet circiter mīlia
passuum D.   5

Alterum [1] vergit ad Hispāniam atque occidentem sōlem;
quā ex parte est Hibernia, dīmidiō minor, ut exīstimātur, quam
Britannia, sed parī spatiō trānsmissūs atque ex Galliā est in
Britanniam. [2] In hōc mediō cursū est īnsula, quae appellātur
Mona; complūrēs praetereā minōrēs subiectae īnsulae exīsti- 10

mantur; dē quibus īnsulīs nōn nūllī scrīpsērunt diēs continuōs xxx sub brūmam esse noctem.   Nōs nihil dē eō percontātiōnibus reperiēbāmus, nisi certīs ex aquā [3] mēnsūrīs breviōrēs esse quam in continentī noctēs vidēbāmus.   Huius est longitūdō lateris, 15 ut fert illōrum opīniō,[4] DCC mīlium.

Tertium est contrā septentriōnēs; cui partī nūlla est obiecta terra, sed eius angulus lateris maximē ad Germāniam spectat. Hoc mīlia passuum DCCC in longitūdinem esse exīstimātur.

Ita omnis īnsula est in circuitū vīciēs [5] centum mīlium passuum.

1. Alterum (latus): *the second side.*   **2. parī spatiō . . . Britanniam:** he says that the distance between Ireland and Britain is equal to that between Britain and Gaul.   **3. ex aquā:** *of the water clock;* the Romans used water instead of sand in their hourglasses.   **4. ut . . . opīniō:** translate *according to their report.*   **5. vīciēs:** Caesar's description is as accurate as could be expected in view of the fact that the Romans had not yet explored or sailed around the island.

Customs of the Britons

14. Ex hīs omnibus longē sunt hūmānissimī quī Cantium incolunt, quae regiō est maritima omnis, neque multum ā Gallicā differunt cōnsuētūdine. Interiōrēs plērīque [1] frūmenta nōn serunt, sed lacte et carne vīvunt pellibusque sunt vestītī.

5   Omnēs vērō sē Britannī vitrō īnficiunt, quod caeruleum efficit colōrem, atque hōc [2] horridiōrēs sunt in pugnā aspectū; [3] capillōque [4] sunt prōmissō atque omnī parte corporis rāsā praeter caput et labrum superius.

1. Interiōrēs plērīque: *the majority of the people living in the interior.*   **2. hōc:** ablative of cause.   **3. aspectū:** ablative of specification.   **4. capillō:** ablative of description.

The story of Chapters 15–23

In a number of skirmishes the Britons show themselves to be spirited and resourceful.   Both the heavily armed Roman infantry and even the more mobile Roman cavalry are at a disadvantage when confronted by the tactics of the charioteers and cavalry of the Britons.

In an attack on three legions, which are on a foraging expedition, the Britons, however, are defeated so decisively that they do not again attempt

REMAINS OF ROMAN FORT IN ENGLAND

This part of a Roman fort is still standing near Portchester.

a pitched battle. Thereafter they content themselves with guerrilla warfare, using their war chariots. Caesar crosses the Thames, scatters the forces of the enemy, receives the submission of several tribes, takes by storm a stronghold, captures great numbers of cattle, kills many men, takes captives, and devastates the country. This rapid and energetic campaign served to give information about Britain to the civilized world and to open the way for future invasions and the Romanization of Britain.

Marcus Cicero, a contemporary of Caesar, in a letter to a friend thus summarizes Caesar's achievements: " On the twenty-fourth of October I received a letter from my brother Quintus and from Caesar, dated from the nearest point on the coast of Britain on the twenty-fifth of September. Britain is settled, hostages taken, no booty, but a tribute imposed, and they are bringing back the army from that place."

The story of Chapters 24–29

On account of the shortage of the crops that summer, Caesar, on his return to Gaul, distributes his forces in various places, unusually far apart but within a radius of one hundred miles. One legion and five cohorts under Sabinus and Cotta are stationed among the Eburones; another under Quintus Cicero, among the Nervii; a third under Labienus, among the Remi. This distribution of the troops invites attacks from rebellious Gauls.

Under Ambiorix and Catuvolcus, the Eburones lead an attack against

the winter quarters of Sabinus and Cotta. Unsuccessful in their attack
on the camp, they call for a parley. In this conference Ambiorix, posing
as a friend because of favors he has received from the Romans, warns them
that the changeable Gauls are planning to attack all the winter camps on
that very day, and he advises the Romans to retire from this place and
join the forces of Cicero or of Labienus. As an expression of his gratitude
to Caesar, he offers to conduct them to safety.

At a council of war, Cotta and some of the leaders protest against taking
advice from any enemy and vigorously affirm their belief that there is no
need of abandoning their camp. A violent altercation ensues. Sabinus
with some of the others trusts Ambiorix and insists that they start out at
once.

Sabinus throws the responsibility of remaining in camp on Cotta

30. Hāc in utramque partem disputātiōne habitā, cum ā
Cottā prīmīsque ōrdinibus [1] ācriter resisterētur :

"Vincite," inquit, "sī ita vultis," Sabīnus, et id clāriōre
vōce, ut magna pars mīlitum exaudīret, "neque is sum,"
5 inquit, "quī gravissimē ex vōbīs mortis perīculō terrear.[2] Hī
sapient ; sī gravius quid acciderit,[3] abs tē ratiōnem reposcent ;
quī, sī per tē liceat,[4] perendinō diē cum proximīs hībernīs con-
iūnctī commūnem cum reliquīs bellī cāsum sustineant, nōn
reiectī et relēgātī longē ā cēterīs aut ferrō aut famē intere-
10 ant."

1. **prīmīsque ōrdinibus :** translate *and the senior centurions*. 2. **quī . . . terrear :**
relative result clause (**587**). 3. **sī . . . acciderit :** for this type of condition, see
607. 4. **sī . . . liceat :** *if you should permit it* (**608**). Write Sabinus' speech
in the indirect form. To whom was Sabinus really speaking? Give reasons for
your answer.

Cotta yields to Sabinus

31. Cōnsurgitur ex cōnsiliō ; comprehendunt utrumque et
ōrant nē suā dissēnsiōne et pertināciā rem in summum perīculum
dēdūcant : facilem esse rem, seu maneant seu proficīscantur,
sī modo ūnum omnēs sentiant ac probent ; contrā in dissēnsiōne
5 nūllam sē salūtem perspicere.

Rēs disputātiōne ad mediam noctem perdūcitur. Tandem

dat Cotta permōtus manūs; superat sententia Sabīnī. Prō-
nūntiātur prīmā lūce itūrōs.

Cōnsūmitur vigiliīs reliqua pars noctis, cum sua quisque
mīles circumspiceret quid sēcum portāre posset, quid ex īnstrū- 10
mentō hībernōrum relinquere cōgerētur. Omnia excōgitantur
quārē nec sine perīculō maneātur et languōre mīlitum et vigiliīs
perīculum augeātur.[1]

Prīmā lūce sīc ex castrīs proficīscuntur ut quibus esset persuāsum[2] nōn ab hoste, sed ab homine amīcissimō cōnsilium 15
datum,[3] longissimō agmine maximīsque impedīmentīs.

1. quārē . . . augeātur: *why they could not remain without danger and (why)
the danger would be augmented by the exhaustion and lack of sleep of the soldiers.*
2. ut . . . persuāsum: *since they were convinced that.*   3. datum: esse is understood.

The story of Chapters 32–39

The Romans set out early the next morning and soon find themselves
ambushed by the forces of the traitorous Gauls. They abandon their
baggage and try to form a hollow square. All is confusion and disorder;
soldiers shout, weep, and desert their standards. In this unexpected crisis,
Sabinus also is panic stricken, but Cotta looks out for the safety of the soldiers
and " does his duty as a commander and a soldier." Many of the soldiers
and officers are wounded. Cotta is hit full in the face by a sling shot.
Caesar says, " They did nothing unworthy of themselves."

Sabinus parleys with Ambiorix for safe conduct, an offer which Cotta
refuses. Sabinus is treacherously slain, and Cotta falls fighting bravely in
the midst of his troops, most of whom are slaughtered. The remnant who
survive either kill themselves or escape to the camp of Labienus.

A Roman historian, Suetonius, says that Caesar let his hair and beard
grow until he avenged this greatest loss of the Gallic war.

The defeat of the forces of Sabinus and Cotta encourages Ambiorix to
organize a more widespread revolt. He induces the Atuatuci, Nervii,
and surrounding states to join his forces in an attack upon the camp of
Cicero.

Cicero is in winter quarters among the Nervii. His brother Marcus
writes to a friend as follows in November of 54 B.C.: " The choice of army
winter quarters has just been given Quintus. . . . If one does not fall in
love with such a man (Caesar), which of the others could one love? "

Quintus Cicero's valiant defense of his besieged camp

40. Mittuntur ad Caesarem[1] cōnfestim ā Cicerōne litterae,
magnīs prōpositīs praemiīs, sī pertulissent;[2] obsessīs omnibus
viīs, missī[3] intercipiuntur. Noctū ex eā māteriā quam mūnītiōnis causā comportāverant turrēs admodum cxx excitantur;
5 incrēdibilī celeritāte quae deesse operī vidēbantur perficiuntur.

Hostēs posterō diē, multō maiōribus coāctīs cōpiīs, castra
oppugnant, fossam complent. Eādem ratiōne quā prīdiē ā
nostrīs resistitur.

Hoc idem reliquīs deinceps fit diēbus.[4] Nūlla pars nocturnī
10 temporis ad labōrem intermittitur; nōn aegrīs, nōn vulnerātīs
facultās quiētis datur. Quaecumque ad proximī diēī oppugnā-
tiōnem opus sunt noctū comparantur; multae praeustae[5]
sudēs, magnus mūrālium pīlōrum numerus īnstituitur; turrēs
contabulantur, pinnae lōrīcaeque ex crātibus attexuntur.[6]
15 Ipse Cicerō, cum tenuissimā valētūdine esset,[7] nē nocturnum
quidem sibi tempus ad quiētem relinquēbat, ut ultrō mīlitum
concursū ac vōcibus sibi parcere cōgerētur.[8]

1. ad Caesarem: Caesar was at Samarobriva (*Amiens*). 2. pertulissent: the
object is litterās understood; why subjunctive (624)? 3. missī: (*the messengers*)
sent. 4. reliquīs deinceps, diēbus: *for several successive days.* 5. praeustae:
hardened at the end by burning. 6. pinnae . . . attexuntur: *i.e.,* interwoven
branches were attached to the towers as breastworks. 7. cum . . . esset: *although
he was in very poor health.* 8. ut . . . cōgerētur: *so that, by the soldiers who ran up
and pleaded with him, he was actually forced to spare himself.* That Caesar appreciated
Quintus Cicero's services may be seen in an extract from a letter written by Marcus
Cicero, " He loads my Quintus with honors, dignities, and favors."

Cicero scorns the protection offered by the crafty Nervii

41. Tunc ducēs prīncipēsque Nerviōrum, quī aliquem ser-
mōnis aditum[1] causamque amīcitiae cum Cicerōne habēbant,
colloquī sēsē velle dīcunt. Factā potestāte, eadem quae Ambiorīx cum Titūriō ēgerat commemorant: omnem Galliam esse
5 in armīs; Germānōs Rhēnum trānsīsse; Caesaris reliquōrum-
que hīberna oppugnārī.

Addunt etiam dē Sabīnī morte; Ambiorīgem ostentant fideī faciundae causā.[2] Errāre eōs[3] dīcunt, sī quicquam ab hīs praesidī spērent quī suīs rēbus diffīdant; sēsē tamen hōc esse in Cicerōnem populumque Rōmānum animō,[4] ut nihil nisi 10 hīberna recūsent, atque hanc inveterāscere cōnsuētūdinem nōlint; licēre illīs per sē incolumibus ex hībernīs discēdere[5] et quāscumque in partēs velint sine metū proficīscī.

Cicerō ad haec ūnum modo respondit: Nōn esse cōnsuētūdinem populī Rōmānī accipere ab hoste armātō condiciōnem; sī ab 15 armīs discēdere velint, sē adiūtōre ūtantur lēgātōsque ad Caesarem mittant; spērāre prō eius iūstitiā quae petierint impetrātūrōs.

1. **aliquem . . . aditum:** *some excuse for an interview.* 2. **ostentant . . . causā:** *to inspire confidence they point to.* 3. **eōs:** refers to Cicero and his men. 4. **sēsē, hōc esse, animō:** *they* (*the Nervii*) *had this feeling* (**544**). 5. **licēre . . . discēdere:** *they* (*Cicero's forces*) *might retire from winter quarters unharmed, so far as they* (*the Nervii*) *were concerned.* To what did the Nervii chiefly object?

The disappointed Nervii adopt Roman methods in besieging the camp

42. Ab hāc spē repulsī Nerviī vāllō pedum decem et fossā pedum quīndecim hīberna cingunt. Haec et superiōrum an- nōrum cōnsuētūdine ā nōbīs cognōverant et, quōsdam dē exercitū nactī captīvōs, ab hīs docēbantur; sed, nūllā ferrāmentōrum cōpiā quae esset ad hunc ūsum idōnea, gladiīs caespitēs cir- 5 cumcīdere, manibus sagulīsque terram exhaurīre[1] cōgēbantur.

Quā quidem ex rē hominum multitūdō cognōscī potuit; nam minus hōrīs tribus mīlium passuum trium in circuitū mūnī- tiōnem perfēcērunt. Reliquīs diēbus turrēs ad[2] altitūdinem vāllī, falcēs testūdinēsque, quās īdem captīvī docuerant, parāre ac 10 facere coepērunt.

1. **manibus . . . exhaurīre:** translate *to dig up the earth with their hands and to take* (*it*) *out with their military cloaks.* 2. **ad:** *in proportion to.*

The Romans are undismayed by blazing darts and fire

43. Septimō oppugnātiōnis diē, maximō coortō ventō, fer- ventēs fūsilī ex argillā glandēs[1] fundīs et fervefacta iacula in

casās,[2] quae mōre Gallicō strāmentīs erant tēctae, iacere coepērunt. Hae celeriter ignem comprehendērunt et ventī magnitū-
5 dine in omnem locum castrōrum distulērunt. Hostēs maximō
clāmōre, sīcutī partā iam atque explōrātā victōriā, turrēs testūdinēsque agere et scālīs vāllum ascendere coepērunt.

At tanta mīlitum virtūs atque ea praesentia animī fuit ut,
cum [3] undique flammā torrērentur maximāque tēlōrum multi-
10 tūdine premerentur suaque omnia impedīmenta atque omnēs
fortūnās cōnflagrāre intellegerent, nōn modo dēmigrandī causā
dē vāllō dēcēderet nēmō, sed paene nē respiceret quidem quisquam, ac tum omnēs ācerrimē fortissimēque pugnārent.

Hic diēs nostrīs longē gravissimus fuit; sed tamen hunc
15 habuit ēventum, ut eō diē maximus numerus hostium vul-
nerārētur atque interficerētur, ut sē sub ipsō vāllō cōnstīpāverant [4] recessumque prīmīs ultimī nōn dabant.[5]

Paulum quidem intermissā flammā et quōdam locō turrī
adāctā et contingente vāllum, tertiae cohortis centuriōnēs
20 ex eō quō stābant locō recessērunt suōsque omnēs remōvērunt,
nūtū [6] vōcibusque hostēs, sī introīre vellent, vocāre coepērunt;
quōrum prōgredī ausus est nēmō. Tum ex omnī parte lapidibus
coniectīs dēturbātī, turrisque succēnsa est.

1. **ferventēs** . . . **glandēs**: *red-hot bullets of molded clay.* 2. **casās**: the word
casa, meaning *hut* or *shack*, is also the word for *house* in Italian and Spanish.
3. **cum**: introduces three concessive clauses. 4. **ut** . . . **cōnstīpāverant**: *as
they had crowded themselves close to the rampart.* 5. **recessumque** . . . **dabant**:
and the rear did not give the van a chance to retire. 6. **nūtū**: why with signs?

CAESAR'S BULLET

Leaden slugs used by slingers often had on them the word **ferī**, *strike.* A few
have been found inscribed, as this one is, with the name of the person for whom
it was intended. **IMP** stands for **imperātor**, *victorious general.*

Trajan's Column, Rome
FIRST AID

The story of two brave rival centurions

44. Erant in eā legiōne fortissimī virī, centuriōnēs, quī prīmīs
ōrdinibus appropinquārent,[1] T. Pullō et L. Vorēnus. Hī per-
petuās inter sē contrōversiās habēbant uter alterī anteferrētur,
omnibusque annīs dē locō summīs simultātibus contendēbant.

Ex hīs Pullō, cum ācerrimē ad mūnītiōnēs pugnārētur, " Quid 5
dubitās," inquit, " Vorēne, aut quem locum tuae probandae
virtūtis exspectās? Hic diēs dē nostrīs contrōversiīs iūdicābit."

Haec cum dīxisset, prōcēdit extrā mūnītiōnēs, quaeque pars
hostium cōnfertissima est vīsa, in eam irrumpit.

Nē Vorēnus quidem sēsē tum vāllō continet, sed omnium 10
veritus exīstimātiōnem subsequitur.

Mediocrī spatiō relictō, Pullō pīlum in hostēs immittit atque
ūnum ex multitūdine prōcurrentem trāicit; quō percussō et
exanimātō, hunc scūtīs prōtegunt hostēs, in illum ūniversī tēla
coniciunt neque dant prōgrediendī facultātem. Trānsfīgitur 15
scūtum Pullōnī [2] et verūtum [3] in balteō dēfīgitur. Āvertit hic
cāsus vāgīnam et gladium ēdūcere cōnantī dextram morātur
manum, impedītumque hostēs circumsistunt. Succurrit inimīcus
illī Vorēnus et labōrantī subvenit.

20 Ad hunc sē cōnfestim ā Pullōne omnis multitūdō convertit;
illum verūtō trānsfīxum arbitrantur. Vorēnus gladiō rem comminus gerit atque, ūnō interfectō, reliquōs paulum prōpellit;
dum cupidius īnstat, in locum dēiectus īnferiōrem concidit.
Huic rūrsus circumventō subsidium fert Pullō, atque ambō
25 incolumnēs, complūribus interfectīs, summā cum laude sēsē
intrā mūnītiōnēs recipiunt.

Sīc fortūna in contentiōne et certāmine utrumque versāvit[4]
ut alter alterī inimīcus auxiliō salūtīque esset, neque dīiūdicārī
posset uter utrī virtūte anteferendus vidērētur.

> **1. quī . . . appropinquārent:** *i.e.*, they were ready for promotion to the first
> rank of centurions. **2. scūtum Pullōnī:** *Pullo's shield;* **Pullōnī,** dative of refer-
> ence. **3. verūtum:** *i.e.*, the dart that had pierced Pullo's shield struck the sword
> belt in such a way that the scabbard was pushed backward so that he could not
> easily draw his sword. **4. fortūna, utrumque versāvit:** translate *the fortune of both
> changed*.

Cicero finally gets a dispatch through to Caesar

45. Quantō[1] erat in diēs gravior atque asperior oppugnātiō,
et maximē quod, magnā parte mīlitum cōnfectā vulneribus, rēs
ad paucitātem dēfēnsōrum pervēnerat, tantō[1] crēbriōrēs litterae
nūntiīque ad Caesarem mittēbantur; quōrum pars dēprehēnsa
5 in cōnspectū nostrōrum mīlitum cum cruciātū necābātur.

Erat ūnus intus Nervius, nōmine Verticō, locō nātus honestō,
quī ā prīmā obsidiōne ad Cicerōnem perfūgerat suamque eī
fidem praestiterat. Hic servō spē lībertātis magnīsque persuādet
praemiīs ut litterās ad Caesarem dēferat. Hās ille in iaculō
10 illigātās effert[2] et, Gallus inter Gallōs sine ūllā suspīciōne versātus, ad Caesarem pervenit. Ab eō dē perīculīs Cicerōnis
legiōnisque cognōscitur.

> **1. Quantō, tantō:** (550). **2. Hās . . . effert:** just how did he carry the
> letter?

The Story of Chapters 46–47

Caesar marches to the rescue and is joined by Crassus and Fabius with
one legion each. Labienus fails to join him because of the approach of the
Treveri.

A letter from Caesar brings hope of relief to Cicero

48. Caesar, cōnsiliō eius [1] probātō, etsī opīniōne trium legiōnum dēiectus ad duās redierat, tamen ūnum commūnī salūtī auxilium in celeritāte pōnēbat. Vēnit magnīs itineribus in Nerviōrum fīnēs.

Ibi ex captīvīs cognōscit quae apud Cicerōnem gerantur 5 quantōque in perīculō rēs sit. Tum cuidam ex equitibus Gallīs magnīs praemiīs persuādet utī ad Cicerōnem epistulam dēferat.

Hanc Graecīs [2] cōnscrīptam litterīs mittit, nē, interceptā epistulā, nostra ab hostibus cōnsilia cognōscantur. Sī adīre nōn possit, monet ut trāgulam cum epistulā ad ammentum 10 dēligātā intrā mūnītiōnēs castrōrum abiciat. In litterīs scrībit sē cum legiōnibus profectum celeriter affore; [3] hortātur ut prīstinam virtūtem retineat.

Gallus perīculum veritus, ut erat praeceptum, trāgulam mittit. Haec cāsū ad turrim adhaesit, neque ā nostrīs bīduō 15 animadversa, tertiō diē ā quōdam mīlite cōnspicitur; dēmpta ad Cicerōnem dēfertur. Ille perlēctam in conventū mīlitum recitat maximāque omnēs laetitiā afficit. Tum fūmī incendiōrum [4] procul vidēbantur; quae rēs omnem dubitātiōnem adventūs legiōnum expulit.   20

1. **eius:** *i.e.*, Labienus. 2. **Graecīs:** why did Caesar use Greek letters instead of Roman? 3. **affore:** future infinitive of **adsum.** 4. **incendiōrum:** *i.e.*, Caesar burns buildings and crops as he advances.

The Gauls turn from the siege of Cicero's camp to attack Caesar

49. Gallī, rē cognitā per explōrātōrēs, obsidiōnem relinquunt; ad Caesarem omnibus cōpiīs contendunt. Haec erant armāta circiter mīlia LX.

Cicerō, datā facultāte, Gallum ab eōdem Verticōne, quem suprā dēmōnstrāvimus, repetit quī litterās ad Caesarem dēferat; 5 hunc [1] admonet iter cautē dīligenterque faciat; perscrībit in litterīs hostēs ab sē discessisse omnemque ad eum multitūdinem convertisse. Quibus litterīs circiter mediā nocte Caesar

allātīs, suōs facit certiōrēs eōsque ad dīmicandum animō cōn-
10 firmat.

Posterō diē lūce prīmā movet castra; et circiter mīlia passuum quattuor prōgressus trāns vallem magnam et rīvum
multitūdinem hostium cōnspicātur. Erat magnī perīculī rēs
tantulīs cōpiīs inīquō locō dīmicāre; tum, quoniam obsidiōne
15 līberātum Cicerōnem sciēbat, aequō animō remittendum dē
celeritāte [2] exīstimābat. Cōnsīdit et quam aequissimō potest
locō castra commūnit, atque haec,[3] etsī erant exigua per sē,
vix hominum mīlium septem,[4] praesertim nūllīs cum impedīmentīs, tamen angustiīs viārum quam maximē potest [5] contrahit,
20 eō cōnsiliō, ut in summam contemptiōnem hostibus veniat.[6]
Interim, speculātōribus in omnēs partēs dīmissīs, explōrat quō
commodissimē itinere vallem trānsīre possit.

1. hunc: *i.e.*, Caesar. 2. remittendum . . . celeritāte; translate *that he
should slacken his speed*. 3. haec (castra): object of contrahit. 4. vix . . .
septem: translate *accommodating scarcely 7,000 men* (511). What was the full
quota of a legion? 5. angustiīs . . . potest: translate *by making the streets as
narrow as possible*. 6. eō . . . veniat: *with this purpose, that he may become an
object of supreme contempt to the enemy*.

The story of Chapters 50–51

Caesar, by making a pretense of fear, lures the Gauls to attack him on
his own ground. He takes them by surprise and routs them with great
slaughter.

Caesar commends the gallant conduct of Cicero and his men

52. Longius prōsequī veritus, quod silvae palūdēsque inter-
cēdēbant, omnibus suīs incolumibus, eōdem diē ad Cicerōnem
pervēnit.

Īnstitūtās turrēs, testūdinēs mūnītiōnēsque hostium ad-
5 mīrātur; prōductā legiōne, cognōscit nōn decimum quemque [1]
esse reliquum mīlitem sine vulnere; ex hīs omnibus iūdicat
rēbus quantō cum perīculō et quantā cum virtūte rēs sint ad-
ministrātae. Cicerōnem prō eius meritō legiōnemque collaudat;

Museum of St. Germain, France

MODEL OF A TOWER

Caesar was surprised to find the enemy making use of towers and other fortifications similar to those of the Romans.

centuriōnēs singillātim tribūnōsque mīlitum appellat, quōrum ēgregiam fuisse 10 virtūtem testimōniō Cicerōnis cognōverat.

Dē cāsū Sabīnī et Cottae certius ex captīvīs cognōscit. Posterō diē, cōntiōne habitā, rem gestam prōpōnit, mīlitēs cōn- 15 sōlātur et cōnfirmat; quod dētrīmentum culpā et temeritāte lēgātī sit acceptum, hōc aequiōre animō ² ferendum ³ docet, quod, beneficiō deōrum immortālium et virtūte eōrum expiātō incommodō, neque 20 hostibus diūtina laetitia neque ipsīs longior dolor relinquātur.

1. nōn . . . quemque: *not one in ten.* 2. hōc . . . animō: *with greater equanimity on this account.* 3. ferendum (esse): the subject is quod . . . acceptum, a substantive clause of fact (594).

The story of Chapters 53–58

Although Caesar holds in submission a great part of Gaul, there is still a deep undercurrent of insubordination. He therefore decides to spend the winter with his troops.

The Treveri under Indutiomarus solicit other states to join them in collecting armed forces to make an attack on the camp of Labienus. Informed of this, Labienus in a well fortified camp awaits the attack while giving out the impression of great fear. Indutiomarus, thus lured on, approaches the Roman camp with insults and challenges to battle. The Roman cavalry makes a sudden rush from the camp with orders to kill Indutiomarus first of all. They bring his head back into camp. Their leader lost, the Gauls are routed and return home. Caesar closes the story with the comment that after this Gaul was more peaceful.

Detailed reports of Caesar's success in the exciting campaign of 54 B.C. must have been sent to Rome. Marcus Cicero writes to Trebatius, one of Caesar's staff: " I am not surprised at your not having written anything to me since you are in the midst of such exciting events. . . . I greatly fear that you will freeze in your winter quarters. I advise you to keep a

A ROMAN SEPUL-
CHRAL MONUMENT

This monument
erected by the Ro-
mans is still stand-
ing at Trier in what
was the country of
the Treveri.

good fire going since there is a shortage of military
cloaks, yet I hear that you are having a hot enough
time there, news which makes me greatly fear for you."

462. **COMPREHENSION — LIBER V**

1. What error did Caesar make in his statements
concerning the mines and trees in Britain? Account
for this. **2.** How nearly accurate was Caesar's idea
of the geography of Britain? **3.** What was an important result of the Roman invasion of Britain?
4. How did Sabinus force Cotta to take advice from
the enemy? **5.** Why were the soldiers not in condition to start on an expedition? **6.** What kind of a
commander was Cicero? Give reasons for your answer. **7.** How did Cicero's reply to the Nervii show
him to be a true Roman? **8.** How did the Nervii
learn Roman engineering methods? Describe in detail their method of attack.
9. Tell the story of Pullo and Vorenus. **10.** Why
did Caesar insert this story in his narrative? **11.** How
did Cicero get a letter through to Caesar? **12.** How
was Caesar's reply delivered to Cicero? **13.** Why did
he write in Greek? **14.** What appreciation did Caesar
show of the brave defense of the camp by Cicero and
his men? **15.** What effect do you think this had
upon the soldiers' attitude toward Caesar? **16.** Give
examples from **Liber V** and preceding books which set
forth the Roman ideal of courage, **fortitūdō.**

463. **VERBA — LIBER V**

Required Vocabulary: addō, admodum, aeger,
aequus, augeō, circumspiciō, dētrīmentum, intereō,
interior, laus, mediocris, metus, obsideō, obsidiō,
accidō, pār, pecus, praesertim, prīdiē, prōnūntiō, recūsō, terreō, ultimus.

Word Study. Define the following words derived from **carō** : *carnage,
carnal, carnelian, carnation, carnival, carniverous, incarnate.*

Trajan's Column, Rome

ROMAN BRIDGE

Caesar built a bridge across the Rhine before each of his expeditions into Germany, although he usually crossed streams over pontoon bridges. He wished to impress the Germans with the Romans' superior knowledge of scientific method. He destroyed the first bridge but left the second, except the part that touched the east bank, standing as a warning. Both bridges were built in a few days and were not like the usual massive structures characteristic of Roman architecture.

LIBER SEXTUS

THE SECOND INVASION OF GERMANY

53 B.C.

The story of Chapters 1-8

Caesar adds three more legions to his forces in the winter of 53 B.C. because he sees signs of a more serious revolt. He plans for an earlier campaign than usual because the rebellion is increasing, especially among the Treveri and Nervii, together with their allies, and the Germans on this side of the Rhine. He marches against the Nervii, devastates their territory, and receives their surrender, after which he goes into winter quarters.

In the spring his first expedition is against the Senones, who with the Carnutes surrender without a struggle. Caesar now turns to the Treveri and their leader, Ambiorix, against whom he sends Labienus. Caesar himself forces their allies, the Menapii, to surrender and sends reinforcements to Labienus. The latter leads the Treveri to believe that he is retiring and, when they follow him, he turns and defeats them. Germans, coming to the aid of the Treveri, return home.

Caesar crosses the Rhine. The Ubii sue for peace

9. Caesar postquam ex Menapiīs in Trēverōs vēnit, duābus dē causīs Rhēnum trānsīre cōnstituit; quārum ūna erat quod Germānī auxilia contrā sē Trēverīs mīserant, altera, nē ad eōs Ambiorīx [1] receptum habēret. Hīs cōnstitūtīs rēbus, paulum

349

Copy in Museum of St. Germain, France

A UBIAN CAVALRYMAN

This relief of a mounted soldier is carved on his tombstone. An inscription below says that he was a Ubian who had served in the army for twelve years and was thirty-five years of age.

5 suprā eum locum quō ante exercitum trādūxerat facere pontem īnstituit. Nōtā atque īnstitūtā ratiōne,[2] magnō mīlitum studiō, paucīs diēbus opus efficitur. Firmō in Trēverīs ad pontem praesidiō relictō, nē quis ab hīs subitō mōtus orerētur,[3] reliquās cōpiās equitātumque trādūcit.

10   Ubiī, quī ante obsidēs dederant atque in dēditiōnem vēnerant, pūrgandī suī causā[4] ad eum lēgātōs mittunt quī doceant neque auxilia ex suā cīvitāte in Trēverōs missa neque ab sē fidem laesam ; petunt atque ōrant ut sibi parcat, nē commūnī odiō Germānōrum innocentēs prō nocentibus poenās pendant ; sī amplius

15 obsidum velit darī, pollicentur. Cognitā Caesar[5] causā reperit ab Suēbīs auxilia missa esse ; Ubiōrum satisfactiōnem accipit, aditūs viāsque in Suēbōs perquīrit.

    1. Ambiorīx: the previous year, through the treachery of Ambiorix, the Roman army had suffered the most serious loss incurred during the whole Gallic War. For this defeat Caesar had vowed vengeance. (V, *The story of Chapters 32–39*.)

    2. Nōtā . . . ratiōne: *since the plan (of such a bridge) was familiar and had been*

tried. Caesar had bridged the Rhine in 55 B.C.; IV, 17. **3. nē** . . . **orerētur:** *that no uprising suddenly originate from them.* **4. pūrgandī** . . . **causā:** *for the purpose of excusing themselves;* **suī:** (486). **5. Caesar:** the subject of **reperit;** note that it is here incorporated in an ablative absolute.

The Suebi mass their forces in the forests

10. Interim paucīs post diēbus fit ab Ubiīs certior [1] Suēbōs omnēs in ūnum locum cōpiās cōgere atque eīs nātiōnibus quae sub eōrum sint imperiō dēnūntiāre ut auxilia peditātūs equitātūsque mittant. Hīs cognitīs rēbus, rem frūmentāriam prōvidet, castrīs idōneum locum dēligit ; Ubiīs imperat ut pecora dēdūcant 5 suaque omnia ex agrīs in oppida cōnferant, spērāns barbarōs atque imperītōs hominēs inopiā cibāriōrum adductōs ad inīquam pugnandī condiciōnem posse dēdūcī ; mandat ut crēbrōs explōrātōrēs in Suēbōs mittant quaeque [2] apud eōs gerantur cognōscant.

Illī imperāta faciunt et, paucīs diēbus intermissīs, referunt : 10 Suēbōs omnēs, posteāquam certiōrēs nūntiī dē exercitū Rōmānōrum vēnerint,[3] cum omnibus suīs sociōrumque cōpiīs, quās coēgissent,[4] penitus ad extrēmōs fīnēs sē recēpisse ; silvam esse ibi īnfīnītā magnitūdine, quae appellātur Bacēnis ; hanc longē intrōrsus pertinēre et, prō nātīvō mūrō obiectam, Cheruscōs 15 ab Suēbōrum Suēbōsque ab Cheruscōrum iniūriīs incursiōnibusque prohibēre ; ad eius silvae initium Suēbōs adventum Rōmānōrum exspectāre cōnstituisse.

1. fit, certior: Caesar is the subject understood. **2. quaeque:** *i.e.,* quae + que ; que connects **mittant** and **cognōscant.** **3. vēnerint:** what is the tense? Why? **4. coēgissent:** why is this tense used (**623**)?

Factions among the Gauls

11. Quoniam ad hunc locum perventum est, nōn aliēnum [1] esse vidētur dē Galliae Germāniaeque mōribus et quō [2] differant hae nātiōnēs inter sēsē prōpōnere.

In Galliā nōn sōlum in omnibus cīvitātibus atque in omnibus pāgīs partibusque, sed paene etiam in singulīs domibus factiōnēs 5 sunt, eārumque factiōnum prīncipēs sunt quī summam auctōri-

tātem eōrum iūdiciō ³ habēre exīstimantur, quōrum ad arbitrium
iūdiciumque summa omnium rērum cōnsiliōrumque redeat.

Idque eius reī causā ⁴ antīquitus īnstitūtum vidētur, nē quis ex
10 plēbe contrā potentiōrem auxilī ⁵ egēret; suōs enim quisque op-
primī et circumvenīrī nōn patitur, neque, aliter sī faciat,⁶ ūllam
inter suōs habeat auctōritātem. Haec eadem ratiō est in summā
tōtīus Galliae; namque omnēs cīvitātēs dīvīsae sunt in duās partēs.

1. aliēnum: *out of place.* 2. quō: *how;* ablative of respect. 3. eōrum iūdiciō:
in their judgment. 4. eius . . . causā: *for this purpose;* explained by the nē . . .
egēret clause. 5. auxilī: genitive with egēret. 6. sī faciat: (608).

Caesar supports the Aeduan faction in its struggle for supremacy

12. Cum ¹ Caesar in Galliam vēnit, alterīus factiōnis prīncipēs erant Aeduī, alterīus Sēquanī. Hī ² cum per sē minus
valērent, quod summa auctōritās antīquitus erat in Aeduīs
magnaeque eōrum erant clientēlae, Germānōs atque Ario-
5 vistum sibi adiūnxerant eōsque ad sē magnīs iactūrīs ³ pollicitā-
tiōnibusque perdūxerant.

Proeliīs vērō complūribus factīs secundīs,⁴ atque omnī nōbilitāte Aeduōrum interfectā, tantum potentiā antecesserant ⁵ ut
magnam partem clientium ab Aeduīs ad sē trādūcerent obsidēs-
10 que ab eīs prīncipum fīliōs acciperent, et pūblicē iūrāre cōgerent
nihil sē contrā Sēquanōs cōnsilī initūrōs, et partem fīnitimī agrī
per vim occupātam possidērent Galliaeque tōtīus prīncipātum
obtinērent. Quā necessitāte adductus Dīviciācus auxilī petendī
causā Rōmam ad senātum profectus, īnfectā rē,⁶ redierat.
15 Adventū Caesaris factā commūtātiōne ⁷ rērum, obsidibus
Aeduīs redditīs, veteribus clientēlīs restitūtīs, novīs per Caesarem
comparātīs, quod eī quī sē ad eōrum amīcitiam aggregāverant
meliōre condiciōne ⁸ atque aequiōre imperiō sē ūtī vidēbant,
reliquīs rēbus ⁹ eōrum grātiā dignitāteque amplificātā, Sēquanī
20 prīncipātum dīmīserant.

In eōrum locum Rēmī successerant; quōs quod adaequāre
apud Caesarem grātiā intellegēbātur,¹⁰ eī quī propter veterēs

inimīcitiās nūllō modō cum Aeduīs coniungī poterant sē Rēmīs
in clientēlam dicābant.[11] Hōs illī dīligenter tuēbantur; ita
et novam et repente collēctam auctōritātem tenēbant. Eō 25
tum statū rēs erat ut longē prīncipēs habērentur Aeduī, secundum locum dignitātis Rēmī obtinērent.

1. Cum: *at the time when;* why indicative (**596**)? **2. Hī:** *the latter.* **3. magnīs
iactūrīs:** *through great sacrifices.* **4. secundīs:** what two meanings of **secundus**
are found in this chapter? **5. tantum . . . antecesserant:** *they had so far out-
stripped them in power.* **6. īnfectā rē:** translate *with his purpose not accomplished.*
7. commūtātiōne: *i.e.,* through Caesar's defeat of Ariovistus. See p. 253. **8. condiciōne:** ablative with **ūtī,** *enjoyed.* **9. reliquīs rēbus:** *in other respects.* **10. quōs
. . . intellegēbātur:** translate *since it was evident that these stood equally well in
Caesar's favor.* **11. Rēmīs . . . dicābant:** translate *they proclaimed themselves
dependencies of the Remi.*

Classes of society, common people, knights, and Druids

Caesar now interrupts his narrative of the war to give some observations
concerning his impressions of the Gauls and Germans. Caesar has little
to tell in the way of achievements this year, and this may account for his
including this description here. It may be, too, that because he has a
scholar's interest in new facts, he wishes to pass them on to the Romans.
At any rate, future generations have found his account a valuable source of
information on the customs of the ancient Gauls and Germans.

13. In omnī Galliā eōrum hominum quī aliquō sunt numerō [1] atque honōre genera sunt duo; nam plēbēs paene ser-
vōrum habētur locō, quae nihil audet per sē, nūllī adhibētur
cōnsiliō. Plērīque, cum aut aere aliēnō [2] aut magnitūdine tribū-
tōrum aut iniūriā potentiōrum premuntur, sēsē in servitūtem 5
dicant nōbilibus; quibus [3] in hōs eadem omnia sunt iūra quae
dominīs [3] in [4] servōs.

Sed dē hīs duōbus generibus alterum est druidum,[5] alterum
equitum. Illī [6] rēbus dīvīnīs intersunt, sacrificia pūblica ac prīvāta
prōcūrant, religiōnēs interpretantur; [6] ad hōs magnus adulēscen- 10
tium numerus disciplīnae causā concurrit, magnōque hī sunt
apud eōs honōre. Nam ferē dē omnibus contrōversiīs pūblicīs
prīvātīsque cōnstituunt, et, sī quod [7] est facinus admissum, sī

caedēs facta, sī dē hērēditāte, dē fīnibus contrōversia est, īdem [8]
15 dēcernunt, praemia poenāsque cōnstituunt; sī quī aut prīvātus
aut populus eōrum dēcrētō nōn stetit, sacrificiīs interdīcunt.[9]

Haec poena apud eōs est gravissima. Quibus ita est inter-
dictum, hī numerō impiōrum ac scelerātōrum habentur, hīs
omnēs dēcēdunt, aditum eōrum sermōnemque dēfugiunt, nē
20 quid ex contāgiōne incommodī [10] accipiant, neque hīs petentibus
iūs redditur neque honōs ūllus commūnicātur.

Hīs autem omnibus druidibus praeest ūnus, quī summam
inter eōs habet auctōritātem. Hōc mortuō, aut, sī quī ex reliquīs
excellit dignitāte, succēdit, aut, sī sunt plūrēs parēs, suffrāgiō
25 druidum, nōn numquam etiam armīs, dē prīncipātū contendunt.
Hī certō annī tempore in fīnibus Carnutum, quae regiō tōtīus
Galliae media habētur, cōnsīdunt in locō cōnsecrātō. Hūc omnēs
undique quī contrōversiās habent conveniunt eōrumque dēcrētīs
iūdiciīsque pārent. Disciplīna [11] in Britanniā reperta atque
30 inde in Galliam trānslāta esse exīstimātur, et nunc quī dīligentius
eam rem cognōscere volunt plērumque illō discendī causā pro-
fīciscuntur.

1. **aliquō, numerō**: *of any importance.* 2. **aere aliēnō**: *debt.* 3. **quibus,
dominīs**: datives of possession with **sunt.** 4. **in**: *over.* 5. **druidum**: *of Druids;*
many huge stones found in Brittany have been thought by some to have been
connected with the Druid worship. Caesar is the best source of information on
Druidism. 6. **Illī . . . interpretantur**: *the former are in charge of religious observ-
ances, regulate sacrifices, public and private, and settle religious controversies.* 7. **sī
quod**: *if any.* 8. **īdem**: *they likewise* (561, *d*). 9. **sī quī . . . interdīcunt**: *if
any person or people does not stand by this decree of theirs, they forbid him to participate
in religious ceremonies.* 10. **incommodī**: modifies **quid**; translate *some harm.*
11. **Disciplīna**: *religious system (of the Druids)*; the statement made here is open to
question.

Exemptions granted to Druids. Their teachings

14. Druidēs ā bellō abesse cōnsuērunt neque tribūta ūnā cum
reliquīs pendunt, mīlitiae vacātiōnem omniumque rērum habent
immūnitātem. Tantīs excitātī praemiīs [1] et suā sponte multī in
disciplīnam conveniunt et ā parentibus propinquīsque mittuntur.

IN THE LAND OF THE DRUIDS

The remains of huge stone structures found in Brittany are thought to have
been connected with the worship of a prehistoric people.

Magnum ibi numerum versuum [2] ēdiscere [3] dīcuntur. Itaque [5]
annōs nōn nūllī vīcēnōs in disciplīnā permanent. Neque fās
esse exīstimant ea litterīs mandāre,[4] cum [5] in reliquīs ferē rēbus,
pūblicīs prīvātīsque ratiōnibus, Graecīs litterīs ūtantur. Id
mihi duābus dē causīs īnstituisse videntur, quod [6] neque in vulgus
disciplīnam efferrī velint, neque eōs quī discunt litterīs cōn- [10]
fīsōs minus memoriae studēre; [7] quod ferē plērīsque accidit, ut
praesidiō litterārum dīligentiam in perdiscendō [8] ac memoriam
remittant.

In prīmīs hoc volunt persuādēre,[9] nōn interīre animās, sed ab
aliīs post mortem trānsīre ad aliōs; atque hōc maximē ad [15]
virtūtem excitārī [10] putant, metū mortis neglēctō. Multa
praetereā dē sīderibus atque eōrum mōtū, dē mundī ac terrārum
magnitūdine, dē rērum nātūrā, dē deōrum immortālium vī ac
potestāte disputant et iuventūtī trādunt.

1. **Tantīs . . . praemiīs:** *i.e.*, exemption from civil and military duties. 2. **Magnum . . . versuum:** why do they learn poetry instead of prose? 3. **ēdiscere:**
translate *commit to memory.* 4. **ea . . . mandāre:** *to put these* (*teachings*) *into
writing.* 5. **cum:** concessive. 6. **quod:** the use of the subjunctive with **quod**

shows that the reason given is not the author's (**630,** *a*).   **7. velint . . . studēre:** *and they do not wish those who are learning, by trusting to written forms, to give less attention to the memory.*   **8. perdiscendō:** in what way do **perdiscō** and **ēdiscō** differ from **discō** in meaning?   **9. persuādēre:** *to teach.*   **10. excitārī:** **hominēs** understood is the subject.

The knights

15. Alterum genus est equitum. Hī, cum est ūsus atque aliquod bellum incidit (quod ferē ante Caesaris adventum quotannīs accidere solēbat, utī aut ipsī iniūriās īnferrent aut illātās prōpulsārent), omnēs in bellō versantur, atque eōrum ut
5 quisque est genere cōpiīsque amplissimus, ita plūrimōs circum sē ambactōs clientēsque habet. Hanc ūnam grātiam potentiamque nōvērunt.

Superstition and sacrifices of the Gauls

16. Nātiō est omnis Gallōrum admodum dēdita religiōnibus, atque ob eam causam quī [1] sunt affectī graviōribus morbīs quīque in proeliīs perīculīsque versantur, aut prō victimīs hominēs [2] immolant aut sē immolātūrōs vovent, administrīsque [3]
5 ad ea sacrificia druidibus ūtuntur, quod, prō vītā hominis nisi hominis vīta reddātur, nōn posse deōrum immortālium nūmen plācārī arbitrantur; pūblicēque eiusdem generis habent īnstitūta [4] sacrificia.

Aliī immānī magnitūdine simulācra habent, quōrum contexta vīminibus membra vīvīs hominibus complent; quibus
10 succēnsīs, circumventī flammā exanimantur hominēs.

Supplicia eōrum quī in fūrtō aut latrōciniō aut aliquā noxiā sint comprehēnsī grātiōra dīs immortālibus esse arbitrantur; sed, cum eius generis cōpia dēficit, etiam ad innocentium sup-
15 plicia dēscendunt.

1. quī: (eī) quī.   The antecedent of a relative pronoun is often omitted (**560,** *b*).
2. prō . . . hominēs: *human beings as sacrifices;* **hominēs** is the object of **immolant** and of **immolātūrōs.**   **3. administrīsque:** (*as*) *ministers.*   **4. habent īnstitūta:** this use of **habeō** with the perfect participle has the force of a perfect or past perfect tense with emphasis on the existing state of affairs.

Villa Farnesina,   *From a painting by*
Rome   *Peruzzi*

MERCURY AND MARS

Note the winged cap, **petasus**, and the wand, **cādūceus**. Wings are on the
god's ankles instead of being attached to sandals, as is often pictured.

The five gods of the Gauls

17. Deōrum [1] maximē Mercurium [2] colunt. Huius sunt
plūrima simulācra; hunc omnium inventōrem artium ferunt,[3]
hunc viārum atque itinerum ducem, hunc ad quaestūs pecūniae
mercātūrāsque habēre vim maximam arbitrantur; post hunc
Apollinem [4] et Mārtem et Iovem et Minervam. 5

Dē hīs eandem ferē quam reliquae gentēs habent opīniōnem:
Apollinem morbōs dēpellere, Minervam operum atque arti-
ficiōrum initia trādere, Iovem imperium caelestium tenēre,
Mārtem bella regere.

Huic, cum proeliō dīmicāre cōnstituērunt, ea quae bellō cēpe- 10
rint [5] plērumque dēvovent; cum superāvērunt, animālia capta
immolant reliquāsque rēs in ūnum locum cōnferunt. Multīs in
cīvitātibus hārum rērum exstrūctōs tumulōs locīs cōnsecrātīs
cōnspicārī licet; neque saepe accidit ut neglēctā quispiam religi-
ōne aut capta apud sē occultāre aut posita tollere audēret,[6] gra- 15
vissimumque eī reī supplicium cum cruciātū cōnstitūtum est.

1. **Deōrum:** many crude images of Gallic gods have been found in France and
are to be seen in museums in the provinces. 2. **Mercurium:** *Mercury,* the Roman

Street of Abundance, Pompeii

MERCURY

This Mercury on the outside wall of a house in Pompeii represents the typical Roman Mercury as the god of gain. Note the purse in his hand.

name which Caesar gave to the Gallic god who, as he thought, corresponded to the Roman god of that name. He follows this practice with all the Gallic gods whom he mentions. **3. ferunt:** *they call.* **4. Apollinem:** object of **colunt** understood. **5. cēperint:** subjunctive in a subordinate clause in implied indirect discourse. **6. ut . . . audēret:** *that anyone disregarding religious scruples dared to hide at his house the things which had been captured or to take away what had been placed (on the mound of booty).*

Origin of the Gauls' unusual customs

18. Gallī sē omnēs ab Dīte patre [1] prōgnātōs praedicant idque ab druidibus prōditum dīcunt. Ob eam causam spatia omnis temporis nōn numerō diērum sed noctium fīniunt; diēs nātālēs et mēnsium et annōrum initia sīc observant ut noctem 5 diēs subsequātur. [2]

In reliquīs vītae īnstitūtīs hōc ferē ab reliquīs differunt, quod suōs līberōs, nisi cum adolēvērunt ut mūnus mīlitiae sustinēre possint, palam ad sē adīre nōn patiuntur, fīliumque puerīlī aetāte in pūblicō in cōnspectū patris assistere turpe dūcunt. [3]

1. ab Dīte patre: *from Father Dis,* later known as Pluto, the god of darkness.
2. ut . . . subsequātur: instead of reckoning time by days, the Gauls reckoned

Pluto How did Gauls measure time?
what does our word fortnight?

53 B.C.] THE SECOND INVASION OF GERMANY 359

it by nights. **3. fīliumque . . . dūcunt:** *and they consider it disgraceful for a son of youthful age to appear in public in the presence (sight) of his father;* a practice very unlike that of the Romans.

Gallic marriages and funerals

19. Virī,[1] quantās pecūniās[2] ab uxōribus dōtis nōmine accēpērunt, tantās ex suīs bonīs, aestimātiōne factā, cum dōtibus commūnicant.[3] Huius omnis pecūniae coniūnctim ratiō habētur, frūctūsque servantur;[4] uter eōrum vītā superāvit, ad eum pars utrīusque cum frūctibus superiōrum temporum pervenit. 5

Virī in[5] uxōrēs, sīcutī in līberōs, vītae necisque habent potestātem; et cum pater familiae illūstriōre locō nātus dēcessit, eius propinquī conveniunt et, dē morte sī rēs in suspīciōnem vēnit, dē uxōribus in servīlem modum quaestiōnem habent[6] et, sī compertum est, ignī atque omnibus tormentīs excruciātās 10 interficiunt.

Fūnera sunt prō cultū Gallōrum magnifica et sūmptuōsa; omniaque quae vīvīs cordī[7] fuisse arbitrantur in ignem īnferunt, etiam animālia, ac paulō suprā hanc memoriam[8] servī et clientēs quōs ab eīs dīlēctōs esse cōnstābat, iūstīs[9] fūnebribus 15 cōnfectīs, ūnā cremābantur.

1. Virī: *their men,* translate *husbands;* this corresponds to the provincial use of *my man* for *husband.* **2. pecūniās:** *property;* what is the meaning of the root of this word? **3. aestimātiōne . . . commūnicant:** *they make a calculation and add to the dowry an equal amount.* **4. coniūnctim . . . servantur:** *a joint account is kept and the income saved.* **5. in:** has what meaning here? The Roman head of the house also had the power of life and death over his family. **6. dē uxōribus . . . habent:** *they examine the wives according to the way they deal with slaves;* i.e., by torture. **7. vīvīs cordī:** translate *dear to them when alive.* **8. paulō . . . memoriam:** translate *a little before the present time.* **9. iūstīs:** *regular.* How does the word get this meaning?

News censored. Freedom of speech forbidden

20. Quae cīvitātēs commodius suam rem pūblicam administrāre exīstimantur habent lēgibus sānctum,[1] sī quis quid dē rē pūblicā ā fīnitimīs rūmōre aut fāmā accēperit, utī ad magis-

what power did a Roman pater
familias have over the member of his
family (Johnson—private life of the Romans
31-132

trātum dēferat nēve cum quō aliō commūnicet, quod saepe homi-
5 nēs temerāriōs atque imperītōs falsīs rūmōribus terrērī et ad facinus impellī et dē summīs rēbus cōnsilium capere cognitum est.

Magistrātūs quae vīsa sunt occultant,[2] quaeque esse ex
ūsū iūdicāvērunt multitūdinī prōdunt. Dē rē pūblicā nisi
per [3] concilium loquī nōn concēditur.

1. Quae . . . sānctum: *the states which are thought to conduct their public affairs
unusually well have it enacted by law;* explained by ūtī . . . commūnicet. **2. Magistrātūs . . . occultant;** *the magistrates conceal what seems (best).* **3. per:** *at.*

The Germans, their religion and manner of living

21. Germānī multum ab hāc cōnsuētūdine differunt. Nam
neque druidēs habent quī rēbus dīvīnīs praesint, neque sacrificiīs
student. Deōrum numerō eōs sōlōs dūcunt quōs cernunt et
quōrum apertē opibus iuvantur, Sōlem et Vulcānum et Lūnam; [1]
5 reliquōs nē fāmā quidem accēpērunt.[2]

Vīta omnis in vēnātiōnibus atque in studiīs reī mīlitāris cōn-
sistit; ā parvīs labōrī ac dūritiae student.[3]

*Historical Museum, Frankfort-
on-the-Main, Germany
Courtesy of German Tourist Information Office*

A GERMAN JUNO AND JUPITER

Although Caesar says that the Germans had no gods except those whom they
could see, other gods may have come in under the influence of the Romans, or
this relief may be wrongly named.

1. Sōlem . . . Lūnam: how do their gods differ from the Gallic gods? For their superstition about the moon see p. 253.   **2. reliquōs . . . accēpērunt:** translate *they have not even heard of the others.* A hundred years later Tacitus, a Roman historian, in his **Dē Germāniā** says that Mercury was their chief god and names Hercules, Mars, and Isis as other divinities.   **3. ā . . . student:** translate *from childhood they are inured to labor and hardship.*

Agriculture among the early Germans

22. Agricultūrae nōn student, maiorque pars eōrum vīctūs in lacte, cāseō, carne cōnsistit. Neque quisquam agrī modum certum aut fīnēs habet propriōs; [1] sed magistrātūs ac prīncipēs in annōs singulōs gentibus cognātiōnibusque hominum, quīque ūnā coiērunt, quantum et quō locō vīsum est agrī attribuunt,[2] atque annō post aliō [3] trānsīre cōgunt.

Eius reī multās [4] afferunt causās: nē assiduā cōnsuētūdine captī [5] studium bellī gerendī agricultūrā [6] commūtent; nē lātōs fīnēs parāre studeant, potentiōrēsque humiliōrēs [7] possessiōnibus expellant; nē accūrātius ad frīgora atque aestūs vītandōs aedifi- 10 cent; nē qua [8] oriātur pecūniae cupiditās, quā ex rē factiōnēs dissēnsiōnēsque nāscuntur; ut animī aequitāte plēbem conti- neant,[9] cum suās quisque opēs cum potentissimīs aequārī videat.

1. propriōs: *of his own.* In Caesar's day the Germans were nomads. **2. in annōs . . . attribuunt:** *distribute for a year at a time to the clans and to bands of kinsmen and those who have united (for the purpose), as much ground and in whatever place seems best.* **3. aliō:** an adverb. **4. multās:** what five reasons are given? **5. nē . . . captī:** *that, pleased with a permanent mode of life, they may not.* **6. agri- cultūrā:** *for agriculture;* an ablative of price (**548**). **7. humiliōrēs:** object of **expellant.** **8. qua:** *any;* modifies **cupiditās.** **9. ut . . . contineant:** *so that they may hold the common people through contentment (of mind).*

Museum at Sens, France   ANCIENT BASKETS AND TUBS

The German frontiers, magistrates, brigandage, treason, hospitality

23. Cīvitātibus maxima laus est quam lātissimē circum sē, vāstātīs fīnibus, sōlitūdinēs habēre. Hoc proprium virtūtis exīstimant, expulsōs agrīs fīnitimōs cēdere, neque quemquam prope audēre cōnsistere; simul hōc sē fore tūtiōrēs arbitrantur,
5 repentīnae incursiōnis timōre sublātō.

Cum bellum cīvitās aut illātum dēfendit aut īnfert, magistrātūs quī eī bellō praesint et vītae necisque habeant potestātem dēliguntur. In pāce nūllus est commūnis magistrātus, sed prīncipēs regiōnum atque pāgōrum inter suōs iūs dīcunt contrō-
10 versiāsque minuunt.

Latrōcinia nūllam habent [1] īnfāmiam quae extrā fīnēs cuiusque cīvitātis fīunt, atque ea [2] iuventūtis exercendae ac dēsidiae minuendae causā fierī praedicant. Atque ubi quis [3] ex prīncipibus in conciliō dīxit sē ducem fore, quī sequī velint pro-
15 fiteantur,[4] cōnsurgunt eī quī et causam et hominem probant suumque auxilium pollicentur atque ā multitūdine collaudantur; quī ex hīs secūtī nōn sunt in dēsertōrum ac prōditōrum numerō dūcuntur, omniumque hīs rērum posteā fidēs dērogātur.[5]
20 Hospitem violāre fās nōn putant; quī quācumque dē causā ad eōs vēnērunt ab iniūriā prohibent, sānctōs [6] habent hīsque omnium domūs patent vīctusque commūnicātur.

1. **habent:** *regard.* 2. **ea:** refers to **latrōcinia** and is the subject of **fierī**; translate *these raids are engaged in.* 3. **quis:** the indefinite pronoun *anyone.* 4. **sē . . . profiteantur:** *i.e.,* he makes this statement, " I will be leader, let those volunteer who wish to follow." 5. **omniumque . . . dērogātur:** translate *confidence is denied them afterwards in all matters.* 6. **sānctōs:** *inviolate ;* the protection of a guest was regarded by many primitive peoples as a sacred obligation.

The story of Chapter 24

Caesar says that although the Gauls were originally superior to the Germans, because of their nearness to the Roman province, they have become softened through contact with civilization, its vices and luxuries.

Chapters 25–28

There is a question as to whether Caesar wrote these chapters describing the Hercynian forest and its strange animals. They were probably added later.

The story of Chapters 29–37

Caesar now returns to his story of his expedition into Germany in pursuit of the Suebi. He cuts down the end of the bridge on the German side, leaves a garrison to guard the Gallic side, and starts in pursuit of Ambiorix and the Eburones, who had ambushed and annihilated the forces of Sabinus and Cotta in the preceding year. He captures all the possessions of Ambiorix, but the chieftain himself escapes into the forest of the Ardennes. His followers are scattered and find refuge in inaccessible places.

Caesar leaves Quintus Tullius Cicero with one legion in charge of the baggage at Atuatuca, a town near the center of the territory of the Eburones, while he himself sets out against Ambiorix. He announces that he will be back in seven days. Because of the difficulties and dangers that his men would encounter in unknown woods and swamps, he invites neighboring tribes to help lay waste the land of the Eburones. The Sugambri, a German tribe across the Rhine, join the Gauls in these raids, but hearing of the baggage stored at Atuatuca, eager for booty, they hasten toward that place.

Although Caesar has given orders that no one is to leave camp, Cicero on the seventh day allows five cohorts and many camp followers to go out foraging. The Sugambri arrive in their absence and make a sudden attack upon the camp. Wild panic ensues but the day is saved by the heroism of Publius Sextius Baculus.

Publius Sextius Baculus gets honorable mention

38. Erat aeger in praesidiō relictus P. Sextius Baculus,[1] quī prīmum pīlum [2] apud Caesarem dūxerat, cuius mentiōnem superiōribus proeliīs fēcimus, ac diem iam quīntum cibō caruerat.

Hic diffīsus suae atque omnium salūtī inermis ex taber-nāculō prōdit; videt imminēre hostēs atque in summō rem 5 esse discrīmine; [3] capit arma ā proximīs atque in portā cōn-sistit. Cōnsequuntur hunc centuriōnēs eius cohortis quae in statiōne erat; paulisper ūnā proelium sustinent.

Relinquit animus Sextium, gravibus acceptīs vulneribus;

Trajan's Column, Rome

A BRAVE MAN FALLS

A wounded soldier is being carried to safety by his comrade.

10 aegrē per manūs trāditus servātur.[4] Hōc spatiō interpositō,[5]
reliquī sēsē cōnfirmant tantum ut in mūnītiōnibus cōnsistere
audeant speciemque dēfēnsōrum praebeant.

1. P. Sextius Baculus: He had been seriously wounded in the battle of the
Nervii; II, 25. **2. prīmum pīlum:** *first centurion.* **3. in . . . discrīmine:**
translate *the situation had reached a crisis.* **4. relinquit . . . servātur:** Sextius
fainted and was passed from hand to hand to safety. **5. hōc . . . interpositō:**
this respite gave the others enough confidence to return to their places.

The story of Chapters 39–44

Inspired by the bravery of Baculus, the soldiers rally. The Sugambri
despair of taking the camp but attack and inflict severe losses upon the
foragers who, having heard the confusion, try to return to camp. Caesar
arrives that night and finds the camp in a state of panic, which is soon
quieted by his presence. He then continues his devastation of the homes and
crops of the Eburones, so that famine may complete the work of the army.

Meanwhile, Ambiorix continues to elude the closely pursuing horsemen.
Caesar gives up the pursuit, puts his army into winter quarters in three
places, and returns to Italy to hold court. The campaign of this year
was Caesar's least successful venture. He must have been greatly dis-
appointed in his failure to capture Ambiorix.

464. COMPREHENSION — LIBER VI

1. What two reasons impelled Caesar to invade Germany a second time?
2. Of what advantage to the Romans was the factional strife of the Gauls?
3. What was the Druid teaching with respect to memorization and to immortality? 4. What gods did the Gauls have corresponding to those of the Romans? 5. Why did the Gauls reckon time by nights instead of by days? 6. Why did Gallic magistrates censor all rumors concerning public affairs? 7. Why were the early Germans not permitted to own land? 8. Why did Caesar interrupt his narrative of the war to tell of the customs of the people? 9. Why was Sextius Baculus given honorable mention? 10. How did the results of the campaign of 53 B.C. compare with those of other years?

465. VERBA — LIBER VI

Required Vocabulary: adhibeō, aequō, caedēs, cernō, commūnicō, exerceō, exstruō, factiō, fīniō, firmus, humilis, iūrō, iūstus, mēnsis, minuō, mōtus (noun), mūnus, parcō, parum, pendō, plēbs, plērumque, possideō, prōdō, quoniam, regō, religiō, repente, sīcut, tueor, vulgus.

Word Study. Define the following words, showing by your definition that they are related to cor: *accord, concord, cordial, core, discordant, encourage, recorder.*

Give Latin words formed from the present or the perfect stem of regō with at least five different suffixes; with five different prefixes. Give the meaning of each word thus formed, and, if possible, an English derivative.

Farm is derived from firmus, *firm* or *fixed.* It originally meant a piece of land held under lease for cultivation for which a *fixed* sum was paid. From this it has come to mean any tract of land devoted to agriculture. Define on the basis of their derivation: *affirmative, confirm, firmament, infirmary, infirmity.*

A ROMAN WINGED VICTORY

This lovely winged figure, represented as Victory carrying a helmet, was part of the decoration on the wall of a Roman house.

LIBER SEPTIMUS

The Defeat of the United Gauls Under Vercingetorix
52 b.c.

The Gauls unite in a final struggle for freedom

1. QUIĒTĀ Galliā,[1] Caesar, ut cōnstituerat, in Italiam ad conventūs agendōs proficīscitur. Ibi cognōscit dē P. Clōdī[2] caede; dē senātūsque cōnsultō[3] certior factus, ut omnēs iūniōrēs Italiae coniūrārent, dīlēctum tōtā prōvinciā habēre īnstituit. Eae rēs in Galliam Trānsalpīnam celeriter perferuntur. Ad-5 dunt ipsī et affingunt rūmōribus Gallī, quod rēs poscere vidē-bātur, retinērī urbānō[4] mōtū Caesarem neque in tantīs dis-sēnsiōnibus ad exercitum venīre posse.

Hāc impulsī occāsiōne, quī iam ante sē populī Rōmānī im-periō subiectōs dolērent, līberius atque audācius dē bellō cōnsilia 10 inīre incipiunt. Indictīs inter sē prīncipēs Galliae conciliīs silvestribus ac remōtīs locīs queruntur dē Accōnis[5] morte; hunc cāsum ad ipsōs recidere posse dēmōnstrant; miserantur com-mūnem Galliae fortūnam; omnibus pollicitātiōnibus ac prae-miīs dēposcunt quī bellī initium faciant et suī capitis perīculō 15 Galliam in lībertātem vindicent. In prīmīs ratiōnem esse habendam dīcunt, priusquam eōrum clandestīna cōnsilia effe-rantur, ut Caesar ab exercitū interclūdātur:

Id esse facile, quod neque legiōnēs audeant, absente im-perātōre, ex hībernīs ēgredī, neque imperātor sine praesidiō 20 ad legiōnēs pervenīre possit; postrēmō in aciē praestāre interficī[6] quam nōn veterem bellī glōriam lībertātemque quam ā maiōribus accēperint recuperāre.

1. **Quiētā Galliā**: the peace was only on the surface. All Gaul had been con-quered, but its spirit had not been broken. The only hope of throwing off the yoke

of Rome was in union under a capable leader. **2. Clōdī:** Clodius, a follower of
Caesar, was murdered in 52 B.C. by gangsters under Milo, a supporter of Pompey.
The Gauls hoped the disturbed condition of affairs at Rome would distract Caesar's
attention. **3. dē . . . cōnsultō:** the substance of this decree of the senate is
given in the **ut** clause, which says that all the men of military age (**iūniōrēs**,
between the ages of 17 and 46) should enlist (take the oath). **4. urbānō:** *i.e.*,
Rome. **5. Accōnis:** Acco, a leader of the rebellion of the Senones in 53 B.C., had
been put to death by Caesar. **6. in . . . interficī:** *it is better to be killed in line of
battle* (*they said*).

The story of Chapters 2–3

The Carnutes volunteer to take the initiative in the revolt. The other
states with solemn ceremonies pledge their support and fidelity.

The Carnutes start the rebellion by the massacre of one of Caesar's
officers and some Roman traders at Cenabum (*Orleans*). The news of this
is spread by the Gallic custom of shouting from field to field and tribe to
tribe. Caesar says, " Although the murder occurred at sunrise, the news
had travelled by nightfall to the land of the Arverni, a distance of one
hundred and sixty miles."

Vercingetorix, a brave and able leader, instigates a general revolt

4. Similī ratiōne ibi Vercingetorīx, Celtillī fīlius, Arvernus,
summae potentiae adulēscēns, cuius pater prīncipātum tōtīus
Galliae obtinuerat et ob eam causam, quod rēgnum appetēbat,
ā cīvitāte erat interfectus, convocātīs suīs clientibus, facile
5 incendit. Cognitō eius cōnsiliō, ad arma concurritur. Pro-
hibētur ā Gobannitiōne, patruō suō, reliquīsque prīncipibus,
quī hanc temptandam fortūnam nōn exīstimābant; expellitur
ex oppidō Gergoviā; nōn dēstitit tamen atque in agrīs habet
dīlēctum egentium ac perditōrum.
10   Hāc coāctā manū, quōscumque adit ex cīvitāte ad suam
sententiam perdūcit; hortātur ut commūnis lībertātis causā
arma capiant, magnīsque coāctīs cōpiīs, adversāriōs suōs, ā
quibus paulō ante erat ēiectus, expellit ex cīvitāte. Rēx ab
suīs appellātur. Dīmittit quōqueversus [1] lēgātiōnēs; obtes-
15 tātur ut in fidē maneant.
    Celeriter sibi Senonēs, Parīsiōs, Pictonēs, Cadūrcōs, Turonōs,

Aulercōs, Lemovīcēs, Andēs reliquōsque omnēs quī Ōceanum attingunt adiungit; omnium cōnsēnsū ad eum dēfertur imperium.   Quā oblātā potestāte, omnibus hīs cīvitātibus obsidēs imperat, 20 certum numerum mīlitum ad sē celeriter addūcī iubet, armōrum quantum quaeque cīvitās domī quodque ante tempus efficiat [2] cōnstituit; in prīmīs equitātuī studet. 25

Summae dīligentiae summam imperī sevēritātem addit; magnitūdine supplicī dubitantēs cōgit. Nam, maiōre commissō dēlictō, ignī atque omnibus tormentīs ne- 30 cat; leviōre dē causā auribus dēsectīs aut singulīs effossīs oculīs, domum remittit ut sint reliquīs documentō [3] et magnitūdine poenae perterreant aliōs.   35

1. quōqueversus: *in every direction.*
2. armōrum . . . efficiat: *how large a quantity of arms each state should prepare at home and before what time.* 3. ut . . . documentō: *that they might be an example to the rest.*

Statue by F. Millet   Courtesy of George R. Swain

VERCINGETORIX

On the site of ancient Alesia stands this statue of a national hero, inspired by the vision of a free Gaul " whose unanimity not even the world can resist."

The story of Chapters 5–14

The Bituriges, attacked by Vercingetorix, surrender and join the uprising. The revolt continues to spread. A large force of the enemy under Lucterius starts for the Province.

Caesar leaves Italy, rushes to Narbo, and establishes new garrisons for the protection of the Province. Then he crosses the Cevennes Mountains through deep snow and attacks the Arverni, to whose rescue Vercingetorix comes. Caesar, leaving Decimus

Vienne, France

A ROMAN TEMPLE IN THE PROVINCE

Caesar waited for reinforcements at **Vienna** (*Vienne*), where this temple of the first century A.D., dedicated to Augustus and Livia, still stands.

Brutus to raid the country of the Arverni, hastens to Vienne for cavalry reinforcements, and from there to his two legions among the Lingones.

When Vercingetorix hears this, he attacks Gorgobina, a town of the Boii. Caesar sets out to the relief of the town and en route captures Vellaunodunum, burns Cenabum, and receives the surrender of Noviodunum (*Nevers*). From there he marches toward Avaricum (*Bourges*), the largest and best fortified town of the Bituriges. Vercingetorix calls a council and urges the Gauls not to attempt to meet the Romans in open battle but to burn their towns and supplies and by this means starve and wear out the enemy.

The Bituriges burn all their towns except beautiful Avaricum

15. Omnium cōnsēnsū hāc sententiā[1] probātā, ūnō diē amplius xx urbēs Biturīgum incenduntur. In omnibus partibus incendia cōnspiciuntur; quae etsī magnō cum dolōre omnēs ferēbant, tamen hoc sibi sōlācī prōpōnēbant, quod sē, prope
5 explōrātā victōriā,[2] celeriter āmissa recuperātūrōs cōnfīdēbant.

Dēlīberātur dē Avaricō[3] in commūnī conciliō, incendī placeat an dēfendī.[4] Prōcumbunt omnibus Gallīs ad pedēs Biturīgēs,[5]

nē pulcherrimam prope tōtīus Galliae urbem, quae praesidiō
et ōrnāmentō sit cīvitātī, suīs manibus succendere cōgantur;
facile sē locī nātūrā dēfēnsūrōs dīcunt, quod, prope ex omnibus 10
partibus flūmine et palūde circumdata, ūnum habeat et per-
angustum aditum.

Datur petentibus venia, dissuādente prīmō Vercingetorīge,
post concēdente [6] et precibus ipsōrum et misericordiā vulgī.
Dēfēnsōrēs oppidō idōneī dēliguntur. 15

1. hāc sententiā: refers to the proposal made by Vercingetorix at the council.
2. prope . . . victōriā: *that with victory almost assured.* 3. Avaricō: Avaricum
is modern Bourges; find it on a map of France. 4. incendī . . . dēfendī: translate *whether it seems best to burn, or defend* (*Avaricum*). 5. Prōcumbunt . . . Biturīgēs: *the Bituriges throw themselves at the feet of all the Gauls* (*begging*); Gallīs,
dative of reference. 6. dissuādente . . . concēdente: this yielding was a fatal
error on the part of Vercingetorix; the capture of this town with its stores saved
the Romans from starvation and lost the war for the Gauls.

The story of Chapters 16–24 and part of 25

Caesar, advancing to Avaricum, is followed and harassed by Vercingetorix, who establishes his camp sixteen miles away. Although the Boii
and the Aeduans fail to furnish the Romans with the supplies promised,
Caesar begins the siege of Avaricum. The soldiers are without food.
" Yet," says Caesar, " no word was heard unworthy of the majesty of the
Roman people and their former victories." Caesar suggests that they
retire, but the starving army refuses to incur the disgrace of abandoning
the siege unfinished.

Vercingetorix draws near Avaricum and diverts Caesar from the siege.
Caesar finds him so strongly established on a hill surrounded by a marsh
that he does not risk an encounter, but returns to the siege. The Gauls
throw their whole strength and ingenuity into the defense of Avaricum.
Their walls are so constructed as to withstand battering-ram and fire.
They make a sally, setting Caesar's agger on fire with great danger to his
siegeworks.

An example cited of the bravery of the Gauls

25. Cum in omnibus locīs, cōnsūmptā iam reliquā parte
noctis, pugnārētur semperque hostibus spēs victōriae redinte-
grārētur, eō magis, quod deustōs pluteōs turrium vidēbant nec

facile adīre apertōs ad auxiliandum animadvertēbant, semperque
5 ipsī recentēs [1] dēfessīs succēderent omnemque Galliae salūtem
in illō vēstīgiō temporis positam arbitrārentur, accidit, īnspec-
tantibus nōbīs,[2] quod dignum memoriā vīsum [3] praetereundum
nōn exīstimāvimus.

Quīdam ante portam oppidī Gallus per manūs sēbī ac picis
10 trāditās glēbās [4] in ignem ē regiōne turris prōiciēbat; scorpiōne [5]
ab latere dextrō trāiectus exanimātusque concidit. Hunc ex
proximīs ūnus iacentem trānsgressus [6] eōdem illō mūnere fungē-
bātur; eādem ratiōne, ictū scorpiōnis exanimātō alterō, successit tertius, et tertiō quārtus, nec prius ille est ā prōpugnātōribus
15 vacuus relictus locus quam, restīnctō aggere atque omnī ex
parte summōtīs hostibus, fīnis est pugnandī factus.[7]

1. **recentēs:** *those who were fresh;* the Gauls, implied in **ipsī.** **2. nōbīs:** a
personal touch which shows Caesar's admiration for bravery even in an enemy.
3. quod . . . vīsum: *(a thing) which (as it) seemed worthy of memory.* **4. per . . .
glēbās:** *balls of suet and pitch, passed along by hand.* **5. scorpiōne:** the Roman
machine gun, a catapult for throwing large arrows and darts. **6. Hunc . . .
trānsgressus:** *one of those standing near stepped over the one who had fallen.* **7. prius
. . . quam . . . factus:** for the indicative, see **598.**

The story of Chapters 26–50

Avaricum finally falls after a courageous and determined defense. Only
eight hundred of the forty thousand inhabitants reach the camp of Vercingetorix in safety. The loss of Avaricum is a heavy blow to the Gauls,
but Vercingetorix undaunted calls a council. With youthful enthusiasm
and intense patriotism he inspires the Gauls with his belief that, " Gaul
united can resist the whole world."

The capture of Avaricum gives Caesar an abundant supply of provisions
and saves his army from starvation. This, together with the approach of
spring, leads Caesar to continue the campaign with renewed vigor. Labienus
is sent north with four legions against the Senones and Parisii. Caesar
moves south with six legions and fortifies two camps near Gergovia. Vercingetorix hastens to encamp on the hill opposite the town.

Caesar is called away by a report that some of the Aeduans, who pose as
loyal supporters, are inciting their people to join the "League of the Gauls."
He meets with them and persuades them to remain loyal to the Romans and
to turn their allegiance to him. Thus, temporarily he checks their revolt.

Returning to Gergovia in time to save his two camps, which had been attacked by the Gauls, Caesar realizes that there is danger of a general Gallic uprising and therefore plans to retire from Gergovia and unite his forces with those of Labienus.

In order to withdraw without giving an appearance of flight, Caesar makes a surprise attack and captures three camps of the enemy. Having accomplished his purpose, he orders his soldiers to retreat, but, excited by victory, they push on and even climb upon the enemies' walls.

Caesar pauses in his narrative to tell the following story:

The brave self-sacrifice of Marcus Petronius

50. M. Petrōnius, eiusdem legiōnis centuriō, cum portās excīdere cōnātus esset, ā multitūdine oppressus ac sibi dēspērāns, multīs iam vulneribus acceptīs, manipulāribus suīs quī illum secūtī erant:

" Quoniam," inquit, " mē ūnā vōbīscum servāre nōn possum, 5 vestrae quidem certē vītae prōspiciam, quōs cupiditāte glōriae adductus in perīculum dēdūxī. Vōs, datā facultāte, vōbīs cōnsulite."

Simul in mediōs hostēs irrūpit, duōbusque interfectīs, reliquōs ā portā paulum summōvit. Cōnantibus auxiliārī suīs : 10

" Frūstrā," inquit, " meae vītae subvenīre cōnāminī, quem iam sanguis vīrēsque dēficiunt. Proinde abīte, dum est facultās, vōsque ad legiōnem recipite."

Ita pugnāns post paulum concidit ac suīs salūtī fuit.

The story of Chapters 51–62

In this engagement the Romans lose forty-six officers and seven hundred men. The next day Caesar reviews his troops and in an address criticizes their disobedience. He mingles equal praise with just criticism, saying that obedience and self-restraint are as essential qualities of a soldier as is bravery.

The withdrawal from Gergovia was the only serious failure that the forces led by Caesar in person suffered during the war. After his evacuation of Gergovia, Caesar withdraws to the country of the Aeduans, who now revolt and join Vercingetorix in a final struggle to drive the Romans from Gaul. They burn the town of Noviodunum, where Caesar had concentrated

ROMAN ARENA IN PARIS

This reminder of the Roman occupation of Gaul perpetuates the name of the ancient capital of the Parisii, **Lutecia.** It is called the Arène Lutèce.

supplies, hostages, and baggage. When he learns of this, Caesar advances north at full speed and moves on to the territory of the Senones.

In the meantime, Labienus advances to capture Lutecia (*Paris*), a town of the Parisii on an island in the River Seine. With indomitable spirit the Parisii cut down the bridge and burn their town rather than have it fall into the hands of the Romans.

Labienus now learns of Caesar's retirement from Gergovia and of the defection of the Aeduans. He himself, beset by the Parisii and the Bellovaci, wins a decisive victory but, because of the prospect of a general Gallic uprising, he decides to join Caesar.

All Gaul in revolt.   Vercingetorix is made commander-in-chief

63. Dēfectiōne Aeduōrum cognitā, bellum augētur. Lēgā-tiōnēs in omnēs partēs circummittuntur; quantum grātiā, auctōritāte, pecūniā valent,[1] ad sollicitandās cīvitātēs nītuntur; nactī obsidēs quōs Caesar apud eōs [2] dēposuerat, hōrum sup-
5 pliciō dubitantēs territant. Petunt ā Vercingetorīge Aeduī ut ad sē veniat ratiōnēsque bellī gerendī commūnicet. Rē impe-trātā, contendunt ut ipsīs summa imperī trādātur, et, rē in con-trōversiam dēductā, tōtīus Galliae concilium Bibracte indīcitur.

Eōdem conveniunt undique frequentēs. Multitūdinis suf-
10 frāgiīs rēs permittitur; ad ūnum [3] omnēs Vercingetorīgem pro-bant imperātōrem.

Ab hōc conciliō Rēmī, Lingonēs, Trēverī āfuērunt : illī, quod
amīcitiam Rōmānōrum sequēbantur; Trēverī, quod aberant
longius et ā Germānīs premēbantur, quae fuit causa quārē tōtō
abessent bellō et neutrīs auxilia mitterent.   15

Magnō dolōre Aeduī ferunt sē dēiectōs prīncipātū ; queruntur
fortūnae commūtātiōnem et Caesaris in sē indulgentiam requī-
runt, neque tamen, susceptō bellō, suum cōnsilium ab reliquīs
sēparāre audent. Invītī summae speī[4] adulēscentēs, Eporēdorīx et Viridomārus, Vercingetorīgī pārent.   20

1. **quantum . . . valent:** translate *with all the influence, prestige, and money that
they have.* **2. eōs:** *i.e.,* the people of Noviodunum. **3. ad ūnum:** *to a man.* **4. speī:**
of ambition.

Vercingetorix plans his campaign

64. Ille imperat reliquīs cīvitātibus obsidēs itemque eī reī
cōnstituit diem; omnēs equitēs, xv mīlia numerō, celeriter
convenīre iubet. Peditātū[1] quem anteā habuerit sē fore contentum dīcit, neque fortūnam temptātūrum aut in aciē dīmicā-
tūrum; sed, quoniam abundet equitātū, perfacile esse factū 5
frūmentātiōnibus pābulātiōnibusque Rōmānōs prohibēre ; aequō
modo animō sua ipsī frūmenta corrumpant[2] aedificiaque in-
cendant, quā reī familiāris iactūrā[3] perpetuum imperium
lībertātemque sē cōnsequī videant.

Hīs cōnstitūtīs rēbus, Aeduīs Segusiāvīsque, quī sunt fīnitimī 10
Prōvinciae, decem mīlia peditum imperat; hūc addit equitēs
DCCC. Hīs praeficit frātrem Eporēdorīgis bellumque īnferre Allobrogibus iubet. Alterā ex parte Gabalōs proximōsque pāgōs
Arvernōrum in Helviōs, item Rutēnōs Cadūrcōsque ad fīnēs Vol-
cārum Arecomicōrum dēpopulandōs mittit. Nihilō minus clandes- 15
tīnīs nūntiīs lēgātiōnibusque Allobrogēs sollicitat, quōrum mentēs
nōndum ab superiōre bellō resēdisse spērābat. Hōrum prīncipibus
pecūniās, cīvitātī autem imperium tōtīus Prōvinciae pollicētur.

1. **Peditātū:** with **contentum. 2. aequō . . . corrumpant:** translate as a
direct statement *just destroy your own grain without concern.* **3. quā . . . iactūrā:**
since by this sacrifice of property.

Avignon, France   © *Ewing Galloway*

IN THE PROVINCE

This ancient bridge over the Rhone is at Avignon.

Caesar sends to Germany for cavalry

65. Ad hōs omnēs cāsūs prōvīsa erant praesidia cohortium
XXII, quae ex ipsā coācta Prōvinciā ab L. Caesare ¹ lēgātō ad
omnēs partēs oppōnēbantur. Helviī suā sponte cum fīnitimīs
proeliō congressī pelluntur et, C. Valeriō Donnotaurō, Cabūrī
5 fīliō, prīncipe cīvitātis, complūribusque aliīs interfectīs, intrā
oppida mūrōsque compelluntur. Allobrogēs, crēbrīs ad Rhodanum dispositīs praesidiīs, magnā cūrā et dīligentiā suōs fīnēs
tuentur.

Caesar, quod hostēs equitātū superiōrēs esse intellegēbat
10 et, interclūsīs omnibus itineribus, nūllā rē ex Prōvinciā atque
Ītaliā sublevārī poterat, trāns Rhēnum in Germāniam mittit
ad eās cīvitātēs quās superiōribus annīs pācāverat equitēsque
ab hīs accessit et levis armātūrae peditēs quī inter eōs proeliārī
cōnsuērant. Eōrum adventū, quod minus idōneīs ² equīs ūtē-
15 bantur, ā tribūnīs ³ mīlitum reliquīsque equitibus Rōmānīs
atque ēvocātīs ⁴ equōs sūmit Germānīsque distribuit.

1. L. Caesare: a cousin of Julius Caesar.   **2. idōneīs:** these are described
in IV, 2.   **3. tribūnīs:** why is this in the ablative case? Explain the case of :
sponte, l. 3; **fīliō,** l. 5; **praesidiīs,** l. 7; **cūrā,** l. 7; **equitātū,** l. 9; **annīs,** l. 12;
equīs, l. 14.   **4. ēvocātīs:** the *ēvocātī* were soldiers who, having served their time
of twenty years, had again enlisted. They seem to have been granted the privilege of having a horse. Since Caesar saw that the German cavalry with their
small horses would not be a match for the well-mounted troops of Vercingetorix,
he remounted the Germans on horses taken from his own forces.

Caesar marches toward the Province.　Vercingetorix plans an attack

66. Intereā, dum haec geruntur, hostium cōpiae ex Arvernīs equitēsque quī tōtī Galliae erant imperātī conveniunt. Magnō hōrum coāctō numerō, cum Caesar in Sēquanōs per extrēmōs Lingonum fīnēs iter faceret, quō facilius subsidium Prōvinciae ferrī posset, circiter mīlia passuum decem ab Rōmānīs trīnīs 5 castrīs Vercingetorīx cōnsēdit, convocātīsque ad concilium praefectīs equitum, vēnisse tempus victōriae dēmōnstrat :

Fugere in Prōvinciam Rōmānōs Galliāque excēdere. Id sibi ad praesentem [1] obtinendam lībertātem satis esse ; ad reliquī temporis [2] pācem atque ōtium parum prōficī ; [3] maiōribus enim 10 coāctīs cōpiīs reversūrōs neque fīnem bellandī factūrōs.

Proinde in agmine impedītōs adoriantur.[4] Sī peditēs suīs auxilium ferant atque in eō [5] morentur, iter facere nōn posse ; sī, id quod magis futūrum cōnfīdat, relictīs impedīmentīs, suae salūtī cōnsulant, et ūsū rērum necessāriārum et dignitāte spoliā- 15 tum īrī.[6] Nam dē equitibus hostium, quīn nēmō eōrum prōgredī modo extrā agmen audeat,[7] nē ipsōs quidem dēbēre dubitāre. Id quō maiōre faciant animō, cōpiās sē omnēs prō castrīs habitūrum et terrōrī hostibus futūrum.

Conclāmant equitēs sānctissimō iūre iūrandō cōnfirmārī opor- 20 tēre nē tēctō recipiātur, nē ad līberōs, nē ad parentēs, nē ad uxōrem aditum habeat quī nōn bis per agmen hostium perequitārit.[8]

---

1. praesentem : *temporary.* **2. reliquī temporis :** *the future.* **3. parum prōficī :** *i.e.,* little will be gained by the withdrawal of the Romans because they will return with greater forces if they once reach the Province. **4. adoriantur :** the subjunctive represents an imperative of the direct discourse. **5. in eō :** *i.e.,* in supporting their comrades. **6. ūsū . . . īrī :** *they would be deprived of necessary things and of their prestige.* What form of the infinitive is used here ? **7. quīn . . . audeat :** object of **dubitāre (591). 8. sānctissimō . . . perequitārit :** *that they ought to bind themselves by a most solemn oath that no man shall be received under a roof, or visit his children, his parents, or his wife, who has not twice ridden through the line of the enemy ;* **perequitāret = perequitāverit,** the perfect subjunctive. In the engagement that followed, the cavalry, striving in vain to keep the vow that they had sworn, fought on without support, while the infantry fell back to the camps.

The Gauls are defeated by the cavalry

67. Probātā rē atque omnibus iūre iūrandō adāctīs, posterō diē in trēs partēs distribūtō equitātū, duae sē aciēs ab duōbus

Cologne, Germany

THE TOMBSTONE OF A
CAVALRYMAN

lateribus ostendunt, ūna ā prīmō agmine iter impedīre coepit. Quā rē nūntiātā, Caesar suum quoque equitātum tripertītō dīvīsum contrā hostem īre iubet.

Pugnātur ūnā omnibus in partibus. Cōnsistit agmen; impedīmenta intrā legiōnēs recipiuntur. Sī quā in parte nostrī labōrāre aut gravius premī vidēbantur, eō signa īnferrī Caesar aciemque cōnstituī iubēbat; quae rēs et hostēs ad īnsequendum tardābat et nostrōs spē auxilī cōnfirmābat.

Tandem Germānī ab dextrō latere summum iugum nactī hostēs locō dēpellunt; fugientēs usque ad flūmen, ubi Vercingetorīx cum pedestribus cōpiīs cōnsēderat, persequuntur complūrēsque interficiunt. Quā rē animadversā, reliquī, nē circumīrentur veritī, sē fugae mandant. Omnibus locīs fit caedēs.

Trēs nōbilissimī Aeduī captī ad Caesarem perdūcuntur: Cotus, praefectus equitum, et Cavarillus, et Eporēdorīx.

Vercingetorix takes refuge in Alesia. Caesar follows him

68. Fugātō omnī equitātū, Vercingetorīx cōpiās suās, ut prō castrīs collocāverat, redūxit prōtinusque Alesiam, quod est oppidum Mandubiōrum, iter facere coepit celeriterque impedīmenta ex castrīs ēdūcī et sē subsequī iussit.

5   Caesar, impedīmentīs in proximum collem dēductīs, duābus legiōnibus praesidiō relictīs, secūtus hostēs quantum diēī tempus est passum, circiter tribus mīlibus ex novissimō agmine interfectīs, alterō diē ad Alesiam castra fēcit.

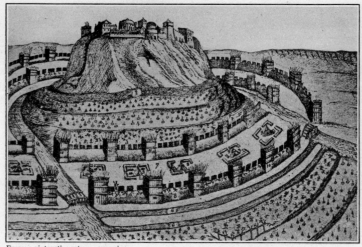

From a sixteenth-century engraving

ALESIA AND THE ROMAN SIEGE WORKS

This old drawing shows Alesia on the hill and Caesar's two lines of fortification, an inner to protect his army from the Alesian forces in the town, an outer as a defense against the Gallic army of relief.

Perspectō urbis sitū perterritīsque hostibus, quod equitātū, quā maximē parte exercitūs cōnfīdēbant, erant pulsī, adhortātus 10 ad labōrem mīlitēs circumvāllāre īnstituit.

The location of Alesia and Caesar's fortification of it

69. Ipsum erat oppidum Alesia [1] in colle summō admodum ēditō locō, ut nisi obsidiōne expugnārī nōn posse vidērētur. Cuius collis rādīcēs [2] duo duābus ex partibus flūmina [3] subluēbant.

Ante oppidum plānitiēs circiter mīlia passuum tria in longitūdinem patēbat; reliquīs ex omnibus partibus collēs, mediocrī 5 interiectō spatiō, parī altitūdinis fastīgiō oppidum cingēbant.[4]

Sub mūrō, quae pars collis ad orientem sōlem spectābat, hunc omnem locum cōpiae Gallōrum complēverant fossamque et māceriam in altitūdinem sex pedum praedūxerant.

Model in Museum at St. Germain, France

CAESAR'S SIEGE WORKS AT ALESIA

The towers and palisades are on the rampart, which is also protected by a row of pointed stakes projecting horizontally near the top. To the right of the rampart are two ditches, sharp posts hidden by an entanglement of brushwork, and wolf-holes. These are holes in which sharp-pointed stakes are imbedded and covered with brush and brambles.

10   Eius mūnītiōnis quae ab Rōmānīs īnstituēbātur circuitus XI mīlia passuum tenēbat. Castra [5] opportūnīs locīs erant posita ibique castella XXIII facta; quibus in castellīs interdiū statiōnēs pōnēbantur, nē qua subitō ēruptiō fieret; haec eadem noctū excubitōribus ac firmīs praesidiīs tenēbantur.

1. Alesia: this name still survives in *Alise-Sainte-Reine,* a town on one of the slopes of the hill which today bears the name of *Mont Auxois.* **2. rādīcēs:** *the foot;* direct object of **subluēbant. 3. duo, flūmina:** the Ose and the Oserain. **4. reliquīs . . . cingēbant:** *on all the other sides a short distance away, hills of equal height encircled the town.* **5. Castra:** here refers to more than one camp as is shown by **locīs.** Traces of eight have been found.

The story of Chapters 70–87

The Gauls attempt to thwart the Romans' siege preparations, but are routed with great slaughter by the German cavalry. Vercingetorix sends out a call to all Gaul for aid. In preparation for the siege he assumes a food dictatorship, since he has barely thirty days' provisions.

Caesar builds an inner line of siegeworks to hold Vercingetorix in Alesia; he builds an outer line to defend his army from attack, in both of which he makes use of brushwood entanglements and wolf-holes. A device similar to this was used in the World War.

In a national assembly the Gauls assign the quotas for which each state is made responsible. Two hundred and fifty thousand infantry and eight thousand cavalry march confidently to the relief of Alesia under the command of four great leaders: Commius, an Atrebatian; Viridomarus and Eporedorix, Aeduans; and Vercassivellanus, an Arvernian, a cousin of Vercingetorix. These are supported by a council elected from the various tribes.

In the meantime, at Alesia, the army of relief has not arrived, supplies are exhausted, and a council of war is called. Some advocate surrender, some a sortie. Critognatus, in a vigorous and eloquent speech, urges them to stand firm. Women, children, and the sick are driven out of the town. They appeal to Caesar, who refuses to give them food.

Meanwhile, the army of relief for the besieged arrives and encamps on a hill near Caesar's lines. The next day the Gallic cavalry descends into the open plain filling a space of three miles. The Roman cavalry advances to meet them. Fierce war cries fill the air. The Roman legionaries on the hill watch the hotly contested cavalry battle, which rages till sunset, when a last furious charge upon the Gauls drives them back into their fortifications.

Two days later the enemy make a concerted attack upon both the inner and outer lines, but are repulsed by the Romans. Not thwarted by this defeat, sixty thousand Gauls, supported by cavalry, make a last desperate attack. Caesar watches the conflict while both sides strain every nerve. The situation is critical for the Romans. Noting this, Caesar sends Labienus to the rescue, and he himself leads a body of reserves into the battle.

A vivid description of the battle, flight, pursuit, and slaughter

88. Eius adventū ex colōre [1] vestītūs cognitō, quō īnsignī in proeliīs ūtī cōnsuērat, turmīsque equitum et cohortibus vīsīs quās sē sequī iusserat, ut dē locīs superiōribus haec dēclīvia et dēvexa cernēbantur, hostēs proelium committunt.

Utrimque clāmōre sublātō, excipit [2] rūrsus ex vāllō atque omnibus mūnītiōnibus clāmor. 5

Nostrī, omissīs pīlīs, gladiīs rem gerunt.

Repente post tergum equitātus cernitur; cohortēs aliae appropinquant.

10 Hostēs terga vertunt; fugientibus equitēs occurrunt. Fit magna caedēs.

Sedulius, dux et prīnceps Lemovīcum, occīditur; Vercassivellaunus Arvernus vīvus in fugā comprehenditur; signa mīlitāria LXXIIII ad Caesarem referuntur; paucī ex tantō numerō 15 sē incolumēs in castra recipiunt. Cōnspicātī ex oppidō caedem et fugam suōrum, dēspērātā salūte, cōpiās ā mūnītiōnibus redūcunt.

Fit prōtinus, hāc rē audītā, ex castrīs Gallōrum fuga. Quod [3] nisi crēbrīs subsidiīs ac tōtīus diēī labōre mīlitēs essent dēfessī, 20 omnēs hostium cōpiae dēlērī potuissent.[4] Dē mediā nocte missus equitātus novissimum agmen cōnsequitur; magnus numerus capitur atque interficitur; reliquī ex fugā in cīvitātēs discēdunt.

1. colōre: the general wore a scarlet cloak. The enemy recognized Caesar by this. **2. excipit:** *follows.* **3. Quod:** translate *and.* **4. dēlērī potuissent:** *might have been destroyed* **(609).**

Caesar receives the surrender of the great-hearted Vercingetorix

89. Posterō diē Vercingetorīx,[1] conciliō convocātō, id bellum sē suscēpisse nōn suārum necessitātum, sed commūnis lībertātis causā dēmōnstrat, et quoniam sit fortūnae cēdendum, ad utramque rem sē illīs offerre, seu morte suā Rōmānīs satisfacere seu 5 vīvum trādere velint.

Mittuntur dē hīs rēbus ad Caesarem lēgātī. Iubet arma trādī, prīncipēs prōdūcī. Ipse in mūnītiōne prō castrīs cōnsīdit; eō ducēs prōdūcuntur. Vercingetorīx dēditur, arma prōiciuntur.

Reservātīs Aeduīs atque Arvernīs, sī per eōs cīvitātēs recu- 10 perāre posset, ex reliquīs captīvīs tōtī exercituī capita singula praedae nōmine distribuit.

1. Vercingetorīx: with great dignity he makes his surrender to Caesar. He is sent to Rome as a captive. There he remains in prison for six years, saved to grace Caesar's triumph in the Civil War. He is led in chains before the victor's car in the procession, after which he is executed. Plutarch says, " He was every inch a king."

Trajan's Column, Rome

SOLDIER WITH BOOTY

The soldier's saddle bags are filled with various small articles that suggest booty. After the fall of Alesia each soldier was given a captive as booty.

The story of Chapter 90

The last tribes submit. Caesar sends his troops into winter quarters. A twenty days' thanksgiving is declared at Rome in honor of his victory.

466. COMPREHENSION — LIBER VII

1. How did the Gauls send wireless messages? **2.** What qualities made Vercingetorix a capable leader of the Gauls? **3.** What was the result of Vercingetorix' consenting to save Avaricum? **4.** What example of the bravery of the Gauls at the siege of Avaricum does Caesar record? Of a Roman at the siege of Gergovia? **5.** Give examples from **Liber VII** and preceding books which set forth the Roman ideals of *discipline*, **disciplīna**, *manliness*, **virtūs**, and *courage*, **fortitūdō**.

6. What was Vercingetorix' plan of campaign as commander-in-chief of all Gaul? **7.** What advantages had Alesia as a stronghold? **8.** What preparations did Caesar make to lay siege to Alesia? **9.** What was the final outcome? **10.** Why is Vercingetorix regarded as a national hero?

11. Point out five modern French cities whose names are derived from the Latin names of Gallic tribes. **12.** What was the most far-reaching effect of Caesar's conquest of Gaul?

467.   VERBA — LIBER VII

Required Vocabulary: an, bis, compellō, congredior, ēruptiō, indīcō, occultus, praesēns, prōficiō, quiētus, recuperō, semper, trānsgredior.

Word Study. Define the following words, showing by your definition that they are related to **manus** : *amanuensis, emancipate, legerdemain, manacle, management, manufacturer, manifest, manumission.*

To what Latin word in **Liber VII** do you think each of the following is related by derivation?

Spanish	French	Italian	English
cautivo	captif	cattivo	*captive*
clamor	clameur	clamore	*clamor*
copia	copie	copia	*copious*
deber	devoir	debito	*debit*
diestra	dextre	destra	*dexterity*
gracia	grâce	grazia	*grace*
hueste	hostile	ostile	*hostile*
nombre	nom	nome	*nominal*
satisfacer	satisfaire	soddisfare	*satisfaction*
victoria	victoire	vittoria	*victory*

FĪNIS

Caesar ends his account of the Gallic War with this book. One of his generals, Aulus Hirtius, wrote an eighth book giving the history of the last two years, in which Caesar completed the subjugation of all Gaul. He quelled minor uprisings and inspired allegiance by his generous treatment of the conquered and the establishment of efficient government.

The conquest of Gaul settled the question of Teuton or Roman supremacy in southwestern Europe and opened the way to the establishment in the western world of Roman civilization, which found expression in the art, architecture, government, literature, and the speech of the people. The impress of Roman civilization still lives on.

THE AMPHITHEATER AT NÎMES

This is a well-preserved example of Roman architecture, situated at Nîmes, a town in southern France noted for its Roman remains. It accommodated about 24,000 spectators. Dramatic performances and even bullfights are still given in this arena.

JULIUS AND AUGUSTUS CAESAR

A bronze coin with the laureled head of Julius Caesar as a god (**DIVOS IVLIVS**) on one side, and that of his adopted son [**CAESAR DIVI F**(ilius)], Augustus, on the other.

FORMS FOR REFERENCE

"Nōmina dēclīnāre et verba in prīmīs sciant; neque enim aliter pervenīre ad intellēctum sequentium possunt, *Children should learn to inflect nouns and especially verbs; for in no other way can they come to an understanding of what they study later.*" QUINTILIAN

NOUNS

468.   FIRST DECLENSION

terra, *f.* land

	Singular	*Plural*
Nom.	terra	terrae
Gen.	terrae	terrārum
Dat.	terrae	terrīs
Acc.	terram	terrās
Abl.	terrā	terrīs

The stem ends in -ā. This is short in the nominative singular, -a, and also in the accusative singular, -am.

The gender is regularly feminine. Among the exceptions are: **Matrona**, m., *the (river) Marne;* **nauta**, m., *sailor.*

The vocative case has the same form as the nominative. The locative singular ends in **-ae**: **Rōmae**, *at Rome;* the plural ends in **-īs**: **Athēnīs**, *at Athens.* The dative and ablative plural of **dea** and **fīlia** usually ends in **-ābus**.

469.   SECOND DECLENSION

equus, *m.* horse   **puer**, *m.* boy   **ager**, *m.* field   **vir**, *m.* man   **oppidum**, *n.* town

Singular

Nom.	equus	puer	ager	vir	oppidum
Gen.	equī	puerī	agrī	virī	oppidī
Dat.	equō	puerō	agrō	virō	oppidō
Acc.	equum	puerum	agrum	virum	oppidum
Abl.	equō	puerō	agrō	virō	oppidō

Plural

Nom.	equī	puerī	agrī	virī	oppida
Gen.	equōrum	puerōrum	agrōrum	virōrum	oppidōrum
Dat.	equīs	puerīs	agrīs	virīs	oppidīs
Acc.	equōs	puerōs	agrōs	virōs	oppida
Abl.	equīs	puerīs	agrīs	virīs	oppidīs

The stem ends in **-o**.

Second declension nouns ending in **-us, -er, -ir** are regularly masculine; those ending in **-um** are neuter.

The genitive singular of nouns in **-ius** and **-ium** regularly appears as **-ī**, instead of **-iī**, with the accent on the penult: **fī′lī**, *of a son;* **auxi′lī**, *of aid.*

The vocative singular of nouns in **-us** has the ending **-e**: **Mārce**, *O, Marcus;* of nouns in **-ius, -ī**: **fīlī**, *O, son;* the vocative form of all other nouns is the same as the nominative.

The locative case in the singular ends in **-ī**; in the plural in **-īs**: **Cēnabī**, *at Cenabum;* **Pompeiīs**, *at Pompeii.*

The plural of **deus** has irregular forms: *nom.,* **deī, diī, dī;** *gen.,* **deōrum, deum;** *dat.* and *abl.,* **deīs, diīs, dīs.**

THIRD DECLENSION

470.   (1) CONSONANT STEMS

a. MASCULINE OR FEMININE

	dux, *m.*	cōnsul, *m.*	ōrātor, *m.*	lēx, *f.*	ōrātiō, *f.*
	leader	consul	orator	law	speech

Singular

Nom.	dux	cōnsul	ōrātŏr	lēx	ōrātiō
Gen.	ducis	cōnsulis	ōrātōris	lēgis	ōrātiōnis
Dat.	ducī	cōnsulī	ōrātōrī	lēgī	ōrātiōnī
Acc.	ducem	cōnsulem	ōrātōrem	lēgem	ōrātiōnem
Abl.	duce	cōnsule	ōrātōre	lēge	ōrātiōne

Plural

Nom.	ducēs	cōnsulēs	ōrātōrēs	lēgēs	ōrātiōnēs
Gen.	ducum	cōnsulum	ōrātōrum	lēgum	ōrātiōnum
Dat.	ducibus	cōnsulibus	ōrātōribus	lēgibus	ōrātiōnibus
Acc.	ducēs	cōnsulēs	ōrātōrēs	lēgēs	ōrātiōnēs
Abl.	ducibus	cōnsulibus	ōrātōribus	lēgibus	ōrātiōnibus

b. NEUTER

flūmen, *n.* river   corpus, *n.* body

	Singular	*Plural*	*Singular*	*Plural*
Nom.	flūmen	flūmina	corpus	corpora
Gen.	flūminis	flūminum	corporis	corporum
Dat.	flūminī	flūminibus	corporī	corporibus
Acc.	flūmen	flūmina	corpus	corpora
Abl.	flūmine	flūminibus	corpore	corporibus

471.   (2) I-STEMS

a. MASCULINE OR FEMININE   *b.* NEUTER

cīvis, *m.*	urbs, *f.*	animal, *n.*	mare, *n.*
citizen	city	animal	sea

	Singular		*Singular*	
Nom.	cīvis	urbs	animal	mare
Gen.	cīvis	urbis	animālis	maris
Dat.	cīvī	urbī	animālī	marī
Acc.	cīvem	urbem	animal	mare
Abl.	cīve	urbe	animālī	marī

	Plural		*Plural*	
Nom.	cīvēs	urbēs	animālia	maria
Gen.	cīvium	urbium	animālium	——
Dat.	cīvibus	urbibus	animālibus	maribus
Acc.	cīvēs, -īs	urbēs, -īs	animālia	maria
Abl.	cīvibus	urbibus	animālibus	maribus

The stem ends in a consonant or -i. I-stems include the following: nouns ending in -is or -ēs and having the same number of syllables in the genitive, **nāvis**; nouns ending in **-ns** or **-rs**, **adulēscēns, ars**; neuters ending in -e, -al, or -ar, **vectīgal**; and monosyllables ending in -s or -x preceded by a consonant, **urbs, arx**.

The locative singular regularly ends in -ī: **rūrī,** *in the country.*

Turris and a few proper nouns may have an accusative singular in **-im.**

Ignis, turris, nāvis, fīnis, and a few other i-stems may have either -ī or -e in the ablative singular.

472.   (3) NOUNS OF IRREGULAR DECLENSION

vīs, *f.*	**iter,** *n.*	**senex,** *m.*	**Iuppiter,** *m.*	**nēmō,** *m.*
strength	road	old man	Jupiter	no one

			Singular		
Nom.	vīs	iter	senex	Iuppiter	nēmō
Gen.	(vīs)	itineris	senis	Iovis	(nūllīus)
Dat.	(vī)	itinerī	senī	Iovī	nēminī
Acc.	vim	iter	senem	Iovem	nēminem
Abl.	vī	itinere	sene	Iove	(nūllō)

			Plural		
Nom.	vīrēs	itinera	senēs	——	——
Gen.	vīrium	itinerum	senum	——	——
Dat.	vīribus	itineribus	senibus	——	——
Acc.	vīrēs, -īs	itinera	senibus	——	——
Abl.	vīribus	itineribus	senēs	——	——

473.   FOURTH DECLENSION

exercitus, *m.* exercise   **domus,** *f.* house   **cornū,** *n.* horn

		Singular	
Nom.	exercitus	domus	cornū
Gen.	exercitūs	domūs, -ī	cornūs
Dat.	exercituī	domuī, -ō	cornū
Acc.	exercitum	domum	cornū
Abl.	exercitū	domū, -ō	cornū

Plural

Nom.	exercitūs	domūs	cornua
Gen.	exercituum	domuum, -ōrum	cornuum
Dat.	exercitibus	domibus	cornibus
Acc.	exercitūs	domūs, -ōs	cornua
Abl.	exercitibus	domibus	cornibus

The stem ends in -u.
Fourth declension nouns ending in -us are regularly masculine except **domus**, **Īdūs**, and **manus**; those in -ū are neuter.
The locative of **domus** is **domī**.

474. FIFTH DECLENSION

diēs, *m.* day   rēs, *f.* thing

	S.	Pl.	S.	Pl.
Nom.	diēs	diēs	rēs	rēs
Gen.	diēī	diērum	reī	rērum
Dat.	diēī	diēbus	reī	rēbus
Acc.	diem	diēs	rem	rēs
Abl.	diē	diēbus	rē	rēbus

The stem ends in -ē.
The gender is regularly feminine. **Diēs** is masculine or feminine in the singular, but feminine only when used in the sense of an appointed day.
The genitive and dative singular ending -ēī becomes -eī when preceded by a consonant: **fideī**.

ADJECTIVES

475. FIRST AND SECOND DECLENSIONS

a. ADJECTIVES ENDING IN *-US, -A, -UM*

lātus wide

	Singular			Plural		
	MASC.	FEM.	NEUTER	MASC.	FEM.	NEUTER
Nom.	lātus	lāta	lātum	lātī	lātae	lāta
Gen.	lātī	lātae	lātī	lātōrum	lātārum	lātōrum
Dat.	lātō	lātae	lātō	lātīs	lātīs	lātīs
Acc.	lātum	lātam	lātum	lātōs	lātās	lāta
Abl.	lātō	lātā	lātō	lātīs	lātīs	lātīs

b. ADJECTIVES ENDING IN *-ER, -ERA, -ERUM*

līber free

	Singular			Plural		
	MASC.	FEM.	NEUTER	MASC.	FEM.	NEUTER
Nom.	līber	lībera	līberum	līberī	līberae	lībera
Gen.	līberī	līberae	līberī	līberōrum	līberārum	līberōrum
Dat.	līberō	līberae	līberō	līberīs	līberīs	līberīs
Acc.	līberum	līberam	līberum	līberōs	līberās	lībera
Abl.	līberō	līberā	līberō	līberīs	līberīs	līberīs

c. ADJECTIVES ENDING IN -ER, -RA, -RUM

pulcher beautiful

	Singular			Plural	
	MASC.	FEM.	NEUTER	MASC.	FEM.	NEUTER
Nom.	pulcher	pulchra	pulchrum	pulchrī	pulchrae	pulchra
Gen.	pulchrī	pulchrae	pulchrī	pulchrōrum	pulchrārum	pulchrōrum
Dat.	pulchrō	pulchrae	pulchrō	pulchrīs	pulchrīs	pulchrīs
Acc.	pulchrum	pulchram	pulchrum	pulchrōs	pulchrās	pulchra
Abl.	pulchrō	pulchrā	pulchrō	pulchrīs	pulchrīs	pulchrīs

476.   THIRD DECLENSION

a. ADJECTIVES OF THREE ENDINGS

ācer keen, sharp

	Singular			Plural	
	MASC.	FEM.	NEUTER	MASC.	FEM.	NEUTER
Nom.	ācer	ācris	ācre	ācrēs	ācrēs	ācria
Gen.	ācris	ācris	ācris	ācrium	ācrium	ācrium
Dat.	ācrī	ācrī	ācrī	ācribus	ācribus	ācribus
Acc.	ācrem	ācrem	ācre	ācrēs, -īs	ācrēs, -īs	ācria
Abl.	ācrī	ācrī	ācrī	ācribus	ācribus	ācribus

b. ADJECTIVES OF TWO ENDINGS

omnis all

	Singular		Plural	
	MASC. OR FEM.	NEUTER	MASC. OR FEM.	NEUTER
Nom.	omnis	omne	omnēs	omnia
Gen.	omnis	omnis	omnium	omnium
Dat.	omnī	omnī	omnibus	omnibus
Acc.	omnem	omne	omnēs, -īs	omnia
Abl.	omnī	omnī	omnibus	omnibus

c. ADJECTIVES OF ONE ENDING

audāx bold

	Singular		Plural	
	MASC. OR FEM.	NEUTER	MASC. OR FEM.	NEUTER
Nom.	audāx	audāx	audācēs	audācia
Gen.	audācis	audācis	audācium	audācium
Dat.	audācī	audācī	audācibus	audācibus
Acc.	audācem	audāx	audācēs, -īs	audācia
Abl.	audācī	audācī	audācibus	audācibus

potēns powerful

	Singular		Plural	
	MASC. OR FEM.	NEUTER	MASC. OR FEM.	NEUTER
Nom.	potēns	potēns	potentēs	potentia
Gen.	potentis	potentis	potentium	potentium
Dat.	potentī	potentī	potentibus	potentibus
Acc.	potentem	potēns	potentēs, -īs	potentia
Abl.	potentī, -e	potentī, -e	potentibus	potentibus

477. DECLENSION OF PRESENT ACTIVE PARTICIPLES

portāns carrying

	Singular		*Plural*	
	MASC. OR FEM.	NEUTER	MASC. OR FEM.	NEUTER
Nom.	portāns	portāns	portantēs	portantia
Gen.	portantis	portantis	portantium	portantium
Dat.	portantī	portantī	portantibus	portantibus
Acc.	portantem	portāns	portantēs, -īs	portantia
Abl.	portante, -ī	portante, -ī	portantibus	portantibus

The ablative singular of a present participle, when used as an adjective, ends in -ī.

478. ADJECTIVES OF SPECIAL DECLENSION

ūnus one   alter the other

	Singular			*Singular*		
	MASC.	FEM.	NEUTER	MASC.	FEM.	NEUTER
Nom.	ūnus	ūna	ūnum	alter	altera	alterum
Gen.	ūnīus	ūnīus	ūnīus	alterīus	alterīus	alterīus
Dat.	ūnī	ūnī	ūnī	alterī	alterī	alterī
Acc.	ūnum	ūnam	ūnum	alterum	alteram	alterum
Abl.	ūnō	ūnā	ūnō	alterō	alterā	alterō

Nine adjectives have -īus in the genitive singular and -ī in the dative singular : alius, alia, aliud ; alter, altera, alterum ; neuter, neutra, neutrum ; nūllus, -a, -um ; sōlus, -a, -um ; tōtus, -a, -um ; ūllus, -a, -um ; ūnus, -a, -um ; and uter, utra, utrum. They are declined in the plural like lātus.

vetus old   plūs more

	Singular		*Plural*		*Singular*	*Plural*	
	MASC. OR FEM.	NEUTER	MASC. OR FEM.	NEUTER	NEUTER	MASC. OR FEM.	NEUTER
Nom.	vetus	vetus	veterēs	vetera	plūs	plūrēs	plūra
Gen.	veteris	veteris	veterum	veterum	plūris	plūrium	plūrium
Dat.	veterī	veterī	veteribus	veteribus	——	plūribus	plūribus
Acc.	veterem	vetus	veterēs	vetera	plūs	plūrēs	plūra
Abl.	vetere	vetere	veteribus	veteribus	plūre	plūribus	plūribus

duo two   trēs three   mīlle thousand

	Plural			*Plural*		*Singular*	*Plural*
	MASC.	FEM.	NEUTER	MASC. OR FEM.	NEUTER		
Nom.	duo	duae	duo	trēs	tria	mīlle	mīlia
Gen.	duōrum	duārum	duōrum	trium	trium	mīlle	mīlium
Dat.	duōbus	duābus	duōbus	tribus	tribus	mīlle	mīlibus
Acc.	duōs	duās	duo	trēs, trīs	tria	mīlle	mīlia
Abl.	duōbus	duābus	duōbus	tribus	tribus	mīlle	mīlibus

In the singular plūs has no masculine or feminine forms.

479.   REGULAR COMPARISON OF ADJECTIVES

Positive	Comparative	Superlative
lātus, -a, -um wide	lātior, lātius wider	lātissimus, -a, -um widest
fortis, -e brave	fortior, fortius braver	fortissimus, -a, -um bravest
audāx bold	audācior, audācius bolder	audācissimus, -a, -um boldest
potēns powerful	potentior, potentius more powerful	potentissimus, -a, -um most powerful
līber, -era, -erum free	līberior, līberius freer	līberrimus, -a, -um freest
pulcher, pulchra, pulchrum beautiful	pulchrior, pulchrius more beautiful	pulcherrimus, -a, -um most beautiful
ācer, ācris, ācre sharp	ācrior, ācrius sharper	ācerrimus, -a, -um sharpest
facilis, -e easy	facilior, facilius easier	facillimus, -a, -um easiest

Adjectives ending in -er are compared like **līber**.
Difficilis, dissimilis, humilis, and **similis** are compared like **facilis.**

480.   IRREGULAR COMPARISON OF ADJECTIVES

Positive	Comparative	Superlative
bonus, -a, -um good	melior, melius better	optimus, -a, -um best
malus, -a, -um bad	peior, peius worse	pessimus, -a, -um worst
magnus, -a, -um great	maior, maius greater	maximus, -a, -um greatest
parvus, -a, -um small	minor, minus smaller	minimus, -a, -um smallest
multus, -a, -um much	——, plūs more	plūrimus, -a, -um most

The irregular comparison of other adjectives is indicated in the LATIN-ENGLISH VOCABULARY.

481.   DECLENSION OF THE COMPARATIVE OF ADJECTIVES

audācior bolder

	Singular		Plural	
	MASC. OR FEM.	NEUTER	MASC. OR FEM.	NEUTER
Nom.	audācior	audācius	audāciōrēs	audāciōra
Gen.	audāciōris	audāciōris	audāciōrum	audāciōrum
Dat.	audāciōrī	audāciōrī	audāciōribus	audāciōribus
Acc.	audāciōrem	audācius	audāciōrēs	audāciōra
Abl.	audāciōre	audāciōre	audāciōribus	audāciōribus

ADVERBS

482.   REGULAR COMPARISON OF ADVERBS

Positive	Comparative	Superlative
lātē widely	lātius	lātissimē
miserē miserably	miserius	miserrimē
pulchrē beautifully	pulchrius	pulcherrimē
fortiter bravely	fortius	fortissimē
ācriter sharply	ācrius	ācerrimē
facile easily	facilius	facillimē

483. IRREGULAR COMPARISON OF ADVERBS

Positive		Comparative		Superlative	
bene	well	melius	better	optimē	best
male	badly	peius	worse	pessimē	worst
magnopere	greatly	magis	more	maximē	most
multum	much	plūs	more	plūrimum	most
parum	little	minus	less	minimē	least
diū	long (*in time*)	diūtius	longer	diūtissimē	longest
prope	near	propius	nearer	proximē	next
saepe	often	saepius	oftener	saepissimē	oftenest

484. NUMERALS

ROMAN NUMERALS	CARDINALS		ORDINALS	
I	ūnus, -a, -um	one	prīmus, -a, -um	first
II	duo, duae, duo	two	secundus, -a, -um; *or*	
			alter, altera, alterum	second
III	trēs, tria	three	tertius, -a, -um	third
IV	quattuor	four	quārtus, -a, -um	fourth
V	quīnque	five	quīntus, -a, -um	fifth
VI	sex	etc.	sextus	etc.
VII	septem		septimus	
VIII	octō		octāvus	
IX	novem		nōnus	
X	decem		decimus	
XI	ūndecim		ūndecimus	
XII	duodecim		duodecimus	
XIII	tredecim		tertius decimus	
XIV	quattuordecim		quārtus decimus	
XV	quīndecim		quīntus decimus	
XVI	sēdecim		sextus decimus	
XVII	septendecim		septimus decimus	
XVIII	duodēvīgintī		duodēvīcēsimus	
XIX	ūndēvīgintī		ūndēvīcēsimus	
XX	vīgintī		vīcēsimus	
XXI	vīgintī ūnus		vīcēsimus prīmus	
XXX	trīgintā		trīcēsimus	
XL	quadrāgintā		quadrāgēsimus	
L	quīnquāgintā		quīnquāgēsimus	
LX	sexāgintā		sexāgēsimus	
LXX	septuāgintā		septuāgēsimus	
LXXX	octōgintā		octōgēsimus	
XC	nōnāgintā		nōnāgēsimus	
C	centum		centēsimus	
CI	centum (et) ūnus		centēsimus (et) prīmus	
CXXI	centum vīgintī ūnus		centēsimus vīcēsimus prīmus	
CC	ducentī, -ae, -a		ducentēsimus	
CCC	trecentī		trecentēsimus	

Roman Numerals	Cardinals	Ordinals
CCCC	quadringentī	quadringentēsimus
D	quīngentī	quīngentēsimus
DC	sescentī	sescentēsimus
DCC	septingentī	septingentēsimus
DCCC	octingentī	octingentēsimus
DCCCC	nōngentī	nōngentēsimus
M	mīlle	mīllēsimus
MC	mīlle centum	mīllēsimus centēsimus
MM	duo mīlia	bis (= twice) mīllēsimus

PRONOUNS

485.   PERSONAL   **486.** REFLEXIVE

ego I   tū you   suī of himself, etc.

	Sing.	Pl.	Sing.	Pl.	Sing.	Pl.
Nom.	ego	nōs	tū	vōs	——	——
Gen.	meī	nostrum, -trī	tuī	vestrum, -trī	suī	suī
Dat.	mihi	nōbīs	tibi	vōbīs	sibi	sibi
Acc.	mē	nōs	tē	vōs	sē, sēsē	sē, sēsē
Abl.	mē	nōbīs	tē	vōbīs	sē, sēsē	sē, sēsē

The demonstrative **is,** *he,* **ea,** *she,* **id,** *it* (**561,** *b*) is used as the personal pronoun of the third person.

Reflexive pronouns have no nominative. In the first and second persons, they have the same forms as the gen., dat., acc., and abl. of the personal pronouns.

Meus, noster, tuus, vester, and **suus,** the possessive forms of the personal and reflexive pronouns, are declined like adjectives of the first and second declensions.

487.   DEMONSTRATIVE

is this, that, he, she, it

	Singular			*Plural*		
	Masc.	Fem.	Neuter	Masc.	Fem.	Neuter
Nom.	is	ea	id	eī	eae	ea
Gen.	eius	eius	eius	eōrum	eārum	eōrum
Dat.	eī	eī	eī	eīs (iīs)	eīs (iīs)	eīs (iīs)
Acc.	eum	eam	id	eōs	eās	ea
Abl.	eō	eā	eō	eīs (iīs)	eīs (iīs)	eīs (iīs)

hic this

	Singular			*Plural*		
	Masc.	Fem.	Neuter	Masc.	Fem.	Neuter
Nom.	hic	haec	hoc	hī	hae	haec
Gen.	huius	huius	huius	hōrum	hārum	hōrum
Dat.	huic	huic	huic	hīs	hīs	hīs
Acc.	hunc	hanc	hoc	hōs	hās	haec
Abl.	hōc	hāc	hōc	hīs	hīs	hīs

ille that

	Singular			*Plural*		
	MASC.	**FEM.**	**NEUTER**	**MASC.**	**FEM.**	**NEUTER**
Nom.	ille	illa	illud	illī	illae	illa
Gen.	illīus	illīus	illīus	illōrum	illārum	illōrum
Dat.	illī	illī	illī	illīs	illīs	illīs
Acc.	illum	illam	illud	illōs	illās	illa
Abl.	illō	illā	illō	illīs	illīs	illīs

Iste, ista, istud, *that (of yours)*, is declined like ille, illa, illud.

īdem the same

	Singular			*Plural*		
	MASC.	**FEM.**	**NEUTER**	**MASC.**	**FEM.**	**NEUTER**
Nom.	īdem	eadem	idem	eīdem, īdem	eaedem	eadem
Gen.	eiusdem	eiusdem	eiusdem	eōrundem	eārundem	eōrundem
Dat.	eīdem	eīdem	eīdem	eīsdem (īsdem)	eīsdem (īsdem)	eīsdem (īsdem)
Acc.	eundem	eandem	idem	eōsdem	eāsdem	eadem
Abl.	eōdem	eādem	eōdem	eīsdem (īsdem)	eīsdem (īsdem)	eīsdem (īsdem)

488. INTENSIVE

ipse self

	Singular			*Plural*		
	MASC.	**FEM.**	**NEUTER**	**MASC.**	**FEM.**	**NEUTER**
Nom.	ipse	ipsa	ipsum	ipsī	ipsae	ipsa
Gen.	ipsīus	ipsīus	ipsīus	ipsōrum	ipsārum	ipsōrum
Dat.	ipsī	ipsī	ipsī	ipsīs	ipsīs	ipsīs
Acc.	ipsum	ipsam	ipsum	ipsōs	ipsās	ipsa
Abl.	ipsō	ipsā	ipsō	ipsīs	ipsīs	ipsīs

489. RELATIVE

quī who, which, that

	Singular			*Plural*		
	MASC.	**FEM.**	**NEUTER**	**MASC.**	**FEM.**	**NEUTER**
Nom.	quī	quae	quod	quī	quae	quae
Gen.	cuius	cuius	cuius	quōrum	quārum	quōrum
Dat.	cui	cui	cui	quibus	quibus	quibus
Acc.	quem	quam	quod	quōs	quās	quae
Abl.	quō	quā	quō	quibus	quibus	quibus

490. INTERROGATIVE

quis who? which? what?

Singular

MASC. OR FEM.		NEUTER
Nom.	quis	quid
Gen.	cuius	cuius
Dat.	cui	cui
Acc.	quem	quid
Abl.	quō	quō

The plural of the interrogative **quis** is like that of the relative **quī**.
The interrogative adjective is **quī, quae, quod.** It is declined like the relative **quī.**

491. INDEFINITE

	Singular			*Plural*	
MASC. OR FEM.	NEUTER	MASC.	FEM.	NEUTER
Nom. aliquis	aliquid	aliquī	aliquae	aliqua
Gen. alicuius	alicuius	aliquōrum	aliquārum	aliquōrum
Dat. alicui	alicui	aliquibus	aliquibus	aliquibus
Acc. aliquem	aliquid	aliquōs	aliquās	aliqua
Abl. aliquō	aliquō	aliquibus	aliquibus	aliquibus

Singular

	MASC.	FEM.	NEUTER
Nom.	quīdam	quaedam	quiddam
Gen.	cuiusdam	cuiusdam	cuiusdam
Dat.	cuidam	cuidam	cuidam
Acc.	quendam	quandam	quiddam
Abl.	quōdam	quādam	quōdam

Plural

Nom.	quīdam	quaedam	quaedam
Gen.	quōrundam	quārundam	quōrundam
Dat.	quibusdam	quibusdam	quibusdam
Acc.	quōsdam	quāsdam	quaedam
Abl.	quibusdam	quibusdam	quibusdam

	Singular			*Singular*	
MASC. OR FEM.	NEUTER	MASC. OR FEM.	NEUTER
Nom. quisquam	quicquam	quisque	quidque
Gen. cuiusquam	cuiusquam	cuiusque	cuiusque
Dat. cuiquam	cuiquam	cuique	cuique
Acc. quemquam	quicquam	quemque	quidque
Abl. quōquam	quōquam	quōque	quōque

The indefinite pronouns are **aliquis, quīdam, quīlibet, quispiam, quisquam, quisque,** and **quīvīs.**

Quis and **quid** are used as indefinites after **sī, nisi, nē,** and **num.** They are declined like the interrogative **quis.** Their corresponding adjective form **quī** is declined like the relative **quī**, but the adjective form usually has **qua** for **quae** except in the nominative plural feminine.

The adjective form of **aliquis, -quid** is **aliquī, -qua, -quod.**

Quoddam is the adjective form of **quiddam.**

Quisquam has no plural. **Quisque** is seldom used in the plural. When used as an adjective, its form is **quisque, quaeque, quodque.**

CONJUGATION OF VERBS

492.
REGULAR VERBS

	Principal Parts		*Stems*
1st Conj.:	portō, portāre, portāvī, portātus	carry	portā-; portāv-; portāt-
2nd Conj.:	videō, vidēre, vīdī, vīsus	see	vidē-; vīd-; vīs-
3rd Conj.:	mittō, mittere, mīsī, missus	send	mittē-; mīs-; miss-
3rd Conj. (-iō):	capiō, capere, cēpī, captus	take	cape-; cēp-; capt-
4th Conj.:	audiō, audīre, audīvī, audītus	hear	audī-; audīv-; audīt-

INDICATIVE

Active Voice

Present Tense

I carry, am carrying, etc.	I see, am seeing, etc.	I send, am sending, etc.	I take, am taking, etc.	I hear, am hearing, etc.
portō	videō	mittō	capiō	audiō
portās	vidēs	mittis	capis	audīs
portat	videt	mittit	capit	audit
portāmus	vidēmus	mittimus	capimus	audīmus
portātis	vidētis	mittitis	capitis	audītis
portant	vident	mittunt	capiunt	audiunt

Imperfect Tense

I carried, was carrying, etc.	I saw, was seeing, etc.	I sent, was sending, etc.	I took, was taking, etc.	I heard, was hearing, etc.
portābam	vidēbam	mittēbam	capiēbam	audiēbam
portābās	vidēbās	mittēbās	capiēbās	audiēbās
portābat	vidēbat	mittēbat	capiēbat	audiēbat
portābāmus	vidēbāmus	mittēbāmus	capiēbāmus	audiēbāmus
portābātis	vidēbātis	mittēbātis	capiēbātis	audiēbātis
portābant	vidēbant	mittēbant	capiēbant	audiēbant

Future Tense

I shall carry, etc.	I shall see, etc.	I shall send, etc.	I shall take, etc.	I shall hear, etc.
portābō	vidēbō	mittam	capiam	audiam
portābis	vidēbis	mittēs	capiēs	audiēs
portābit	vidēbit	mittet	capiet	audiet
portābimus	vidēbimus	mittēmus	capiēmus	audiēmus
portābitis	vidēbitis	mittētis	capiētis	audiētis
portābunt	vidēbunt	mittent	capient	audient

PERFECT TENSE

I have carried, carried, etc.	I have seen, saw, etc.	I have sent, sent, etc.	I have taken, took, etc.	I have heard, heard, etc.
portāvī	vīdī	mīsī	cēpī	audīvī
portāvistī	vīdistī	mīsistī	cēpistī	audīvistī
portāvit	vīdit	mīsit	cēpit	audīvit
portāvimus	vīdimus	mīsimus	cēpimus	audīvimus
portāvistis	vīdistis	mīsistis	cēpistis	audīvistis
portāvērunt, -ēre	vīdērunt, -ēre	mīsērunt, -ēre	cēpērunt, -ēre	audīvērunt, -ēre

PAST PERFECT TENSE

I had carried, etc.	I had seen, etc.	I had sent, etc.	I had taken, etc.	I had heard, etc.
portāveram	vīderam	mīseram	cēperam	audīveram
portāverās	vīderās	mīserās	cēperās	audīverās
portāverat	vīderat	mīserat	cēperat	audīverat
portāverāmus	vīderāmus	mīserāmus	cēperāmus	audīverāmus
portāverātis	vīderātis	mīserātis	cēperātis	audīverātis
portāverant	vīderant	mīserant	cēperant	audīverant

FUTURE PERFECT TENSE

I shall have carried, etc.	I shall have seen, etc.	I shall have sent, etc.	I shall have taken, etc.	I shall have heard, etc.
portāverō	vīderō	mīserō	cēperō	audīverō
portāveris	vīderis	mīseris	cēperis	audīveris
portāverit	vīderit	mīserit	cēperit	audīverit
portāverimus	vīderimus	mīserimus	cēperimus	audīverimus
portāveritis	vīderitis	mīseritis	cēperitis	audīveritis
portāverint	vīderint	mīserint	cēperint	audīverint

SUBJUNCTIVE

Active Voice

PRESENT TENSE

portem	videam	mittam	capiam	audiam
portēs	videās	mittās	capiās	audiās
portet	videat	mittat	capiat	audiat
portēmus	videāmus	mittāmus	capiāmus	audiāmus
portētis	videātis	mittātis	capiātis	audiātis
portent	videant	mittant	capiant	audiant

IMPERFECT TENSE

portārem	vidērem	mitterem	caperem	audīrem
portārēs	vidērēs	mitterēs	caperēs	audīrēs
portāret	vidēret	mitteret	caperet	audīret
portārēmus	vidērēmus	mitterēmus	caperēmus	audīrēmus
portārētis	vidērētis	mitterētis	caperētis	audīrētis
portārent	vidērent	mitterent	caperent	audīrent

PERFECT TENSE

portāverim	vīderim	mīserim	cēperim	audīverim
portāveris	vīderis	mīseris	cēperis	audīveris
portāverit	vīderit	mīserit	cēperit	audīverit
portāverīmus	vīderīmus	mīserīmus	cēperīmus	audīverīmus
portāverītis	vīderītis	mīserītis	cēperītis	audīverītis
portāverint	vīderint	mīserint	cēperint	audīverint

PAST PERFECT TENSE

portāvissem	vīdissem	mīsissem	cēpissem	audīvissem
portāvissēs	vīdissēs	mīsissēs	cēpissēs	audīvissēs
portāvisset	vīdisset	mīsisset	cēpisset	audīvisset
portāvissēmus	vīdissēmus	mīsissēmus	cēpissēmus	audīvissēmus
portāvissētis	vīdissētis	mīsissētis	cēpissētis	audīvissētis
portāvissent	vīdissent	mīsissent	cēpissent	audīvissent

IMPERATIVE

PRESENT

Singular

portā carry (thou)	vidē see (thou)	mitte send (thou)	cape take (thou)	audī hear (thou)

Plural

portāte carry (ye)	vidēte see (ye)	mittite send (ye)	capite take (ye)	audīte hear (ye)

FUTURE

Singular

2nd portātō thou shalt carry	vidētō thou shalt see	mittitō thou shalt send	capitō thou shalt take	audītō thou shalt hear
3rd portātō he shall carry	vidētō he shall see	mittitō he shall send	capitō he shall take	audītō he shall hear

Plural

2nd portātōte ye shall carry	vidētōte ye shall see	mittitōte ye shall send	capitōte ye shall take	audītōte ye shall hear
3rd portantō they shall carry	videntō they shall see	mittuntō they shall send	capiuntō they shall take	audiuntō they shall hear

INFINITIVE

PRESENT

portāre to carry	vidēre to see	mittere to send	capere to take	audīre to hear

PERFECT

portāvisse to have carried	vīdisse to have seen	mīsisse to have sent	cēpisse to have taken	audīvisse to have heard

FUTURE

portātūrus esse to be about to carry	vīsūrus esse to be about to see	missūrus esse to be about to send	captūrus esse to be about to take	audītūrus esse to be about to hear

PARTICIPLE

PRESENT

portāns, -antis carrying	vidēns, -entis seeing	mittēns, -entis sending	capiēns, -entis taking	audiēns, -entis hearing

FUTURE

portātūrus, -a, -um about to carry	vīsūrus, -a, -um about to see	missūrus, -a, -um about to send	captūrus, -a, -um about to take	audītūrus, -a, -um about to hear

GERUND

Gen.	portandī of carrying	videndī of seeing	mittendī of sending	capiendī of taking	audiendī of hearing
Dat.	portandō for carrying	videndō for seeing	mittendō for sending	capiendō for taking	audiendō for hearing
Acc.	portandum carrying	videndum seeing	mittendum sending	capiendum taking	audiendum hearing
Abl.	portandō by carrying	videndō by seeing	mittendō by sending	capiendō by taking	audiendō by hearing

SUPINE

Acc.	portātum to carry	vīsum to see	missum to send	captum to take	audītum to hear
Abl.	portātū to carry	vīsū to see	missū to send	captū to take	audītū to hear

INDICATIVE

Passive Voice

PRESENT TENSE

I am carried, etc.	I am seen, etc.	I am sent, etc.	I am taken, etc.	I am heard, etc.
portor	videor	mittor	capior	audior
portāris, -re	vidēris, -re	mitteris, -re	caperis, -re	audīris, -re
portātur	vidētur	mittitur	capitur	audītur
portāmur	vidēmur	mittimur	capimur	audīmur
portāminī	vidēminī	mittiminī	capiminī	audīminī
portantur	videntur	mittuntur	capiuntur	audiuntur

pleorothyallthaus (handwritten)

IMPERFECT TENSE

I was carried, etc.	I was seen, etc.	I was sent, etc.	I was taken, etc.	I was heard, etc.
portābar	vidēbar	mittēbar	capiēbar	audiēbar
portābāris, -re	vidēbāris, -re	mittēbāris, -re	capiēbāris, -re	audiēbāris, -re
portābātur	vidēbātur	mittēbātur	capiēbātur	audiēbātur
portābāmur	vidēbāmur	mittēbāmur	capiēbāmur	audiēbāmur
portābāminī	vidēbāminī	mittēbāminī	capiēbāminī	audiēbāminī
portābantur	vidēbantur	mittēbantur	capiēbantur	audiēbantur

FUTURE TENSE

I shall be carried, etc.	I shall be seen, etc.	I shall be sent, etc.	I shall be taken, etc.	I shall be heard, etc.
portābor	vidēbor	mittar	capiar	audiar
portāberis, -re	vidēberis, -re	mittēris, -re	capiēris, -re	audiēris, -re
portābitur	vidēbitur	mittētur	capiētur	audiētur
portābimur	vidēbimur	mittēmur	capiēmur	audiēmur
portābiminī	vidēbiminī	mittēminī	capiēminī	audiēminī
portābuntur	vidēbuntur	mittentur	capientur	audientur

PERFECT TENSE

I have been (was) carried, etc.	I have been seen, etc.	I have been sent, etc.	I have been taken, etc.	I have been heard, etc.
portātus sum	vīsus sum	missus sum	captus sum	audītus sum
portātus es	vīsus es	missus es	captus es	audītus es
portātus est	vīsus est	missus est	captus est	audītus est
portātī sumus	vīsī sumus	missī sumus	captī sumus	audītī sumus
portātī estis	vīsī estis	missī estis	captī estis	audītī estis
portātī sunt	vīsī sunt	missī sunt	captī sunt	audītī sunt

PAST PERFECT TENSE

I had been carried, etc.	I had been seen, etc.	I had been sent, etc.	I had been taken, etc.	I had been heard, etc.
portātus eram	vīsus eram	missus eram	captus eram	audītus eram
portātus erās	vīsus erās	missus erās	captus erās	audītus erās
portātus erat	vīsūs erat	missus erat	captus erat	audītus erat
portātī erāmus	vīsī erāmus	missī erāmus	captī erāmus	audītī erāmus
portātī erātis	vīsī erātis	missī erātis	captī erātis	audītī erātis
portātī erant	vīsī erant	missī erant	captī erant	audītī erant

FUTURE PERFECT TENSE

I shall have been carried, etc.	I shall have been seen, etc.	I shall have been sent, etc.	I shall have been taken, etc.	I shall have been heard, etc.
portātus erō	vīsus erō	missus erō	captus erō	audītus erō
portātus eris	vīsus eris	missus eris	captus eris	audītus eris
portātus erit	vīsus erit	missus erit	captus erit	audītus erit
portātī erimus	vīsī erimus	missī erimus	captī erimus	audītī erimus
portātī eritis	vīsī eritis	missī eritis	captī eritis	audītī eritis
portātī erunt	vīsī erunt	missī erunt	captī erunt	audītī erunt

SUBJUNCTIVE

Passive Voice

PRESENT TENSE

porter	videar	mittar	capiar	audiar
portēris, -re	videāris, -re	mittāris, -re	capiāris, -re	audiāris, -re
portētur	videātur	mittātur	capiātur	audiātur
portēmur	videāmur	mittāmur	capiāmur	audiāmur
portēminī	videāminī	mittāminī	capiāminī	audiāminī
portentur	videantur	mittantur	capiantur	audiantur

IMPERFECT TENSE

portārer	vidērer	mitterer	caperer	audīrer
portārēris, -re	vidērēris, -re	mitterēris, -re	caperēris, -re	audīrēris, -re
portārētur	vidērētur	mitterētur	caperētur	audīrētur
portārēmur	vidērēmur	mitterēmur	caperēmur	audīrēmur
portārēminī	vidērēminī	mitterēminī	caperēminī	audīrēminī
portārentur	vidērentur	mitterentur	caperentur	audīrentur

PERFECT

portātus sim	vīsus sim	missus sim	captus sim	audītus sim
portātus sīs	vīsus sīs	missus sīs	captus sīs	audītus sīs
portātus sit	vīsus sit	missus sit	captus sit	audītus sit
portātī sīmus	vīsī sīmus	missī sīmus	captī sīmus	audītī sīmus
portātī sītis	vīsī sītis	missī sītis	captī sītis	audītī sītis
portātī sint	vīsī sint	missī sint	captī sint	audītī sint

PAST PERFECT TENSE

portātus essem	vīsus essem	missus essem	captus essem	audītus essem
portātus essēs	vīsus essēs	missus essēs	captus essēs	audītus essēs
portātus esset	vīsus esset	missus esset	captus esset	audītus esset
portātī essēmus	vīsī essēmus	missī essēmus	captī essēmus	audītī essēmus
portātī essētis	vīsī essētis	missī essētis	captī essētis	audītī essētis
portātī essent	vīsī essent	missī essent	captī essent	audītī essent

IMPERATIVE

PRESENT

Singular

portāre be (thou) carried	vidēre be (thou) seen	mittere be (thou) sent	capere be (thou) taken	audīre be (thou) heard

Plural

portāminī be (ye) carried	vidēminī be (ye) seen	mittiminī be (ye) sent	capiminī be (ye) taken	audīminī be (ye) heard

FUTURE

Singular

2nd **portātor** thou shalt be carried	**vidētor** thou shalt be seen	**mittitor** thou shalt be sent	**capitor** thou shalt be taken	**audītor** thou shalt be heard
3rd **portātor** he shall be carried	**vidētor** he shall be seen	**mittitor** he shall be sent	**capitor** he shall be taken	**audītor** he shall be heard

Plural

3rd **portantor** they shall be carried	**videntor** they shall be seen	**mittuntor** they shall be sent	**capiuntor** they shall be taken	**audiuntor** they shall be heard

INFINITIVE

PRESENT

portārī to be carried	**vidērī** to be seen	**mittī** to be sent	**capī** to be taken	**audīrī** to be heard

PERFECT

portātus esse to have been carried	**vīsus esse** to have been seen	**missus esse** to have been sent	**captus esse** to have been taken	**audītus esse** to have been heard

FUTURE

portātum īrī to be about to be carried	**vīsum īrī** to be about to be seen	**missum īrī** to be about to be sent	**captum īrī** to be about to be taken	**audītum īrī** to be about to be heard

PARTICIPLE

PERFECT

portātus, -a, -um having been carried	**vīsus, -a, -um** having been seen	**missus, -a, -um** having been sent	**captus, -a, -um** having been taken	**audītus, -a, -um** having been heard

FUTURE

portandus, -a, -um to be carried	**videndus, -a, -um** to be seen	**mittendus, -a, -um** to be sent	**capiendus, -a, -um** to be taken	**audiendus, -a, -um** to be heard

493.

DEPONENT VERBS

Principal Parts		*Stems*
1st Conj.:	**cōnor, cōnārī, cōnātus sum** try	cōnā-; cōnāt-
2nd Conj.:	**vereor, verērī, veritus sum** fear	verē-; verit-
3rd Conj.:	**sequor, sequī, secūtus sum** follow	seque-; secūt-
4th Conj.:	**orior, orīrī, ortus sum** rise	orī-; ort-

INDICATIVE

Pres.	cōnor	vereor	sequor	orior
	cōnāris, -re	verēris, -re	sequeris, -re	orīris, -re
	cōnātur	verētur	sequitur	orītur
	cōnāmur	verēmur	sequimur	orīmur
	cōnāminī	verēminī	sequiminī	orīminī
	cōnantur	verentur	sequuntur	oriuntur
Imperf.	cōnābar, etc.	verēbar, etc.	sequēbar, etc.	oriēbar, etc.
Fut.	cōnābor	verēbor	sequar	oriar
Perf.	cōnātus sum	veritus sum	secūtus sum	ortus sum
Past Perf.	cōnātus eram	veritus eram	secūtus eram	ortus eram
Fut. Perf.	cōnātus erō	veritus erō	secūtus erō	ortus erō

SUBJUNCTIVE

Pres.	cōner, etc.	verear, etc.	sequar, etc.	oriar, etc.
Imperf.	cōnārer	verērer	sequerer	orīrer
Perf.	cōnātus sim	veritus sim	secūtus sim	ortus sim
Past Perf.	cōnātus essem	veritus essem	secūtus essem	ortus essem

IMPERATIVE

Pres.	cōnāre	verēre	sequere	orīre
Fut.	cōnātor	verētor	sequitor	orītor

INFINITIVE

Pres.	cōnārī	verērī	sequī	orīrī
Perf.	cōnātus esse	veritus esse	secūtus esse	ortus esse
Fut. Active	cōnātūrus esse	veritūrus esse	secūtūrus esse	ortūrus esse

PARTICIPLE

Pres. Active	cōnāns	verēns	sequēns	oriēns
Fut. Active	cōnātūrus	veritūrus	secūtūrus	ortūrus
Perf.	cōnātus	veritus	secūtus	ortus
Fut.	cōnandus	verendus	sequendus	oriendus

GERUND

Gen.	cōnandī, etc.	verendī, etc.	sequendī, etc.	oriendī, etc.

SUPINE

Acc.	cōnātum	veritum	secūtum	ortum
Abl.	cōnātū	veritū	secūtū	ortū

Note that deponent verbs have the following active forms: future infinitive, present participle, future participle, gerund, and supine. The future passive participle retains its passive meaning and sometimes the perfect passive participle does.

Future active, future passive, and perfect passive participles are declined like **lātus, -a, -um.**

494. ## SEMI-DEPONENT VERBS

Semi-deponent verbs have active forms in the tenses formed on the present system and passive forms with active meanings in those formed on the perfect system: **audeō, audēre, ausus sum.**

495. ## IRREGULAR VERBS

sum be

Principal Parts: **sum, esse, fuī, futūrus**
Stems:　　　　**es- *; fū; fut-**

INDICATIVE

PRESENT	IMPERFECT	FUTURE	PERFECT	PAST PERFECT	FUT. PERFECT
sum	eram	erō	fuī	fueram	fuerō
es	erās	eris	fuistī	fuerās	fueris
est	erat	erit	fuit	fuerat	fuerit
sumus	erāmus	erimus	fuimus	fuerāmus	fuerimus
estis	erātis	eritis	fuistis	fuerātis	fueritis
sunt	erant	erunt	fuērunt, -ēre	fuerant	fuerint

SUBJUNCTIVE

PRESENT	IMPERFECT	PERFECT	PAST PERFECT
sim	essem	fuerim	fuissem
sīs	essēs	fuerīs	fuissēs
sit	esset	fuerit	fuisset
sīmus	essēmus	fuerīmus	fuissēmus
sītis	essētis	fuerītis	fuissētis
sint	essent	fuerint	fuissent

	IMPERATIVE		INFINITIVE		PARTICIPLE
	Sing.	*Pl.*			
Pres. 2nd	es	este	*Pres.*	esse	*Pres.* ——
Fut. 2nd	estō	estōte	*Perf.*	fuisse	*Perf.* ——
3rd	estō	suntō	*Fut.*	futūrus esse, fore	*Fut.* futūrus

496.　　　　　**possum** be able, can

Principal Parts: **possum, posse, potuī, ——**

* The stem **es-** changes to **er-** before a vowel: **erō.**

	INDICATIVE		SUBJUNCTIVE	
	Sing.	*Pl.*	*Sing.*	*Pl.*
Pres.	possum	possumus	possim	possīmus
	potes	potestis	possīs	possītis
	potest	possunt	possit	possint
Imperf.	poteram, etc.	poterāmus, etc.	possem, etc.	possēmus, etc.
Fut.	poterō	poterimus	——	——
Perf.	potuī	potuimus	potuerim	potuerīmus
Past Perf.	potueram	potuerāmus	potuissem	potuissēmus
Fut. Perf.	potuerō	potuerimus	——	——

INFINITIVE

Pres. posse   *Perf.* potuisse

PARTICIPLE

Pres. potēns

497.   ferō   bear, carry, endure

Principal Parts: **ferō, ferre, tulī, lātus**
Stems: **fer-; tul-; lāt-**

Active   Passive

INDICATIVE

	Sing.	*Pl.*	*Sing.*	*Pl.*
Pres.	ferō	ferimus	feror	ferimur
	fers	fertis	ferris, -re	feriminī
	fert	ferunt	fertur	feruntur
Imperf.	ferēbam, etc.		ferēbar, etc.	
Fut.	feram, ferēs, etc.		ferar, ferēris, etc.	
Perf.	tulī		lātus sum	
Past Perf.	tuleram		lātus eram	
Fut. Perf.	tulerō		lātus erō	

SUBJUNCTIVE

Pres.	feram, ferās, etc.		ferar, ferāris, etc.	
Imperf.	ferrem		ferrer	
Perf.	tulerim		lātus sim	
Past Perf.	tulissem		lātus essem	

IMPERATIVE

Pres. 2nd	fer	ferte	ferre	feriminī	
Fut. 2nd	fertō	fertōte	fertor	——	
3rd	fertō	feruntō	fertor	feruntor	

INFINITIVE

Pres.	ferre	ferrī	
Perf.	tulisse	lātus esse	
Fut.	lātūrus esse	lātum īrī	

	Active		Passive

PARTICIPLE

Pres.	ferēns	*Perf.*	lātus
Fut.	lātūrus	*Fut.*	ferendus

GERUND		SUPINE
Gen.	ferendī, etc.	lātum, -ū

498.   fīō be made, become, happen (passive of faciō)

> *Principal Parts:* fīō, fierī, factus sum
> *Stems:*   fī- ; fact-

INDICATIVE			SUBJUNCTIVE		
	Sing.	*Pl.*		*Sing.*	*Pl.*
Pres.	fīō	fīmus	*Pres.*	fīam	fīāmus
	fīs	fītis		fīās	fīātis
	fit	fīunt		fīat	fīant
Imperf.	fīēbam, etc.		*Imperf.*	fierem, etc.	
Fut.	fīam				
Perf.	factus sum		*Perf.*	factus sim	
Past Perf.	factus eram				
Fut. Perf.	factus erō		*Past Perf.*	factus essem	

IMPERATIVE			INFINITIVE		PARTICIPLE	
	Sing.	*Pl.*	*Pres.*	fierī	*Pres.*	——
Pres.	fī	fīte	*Perf.*	factus esse	*Perf.*	factus
			Fut.	factum īrī	*Fut.*	faciendus

GERUND

faciendī, etc.

499.   volō   nōlō   mālō

> *Principal Parts:* volō, velle, voluī, —— be willing, will, wish
> nōlō, nōlle, nōluī, —— be unwilling, will not
> mālō, mālle, māluī, —— be more willing, prefer

INDICATIVE

Pres.	volō	nōlō	mālō
	vīs	nōn vīs	māvīs
	vult	nōn vult	māvult
	volumus	nōlumus	mālumus
	vultis	nōn vultis	māvultis
	volunt	nōlunt	mālunt
Imperf.	volēbam, etc.	nōlēbam, etc.	mālēbam, etc.

Fut.	volam, volēs, etc.	nōlam, nōlēs, etc.	mālam, mālēs, etc.
Perf.	voluī	nōluī	māluī
Past Perf.	volueram	nōlueram	mālueram
Fut. Perf.	voluerō	nōluerō	māluerō

SUBJUNCTIVE

Pres.	velim	nōlim	mālim
Imperf.	vellem	nōllem	māllem
Perf.	voluerim	nōluerim	māluerim
Past Perf.	voluissem	nōluissem	māluissem

IMPERATIVE

Pres.	*2nd*	*Sing.*	——	nōlī	——
	2nd	*Pl.*	——	nōlīte	——

INFINITIVE

Pres.	velle	nōlle	mālle
Perf.	voluisse	nōluisse	māluisse

PARTICIPLE

Pres.	volēns	nōlēns	——

500.

eō   go

Principal Parts: eō, īre, iī or īvī, itus
Stems: ī-; i- or īv-; it-

INDICATIVE			SUBJUNCTIVE	IMPERATIVE		
	Sing.	*Pl.*			*Sing.*	*Pl.*
Pres.	eō	īmus	eam, etc.	*2nd Pers.*	ī	īte
	īs	ītis				
	it	eunt				
Imperf.	ībam, etc.		īrem			
Fut.	ībō			*2nd Pers.*	ītō	ītōte
Perf.	iī		ierim	*3rd Pers.*	ītō	euntō
Past Perf.	ieram		īssem			
Fut. Perf.	ierō					

INFINITIVE

Pres.	īre
Perf.	īsse
Fut.	itūrus esse

PARTICIPLE

Active		*Passive*	
Pres.	iēns, euntis	*Perf.*	itus
Fut.	itūrus	*Fut.*	eundus

GERUND

Gen. eundī, etc.

SUPINE

itum, -ū

501.   PERIPHRASTIC CONJUGATION

The active periphrastic conjugation is formed by combining the future active participle with forms of **sum.**   It expresses future or intended action: **portātūrus sum,** *I am going to carry;* **portātūrus eram,** *I was going to carry,* etc.

The passive periphrastic conjugation is formed by combining the future passive participle with forms of **sum.**   It expresses obligation or necessity: **portandus est,** *he ought to be carried;* **portandus erat,** *it was necessary for him to be carried,* etc.

502.   IMPERSONAL VERBS

Some verbs are used in the third person singular and in the infinitive without a personal subject: **pluit,** *it rains;* **oportet,** *it is necessary.*   Other verbs always used in this way are: **decet, libet, licet, miseret, paenitet, piget, pudet, refert, taedet.**

Intransitive verbs are often used impersonally in the passive, third person singular: **ventum est,** (*it was come*) *they came;* **pugnātum est,** (*it was fought*) *they fought.*

503.   DEFECTIVE VERBS

Defective verbs lack certain forms.   **Coepī** is used only in the perfect system. Its present is supplied by **incipiō.**   **Meminī** and **ōdī** are perfect in form but present in meaning.   Some forms of **aiō** are lacking, but the following ones are in common use: **aiō, ais, ait, aiunt.**   **Inquam** is also defective.   It is rarely used except in the forms **inquam, inquis, inquit, inquiunt.**

504.   CONTRACTED FORMS

Forms of the perfect system in **-āvī, -ēvī,** or **-ōvī** sometimes drop **-v-** and the following vowel before **-r** or **-s:** **portāvistī, portāstī; portāvērunt, portārunt.** Similar forms in **-īvī** drop **-v-** and the following vowel before **-s,** but only **-v-** before **-r: audīvistī, audīstī; audīvērunt, audiērunt.**

SYNTAX FOR REFERENCE

THE NOUN

THE APPOSITIVE

505. A noun explaining or describing the object represented by another noun or a pronoun denoting the same person or thing is called an appositive. An appositive always agrees in case with the noun or pronoun it explains: **Persuādet Casticō,** *Sēquanō, he persuades Casticus, the Sequanian,* I, 3.

THE VOCATIVE CASE

506. The vocative case is used to name the person or thing directly addressed: "**Habētis,**" **inquit,** "*mīlitēs,* **quam petīstis facultātem,**" "*Soldiers,*" *he says,* "*you have the opportunity which you have sought,*" VI, 8; "**Quid dubitās,**" **inquit,** "*Vorēne?*" "*Why,*" *he says,* "*do you hestitate, Vorenus?*" V, 44.

THE NOMINATIVE CASE

507. The subject. The subject of a finite verb is in the nominative case. The subject of a historical infinitive is also in the nominative case: **Hostēs terga vertunt,** *the enemy flee,* VII, 88; **Hostēs ex omnibus partibus dēcurrere,** *the enemy rushed down from all directions,* III, 4.

508. The predicate nominative. A predicate nominative is connected with the subject by a form of the verb **sum** or a verb meaning *to become, to be made, to appear.* It is also used with the passive voice of verbs meaning *to call, to choose, to name,* and the like: **Fortissimī sunt Belgae,** *the Belgians are the bravest,* I, 1; **Caesar** *certior* **factus est,** *Caesar was informed (made certain),* I, 2; **Is pāgus appellābātur** *Tigurīnus, this canton was called Tigurinus,* I, 12.

THE GENITIVE CASE

509. The possessive genitive. The genitive is used to denote the possessor: **In** *Aeduōrum* **fīnēs pervēnerant,** *they had come into the territories of the Aeduans,* I, 11.

a. The genitive with **causā** and **grātiā** is of possessive origin: **Eius** *reī* **causā moram interpōnī arbitrābātur,** *he thought a delay was interposed on account of this thing,* IV, 9.

b. The possessive genitive is sometimes used in the predicate with **sum** or **faciō** : **Neque sē iūdicāre, Galliam esse *Ariovistī*,** *and (he said) that he did not consider that Gaul belonged to Ariovistus (was of Ariovistus),* I, 45.

Note 1. The possessive adjective is regularly used instead of the possessive genitive of a personal or a reflexive pronoun : **Suās cīvitātisque fortūnās eius fideī permissūrum,** *that he would entrust his own fortunes and those of the state to his protection,* V, 3.

Note 2. Instead of the possessive genitive of **alius,** the adjective **aliēnus** is used : **Suum perīculum in *aliēnā* vident virtūte cōnstāre,** *they see that their own safety (danger) depends upon the courage of others,* VII, 84.

510. The genitive of the whole. The genitive of the whole is used to designate the whole of which a part is indicated by a noun, pronoun, adjective, or adverb which this genitive modifies : **Mīlibus *passuum* sex ā Caesaris castrīs sub monte cōnsēdit,** *he encamped at the foot of a mountain six miles (six thousand of paces) from Caesar's camp,* I, 48; **Quid ergō meī *cōnsilī* est?** *What then is my plan?* VII, 77.

a. Instead of the genitive of the whole, the ablative with **ē, ex,** or **dē** is used with cardinal numerals and **quīdam** : **Quīdam *ex mīlitibus* decimae legiōnis dīxit,** *a certain soldier of the Tenth Legion said,* I, 42.

511. The genitive of description (quality). The genitive modified by an adjective may be used to *describe* or *denote a quality:* **Lucterium Cadūrcum, *summae* hominen *audāciae,* mittit,** *he sends Lucterius Cadurcus, a man of very great courage,* VII, 5.

a. The genitive of description is used to denote *measure* with words of *width, depth,* and similar ideas : **Flūminis erat altitūdō *pedum* circiter trium,** *the depth of the river was (of) about three feet,* II, 18.

b. The genitive of description is sometimes used in the predicate : **Erat magnī *perīculī* rēs,** *the thing was extremely dangerous (of great danger),* V, 49.

c. The genitive of description is sometimes used in the predicate to express *indefinite value:* **Cuius auctōritās *magnī* habēbātur,** *his authority was considered great (of great value),* IV, 21.

512. The objective genitive. The genitive is used to denote the *object of an action* implied in a noun or adjective : **Augēbātur *auxiliōrum* cotīdiē spēs,** *the hope of aid was increasing daily,* VI, 7.

Note. This should not be confused with the *subjective genitive,* which denotes the subject of an action : **amor *parentum,*** *love of parents.* This is subjective if it means the love felt *by* parents. If it means the love felt *for* parents, it is an objective genitive.

513. The genitive with adjectives (specification). The genitive is used to limit the application of many adjectives denoting *skill, desire, knowledge,* *fullness, memory, similarity, connection,* and their *opposites:* **reī mīlitāris peritissimus,** *most skilled in the art of war,* I, 21.

514. The genitive with verbs meaning *to remember* and *to forget.* The genitive is used with **meminī** and **reminīscor** when meaning *to be mindful of,* and **oblīvīscor,** *to be unmindful of:* **Cohortātus est Aeduōs ut contrōversiārum ac dissēnsiōnis oblīvīscerentur,** *he urged the Aeduans to forget disagreements and discord,* VII, 34.

515. The genitive with *potior.* The genitive is sometimes used with **potior :** **Tōtīus** *Galliae* **sēsē potīrī posse spērant,** *they hope they can get possession of all Gaul,* I, 3.

THE DATIVE CASE

516. The dative of indirect object. The dative of indirect object is used to denote *to,* or *toward whom* or *what* something is said, given, done, or felt. This use is found in connection with a direct object : **Alteram partem eius vīcī** *Gallīs* **concessit, alteram** *cohortibus* **attribuit,** *one part of this village he granted to the Gauls, the other he assigned to his cohorts,* III, 1.

517. The dative with special verbs. The dative of indirect object is used with many intransitive verbs denoting a mental attitude or action; for example, verbs meaning *to help, injure, please, displease, persuade, believe, command, obey, trust, distrust, favor, serve, resist, pardon, spare, envy, be angry,* and *threaten:* **Facile hāc ōrātiōne *Nerviīs* persuādet,** *with this speech he easily persuades the Nervii,* V, 38 ; *Agricultūrae* **nōn student,** *they do not pay attention to agriculture,* VI, 22.

Note. Such verbs used in the passive are impersonal and retain the dative : **Intellēxit neque *eīs* nocērī posse,** *and he knew that they could not be harmed,* III, 14.

518. The dative with compound verbs. The dative of indirect object is used with many verbs compounded with the prepositions **ad, ante, con, in, inter, ob, post, prae, prō, sub, super,** and sometimes **circum : Eī mūnītiōnī T. Labiēnum lēgātum praefēcit,** *he placed Labienus, the chief of staff, in command of this fortification,* I, 10.

519. The dative of reference. The dative of reference is used to denote the person or thing to whom a statement refers, or to whom it is of interest. This dative very often occurs with a dative of purpose : **Quae rēs magnō ūsuī** *nostrīs* **fuit,** *this method was of great advantage to our men,* IV, 25 ; **Praeterita sē *Dīviciācō frātrī* condōnāre dīcit,** *he says he forgives the past for the sake of his brother Diviciacus,* I, 20.

a. The dative of reference often has the force of a possessive genitive : **Trānsfīgitur scūtum *Pullōnī*,** *Pullo's (for Pullo) shield is pierced through,* V, 44.

520. The dative of separation. A variation of the dative of reference, called the dative of separation, is used with verbs meaning *to take away*, usually compounds, instead of the ablative of separation : *Hostibus* spēs potiundī oppidī discessit, *hope of getting possession of the town left the enemy,* II, 7.

521. The dative of possession. The dative is used with forms of sum to denote the *possessor :* In mūrō cōnsistendī potestās erat *nūllī, no one could (there was power to no one) stand on the wall,* II, 6.

522. The dative of agent. The dative is used with the passive periphrastic conjugation to denote the *agent :* Quārum rērum omnium *nostrīs nāvibus* cāsus erat extimēscendus, *the risk of all these things was greatly to be feared by (for) our ships,* III, 13.

523. The dative of purpose or tendency. The dative is often used to express *purpose.* This dative usually occurs in combination with a dative of reference : *Praesidiō* impedīmentīs erant, *they were (for) a protection to the baggage,* II, 19.

524. The dative with adjectives. The dative is used with many adjectives denoting *fitness, likeness, nearness, service,* and their *opposites :* Helvētiīs erat amīcus, *he was friendly to the Helvetians,* I, 9.

THE ACCUSATIVE CASE

525. The direct object. The direct object of a finite verb is in the accusative case and denotes that which is produced or that which is affected by the action of the verb : *Castra* ex eō locō movent, *they move the camp from that place,* I, 15.

526. Two accusatives. Verbs meaning *to make, to choose, to call,* and the like may have a *direct object* and a *predicate accusative :* Quōs stimulōs nōminābant, *they called these goads,* VII, 73.

527. The accusative of the person and the thing. Verbs meaning *to inquire, to demand, to teach,* or *to conceal* may have *two accusatives,* one of the person, and the other of the thing : Caesar *Aeduōs frūmentum* flāgitāre, *Caesar asked the Aeduans for grain,* I, 16.

528. The accusatives with compounds. Verbs compounded with circum and trāns may have *two objects,* one as object of the verb, the other, of the preposition. The accusative with the preposition is retained in the passive voice, and the accusative with the verb becomes the subject. *Exercitum Ligerim* trādūcit, *he leads his army across the Loire,* VII, 11.

529. The accusative of place to which (limit of motion). *Place to which* is expressed by the accusative with the prepositions ad, in, or sub. With domus, rūs, and names of towns and small islands, the accusative is used without a preposition : In *Italiam* profectus est, *he set out for Italy,* II, 35 ; *Viennam* pervenit, *he arrives at Vienne,* VII, 9.

530. The accusative of extent. *Extent of time* (*duration*) and *of space* is expressed by the accusative case: **Secūtae sunt complūrēs *diēs* tempestātēs,** *storms followed for several days*, IV, 34; **Perpetuae fossae quīnōs *pedēs* altae dūcēbantur,** *continuous ditches, each five feet deep, were made*, VII, 73.

a. A neuter pronoun or an adjective of quantity is used as an accusative of extent to express *degree*: ***Multum* in rē mīlitārī potest fortūna,** *fortune is very powerful in military affairs*, VI, 30. **Maximam partem** is sometimes used to express degree: ***Maximam partem* lacte atque pecore vīvunt,** *they live chiefly on milk and flesh*, IV, 1.

531. The accusative subject of an infinitive. The subject of an infinitive (not historical) is in the accusative case: **Iubet *arma* trādī,** *he orders arms to be given up*, VII, 89.

532. The accusative of exclamation. The accusative is often used in exclamations: **Heu mē miserum,** *alas, wretch that I am!*

533. The accusative with prepositions. The accusative is used with the prepositions **ad, ante, circum, contrā, inter, intrā, ob, per, post, prope, propter, super, trāns,** and **ultrā.** The accusative is used with **in** and **sub** with verbs of motion.

THE ABLATIVE CASE

534. The ablative of separation. The ablative, with or without the preposition **ā, ab, ē,** or **ex,** is used to express *separation*: **Mūrus dēfēnsōribus nūdātus est,** *the wall was stripped of defenders*, II, 6.

535. The ablative of place from which. *Place from which* with verbs of motion is expressed by the ablative with a preposition. With **domus, rūs,** and names of towns and small islands, the ablative is used without a preposition: **Hostēs item suās cōpiās *ex castrīs* īnstrūxērunt,** *the enemy also led their forces forth from the camp*, II, 8; ***Domō* excesserant,** *they had set out from home*, IV, 14.

536. The ablative of source. *Source* is expressed by the ablative, with or without the preposition **ā, ab, dē, ē,** or **ex,** but usually without a preposition: **Amplissimō *genere* nātus,** *sprung from a most illustrious family*, IV, 12.

537. The ablative of accordance. The ablative is used with or without a preposition, **dē** or **ex,** to express the idea *in accordance with*: **Tum suō mōre conclāmāvērunt,** *then according to their custom they shouted*, IV, 26.

538. The ablative of agent. The ablative with **ā** or **ab** is used with a passive verb to denote the *agent*: **Ā senātū populī Rōmānī amīcus appellātus erat,** *he had been called by the Senate a friend of the Roman people*, I, 3.

Note. **Per** with the accusative is sometimes used instead of an ablative, when the agent is thought of as a means: **Haec quoque *per explōrātōrēs***

ad hostēs dēferuntur, *these things, too, are reported to the enemy by (through) scouts,* VI, 7.

539. The ablative of comparison. The ablative may be used with a comparative instead of **quam** with a nominative or accusative : **Castra amplius mīlibus passuum octō in lātitūdinem patēbant,** *the camp extended more than eight miles in width,* II, 7.

Note. With the comparatives **plūs, minus, amplius,** or **longius,** without **quam,** a word of measure or number is often used with no change in the case : **Spatium est nōn amplius *pedum* sescentōrum,** *the distance is not more than six hundred feet,* I, 38.

540. The ablative of cause. The ablative, generally without a preposition, is used to express *cause* : **Levitāte animī novīs imperiīs studēbant,** *they were eager for new forms of government because of their instability of mind,* II, 1 ; **Reī frūmentāriae commeātūsque *causā* morātur,** *he delays on account of grain and supplies,* I, 39.

541. The ablative of accompaniment. The ablative with **cum** is used to express *accompaniment* and other ideas of *connection* : **Germānī *magnā cum multitūdine* flūmen trānsiērunt,** *the Germans with a great number crossed the river,* IV, 1 ; **Cum Germānīs contendunt,** *they struggle with the Germans,* I, 1 ; **Parvulīs proeliīs *cum nostrīs* contendēbant,** *they fought in minor battles with our men,* II, 30.

Note. In military phrases **cum** is often omitted if the ablative is modified by any other than a numerical adjective : **Ipse eō *pedestribus cōpiīs* contendit,** *he himself hurried there with infantry,* III, 11.

542. The ablative of manner. The ablative, with or without **cum,** is used to express the *manner* in which an act is performed. If the ablative has an adjective modifier, **cum** may be omitted : **Incrēdibilī celeritāte dē victōriā Caesaris fāma perfertur,** *the report concerning Caesar's victory spread with incredible speed,* V, 53.

543. The ablative of attendant circumstance. The ablative, usually without **cum,** is used to denote a *circumstance attending the action* expressed by a verb : **Intellegēbat *magnō cum perīculō* Prōvinciae futūrum,** *he knew that it would be very dangerous (with great danger) to the Province,* I, 10.

544. The ablative of description (quality). The ablative with a qualifying word is used to *describe* or to *denote quality.* The ablative is regularly used to describe *physical qualities,* the genitive for measure : **Ēgregiā virtūte erant cognitī,** *they were known (as men) of marked courage,* I, 28 ; **Capillō sunt prōmissō,** *they let their hair grow (they are of long hair),* V, 14.

545. The ablative absolute. The equivalent of a clause may be expressed by a phrase consisting of the ablative of a noun or pronoun with a participle or adjective in agreement with it, or with another noun in the ablative case.

This phrase, called the *ablative absolute*, may express a variety of ideas: *time*, *cause*, *condition*, *manner*, *opposition*, and *attendant circumstance*. This construction should be translated by a clause expressing the idea which fits the context:

Rēgnō occupātō, tōtīus Galliae sēsē potīrī posse spērant, *they hope that after they have seized the royal power* (*the royal power having been seized*) *they can get possession of all Gaul*, I, 3.

L. Pīsōne, A. Gabīniō cōnsulibus, when *Lucius Piso and Aulus Gabinius were consuls* (*L. Piso and A. Gabinius being consuls*), I, 6.

Quā, Sēquanīs invītīs, īre nōn poterant, *through this* (*way*) *they could not go if the Sequanians were unwilling*, I, 9.

Paucīs dēfendentibus, expugnāre nōn potuit, *although there were but few defenders, he was not able to take it* (*the town*) *by storm*, II, 12.

546. The ablative of means. The ablative without a preposition is used to denote the *means* by which an act is performed: **Eum locum *vāllō fossāque* mūnīvit**, *he fortified this place with a wall and a ditch*, III, 1.

547. The ablative with special deponent verbs. The ablative is used with **ūtor, fruor, fungor, potior**, and **vēscor**, and their compounds: **Sine contentiōne *oppidō* potītur**, *he gets possession of the town without a struggle*, VII, 58.

548. The ablative of price. The ablative is used to denote *definite price* or *value*, and *indefinite price* or *value* with **pretiō** or a word of similar meaning, modified by an adjective: **Quae *impēnsō* parant *pretiō***, *these they obtain at an extravagant price*, IV, 2.

549. The ablative of the way by which. The ablative is used to denote the *road by which one goes*: **Erant omnīnō itinera duo *quibus itineribus* domō exīre possent**, *there were only two routes by which they could go from home*, I, 6.

550. The ablative of measure (degree) of difference. The ablative is used with comparatives and other words which imply comparison to denote the *measure of difference*: **Alterum (iter) per prōvinciam nostram, *multō* facilius atque expedītius (erat)**, *the other way was through our province, much easier* (*easier by much*) *and more unobstructed*, I, 6.

551. The ablative of specification. The ablative is used to denote that *in respect to which* a statement is made: **Erat Rōmānīs nec *locō* nec *numerō* aequa contentiō**, *neither in place nor in number was it a fair contest for the Romans*, VII, 48.

    a. The ablative of specification is used with **dignus** and **indignus**: **Accidit, īnspectantibus nōbīs, quod dignum *memoriā* vīsum**, *there happened in our sight something which seemed worthy of memory*, VII, 25.

552. The ablative of place where. The ablative with the preposition **in** is regularly used to express *place where*: **Quae cīvitās est *in Prōvinciā***, *a state which is in the Province*, I, 10.

a. **Locus, pars,** and several other nouns may be used in the ablative without a preposition to denote *place where.* A preposition is rarely used with any noun modified by **tōtus**: **Vulgō *tōtīs castrīs* testāmenta obsignābantur,** *everywhere in the whole camp wills were being signed,* I, 39.

b. With the names of towns and small islands and with **domus** and **rūs,** the locative case is used.

553. The ablative of time. The ablative without a preposition is used to express *time when* or *time within which:* **Diē septimō pervenit,** *he arrives on the seventh day,* I, 10; **Castra movet *diēbusque* circiter quīndecim ad fīnēs Belgārum pervenit,** *he moves camp and within about fifteen days reaches the territory of the Belgians,* II, 2.

a. *Duration of time* is sometimes expressed by the ablative instead of the accusative: **Omnibusque *annīs* dē locō summīs simultātibus contendēbant,** *through all the years with the greatest rivalry they had striven for the place,* V, 44.

554. The ablative with prepositions. The ablative is used with the prepositions **ab, absque, cōram, cum, dē, ex, prae, prō, sine.**

THE LOCATIVE CASE

555. The locative case is used to express *place where* with the names of towns and small islands and with **domus** and **rūs.** In the singular of nouns of the first and second declensions, it has the same form as the genitive. Elsewhere, it has the same form as the ablative: **Rōmae diērum vīgintī supplicātiō redditur,** *a thanksgiving of twenty days is proclaimed at Rome,* VII, 90; **Illī *domī* remanent,** *they remain at home,* IV, 1.

THE PRONOUN

556. The personal pronoun. A personal pronoun is used as the subject of a finite verb only to express *emphasis* or *contrast:* **Ego certē meum reī pūblicae atque imperātōrī officium praestiterō,** *I shall at least have done my duty to my country and to my general,* IV, 25.

a. The lack of a personal pronoun of the third person is supplied by a demonstrative, a relative, or the reflexive **suī**: **Ad eum in castra vēnērunt *suī* pūrgandī causā,** *they came into camp to him for the purpose of excusing themselves,* IV, 13.

557. The reflexive pronoun. The reflexive pronoun in an independent clause regularly refers to the grammatical or to the logical subject of the clause: **Sē suaque omnia sine morā dēdidērunt,** *they surrendered themselves and all their (possessions) without delay,* II, 15.

a. In a dependent clause the reflexive pronoun may refer to the subject of the principal clause, if the subordinate clause expresses the thought of the person denoted by the subject of the main clause. When so used it is called an *indirect reflexive:* **Ōrant ut sibi parcat,** *they beg that he spare them,* VI, 9.

558. The intensive pronoun. The intensive pronoun **ipse** is used alone or in apposition with a substantive to add *emphasis.* Often it may be translated by *self,* or *very own,* or some other expression which fits the context: *Ipse* **adit reliquōs,** *he himself goes to the others,* VII, 86.

Note. The intensive **ipse** may be used in a subordinate clause as an indirect reflexive: **Nihil quod ipsīs esset indignum committēbant,** *they did nothing which was unworthy of themselves,* V, 35.

559. The indefinite pronoun and adjective. **Quīdam,** *a certain one,* refers to a person or thing known but not necessary to name; **quis** or **quī,** *someone,* is very indefinite and used in Caesar only with **sī, nisi, nē,** and some interrogative words; **aliquis,** *someone,* is more definite; **quisquam,** *anyone,* and **ūllus,** *anyone,* are used in negative sentences or interrogative sentences implying a negative: **Quīdam ex hīs nocte ad Nerviōs pervēnērunt,** *certain ones of (from) these came by night to the Nervii,* II, 17; **Sī quī eōrum dēcrētō nōn stetit, sacrificiīs interdīcunt,** *if anyone has not abided by their decrees, they exclude him from the sacrifices,* VI, 13; **Neque hominum memoriā repertus est quisquam,** *nor within the memory of man has anyone been found,* III, 22.

560. The relative pronoun and adjective. The relative pronoun refers to an antecedent with which it agrees in gender and number. Its case is determined by its use in the clause in which it stands: **Hominēs id quod volunt crēdunt,** *men believe that which they wish (to believe),* III, 18.

a. The relative pronoun is never omitted; sometimes its antecedent is repeated or incorporated in the relative clause in the same case as the relative pronoun: **Diem dīcunt quā diē ad rīpam Rhodanī omnēs conveniant,** *they name a day when (on which day) all are to assemble on the banks of the Rhone,* I, 6.

b. The antecedent of a relative pronoun is often omitted: **Quod iussī sunt faciunt,** *they do that which they have been ordered,* III, 6.

c. The antecedent of a relative pronoun may be the idea expressed in a clause: **Diērum quīndecim supplicātiō dēcrēta est, quod ante id tempus accidit nūllī,** *a thanksgiving of fifteen days was decreed, (a thing) which before this time has happened to no one,* II, 35.

d. When a relative clause contains a predicate noun indicating the same person or thing as the antecedent, the relative pronoun usually agrees with the predicate noun: **Eā quae secūta est hieme, quī fuit annus, Cn. Pompeiō M. Crassō cōnsulibus, Usipetēs Rhēnum trānsiērunt,** *during that winter which followed, which was the year that Gnaeus Pompeius and Marcus Crassus were consuls, the Usipetes crossed the Rhine,* IV, 1.

e. A relative pronoun is often used at the beginning of a sentence to connect with and refer to an antecedent or an idea in the preceding sentence. A relative so used should be translated by a demonstrative or a personal pronoun: *Quod ubi audītum est, conclāmant omnēs, when this was heard, they all shouted,* III, 18.

561. The demonstrative pronoun and adjective. The demonstrative pronouns are hic, is, ille, iste, and īdem. They may also be used as adjectives.

a. **Hic,** *this,* refers to what is near the speaker in time, place, or thought; **ille,** *that,* to what is remote. When used to point out a contrast, **hic** refers to the *latter* and **ille** to the *former: Hōs illī* **dīligenter tuēbantur,** *the former guarded the latter diligently,* VI, 12 ; **Id quod volunt,** *that which they wish,* III, 18.

b. **Is,** *this* or *that,* is more indefinite in its reference than **hic** or **ille.** It takes the place of the personal pronoun of the third person and often is used as the antecedent of a relative: *Id eā* **maximē ratiōne fēcit,** *he did it especially for this reason,* I, 28.

c. **Iste,** *that of yours,* refers to that which is near the person addressed or which concerns him. It often has a contemptuous force: **Animī est** *ista* **mollitia,** *that is weakness of mind on your part (that weakness of mind of yours),* VII, 77.

d. **Īdem,** *the same,* is often used with the force of *also* and *likewise:* **Haec** *eadem* **mandābant,** *they demanded these (same things) too,* VII, 17.

e. **Alius . . . alius** is often used idiomatically as a condensed expression for *one . . . one . . . another . . . another:* **Aliī** *aliam* **in partem perterritī ferēbantur,** *some terrified were borne in one direction and others in another,* II, 24.

THE ADJECTIVE

562. An adjective or any word used as an adjective agrees in gender, number, and case with the noun or pronoun which it modifies. An adjective modifying two or more nouns may be plural or agree with the nearest noun.

563. The participial adjective. A participle which modifies a noun is classified as an adjective and agrees with the noun in gender, number, and case: **In nostrōs** *venientēs* **tēla coniciēbant,** *they threw weapons on our men as they came (coming),* I, 26 ; **Hāc ōrātiōne** *adductī* **inter sē fidem et iūs iūrandum dant,** *influenced by this speech they pledge their word and take an oath,* I, 3.

564. The possessive adjective. A possessive adjective is used only to make the meaning clear, to give emphasis, or to indicate contrast: **Caesar** *suās* **cōpiās in proximum collem subdūcit,** *Caesar leads his forces to the nearest hill,* I, 22.

a. *His, her, its,* and *their,* when not reflexive, are expressed by the genitive of the demonstrative pronoun, not by **suus: Dē** *eius* **adventū Helvētiī certiōrēs factī sunt,** *the Helvetians were informed about his arrival,* I, 7.

565. The adjective and participle used substantively. Adjectives and participles are frequently used as *substantives:* **Recessum** *prīmīs ultimī* **nōn dabant,** *those in the rear ranks did not give those in the front ranks a chance to withdraw,* V, 43.

566. The comparative and superlative. The comparative of an adjective is sometimes translated by the positive with *quite, rather, too,* or *somewhat,* and the superlative by the positive with *very.* The superlative with **quam** denotes the highest degree possible : *Horribiliōrēs* **sunt in pugnā aspectū,** *they are quite frightful-looking in battle,* V, 14 ; **Cōnstituērunt sēmentēs** *quam maximās* **facere,** *they decided to make as large sowings as possible,* I, 3.

567. Special uses of the adjective. *a.* An adjective is sometimes used to designate a part of the object to which it refers. The adjectives very commonly used in this way are **summus, īnfimus, medius, prīmus,** and **reliquus : summus mōns,** *the top of the mountain;* **īnfimus collis,** *the foot of the hill:* **ipse interim in colle** *mediō* **triplicem aciem īnstrūxit,** *meanwhile he himself drew up a triple line of battle half way up the hill,* I, 24.

b. In Latin an adjective is often used when in English an adverb would be used : **Eīs quī** *prīmī* **mūrum ascendissent praemia prōposuit,** *to those who first ascended the wall he offered rewards,* VII, 27.

THE VERB

AGREEMENT

568. The agreement of the verb with its subject. A finite verb and its subject agree in person and number. The participle of a compound tense form of a verb agrees with the subject in number, case, and gender : **Quō proeliō** *bellum* **Venetōrum** *cōnfectum est,* *by this battle the war of the Veneti was finished,* III, 16.

a. A verb with a compound subject may be plural or agree with the nearest subject. Two or more subjects may have a singular verb when they are thought of together, that is, as a unit : **Reliquōs aditūs** *locus* **ipse per sē** *mūnītiōque* **dēfendit,** *the place itself and the fortification defends the other approaches,* VI, 37.

b. A collective noun may have a singular or a plural verb ; if the individuals are thought of, it is plural : *Multitūdō* **in oppidum** *convēnit,* *a great number assembled in the town,* II, 12 ; **Cīvitātī persuāsit ut dē fīnibus suīs cum omnibus cōpiīs** *exīrent,* *he persuaded the citizens (the state) to go out from their territories with all their supplies,* I, 2.

569. The impersonal use of verbs. Intransitive verbs may be used impersonally: **Ut erat eī praeceptum,** *as he had been ordered* (*as had been ordered to him*), I, 22.

THE TENSES OF THE INDICATIVE

570. The present tense. The present tense corresponds to the English present tense: **Gallī appellantur,** *they are called Gauls,* I, 1.

a. The *historical present* is used in narrative for the sake of vividness to express a past act as present. It is often best translated by a past tense: **Oppida mūniunt,** *they fortified* (*fortify*) *the towns,* III, 9.

571. The imperfect tense. The imperfect tense represents an action as continuing, customary, repeated, or attempted in the past: **Multa Caesarem ad id bellum incitābant,** *many things were urging Caesar to this war,* III, 10; **Crēbrās ex oppidō excursiōnēs faciēbant,** *they kept making frequent sallies from the town,* II, 30; **Nostrōs intrā mūnītiōnēs ingredī prohibēbant,** *they were trying to keep our men from advancing inside the fortifications,* V, 9. The imperfect is also used to denote *situation* under which a main act occurred: **Causa mittendī fuit, quod iter patefierī volēbat,** *His reason for sending was because he wished a road opened,* III, 1.

572. The future tense. The Latin future tense corresponds to the English future tense, but, since in Latin time is expressed with much more exactness than in English, the future tense is often used when in English the present tense is used: **Hic diēs dē nostrīs contrōversiīs iūdicābit,** *this day will decide our quarrel,* V, 44.

Note. Future time is sometimes expressed by the active periphrastic conjugation. See **501.**

573. The perfect tense. The perfect tense corresponds to the (1) present perfect tense (*has, have*) in English, which represents an action completed at the present time, and (2) the past tense in English, which represents an action completed at an indefinite past time: **Neque enim umquam aliā condiciōne bella gessērunt,** *for they have never waged war on other terms,* VII, 77; **Caesar in Galliam vēnit,** *Caesar came into Gaul,* VI, 12.

574. The past perfect (pluperfect) tense. The past perfect tense corresponds to the past perfect tense in English, which represents an action as completed at or before a past time: **Ultrā eum locum quō in locō Germānī cōnsēderant castrīs idōneum locum dēlēgit,** *beyond that place in which the Germans had settled he chose a place suitable for a camp,* I, 49.

575. The future perfect tense. The future perfect tense corresponds to the future perfect tense in English, but is used with much more precision and frequency than in English. It represents an action completed before some future time: **Meum reī pūblicae atque imperātōrī officium praestiterō,** *I shall have done my duty to my state and to my general,* IV, 25.

576. The verbs with incomplete tenses. The perfect and past perfect tenses of **nōscō, cognōscō, cōnsuēscō,** and the defectives **meminī** and **ōdī** represent a state resulting from an action and are translated by the present and imperfect respectively: **Temperantiam Dīviciācī *cognōverat,*** *he knew the self-control of Diviciacus,* I, 19.

SEQUENCE OF TENSES

577. The tense groups. Primary or principal tenses are those which denote present or future time. In the indicative they are the present, present perfect (definite time), future, and future perfect tenses. In the subjunctive they are the present to express incomplete action, and the perfect to express completed action.

Secondary or historical tenses are those which denote past time. In the indicative they are the imperfect, perfect (indefinite time), and past perfect tenses. In the subjunctive they are the imperfect to express incomplete action, and the past perfect to express completed action.

578. The rules of sequence. In general, a primary tense in the principal clause is followed by a primary tense of the subjunctive in the subordinate clause; a secondary tense, by a secondary tense: **Veniunt quī *polliceantur* obsidēs dare,** *they come promising (to promise) to give hostages,* IV, 21; **Cum ab eīs quae cīvitātēs in armīs *essent,* sīc *reperiēbat,*** *when he asked them what states were in arms, he found this,* II, 4.

a. **In a result clause.** In a result clause depending upon a secondary tense, the perfect tense is sometimes used: **Fuit hostiumque tam parātus ad dīmicandum animus ut ad īnsignia accommodanda tempus *dēfuerit,*** *the mind of the enemy was so prepared for fighting that time was lacking for fitting on their decorations,* II, 21.

b. **The historical present.** The historical present, which is considered sometimes a primary tense and sometimes a secondary tense, is found with either the primary or secondary sequence, usually secondary: **Huic *mandat* Rēmōs reliquōsque Belgās *adeat,*** *he commands him to go to the Remi and the rest of the Belgians,* III, 11; **Dumnorīgī ut idem *cōnārētur persuādet,*** *he persuaded Dumnorix to attempt the same,* I, 3.

MOOD

THE INDICATIVE MOOD

579. The indicative mood is used to state a fact or to ask a question of fact: **Vēnī, vīdī, vīcī,** *I came, I saw, I conquered,* SUETONIUS, *Life of Julius Caesar;* **Quid dubitās,** *why do you hestitate?* V, 44.

THE SUBJUNCTIVE MOOD IN INDEPENDENT CLAUSES

580. The volitive subjunctive. The subjunctive is used to express an act as *willed* or *desired*. The negative is **nē**.

a. **A command.** The volitive subjunctive is used to express a command in the first and third persons. In conversational Latin it is sometimes used in the second person instead of the imperative. See *Imperative*, **611.** In **cōnsiliō capiendō omnem Galliam** *respiciāmus, in adopting a plan let us consider all Gaul,* VII, 77 ; **Sibi** *habeant* **arma,** *let them have their arms,* CICERO, **Dē Senectūte,** 58.

b. **The deliberative question.** The volitive subjunctive is used in questions of deliberation, perplexity or indignation, or questions asking the will or advice of the one addressed : **Quid** *faciam, What shall I do?* TERENCE, **Phormio,** 199.

581. The optative subjunctive. The subjunctive is used to express a *wish.* It is often introduced by **utinam** ; the negative is **nē**. A wish that is thought of as impossible of realization is in the imperfect or the past perfect tense. **Ad senectūtem** *utinam perveniātis, may you come to old age,* CICERO, **Dē Senectūte,** 85 ; **Utinam Clōdius vīveret,** *I wish Clodius were alive.*

582. The potential subjunctive. The subjunctive is used to express a possibility. The negative is **nōn**. *Errāverim* **fortasse quī mē aliquid putāvī,** *perhaps I may have made a mistake in thinking I was somebody,* PLINY, **Epistula,** I, 23.

a. The potential subjunctive is often used in the second person with indefinite force to express the idea *one (you) can :* **Videās,** *one can see;* **audīrēs,** *one could hear.*

THE INDICATIVE AND THE SUBJUNCTIVE IN DEPENDENT CLAUSES

THE RELATIVE CLAUSE

583. Determinative. The verb in a relative clause which merely points out *who* or *what* object is meant by an antecedent otherwise incomplete, or which states a fact about a definite antecedent, is in the indicative : **Proximī sunt Germānīs, quī trāns Rhēnum** *incolunt, they are nearest to the Germans, who live across the Rhine,* I, 1.

584. Descriptive (characteristic). The verb in a relative clause that *describes* or gives a *characteristic* of the object named by an indefinite antecedent is in the subjunctive. Such a clause answers the question *what sort of* and follows indefinite expressions : **Sunt quī dīcant,** *there are those who* *say;* **Nec fuit quisquam quī praedae** *studēret, nor was there anyone who was eager for booty,* VII, 28.

a. A relative descriptive clause may express cause, concession, or condition: **Titūrius, quī nihil ante** *prōvīdisset,* **trepidāre,** *Titurius, since he had provided nothing beforehand, was frightened,* V, 33.

585. Purpose. The verb in a relative clause expressing *purpose* is in the subjunctive: **Dēposcunt quī bellī initium** *faciant, they call for (men) to begin the war,* VII, 1.

a. The ablative **quō** is frequently used as the introductory word of a purpose clause containing an adjective or adverb in the comparative: **Lēgātōs mittunt subsidium rogātum, quō facilius hostium cōpiās sustinēre** *possint, they send ambassadors to ask aid that they may more easily withstand the attack of the enemy,* VII, 5.

THE ADVERBIAL CLAUSE OF PURPOSE

586. Purpose is generally expressed by a clause introduced by **ut,** *that,* or **nē,** *that not,* with its verb in the subjunctive: **Accelerat Caesar** *ut* **proeliō** *intersit, Caesar hastens that he may take part in the battle,* VII, 87; **Praesidiō relictō** *nē* **quis ab hīs subitō mōtus** *orerētur, a garrison had been left for fear that (in order that . . . not) some uprising might suddenly start from them,* VI, 9.

THE CLAUSE OF RESULT

587. Result is regularly expressed by a clause introduced by **ut,** *that,* or **ut nōn,** *that not,* with its verb in the subjunctive: **Tanta rērum commūtātiō est facta** *ut* **nostrī proelium** *redintegrārent, so great a change of affairs was made that our men renewed the battle,* II, 27. A result clause may also be introduced by a relative pronoun.

THE SUBSTANTIVE CLAUSE

588. A substantive clause is a clause which is used as a noun. It may be the subject of a verb or used in any other noun relation.

589. The substantive volitive clause. A clause used as the object of a verb expressing will or desire, meaning *to command, induce, advise, ask, allow,* or *strive,* has its verb in the subjunctive. The introductory word is **ut** or **nē**: **Ūniversī ab eō** *nē* **id** *faceret* **petēbant,** *all begged him not to do it,* VII, 17.

Note. With **iubeō,** *I order,* and **vetō,** *I forbid,* the infinitive with subject accusative is used: **Titum Labiēnum summum iugum montis ascendere iubet,** *he orders Titus Labienus to climb to the highest crest of the mountain,* I, 21.

590. The substantive clause of hindering. A clause introduced by **nē, quīn,** or **quōminus,** dependent upon a verb meaning *to hinder, prevent,* or *refuse*, has its verb in the subjunctive: **Nāvēs ventō tenēbantur *quōminus* in portum venīre *possent*,** *the ships were kept by the wind from being able to come into the port,* IV, 22.

Note. Caesar uses **prohibeō** with an infinitive.

591. The substantive clause of doubting. A clause dependent upon a word denoting *doubt* or *ignorance* in which a negative is expressed or implied has its verb in the subjunctive. It is introduced by **quīn : Nōn dubitāre *quīn* gravissimum supplicium *sūmat*,** (*he says that*) *he does not doubt that he will inflict very severe punishmnet,* I, 31.

Note. With **dubitō** meaning *to hesitate*, the infinitive is regularly used.

592. The substantive clause of fearing. A clause used as the object of a verb meaning *to fear* has its verb in the subjunctive. It is introduced by **ut,** *that not*, or **nē**, *that : * **Nē Dīviciācī animum offenderet verēbātur,** *he was afraid that he would offend the feelings of Diviciacus,* I, 19.

593. The substantive clause of result. The subjunctive is used in a substantive clause as the object of a verb meaning *to bring about* or *to accomplish*, or as the subject of an impersonal verb meaning *to happen : * **Fēcērunt *ut* cōnsimilis fugae profectiō *vidērētur*,** *they brought it about that their departure seemed like flight,* II, 11 ; **Quod ferē plērīsque accidit *ut* praesidiō litterārum memoriam *remittant*,** *this, as a rule, happens to many, that through their reliance upon written records they lose their memories,* VI, 14.

a. An **ut** clause in apposition with an expression such as **iūs est, mōs est,** or **cōnsuētūdō est,** or with a neuter pronoun or noun, has its verb in the subjunctive : **Est enim hoc Gallicae cōnsuētūdinis *utī* viātōrēs etiam invītōs cōnsistere *cōgant*,** *for this is (of) a Gallic custom to force travelers to stop, even against their wills,* IV, 5.

594. The *quod* clause of fact. A substantive clause with its verb in the indicative introduced by **quod,** *the fact that*, may be used as subject, predicate, object, or appositive : **Accēdēbat *quod dolēbant*,** *there was added the fact that they grieved,* III, 2.

THE INDIRECT QUESTION

595. An indirect question has its verb in the subjunctive. It is a substantive clause dependent upon a verb meaning *to ask* or *to inquire* or other expression suggestive of an interrogative idea. It is introduced by an interrogative pronoun, adjective, adverb, or particle : **Quid fierī *velit* ēdocet,** *he shows what he wishes to be done,* III, 18.

THE TEMPORAL CLAUSE

596. *Cum* with the indicative. A **cum** clause used to point out a *definite time*, often with **tum, eō tempore,** or a similar expression of time, has its verb in the indicative mood. **Cum prīmum,** *as soon as,* is used in the same way : *Cum prīmum per annī tempus potuit,* ad exercitum contendit, *as soon as the time of year made it possible, he hastened to the army,* III, 9 ; **Cum omnis iuventūs eō convēnerant, tum nāvium quod ubīque fuerat coēgerant,** *not only had all the young men gathered there, but they had also gathered together all the ships they had anywhere,* III, 16 ; *Cum* Caesar in Galliam *vēnit,* alterīus factiōnis prīncipēs erant Aeduī, *when Caesar came into Gaul, the Aeduans were leaders of the one faction,* VI, 12.

a. **Repeated action.** A cum clause with its verb in the indicative may express repeated action, *whenever:* **Cum eius generis cōpia dēficit,** etiam ad innocentium supplicia dēscendunt, *whenever a supply of this kind fails, they even resort to the punishment of the innocent,* VI, 16.

597. *Cum* **with the subjunctive (*Cum*-circumstantial).** A cum clause which gives the *situation* or *circumstance* under which the action of the main verb occurred has its verb in the subjunctive. The tense used is the imperfect or the past perfect : *Cum esset* Caesar in citeriōre Galliā, crēbī ad eum rūmōrēs afferēbantur, *when Caesar was in hither Gaul, frequent rumors kept coming to him,* II, 1.

598. *Antequam* **or** *priusquam* **with the indicative.** A clause introduced by **antequam** or **priusquam** which states an actual fact has its verb in the indicative. These conjunctions are often written as two words, **ante** or **prius** in the principal clause and **quam** in the dependent : **Nec *prius* ille est relictus locus *quam* fīnis *est* pugnandī *factus,*** *that place was not abandoned before an end of fighting was made,* VII, 25.

599. *Antequam* **or** *priusquam* **with the subjunctive.** A clause introduced by **antequam** or **priusquam** has its verb in the subjunctive when it expresses an act as *anticipated* or *foreseen :* **Prius omnēs in ūnum locum cōgit *quam* dē eius adventū Arvernīs nūntiārī *posset,*** *he collected all into one place before his arrival could be reported to the Arverni,* VII, 9.

600. *Dum* **with the indicative.** A clause introduced by **dum, quoad, quam diū,** or **dōnec,** when the introductory word means *as long as, while,* or *until,* has its verb in the indicative : **Proinde abīte *dum est* facultās,** *go then while there is an opportunity,* VII, 50.

Note. A clause introduced by **dum,** meaning *while* in the sense of *the time during which,* regularly has its verb in the present indicative regardless of the tense of the verb in the main clause : **Dum haec *geruntur,*** discessērunt, *while these things were (are) being done, they departed,* IV, 34.

601. *Dum* **with the subjunctive.** A clause introduced by **dum,** *until,* expressing anticipation or intention, has its verb in the subjunctive : **Dum reliquae nāvēs eō *convenīrent,* ad hōram nōnam exspectāvit,** *he waited up to the ninth hour until the rest of the ships should assemble at that place,* IV, 23.

602. *Postquam* **with the indicative.** A clause introduced by **postquam, simul, simul atque (ac), ubi,** or **ut** meaning *as* or *when*, has its verb in the indicative, usually in the historical present or the perfect tense: **Postquam id animadvertit, cōpiās suās Caesar in proximum collem subdūxit,** *after he noticed this, Caesar led his forces to the nearest hill,* I, 24; **Ubi ea diēs venit, Carnutēs Cēnabum concurrunt,** *when that day arrives, they rush to Cenabum,* VII, 3; **Dē quārtā vigiliā, ut dīxerat, profectus est,** *about the fourth watch he set out, as he had said (that he would do),* I, 41.

THE CAUSAL CLAUSE

603. The causal clause with *quod.* A clause introduced by **quod, quia,** or **quoniam** has its verb in the indicative when it states the reason of the writer or speaker: **Quod hostibus** *appropinquābat,* **cōnsuētūdine suā Caesar sex legiōnēs expedītās dūcēbat,** *because he was nearing the enemy, according to his custom Caesar led six legions without baggage,* II, 19.

a. A causal clause giving the reason of someone other than the speaker or writer has its verb in the subjunctive: **Quod** *sit* **dēstitūtus queritur,** *he complains because he was abandoned,* I, 16.

b. **Nōn quod,** *not because,* and **quam quō,** *than because,* suggest a cause as to the truth of which a denial is made or implied.

604. The causal clause with *cum.* **Cum** meaning *since* introduces a clause with its verb in the subjunctive: **Aeduī,** *cum* **sē suaque ab eīs dēfendere nōn** *possent,* **lēgātōs ad Caesarem mittunt,** *the Aeduans, since they could not defend themselves and their property from these, sent envoys to Caesar,* I, 11.

THE ADVERSATIVE (CONCESSIVE) CLAUSE

605. With the indicative. **Quamquam** or **etsī** introduces a concessive clause with its verb in the indicative: **Eī,** *quamquam sunt* **eiusdem generis, sunt cēterīs hūmāniōrēs,** *although they are of the same class, they are more civilized than the rest,* IV, 3.

606. With the subjunctive. **Cum, quamvīs, licet,** or **ut,** with the concessive or adversative meaning *although,* introduces a clause with its verb in the subjunctive: **Cicerō,** *cum* **tenuissimā valētūdine** *esset,* **nē nocturnum quidem sibi tempus ad quiētem relinquēbat,** *Cicero, although he was in very poor health, did not leave himself time for rest even at night,* V, 40.

THE CONDITIONAL SENTENCE

The two parts of a conditional sentence are called the condition (protasis) and the conclusion (apodosis). The usual introductory word of the condition is **sī, nisi,** or **sīn.** There are three types of conditions.

607. The condition of fact. A conditional sentence which assumes a fact to be true in present, past, or future time regularly has the verb in the indicative in both the condition and the conclusion. In the future and future perfect tenses, this condition is sometimes called the *future more vivid:* Sī gravius quid *acciderit,* abs tē ratiōnem *reposcent, if anything too serious shall have happened, they will demand an account from you,* V, 30.

608. The condition of possibility (*should . . . would*). A conditional sentence which denotes a *possibility* in future time regularly has the verb in both clauses in the present or perfect subjunctive. This type of condition is sometimes called *future less vivid:* Neque, aliter sī *faciat,* üllam inter suōs habeat auctōritātem, *and if he should do otherwise, he would not have any authority among his people,* VI, 11.

609. The contrary to fact condition. A conditional sentence in which the idea of the condition and conclusion is represented as being *contrary to fact* has its verb in the subjunctive in both the condition and the conclusion. The tenses in a contrary to fact conditional sentence do not follow the rule for sequence of tenses. The imperfect tense regularly denotes present time and the past perfect, past time: Ego hanc sententiam *probārem,* sī nūllam praeterquam vītae nostrae iactūram *vidērem, I would approve of this opinion, if I saw no other loss than that of our lives,* VII, 77; Ego hanc sententiam *probāvissem,* sī nūllam praeterquam vītae nostrae iactūrum *vīdissem, I would have approved of this opinion, if I had seen no other loss than that of our lives.*

THE SUBJUNCTIVE BY ATTRACTION

610. A clause dependent upon another clause, the verb of which is in the subjunctive and forms an essential part of the whole idea, often has its verb in the subjunctive: Huic imperat quās *possit* adeat cīvitātēs, *he orders him to visit as many states as possible,* IV, 21.

THE IMPERATIVE MOOD

611. The imperative mood is used to express a command in the second person: Vōbīs cōnsulite, *look out for yourselves,* VII, 50. (In Latin, there is a third person in the future imperative, which is rarely used.) For the *Volitive Subjunctive,* see **580.**

   a. The imperative of nōlō (nōlī, nōlīte) with a complementary infinitive is regularly used to express a negative command: *Nōlīte* hōs vestrō auxiliō exspoliāre, *do not (be unwilling) rob them of your help,* VII, 77.

THE INFINITIVE

612. The infinitive, like a finite verb, has voice and tense and may be modified by an adverb. Its tenses are the present, the perfect, and the future.

613. The infinitive as subject or object. Like a noun, the infinitive is often used as the subject or object of a verb and may be modified by a neuter adjective. It is used (usually in the present) with impersonal verbs and verbal phrases, such as **decet, libet, oportet, placet, praestat, fās est, opus est,** and **tempus est :** Hospitem violāre fās (esse) nōn putant, *they do not think it is right to harm a guest,* VI, 23.

The infinitive with subject accusative is used as the object of verbs of saying, knowing, and similar meanings. For this use, see Indirect Discourse, **616–620.**

614. Complementary. Many verbs such as **possum, cōnor,** and **coepī** have their meaning completed by a present infinitive : Iter in ea loca *facere* coepit, *he began to make a journey into those places,* IV, 7.

615. Historical. The present infinitive, with a subject nominative, may be used in vivid narrative with the force of a past tense : Diem ex diē Aeduī *dūcere, the Aeduans put him off from day to day,* I, 16.

INDIRECT DISCOURSE

616. Indirect discourse is dependent on a verb of *saying, perceiving, ascertaining, thinking, knowing,* or *remembering.* It represents the words or thoughts of someone, in indirect form, without quoting the exact words.

The direct quotation in the sentence, *He said, " I am going,"* when changed to the indirect, (*He said*) *that he was going,* shows that in English changes of pronoun, person, and tense must be made in quoting indirectly. In Latin, indirect discourse also involves these changes. Indirect discourse is easier to understand if it is turned into the direct form and translated as direct speech instead of indirect.

THE TENSE OF THE INFINITIVE IN INDIRECT DISCOURSE

617. The present infinitive usually denotes an action going on at the same time as that indicated by the verb on which it depends : Dīcit sē vidēre, *he says that he sees;* Dīxit sē vidēre, *he said that he saw.*

618. The perfect infinitive denotes an action that is complete at the time indicated by the verb on which it depends : Dīcit sē vīdisse, *he says that he saw;* Dīxit sē vīdisse, *he said that he had seen.*

619. The future infinitive denotes an action that is to take place after the time indicated by the verb on which it depends: **Dīcit sē vīsūrum esse,** *he says that he will see;* **Dīxit sē vīsūrum esse,** *he said that he would see.*

THE PRINCIPAL CLAUSE IN INDIRECT DISCOURSE

620. The indirect statement. The verb in a principal clause of a declarative sentence becomes an infinitive (with subject accusative) in indirect discourse: **(Dīcunt) id esse facile,** *(they say) this is easy,* VII, 1.

621. The indirect question. The verb of a real (not rhetorical) question is in the subjunctive in indirect discourse: **Cum quaereret quae cīvitātēs quantaeque in armīs essent,** sic **reperiēbat,** *when he asked what and how great states were in arms, he found out this,* II, 4.

622. The indirect command. The verb of a command or order, expressed by an imperative or by a volitive subjunctive in the direct discourse, is in the subjunctive in indirect discourse: **Nē sē armīs dēspoliāret,** *(they begged that) he should not despoil them of their arms,* II, 31. The direct form would be, **Nōlī nōs armīs dēspoliāre,** *do not despoil us of our arms.*

The tenses of the subjunctive follow the regular rule of sequence of tenses.

623. The subordinate clause in indirect discourse. The verb in a subordinate, or dependent, clause in indirect discourse is in the subjunctive mood. Its sequence is determined by the verb governing the indirect discourse, except in the case of a clause dependent upon a perfect infinitive in which case the sequence is secondary. **(Dīxērunt) sēsē habēre quāsdam rēs quās ab eō petere vellent,** *they said that they had certain things that they wished to ask him,* I, 30.

If a subordinate clause is not a part of the indirect discourse, but is introduced by the author to explain or emphasize a fact, its verb is in the indicative.

a. **The conditional sentence.** The tense of the verb of a condition, except in a contrary to fact condition, in which the tense *never* changes, is governed by that of the verb on which the indirect discourse depends. The verb of the conclusion appears as an infinitive:

INDIRECT (*Dīcit*) **sī quid ille sē velit,** illum ad sē venīre *oportēre,* *that if he (Caesar) wishes anything of him, it is fitting for that one (Caesar) to come to him,* I, 34.

(*Dīxit*) **sī quid ille sē vellet,** illum ad sē venīre oportēre, *that if he wished anything of him, it was fitting for that one to come to him.*

DIRECT **Sī quid ille mē vult,** illum ad mē venīre oportet, *if he wishes anything of me, it is fitting for him to come to me.*

Note. A future perfect indicative becomes a perfect subjunctive when dependent on a primary tense, and a past perfect subjunctive when dependent on a secondary tense:

INDIRECT Dīviciācus *facit* verba : quod sī fēcerit, Aeduōrum auctōritātem apud onmēs Belgās *amplificātūrum* (*esse*), *Diviciacus says that if he should do this, he would increase the influence of the Aeduans among all the Belgians,* II, 14.

DIRECT Quod sī fēceris, . . . amplificābis, *if you do* (*shall have done*) *this, you will increase.* . . .

INDIRECT Caesar respondit : sē cīvitātem *cōnservātūrum* (*esse*), sī priusquam mūrum ariēs attigisset, sē dēdidissent, *Caesar replied that he would spare the state, if they* (*should have*) *surrendered before the battering ram* (*should have*) *touched the wall,* II, 32.

DIRECT Cīvitātem cōnservābō, sī . . . vōs dēdideritis, *I will save the state, if you will have surrendered.* . . .

624. Implied indirect discourse. The subjunctive is often used instead of the indicative in a subordinate clause to indicate that the thought expressed is that of someone other than the writer or speaker : **Veniēbant Aeduī questum, quod Harūdēs fīnēs eōrum *populārentur,*** *the Aeduans came to complain because* (*as they said*) *the Harudes were devastating their territory,* I, 37.

THE PARTICIPLE

625. The tense and use of the participle. A participle is a verbal adjective denoting time relative to that of the verb in its clause. It may express, according to the context, a variety of ideas, such as *time, manner, means, situation, opposition,* and *condition:* Ibi L. Cotta *pugnāns* interficitur, *there L. Cotta is killed while fighting,* V. 37 ; *Repulsī* ab equitātū sē in silvās abdidērunt, (*having been*) *driven back by the cavalry, they hid in the woods,* V, 9.

626. The perfect participle equivalent to the present participle. The perfect participle of some deponent verbs is used with a present meaning, veritus, arbitrātus, cōnātus, secūtus, ūsus, cōnfīsus, and gāvīsus : Quōs sibi Caesar oblātōs gāvīsus illōs retinērī iussit, *Caesar, rejoicing that these had come into his power, ordered them to be held,* IV, 13.

627. The perfect participle equivalent to a coördinate clause. The perfect participle is often equivalent to a coördinate clause : Equitātū *circumventōs* interfēcērunt, *they surrounded* (*them*) *with the cavalry and killed them* (*they killed them having been surrounded*), II, 10.

628. The future participle. See *Active Periphrastic Conjugation,* **501,** *Passive Periphrastic Conjugation,* **501,** and *Gerundive,* **630.**

THE GERUND

629. The gerund is a verbal noun, active in meaning, used in the neuter singular, and lacking the nominative case.   It is never used as the subject or object of a verb.   It may have an object except when it is dependent upon a preposition or is in the dative case : **Certam diem** *conveniendī* **dīcit,** *he sets a definite day of meeting,* V, 57 ; **Aliōs** *territandō* **aliōs** *cohortandō* **magnam partem Galliae in officiō tenuit,** *by terrifying some and by urging others, he kept a great part of Gaul in allegiance,* V, 54.

a. The accusative of the gerund is used as the object of a preposition, usually **ad,** to express purpose : **Lēgātīs respondit diem sē ad** *dēlīberandum* **sūmptūrum,** *he replied to the envoys that he would take time (a day) for deliberating,* I, 7.

b. The genitive of the gerund with **causā** also expresses purpose: **speculandī causā,** *for the purpose of spying,* I, 47.

THE GERUNDIVE

630. The gerundive is the future passive participle, used as a verbal adjective agreeing with a noun, and expressing the leading idea of the phrase of which it is a part.   It is translated like a gerund with a direct object : **Erant hae difficultātēs bellī** *gerendī,* *these were the difficulties of waging war,* III, 10.

a. The gerundive modifying a noun in the genitive case with **causā** or in the accusative case with **ad** is used to express *purpose:* **Commeātūs** *petendī* **causā missī erant,** *they had been sent for the purpose of getting grain,* III, 2 ; **Ad quōs** *cōnsectandōs* **Caesar equitātum mīsit,** *Caesar sent the cavalry to pursue them,* IV, 14.

b. The gerundive also expresses *purpose* when used to modify the object of certain verbs, **cūrō, dō, dēdō** : **Caesar exercitum** *trānsportandum* **cūrāverat,** *Caesar had had the army transported,* IV, 29.

THE SUPINE

631. The supine is a verbal noun of the fourth declension with two forms only, the accusative and the ablative.

a. The supine in -um is used with verbs of motion to express *purpose:* **Ad Caesarem grātulātum convēnērunt,** *they came to Caesar to congratulate him,* I, 30.

b. The supine in -ū is used with some adjectives to express *specification:* **Optimum factū esse dūxērunt,** *they decided that it was the best thing to do,* IV, 30.

THE ROMAN CALENDAR

632. The Roman year was regularly indicated by the names of the consuls in the ablative absolute construction: **M. Messālā, M. Pīsōne cōnsulibus,** *in the year when Marcus Messala and Marcus Piso were consuls.*

633. The year was divided into twelve months, and the number of days in each month, after Caesar's revision of the calendar in 46 B.C., was the same as today. Originally the Roman year began in March. Although the beginning of the year was later changed to January, the numerical names of the months remained the same, except **Quīntīlis** and **Sextīlis** which, in 44 B.C., were renamed in honor of Julius Caesar and Augustus respectively.

The Roman names of the months were: **Iānuārius, Februārius, Mārtius, Aprīlis, Maius, Iūnius, Quīntīlis (Iūlius), Sextīlis (Augustus), September, Octōber, November, December.** These words are adjectives and are used to modify the names of the three days in the month from which the Romans counted: **Kalendae** (the *Calends*), **Nōnae** (the *Nones*), and **Īdūs** (the *Ides*).

634. The Calends were the first day of the month, the Nones the fifth, the Ides the thirteenth, except that in March, May, July, and October, the Nones were on the seventh day and the Ides on the fifteenth.

635. The Calends, Nones, and Ides were the days from which all other dates were reckoned. The day before was designated by **prīdiē** and the accusative: **prīdiē Īdūs Iānuāriās (prīd. Īd. Iān.),** *the twelfth of January.* Other days were indicated by **ante diem** with an ordinal and the accusative: **ante diem quārtum Nōnās Aprīlēs (a.d. IIII Nōn. Apr.),** *the second day of April.*

The Romans always counted both the first day and the last day of a given period. Thus, to turn a Roman date into an English date, add one, in the case of the Ides or Nones, to the date on which they fall, and subtract the given number; for the Calends, add two to the number of days in the preceding month, and subtract the given number. For example: **A.d. VI Kal. Apr.,** add two to thirty-one, the number of days in March, and subtract six, and the date is *March twenty-seventh;* **A.d. III Nōn. Apr.,** add one to the date of the Nones in April, the fifth, and subtract three, and the date is *April third.*

636. A Roman day was the period between sunrise and sunset. This space of time was divided into twelve hours. In different seasons, therefore, the length of an hour varied greatly. In the army the term **vigilia** was used for one of the four watches into which the night was divided. **Prīma vigilia,** *the first watch,* began at sunset.

PREFIXES AND SUFFIXES FOR REFERENCE

637. Prefixes. Consult the LATIN-ENGLISH VOCABULARY for the meaning of prefixes. When a prefix ending in a consonant is affixed to a word beginning with a consonant, the final consonant of the prefix is assimilated, that is, made like the following consonant: thus, **ad** + **currō** becomes **accurrō**.

638. Vowel changes. A short **a** or **e** in the stem of a verb compounded with a preposition is sometimes changed to short **i**: thus, **ex** + **faciō** becomes **efficiō**. Short **a** in such compounds usually becomes short **e** before two consonants: **per** + **factus** becomes **perfectus**.

639. Suffixes.

-ālis, *pertaining to*, rēg + ālis; adjective from noun

-ānus, -ēnus, -īnus, -nus, *pertaining to*, urb + ānus; adjective from noun

-āris, -ārius, *pertaining to*, popul + āris, legiōn + ārius; adjective from noun

-ārium, -ōrium, *place where*, aqu + ārium, audit + ōrium; noun from noun or verb

-ātus, *official position*, magistr + ātus; noun from noun

-bilis, -ilis, *able or capable of*, amā + bilis; adjective from verb

-ia, -cia, -tia, -antia, -entia, *quality of* or *condition*, victōr + ia; noun from noun or adjective

-icus, -ius, -nus, -ēnsis, *pertaining to*, Gall + icus, Hispāni + ēnsis; adjective or noun from noun

-idus, *state of* or *condition*, cup + idus; adjective from verb

-īlis, -lis, *able to be*, cīv + īlis; adjective from noun

-īnus, *pertaining to*, dīv + īnus; adjective from adverb, adjective, or noun

-iō, -siō, -tiō, *action or state of*, ōrā + tiō; noun from verb

-ium, -cium, -tium, *action in progress*, sacrific + ium; noun from verb

-īvus, *pertaining to*, fugit + īvus; adjective from noun or verb

-men, -mentum, *means of*, ōrnā + mentum; noun from verb

-olus, -culus, -ellus, -lus, -ulus, *little*, nāvi + cula; noun from noun

-or, *state of*, am + or; noun from verb

-ōsus, *full of*, perīcul + ōsus; adjective from noun

-tās, *state of* līber + tās; noun from adjective

-tor, -sor, *actor, agent*, vic + tor; noun from verb

-tūdō, *state of*, multi + tūdō; noun from adjective

-tus, -sus, *action, result of action*, impe + tus; noun from verb

-ulum, -bulum, -culum, *means* or *instrument*, vehi + culum; noun from verb

-ūra, -sūra, -tūra, *action, result of action*, sepul + tūra; noun from verb

Compounds of many words are formed by the combination of two words; **faciō** is frequently used in this way, **ampli** + **faciō**, **amplificō**.

LATIN–ENGLISH VOCABULARY

The words starred are those specified by the College Entrance Examination Board and the New York State Tentative Syllabus in Ancient Languages (1928 Revision) to be learned in the first and second years.

The principal parts of a verb of the first conjugation that is regular are not given but are indicated by the figure **1**. The infinitive of a regular verb of the second, third, or fourth conjugation is not given, but the conjugation to which it belongs is indicated by the figure **2**, **3**, or **4** respectively.

A verb used intransitively in this book is indicated by *intr.;* one used both transitively and intransitively by *tr. or intr.;* one used transitively is not indicated in any way.

A., *abbr. for* **Aulus** Au'lus, Roman praenomen

* **ā, ab, abs** (ā *before consonants;* **ab** *before vowels and consonants;* **abs** *in some compounds*), *prep. w. abl.* from, away from, at, on, in, after, by, away

a.d., *abbr. for* **ante diem**

* **abdō, 3, –didī, –ditus** [ab + dō] put away, hide

abdūcō, 3, –dūxī, –ductus lead away, take away

abeō, –īre, –iī (–īvī), –itus, *intr.* go away

abiciō, 3, –iēcī, –iectus [ab + iaciō] throw away, throw down, hurl

abiēs, –ietis, *f.* fir, spruce

abrogō, 1 repeal

abscīdō, 3, –cīdī, –cīsus [abs + caedō] cut away, cut off

absēns, –entis, *see* **absum**

absimilis, –e unlike

absistō, 3, –stitī, —, *intr.* withdraw, go away

abstineō, 2, –tinuī, –tentus, *intr.* hold away, keep away, refrain, abstain

* **absum, abesse, āfuī, āfutūrus,** *intr.* be away, be absent, be distant, be lacking, be exempt from; *pres. part., as adj.,* **absēns** absent

Absyrtus, –ī, *m.* Absyr'tus, brother of Medea

abundō, 1, *intr.* overflow, abound

* **ac,** *see* **atque**

acadēmia, –ae, *f.* school

Acastus, –ī, *m.* Acas'tus, son of Pelias

* **accēdō, 3, –cessī, –cessus,** *intr.* move towards, approach, come, be added; *w.* **ut** *or* **quod** besides

accersō, *see* **arcessō**

* **accidō, 3, –cidī, —** [ad + cadō] *intr.* fall to, fall, happen; **accidit** it happens

* accipiō, 3, –cēpī, –ceptus [ad + capiō] take, receive, get, suffer, learn

Accō, –ōnis, *m.* Ac′co, a chief of the Senones

accommodō, 1 fit on, adjust

accumbō, 3, –cubuī, –cubitus, *intr.* to recline *or* sit at table

accūrātius, *comp. of* accūrātē, *adv.* carefully

accurrō, 3, –currī *or* –cucurrī, –cursus, *intr.* run to, hasten to

accūsō, 1 [ad + causa] blame, chide

* ācer, ācris, ācre sharp, piercing

acerbē, *adv.* bitterly

acerbus, –a, –um bitter, sharp

ācerrimē, *sup. of* ācriter

* aciēs, –ēī, *f.* sharp edge, battle-line, army, battle

ācriter, *adv.* sharply, fiercely, courageously

āctor, –ōris, *m.* doer

āctus, *p. p. of* agō

* acūtus, –a, –um sharp, pointed

* ad, *prep. w. acc.* toward, to the vicinity of, near, at, to, until, by; *w. gerund or gerundive* for the purpose of; *w. numerals, adv.* about

adāctus, *p. p. of* adigō

adaequō, 1 make equal, level

addō, 3, –didī, –ditus put to, add, join

* addūcō, 3, –dūxī, –ductus lead to, lead, draw tight; *in pass.* influenced

* adeō, *adv.* to that point, to such a degree, so, so much, even

* adeō, –īre, –iī (-īvī), –itus, *tr. or intr.* go to, approach, visit

adhaereō, 2, –haesī, –haesūrus, *intr.* stick to, cling

* adhibeō, 2, –uī, –itus [ad + habeō] hold to, summon, admit, use

adhortor, 1, *dep.* encourage

adhūc, *adv.* to this point, thus far, hitherto, still

* adiciō, 3, –iēcī, –iectus [ad + iaciō] throw to, throw up, add

* adigō, 3, –ēgī, –āctus [ad + agō] drive to, bring to, hurl to

adimō, 3, –ēmī, –ēmptus [ad + emō] take away, destroy

* aditus, –ūs, *m.* approach, way of approach, access

adiungō, 3, –iūnxī, –iūnctus join to, win over, annex

adiūtor, –ōris, *m.* helper, mediator

adiuvō, 1, –iūvī, –iūtus help, support, aid

administer, –trī, *m.* assistant

* administrō, 1 manage, perform, carry out

* admīror, 1, *dep.* wonder at, admire

* admittō, 3, –mīsī, –missus send to, let in, permit, incur, commit

* admodum, *adv.* to the limit, very, especially, at least, fully

admoneō, 2, –uī, –itus warn, advise

admoveō, 2, –mōvī, –mōtus move to, apply, bring near

adolēscō, 3, –olēvī, –ultus, *intr.* grow up

* adorior, 4, –ortus sum, *dep.* rise, rise against, attack

* adsum, –esse, affuī, affutūrus, *intr.* be near, be present, stand by, help

* adulēscēns, –entis, *m.* young man

adulēscentia, –ae, *f.* youth

adulterium, –ī, *n.* adultery

adveniō, 4, –vēnī, –ventus, *intr.* arrive

* **adventus, –ūs,** *m.* arrival, coming, approach

adversārius, –a, –um [adversus] opposing; *as noun, m.* opponent

* **adversus, –a, –um** turned against, opposing, opposite, unfavorable; **adversā nocte** in the face of the night

* **advertō, 3, –tī, –versus** turn, turn towards

advocō, 1 call to, call, summon

aedēs, –is, *f.* temple; *pl.* house, building, dwelling

* **aedificium, –ī,** *n.* building, house

aedificō, 1 build

Aeduī, –ōrum, *m., pl.* the Aedui or Aeduans (Ed'uans), a powerful Gallic tribe

Aeētēs, –ae, *m.* Aeëtes (Eē'tēs), king of Colchis

* **aeger, –gra, –grum** sick, weak, suffering

* **aegrē,** *adv.* painfully, with difficulty

aegrōtō, 1, *intr.* be sick

Aemilius, –ī, *m.* Lucius Aemilius (Ēmil'ius), a decurion of cavalry in Caesar's army

aēneus, –a, –um of copper, bronze

aequinoctium, –ī, *n.* the time when day and night are equal, equinox

aequitās, –tātis, *f.* firmness, intention, equality, justice

* **aequō, 1** [aequus] make level *or* equal

* **aequus, –a, –um** level, plain, equal, favorable, just; **aequō animō** with equanimity

āēr, āeris (*acc.* āera) *m.* air

aerumna, –ae, *f.* hardship, trouble, labor

* **aes, aeris,** *n.* copper, bronze, money; **aes aliēnum** debt (*another's money*)

Aesōn, –onis, *m.* Aeson (Ē'son), father of Jason

* **aestās, –tātis,** *f.* heat, summer

aestimātiō, –ōnis, *f.* valuation

* **aestus, –ūs,** *m.* heat, tide

* **aetās, –tātis,** *f.* time of life, age

aeternus, –a, –um everlasting

* **afferō, –ferre, attulī, allātus** [ad + ferō] bring to, announce, cause

* **afficiō, 3, –fēcī, –fectus** do to, treat

affīgō, 3, –fīxī, –fīxus fasten to, attach

affingo, 3, –fīnxī, –fictus add falsely

affīnitās, –tātis, *f.* relationship by marriage, alliance

afflīctō, 1 dash against, strand, wreck

afflīgō, 3, –flīxī, –flīctus strike against, damage, overthrow

affore = affutūrus esse, *fut. inf. of* **adsum**

Āfrica, –ae, *f.* Africa

āfuisse, āfutūrus, *see* **absum**

* **ager, agrī,** *m.* land, country, field, territory

* **agger, –eris** [ad + gerō] *m.* mound, dike, rampart

* **aggredior, 3, –gressus sum,** *dep.* move towards, attack

aggregō, 1 join

agitātor, –ōris, *m.* driver

* **agmen, agminis** [agō] *n.* marching army, column, line of march

agnōscō, 3, –gnōvī, –gnitus recognize

agnus, –ī, *m.* lamb

* **agō, 3, ēgī, āctus** set in motion, drive, lead, push forward, discuss, do, build

* **agricola, –ae,** *m.* farmer

agricultūra, –ae, *f.* agriculture

aiō, *defective,* **aiō, ais, ait, aiunt** say

āla, –ae, *f.* wing

* **alacer, –cris, –cre** lively, eager, ready

alacritās, –tātis, *f.* eagerness, spirit

Albānus, –a, –um Alban

albus, –a, –um white

Alesia, –ae, *f.* Alē′sia (*Alise-Sainte-Reine*), a town of the Mandubii

alibī, *adv.* elsewhere, at another place

* **aliēnus, –a, –um** [alius] another's, unfavorable, hostile

aliō, *adv.* to another place

aliquamdiū, *adv.* for some time, for a time

aliquandō, *adv.* at some time or other, once at length

* **aliquis (–quī), –qua, –quid (–quod),** *indef. pron. or adj.* someone, any one, something, anything, some, any

aliquot, *indecl. adj.* some, several, a few

* **aliter,** *adv.* in another way, otherwise; **aliter ac** otherwise than

* **alius, –a, –ud** another, other; **alius . . . alius** one . . . another; *pl.* some . . . others

allātus, *p. p. of* **afferō**

alligō, 1 tie up, fetter

Allobrogēs, –um, *m. pl.* the Allobroges (Alob′rojēz), a Gallic tribe

* **alō, 3, –uī, altus (alitus)** feed, support, raise

Alpēs, –ium, *f. pl.* the Alps

* **alter, –era, –erum** the other, second, another; **alter . . . alter** the one . . . the other

alternus, –a, –um one after the other, alternate

* **altitūdō, –inis** [altus] *f.* height, depth, thickness

* **altus, –a, –um** (*p. p. of* **alō**) high, tall, deep; *as noun, n.* the sea

Amāzōn, –onis, *f.* Amazon, a woman warrior

ambactus, –ī, *m.* dependent, slave

ambāgēs, –um, *f. pl.* windings

Ambarrī, –ōrum, *m. pl.* Ambar′rī, a Gallic tribe

Ambiānī, –ōrum, *m. pl.* the Ambiā′nī, a Belgian tribe

Ambiorīx, –īgis, *m.* Ambi′orix, king of the Eburones

ambō, –ae, –ō, both

ambulātor, –ōris, *m.* one who walks about, idler, lounger

ambulātrīx, –īcis, *f.* gadabout, lounger

ambulō, 1, *intr.* walk, traverse

āmentia, –ae, *f.* madness, insanity

* **amīcitia, –ae,** *f.* friendship

* **amīcus, –a, –um** [amō] friendly, devoted; *as noun, m.* friend

* **āmittō, 3, –mīsī, –missus** let go away, send away, lose

ammentum, –ī, *n.* strap, thong

* **amō, 1** love, like; *present participle as noun,* **amāns, –tis,** *m. or f.* lover

amor, –ōris, *m.* love

amphora, –ae, *f.* a large jar

amplificō, 1 increase, extend

* **amplius,** *comp. adv.* more; *as noun, n.* more

* **amplus, –a, –um** of great extent, ample, abundant

* **an,** *conj.* or; **utrum (–ne) . . . an** whether . . . or

anceps, –cipitis [ambi + caput] with two heads, double, doubtful

ancilla, –ae, f. maid-servant

* **ancora, –ae, f.** anchor

Ancus, see **Mārcius**

Andebrogius, –ī, m. Andebro'gius, a leader of the Remi

Andēs, –ium, m. pl. the An'dēs, a Gallic tribe north of the Liger River (the *Loire*)

angulus, –ī, m. angle, corner, bend

* **angustiae, –ārum, f. pl.** narrowness, narrow place, defile, difficulty

* **angustus, –a, –um** narrow, difficult; **in angustō** at a crisis

* **animadvertō, 3, –vertī, –versus, tr. or intr.** turn attention to, notice; **animadvertere in** punish, attend to

animal, –ālis, n. living being, animal

* **animus, –ī, m.** spirit, feelings, thoughts, will, courage, pluck, consciousness, mind

Aniō, Aniēnis, m. the An'io River, a tributary of the Tiber River

annōn = an + nōn

annōna, –ae, f. food supply

annuō, 3, –uī, —, intr. nod assent

* **annus, –ī, m.** year

ānser, –eris, m. goose

* **ante, adv.** before, previously; **prep. w. acc.** before, in front of

* **anteā [ante + is] adv.** formerly, once

* **antecēdō, 3, –cessī, –cessus, tr. or intr.** go before, march in advance, surpass

anteferō, –ferre, –tulī, –lātus bear before, place before, prefer

antemna, –ae, f. sail-yard

antequam, conj. before

antīquitus, adv. from ancient times, in old times

* **antīquus, –a, –um** ancient, former

antistō, 1, –stetī, —, intr. excel, surpass

ānulus, –ī, m. ring

anus, –ūs, f. an old woman; *as adj.* old

ānxius, –a, –um troubled, anxious

aper, aprī, m. wild boar

* **aperiō, 4, –uī, apertus** open, uncover

apertē, adv. openly

* **apertus, –a, –um (p. p. of aperiō)** open, unprotected, exposed

Apollō, –inis, m. Apollo, god of the sun, music, poetry, and medicine

appāreō, 2, –uī, –itūrus appear

apparō, 1 prepare, get ready

* **appellō, 1** speak to, call by name, call

appellō, 3, –pulī, pulsus move up, bring along

appetō, 3, –petīvī (–iī), –petītus, tr. or intr. seek for, desire, approach

appōnō, 3, –posuī, –positus place near

* **appropinquō, 1** approach

Aprīlis, –e of April

aptō, 1 fit, adjust

aptus, –a, –um ready

* **apud, prep. w. acc.** in the presence of, before, at the house of, among, with, near

* **aqua, –ae, f.** water

* **aquila, –ae, f.** eagle, standard of a legion, a silver eagle mounted on a staff

Aquileia, –ae, f. Aquilē'ia, a town in Cisalpine Gaul

aquilō, –ōnis, m. the north wind

Aquītānia, –ae, *f.* Aquitā'nia, the southwestern part of Gaul between the Garonne and the Pyrenees

Aquītānus, –a, –um belonging to Aquitā'nia ; *as noun, m.* an Aquitā'nian ; *pl.* the Aquitā'nī *or* Aquitanians

āra, –ae, *f.* altar

Arar, –aris, *acc.* **–im,** *m.* the Arar River (the *Saône*)

arbitrium, –ī, *n.* judgment, pleasure

*** arbitror, ī,** *dep., tr. or intr.* believe, think, consider

*** arbor, -oris,** *f.* tree

arca, –ae, *f.* ark, chest, box

Arcadia, –ae, *f.* Arcadia

*** arcessō, 3, –īvī, –ītus** send for, invite, summon

Arecomicī, –ōrum, *m. pl.,* see **Volcae**

arēna, –ae, *f.* sand, arena

argentum, –ī, *n.* silver, silverware

argilla, –ae, *f.* white clay

Argō, –ūs, *f.* the ship *Argo*

Argonautae, –ārum, *m. pl.* Argonauts, the crew of the *Argo*

Argus, –ī, *m.* Argus, builder of the *Argo*

āridus, –a, –um dry ; *as noun, n.* dry land

ariēs, –ietis, *m.* battering ram

Arīminum, –ī, *n.* Arīm'inum (*Rimini*), a town in northeastern Italy

Ariovistus, –ī, *m.* Ariovis'tus, a German chief

*** arma, –ōrum,** *n. pl.* arms, weapons, armor, rigging

armāmenta, –ōrum, *n. pl.* implements, equipment

armātūra, –ae, *f.* armor, equipment

*** armō, ī** arm, equip ; **armātus, –a,**

–um, *p. p. as adj.* armed, equipped ; *m. pl. as noun* armed men

arō, ī plough

Arria, –ae, *f.* Ar'ria, a Roman woman

arripiō, 3, –uī, –reptus seize, snatch

ars, artis, *f.* skill, art

artifex, –icis, *m.* architect, builder

artificium, –ī, *n.* handicraft, skill, artifice, trade

Arvernus, –a, –um Arver'nian ; *as noun, m. pl.* the Arvernians *or* Arverni, a Gallic tribe

ās, assis, *m.* a penny

ascendō, 3, –scendī, –scēnsus, *tr. or intr.* climb, go aboard

ascēnsus, –ūs, *m.* ascent, way up

ascīscō, 3, –scīvī, –scītus attach (*to oneself*), receive

asellus, –ī, *m.* donkey

aspectus, –ūs, *m.* seeing, sight, look, aspect, appearance

asper, –era, –erum rough, hard

aspiciō, 3, –spexī, –spectus see

assector, ī, *dep.* follow

assiduus, –a, –um constant, continual

assistō, 3, astitī, —, *intr.* take a stand, stand near, assist

assuēfaciō, 3, –fēcī, –factus, *tr. or intr.* to accustom

astō, ī, astitī, —, *intr.* stand at, stand near

*** at,** *conj.* but, but yet, at least, at any rate

Athēnae, –ārum, *f. pl.* Athens

Atlās, Atlantis, *m.* Atlas, a giant who held the world on his shoulders

*** atque, ac,** *conj.* and, and also, and besides, and even ; **alius atque** other than ; **aliter ac** otherwise than ; **simul atque** as soon as

Atrebās, –ātis, *m.* an Atrebatian (Atrebā'shian); *pl.*, the Atrebā'tes *or* Atrebatians, a Belgian tribe

atrōciter, *adv.* cruelly

attexō, 3, –uī, –tus weave to, join on

* **attingō, 3, –tigī, –tāctus** [ad + tangō] arrive at, border on, get

attribuō, 3, –uī, –ūtus assign, give in charge, allot

attrītus, –a, –um rubbed

attulī, *see* **afferō**

* **auctor, –ōris** [augeō] *m.* promoter, leader, adviser

* **auctōritās, –tātis,** *f.* influence, power, authority, dignity

audācia, –ae, *f.* boldness, recklessness

* **audācter,** *adv.* boldly, recklessly

* **audāx, –ācis** bold, brave

* **audeō, 2, ausus sum,** *semi-dep.*, *tr. or intr.* dare

* **audiō, 4, –īvī, –ītus** hear, hear of, listen to, obey, be obedient to

auferō, –ferre, abstulī, ablātus [ab + ferō] carry off

aufugiō, 3, –fūgī, —, *intr.* run away, escape

Augēas, –ae, *m.* Augeus (Âjē'as), king of Elis

* **augeō, 2, auxī, auctus** increase

Augustus, –ī, *m.* Augustus, a title of Octavius Caesar as emperor; *as adj.* of Augustus

Aulercī, –ōrum, *m. pl.* the Aulerci (Auler'sī), a Gallic tribe

aura, –ae, *f.* air, wind

aureolus, –a, –um golden

aureus, –a, –um of gold, golden

aurīga, –ae, *m.* charioteer, driver

auris, –is, *f.* ear

aurītus, –a, –um having ears; *w.* **testis** earwitness

aurum, –ī, *n.* gold

Aurunculeius, –ī, *m.* Lū'cius Aurunculē'ius Cotta, one of Caesar's legates

ausus, –a, –um, *p. p. of* **audeō**

* **aut,** *conj.* or; **aut . . . aut** either . . . or

* **autem,** *conj.* on the other hand, but, furthermore, now, moreover

auxilior, 1, *dep., intr.* give aid, help

* **auxilium, –ī** [augeō] *n.* aid, support; *pl.* auxiliaries, reserves

Avaricum, –ī, *n.* Avar'icum (*Bourges*), a town of the Bituriges

avāritia, –ae, *f.* greed, avarice

āvehō, 3, –vexī, –vectus carry away

Aventīnus, –a, –um Av'entīne; *w.* **mōns** one of the seven hills of Rome

āversus, –a, –um turned, in the rear, retreating

āvertō, 3, –tī, –versus turn away, alienate

avidus, –a, –um greedy

avis, –is, *f.* bird

Avītus, –ī, *m.* Avī'tus, Roman cognomen

avus, –ī, *m.* grandfather

Axona, –ae, *m.* the Ax'ona River, (the *Aisne*)

Babylōnia, –ae, *f.* Babylon

Bacchus, –ī, *m.* Bacchus, god of wine

Bacēnis, –is, *f.* Bacenis (Basē'nis), a forest in Germany

Baculus, –ī, *m., see* **Sextius**

Balbus, –ī, *m.* Cornelius Balbus, an intimate friend of Caesar

Baleāris, -e Balearic, of the Balearic Islands. The best slingers came from this island

balteus, -ī, m. sword-belt

* **barbarus, -a, -um** (*not Greek or Roman*), barbarous, uncivilized; *as noun, m.* native, barbarian

basilica, -ae, f. a public building used for business and courts

beātus, -a, -um blessed, happy

Belgae, -ārum, m. pl. the Belgians

Belgium, -ī, n. Belgium

bellicōsus, -a, -um warlike, fond of war

bellicus, -a, -um warlike

bellō, 1, intr. carry on war, fight

Bellovacī, -ōrum, m. pl. the Bellovaci (Bellov'asī), a powerful tribe of the Belgians

* **bellum, -ī, n.** war

* **bene, adv.** well, successfully

* **beneficium, -ī [bene + faciō] n.** favor, kindness, service, benefit

bēstia, -ae, f. beast

bi-, bis-, insep. prefix two

bibō, 3, bibī, —, tr. or intr. drink

Bibracte, -is, n. Bibrac'te, the chief town of the Aeduans

Bibrax, -actis, f. Bī'brax, a town of the Remi

biceps, bicipitis [bi + caput] two-headed

* **bīduum, -ī [bis + diēs] n.** period of two days, two days

biennium, -ī [bi + annus] n. two years

* **bīnī, -ae, -a [bis] pl. adj.** two at a time, two apiece

bipertītō, adv. in two divisions

* **bis, adv.** twice

Biturīgēs, -um, m. pl. the Bituriges (Biturī'jēz), a tribe of central Gaul

Boiī, -ōrum, m. pl. the Boi'ī, a Gallic tribe

bonitās, -tātis [bonus] f. goodness, fertility

* **bonus, -a, -um** good, faithful, reliable, favorable, friendly, kindly

bōs, bovis, m. or f. ox, cow; *pl.* cattle

bracchium, -ī, n. forearm, arm

Bratuspantium, -ī, n. Bratuspantium (Bratuspan'shium), a town of the Bellovaci

* **brevis, -e** short, brief

brevitās, -tātis, f. shortness, brevity

Britannī, -ōrum, m. pl. the Britons

Britannia, -ae, f. Britain

brūma, -ae, f. winter solstice, winter

Brūtus, -ī [brutus, dull] m. Decimus Junius Brutus, an able officer under Caesar, but later one of his assassins; Lucius Junius Brutus, first consul; Marcus Junius Brutus, also one of Caesar's assassins

C., abbr. for Gāius Gā'ius, a Roman praenomen

Cabūrus, -ī, m., see Valerius

cadāver, -eris [cadō] n. corpse

* **cadō, 3, cecidī, cāsūrus, intr.** fall, be slain

Cadūrcī, -ōrum, m. pl. the Caduci (Kader'sī), a Gallic tribe near the Province

Caeciliānus, -ī, m. Caecilianus (Sēsiliā'nus), a Roman cognomen

Caecīna, -ae, m. Caecina Paetus (Sēsī'na Pē'tus), husband of Arria

caecus, -a, -um blind

* **caedēs, -is, f.** cutting down, killing, massacre

* **caedō, 3, cecīdī, caesus** cut, cut down, kill
caelestis, -e of heaven, heavenly; *as noun, m. pl.* gods
Caelius, -a, -um Caelian (Sē'lian); *w.* mōns one of the hills of Rome
caelum, -ī, n. sky, heaven
caeruleus, -a, -um sky-blue, blue
Caesar, -aris, m. Gaius Julius Caesar, the conqueror of Gaul and author of the *Commentaries*
caespes, -itis, m. cut sod, turf
* **calamitās, -tātis, f.** loss, disaster, defeat
calcar, -āris, n. spur
calceus, -ī, m. shoe
calidus, -a, -um warm
callidus, -a, -um cunning, shrewd
cālō, -ōnis, m. servant, camp-follower, driver
* **campus, -ī, m.** open country, field, plain
candidus, -a, -um white
candor, -ōris, m. splendor, brilliancy
canis, -is, m. or f. dog
Cannae, -ārum, f. pl. Cannae (Can'ē), a town in Italy
canō, 3, cecinī, cantus, tr. or intr. sound, sing
Cantium, -ī, n. Cantium (*Kent*), a district in England
cantō, 1, tr. or intr. sing
capillus, -ī, m. hair
* **capiō, 3, cēpī, captus** take, receive, seize, capture, deceive, reach, arrive at, move
Capitōlium, -ī, n. the Capitoline, one of the hills of Rome
capra, -ae, f. goat
* **captīvus, -a, -um** taken, captured; *as noun, m.* captive

* **caput, -itis, n.** head, mouth (*of a river*), life
careō, 2, -uī, -itūrus intr. be without, go without
carmen, -inis, n. song, prophecy
Carnutēs, -um, m. pl. the Car'nutēs, a Gallic tribe
carō, carnis, f. flesh, meat
carpō, 3, carpsī, carptus pick, blame, divide
* **carrus, -ī, m.** cart
Carthāginiēnsis, -e Carthaginian
Carthāgō, -inis, f. Carthage
cārus, -a, -um dear, beloved
casa, -ae, f. hut, cabin
Casca, -ae, m. Cas'ca, a Roman cognomen
cāseus, -ī, m. cheese
Cassiānus, -a, -um [Cassius] of Cassius
Cassius, -ī, m. Lucius Cassius Longinus (Lū'shius Cash'ius Lonjī'nus), consul in 107 B.C.
* **castellum, -ī, n.** little fort, post, fortress, small camp
Casticus, -ī, m. Cas'ticus, a chief of the Sequanians
Castor, -oris, m. Castor, brother of Pollux
* **castra, -ōrum, n. pl.** camp
* **cāsus, -ūs [cadō] m.** fall, chance, calamity, fate, emergency
catēna, -ae, f. chain, fetter
Caturīgēs, -um, m. pl. the Caturiges (Caturī'jēs), a tribe in the Alps
cauda, -ae, f. tail
caupō, -ōnis, m. innkeeper
* **causa, -ae, f.** cause, reason; **causā**, *with a preceding genitive* for the sake of, for the purpose of

causātus (*p. p. of* causor) giving as reason

causidicus, –ī, *m.* pleader

cautē, *adv.* carefully

Cavarillus, –ī, *m.* Cavaril′lus, a chieftain of the Aeduans

caveō, 2, cāvī, cautus, *tr. or intr.* take care, be on guard, be cautious

caverna, –ae, *f.* cave

* cēdō, 3, cessī, cessus, *intr.* move, retreat, obey

celebrō, 1 celebrate

* celer, –eris, –ere swift, sudden

* celeritās, –tātis, *f.* swiftness, speed

celeriter, *adv.* quickly, swiftly

cēlō, 1 hide, conceal

Celtillus, –ī, *m.* Celtillus (Seltil′us), an Arvernian, father of Vercingetorix

cēna, –ae, *f.* dinner

Cēnabum, –ī, *n.* Cenabum (Sen′abum), (*Orleans*), a city of the Carnutes

* cēnseō, 2, cēnsuī, cēnsus estimate, think, decree, be of an opinion

cēnsus, –ūs, *m.* enumeration, census

Centaurus, –ī, *m.* Centaur, a creature half man and half horse

* centum, *indecl. adj.* one hundred

* centuriō, –ōnis, *m.* commander of a century, captain, centurion

cēra, –ae, *f.* wax

Cerberus, –ī, *m.* Cerberus, the dog guarding the door of Hades

Cerēs, –eris, *f.* Ceres, goddess of fruits and grains

* cernō, 3, crēvī, crētus [certus] separate, discern, see

certāmen, –inis [certō, *struggle*] *n.* battle, contest, rivalry

certē, *adv.* surely, at least

* certus, –a, –um determined, definite, sure, appointed, well-established; certiōrem facere inform

cervīx, –īcis, *f.* neck

cervus, –ī, *m.* stag

* cēterī, –ae, –a, *pl.* the others, the rest

certē, *adv.* surely, at least

Ceutronēs, –um, *m. pl.* the Ceutrones (Sū′tronēz), a Gallic tribe in the Province

Cheruscī, –ōrum, *m. pl.* the Cherusci (Kerus′ī), a German tribe

Christiānus, –ī, *m.* a Christian

Christus, –ī, *m.* Christ

cibārius, –a, –um relating to food; *as noun, n. pl.* food, supplies

* cibus, –ī, *m.* food

Cicerō, –ōnis, *m.* Quintus Tullius Cicero (Sis′ero), brother of Cicero the orator, was one of Caesar's officers

Cimber, –brī, *m.* Cimber (Sim′ber), one of the assassins of Caesar

Cimbrī, –ōrum, *m. pl.* the Cimbri (Sim′brī), a German tribe

Cincinnātus, –ī, *m.* Lucius Quinctius Cincinnatus (Sinsinā′tus), a famous Roman

cingō, 3, cīnxī, cīnctus surround, inclose, invest

cinis, –eris, *m.* ashes

* circiter [circus, *circle*] *adv.* about; *prep. w. acc.* around, near

circuitus, –ūs, *m.* going around, distance around, circuit

* circum, *prep. w. acc.* around, about, near

circumagō, 3, –ēgī, –āctus go out of the way

circumcīdō, 3, –cīdī, –cīsus cut around

* circumdō, 1, –dedī, –datus put around, surround, encompass

circumeō, –īre, –iī (–īvī), –itus *tr.* or *intr.* go around, surround, visit

circumiciō, 3, –iēcī, –iectus [circum + iaciō] throw around, place around

circummittō, 3, –mīsī, –missus send around

* circumsistō, 3, –stetī, — take a stand around, surround

circumspiciō, 3, –spexī, –spectus look around at, consider, examine

circumvāllō, 1 surround with a rampart, blockade

* circumveniō, 4, –vēnī, –ventus come around, beset, circumvent, deceive

cis, *prep. w. acc.* this side, on this side of

* citerior, –ius, *adj.*, *comp.* on this side, nearer, hither

cithara, –ae, *f.* cithara, lute

citharoedus, –ī, *m.* harpist

citissimē, *sup. of* citō, *adv.* most swiftly

citō, *adv.* quickly

citrā, *prep. w. acc.* on this side

* cīvis, –is, *m. or f.* citizen, fellow-citizen

* cīvitās, –tātis [cīvis] *f.* citizenship, state, nation, city

* clam, *adv.* secretly

clāmitō, 1 call repeatedly, cry out

* clāmō, 1 call out

* clāmor, –ōris, *m.* shout, uproar, clamor

clandestīnus, –a, –um secret, clandestine

clārus, –a, –um clear, bright, loud

* classis, –is, *f.* fleet

Claudius, –ī, *m.* Claudius, a Roman emperor; Appius Claudius Pulcher, consul in 54 B.C.

* claudō, 3, clausī, clausus shut, close

clāvis, –is, *f.* key, lock

clēmentia, –ae, *f.* mercy, kindness

* cliēns, –entis, *m.* dependent, client

clientēla, –ae, *f.* clientship, protection

cloāca, –ae, *f.* sewer

Clōdius, –ī, *m.* Publius Clodius Pulcher, who was killed by Milo in 52 B.C.

Cn., *abbr. for* Gnaeus Gnaeus (Nē′us), Roman praenomen

coacervō, 1 heap together, pile up

coāctus, *p. p. of* cōgō

coccinus, –a, –um scarlet

coctus, *p. p. of* coquō

coemō, 3, –ēmī, –ēmptus purchase, buy up

coeō, –īre, –iī (–īvī), –itus, *intr.* go together, come together

* coepī, coepisse, coeptus, *defective* (*used in perfect system only*) *tr.* or *intr.* began, undertook

coerceō, 2, –ercuī, –ercitus restrain, hold in check

coetus, –ūs, *m.* assembly

* cōgitō, 1 consider thoroughly, think, plan

cognātiō, –ōnis, *f.* blood-relationship

* cognōscō, 3, –gnōvī, –gnitus learn, find out about, investigate; *in perf. system* know

* cōgō, 3, coēgī, coāctus [con + agō] drive together, bring together, get together, collect, compel, oblige, force

* cohors, –ortis, *f.* cohort, company

cohortātiō, –ōnis, *f.* encouragement

cohortor, 1, *dep.* encourage, address

Colchī, –ōrum, *m. pl.* Colchians (Kol′kians), inhabitants of Colchis

Colchis, –idis (*acc.* –ida) *f.* Colchis (Kol′kis), a country east of the Black Sea

collātus, *p. p. of* cōnferō

collaudō, 1 praise

colligō, 1 tie together, fasten together

* colligō, 3, –lēgī, –lēctus gather together, collect

* collis, –is, *m.* hill

* collocō, 1 place, station, settle

* colloquium, –ī, *n.* conference, interview, conversation

* colloquor, 3, –locūtus sum, *dep., intr.* talk, converse, confer

colō, 3, –uī, cultus till, cherish, worship

colōnia, –ae, *f.* colony

color, –ōris, *m.* color

columba, –ae, *f.* dove

coma, –ae, *f.* hair, rays

combūrō, 3, –ussī, –ustus burn up, consume

comedō, 3, –ēdī, –ēsus *or* –ēstus eat, consume

comes, –itis, *m.* companion

comitia, –ōrum, *n. pl.* assembly of the people for voting, election

comitor, 1, *dep.* accompany, follow

* commeātus, –ūs, *m.* going to and fro, trip, supplies

* commemorō, 1 bring to mind, mention

commendātiō, –ōnis, *f.* recommendation

* commendō, 1 put under one's protection, intrust

commeō, 1, *intr.* go back and forth, go about, go

commīlitō, –ōnis, *m.* fellow-soldier

comminus, *adv.* hand to hand, at close range

* committō, 3, –mīsī, –missus put together, join, unite, risk, intrust, allow, admit

Commius, –ī, *m.* Com′mius, an Atrebatian

commodē, *adv.* well, suitably, conveniently, easily

commodum, –ī, *n.* convenience, profit, blessing

* commodus, –a, –um suitable, convenient, favorable, easy, useful

* commoror, 1, *dep., intr.* delay, stay

* commoveō, 2, –mōvī, –mōtus disturb, excite, agitate, impel

* commūnicō, 1 communicate, impart, share, unite, consult

commūniō, 4, –īvī, –ītus fortify on all sides, build

* commūnis, –e common, belonging to all

commūtātiō, –ōnis, *f.* change, reversal

commūtō, 1 change wholly, exchange, replace

* comparō, 1 prepare, procure, buy

* compellō, 3, –pulī, –pulsus drive together, collect

* comperiō, 4, –perī, –pertus learn, detect, find out

complector, 3, –plexus sum, *dep.* embrace, include

* compleō, 2, –ēvī, –ētus fill up, fill, crowd

* complūrēs, –a *or* –ia, *pl. adj.* many, several

comportō, 1 carry together, collect, bring in

* comprehendō, 3, –dī, –hēnsus lay hold of, seize

compulsus, –a, –um, *p. p. of* compellō

con– [cum] *prefix* with, completely

cōnātus, –ūs, *m.* attempt

* concēdō, 3, –cessī, –cessus, *tr. or intr.* go away, grant, submit

concidō, 3, –cidī, —, *intr.* fall down, be slain

* concīdō, 3, –cīdī, –cīsus cut to pieces, intersect, kill

conciliō, 1 call together, reconcile, win over, gain

* concilium, –ī, *n.* assembly, meeting

concinō, 3, –uī, —, *tr. or intr.* sing in concert

concitō, 1 rouse, incite

conclāmō, 1, *tr. or intr.* cry out, shout

concordia, –ae, *f.* harmony, concord

concrēdō, 3, —idī, –itus intrust

concurrō, 3, –currī *or* –cucurrī, –cursus run together, run up, hurry

concursus, –ūs, *m.* running together, encounter, collision, attack

* condiciō, –ōnis, *f.* terms, proposition, situation

condō, 3, –didī, –ditus found, put away

condūcō, 3, –dūxī, –ductus lead together, assemble, hire

* cōnferō, –ferre, contulī, collātus bring together, consider, collect, convey, put off, ascribe; sē cōnferre betake oneself, go

* cōnfertus, –a, –um crowded, dense

* cōnfestim, *adv.* at once, immediately

* cōnficiō, 3, –fēcī, –fectus complete, finish, exhaust

* cōnfīdō, 3, –fīsus sum, *semi-dep., intr.* have confidence in, rely upon, trust, believe, hope

* cōnfirmō, 1 strengthen, encourage, state, appoint, establish

cōnfīsus, *p. p. of* cōnfīdō

cōnflagrō, 1, *intr.* be on fire, burn

* cōnflīgō, 3, –flīxī, –flīctus, *intr.* fight together, contend

* congredior, 3, –gressus sum, *dep., intr.* meet, meet in arms

* coniciō, 3, –iēcī, –iectus throw together, hurl, station, put

coniūnctim, *adv.* together, jointly

* coniungō, 3, –iūnxī, –iūnctus join together, unite

coniūnx, –iugis, *m. or f.* husband, wife

coniūrātiō, –ōnis, *f.* conspiracy, plot

* coniūrō, 1, *intr.* take oath together, conspire, plot

Conōn, –ōnis, *m.* Cō'non

* cōnor, 1, *dep., tr. or intr.* attempt, try

* conquīrō, 3, –quīsīvī, –quīsītus seek for, hunt up, bring together

cōnsanguineus, –a, –um related by blood; *as noun, m.* kinsman

* cōnscendō, 3, –scendī, –scēnsus climb, scale, embark

cōnscīscō, 3, –scīvī, –scītus approve of, decide upon, decree

* cōnscrībō, 3, –scrīpsī, –scrīptus write, levy, enlist

cōnsecrātus, –a, –um sacred, hallowed

cōnsector, 1, *dep.* follow closely, overtake, pursue

cōnsēnsus, –ūs, *m.* consent, agreement

* cōnsentiō, 4, –sēnsī, –sēnsus, *intr.* agree together, conspire

* cōnsequor, 3, –secūtus sum, *dep.* follow up, overtake, attain, pursue, follow

cōnservō, 1 spare, protect

Cōnsidius, –ī, *m.* Pub′lius Consid′ius, an officer in Caesar's army

* cōnsīdō, 3, –sēdī, –sessus, *intr.* take a seat, settle, pitch camp

* cōnsilium, –ī, *n.* plan, decision, purpose, design, consent, authority, judgment, council

cōnsimilis, –e very similar, much like

* cōnsistō, 3, –stitī, —, *intr.* take a stand, be stationed, halt, stay, settle, ground, anchor, depend, be

cōnsōlor, 1, *dep.* comfort, encourage

* cōnspectus, –ūs, *m.* sight, appearance

* cōnspiciō, 3, –spexī, –spectus get sight of, see

* cōnspicor, 1, *dep.* get sight of, see, notice

cōnspīrō, 1 agree together, conspire

cōnstanter, *adv.* unanimously, firmly

cōnstīpō, 1 crowd together, pack

* cōnstituō, 3, –stituī, –stitūtus station, put, set up, halt, anchor, appoint, make, finish, form, decide

* cōnstō, 1, –stitī, –stātūrus, *intr.* stand together, be agreed, appear, cost; *impers.*, * cōnstat it is agreed, known, certain

* cōnsuēscō, 3, –suēvī, –suētus, *intr.* become accustomed; *in perf. system* be accustomed

* cōnsuētūdō, –inis, *f.* custom, habit, way of life

* cōnsul, –ulis, *m.* consul, the highest magistrate of the Roman state

cōnsulātus, –ūs, *m.* consulship

* cōnsulō, 3, –suluī, –sultus, *tr. or intr.* hold a consultation, consult for, spare

cōnsultō, 1, *tr. or intr.* take counsel, deliberate, consult

cōnsultum, –ī, *n.* decree, decision

* cōnsūmō, 3, –sūmpsī, –sūmptus use up, consume, waste, destroy, spend

cōnsurgō, 3, –surrēxī, –surrēctus, *intr.* rise, stand up

contabulō, 1 build of boards, erect

contāgiō, –ōnis, *f.* contact, evil association

* contemnō, 3, –tempsī, –temptus despise

contemptiō, –ōnis, *f.* scorn, contempt

* contendō, 3, –tendī, –tentus, *tr. or intr.* strain, strive for, press forward, fight, insist

contentiō, –ōnis, *f.* effort, struggle, rivalry

conterō, 3, –trīvī, –trītus use up

contestor, 1, *dep.* call to witness, invoke

contexō, 3, –uī, –tus join together, weave

continēns, –entis contiguous, continuous; *as noun, f.* continent

continenter, *adv.* continuously, continually

continentia, –ae, *f.* self-control, moderation

* contineō, 2, –uī, –tentus hold together, keep, check, hem in, bound, hold, comprise, fill; sē continēre stay, remain

contingō, 3, –tigī, –tāctus, *tr. or intr.* touch, reach, extend to, happen

* continuus, –a, –um continuous, successive, without interruption

cōntiō, –ōnis, *f.* speech, assembly

* **contrā**, *adv.* fronting, on the other hand, in opposition; **contrā atque** opposite to, otherwise than; *prep. w. acc.* contrary to, opposite, against, facing, in spite of, in reply to, towards

contrahō, 3, **–trāxī**, **–tractus** bring together, collect, contract

contrārius, **–a**, **–um** on the other side, opposite, opposing

*__controversia__, **–ae**, *f.* dispute, quarrel

* **contumēlia**, **–ae**, *f.* insult, abuse, disgrace, outrage

* **conveniō**, 4, **–vēnī**, **–ventus**, *tr. or intr.* come together, assemble, be suitable, meet, agree upon; *impers.* **convenit** it is agreed

conventus, **–ūs**, *m.* meeting, assembly, court

conversiō, **–ōnis**, *f.* revolution

* **convertō**, 3, **–vertī**, **–versus**, *tr. or intr.* turn, turn about; **conversa signa īnferre** wheel and charge

Convictolitāvis, **–is**, *m.* Convictolitā'vis, a prominent Aeduan

convocō, 1 call together, summon

coorior, 4, **–ortus sum**, *dep., intr.* arise, break out, spring up

cophinus, **–ī**, *m.* casket

* **cōpia**, **–ae** [co– + ops] *f.* plenty, abundance, supply; *pl.* supplies, resources, soldiers, forces

cōpiōsus, **–a**, **–um** abundantly supplied, rich

coquō, 3, **coxī**, **coctus** cook

cor, **cordis**, *n.* heart

cōram [co– + ōs] *adv.* present, face to face, in person

Corinthus, **–ī**, *f.* Corinth, a city in Greece

Coriolānus, **–ī**, *m.* Coriolā'nus

* **cornū**, **–ūs**, *n.* horn, antler, wing (*of an army*), flank

corōna, **–ae**, *f.* wreath, circle (*of men*); **sub corōnā** at auction

* **corpus**, **–oris**, *n.* body, person, corpse

corrumpō, 3, **–rūpī**, **–ruptus** break up, destroy, spoil

corvus, **–ī**, *m.* raven

* **cotīdiānus**, **–a**, **–um** daily, usual

* **cotīdiē** [quot + diēs] *adv.* daily, every day

Cotta, **–ae**, *m.* a Roman cognomen; *see* **Aurunculeius**

Cotus, **–ī**, *m.* Cō'tus, a prominent Aeduan

coxī, *see* **coquō**

Crassus, **–ī**, *m.* Marcus Licinius Crassus, triumvir with Caesar, 55 B.C.; Publius Licinius Crassus, one of Caesar's officers

crātis, **–is**, *f.* faggot; *pl.* wickerwork

* **crēber**, **–bra**, **–brum** thick, crowded, frequent, numerous

* **crēdō**, 3, **crēdidī**, **crēditus**, *tr. or intr.* intrust, trust, believe, consider, think

cremō, 1 burn, consume

creō, 1 appoint, elect

Creōn, **–ontis**, *m.* Crē'on, king of Corinth

crēscō, 3, **crēvī**, **crētus**, *intr.* grow, increase

crēta, **–ae**, *f.* chalk

Crēta, **–ae**, *f.* Crete, an island

Crētēnsēs, **–ium**, *m. pl.* Cretans

Crēticus, **–a**, **–um** Cretan

* **cruciātus**, **–ūs**, *m.* torment, torture

crūdēlis, **–e** cruel

cubiculum, **–ī**, *n.* bedroom

cubō, 1, –uī, –itus, *intr.* recline, lie sick

culpa, –ae, *f.* fault, error, blame

cultūra, –ae, *f.* tillage, cultivation

cultus, –ūs, *m.* care, way of living, civilization

* **cum,** *prep. w. abl.* with

* **cum,** *conj.* when, while, after, at the time when, whenever, as often as, as, since, because, although, while; **cum prīmum** as soon as; * **cum . . . tum** as . . . so, both . . . and, not only . . . but also

cūnābula, –ōrum, *n. pl.* cradle

cūnctor, 1, *dep., intr.* hesitate

cūnctus, –a, –um all collectively, all

cupidē, *adv.* eagerly, ardently

* **cupiditās, –tātis,** *f.* eagerness, greed, desire

cupīdō, –inis, *f.* desire, eagerness

Cupīdō, –inis, *m.* Cupid, god of love

* **cupidus, –a, –um** eager, desirous

* **cupiō, 3, –īvī, –ītus,** *tr. or intr.* desire, wish, long for

* **cūr,** *interr. adv.* why? wherefore?

* **cūra, –ae,** *f.* care, anxiety, diligence

cūria, –ae, *f.* senate house

Curius, –ī, *m.* M'. Curius Dentatus (Manius Cu'rius Dentā'tus), victor over the Samnites

* **cūrō, 1** take care of, see to, cause

* **currō, 3, cucurrī, cursus,** *intr.* run

currus, –ūs, *m.* cart, wagon, chariot

* **cursus, –ūs,** *m.* running, speed, course

custōdia, –ae, *f.* watch, guard

custōdiō, 4, –īvī, –ītus guard, hold in custody

* **custōs, –ōdis,** *m.* guard, sentinel

Cyzicus, –ī, *f.* Cyzicus (Siz'ikus), a city in Asia Minor

D., *abbr. for* **Decimus** Decimus (Des'imus), Roman praenomen

Daedalus, –ī, *m.* Daedalus (Ded'-alus), first flier

damnō, 1 find guilty, convict

damnōsus, –a, –um injurious, destructive

* **dē,** *prep. w. abl.* down from, from, down, away from, out of, about, concerning, of, during, in regard to, because of, in consequence of, for

dea, –ae, *f.* goddess

* **dēbeō, 2, –uī, –itus** owe; *w. inf.* ought, should, must; *pass.* be due

dēcēdō, 3, –cessī, –cessus, *intr.* go away, withdraw, die

* **decem,** *indecl. adj.* ten

* **dēcernō, 3, –crēvī, –crētus,** *tr. or intr.* decide, determine, resolve

* **dēcertō, 1,** *intr.* fight, fight to a finish, decide by battle

dēcessus, –ūs, *m.* going away, ebbing, death

dēcidō, 3, –cidī, —, *intr.* fall down, fall off

* **decimus, –a, –um** tenth

dēcipiō, 3, –cēpī, –ceptus deceive

* **dēclīvis, –e** sloping, downward; *as noun, n. pl.* slopes

decōrus, –a, –um beautiful

dēcrēscō, 3, –crēvī, –crētus, *intr.* decrease, grow less

dēcrētum, –ī, *n.* decree, decision

dēcrētus, –a, –um, *p. p. of* **dēcernō**

decuriō, –ōnis, *m.* decurion, commander of a troop of ten horsemen

dēcurrō, 3, –cucurrī *or* **–currī, –cursus,** *intr.* run down, hurry

dēdecus, –oris, *n.* disgrace, reproach

dēditīcius, –a, –um surrendered; *as noun, m. pl.* captives

* **dēditiō, -ōnis,** *f.* surrender
* **dēdō, 3, -didī, -ditus** give up, surrender, devote
* **dēdūcō, 3, -dūxī, -ductus** lead down, draw out, launch, mislead
dēfatīgō, 1 tire out, exhaust
dēfectiō, -ōnis, *f.* desertion, revolt, rebellion
* **dēfendō, 3, -fendī, -fēnsus** drive off, avert, protect
dēfēnsiō, -ōnis, *f.* defense
* **dēfēnsor, -ōris,** *m.* protector; *pl.* guards, defenses
* **dēferō, -ferre, -tulī, -lātus** carry off, drive down, bring, carry, confer, offer, report, propose; *pass.* drift, be turned aside
* **dēfessus, -a, -um** worn out
* **dēficiō, 3, -fēcī, -fectus,** *tr. or intr.* revolt, fail, cease; **dēficere ab** desert
dēfīgō, 3, -fīxī, -fīxus set, fasten, drive down
dēfodiō, 3, -fōdī, -fossus dig down, bury
dēfōrmis, -e deformed, ugly
dēfugiō, 3, -fūgī, — run away, flee from, avoid
dēfungor, 3, dēfūnctus sum, *dep.,* *intr.* finish, die
dēiciō, 3, -iēcī, -iectus throw down, hurl, destroy, drive away
dēiectus, -ūs, *m.* declivity, descent
deinceps, *adv.* successively
* **deinde,** *adv.* afterwards, next, then
dēlābor, 3, -lāpsus sum, *dep., intr.* sink, descend
dēlātus, *p. p. of* **dēferō**
dēlectō, 1 delight, please
dēlēctus, *see* **dīlēctus**

* **dēleō, 2, -ēvī, -ētus** blot out, destroy, annihilate
dēlīberō, 1, *tr. or intr.* consider, discuss
dēlictum, -ī, *n.* fault, crime
dēligō, 1 tie down, fasten, moor
* **dēligō, 3, -lēgī, -lēctus** select
dēlitēscō, 3, -lituī, —, *intr.* hide away
Delphī, -ōrum, *m. pl.* Delphi, a city in Greece, the home of the oracle of Apollo
dēmetō, 3, -messuī, -messus harvest, gather
dēmigrō, 1, *intr.* move away, go from home
dēmō, 3, dēmpsī, dēmptus take down, remove
* **dēmōnstrō, 1** show, designate, explain
dēmum, *adv.* at last, finally
dēnique, *adv.* finally, after all, at least
* **dēns, dentis,** *m.* tooth
dēnsus, -a, -um thick, crowded
dēnūntiō, 1 announce, order, threaten
deorsum, *adv.* down
dēpellō, 3, -pulī, -pulsus drive away, avert
dēpendeō, 2, -dī, —, *intr.* hang from, hang down, be dependent on
* **dēpōnō, 3, -posuī, -positus** lay down, lay aside, give up
dēpopulor, 1, *dep.* lay waste, plunder
dēportō, 1 carry away
dēposcō, 3, -poposcī, — call for, demand
dēprecātor, -ōris, *m.* intercessor
dēprehendō, 3, -dī, -hēnsus seize, catch, overtake
dēripiō, 3, -uī, -reptus snatch, tear away

dērogō, 1 take away

dēscendō, 3, **−dī, −scēnsus,** *intr.* climb down, descend, lower oneself, resort to

dēsecō, 1, **−uī, −sectus** cut off

* **dēserō,** 3, **−uī, −tus** leave, abandon, fail

* **dēsīderō,** 1 desire, wish for, demand, miss; *pass.* be lost

dēsidia, −ae, *f.* idleness

dēsīdō, 3, **−dī, —,** *intr.* fall

dēsiliō, 4, **−uī, −sultus,** *intr.* jump down, dismount

dēsinō, 3, **−siī, −situs,** *intr.* desist, stop

* **dēsistō,** 3, **−stitī, −stitus,** *intr.* stand away, desist, give up, cease

dēspectus, −ūs, *m.* downward look, view

* **dēspērō,** 1, *intr.* be hopeless, despair of

* **dēspiciō,** 3, **−spexī, −spectus** look down on, despise

dēstinō, 1 make fast, bind, appoint

dēstringō, 3, **−strīnxī, −strictus** unsheathe

***dēsum, −esse, −fuī, −futūrus,** *intr.* fail, be lacking, be needed

dēsuper, *adv.* from above

dēterreō, 2, **−uī, −itus** frighten off, hinder, prevent

dētrahō, 3, **−trāxī, −tractus** take off, pull off, detract, remove

* **dētrīmentum, −ī,** *n.* loss, injury, defeat

dēturbō, 1 drive down, overthrow, dislodge

Deucaliōn, −ōnis, *m.* Deucā'lion, Greek survivor of the flood

deūrō, 3, **−ussī, −ustus** burn down

* **deus, −ī,** *m.* god, deity

dēvehō, 3, **−vexī, −vectus** carry down, carry away, bring, convey

dēveniō, 4, **−vēnī, −ventus,** *intr.* come, arrive

dēvertō, 3, **−tī, —,** *tr. or intr.* turn aside, lodge

dēvexus, −a, −um sloping; *as noun, n. pl.* slopes, hillside

dēvoveō, 2, **−vōvī, −vōtus** sacrifice

* **dexter, −tra, −trum** on the right, right; *as noun, f.* **dextra, −ae** (*sc.* **manus**) right hand

Diāna, −ae, *f.* Diana, goddess of the moon and the chase

dicō, 1 dedicate, offer

* **dīcō,** 3, **dīxī, dictus** speak, say, plead, appoint, set; **iūs dīcere** pronounce judgment

dictātor, −ōris, *m.* dictator

* **diēs, −ēī,** *m. or f.* day, daytime; **in diēs** from day to day

* **differō, −ferre, distulī, dīlātus,** *tr. or intr.* spread, scatter, put off, differ

* **difficilis, −e** hard, laborious, perilous

* **difficultās, −tātis,** *f.* difficulty, hardship

diffīdō, 3, **−fīsus sum,** *semi-dep.,* *intr.* distrust, despair

diffundō, 3, **−fūdī, −fūsus** spread out, extend

* **digitus, −ī,** *m.* finger

* **dignitās, −tātis,** *f.* worth, character, honor, authority, prestige

* **dignus, −a, −um** worthy, deserving

diiūdicō, 1 decide

dīlēctus, −ūs, *m.* selection, levy, conscription, choice

* **dīligēns, −entis** industrious, faithful

dīligenter, *adv.* with pains, carefully

dirus, a, um — dire,

dīligentia, –ae, f. industry, care

dīligō, 3, –lēxī, –lēctus single out, value, love

dīluvium, –ī, n. flood

* dīmicō, 1, intr. fight

dīmidius, –a, –um half; as noun, n. half

* dīmittō, 3, –mīsī, –missus send in different directions, send out, send away, let slip, give up

Diomēdēs, –is, m. Diomedes (Dīomē'dēz), a king of Thrace

* dīrigō, 3, –rēxī, –rēctus drive

* dīripiō, 3, –uī, –reptus tear to pieces, plunder

dis–, insep. prefix apart, not

Dīs, Dītis, m. Dis or Pluto, the god of the underworld

* discēdō, 3, –cessī, –cessus, intr. go away, open; w. ab abandon

discessus, –ūs, m. departure, marching away

* disciplīna, –ae, f. instruction, training, education, doctrine

discipulus, –ī, m. pupil

discō, 3, didicī, —, tr. or intr. learn, be taught

Discordia, –ae, f. Discor'dia, goddess of discord

discrīmen, –inis, n. decisive movement, crisis

* dispergō, 3, –spersī, –spersus scatter, disperse

dispōnō, 3, –posuī, –positus place, arrange, post, station here and there

disputātiō, –ōnis, f. argument, discussion

disputō, 1 discuss, argue

dissēnsiō, –ōnis, f. difference of opinion, strife

dissuādeō, 2, –suāsī, –suāsus, tr. or intr. advise against, dissuade

distineō, 2, –uī, –tentus keep apart, hold back, hinder

* distribuō, 3, –uī, –ūtus divide, assign

distulī, see differō

disyllabus, –a, –um of two syllables

dītissimus, –a, –um, sup. of dīves richest, very rich

* diū, adv. a long time; quam diū as long as

diūtinus, –a, –um permanent

diūtius, diūtissimē, comp. and sup. of diū

diūturnus, –a, –um long, enduring

* dīversus, –a, –um scattered, separate, distant, different

dīves, –itis rich

Dīviciācus, –ī, m. Diviciacus (Divishiā'kus), an Aeduan, friendly to the Romans; a king of the Suessiones

Dīvicō, –ōnis, m. Div'ico, a leader among the Aeduans

* dīvidō, 3, –vīsī, –vīsus separate, scatter, divide

dīvīnus, –a, –um belonging to the gods, sacred, divine

dīvus, –a, –um deified, holy; Dīvus Salvātor San Salvador

* dō, dare, dedī, datus give, grant, assign, allot, cause, give up; inter sē dare exchange

* doceō, 2, –uī, doctus teach, show, tell

doctrīna, –ae, f. knowledge, learning

doctus, –a, –um learned; as noun, m. learned man, sage

documentum, –ī, n. lesson, example, warning

* **doleō, 2, -uī, -itūrus,** *intr.* suffer, grieve, lament
dolor, -ōris, *m.* pain, grief, annoyance, indignation
dolus, -ī, *m.* device, deceit, trickery
domesticus, -a, -um belonging to a home, civil, native
domina, -ae, *f.* mistress
dominicus, -a, -um belonging to the master; *w.* **diēs** Sunday
dominor, 1, *dep., intr.* master
* **dominus, -ī,** *m.* master, lord
* **domus, -ūs,** *f.* house, family, home, country; **domī,** *loc.* at home
dōnec, *conj.* until
Donnataurus, -ī, *m.* Donnatau'rus; *see* **Valerius**
dōnum, -ī, *n.* gift, present, bribe
dormiō, 4, -īvī, -ītus *intr.* sleep
dorsum, -ī, *n.* back, ridge
dōs, dōtis [dō], *f.* marriage portion, dowry
dracō, -ōnis, *m.* dragon
Druidēs, -um, *m. pl.* Druids, priests of Gaul and Britain
dubitātiō, -ōnis, *f.* doubt, hesitancy
* **dubitō, 1,** *tr. or intr.* doubt, be uncertain, hesitate
dubius, -a, -um doubtful
ducentī, -ae, -a, *pl.* two hundred
* **dūcō, 3, dūxī, ductus** lead, lead out, bring, take, construct, extend, put off, consider; **in mātrimōnium dūcere** marry
dulce, *adv.* agreeably, delightfully
dulcis, -e sweet
* **dum,** *conj.* while, as long as, until
Dumnorīx, -īgis, *m.* Dum'norix, an Aeduan, brother of Diviciacus
* **duo, -ae, -o** two

duodecim, *indecl. adj.* twelve
duodecimus, -a, -um twelfth
duodēvīgintī, *indecl. adj.* eighteen
duplicō, 1 double
dūritia, -ae, *f.* hardness, hardship
* **dūrus, -a, -um** hard, severe, adverse
* **dux, ducis,** *m.* leader, guide, commander

* **ē,** *see* **ex**
Ēchō, Echūs, *f.* Echo, a nymph who pined way for love of Narcissus
ecquis, -quid, *interr. pron.* anyone, anything
ēdiscō, 3, -didicī, — learn thoroughly
* **ēditus, -a, -um** elevated, rising high
* **ēdō, 3, -didī, -ditus** put forth, display
edō, 3, ēdī, ēsus eat
ēdūcō, 3, -dūxī, -ductus lead out, lead forth
effector, -ōris, *m.* a maker, producer
effēminō, 1 make effeminate, weaken
* **efferō, -ferre, extulī, ēlātus** carry out, take away, make public, report, tell, lift up, raise, encourage, elate
effervēscō, 3, -ferbuī, —, *intr.* boil
* **efficiō, 3, -fēcī, -fectus** do, finish, complete, effect, bring about, produce, make, construct, muster, furnish
effodiō, 3, -fōdī, -fossus dig out, tear out
* **effugiō, 3, -fūgī, —,** *tr. or intr.* escape, shun
effundō, 3, -fūdī, -fūsus pour out

egēns, –entis needy; *as noun, pl.* the poor, the destitute

egeō, 2, eguī, —, *intr.* be in want, lack, need

ēgerō, 3, –gessī, –gestus carry out

* **ego, meī,** *pers. pron.* I

* **ēgredior, 3, –gressus sum,** *dep., tr. or intr.* go out, march out, leave, disembark, land

ēgregiē, *adv.* excellently

* **ēgregius, –a, –um** excellent, admirable, remarkable

ēgressus, *p. p. of* ēgredior

ēiciō, 3, –iēcī, –iectus drive out, expel, banish, strand; **sē ēicere** rush out, break out

ēlātus, *p. p. of* efferō

ēligō, 3, –lēgī, –lēctus choose

ēloquor, 3, ēlocūtus sum, *dep.* declare

ēmineō, 2, –minuī, —, *intr.* stand out, project

ēmittō, 3, –mīsī, –missus send forth, throw, let go

* **emō, 3, ēmī, ēmptus** buy

ēmptor, –ōris, *m.* buyer, purchaser

* **enim,** *conj.* in fact, to be sure, for

Ennius, –ī, *m.* En'nius, an early Roman poet

* **ēnūntiō, 1** tell in public, announce

* **eō, īre, iī (īvī), itus,** *intr.* go, walk, march, travel

* **eō,** *adv.* thither, to that place, so, far, there, thereon, to this *or* that end

* **eōdem,** *adv.* to the same place, to the same end

ephippiātus, –a, –um using saddles

ephippium, –ī, *n.* saddle-cloth, saddle

epistula, –ae, *f.* letter

Eporēdorīx, –īgis, *m.* Eporē'dorix, an Aeduan general

* **eques, –itis,** *m.* horseman, member of the equestrian order, knight; *pl.* cavalry

* **equester, –tris, –tre** equestrian, cavalry

equidem, *adv.* truly, indeed

* **equitātus, –ūs,** *m.* cavalry, body of horsemen

equitō, 1, *tr. or intr.* ride

* **equus, –ī,** *m.* horse

ērēctus, –a, –um upright, lofty

ergō, *adv.* then

Eridanus, –ī, *m.* Erid'anus (River)

* **ēripiō, 3, –uī, –reptus** tear away, seize, rescue; *pass.* be lost, be destroyed

errō, 1, *intr.* wander, be mistaken

* **ēruptiō, –ōnis,** *f.* breaking forth, sally, rush

Erymanthius, –a, –um Eryman'thian, of Eryman'thus, a chain of mountains in Greece

Ēsquilīnus, –a, –um Es'quilīne; *w.* **mōns** one of the hills of Rome

essedārius, –ī, *m.* fighter in an essedum, charioteer

essedum, –ī, *n.* war chariot used by the Britons

* **et,** *conj.* and; *after a negative* but, also, even; **et . . . et** both . . . and, not only . . . but also

etenim, *conj.* because, since, for

* **etiam,** *adv.* even now, still, also, besides, even

* **etsī,** *conj.* even if, although

Eucliō, –ōnis, *m.* Euclio (Ū'clio), a miser

Eurystheus, –ī, *m.* Eurystheus (Ūris'thoos), king of Mycenae ēvādō, 3, -vāsī, -vāsus, *intr.* go out, escape, evade

ēvellō, 3, -ī, -vulsus pull out

ēveniō, 4, -vēnī, -ventus, *intr.* come out, turn out, happen

* ēventus, -ūs, *m.* outcome, event, result, accident; Bonus Ēventus god of good fortune

ēvocō, 1 call away, summon, invite, challenge

* ex, ē (ē *before consonants*, ex *before vowels and consonants*) *prep. w. abl.* out of, from, from among, of, after, since, in accordance with, in consequence of, by, of (*made of*), in, on

exāctus, *p. p. of* exigō

exagitō, 1 drive about, harass

exāminō, 1 weigh, test

* exanimō, 1 exhaust, kill

exārdēscō, 3, -ārsī, -ārsus, *intr.* blaze forth, rage

exaudiō, 4 -īvī, -ītus hear clearly, hear

* excēdō, 3, -cessī, -cessus, *intr.* go forth, withdraw, depart, retire

excellō, 3, -celluī, -celsus, *intr.* be eminent, be superior, surpass

excīdō, 3, -dī, -cīsus cut out, destroy

* excipiō, 3, -cēpī, -ceptus, *tr. or intr.* take out, capture, intercept, receive

excitō, 1 call forth, rouse, incite, build up, raise

exclūdō, 3, -clūsī, -clūsus shut out, hinder, prevent

excōgitō, 1 think out, consider

excruciō, 1 torture, rack

excubitor, -ōris, *m.* watchman, sentinel

excūsō, 1 excuse

exemplum, -ī, *n.* example, precedent, way, manner

exeō, -īre, -iī (-īvī), -itus, *intr.* go out, march out, depart

* exerceō, 2, -uī, -itus drive on, occupy, train, exercise

* exercitātiō, -ōnis, *f.* exercise, training, experience, skill, practice

exercitātus, -a, -um trained, experienced

* exercitus, -ūs, *m.* army, infantry

exhauriō, 4, -hausī, -haustus draw out, remove

exigō, 3, -ēgī, -āctus drive out, spend, pass

exiguitās, -tātis, *f.* scantiness, shortness, smallness

* exiguus, -a, -um small, short

eximius, -a, -um distinguished, uncommon

exīstimātiō, -ōnis, *f.* judgment, opinion, thought, repute

* exīstimō, 1 think, suppose, estimate, consider

exitium, -ī, *n.* destruction

* exitus, -ūs, *m.* departure, exit, end, conclusion, outcome

* expediō, 4, -īvī, -ītus extricate, make ready, put in order

expedītus, -a, -um light-armed, without luggage

expellō, 3, -pulī, -pulsus drive out, remove

* experior, 4, -pertus sum, *dep.* try, experience

expiō, 1 atone for, expiate

* explōrātor, -ōris, *m.* explorer, scout

* explōrō, 1 search out, explore, investigate, reconnoiter

* expōnō, 3, -posuī, -positus put
out, disembark, expose, set forth,
tell, show

exprimō, 3, -pressī, -pressus force
out, extort

* expugnō, 1 take by storm, capture,
overcome

exsequor, 3, -secūtus sum, ' dep.
follow up, enforce

exsiliō, 4, -siluī, —, intr. leap up

exsistō, 3, -stitī, —, intr. come forth,
appear, arise, spring up

* exspectō, 1 look out for, await,
wait for, expect, hope for, wait

* exstruō, 3, -strūxī, -strūctus pile
up, heap up, build

extendō, 3, -tendī, -tentus extend,
spread out

* extrā, prep. w. acc. outside of,
beyond

extrahō, 3, -trāxī, -tractus draw
out, waste in delay

* extrēmus, -a, -um [sup. of exterus]
most distant, farthest, last, extreme, frontier

extrūdō, 3, -trūsī, -trūsus thrust
out, shut out

Fabius, -ī, m. Gaius Fā′bius, a
lieutenant in Caesar's army;
Lucius Fabius, a centurion of the
Eighth Legion

fābula, -ae, f. story

* facile, adv. easily, safely

* facilis, -e easy to do, practicable

facinus, -oris, n. deed, crime

* faciō, 3, fēcī, factus (for pass. see
fiō) tr. or intr. make, do, act, cause,
incite, appoint

* factiō, -ōnis, f. faction, party

* factum, -ī, n. deed, act, measure

* facultās, -tātis, f. ability, occasion,
leave, supply; pl. resources

fācundus, -a, -um eloquent, fluent

fāgus, -ī, f. beech tree

falcātus, -a, -um cut with a scythe

* fallō, 3, fefellī, falsus deceive, fail

falsus, -a, -um false, groundless

falx, falcis, f. wall-hook

* fāma, -ae [for, speak] f. story,
report, reputation

* famēs, -is, abl. famē, f. hunger,
want

* familia, -ae, f. collection of slaves,
household, family

* familiāris, -e belonging to a house
or family, private; as noun, m.
friend

fās, found only in nom. and acc.
[for, speak] n. justice, right

fascis, -is, m. bundle

fastīgātus, -a, -um sloping, de-
scending

fastīgium, -ī, n. summit, slope

fātum, -ī [for, speak] n. destiny, fate,
ill fortune

faucēs, -ium, f., pl. throat, jaws

faveō, 2, fāvī, fautus, intr. well
disposed toward, favor

fax, facis, f. torch, firebrand

febris, -is, f. fever

fēlīcitās, -tātis, f. good fortune,
happiness

fēlīciter, adv. fortunately, happily

fēlis (fēlēs), -is, f. cat

fēlīx, -īcis happy, fortunate

* fēmina, -ae, f. woman, female

fenestra, -ae, f. window

* ferē, adv. almost, about, generally

* ferō, ferre, tulī, lātus, tr. or intr.
bear, carry, endure, suffer, win,

report, offer; *pass.* rush, flow;
signa ferre advance

ferrāmenta, −ōrum, *n. pl.* tools
made of iron

ferreus, −a, −um made of iron

* **ferrum, −ī,** *n.* iron, sword

fertilitās, −tātis, *f.* fertility

* **ferus, −a, −um** wild, savage, cruel

fervefaciō, 3, −fēcī, −factus make
hot

fervēns, −entis red-hot, hot

fēstus, −a, −um festal; *w.* **diēs**
holiday

fictus, *p. p. of* **fingō**

ficus, −ī, *m. or f.* fig

* **fidēlis, −e** trustworthy, faithful

* **fidēs, −eī,** *f.* trust, faith, loyalty,
protection, word, pledge

* **fīdūcia, −ae,** *f.* trust, confidence

fīdus, −a, −um faithful

* **figō, 3, fīxī, fīxus** drive, affix

figūra, −ae, *f.* form

* **fīlia, −ae,** *f.* daughter

* **fīlius, −ī,** *m.* son

fingō, 3, fīnxī, fictus make, imagine

* **fīniō, 4, −īvī, −ītus** bound, end,
mark off, define

* **fīnis, −is,** *m.* boundary, end; *pl.*
borders, territory

* **fīnitimus, −a, −um,** adjacent, neighboring; *as noun, m. pl.* neighbors

* **fīō, fierī, factus sum,** *pass. of* **faciō**
be made, be done, happen, result;
certior fierī be informed

firmiter, *adv.* steadfastly, immovably

* **firmus, −a, −um** strong, stable,
firm

Flāminius, −a, −um Flāmin′ian

flamma, −ae, *f.* flame, fire

flammeum, −ī, *n.* flame-colored
bridal veil

flectō, 3, flexī, flexus bend, turn

* **fleō, 2, flēvī, flētus,** *intr.* weep,
bewail

Flōra, −ae, *f.* Flora, goddess of
flowers

flōrēns, −entis flourishing, influential

flōreō, 2, −uī, — blossom, flourish

flōs, flōris, *m.* blossom, flower

flūctus, −ūs, *m.* wave

* **flūmen, −inis,** *n.* running water,
river

* **fluō, 3, flūxī, flūxus,** *intr.* flow

focus, −ī, *m.* hearth

fōns, fontis, *m.* fountain, source

forceps, −cipis, *f.* shears

fore = futūrus esse, *see* **sum**

foris, −is, *f.* door; **forīs,** *adv.* out
of doors

* **fōrma, −ae,** *f.* beauty, shape, appearance

formīca, −ae, *f.* ant

* **fors, fortis,** *f.* chance, fortune

fortasse, *adv.* perhaps

forte [fors] *adv.* by chance

* **fortis, −e** brave, manly

fortiter, *adv.* bravely

fortitūdō, −inis, *f.* courage, bravery

* **fortūna, −ae,** *f.* fortune, chance,
fate, good fortune; *pl.* possessions

forum, −ī, *n.* public square, market-
place

* **fossa, −ae,** *f.* ditch, trench

* **frangō, 3, frēgī, frāctus** break,
dash to pieces

* **frāter, −tris,** *m.* brother; *pl.* allies

fraus, fraudis, *f.* deceit, imposition

frequēns, −entis in great numbers

frētus, −a, −um relying on, trusting in

frīgidus, –a, –um cold

frīgus, –oris, n. cold, frost, wintry weather; pl. cold seasons

* frōns, frontis, f. forehead, front

frūctus, –ūs, m. enjoyment, fruit, interest, reward

frūgī, indec. adj. honest, frugal

* frūmentārius, –a, –um of grain, abounding in grain, fertile; * rēs frūmentāria grain supply, provisions

frūmentātiō, –ōnis, f. foraging

frūmentor, 1, dep., intr. collect grain, forage

* frūmentum, –ī, n. grain; pl. standing grain, grain crop

fruor, 3, frūctus sum, dep., intr. enjoy

* frūstrā, adv. in vain

frūx, frūgis, f. fruit, produce; pl. crops

* fuga, –ae, f. flight, rout; sē fugae mandāre take to flight; in fugam dare put to flight, rout

* fugiō, 3, fūgī, fugitūrus, tr. or intr. flee, shun, avoid

fugitīvus, –a, –um fugitive; as noun, m. runaway, deserter

fugō, 1 put to flight, rout

fulgor, –ōris, m. lightning, splendor

fulmen, –inis, n. thunderbolt

fūmus, –ī, m. smoke

funda, –ae, f. sling, sling-stone

* funditor, –ōris, m. slinger

* fundō, 3, fūdī, fūsus pour, scatter

fūnebris, –e of a funeral

fungor, 3, fūnctus sum, dep. perform, execute

fūnis, –is, m. rope

fūnus, –eris, n. funeral, funeral rites

fūr, fūris, m. thief

furor, –ōris, m. madness, frenzy

fūrtum, –ī, n. theft

fūsilis, –e molten, red-hot

futūrus, see sum

Gabalī, –ōrum, m. the Gab'alī, a tribe in southern Gaul

Gabīnius, –ī, m. Aulus Gabin'ius, consul in 58 B.C.

Gādēs, –ium, f. pl. Gā'des (Cadiz), a city in Spain

Gāius, –ī, m. Gā'ius, a Roman praenomen

Galba, –ae, m. Ser'vius Sulpicius (Sulpish'ius) Gal'ba, one of Caesar's legates; a king of the Suessiones

galea, –ae, f. helmet

Gallia, –ae, f. Gaul

Gallicus, –a, –um Gallic

gallīna, –ae, f. hen

Gallus, –ī, m. a Gaul; pl. the Gauls

garriō, 4, —, — chatter

Garumna, –ae, m. the Garum'na (Garonne), a river in Gaul

gaudeō, 2, gāvīsus sum, semi-dep., intr. rejoice, be glad

gaudium, –ī, n. joy   [name

Gellius, –ī, m. Gellius, a Roman

gelō, 1 chill, freeze

gemitus, –ūs, m. sigh, complaint

gemma, –ae, f. gem, precious stone

gemō, 3, –uī, —, tr. or intr. groan, creak

Genava, –ae, f. Genava (Geneva), a city of the Allobroges

generālis, –e general

* gēns, gentis, f. race, tribe, nation

* genus, –eris, n. descent, race, kind, rank, species, family, nation

Gergovia, -ae, *f.* Gergovia (Jergō'-via), a city of the Arvernians

Germānia, -ae, *f.* Germany

Germānus, -ī, *m.* a German; *pl.* the Germans; *as adj.* **Germānus, -a, -um** German

* **gerō, 3, gessī, gestus** carry, administer, manage, conduct, do, hold; *pass.* go on, take place

Gēryōn, -onis, *m.* Geryon (Jē'rion), a monster with three bodies

gigās, -antis, *m.* a giant

gignō, 3, genuī, genitus give birth to; *pass.* be born, spring up

gladiātōrius, -a, -um of gladiators, gladiatorial

* **gladius, -ī,** *m.* sword

glāns, glandis, *f.* acorn, sling-bullet, missile

Glaucē, -ēs, *f.* Glauce (Glaw'sē)

glēba, -ae, *f.* clod, mass

* **glōria, -ae,** *f.* renown, fame, glory

glōrior, 1, *dep., intr.* boast, take pride

• **Gobannitiō, -ōnis,** *m.* Gobannitio (Gobanish'yo), an Arvernian

Gracchus, -ī, *m.* Gracchus (Grak'us), Roman cognomen

Graecia, -ae, *f.* Greece

Graecus, -a, -um Greek; *as noun, m.* a Greek

Graiocelī, -ōrum, *m. pl.* the Graioceli (Grāyō'selī), a Gallic tribe in the Alps

graphium, -ī, *n.* writing-stylus

* **grātia, -ae,** *f.* gratitude, thanks, favor; **grātiam habēre** feel grateful; **grātiam referre** make return; **grātiās agere** express thanks; **grātiā** *with preceding gen.* for the sake of

* **grātīs,** *adv.* for nothing, free

* **grātulātiō, -ōnis,** *f.* rejoicing, joy

* **grātus, -a, -um** pleasing, grateful; *as noun, n.* favor

* **gravis, -e** heavy, burdensome, serious

graviter, *adv.* heavily, bitterly, severely

gravor, 1, *dep., intr.* be unwilling, hesitate

grūs, gruis, *m. or f.* crane

gustō, 1 taste

gutta, -ae, *f.* drop

Gȳgēs, -ae, *m.* Gyges (Gī'jēz), a shepherd

* **habeō, 2, -uī, -itus** have, hold, possess, regard, consider, count, make (*a speech*)

habitō, 1, *intr.* inhabit

haesitō, 1, *intr.* stick fast, hesitate

Hamilcar, -aris, *m.* Hamil'car, a Carthaginian leader

Hannibal, -alis, *m.* Hannibal, a Carthaginian general

Harpȳiae, -ārum, *f. pl.* Harpies

haruspex, -icis, *m.* soothsayer

Helena, -ae, *f.* Helen, wife of Menelaus

Helvētius, -a, -um Helvetian (Helvē'shian); *as noun, m.,* a Helvetian; *pl.* the Helvetians, a powerful Gallic tribe in what is now Switzerland

Helviī, -ōrum, *m. pl.* the Hel'viī, a small Gallic tribe in the Province

hem, *interj.* indeed, ha

herba, -ae, *f.* grass, herb

herbidus, -a, -um grassy

Herculēs, -is, *m.* Hercules, a Greek hero

hērēditās, –tātis, *f.* inheritance

hērēs, –ēdis, *m.* heir

Hesperidēs, –um, *f. pl.* Hesperides (Hesper'idēz)

hesternus, –a, –um yesterday's

heu, *interj.* alas, oh

Hibērēs, –um *m. pl.* Spaniards

Hibernia, –ae, *f.* Ireland

* hīberna, –ōrum, *n. pl.* winter quarters

Hibērus, –ī, *m.* the river Ebro

* hic, haec, hoc, *dem. pron.* this, this man, he, the following, the latter (*contrasted with* ille)

hīc, *adv.* here, in this place, there, in that place (*of a place just mentioned*), at this point, then

* hiemō, 1, *intr.* winter, be in winter quarters

* hiems, –emis, *f.* winter, storm

Hispānia, –ae, *f.* Spain

Hispānus, –a, –um Spanish

Homērus, –ī, *m.* Homer, celebrated Greek poet

homicīdium, –ī, *n.* homicide, murder

* homō, –inis, *m. or f.* human being; *pl.* men, people

honestē, *adv.* honorably

honestus, –a, –um respected, honorable

* honor (honōs), –ōris, *m.* repute, distinction, office

* hōra, –ae, *f.* hour

Horātius, –ī, *m.* Horatius, the famous Roman poet Horace

horridus, –a, –um savage, frightful

* hortor, 1, *dep.* urge, encourage, impel

hortus, –ī, *m.* garden

hospes, –itis, *m.* guest-friend, guest, host

hospitium, –ī, *n.* tie of hospitality; in hospitiō being entertained

Hostīlius, *see* Tullus

* hostis, –is, *m. or f.* enemy, foe; *pl.* the enemy

* hūc, *adv.* to this place, to this, to these

* hūmānitās, –tātis, *f.* civilization, refinement

hūmānus, –a, –um civilized, refined

* humilis, –e low, humble

humus, –ī, *f.* ground

Hydra, –ae, *f.* Hy'dra

Hylās, –ae, *m.* Hy'las, one of the Argonauts

Hymēn, –enis, *m.* Hy'men, god of marriage

Hymenaeus, –ī, *m.* Hymen

iaceō, 2, iacuī, —, *intr.* lie, lie dead

* iaciō, 3, iēcī, iactus throw, hurl, cast, construct; ancorās iacere cast anchor

iactō, 1 throw, hurl, toss about

iactūra, –ae, *f.* throwing, sacrifice, loss

iaculum, –ī, *n.* dart, javelin

* iam, *adv.* by this time, already, now, at length, even, in fact

* iam dūdum, *adv.* a long time ago

* iam prīdem long ago

Iāniculum, –ī, *n.* Janic'ulum, one of the hills of Rome

iānua, –ae, *f.* door

Iānus, –ī, *m.* Jā'nus, god of doors; Iānus Quirīnus temple of Janus

Iāsōn, –onis, *m.* Jā'son

* ibi, *adv.* there, at that time, then

Īcarus, –ī, *m.* Ic'arus

Īcarius, –a, –um Icarian

Iccius, -ī, m. Iccius (Ic'shius), leader of the Remi

ictus, -ūs, m. stroke, blow, shot

Īda, -ae, f. mountain near Troy

* **īdem, eadem, idem,** *dem. pron.* that same one, the same

ideō, adv. so, therefore

* **idōneus, -a, -um** suitable, fit

Īdūs, -uum, f. pl. the Ides. *See* 634

igitur, conj. then, therefore

* **ignis, -is, m.** fire

ignōrantia, -ae, f. ignorance

* **ignōrō, 1** not know, be ignorant of, overlook

ignōscō, 3, -gnōvī, -gnōtus, intr. overlook, pardon, excuse

* **ignōtus, -a, -um** unknown, strange

illātus, -a, -um, p. p. of īnferō

* **ille, illa, illud, dem. pron.** that, that one, he, she, it, the former (*contrasted with* **hic**)

illīc, adv. in that place, there

illigō, 1 tie to, tie, bind fast

illō, adv. to that place

illūstris, -e splendid, distinguished

Īllyricum, -ī, n. Illyr'icum, a country on the eastern shore of the Adriatic

imāgō, -inis, f. likeness, statue

imber, imbris, m. rain, storm

immānis, -e monstrous, huge

immineō, 2, —, —, intr. hang over, threaten

immittō, 3, -mīsī, -missus send in, insert, let down, send against

immō, adv. on the other hand, no, yes

immolō, 1 offer sacrifice, sacrifice

immortālis, -e immortal

immūnitās, -tātis, f. exemption

* **impedīmentum, -ī, n.** hindrance; *pl.* baggage

* **impediō, 4, -īvī, -ītus [in + pēs]** entangle, obstruct, hinder

* **impellō, 3, -pulī, -pulsus** drive in, drive on, urge, influence

impendeō, 2, —, —, intr. hang over

impēnsa, -ae, f. charge, expense

impēnsus, -a, -um heavy, excessive

imperātor, -ōris, m. leader, general

* **imperātum, -ī, n.** order, command

imperītus, -a, -um unskilled, not experienced

* **imperium, -ī, n.** military authority, power, command, government, control

* **imperō, 1, tr. or intr.** rule, command, order, levy

* **impetrō, 1** accomplish, obtain a request

* **impetus, -ūs, m.** attack, violence, force

impius, -a, -um impious, undutiful, wicked

implicō, 1, -āvī (-uī), -ātus (-itus), enfold, entwine, catch

implōrō, 1 beg, entreat

* **impōnō, 3, -posuī, -positus** put in *or* upon, impose

importō, 1 bring in, import

imprōvīsō, adv. unexpectedly

imprōvīsus, -a, -um not foreseen; dē imprōvīsō suddenly

imprūdentia, -ae, f. ignorance

impulsus, p. p. of impellō

impūne, adv. without punishment

impūnitās, -tātis, f. freedom from punishment

* **in, prep. w. acc.** into, to, against; *w. abl.* in, within, on, among, of, at, in the case of, in the time of, during

in-, insep. prefix not, un-

infundō, ere, infūdī, infūsus — pour in (handwritten at top)

inānis, –e empty, groundless

incēdō, 3, –cessī, –cessus, *intr.* go, proceed

incendium, –ī, *n.* fire

* incendō, 3, –cendī, –cēnsus set fire to, burn, arouse

incertus, –a, –um not certain, doubtful, in disorder, untried

* incidō, 3, –cidī, —, *intr.* fall upon, happen

* incipiō, 3, –cēpī, –ceptus, *tr. or intr.* take hold of, begin

* incitō, 1 hurry on, drive on, rouse, excite

incognitus, –a, –um unknown

incohō, 1 begin

incola, –ae, *f.* inhabitant

* incolō, 3, –uī, —, *tr. or intr.* inhabit, dwell, live in

* incolumis, –e uninjured, safe

incommodum, –ī, *n.* inconvenience, trouble, injury, defeat

incrēdibilis, –e marvelous, wonderful, incredible

increpitō, 1, —, — find fault with, rebuke

incursiō, –ōnis, *f.* invasion, raid

incursus, –ūs, *m.* approach, attack

incūsō, 1 accuse, censure

* inde, *adv.* from there, next, then

indicium, –ī, *n.* information, evidence

* indicō, 1, reveal, point out

indīcō, 3, –dīxī, –dictus declare publicly, proclaim

indictus, –a, –um unsaid

Indicus, –a, –um of India

indignitās, –tātis, *f.* insult, outrage

indignor, 1, *dep., tr. or intr.* be indignant, deem unworthy

indoctus, –a, –um untaught

* indūcō, 3, –dūxī, –ductus lead in, influence

indulgentia, –ae, *f.* indulgence, favor

induō, 3, –duī, –dūtus put on, impale

* ineō, –īre, –iī (–īvī), –itus go into, enter upon, begin, gain

* inermis, –e unarmed

iners, –ertis without skill, lazy

īnfāmia, –ae, *f.* evil repute, disgrace, dishonor

īnfandus, –a, –um unspeakable

īnfāns, –antis not speaking; *as noun, m. or f.* little child, infant

īnfectus, –a, –um not done

īnfēlīx, –īcis unhappy

* īnferior, –ius, *comp. of* īnferus lower

* īnferō, –ferre, intulī, illātus import, bring, inflict, cause

īnferus, –a, –um low

īnficiō, 3, –fēcī, –fectus stain, paint

* īnfimus (īmus) –a, –um, *sup. of* īnferus lowest; īnfimus collis the foot of the hill

īnfīnītus, –a, –um endless, countless

īnfirmus, –a, –um not strong, weak

īnflectō, 3, –flexī, –flexus bend down, bend

īnfluō, 3, flūxī, –flūxus, *intr.* flow in

* īnfrā, *adv.* below, farther on; *prep. w. acc.* below, smaller than

ingenium, –ī, *n.* nature, disposition

ingēns, –entis not natural, enormous, vast

ingrātus, –a, –um displeasing

* ingredior, 3, –gressus sum, *intr.* enter, advance

iniciō, 3, –iēcī, –iectus throw in, put on, inspire, cause

inimīcitia, –ae, *f.* enmity

* **inimīcus, −a, −um** unfriendly, hostile; *as noun*, *m.* personal enemy

* **inīquus, −a, −um** unequal, unfair, hard

* **initium, −ī,** *n.* entrance, beginning

initus, *p. p. of* ineō

iniungō, 3, −iūnxī, −iūnctus join to, impose on

* **iniūria, −ae,** *f.* injustice, insult, injury

iniussū, *adv.* without orders

innītor, 3, −nīxus (−nīsus) sum, *dep. intr.* rest on

innocēns, −entis harmless, innocent

* **inopia, −ae,** *f.* need, scarcity, lack

inopīnāns, −antis surprised, off one's guard

* **inquam,** *defective* say; **inquit** says, said, says he, said he; *always stands after one or more words in a direct quotation*

inquīrō, 3, −quīsīvī, −quīsītus seek, inquire

īnsciēns, −entis unaware

* **īnsequor, 3, −secūtus sum,** *dep.* follow on, pursue

īnserō, 3, −seruī, −sertus put in, insert

* **īnsidiae, −ārum,** *f. pl.* snare, ambush, treachery

* **īnsignis, −e** remarkable, conspicuous; *as noun*, *n.* emblem, ornament

īnsinuō, 1 wind in

īnsistō, 3, −stitī, —, *tr. or intr.* take a stand upon, stand upon, stand

īnsolenter, *adv.* in an unusual way, haughtily, insolently

īnspectō, 1 look on, watch

īnstabilis, −e unsteady

* **īnstituō, 3, −stituī, −stitūtus** put in position, draw up, begin, decide upon, establish, build, furnish, provide, prepare, teach

* **īnstitūtum, −ī,** *n.* custom, habit

* **īnstō, 1, −stitī, −stātūrus,** *intr.* press on, approach, impend, be near, threaten

īnstrūmentum, −ī, *n.* implement, equipment

* **īnstruō, 3, −strūxī, −strūctus** build, set up, marshal, fit out, draw up

īnsuēfactus, −a, −um accustomed, trained

* **īnsula, −ae,** *f.* island

* **integer, −gra, −grum** [in + tangō] not touched, unhurt, entire, pure

* **intellegō, 3, −lēxī, −lēctus** [inter + legō] find out, come to know, know, understand, see

intentus, −a, −um fixed, intent

* **inter,** *prep. w. acc.* between, among, with, during, within

* **intercēdō, 3, −cessī, −cessus** come between, intervene, pass, occur

intercipiō, 3, −cēpī, −ceptus take on the way, catch up, cut off

* **interclūdō, 3, −clūsī, −clūsus** shut off, cut off, prevent

interdīcō, 3, −dīxī, −dictus, *tr. or intr.* forbid, prohibit, exclude

interdiū [inter + diēs] *adv.* in the daytime

interdum, *adv.* sometimes

* **intereā** [inter + is] *adv.* meanwhile, in the meantime

* **intereō, −īre, −iī (−īvī), −itus** perish, be killed, be destroyed

* **interficiō, 3, −fēcī, −fectus** destroy, kill

intericiō, 3, –iēcī, –iectus throw between, put among, set, intersperse

* interim, *adv.* meanwhile

* interior, –ius inner, interior of, inland; interiōrēs, *as noun, m. pl.* those within

interitus, –ūs, *m.* fall, destruction, death

* intermittō, 3, –mīsī, –missus, *tr. or intr.* let go between, omit, stop, leave vacant, allow to intervene, neglect, interrupt

interpellō, 1 interrupt, interfere with

interpōnō, 3, –posuī, –positus put between, introduce, cause, allege

interpretor, 1, *dep.* explain, interpret

* interrogō, 1 ask, question

interscindō, 3, –scidī, –scissus cut through, break down

* intersum, –esse, –fuī, –futūrus, *intr.* be between, be present, take part, attend to; interest it concerns, it is of advantage

* intervāllum, –ī, *n.* space, distance, interval

interventus, –ūs, *m.* coming between, intervention

* intrā, *prep. w. acc.* within, among, inside, during

intrō, 1 enter

intrō–, *insep. prefix* within

intrōdūcō, 3, –dūxī, –ductus lead in, bring in

introeō, –īre, –iī (–īvī), –itus, *intr.* go in, enter

intrōrsus, *adv.* within, inside

intueor, 2, –tuitus sum, *dep.* look upon

intulī, *see* īnferō

intus, *adv.* within, inside

inundō, 1 overflow

inūsitātus, –a, –um unusual

inūtilis, –e useless

* inveniō, 4, –vēnī, –ventus come upon, find, learn, find out

inventor, –ōris, *m.* discoverer, author

invertō, 3, –vertī, –versus invert, turn about, change, upset

invēstīgō, 1 find out, investigate

inveterāscō, 3, –veterāvī, —, *intr.* grow old, become established

invictus, –a, –um unconquered

invidia, –ae, *f.* envy, ill will

invidus, –a, –um envious

invītō, 1 urge, induce, attract, invite

* invītus, –a, –um against one's will, unwilling

invocō, 1 call upon, invoke

iō, *interj.* ho, hallelujah

Iōhana, –ae, *f.* island of Cuba, named for the Princess Juana (Johanna)

* ipse, ipsa, ipsum, *intensive pron.* self, himself, in person, the very

īra, –ae, *f.* wrath

īrāscor, 3, īrātus sum, *dep., intr.* be angry

īrātus, –a, –um angry

irrīdeō, 2, –rīsī, –rīsum, *tr. or intr.* laugh at

irrumpō, 3, –rūpī, –ruptus, *tr. or intr.* break in

* is, ea, id, *dem. pron.* that, this, he, she, it; *w. comp.* the (by this); eō magis the more

* iste, ista, istud, *demon. pron.* this, that, that of yours, such

istic, istaec, istoc, *demon. pron.* that, that of yours

* ita, *adv.* thus, so, in this way, so far; ita ut just as

Italia, –ae, f. Italy

* itaque, conj. accordingly, consequently, and so

* item, adv. also, besides, likewise

* iter, itineris, n. way, journey, course, road; iter facere march; magnum iter forced march

iterātiō, –ōnis, f. review, repetition

iterum, adv. a second time, again

* iubeō, 2, iussī, iussus order, command

iucundus, –a, –um, adj. delightful

iūdex, –icis, m. or f. judge

iūdicium, –ī, n. judgment, opinion, trial

* iūdicō, 1 judge, form an opinion, decide, think

* iugum, –ī, n. yoke, ridge, summit

Iūlius, –a, –um Julian

Iūlius, –ī, m. Julius; see Caesar

iūmentum, –ī, n. beast of burden

* iungō, 3, iūnxī, iūnctus join, put together

iūnior, –ius younger; as noun, iūniōrēs, –um, m. pl. men of military age

Iūnius, –ī, m. Junius, a Roman nomen; see Brūtus

Iūnō, –ōnis, f. Juno, sister and wife of Jupiter and queen of the gods

Iuppiter, Iovis, m. Jupiter, son of Saturn, king of the gods of the Romans

Iūra, –ae, m. Jura, a range of mountains

iūrātor, -ōris, m. a juror

iūridicus, –a, –um pertaining to court

* iūrō, 1, tr. or intr. take oath, swear

* iūs, iūris, n. constitution, law, rights, authority, right

* iūs iūrandum, iūris iūrandī, n. oath

iūstitia, –ae, f. uprightness

* iūstus, –a, –um lawful, proper, due, regular

iuvenis, –e young; as noun young person, youth

iuventūs, –tūtis, f. youth, young men, men of miltary age

* iuvō, 1, iūvī, iūtus help, aid

iūxtā, adv. close by

Kalendae, –ārum, f. pl. the Calends, the first day of the month. See 634

L., abbr. for Lūcius Lucius (Lū'shius), Roman praenomen

Labiēnus, –ī, m. Titus Atius Labiē'nus, Caesar's most trusted officer in the Gallic War

lābor, 3, lāpsus sum, dep., intr. fall into error

* labor, –ōris, m. work, suffering

labōriōsus, –a, –um laborious, toilsome, full of labor

* labōrō, 1, intr. exert oneself, strive, labor, be troubled, suffer

labrum, –ī, n. lip, edge, brim

labyrinthus, –ī, m. labyrinth

lac, lactis, n. milk

Lacedaemōn, –onis, f. Sparta

lacerna, –ae, f. cloak

* lacessō, 3, –īvī, –ītus harass, attack

lacrima, –ae, f. tear

lacrimō, 1, intr. shed tears, weep

lacus, –ūs, m. lake

laedō, 3, laesī, laesus injure, break, violate

laetitia, –ae, f. joy, delight

laetus, –a, –um joyful, exultant

langueō, 2, —, —, intr. be listless, be sick

languor, –ōris, *m.* feebleness, weariness, sluggishness, languor

lānx, lancis, *f.* dish, scale

* lapis, –idis, *m.* stone

laqueus, –ī, *m.* noose

Lār, Laris, *m.* household god

largĭtiō, –ōnis, *f.* bribery

lassitūdō, –inis, *f.* exhaustion

lassus, –a, –um exhausted, tired out

lātē, *adv.* widely; longē lātēque far and wide

lateō, 2, latuī, —, *intr.* lurk, escape notice

Latīnē, *adv.* in Latin

Latīnus, –a, –um Latin; *as noun,* *m.* a Latin

lātiō, –ōnis, *f.* bearing, bringing

* lātitūdō, –inis, *f.* width, extent

Latobrīgī, –ōrum, *m. pl.* the Latobrigi (Latobrī'jī), a tribe near the Helvetians

lātrō, 1, *tr. or intr.* bark

latrōcinium, –ī, *n.* brigandage, raid

* lātus, –a, –um wide, broad

lātus, *p. p. of* ferō

* latus, –eris, *n.* side, flank, wing (*of an army*)

* laudō, 1 praise

* laus, laudis, *f.* praise, glory, fame

lavō, 1, lāvī, lautus *or* lōtus wash; *pass.* bathe

laxō, 1 extend, open out

lectīca, –ae, *f.* litter, sedan

lectus, –ī, *m.* couch, bed

* lēgātiō, –ōnis, *f.* embassy

* lēgātus, –ī, *m.* envoy, messenger, lieutenant, deputy

* legiō, –ōnis, *f.* body of troops, legion

legiōnārius, –a, –um belonging to a legion, legionary

* legō, 3, lēgī, lēctus select, gather, read

Lemannus, –ī, *m.; w.* lacus Lake Geneva

Lemovīcēs, –um, *m. pl.* the Lemovices (Lemovī'sez), a tribe near the Arvernians

* lēnis, –e soft, gentle, favorable

lēnitās, –tātis, *f.* smoothness, gentleness

lēniter, *adv.* gently, moderately

leō, –ōnis, *m.* lion

lepus, –oris, *m.* hare

Leucī, –ōrum, *m. pl.* the Leuci (Lū'sī)

* levis, –e light, slight, trifling, untrustworthy

levitās, –tātis, *f.* lightness, changeableness

* lēx, lēgis, *f.* statute, law

libenter, *adv.* willingly, gladly

* līber, –era, –erum free, unrestricted, unhindered

Līber, Līberī, *m.* Bacchus, god of wine

* liber, librī, *m.* book

līberālis, –e honorable, liberal

līberāliter, *adv.* kindly, generously

līberē, *adv.* freely, boldly

* līberī, –ōrum, *m. pl.* children

* līberō, 1 free, exempt

* lībertās, –tātis, *f.* freedom, independence, permission

libet, 2, libuit *or* libitum est, *impers., intr.* it is pleasing

lībra, –ae, *f.* pound

* licet, 2, licuit *or* licitum est, *impers., intr.* it is permitted; *w. inf.* may

līmen, –minis, *n.* threshold

Lingonēs, –um, *m. pl.* the Lin'gonēs, a tribe in northeastern Gaul

* lingua, –ae, *f.* tongue, language

linter, –tris, *f.* boat, skiff

linteum, –ī, *n.* linen cloth

liquidus, –a, –um liquid, flowing

līs, lītis, *f.* dispute

Litaviccus, –ī, *m.* Litavic′cus, a young Aeduan noble

lītigō, 1, *intr.* quarrel, dispute

* **littera, –ae,** *f.* letter (*of the alphabet*); *pl.* epistle, letter, message, dispatch, writing

* **lītus, –oris,** *n.* shore, beach

* **locus, –ī,** *m.* (*pl.* **loca, –ōrum,** *n.*) place, station, rank, condition, occasion, region

longē, *adv.* far, at a distance, very much, by far

longinquus, –a, –um distant, protracted

longitūdō, –inis, *f.* length

longurius, –ī, *m.* long pole

* **longus, –a, –um** long

* **loquor, 3, locūtus sum,** *dep.*, *tr. or intr.* talk, speak, say

lōrīca, –ae, *f.* coat of mail, breastwork

lucerna, –ae, *f.* lamp

* **lūdō, 3, lūsī, lūsum,** *intr.* play

Lūdovīcus, –ī, *m.* Louis

lūdus, –ī, *m.* game, public exhibition, sport, school

lūmen, –inis, *n.* light

* **lūna, –ae,** *f.* moon, moon-goddess, Diana

lupus, –ī, *m.* wolf

* **lūx, lūcis,** *f.* light

lūxuria, –ae, *f.* high living, extravagance

Lympha, –ae, *f.* goddess of water

M., *abbr. for* **Mārcus** Marcus, Roman praenomen

M'., *abbr. for* **Mānius** Mā′nius, Roman praenomen

māceria, –ae, *f.* wall

Machāōn, –onis, *m.* a Roman doctor

maculō, 1 spot, stain

maestus, –a, –um sad, despondent

magicus, –a, –um magic

* **magis,** *comp. adv.* more, rather

* **magister, –trī,** *m.* teacher, tutor

* **magistrātus, –ūs,** *m.* public office, magistrate

magnificus, –a, –um splendid

* **magnitūdō, –inis,** *f.* greatness, size, force, might

* **magnopere,** *adv.* greatly

* **magnus, –a, –um** large, great, abundant, important, intense

maior, –ius, *comp. of* **magnus;** **maior nātū** older; *as noun, m. pl.* **maiōrēs, –um** ancestors, forefathers; **maiōrēs nātū** elders

Maius, –ī, *m.* month of May

malacia, –ae, *f.* calm

male, *adv.* badly; unsuccessfully, ill

* **maleficium, –ī,** *n.* wicked deed, harm

* **mālō, mālle, māluī, —,** *tr. or intr.* wish rather, prefer, choose

mālum, –ī, *n.* apple

malum, –ī, *n.* evil, mischief

* **malus, –a, –um** bad

* **mandātum, –ī,** *n.* order, commission, command

* **mandō, 1** intrust, charge, order, command; **fugae sēsē mandāre** take to flight

Mandubiī, –ōrum, *m. pl.* the Mandū′biī, a tribe north of the Aeduans

māne, *adv.* in the morning

* **maneō, 2, mānsī, mānsus,** *intr.* stay, remain, abide (*in or by*)

manipulāris, -e belonging to a maniple; *as noun, m.* soldier of a maniple, comrade

manipulus, -ī, *m.* handful (*of hay*), maniple

mānsuētūdō, -inis, *f.* kindness, mercy

* manus, -ūs, *f.* hand, hold, grasp, power, band, force, division of an army

Mārcellus, -ī, *m.* Marcellus, a Roman cognomen

Mārcius, -a, -um Marcian (Mar'shian)

Mārcius, -ī, *m.* Ancus Marcius, fourth king of Rome

* mare, maris, *n.* sea; mare nostrum the Mediterranean

* maritimus, -a, -um maritime, naval, bordering on the sea

marītus, -ī, *m.* husband

Marō, -ōnis, *m.* Mā'rō, a Roman cognomen

Mārs, Mārtis, *m.* Mars, the war god of the Romans

mās, maris masculine; *as noun* male

matara, -ae, *f.* javelin, spear

* māter, -tris, *f.* mother

* māteria, -ae, *f.* timber, matter

mātrimōnium, -ī, *n.* marriage

mātrōna, -ae, *f.* wife, woman

Matrona, -ae, *m.* the Mat'rona (River) (the *Marne*)

mātūrō, ɪ, *tr. or intr.* hurry

* mātūrus, -a, -um ripe, early

māvolō = mālō

maximē, *adv., sup. of* magis most, in the highest degree, especially, exceedingly, chiefly, very

maximus, *sup. of* magnus greatest, largest

Maymundus, -ī, *m.* Maymun'dus

mēcum = cum mē

Mēdēa, -ae, *f.* Mēdē'a

medicīna, -ae, *f.* medicine

medicus, -ī, *m.* physician

* mediocris, -e moderate, ordinary

mediterrāneus, -a, -um inland

* medius, -a, -um middle; in mediō colle half-way up the hill

mel, mellis, *n.* honey

melior, -ius, *comp. of* bonus better

melius, *adv., comp. of* bene more successfully

membrum, -ī, *n.* limb, member

meminī, meminisse, *defective* (*perf. translated as pres.*) remember, keep in mind

memor, -oris mindful

* memoria, -ae, *f.* recollection, remembrance

Menapiī, -ōrum, *m. pl.* the Menā'piī, a Belgian tribe

mendācium, -ī, *n.* falsehood

Menelāus, -ī, *m.* Menelā'us, king of Sparta, husband of Helen

* mēns, mentis, *f.* mind, thought, sense

* mēnsa, -ae, *f.* table

* mēnsis, -is, *m.* month

mēnsūra, -ae, *f.* measure

mentiō, -ōnis, *f.* mention

* mercātor, -ōris, *m.* trader

mercātūra, -ae, *f.* trade

mercēs, -ēdis, *f.* pay, hire

Mercurius, -ī, *m.* Mercury, the god of trade and gain, patron of merchants; he was also the messenger of the gods, especially of Jupiter

* mereō, 2, -uī, -itus; *also dep.* mereor, -ērī, -itus sum merit, deserve, earn

* **merīdiēs**, *defect.*, *acc.* –**em**, *abl.*
–**ē**, *m.* midday, noon, south

meritō, *adv.* deservedly

meritum, –**ī**, *n.* worth, deserts, kindness, service, fault

meritus, –**a**, –**um** deserved, fit

Messāla, –**ae**, *m.* Marcus Valerius Messā'la, consul in 61 B.C.

metallum, –**ī**, *n.* metal

Metellus, –**ī**, *m.* Metellus, a Roman family name

* **mētior**, 4, **mēnsus sum**, *dep.* measure

Mētius, –**ī**, *m.* Marcus Metius (Mē'shius), whom Caesar sent as an envoy to Ariovistus

metō, 3, **messuī**, **messus** reap, harvest

* **metus**, –**ūs**, *m.* fear, dread, terror

* **meus**, –**a**, –**um** my, mine

mī = **mihi**

Midās, –**ae**, *m.* Mī'das, a Phrygian king

* **mīles**, –**itis**, *m.* soldier

mīlia, *see* **mīlle**

* **mīlitāris**, –**e** of a soldier, belonging to military service, military; * **rēs mīlitāris** the art of war, military science

mīlitia, –**ae**, *f.* military service, warfare

* **mīlle** (M), *indecl. adj. in sing.* thousand; *as noun*, **mīlia**, –**ium**, *n. pl.* thousands; **mīlia passuum** thousands of paces, miles

Minerva, –**ae**, *f.* Minerva, goddess of wisdom

minimē, *adv.*, *sup. of* **parum** least, by no means

minimus, –**a**, –**um**, *sup. of* **parvus** smallest, least; **quam minimum** as little as possible

minor, 1, *dep.*, *tr. or intr.* threaten

minor, **minus**, *comp. of* **parvus** smaller, less; **minor nātū** younger

Mīnōs, **Mīnōis**, *m.* Mī'nos, king of Crete

Mīnōtaurus, –**ī**, *m.* the Min'ōtaur

Minucius, –**a**, –**um** Minucian (Minū'shian)

* **minuō**, 3, **minuī**, **minūtus** lessen, reduce, ebb

minus, *adv.*, *comp. of* **parum** less, not; **nihilō minus** no less, still, nevertheless

mīrāculum, –**ī**, *n.* miracle, wonder

* **mīror**, 1, *dep.*, *tr. or intr.* wonder at

* **mīrus**, –**a**, –**um** wonderful, strange

* **miser**, –**era**, –**erum** wretched, unhappy, poor, insignificant

miserē, *adv.* wretchedly

misericordia, –**ae**, *f.* pity, compassion, mercy

miseror, 1, *dep.* deplore, lament

* **mittō**, 3, **mīsī**, **missus** let go, send, throw, hurl

mōbilitās, –**tātis**, *f.* ease of movement, quickness, changeableness

moderātor, –**ōris**, *m.* ruler, director

moderor, 1, *dep.* guide, control, check

* **modo**, *adv.* simply, only, merely, even, just now, lately, now; * **nōn modo . . . sed etiam** not only . . . but also

* **modus**, –**ī**, *m.* amount, extent, capacity, measure, manner, method, kind; **quem ad modum** how, as

moenia, –**ium**, *n. pl.* walls of defense, city walls, walls

molestē, *adv.* with vexation; **mo-**

lestē ferre be annoyed at, be indignant

molestia, –ae, *f.* nuisance, annoyance, trouble

molestus, –a, –um annoying

molō, 3, –uī, –itus grind

Mona, –ae, *f.* Mō'na, an island near England

* moneō, 2, –uī, –itus remind, warn, advise

* mōns, montis, *m.* mountain

mōnstrō, 1 show

mōnstrum, –ī, *n.* monster

* mora, –ae, *f.* delay, hesitation

mōrātus, –a, –um constituted, mannered

morbus, –ī, *m.* illness, disease

Morinī, –ōrum, *m. pl.* the Mor'inī, a Belgian tribe on the seacoast

morior, 3, mortuus sum, *dep., intr.* die

* moror, 1, *dep., tr. or intr.* delay, wait, stay, check

* mors, mortis, *f.* death

mortālis, –e, *adj.* subject to death; *as noun, m. or f.* man, human being

mortifer, –a, –um death-bringing, deadly

mortuus, –a, –um [morior] dead

mōrum, –ī, *n.* mulberry

mōrus, –ī, *f.* mulberry tree

*mōs, mōris, *m.* custom; *in pl.* manners, character

* mōtus, –ūs, *m.* moving, political movement, disturbance, uprising

* moveō, 2, mōvī, mōtus move, influence, affect

mox, *adv.* soon

* mulier, –eris, *f.* woman

muliercula, –ae, *f.* mere woman

* multitūdō, –inis, *f.* great number, multitude, throng, crowd

multō [*abl. of* multus] *adv.* much, by far

multum, *adv.* much, greatly

* multus, –a, –um much, great; *pl.* many; multā nocte late at night; multum posse (valēre) have much power

mūlus, –ī, *m.* mule

Mulvius, –a, –um Mul'vian (*bridge*)

Munda, –ae, *f.* Mun'da, city in Spain

mundus, –a, –um neat, clean

mundus, –ī, *m.* world, universe

* mūniō, 4, –īvī, –ītus fortify, protect, guard, build; iter mūnīre construct a road

* mūnītiō, –ōnis, *f.* fortifications, ramparts, defensive strength

* mūnus, –eris, *n.* service, duty, favor, gift

mūrālis, –e of a wall

* mūrus, –ī, *m.* wall, city wall, earthwork

mūs, mūris, *m. or f.* mouse

Mūsa, –ae, *f.* Muse

* mūtō, 1, *tr. or intr.* change

mūtuum, –ī, *n.* as a loan

Mȳsia, –ae, *f.* Mys'ia, a district in Asia Minor

nactus, –a, –um, *p. p. of* nancīscor

* nam, *conj.* for

* namque, *conj.* for indeed, for

* nancīscor, 3, nactus *or* nānctus sum, *dep.* get, obtain, secure, meet with, find

nārrō, 1 tell

* nāscor, 3, nātus sum, *dep., intr.* be born, be produced, arise, spring up, be found

nātālis, –e of birth; diēs nātālis birthday

* nātiō, –ōnis, f. race, tribe, people, nation

nātīvus, –a, –um natural, native

natō, 1, intr. swim, float

* nātūra, –ae, f. nature, natural situation, disposition, character

nātus, –a, –um, p. p. of nāscor

* nauta, –ae, m. sailor

nauticus, –a, –um of sailors, of ships, nautical, naval

nāvālis, –e of ships, for ships, naval

nāvicula, –ae, f. small boat, skiff

nāvigātiō, –ōnis, f. sailing, navigation, voyage

nāvigium, –ī, n. vessel, boat

* nāvigō, 1, tr. or intr. sail

* nāvis, –is, f. ship; nāvis longa warship, galley; nāvis onerāria transport

nāvō, 1 do earnestly; operam nāvāre do one's utmost

* nē, adv. not; used with quidem, with the emphasized word or words between not even, not . . . either; nōn modō . . . sed nē . . . quidem not only not . . . but not even; conj. that . . . not, lest; after expressions of fearing that; nē quis that no one

* –ne, enclitic interrog., as adv. sign of a question; as conj. in indirect questions whether

* nec, see neque

necessāriō, adv. unavoidably, inevitably

* necessārius, –a, –um necessary, indispensable; as noun, m. kinsman

* necesse, indecl. adj. necessary, needful, inevitable

necessitās, –tātis, f. necessity, compulsion, need

* necō, 1 slay, destroy

nectar, –aris, n. nectar

nefās, indecl. n. something contrary to divine law, sin, wrong

* neglegō, 3, –lēxī, –lēctus disregard, neglect, overlook

* negō, 1, tr. or intr. say no, say . . . not, refuse, deny

negōtior, 1, dep., intr. carry on business

* negōtium, –ī [nec + ōtium] n. business, affair, concern, trouble, difficulty

Nemea, –ae, f. Nē′mēa, a valley in Greece

* nēmō [nē + homō], dat. nēminī, acc. nēminem, m. or f. no one, nobody, not one; nōn nēmō somebody, some

nepōs, –ōtis, m. grandson

Neptūnus, –ī, m. Neptune

nēquāquam, adv. in no way, not at all

* neque or nec, conj. and not, nor, but not; * neque (nec) . . . neque (nec) neither . . . nor

nequeō, 4 (nequīre), –īvī, —, intr. not be able

nēquīquam, adv. in vain

Nēreis, –idis, f. sea nymph

Nēreus, –eī, m. a sea god, father of Thetis

Nervius, –ī, m. a Nervian; pl. the Ner′viī or Nervians, a powerful tribe of the Belgians

nervus, –ī, m. sinew, muscle; pl. power, resources

nescio, 4, –ii (–īvī), — not know

neu, *see* nēve

* neuter, –tra, –trum neither; *as noun, m. pl.* neither party

* nēve *or* neu, *conj.* and not, nor

nex, necis, *f.* death, murder

niger, nigra, nigrum black

* nihil, *indecl. n.* nothing; *as adv.* not, not at all; nōn nihil somewhat

nihilum, –ī, *n.* nothing; nihilō by nothing; nihilō minus none the less, nevertheless

nīl = nihil

Nīlus, –ī, *m.* Nile River

Nīnus, –ī, *m.* Nī'nus, mythical founder of Babylon

* nisi, *conj.* if not, unless, except, but

nitidus, –a, –um shining

nītor, 3, nīxus *or* nīsus sum, *dep., intr.* strive, endeavor, rely on

nix, nivis, *f.* snow

* nōbilis, –e well known, noted, famous, of high birth; *as noun, m. pl.* nobles

* nōbilitās, –tātis, *f.* nobility, rank, nobles, aristocracy

nocēns, –entis, *adj.* harmful, guilty

* noceō, 2, nocuī, nocitus, *intr.* injure, harm

* noctū, *adv.* in the night

* nocturnus, –a, –um nocturnal, during the night

* nōlō, nōlle, nōluī, —, *tr. or intr.* be unwilling, wish . . . not

* nōmen, –inis, *n.* name, reputation; suō nōmine in his (their) own name

nōminātim, *adv.* by name

nōminō, 1 name

* nōn, *adv.* not, not at all, by no means

Nōnae, –ārum, *f. pl.* Nones, ninth day before the Ides. *See* 634

nōnāgintā (XC), *indecl. adj.* ninety

* nōndum, *adv.* not yet

nōnne, *interrog. adv.* not (*answer "yes" expected*)

* nōnus, –a, –um ninth

Nōricus, –a, –um Nor'ican; *as noun, f.* a Norican woman

nōs, *pl. of* ego

* nōscō, 3, nōvī, nōtus get knowledge of, learn; nōvī I have learned, *hence* I know

* noster, –tra, –trum our, ours; *as noun, m. pl.* our men

* nōtus, –a, –um well known, famous

* novem (VIIII *or* IX), *indecl. adj.* nine

Noviodūnum, –ī, *n.* Nōviōdū'num, the name of several towns in Gaul

novissimus, –a, –um, *sup. of* novus last, latest; *as noun, m. pl.* soldiers in the rear

novitās, –tātis, *f.* newness, strangeness

* novus, –a, –um new, fresh, recently acquired, novel, strange, unusual; novae rēs revolution

* nox, noctis, *f.* night; prīmā nocte at nightfall

noxia, –ae, *f.* wrong act, harm, offense, crime

nūbēs, –is, *f.* cloud, mist

nūbō, 3, nūpsī, nūptus, *intr.* veil oneself, be married (*said of a woman*)

* nūdō, 1 strip, uncover, expose

nūdus, –a, –um naked, bare, unprotected

* nūllus, –a, –um not any, none; *as noun, m.* no one; * nōn nūllus some; *as noun, pl.* some persons

* **num,** *interrog. adv. implying and expecting a negative answer; conj. introducing an indirect question* whether, if

Numa, *see* **Pompilius**

nūmen, −**inis,** *n.* divine will, divinity

* **numerus,** −**ī,** *m.* number, quantity

Numida, −**ae,** *m.* a Numidian, native of Numidia

nummus, −**ī,** *m.* piece of money

* **numquam,** *adv.* never; **nōn numquam** sometimes

numquid, *adv., introducing a question, an emphatic* **num**

* **nunc,** *adv.* now

* **nūntiō,** 1 bring news, tell

* **nūntius,** −**ī,** *m.* messenger, news

nūper, *adv.* lately, recently

nūptus, −**a,** −**um,** *p. p. of* **nūbō;** *as noun, f.* bride

nūptiae, −**ārum,** *f. pl.* marriage

nūptiālis, −**e** of a marriage, nuptial

nusquam, *adv.* nowhere

nūtriō, 4, −**īvī,** −**ītus** nourish, rear

nūtus, −**ūs,** *m.* nod

nympha, −**ae,** *f.* nymph

Ō, *interj.* O, Oh

* **ob,** *prep. w. acc.* before, on account of, because of, for; **quam ob rem** wherefore, therefore, why? *In compounds* toward, against, before

obdūcō, 3, −**dūxī,** −**ductus** lead against, lead to meet; *w.* **fossam** construct

obferō, *see* **offerō**

* **obiciō,** 3, −**iēcī,** −**iectus** throw before, cast in the way, expose, set up, lie opposite

oblātus, *see* **offerō**

oblinō, 3, −**lēvī,** −**litus** daub, smear

oblīvīscor, 3, −**litus sum,** *dep., tr. or intr.* forget, be forgetful of

obsecrō, 1 beseech, implore, beg

observō, 1 observe, watch, respect

* **obses,** −**sidis,** *m. or f.* hostage

* **obsideō,** 2, −**sēdī,** −**sessus** beset, besiege, blockade, occupy

* **obsidiō,** −**ōnis,** *f.* siege

obstringō, 3, −**strīnxī,** −**strictus** bind, lay under obligations

obtemperō, 1 obey, yield to

obtestor, 1, *dep.* call as a witness

* **obtineō,** 2, −**uī,** −**tentus** hold, keep, occupy, maintain, get possession of

obtulī, *see* **offerō**

obvolvō, 3, −**volvī,** −**volūtus** wrap around

* **occāsiō,** −**ōnis,** *f.* [**ob** + **cadō**] opportunity, fit time, surprise

* **occāsus,** −**ūs,** *m.* going down, setting

* **occidō,** 3, −**cidī,** −**cāsus,** *intr.* fall, be killed, set; **sōl occidēns** setting sun, west

* **occīdō,** 3, −**cīdī,** −**cīsus** kill, destroy

* **occultō,** 1 hide, conceal

* **occultus,** −**a,** −**um** covered up, hidden, secret

occupātiō, −**ōnis,** *f.* business, employment

* **occupō,** 1 seize, master, occupy

* **occurrō,** 3, −**currī** *or* −**cucurrī,** −**cursus,** *intr.* run against, meet, resist, occur

Ōceanus, −**ī,** *m.* the ocean

Ocelum, −**ī,** *n.* Ocelum (Os′elum), a town in Cisalpine Gaul

ōcius, *adv.* more quickly

* octāvus, –a, –um eighth

* octō (VIII), *indecl. adj.* eight

octōgintā (LXXX), *indecl. adj.* eighty

oculātus, –a, –um having an eye; *w.* testis eyewitness

* oculus, –ī, *m.* eye

ōdī, ōdisse, ōsūrus, *defective* hate

odium, –ī, *n.* hatred, animosity

* offerō, –ferre, obtulī, oblātus bear to, put in one's power, offer, confer

* officium, –ī, *n.* duty, obligation, allegiance, favor

oleum, oleī, *n.* oil, ointment

ōlim, *adv.* formerly, once on a time

olīvētum, –ī, *n.* olive orchard

ōmen, ōminis, *n.* omen

omittō, 3, –mīsī, –missus lay aside, give up, neglect

* omnīnō, *adv.* wholly, only, at all

* omnis, –e every, all

* onerārius, –a, –um of burden, for freight; nāvis onerāria transport

* onus, oneris, *n.* load, burden, weight

* opera, –ae, *f.* effort, work, services; dare operam exert oneself, do one's utmost

operiō, 4, operuī, opertus cover

* opīniō, –ōnis, *f.* guess, opinion, reputation, renown

opīnor, 1, *dep., intr.* suppose

* oportet, 2, oportuit, *impers., intr.* it is necessary *or* proper, it behooves, it ought

* oppidānus, –a, –um of a town; *as noun, m.* townsman, inhabitant of a town

* oppidum, –ī, *n.* town, stronghold

Oppius, –a, –um Oppian (*of a law proposed by C. Oppius*)

oppōnō, 3, –posuī, –positus oppose

opportūnē, *adv.* opportunely

opportūnitās, –tātis, *f.* fitness, occasion, opportunity

* opportūnus, –a, –um fit, convenient, opportune, fortunate

oppositus, –a, –um (*p. p. of* oppōnō) lying opposite

* opprīmō, 3, –pressī, –pressus burden, overthrow, fall upon, surprise

* oppugnātiō, –ōnis, *f.* assault, siege, method of attacking

* oppugnō, 1 attack, besiege

* ops, opis, *f.* aid, assistance; *pl.* resources, power, influence

optimus, –a, –um, *sup. of* bonus best

* opus, operis, *n.* work, labor, structure, fortification

opus, *indecl. n.* necessity, need

ōra, –ae, *f.* shore, coast

ōrāculum, –ī, *n.* oracle

* ōrātiō, –ōnis, *f.* speech, plea; ōrātiōnem habēre make a speech

ōrātor, –ōris, *m.* speaker, envoy

orbis, –is, *m.* circle; orbis terrārum the whole earth *or* world

Orcus, –ī, *m.* Pluto, the Lower World

* ōrdō, –inis, *m.* row, series, layer, position, class, company of soldiers; prīmī ōrdinēs first centurians

Orgetorīx, –īgis, *m.* Orgetorix (Orjet'orix), a Helvetian nobleman

orīgō, –inis, *f.* beginning; Orīginēs name of a book by M. Porcius Cato

* orior, 4, ortus sum, *intr., dep.* arise, appear, begin, be born; sōl oriēns rising sun, the east ōrnāmentum, –ī, *n.* honor, ornament, decoration

ōrnātus, –ūs, *m.* ornament, decoration

ōrnō, 1 fit out, honor

* ōrō, 1 speak, plead, implore

Orpheus, –ī, *m.* Orpheus, famous musician

ōs, ōris, *n.* mouth, face

os, ossis, *n.* bone

ōsculum, –ī, *n.* kiss

* ostendō, 3, –tendī, –tentus point out, show, declare, make known

ostentō, 1 display

ōtium, –ī, *n.* leisure, quiet, peace

ovis, ovis, *f.* sheep

ōvum, –ī, *n.* egg

P., *abbr. for* Pūblius Pub'lius, Roman praenomen

pābulātiō, –ōnis, *f.* foraging

* pābulor, 1, *dep.*, *intr.* forage, get fodder

* pābulum, –ī, *n.* food, fodder

* pācō, 1 make peaceful, conquer

Pactōlus, –ī, *m.* Pac'tolus River

* paene, *adv.* nearly, almost

Paetus, –ī, *m.* Paetus (Pē'tus), a Roman, husband of Arria

* pāgus, –ī, *m.* district, canton

pāla, –ae, *f.* set gem

palam, *adv.* openly, publicly

palaestra, –ae, *f.* gymnasium

Palātĭnus, –a, –um Palatine; *w.* mōns the Palatine Hill, one of the seven hills of Rome

palla, –ae, *f.* cloak

palma, –ae, *f.* palm, hand, palm tree

* palūs, –ūdis, *f.* swamp, marsh, marshy stream

pandō, 3, –dī, passus spread out, extend

pānis, pānis, *m.* bread

Papīrius, –ī, *m.* Papir'ius, a Roman name

* pār, paris equal, like, same

parātus, –a, –um ready, prepared

* parcō, 3, pepercī, parsus, *intr.* spare, protect

parēns, –entis, *m. or f.* parent

* pāreō, 2, pāruī, — obey, submit, comply

pariēs, –ietis, *m.* partition, wall

pariō, 3, peperī, partus give birth to, produce, gain, effect

Paris, –idis, *m.* Paris, son of Priam

Parīsii, –ōrum, *m. pl.* the Paris'ii, a tribe on the Sequana (*Seine*) near modern Paris

pariter, *adv.* equally, like

Parnāsus, –ī, *m.* Mt. Parnas'sus

* parō, 1 prepare, provide

* pars, partis, *f.* part, portion, faction, direction, respect

* partim, *adv.* partly, in part

partus, –a, –um, *p. p. of* pariō

* parum, *adv.* too little

parvulus, –a, –um very small, petty, slight, young

* parvus, –a, –um small, little

passus, *p. p. of* pandō

* passus, –ūs, *m.* step, double step (*five Roman feet*); mīlle passūs *or* mīlle passuum mile

pāstor, –ōris, *m.* shepherd

patefaciō, 3, –fēcī, –factus lay open, open

patēns, –entis open, accessible, passable

* pateō, 2, –uī, —, *intr.* be open, be accessible, be free, extend

* **pater, –tris,** *m.* father; *pl.* forefathers, ancestors
* **patior, 3, passus sum,** *dep.*, *tr. or intr.* suffer, permit
* **patria, –ae,** *f.* fatherland, native land
patruus, –ī, *m.* paternal uncle
* **paucī, –ae, –a,** *pl. adj.* few, only a few
paucitās, –tātis, *f.* small number, few
* **paulātim,** *adv.* little by little, a few at a time
* **paulisper,** *adv.* for a short time
* **paulō,** *adv.* by a little, somewhat, a little
paululum, *adv.* a very little
* **paulum, –ī,** *n.* a little; *as adv.* a little, somewhat
pauper, –eris poor
* **pāx, pācis,** *f.* treaty of peace
peccō, 1, *intr.* do wrong
pectus, –oris, *n.* breast
* **pecūnia, –ae,** *f.* property, wealth, money
* **pecus, –oris,** *n.* cattle, flock
* **pedes, –itis,** *m.* foot soldier; *pl.* infantry
* **pedester, –tris, –tre** of foot soldiers, of infantry, overland; **pedestrēs cōpiae** infantry
peditātus, –ūs, *m.* foot soldiers, infantry
Pedius, –ī, *m.* Pē′dius, a Roman nomen; Quintus Pedius, one of Caesar's staff
peior, –ius, *comp. of* malus worse
Pēleus, –ī, *m.* Peleus (Pē′leūs), father of Achilles
Peliās, –ae, *m.* Pē′lias, king of Thessaly

pellis, –is, *f.* skin, hide, leather
* **pellō, 3, pepulī, pulsus** drive away, rout, defeat
Penātēs, –ium, *m. pl.* Penates (Pēnā′tēz), the household gods
* **pendō, 3, pependī, pēnsus** hang, weigh, pay
penitus, *adv.* far within
* **per,** *prep. w. acc.* through, across, by means of, on account of, by the agency of, because of, by; *of time* during, along, on; **per vim** by violence; **per sē** of himself (*themselves*), of his (*their*) own accord
pēra, –ae, *f.* bag, wallet
perangustus, –a, –um very narrow
percipiō, 3, –cēpī, –ceptus [per + capiō] get, reap, hear, learn, feel
percontātiō, –ōnis, *f.* questioning, investigation
percurrō, 3, –cucurrī *or* **–currī, –cursus** run through, run along
percutiō, 3, –cussī, –cussus strike through, transfix
perdiscō, 3, –didicī, — learn thoroughly
perditus, –a, –um lost, desperate, corrupt
perdō, 3, –didī, –ditus lose, destroy
* **perdūcō, 3, –dūxī, –ductus** lead through, conduct, persuade, prolong
perendinus, –a, –um after to-morrow
* **pereō, –īre, –iī (–īvī), –itus,** *intr.* die
perequitō, 1 ride through
perfacilis, –e very easy
* **perferō, –ferre, –tulī, –lātus** bear through, bear, endure, suffer, report

* **perficiō, 3,** –fēcī, –fectus make thoroughly, bring about, finish, arrange

* **perfidia,** –ae, *f.* treachery

perfodiō, 3, –fōdī, –fossus pierce through

perfringō, 3, –frēgī, –frāctus break through

* **perfugiō, 3,** –fūgī, —, *intr.* flee for refuge, escape, desert

perfugium, –ī, *n.* refuge, place of safety

pergō, 3, perrēxī, perrēctus, *intr.* press on, proceed

perīclitor, 1, *dep.*, *tr. or intr.* put to the test, try to find out, be endangered

perīculōsus, –a, –um dangerous

* **perīculum,** –ī, *n.* trial, attempt, danger, risk

* **perītus,** –a, –um experienced, acquainted with, skilled

perlātus, *p. p. of* perferō

perlegō, 3, –lēgī, –lēctus read through

* **permaneō, 2,** –mānsī, –mānsūrus, *intr.* remain, continue, hold out

* **permittō, 3,** –mīsī, –missus give up, intrust, permit

* **permoveō, 2,** –mōvī, –mōtus move deeply, influence, induce, disturb, frighten

perpaucī, –ae, –a, *pl. adj.* very few

* **perpetuus,** –a, –um continuous, entire, perpetual; in perpetuum forever

perquīrō, 3, –quīsīvī, –quīsītus inquire about

perrumpō, 3, –rūpī, –ruptus, *tr. or intr.* break through

perscrībō, 3, –scrīpsī, –scrīptus write in full, write out

* **persequor, 3,** –secūtus sum, *dep.*, *tr. or intr.* follow up, hunt down, proceed against, avenge

perservō, 1 preserve

persevērō, 1, *intr.* persist, persevere

persolvō, 3, –solvī, –solūtus pay in full, suffer

* **perspiciō, 3,** –spexī, –spectus look through, examine, perceive, understand

perstō, 1, –stitī, –statūrus, *intr.* stand firmly, persist

* **persuādeō, 2,** –suāsī, –suāsus, *tr. or intr.* persuade, convince

* **perterreō, 2,** –uī, –itus frighten thoroughly, terrify, alarm

pertinācia, –ae, *f.* persistence, obstinacy

* **pertineō, 2,** –uī, —, *intr.* reach, extend, pertain, tend

pertulī, *see* perferō

perturbātiō, –ōnis, *f.* confusion, alarm

* **perturbō, 1** throw into confusion, alarm

pervādō, 3, –vāsī, —, *tr. or intr.* spread through

* **perveniō, 4,** –vēnī, –ventus, *intr.* come through, arrive, come

* **pēs, pedis,** *m.* foot, a foot (*as a measure, slightly shorter than the standard English foot*)

pessimus, –a, –um, *sup. of* malus worst

* **petō, 3,** –īvī, –ītus strive for, seek, beg, ask, aim at, attack

Petrōnius, –ī, *m.* Marcus Petrō′nius, a centurion of the Eighth Legion

Phaethōn, –ontis, *m.* Phaëthon (Fā′ethon), son of Apollo

phalanx, –angis, *f.* phalanx, a compact body of troops in battle array

Phāsis, –idis, *acc.* **–im,** *m.* Phasis (Fā'sis), a river flowing into the Black Sea

Philerōs, –ōtos, *m.* Phil'eros, a man's name

Phīneus, –ī, *m.* Phineus (Fin'ūs), blind king of Thrace

Phrixus, –ī, *m.* Phrixus (Frik'sus), brother of Helle

Phrygia, –ae, *f.* Phrygia, in Asia Minor

Pictonēs, –um, *m. pl.* the Pictones (Pic'tōnēz), a tribe in western Gaul

piger, pigra, pigrum lazy

* **pīlum, –ī,** *n.* javelin

pinna, –ae, *f.* feather, battlement

pīnus, –ūs, *f.* pine, pine tree, ship

piscis, –is, *m.* fish

Pīsō, –ōnis, *m.* (1) Lucius Calpurnius Pī'sō, consul in 58 B.C., father-in-law of Caesar; (2) Lucius Calpurnius Piso, grandfather of (1); (3) Marcus Pupius Piso, consul in 61 B.C.; Piso, an Aquitaian of high rank,

pius, –a, –um pious, devout, kind

pix, picis, *f.* pitch

* **placeō 2, –uī, –itus,** *intr.* please, be pleasing, seem best; **placuit** he *or* they decided

plācō, 1 appease, propitiate, placate

* **plānitiēs, –ēī,** *f.* level ground, plain

plānus, –a, –um even, level, flat

Platō, –ōnis, *m.* Plato, Greek philosopher

* **plēbs, plēbis,** *f.* common people, populace

plēnus, –a, –um, full, complete

* **plērīque, –aeque, –aque,** *pl. adj.* most, majority, a very great part

* **plērumque,** *adv.* for the most part

Plīnius, –ī, *m.* Pliny, a Roman writer

plōrō, 1, *tr. or intr.* weep, wail

plūma, –ae, *f.* feather, down

plumbum, –ī, *n.* lead; **plumbum album** tin

pluō, 3, pluī, —, *impers., intr.* rain

plūrimum, *adv., sup. of* **multum** very much

plūrimus, –a, –um, *sup. of* **multus;** *pl.* very many, a great many; **quam plūrimī** as many as possible; *as noun,* **plurimum, –ī,** *n.* very much, a great deal

plūs, plūris, *comp. of* **multus** more; *in sing., as noun, n.* the greater part; *m. pl.* **plūrēs** more, a good many; **plūs** *is sometimes used as an adverb*

pluteus, –ī, *m.* breastwork

* **poena, –ae,** *f.* punishment, penalty

* **poēta, –ae,** *m.* poet

* **polliceor, 2, pollicitus sum,** *dep.* offer, promise

pollicitātiō, –ōnis, *f.* promise, pledge

pollicitus, p. p. of polliceor

Polyphēmus, –ī, *m.* Polyphemus (Polyfē'mus)

Pompeius, –ī, *m.* Gnaeus Pompē'ius Magnus, the friend and son-in-law and later the rival of Caesar

Pompilius, –ī, *m.* Nū'ma Pompil'ius, second king of Rome

pondus, –eris, *n.* weight, mass

* **pōnō, 3, posuī, positus** put down, place, pitch, make depend (*on*), lay down; *pass.* depend (*on*)

* **pōns, pontis,** *m.* bridge
popīna, –ae, *f.* low tavern
poposcī, *see* **poscō**
populātiō, –ōnis, *f.* laying waste, plundering
* **populor, 1,** *dep.* lay waste, pillage
* **populus, –ī,** *m.* people, nation
pōpulus, –ī, *f.* poplar tree
Porcius, –ī, *m.* Porcius Cato (Por'-shyus Cā'to)
porcus, –ī, *m.* pig
* **porta, –ae,** *f.* gateway, gate
* **portō, 1** bring, carry
* **portus, –ūs,** *m.* harbor, port
* **poscō, 3, poposcī, —** demand, request, call for, need
positus, –a, –um (*p. p. of* **pōnō**) situated
possessiō, –ōnis, *f.* occupation, possession, property
* **possideō, 2, –sēdī, –sessus** have and hold, occupy, own
* **possum, posse, potuī, —,** *intr.* be able, can (*with inf.*); **plūrimum posse** be most powerful
* **post,** *adv.* afterwards; *prep. w. acc.* after, behind
* **posteā,** *adv.* after that, afterwards
* **posteāquam,** *conj.* after
* **posterus, –a, –um** following, next, later; **in posterum** to the next day; *as noun, m. pl.* posterity
posthāc, *adv.* after this
* **postquam,** *conj.* after, when
postrēmō, *adv.* finally, last of all
postrēmus, –a, –um, *sup. of* **posterus** last, final
* **postrīdiē,** *adv.* on the next day
postulātum, –ī, *n.* demand, request
* **postulō, 1** demand, request, require, call for

* **potēns, –entis** powerful, influential
potentia, –ae, *f.* power, authority, influence
* **potestās, –tātis,** *f.* power, civil authority, opportunity, chance
pōtiō, –ōnis, *f.* drink
* **potior, 4, –ītus sum,** *dep., intr.* get possession of, become master of
* **potius,** *adv.* rather, more, sooner
prae, *prep. w. abl.* before, in comparison with
praeacūtus, –a, –um sharpened at the end, pointed
* **praebeō, 2, –uī, –itus** hold out, furnish, present, cause
praecaveō, 2, –cāvī, –cautus, *tr. or intr.* take care beforehand, be on guard against
praecēdō, 3, –cessī, –cessus, *tr. or intr.* go ahead of, surpass
praeceps, –cipitis headlong, steep
praeceptum, –ī, *n.* order, injunction, direction
* **praecipiō, 3, –cēpī, –ceptus** take in advance, anticipate, suspect, order, direct
praecipitō, 1 throw headlong, hurl down
praecipuē, *adv.* especially
praeclārus, –a, –um distinguished, noble
* **praeda, –ae,** *f.* booty, plunder
* **praedicō, 1** announce, assert, boast
praedīcō, 3, –dīxī, –dictus foretell
praedūcō, 3, –dūxī, –ductus lead forward, construct before, construct
* **praefectus,** *p. p. of* **praeficiō**; *as noun, m.* overseer, prefect
praeferō, –ferre, –tulī, –lātus bear before, put before, prefer; **sē praeferre** surpass

* **praeficiō, 3, –fēcī, –fectus** set over, put in command of

* **praemittō, 3, –mīsī, –missus** send ahead, send forward

* **praemium, –ī,** *n.* reward, prize, bribe

praeoptō, 1 choose rather, prefer

praeparō, 1 make ready beforehand, prepare

praepōnō, 3, –posuī, –positus place in front of, set over, put in charge of

praerumpō, 3, –rūpī, –ruptus tear away in front, break off

praesaepe, –is, *n.* manger

praescrībō, 3, –scrīpsī, –scrīptus write beforehand, direct, dictate

* **praesēns, –entis** present, existing

praesentia, –ae, *f.* present, presence

* **praesertim,** *adv.* especially, chiefly

praesideō, 2, –sēdī, —, *tr. or intr.* to sit before, guard

* **praesidium, –ī,** *n.* defense, aid, guard, garrison, station

praestāns, –stantis (*pres. part. of* **praestō**) remarkable

* **praestō, 1, –stitī, –stitus,** *tr. or intr.* stand before, excel, perform, show; **praestat** it is better

praestō, *adv.* at hand, present

* **praesum, –esse, –fuī, —,** *intr.* be before, be set over, be in command of

praesūmō, 3, —, –sūmptus take for granted, presume

* **praeter,** *prep. w. acc.* beyond, except, besides, in addition to

* **praetereā,** *adv.* in addition, furthermore, besides

praetereō, –īre, –iī (–īvī), –itus, *tr. or intr.* pass, disregard, pass over

praetermittō, 3, –mīsī, –missus let go by, overlook, lose

praetextātus, –a, –um wearing the purple bordered toga of youth

praetor, –ōris, *m.* praetor

praeustus, –a, –um charred *or* burned at the end

precor, 1, *tr. or intr.* pray

* **prehendō, 3, –hendī, –hēnsus** grasp, seize

* **premō, 3, pressī, pressus** press hard, crowd, drive, burden

pretiōsus, –a, –um costly, valuable

pretium, –ī, *n.* value, price

* **prex, precis,** *f.* request, prayer

Priamus, –ī, *m.* Prī'am, last king of Troy

* **prīdiē,** *adv.* on the day before

prīmipīlus, –ī, *m.* first centurion (*of a legion*), chief centurion

* **prīmō,** *adv.* at first

* **prīmum,** *adv.* first; **cum prīmum** *or* **ubi prīmum** as soon as; **quam prīmum** as soon as possible

* **prīmus, –a, –um** first, first part of; *as noun, m. pl.* the van; **in prīmīs** among the first things, especially, chiefly

* **prīnceps, –cipis** first, chief; *as noun, m.* leader, noble

* **prīncipātus, –ūs,** *m.* first place, leadership

* **prior, prius** former, in advance, first; *as noun, m. pl.* those in front, the van

Prīscus, *see* **Tarquinius**

* **prīstinus, –a, –um** former, preceding, original, pristine

prius, *adv.* before, earlier

* **priusquam,** *conj.* earlier than, before, sooner than; *also* **prius . . . quam**

* prīvātus, −a, −um personal, individual; as *noun*, *m.* private
  person
* prō, *prep. w. abl.* before, in front
  of, in behalf of, for, in place of,
  instead of, as, just as, because of,
  in return for
* probō, 1 approve, command, show,
  prove
* prōcēdō, 3, −cessī, −cessus, *intr.*
  go forward, advance
* procul, *adv.* at a distance, far away
  prōcumbō, 3, −cubuī, −cubitus, *intr.*
  fall forward, fall, sink down
  prōcūrō, 1 take care of, attend to
  prōcurrō, 3, −cucurrī *or* −currī, −cur-
  sus, *intr.* run forward, charge
  prōditor, −ōris, *m.* traitor
* prōdō, 3, −didī, −ditus give forth,
  hand down, give up, betray
* prōdūcō, 3, −dūxī, −ductus lead out,
  bring forward, produce, protract
  proelior, 1, *dep.*, *intr.* join battle,
  fight
* proelium, −ī, *n.* battle, combat
* profectiō, −ōnis, *f.* setting out,
  departure
  prōferō, −ferre, −tulī, −lātus carry
  out, bring out, postpone
  professor, −ōris, *m.* professor
* prōficiō, 3, −fēcī, −fectus, *tr. or*
  intr. advance, accomplish
* proficīscor, 3, −fectus sum, *dep.*,
  intr. set out, depart, march
  profiteor, 2, −fessus sum, *dep.* avow,
  promise, offer
  profugiō, 3, −fūgī, —, *intr.* flee forth,
  escape
  prōgnātus, −a, −um [prō + (g)nātus,
  p. p. of (g)nāscor] sprung, descended

* prōgredior, 3, −gressus sum, *dep.*,
  intr. advance, proceed
* prohibeō, 2, −uī, −itus hinder,
  check, prevent, keep off, cut off
* prōiciō, 3, −iēcī, −iectus hurl
  forward, throw, throw down,
  abandon, reject, leap
  proinde, *adv.* therefore, so
  prōmittō, 3, −mīsī, −missus let
  go forward, let grow
  prōmoveō, 2, −mōvī, −mōtus move
  forward
* prōnūntiō, 1 announce, pronounce,
  tell, order
  prōpāgō, 1 bring, spread
* prope, *adv.* almost, nearly; *prep.*
  w. acc. near
  prōpellō, 3, −pulī, −pulsus drive
  away, keep off, dislodge
  properō, 1, *intr.* hasten
  propinquitās, −tātis, *f.* nearness,
  vicinity, relationship
* propinquus, −a, −um near, neighboring, at hand, related; as *noun*,
  m. or f. relative
  propius, *adv.* nearer
* prōpōnō, 3, −posuī, −positus place
  before, display, propose, offer,
  present, relate, explain, intend
  proprius, −a, −um individual, belonging to, characteristic
* propter, *prep. w. acc.* on account
  of, because of
* proptereā, *adv.* on that account;
  propereā quod for the reason that,
  because
  prōpugnātor, −ōris, *m.* defender
  prōpugnō, 1, *intr.* fight on the offen-
  sive, repel an attack, resist
  prōpulsō, 1 beat back, repel
  prōra, −ae, *f.* bow, prow

* prōsequor, 3, –secūtus sum, *dep.* follow up, exhort, honor

Prōserpina, –ae, *f.* Proserpine

prōsiliō, 4, –uī, —, *intr.* leap forward, spring up, spring forth

prōspiciō, 3, –spexī, –spectus, *intr.* watch, provide, use foresight

prōsum, prōdesse, prōfuī, —, *intr.* be of advantage, help

prōtegō, 3, –tēxī, –tēctus cover over, protect, shield

* prōtinus, *adv.* immediately

prōvehō, 3, –vexī, –vectus carry forward; *pass.* advance, sail out

prōvideō, 2, –vīdī, –vīsus, *tr. or intr.* foresee, take precautions, provide, prepare

* prōvincia, –ae, *f.* province, territory governed by a magistrate from Rome, official duty

proximē, *adv.* next, most recently, last

proximus, –a, –um, *sup. of* prope nearest, latest, following

* prūdēns, –entis knowing, wise

prūdentia, –ae, *f.* foresight, judgment

Psȳchē, Psȳchēs, *f.* Psyche

pūblicē, *adv.* in the name of the state, publicly

* pūblicus, –a, –um of the people, public, official; *as noun, n.* public place, public view; * rēs pūblica, *f.* public interest, public welfare, the state (*especially Rome*)

pudor, –ōris, *m.* shame, conscientiousness

* puella, –ae, *f.* girl

* puer, –erī, *m.* boy; *pl.* children

puerīlis, –e boyish, childish

* pugna, –ae, *f.* fight, battle

* pugnō, 1, *intr.* fight; *impers. in*

pass., pugnātur it is fought, they fight

pulcher, –chra, –chrum beautiful, honorable, illustrious

pulchritūdō, –inis, *f.* beauty

Pullō, –ōnis, *m.* Titus Pul'lō, a brave centurion in Caesar's army

pullus, –ī, *m. or f.* young animal, young chick

pulsus, *p. p. of* pellō

* pulvis, –eris, *m.* dust, cloud of dust

pūmex, –icis, *m.* rock, pumice stone

pūniō, 4, –īvī, –ītus punish

puppis, –is, *f.* stern, ship

pūrgō, 1 cleanse, excuse, justify

purpura, –ae, *f.* purple

pūrus, –a, –um pure, clean, unstained

puteus, –ī, *m.* well

* putō, 1 consider, judge

Pȳramus, –ī, *m.* Pyr'amus

Pȳrēnaeus, –a, –um; *w.* montēs the Pyrenees Mountains

Pyrrha, –ae, *f.* Pyr'rha, wife of Deucalion

Pyrrhus, –ī, *m.* Pyrrhus, a king of Epirus

Q., *abbr. for* Quīntus Quin'tus, Roman praenomen

* quā (*abl. f. of* quī; = quā viā), *adv.* by which way, where, on which side

quadrāgēsimus, –a, –um fortieth

quadrāgintā (XL), *indecl. adj.* forty

quadringentī, –ae, –a (CCCC), *pl. adj.* four hundred

* quaerō, 3, –sīvī, –sītus seek, inquire, investigate, ask

quaestiō, −ōnis, *f.* questioning, judicial investigation

* quaestor, −ōris, *m.* quaestor

quaestus, −ūs, *m.* gain, profit

quālis, −e of what sort? what? of which kind?

* quam, *adv.* to what degree? how? as, than, rather than; quam *with a superlative with or without some form of* possum in the highest degree, as . . . possible; quam prīmum as soon as possible

quamvīs, *adv.* as you will, however

quandō, *adv.* when?; *after* sī at any time, ever

* quantus, −a, −um how great? how much? as great, as much, as, as great as, as much as; tantus . . . quantus as great . . . as, as much . . . as; quantō . . . tantō by how much . . . by so much, the . . . the

quārē (quā rē), *adv.* wherefore? why? therefore, for that reason

* quārtus, −a, −um fourth

quasi, *conj.* as if, just as if

quassō, 1 shake, toss, shatter

quatiō, 3, —, quassus shake, brandish

* quattuor (IIII *or* IV), *indecl. adj.* four

* −que, *enclitic conj.* and, and in fact

quem ad modum, *interrog. adv.* in what way? how? as

queō, 4 (quīre), quīvī, quitus, *intr.* be able, can

* queror, 3, questus sum, *dep., tr. or intr.* wail, lament

* quī, quae, quod, *rel. pron.* who, which, that

quī, quae, quod, *interrog. adj.* which?

what?; quam ob rem for what reason? why?

quī, quae *or* qua, quod, *indef. adj.*, *used after* sī, nisi, nē, num any, some

quia, *conj.* because

quicquam, *see* quisquam

* quīcumque, quaecumque, quodcumque, *indef. rel. pron. or adj.* whoever, whatever, whichever

quid, *interrog. adv.* why?

* quīdam, quaedam, quiddam (*adj.* quoddam), *indef. pron. or adj.* a certain one, certain, somebody

* quidem, *adv.* certainly, in fact, indeed, yet, however; *nē . . . quidem not even

quidlibet, *n.* anything, everything

quidnam, why in the world?

* quiēs, −ētis, *f.* repose, rest, sleep

* quiētus, −a, −um peaceful, tranquil

quīlibet, quaelibet, quodlibet, *indef. pron.* whom you will, anyone

* quīn, *conj., after neg. expressions of doubt* that . . . not, that; quīn etiam why even, in fact

Quīnctius, *see* Cincinnātus

quīndecim (XV), *indecl. adj.* fifteen

quīngentī, −ae, −a (D), *num. adj.* five hundred

quīnī, −ae, −a, *pl. indecl. adj.* five each, by fives

quīnquāgintā (L), *indecl. adj.* fifty

* quīnque (V), *indecl. adj.* five

quīnquiēns, *adv.* five times

* quīntus, −a, −um fifth

quippe, *adv.* of course

Quirīnālis, −e Quirinal; *w.* collis one of the seven hills of Rome

Quirīnus, -ī, *m.* name given to Romulus; **Iānus Quirīnus** temple of Janus

* **quis, quid,** *interrog. pron.* who? what?; **quid** why? how much?

* **quis, quid,** *indef. pron.* anyone, anything; *after* **sī, nisi, nē, num** anyone, anything, someone, something

quispiam, quaepiam, quidpiam (*adj.* **quodpiam**), *indef. pron. or adj.* anyone, any, someone, some; *as adj.* any

* **quisquam, quicquam,** *indef. pron. or adj.* anyone at all

* **quisque, quaeque, quidque** (*adj.* **quodque**), *indef. pron. or adj.* each, everyone, everybody, all

quīvīs, quaevīs, quidvīs (*adj.* **quodvīs**), *indef. pron. or adj.* any one you please; *adj.* any you please, whatever

* **quō,** *adv. rel.* to which place, as far as; *interrog.* where?; *indef. after* **sī** to any place

quō, *conj.* that, thereby, in order that

quoad, *conj.* until, as long as, as far as

quōcumque, *adv.* wherever

* **quod,** *conj.* that, in that, because, since, as to the fact that, the fact that

* **quod sī,** but if

* **quōminus** *or* **quō minus,** *conj.* that . . . . not, but that, from

quōmodo, *adv.* in what manner, how

* **quoniam,** *conj.* since, because

* **quoque,** *adv.* also, too

quōqueversus, *adv.* in all directions, everywhere

quōquō, *adv.* wherever, to whatever place

quot, *indecl. adj.* how many? as many as, as

quotannīs, *adv.* every year, annually

quotiēns, *adv.* how often? how many times? as often as

rādīx, -īcis, *f.* root, base; *pl.* foot of a hill *or* mountain

rādō, 3, rāsī, rāsus scrape, shave

rāmus, -ī, *m.* branch, bough, prong

rāpa, -ae, *f.* turnip

rapīna, -ae, *f.* robbery, plundering

* **rapiō, 3, rapuī, raptus** seize

rāsilis, -e polished

rāsus, *p. p. of* **rādō**

* **ratiō, -ōnis,** *f.* reckoning, account, list, report, art, science, manner, fashion, reason

ratis, -is, *f.* raft, float

ratus, *p. p. of* **reor**

raucus, -a, -um hoarse

Rauracī, -ōrum, *m. pl.* the Rauraci (Rau'rasī), a Gallic tribe near the Rhine

re- *or* **red-,** *insep. prefix* again, back

rebelliō, -ōnis, *f.* revolt, uprising

recēdō, 3, -cessī, -cessus, *intr.* go back, retire

* **recēns, -entis** fresh, vigorous

receptus, -ūs, *m.* retreat, way of retreat, place of refuge, shelter

recessus, -ūs, *m.* retreat, chance to retreat

recidō, 3, -cidī, -cāsūrus, *intr.* fall back, be thrown back

* **recipiō, 3, -cēpī, -ceptus** take back, lead back, retreat, admit, accept; **sē recipere** recover, betake oneself, retreat

recitō, **1** read aloud, recite

rēctē, *adv.* rightly, well

rēctus, –a, –um straight, direct

recumbō, **3,** –uī, —, *intr.* lie down

* recuperō, **1** get back, recover

* recūsō, **1,** *tr. or intr.* make objections, refuse

redāctus, *p. p. of* redigō

* reddō, **3,** –didī, –ditus give back, restore, give, render, make

* redeō, **4,** –iī (–īvī), –itus, *intr.* go back, return, be referred

* redigō, **3,** –ēgī, –āctus bring down, cause to be, render, make

redimō, **3,** –ēmī, –ēmptus buy back, purchase

redintegrō, **1** make whole, restore, renew, begin again

reditiō, –ōnis, *f.* return

reditus, –ūs, *m.* return

redūcō, **3,** –dūxī, –ductus lead back, draw off, draw back, extend back

refectus, *p. p. of* reficiō

* referō, –ferre, rettulī, relātus carry back, bring, carry, report, refer

* reficiō, **3,** –fēcī, –fectus repair, refresh

refulgeō, **2,** –fulsī, —, *intr.* glisten, shine

rēgia, –ae, *f.* palace

* rēgīna, –ae, *f.* queen

* regiō, –ōnis, *f.* direction, line, region, country

rēgnō, **1,** *intr.* reign

* rēgnum, –ī, *n.* kingly power, kingdom, throne

* regō, **3,** rēxī, rēctus make straight, direct, govern

reiciō, **3,** –iēcī, –iectus [re– + iaciō] throw, hurl *or* drive back, drive away, reject

relanguēscō, **3,** –languī, —, *intr.* become weak

relātus, *p. p. of* referō

relēgō, **1** remove, banish

* religiō, –ōnis, *f.* sense of duty, duty to the gods; *pl.* religious matters, rites

* relinquō, **3,** –līquī, –lictus leave behind, leave, abandon; *pass.* remain

* reliquus, –a, –um remaining, the rest of, the rest, the other; *as noun, n.* the rest

remaneō, **2,** –mānsī, —, *intr.* be left, remain, stay, continue

remedium, –ī, *n.* remedy

Rēmī, –ōrum, *m. pl.* Rē′mī, a Belgian tribe near modern Reims

rēmigō, **1,** *intr.* row

remigrō, **1,** *intr.* remove, return

reminīscor, **3,** —, *dep.* remember

remissus, –a, –um lax, gentle, mild

* remittō, **3,** –mīsī, –missus send back, release, hurl back, relax, remove, resign

remollēscō, **3,** —, —, *intr.* become weak

remōtus, –a, –um remote, retired

* removeō, **2,** –mōvī, –mōtus move back, remove, dismiss

* rēmus, –ī, *m.* oar

Rēmus, –ī, *m.* one of the Remi

Remus, –ī, *m.* brother of Romulus

* renūntiō, **1** bring back word, announce

reor, rērī, ratus sum, *dep.* think, suppose

repellō, **3,** reppulī, repulsus drive back, repel, repulse

* repente, *adv.* suddenly

* repentīnus, –a, –um sudden, unexpected

* **reperiō, 4, repperī, repertus** find, meet with, discover, ascertain, learn

repetō, 3, -iī (-īvī), -ītus seek again

* **repleō, 2, -plēvī, -plētus** replenish, supply fully

reportō, 1 carry back

reposcō, 3, —, — demand back, require

reppulī, see **repellō**

reprimō, 3, -pressī, -pressus drive back, suppress, stop

repudiō, 1 repudiate, divorce

repulsus, p. p. of repellō

requiēscō, 3, -quiēvī, -quiētus, intr. be at rest, repose

requīrō, 3, -quīsīvī, -quīsītus demand

* **rēs, reī, f.** thing, matter, object, affair, event, business, fact, circumstance; **rēs gestae** deeds, occurrences

rescindō, 3, -scidī, -scissus cut down, break down, tear apart

rescīscō, 3, -scīvī, -scītus find out, learn

reservō, 1 keep back, reserve, keep

resīdō, 3, -sēdī, —, intr. settle down again, become calm

* **resistō, 3, -stitī, —, intr.** halt, make a stand, withstand, oppose

respiciō, 3, -spexī, -spectus, tr. or intr. look back, look at, regard, be mindful of, consider

* **respondeō, 2, -spondī, -spōnsus, tr. or intr.** reply

* **respōnsum, -ī, n.** answer

restinguō, 3, -stīnxī, -stīnctus put out, extinguish

restitī, see **resistō**

* **restituō, 3, -uī, -ūtus** restore, renew, reinstate, return, rebuild

retineō, 2, -uī, -tentus hold back, keep, restrain

rettulī, see **referō**

* **revertō, 3, -vertī, —, intr. (regularly in perf. tenses only); revertor, 3, -versus sum, dep., intr.** turn back, go back, return

revocō, 1 recall, call off, call away, invite in return

* **rēx, rēgis, m.** king

Reynardus, -ī, m. Reynard, a name given to a fox

Rhēnus, -ī, m. the Rhine River

Rhodanus, -ī, m. the Rhone River

rīdeō, 2, rīsī, rīsus, intr. smile, laugh

rīma, -ae, f. crack

* **rīpa, -ae, f.** bank

rīte, adv. with due rites

rīvus, -ī, m. stream, brook

rōbīgō, -inis, f. mildew

Rōbīgus, -ī, m. Robī'gus, the god who averted mildew

rōbur, -oris, n. oak, strength

rogātiō, -ōnis, f. proposed law

* **rogō, 1** ask, beg

Rōma, -ae, f. Rome

Rōmānus, -a, -um Roman

Rōmulus, -ī, m. Romulus, founder of Rome

rosa, -ae, f. rose

rōstrum, -ī, n. beak, ship's beak, ram

rota, -ae, f. wheel

ruber, rubra, rubrum red

rubus, -ī, m. bramble

rudis, -e, rude, unpolished

Rūfus, -ī, m. Rufus; see **Sulpicius**

* **rūmor, -ōris, m.** report, hearsay

* **rumpō, 3, rūpī, ruptus** break, destroy

rūpēs, -is, f. cliff, rock

* **rūrsus,** *adv.* again, in turn

rūsticus, -a, -um of the country, rural

rūsticus, -ī, *m.* countryman, rustic

Rutēnī, -ōrum, *m. pl.* the Rutē′nī, a tribe on the borders of the Province

Sabidius, -ī, *m.* Sabid′ius, a Roman name

Sabīnī, -ōrum, *m. pl.* the Sabines

Sabīnus, -ī, *m.* Sabinus; *see* **Titūrius**

sacculus, -ī, *m.* bag

sacer, sacra, sacrum sacred; *as noun,* *n. pl.* sacred rites

sacerdōs, -ōtis, *m. or f.* priest, priestess

sacerdōtium, -ī, *n.* priesthood

sacrāmentum, -ī, *n.* oath

sacrificium, -ī, *n.* sacrifice

sacrōsānctus, -a, -um sacred, inviolable

* **saepe,** *adv.* often; **minimē saepe** very seldom; *comp.* **saepius**; *sup.* **saepissimē**

saevus, -a, -um savage

* **sagitta, -ae,** *f.* arrow

* **sagittārius, -ī,** *m.* bowman, archer

sagulum, -ī, *n.* military cloak, cloak

Salmydēssus, -ī, *m.* Salmydes′sus, a town in Thrace

saltō, 1 dance

saltus, -ūs, *m.* pass, glen

* **salūs, -ūtis,** *f.* health, safety, welfare, prosperity

salūtō, 1 pay respects to

Salvātor, -ōris, *m.* the Saviour

Samnītēs, -ium, *m. pl.* the Sam′nītes, a people of Italy

sānctus, -a, -um sacred, inviolable

sanguis, -inis, *m.* blood

Santonēs, -um, *or* **Santonī, -ōrum,** *m. pl.* the Santones (San′tōnēz), or Santoni, a tribe in western Gaul

sānus, -a, -um sound, well, sensible

sapiēns, -entis wise

sapientia, -ae, *f.* wisdom

sapiō, 3, -īvī, —, *intr.* savor of, taste, be discreet, be wise

sarcina, -ae, *f.* bundle, soldier's pack

Sardanapallus, -ī, *m.* Sardanapal′lus

Sardinia, -ae, *f.* island of Sardinia

* **satis** *or* **sat,** *indecl. adj. and noun, nom. and acc.,* *n.* enough, quite sufficient; *adv.* enough, fully, somewhat

* **satisfaciō, 3, -fēcī, -factus,** *intr.* do enough for, give satisfaction, make restitution, placate

satisfactiō, -ōnis, *f.* apology

Saturnus, -ī, *m.* Saturn, god of agriculture

satus, *p. p. of* serō

* **saxum, -ī,** *n.* large stone, rock

scālae, -ārum, *f. pl.* flight of steps, scaling-ladder

scapha, -ae, *f.* ship's boat, skiff

scelerātus, -a, -um wicked

scelus, -eris, *n.* wicked deed, crime

scientia, -ae, *f.* knowledge, skill

* **sciō, 4, scīvī, scītus** understand, know

scorpiō, -ōnis, *m.* scorpion

* **scrībō, 3, scrīpsī, scrīptus** write

Scrībōniānus, -ī, *m.* Scriboniā′nus

* **scūtum, -ī,** *n.* shield

sē- *or* **sed-,** *insep. prefix* from

sē, *acc. and abl. of* **suī**

sēbum, -ī, *n.* fat, tallow

sēcēdō, 3, -cessī, -cessus, *intr.* withdraw

sēcessiō, -ōnis, *f.* insurrection

sēcum = cum sē

secundum, *prep. w. acc.* following, along, beside, in addition to; secundum nātūram flūminis downstream

* secundus, —a, —um following, second, successful, favorable; secundō flūmine downstream

Secundus, —ī, *m.* Secundus, a Roman name

secūtus, *p. p. of* sequor

* sed, *conj.* but, on the contrary, yet, however, but in fact, but indeed

sēdecim (XVI), *indecl. adj.* sixteen

sedeō, 2, sēdī, sessus, *intr.* sit

sēditiō, —ōnis, *f.* dissention, insurrection

sēdūcō, 3, —dūxī, —ductus draw aside

Sedulius, —ī, *m.* Sedulius, a chieftain of the Lemovices

Segusiāvī, —ōrum, *m. pl.* the Segusiavi (Segūshiā'vī), a Gallic tribe

sella, —ae, *f.* [sedeō] chair

sēmen, —inis, *n.* seed

sēmentis, —is, *f.* sowing; sēmentēs facere sow

sēmita, —ae, *f.* path, byway

* semper, *adv.* always, ever

senātor, —ōris, *m.* senator, councilor

* senātus, —ūs, *m.* senate, council of elders

senectūs, —tūtis, *f.* old age

senex, senis old; *comp.* senior, —ōris older, elder; *as noun* old man, aged person

Senonēs, —um, *m. pl.* the Senones (Sen'onēz), a tribe in central Gaul

sēnsus, —ūs, *m.* feeling, sentiment, sense

*sententia, —ae, *f.* way of thinking, opinion, decision, purpose, official judgment, sentence, vote

sentēs, —ium, *m. pl.* thorns, briers

* sentiō, 4, sēnsī, sēnsus perceive, find out, feel, experience, think, know

sēparātim, *adv.* separately

sēparō, 1 separate, divide

*septem (VII), *indecl. adj.* seven

September, —bris, *m.* of September, of the seventh month

septentriōnēs, —um, *m. pl.* seven plow-oxen, the seven stars of the constellation " Great Bear," north

* septimus, —a, —um seventh

septuāgēsimus, —a, —um seventieth

sepultūra, —ae, *f.* burial

Sēquana, —ae, *f.* the Sequana (Sek'-wana) River (Seine)

Sēquanus, —a, —um Sequā'nian; *as noun, m.* a Sequanian; *pl.* the Sequani (Sek'wanī), *or* Sequanians, a tribe west of the Ural Mountains

* sequor, 3, secūtus sum, *dep., tr. or intr.* pursue, follow, accompany, conform to

sera, —ae, *f.* bar, bolt

sermō, —ōnis, *m.* talk, conversation

serō, 3, sēvī, satus sow, plant

sērō, *adv.* late

serpēns, —entis, *m. or f.* snake, serpent

servīlis, —e of a slave, slavish, servile

serviō, 4, —īvī, —ītus, *intr.* serve

* servitūs, —tūtis, *f.* servitude, slavery, subjection

Servius, —ī, *m.* Servius; Servius Tullius, sixth king of Rome

* servō, 1 protect, preserve, save, lay up, store

servolus, —ī, *m.* slave, young slave

* **servus, -ī,** *m.* slave, servant
sēsē, *acc. and abl. of* **suī**
sēstertius, sēstertī, *m.* sesterce, a small Roman coin worth about five cents
seu, *see* **sīve**
sevēritās, -tātis, *f.* severity, sternness
sēvocō, 1 call aside or away
* **sex (VI),** *indecl. adj.* six
Sextius, -ī, *m.* Publius Sextius Baculus, a brave centurion in Caesar's army
* **sextus, -a, -um** sixth
* **sī,** *conj.* if, whether; **quod sī** but if; * **sī quis,** *see* **quis**
sibi, *dat. of* **suī**
* **sīc,** *adv.* in this way, thus, so; **ut ... sīc as ... so**
siccitās, -tātis, *f.* dryness, drought
siccus, -a, -um dry
* **sīcut** *or* **sīcutī** [**sīc + ut (utī)**], *adv.* just as, as if
Sīdōn, -onis, *f.* Sidon, a Phoenician city
sīdus, -eris, *n.* star, constellation
signifer, -ferī, *m.* standard bearer
* **significō, 1** make signs, indicate
* **signum, -ī,** *n.* sign, signal, military standard
* **silentium, -ī,** *n.* stillness
* **silva, -ae,** *f.* forest, wood
silvestris, -e wooded
* **similis, -e** like, resembling, similar
* **simul,** *adv.* at the same time, also; **simul atque (ac)** as soon as
simulācrum, -ī, *n.* likeness, image, statue
* **simulō, 1** counterfeit, pretend
simultās, -tātis, *f.* rivalry, jealousy
sīn [**sī + ne**], *conj.* but if

* **sine,** *prep. w. abl.* without
singillātim, *adv.* one by one
* **singulāris, -e** single, singular, matchless, one by one
* **singulī, -ae, -a,** *pl. adj.* one at a time, single, one apiece
* **sinister, -tra, -trum** left; *as noun,* *f.* (*sc.* **manus**) left hand
sinō, 3, sīvī, situs be quiet, allow
sitis, sitis, *f.* thirst
situla, -ae, *f.* bucket
situs, -ūs, *m.* situation, site
* **sīve** *or* **seu,** *conj.* or if, or; **sīve (seu) ... sīve (seu)** whether ... or, either ... or
socer, -erī, *m.* father-in-law
* **socius, -ī,** *m.* comrade, ally
* **sōl, sōlis,** *m.* sun
sōlācium, -ī, *n.* comfort, solace
soleō, 2, solitus sum, *semi-dep., intr.* be wont, be accustomed
sōlitūdō, -inis, *f.* loneliness, lonely place, wilderness
solitus, -a, -um accustomed
sollemniter, *adv.* solemnly
* **sollicitō, 1** urge, incite to revolt, excite, rouse
solum, -ī, *n.* bottom, ground, soil
* **sōlum,** *adv.* alone, only; **nōn sōlum ... sed etiam** not only ... but also
* **sōlus, -a, -um** only, alone, single
* **solvō, 3, solvī, solūtus** loose, cast off; *sc.* **nāvem** *or* **nāvīs** set sail
somnium, -ī, *n.* dream
somnus, -ī, *m.* sleep
sonus, -ī, *m.* sound, noise
* **soror, -ōris,** *f.* sister
sors, sortis, *f.* lot, decision by lot
spargō, 3, sparsī, sparsus scatter, fling, sprinkle

* **spatium, -ī, n.** space, length, distance, interval, extent, course

* **speciēs, -ēī, f.** appearance, sight, pretense, show, form

spectāculum, -ī, n. show, public games

* **spectō, 1** look, face, look to, lie, be situated

speculātor, -ōris, m. spy

speculātōrius, -a, -um for observation; **speculātōrium nāvigium** spy boat

* **spērō, 1** hope, look for, expect

* **spēs, speī, f.** hope, expectation

spīritus, -ūs, m. spirit, courage; *pl.* arrogance, pride

spoliō, 1 strip, rob, deprive

spolium, -ī, n. skin; *pl.* spoils, booty

* **sponte, abl. sing., f.** (*nom.* **spōns** *obselete*) free will; * **suā sponte** of his (*their*) own accord

Spūrinna, -ae, m. Spurin'na, a soothsayer

stabilitās, -tātis, f. firmness, stability

stabulum, -ī, n. stable

* **statim, adv.** at once, on the spot

* **statiō, -ōnis, f.** station, post, guard, reserve, sentry, picket

statua, -ae, f. statue

* **statuō, 3, -uī, -ūtus** erect, decide, decree, think

status, -ūs, m. condition

stella, -ae, f. star, planet

* **stīpendium, -ī, n.** [**stips**, *contribution* + **pendō**] tax, tribute

* **stō, 1, stetī, stātus, intr.** stand, stand by

strāgulum, -ī, n. bed-covering

strāmentum, -ī, n. thatch, straw, packsaddle

strangulō, 1 choke, strangle

strepitus, -ūs, m. confused noise, din

stringō, 3, strīnxī, strictus draw tight, bind, compress

struō, 3, strūxī, strūctus, intr. contrive, devise

* **studeō, 2, -uī, —, intr.** give attention to, strive for, wish, care for

* **studium, -ī, n.** eagerness, enthusiasm, zeal, exertion, pursuit, good will, devotion

stultus, -a, -um foolish; *as noun,* *m.* fool

stupeō, 2, stupuī, —, intr. be astounded, be struck

Stymphālicus, -a, -um Stymphā'lian

Stymphālis, -idis, adj. Stymphā'lian, of Stymphalus, a town in Arcadia

Styx, Stygis, f. the River Styx

suāviter, adv. agreeably

* **sub, prep. w. acc.** (*implying motion*) under, beneath, near to, just before, about; *w. abl.* (*implying rest*) under, beneath, at the foot of, near

* **subdūcō, 3, -dūxī, -ductus** lead up, withdraw, beach (a ship)

subeō, -īre, -iī (-īvī), -itus, tr. or intr. go under, enter, come up, approach, submit to, endure, undergo

subiciō, 3, -iēcī, -iectus place under, make subject

subigō, 3, -ēgī, -āctus subdue, constrain

* **subitō, adv.** suddenly

subitus, -a, -um sudden, unexpected, surprising, quick

sublātus, p. p. of tollō

* **sublevō, 1** raise up, support, lighten, assist

subluō, 3, —, -lūtus wash

submergō, 3, -mersī, -mersus plunge under, submerge

subruō, 3, –ruī, –rutus dig under, undermine

* **subsequor, 3, –secūtus sum,** *dep.,* *tr. or intr.* follow up, follow closely

* **subsidium, –ī, *n.*** aid, protection, reserve, auxiliary troops

subsiliō, 4, –uī, —, *intr.* leap up

subsistō, 3, –stitī, —, *intr.* make a stand, stand firm, resist

subsum, –esse, —, —, *intr.* be near or under

subveniō, 4, –vēnī, –ventus, *intr.* come to help, assist, relieve

* **succēdō, 3, –cessī, –cessus, *tr. or intr.*** march up, approach, come next, take the place of, prosper

succendō, 3, –cendī, –cēnsus set on fire

successiō, –ōnis, *f.* succession

successus, –ūs, *m.* advance, approach

succurrō, 3, –currī, –cursus, *intr.* run to help, assist

sūcus, –ī, *m.* juice

sudis, –is, *f.* stake

Suēbus, –a, –um Sueban (Swē′ban); *as noun, m. or f.* a Sueban; *pl.* the Suē′bans *or* Suē′bī, a powerful German tribe

Suessiōnēs, –um, *m. pl.* the Suessiones (Swessiō′nēz), a Belgian tribe

sufficiō, 3, –fēcī, –fectus, *tr. or intr.* be sufficient, suffice

suffrāgium, –ī, *n.* vote

* **suī, *gen. of reflex. pron.*** him, her, it, them, itself, themselves

Sulla, –ae, *m.* Lucius Cornelius Sulla, leader of the aristocratic party

Sulpicius, –ī, *m.* Publius Sulpicius (Sulpish′us) Rufus, one of Caesar's officers

* **sum, esse, fuī, futūrus, *intr.*** be, come to pass, happen, be engaged, belong to, be the duty of

* **summa, –ae, *f.*** leadership, control, whole, amount, sum

sumministrō, 1 aid, hand, supply

* **summittō, 3, –mīsī, –missus** send to help, reinforce, send, submit

summoveō, 2, –mōvī, –mōtus drive off, drive back

* **summus, –a, –um, *sup. of* superus** highest, greatest, summit of, first, best, utmost, extreme, most important, perfect

* **sūmō, 3, sūmpsī, sūmptus** take, obtain, spend, use, assume; **supplicium sūmere de** inflict punishment

sūmptuōsus, –a, –um very expensive, sumptuous

sūmptus, –ūs, *m.* expense, cost

super, *adv.* above, over

* **superior, –ius, *comp. of* superus** higher, former, more distinguished, superior, better, stronger

* **superō, 1, *tr. or intr.*** rise above, surpass, conquer, survive

superscrīptiō, –ōnis, *f.* inscription

supersedeō, 2, –sēdī, –sessus, *intr.* preside over, refrain from, keep from

* **supersum, –esse, –fuī, –futūrus, *intr.*** be left, remain, survive

* **superus, –a, –um** upper

suppetō, 3, –petīvī, –petītus, *intr.* be at hand, be available, be sufficient, hold out

supplicātiō, –ōnis, *f.* public prayer, thanksgiving (*for victory*)

suppliciter, *adv.* suppliantly, humbly

* **supplicium, -ī,** *n.* punishment, penalty, torture, suffering

supplicō, 1, *tr. or intr.* supplicate

suppōnō, 3, -posuī, -positus put under

* **supportō, 1** bring up, convey, supply

* **suprā,** *adv.* above, before; *prep. w. acc.* above, before

suprēmus, -a, -um, *sup. of* superus last

surgō, 3, surrēxī, —, *intr.* rise, get up

surculus, -ī, *m.* twig, branch

* **suscipiō, 3, -cēpī, -ceptus** undertake, take, enter upon

suspendō, 3, -pendī, -pēnsus suspend, hang

* **suspīciō, -ōnis,** *f.* suspicion

* **suspicor, 1,** *dep.* suspect

sustentō, 1, *tr. or intr.* sustain, endure

* **sustineō, 2, -tinuī, -tentus** hold up, check, withstand, sustain, endure, hold out

sustulī, *see* **tollō**

* **suus, -a, -um,** *reflex.* his (her, its, their) own, his, her, its, their; *as noun,* **suī,** *m. pl.* his (their) men; *as noun,* **sua,** *n. pl.* his (their) possessions

Symmachus, -ī, *m.* Sym'machus

Symplēgadēs, -um, *f. pl.* the Sympleg'ades, the Clashing Rocks

T., *abbr. for* **Titus** Tī'tus, Roman praenomen

tabernāculum, -ī, *n.* tent

tabula, -ae, *f.* board, list

taceō, 2, tacuī, tacitus, *tr. or intr.* be silent, keep silent, be silent about, keep secret

tacitus, -a, -um silent

tāctus, -ūs, *m.* touch

tālea, -ae, *f.* stake, rod, block, bar

talentum, -ī, *n.* a talent, about $1100

tālis, -e such, of such a sort

* **tam,** *adv.* so, so very

* **tamen,** *adv.* yet, however, still, nevertheless

tandem, *adv.* at length, finally

* **tangō, 3, tetigī, tāctus** touch, border on

tantulus, -a, -um so little, trifling, unimportant

tantum, *adv.* so far, only

* **tantus, -a, -um** so great, so much; **tantum . . . quantum** so much (*as much*) . . . as

tardē, *adv.* tardily, slowly, late

* **tardō, 1** delay, hinder, check

* **tardus, -a, -um** slow, late

Tarquinius, -ī, *m.* Priscus Tarquin'ius, Tarquin, fifth king of Rome; Lucius Tarquinius Superbus, seventh and last king of Rome

Tartarus, -ī, *m.* Tar'tarus, Hades

taurus, -ī, *m.* bull

tēctum, -ī [tegō], *n.* roof, house

tegimentum, -ī, *n.* covering, cover

* **tegō, 3, tēxī, tēctus** cover, protect, conceal

Tellūs, -ūris, *f.* Tel'lus, earth

* **tēlum, -ī,** *n.* weapon, missile, spear

temerārius, -a, -um rash, heedless, imprudent

* **temerē,** *adv.* without plan, rashly

temeritās, -tātis, *f.* rashness, temerity

tēmō, -ōnis, *m.* pole of a chariot

temperātus, -a, -um moderate, temperate

* **tempestās, -tātis,** *f.* weather, stormy weather, storm tempestīvē, *adv.* in proper season

templum, -ī, *n.* temple

* temptō, 1 try, test, make trial of, attack

* tempus, -oris, *n.* time, season, occasion

Tēncterī, -ōrum, *m. pl.* the Tenc'-terī, a German tribe

* tendō, 3, tetendī, tentus stretch out, pitch (*tents*), encamp

tenebrae, -ārum, *f. pl.* shadows, darkness, gloom

* teneō, 2, -uī, — hold, keep, retain, occupy, control, hold back, check, hold under obligation; sē tenēre stay, remain

tenuis, -e thin, trifling, feeble, poor

ter [trēs], *adv.* three times

* tergum, -ī, *n.* back; ā tergō behind; terga vertere turn in flight

ternī, -ae, -a, *pl. adj.* three at a time, three apiece

* terra, -ae, *f.* earth, land, country

* terreō, 2, -uī, -itus frighten, deter by frightening, prevent

terribilis, -e terrible, frightful

territō, 1 alarm, fill with terror, threaten

* terror, -ōris, *m.* fear, alarm, panic

* tertius, -a, -um third

testāmentum, -ī [testor, *call as a witness*], *n.* will

testimōnium, -ī, *n.* evidence, proof

* testis, -is, *m. or f.* witness

testūdō, -inis, *f.* tortoise, testudo, shed

tetigī, *see* tangō

Teutonēs, -um *or* Teutonī, -ōrum, *m. pl.* the Teu'tōnēs, a people of Germany

theātrum, -ī, *n.* theatre

thēsaurus, -ī, *m.* treasury

Thēseus, -ī, *m.* Theseus, mythical king of Athens

Thessalia, -ae, *f.* Thessaly, in northern Greece

Thetis, -idis, *f.* Thetis, a sea nymph, mother of Achilles

Thisbē, -ēs, *f.* Thisbe

Thrācia, -ae, *f.* Thrace, a country north of Greece

Tiberis, Tiberis, *m.* Tiber River

tībia, -ae, *f.* leg

Tigurīnus, -ī, *m.* Tigurī'nus, one of the cantons of the Helvetians; *pl.* the Tigurī'nī

* timeō, 2, -uī, —, *tr. or intr.* fear, dread

* timidus, -a, -um fearful, timid, afraid, cowardly

* timor, -ōris, *m.* fear, dread

tingō, 3, tīnxī, tīnctus moisten, dye

tintinnābulum, -ī, *n.* bell

Titūrius, -ī, *m.* Quintus Titū'rius Sabī'nus, one of Caesar's officers

* toga, -ae, *f.* toga

tolerō, 1 endure, support

* tollō, 3, sustulī, sublātus take up, lift up, raise, weigh (*anchor*), encourage, carry off, ruin, destroy

Tolōsātēs, -ium, *m. pl.* the Tolosates (Tolosā'tēz), a tribe in the Province

tondeō, 2, totondī, tōnsus shear, clip, mow

* tormentum, -ī, *n.* engine (*for hurling missiles*), artillery

torqueō, 2, torsī, tortus torture

torreō, 2, -uī, tostus parch, scorch, burn

torus, -ī, *m.* couch

* tot, *indecl. adj.* so many

* **totidem,** *indecl. adj.* just as many, the same number

totiēns, *adv.* so often, as many times

* **tōtus, –a, –um** whole, all, entire

* **trabs, trabis,** *f.* beam, timber

* **trādō, 3, –didī, –ditus** give over, pass along, surrender, intrust, yield, leave, transmit, teach, relate

trādūcō, 3, –dūxī, –ductus lead across, bring over, win over

trāgula, –ae, *f.* javelin, dart

* **trahō, 3, trāxī, tractus** drag, drag along

Trāiānus, –ī, *m.* Trajan, Roman Emperor 98–117 A.D.

trāiciō, 3, –iēcī, –iectus, *tr. or intr.* throw across, strike through, transfix

tranquillitās, –tātis, *f.* stillness, calm

tranquillus, –a, –um calm, still; *as noun* peace, tranquillity

* **trāns,** *prep. w. acc.* across, over, beyond

Trānsalpīnus, –a, –um across the Alps, Transalpine

trānscendō, 3, –scendī, —, *tr. or intr.* pass over, board (*a ship*)

* **trānseō, –īre, –iī (–īvī), –itus,** *tr. or intr.* go across, march through, pass by

trānsferō, –ferre, –tulī, –lātus carry over, transfer

trānsfīgō, 3, –fīxī, –fīxus pierce through, transfix

trānsgredior, 3, –gressus sum, *dep.* step across, across

trānsmissus, –ūs, *m.* crossing, passage

trānsportō, 1 carry over, take across, transport

trānsversus, –a, –um crosswise, transverse

Trebātius, –ī, *m.* Gaius Trebatius Testa, a young man on Caesar's staff, an intimate friend of Cicero

trecēnī, –ae, –a three hundred each

trecentī, –ae, –a (CCC) three hundred

trepidō, 1 hurry in alarm, be agitated

* **trēs, tria (III)** three

Trēverī, –ōrum, *m. pl.* the Trev'erī, a tribe in northeastern Gaul

* **tribūnus, –ī,** *m.* tribune

* **tribuō, 3, tribuī, tribūtus** assign, concede, attribute, ascribe, give credit

tribūtum, –ī, *n.* contribution, tribute

trīceps, –cipitis three headed

trīcēsimus, –a, –um thirtieth

* **trīduum, –ī,** *n.* a period of three days

trīgintā (XXX), *indecl. adj.* thirty

trīnī, –ae, –a, *pl. adj.* three at a time, threefold

tripertītō, *adv.* in three parts

triplex, –icis threefold, triple

triquetrus, –a, –um triangular

trīstis, –e sad, sorrowful, gloomy

trīstitia, –ae, *f.* sadness, dejection

triumphus, –ī, *m.* triumph

Trōia, –ae, *f.* Troy

truncus, –ī, *m.* trunk of a tree

* **tū, tuī,** *pers. pron.* thou, you

* **tuba, –ae,** *f.* trumpet

* **tueor, 2, tūtus sum,** *dep.* watch, care for, guard

tulī, *see* **ferō**

Tulingī, –ōrum, *m. pl.* the Tulingi (Tulin'jī), a German tribe north of the Helvetians

Tullius, *see* **Servius**

Tullus, -ī, *m.* Tullus Hostilius, the third king of Rome

* **tum,** *adv.* then, at that time, next, besides; * **cum . . . tum** not only . . . but also, both . . . and

* **tumultus, -ūs,** *m.* uproar, noise, disturbance, revolt

* **tumulus, -ī,** *m.* mound, hill, tomb

tunc, *adv.* then, on that occasion

turba, -ae, *f.* crowd, turmoil, up-roar

turma, -ae, *f.* troop of cavalry

Turonī, -ōrum, *m. pl.* the Tu'ronī, a Gallic tribe

* **turpis, -e,** *adj.* unseemly, disgrace-ful, ugly

turpitūdō, -inis, *f.* disgrace

tūs, tūris, *n.* incense

* **turris, -is,** *f.* tower

* **tūtus, -a, -um** safe, secure

* **tuus, -a, -um** [tū] thy, thine, your, yours

* **ubi,** *adv.* where, in which place; *conj.* when, as; **ubi prīmum** as soon as

Ubiī, -ōrum, *m. pl.* the Ubii, a German tribe

ubīque, *adv.* everywhere, anywhere

ulcīscor, 3, ultus sum, *dep.* take vengeance on, punish, avenge

* **ūllus, -a, -um** any; *as noun, m. or f.* anyone, anybody

* **ulterior, -ius** [ultrā] farther, more distant; **Gallia Ulterior** Trans-alpine Gaul

* **ultimus, -a, -um** [ultrā] farthest, most remote

ultor, -ōris, *f.* avenger

* **ultrā,** *prep. w. acc.* on the farther side of, beyond

* **ultrō,** *adv.* to the farther side, besides, voluntarily

ultus, *p. p. of* ulcīscor

ululātus, -ūs, *m.* yell, wailing

umbra, -ae, *f.* shadow, shade, ghost

umerus, -ī, *m.* shoulder

* **umquam,** *adv.* ever, at any time

* **ūnā,** [*abl. f. of* ūnus], *adv.* at the same time, together; **ūnā cum** together with

ūnanimus, -a, -um beloved, concor-dant, unanimous

* **unde,** *adv.* from which place, whence

* **undique,** *adv.* from all sides, on all sides, everywhere

ūnicus, -a, -um only

* **ūniversus, -a, -um** all together, in a body, whole, entire; *as noun, m. pl.* the whole body, all

* **ūnus, -a, -um** (1) one, alone, sole, only, one and the same

urbānus, -a, -um of the city

* **urbs, urbis,** *f.* city, town

urgeō, 2, ursī, — press, push, press hard

urna, -ae, *f.* urn

ūrō, 3, ussī, ustus burn

Usipetēs, -um, *m. pl.* the Usipetes (Usip'etēz), a German tribe

* **usque,** *adv.* all the way, even, con-tinually

ūsus, *p. p. of* ūtor

* **ūsus, -ūs,** *m.* use, employment, experience, practice, custom, fa-miliarity, necessity

* **ut** *or* **utī,** *adv.* how? as, just as, as if; *conj.* when, as soon as, as, al-though; *with subjunctive of purpose* in order that, that, to; *with sub-junctive of result* so that, that; *with expressions of fear* that . . . not

* uter, utra, utrum, *interrog. adj. or pron.* which (of two)? *indef.* whichever one
* uterque, utraque, utrumque each (*of two*), either, both

ūtī, *see* ūtor

* ūtilis, -e useful, expedient
* ūtor, 3, ūsus sum, *dep., intr.* employ, make use of, accept, abide by, enjoy, have, practise, show

utrimque, *adv.* from each side, on both sides

utrum, *conj.* whether

ūva, -ae, *f.* grape, bunch of grapes

* uxor, -ōris, *f.* wife

vacātiō, -ōnis, *f.* freedom, exemption

vacō, 1, *intr.* be uninhabited, be vacant, lie waste

* vacuus, -a, -um empty, deserted, unoccupied

vādō, 3, —, —, *intr.* go

* vadum, -ī, *n.* shallow place, ford
* vagor, 1, *dep., intr.* wander about, roam

valē, *imperative of* valeō farewell, good-by

* valeō, 2, -uī, -itūrus, *intr.* be strong, have influence, be able, deserve

Valerius, -ī, *m.* Gaius Valē'rius Donnotaurus, a Romanized Gaul; Gaius Valerius Caburus, a Romanized Gaul of high rank

valētūdō, -inis, *f.* health

* vallēs, -is, *f.* valley
* vāllum, -ī, *n.* palisades, rampart, wall

varius, -a, -um different, various

vās, vāsis, *n.* vessel, dish

* vāstō, 1 lay waste, devastate

vāstus, -a, -um unoccupied, waste

-ve, *enclitic conj.* or

* vehemēns, -entis very eager, impetuous
* vehementer, *adv.* vigorously, greatly, exceedingly
* vehō, 3, vexī, vectus bear, carry
* vel [volō], *conj.* or; vel . . . vel either . . . or

vellus, -eris, *n.* fleece

vēlōciter, *adv.* swiftly, quickly

vēlum, -ī, *n.* sail

velut, *adv.* just as, even as, as

vēnātiō, -ōnis, *f.* hunt, hunting expedition

vēndō, 3, -didī, -ditus sell

venēnum, -ī, *n.* poison, magic charm

veneror, 1, *dep.* worship, pray

Venetī, -ōrum, *m. pl.* the Ven'etī, a tribe in western Gaul

Veneticus, -a, -um of the Veneti

venia, -ae, *f.* favor, pardon

* veniō, 4, vēnī, ventus, *intr.* come, arrive; *used impers. in pass.,* ventum est he comes, they come, etc.

ventitō, 1, *intr.* come often, keep coming

* ventus, -ī, *m.* wind

Venus, -eris, *f.* Venus, goddess of love and beauty

Vērānius, -ī, *m.* Verā'nius, a Roman name

verber, -eris, *n.* blow, flogging

Verbigenus, -ī, *m.* Verbigenus (Verbij'enus), a canton of the Helvetians

verbōsus, -a, -um full of words, wordy

* verbum, -ī, *n.* word

Vercassivellaunus, -ī, *m.* Vercassivellau'nus, an Arvernian general

Vercingetorīx, -īgis, *m.* Vercingetorix (Versinjet′orix), an Arvernian noble

vērē, *adv.* truly

* **vereor, 2, veritus sum,** *dep.* fear, be afraid of, dread, be anxious, hesitate, shrink

vergō, 3, —, —, *intr.* turn, slope, lie, be situated

vēritās, -tātis, *f.* truth, sincerity

veritus, *p. p. of* vereor

* **vērō,** *adv.* in truth, in fact, indeed, certainly, but, but in fact, however

versō, 1 keep turning, change the circumstances of

* **versor, 1,** *dep., intr.* busy oneself, be engaged, be busy, live

versus, *adv., or prep. w. acc.* in the direction of, toward

versus, -ūs, *m.* line, verse

Verticō, -ōnis, *m.* Ver′tico, a Nervian

* **vertō, 3, vertī, versus** turn, turn about

* **vērus, -a, -um** true, right, just; *as a noun, n.* truth, faith

verūtum, -ī, *n.* javelin, dart

vēscor, 3, vēscī, —, *dep., intr.* eat, feed upon

* **vesper, -erī (-eris),** *m.* evening

* **vester, -tra, -trum** your, yours

vēstibulum, -ī, *n.* vestibule, entrance

vēstīgium, -ī, *n.* footprint, track, instant; **in vēstīgiō** on the spot, instantly

vestiō, 4, -īvī, -ītus clothe, cover

* **vestis, -is,** *f.* clothing

vestītus, -ūs, *m.* clothing

Vesuvius, -ī, *m.* Mt. Vesuvius

veterānus, -a, -um old, veteran; *as noun, m. pl.* veterans

vetō, 1, -uī, -itus forbid

* **vetus, veteris** old, ancient, former

* **vetustus, -a, -um** aged, old, ancient

vexillum, -ī, *n.* banner, flag

vexō, 1 harass, trouble, ravage

* **via, -ae,** *f.* way, road, pass, march

viātor, -ōris, *m.* traveler

vīcēnī, -ae, -a, *pl.* twenty each

vīcēsimus, -a, -um twentieth

vīciēs, *adv.* twenty times

* **vīcīnus, -a, -um** neighboring; *as noun, m.* a neighbor

vicis, *gen. f.*; **in vicem** in turn

vicissitūdō, -inis, *f.* change, vicissitude

victima, -ae, *f.* sacrifice, victim

* **victor, -ōris,** *m.* conqueror, victor

* **victōria, -ae,** *f.* victory

vīctus, -ūs, *m.* food, way of living, living

* **vīcus, -ī,** *m.* village

* **videō, 2, vīdī, vīsus** see, perceive; *often in pass.* seem, appear, seem good

* **vigilia, -ae,** *f.* wakefulness, keeping guard, watch (*as a measure of time*)

* **vīgintī (XX),** *indecl. adj.* twenty

vīlica, -ae, *f.* housekeeper

vīlicus, -ī, *m.* overseer, manager

* **vīlla, -ae,** *f.* house, villa

vīmen, -inis, *n.* pliant twig, osier

Vīminālis, -e Viminal; *w.* **collis** one of the seven hills of Rome

vinciō, 4, vīnxī, vīnctus bind, fetter

* **vincō, 3, vīcī, victus** conquer, subdue, surpass; **victī, -ōrum,** *m. pl.* the conquered

* **vinculum, -ī,** *n.* chain, fetter, bond

vindicō, 1 assert a claim, maintain, inflict punishment

vīnea, –ae [vīnum] *f.* a shed used in sieges

vīnum, –ī, *n.* wine

violentus, –a, –um violent, vehement

violō, 1 injure, ravage

* vir, virī, *m.* man, husband

vīrēs, *pl. of* vīs

virga, –ae, *f.* twig, wand

virgō, –inis, *f.* maiden, girl

Viridomārus, –ī, *m.* Viridomā'rus, a leader of the Aeduans

* virtūs, –tūtis [vir], *f.* manliness, worth, courage

* vīs, (vīs), *f.* strength, power, force, influence, violence; *pl.*, vīrēs strength

vīsō, 3, vīsī, vīsus see, behold, go to see

vīsus, *p. p. of* videō

* vīta, –ae, *f.* life, mode of living

vītis, –is, *f.* vine

vitium, –ī, *n.* fault, defect

* vītō, 1 avoid, evade

vitrum, –ī, *n.* woad, a plant furnishing a blue dye

* vīvō, 3, vīxī, vīctus, *intr.* live

* vīvus, –a, –um alive, living

* vix, *adv.* with difficulty, scarcely

Vocciō, –ōnis, *m.* Voccio (Vok'shyō), a king of the Norici

* vocō, 1 summon, challenge

Vocontiī, –ōrum, *m. pl.* the Vocontii (Vocon'shyī), in the Province

Volcae, –ārum, *m. pl.* the Volcae (Vol'sē), a Gallic tribe in the Province consisting of two branches,

Arecomici (Arekome'isī) and Tectosages (Tectos'ajēz)

* volō, velle, voluī, —, *tr. or intr.* will, be willing, wish, plan, resolve

volō, 1 fly

Volscī, –ōrum, *m. pl.* the Volsci (Vol'sī), a people south of Rome

* voluntās, –tātis, *f.* will, wish, desire, inclination, good will

voluptās, –tātis, *f.* pleasure, enjoyment

Volusēnus, –ī, *m.* Gaius Volūsē'nus Quadratus, a tribune of soldiers in Caesar's army

Vorēnus, –ī, *m.* Lū'cius Vorē'nus, a brave centurion of Caesar's army

vōs, *pl. of* tū

voveō, 2, vōvī, vōtus promise solemnly, vow

* vōx, vōcis, *f.* voice, cry, word

Vulcānus, –ī, *m.* Vulcan, god of fire and of workers in metal

vulgō, *adv.* commonly, everywhere

* vulgus, –ī, *n.* multitude, crowd, the people

* vulnerō, 1 wound

* vulnus, –eris, *n.* wound, injury, blow

vulpēs, –is, *f.* fox

vultus, –ūs, *m.* countenance, face

Zētēs, –ae, *m.* Zē'tēs, one of the Argonauts

Zōilus, –ī, *m.* Zo'ilus, Roman name

zōna, –ae, *f.* girdle

ENGLISH–LATIN VOCABULARY

Proper nouns and the principal parts of verbs are not given in this vocabulary. They may be found in the LATIN-ENGLISH VOCABULARY.

about, *prep.* circum, circiter, *w. acc.;* dē, *w. abl.*

accident cāsus, –ūs, *m.*

accomplish cōnficiō, faciō

accord, of his (their) own suā sponte, ultrō

accustomed, be cōnsuēscō

admire mīror

advance prōgredior

adversity adversa rēs; calamitās, –tātis, *f.*

advise praecipiō

affect afficiō

after, *prep.* post, *w. acc.; conj.* postquam

afterwards post

again rūrsus

against, *prep.* ad, contrā, in, *w. acc.*

agree cōnsentiō

aid, *verb* iuvō

aid, *noun* subsidium, ī, *n.;* auxilium, –ī, *n.*

air āēr, āeris, *m.*

alive vīvus, –a, –um

all omnis, omne; all together ūniversus, –a, –um

almost paene, ferē

along with, *adv.* ūnā

although etsi, *w. indic.;* cum, *w. subjunctive; sometimes an abl. abs. or participle*

altogether, *adv.* omnīnō

ambassador lēgātus, –ī, *m.*

ambush īnsidiae, –ārum, *f. pl.*

anchor ancora, –ae, *f.*

ancient vetustus, –a, –um

and et, –que, atque

anger īra, –ae, *f.*

animal animal, –ālis, *n.*

any ūllus, –a, –um; anyone, *pron.* ūllus, aliquis, quisquam; (*after* sī) quis

appearance speciēs, –ēī, *f.*

appointed cōnstitūtus, –a, –um

approach, *noun* aditus, –ūs, *m.*

approach, *verb* appropinquō

approve probō

archer sagittārius, –ī, *m.*

arm, equip, *verb* armō

armor, arms arma, –ōrum, *n.*

army exercitus, –ūs, *m.*

arrival adventus, –ūs, *m.*

arrow sagitta, –ae, *f.*

as ut; as soon as simul ac

ask quaerō, rogō; ask for petō

assign attribuō, distribuō

assemble conveniō

at least certē

attack, *verb* adorior, oppugnō, aggredior

attack, *noun* impetus, –ūs, *m.*

attempt cōnor

attribute **tribuō**
authority **auctoritās, -tātis,** *f.*
avail **valeō**
avoid **vītō**

back **tergum, -ī,** *n.*
baggage **impedīmenta, -ōrum,** *n. pl.*
banquet, dinner **cēna, -ae,** *f.*
barbarians **barbarī, -ōrum,** *m. pl.*
battle **proelium, -ī,** *n.;* fight a battle **proelium faciō**
be **sum**; be away **absum**
beach, *verb* **subdūcō**
bear **ferō, vehō**; bear it ill **aegrē ferō**
beautiful **pulcher, -chra, -chrum**
beauty **fōrma, -ae,** *f.*
because **cum, quod, proptereā quod**
become **fīō**
before, *adv.* **ante**; *prep.* **ante,** *w. acc.; conj.* **priusquam**
beg **ōrō, petō**
begin **incipiō, coepī** *def.*
beginning **initium, -ī,** *n.*
behind, *prep.* **post,** *w. acc.*
believe **cōnfīdō**
betake one's self **cōnferō,** *w. reflex.*
between, *prep.* **inter,** *w. acc.;* be between **intersum**
beyond, *prep.* **ultrā,** *w. acc.*
bird **avis, -is,** *f.*
booty **praeda, -ae,** *f.;* get booty **praedam faciō**
boy **puer, -ī,** *m.*
bravery **virtus, -tūtis,** *f.*
bring **afferō, ferō, īnferō, perdūcō, dēferō**; bring back **referō**; bring about **efficiō**
bronze **aes, aeris,** *n.*
build **aedificō**
bury **condō, sepeliō**

but **sed**
buy **emō**
by, *prep.* **ā, ab,** *w. abl. of agent*

call (by name) **appellō**
camp **castra, -ōrum,** *n. pl.*
can **possum**
canton **pāgus, -ī,** *m.*
carry **ferō, portō**; carry out **faciō**
cause **causa, -ae,** *f.*
cavalry **equitātus, -ūs,** *m.;* **equitēs, -um,** *m. pl.*
cave **caverna, -ae,** *f.*
centurion **centuriō, -ōnis,** *m.*
certain one, a **quīdam, quaedam, quiddam**
chain **vinculum, -ī,** *n.;* in chains **ex vinculīs**
chance **cāsus, -ūs,** *m.;* **fors, fortis,** *f.*
change **convertō**
charge, be in **praesum**
chariot **currus, -ūs,** *m.*
children **līberī, -ōrum,** *m. pl.*
city **urbs, urbis,** *f.*
clamor, shout **clāmor, -ōris,** *f.*
clear, be, *verb* **cōnstō**
client **cliēns, -entis,** *m. or f.*
climb on **trānscendō**
cling to **adhaereō**
close **claudō**
cohort **cohors, -hortis,** *f.*
collect **comportō, conquīrō**
come **veniō, perveniō**; come together **concurrō**
command, *noun* **imperātum, -ī,** *n.;* **mandātum, -ī,** *n.*
command, *verb* **imperō**; be in command **praesum**
compact **cōnfertus, a, um**
comrade **socius, -ī,** *m.*
conceal **occultō**

congratulation grātulātiō, –ōnis, *f.*
consent voluntās, –tātis, *f.*
conspire coniūrō
consult cōnsulō
contend contendō
continue permaneō
course cursus, –ūs, *m.*
cover (overflow) inundō
cross trānseō
cry aloud conclāmō
custom mōs, mōris, *m.;* cōnsuētūdō, –inis, *f.*
cut abscīdō ; cut off interclūdō

daily cotīdiānus, –a, –um
danger perīculum, –ī, *n.*
daughter fīlia, –ae, *f.*
day diēs, diēī, *m. or f.;* on the following day postrīdiē
daybreak, at prīmā lūce, ortā lūce
death mors, mortis, *f.*
decide dēcernō, cēnseō, cōnstituō
decorate ōrnō
defender dēfēnsor, –ōris, *m.*
delay, *noun* mora, –ae, *f.*
delay, *verb* moror
deliberate dēlīberō
demand postulō, poscō
depart dēcēdō, excēdō, proficīscor
departure profectiō, –ōnis, *f.*
depth altitūdō, –inis, *f.*
descend dēscendō ; (spring from)
  orior
deserved meritus, –a, –um
desire cupiditās, –tātis, *f.;* studium,
  –ī, *n.*
desire, *verb* dēsīderō
desist dēsistō
despair dēspērō
despise dēspiciō
destruction exitium, –ī, *n.*

devastate vāstō
differ differō
differently aliter
difficult difficilis, –e
difficulty difficultās, –tātis, *f.*
dignity dignitās, –tātis, *f.*
diligence dīligentia, –ae, *f.*
diligent dīligēns, –entis
disaster calamitās, –tātis, *f.;* ēventus, –ūs, *m.*
discover reperiō
disgraceful turpis, –e
do faciō, agō ; do not nōlī, nōlīte,
  w. inf.; do one's duty praestō
  officium
dog canis, –is, *m. or f.*
doubt dubitō
drag trahō
dragon dracō, –ōnis, *m.*
draw up expōnō
dust pulvis, –eris, *m.*
duty officium, –ī, *n.*

each one quisque, quidque
eager alacer, –cris, –cre
eagle aquila, –ae, *f.*
early mātūrus, –a, –um
easily facile
eight octō
eighteen duodēvīgintī
either uterque, –traque, –trumque
either . . . or aut . . . aut, vel
  . . . vel
embassy lēgātiō, –ōnis, *f.*
emergency cāsus, –ūs, *m.*
empty vacuus, –a, –um
encourage hortor, cohortor
end fīnis, –is, *m.*
endure perferō
enemy hostis, hostis, *m.*
enjoy fruor

enlist cōnscrībō
enroll cōnscrībō
entrust permittō, commendō
equestrian equester, –tris, –tre
equip armō
escape ēvādō, effugiō
even, not nē quidem
evening vesper, –erī, m.
ever umquam
everything omnia, –ium, n. pl.
except praeter, w. acc.
excite sollicitō
exercise exercitātiō, –ōnis, f.
expel expellō
extend pateō
eye oculus, –ī, m.

faithful fidēlis, –e
fall cadō
famous clārus, –a, –um
farther longius
father pater, –tris, m.; parēns,
    –entis, m. or f.
favor faveō
fear, noun timor, –ōris, m.
fear, verb vereor, timeō
feed alō
few paucī, –ae, –a
field ager, –grī, m.; campus, –ī, m.
fierce ferus, –a, –um
fight pugnō, contendō, prōpugnō,
    dīmicō ; fight to a finish dēcertō
fill compleō
find inveniō ; find out comperiō,
    reperiō
finger digitus, –ī, m.
finish cōnficiō, perficiō
fire ignis, –is, m.
first, at first, adv. prīmum, prīmō
five quīnque
flee fugiō, perfugiō

fleece vellus, –eris, n.
fleet classis, –is, f.
flesh carō, carnis, f.
flight fuga, –ae, f.
flow fluō
flower flōs, flōris, m.
fly volō, 1
fodder pābulum, –ī, n.
follow sequor, subsequor ; follow
    up cōnsequor
following posterus, –a, –um
food supply rēs frūmentāria, f.
foot pēs, pedis, m.
for, often expressed by the dative case;
    (toward) ad, w. acc.; conj. namque
force cōgō
forced march magnum iter, n.
forces cōpiae, –ārum, f. pl.
ford vadum, –ī, n.
form ineō, capiō, faciō
former vetus, –eris ; prīstinus, –a,
    –um
formerly ōlim, anteā
fortification mūnītiō, –ōnis, f.
fortress praesidium, –ī, n.; cas-
    tellum, –ī, n.
free līberō
friend amīcus, –ī, m.
frighten perterreō
from, prep. ē, ex, ā, ab, dē, w. abl.;
    from a distance, adv. procul ;
    from there inde
front frōns, frontis, f.; in front ā
    fronte ; those in front priōrēs,
    –um, m. pl.; front line prīma
    aciēs, f.

garment vestis, –is, f.
gate porta, –ae, f.
get possession of potior, w. abl. or gen.
gift dōnum, –ī, n.

girl puella, –ae, *f.*

give dō

glory glōria, –ae, *f.*

go eō, iter faciō ; go forth exeō ;
  go to adeō

god deus, –ī, *m.*

goddess dea, –ae, *f.*

gold aurum, –ī, *n.*

golden aureus, –a, –um

gradually paulātim

grain frūmentum, –ī, *n.*

great magnus, –a, –um ; so great
  tantus, –a, –um

grief dolor, –ōris, *m.*

guard statiō, –ōnis, *f.*

happen accidō

happy laetus, –a, –um

have habeō ; *dative of possession*
  with sum

he is, hic, ille

hear audiō

heat aestus, –ūs, *m.*

hero vir, virī, *m.*

hide abdō

himself, herself, *intensive* ipse, ipsa ;
  reflexive suī, sibi, sē

his, hers, theirs eius, eōrum, eārum ;
  reflexive suus, –a, –um

hither citerior, –ius

hold, hold back teneō

home, house domus, –ūs, *f.*

hope, *verb* spērō

hope, *noun* spēs, –eī, *f.*

horrible horribilis, –e

horse equus, –ī, *m.*

hospitality hospitium, –ī, *n.*

hostage obses, –idis, *m. or f.*

hour hōra, –ae, *f.*

house aedificium, –ī, *n.;* domicilium,
  –ī, *n.*

household familia, –ae, *f.*

how quōmodo ; how great quantus,
  –a, –um ; however autem

huge ingēns, –entis

hunger famēs, –is, *f.*

hurl adigō

hurling engine tormentum, –ī, *n.*

husband marītus, –ī, *m.*

I ego, meī

if sī

ill, *adv.* aegrē

immediately statim, prōtinus

impede impediō

impediment impedīmentum, –ī, *n.*

impel impellō

import importō

in in, *w. abl.*

incite incitō

indicate significō

infantry pedestrēs cōpiae, *f. pl.*

inflict īnferō ; inflict punishment
  supplicium sūmō dē

influence moveō, indūcō, addūcō

inform certiōrem faciō

injure noceō

institution īnstitūtum, ī, *n.*

interrupt intermittō

intervene intercēdō, intermittō

into, *prep.* in, *w. acc.*

island īnsula, –ae, *f.*

it id

javelin pīlum, –ī, *n.*

join coniungō

judge iūdicō

keep from prohibeō

kill necō, interficiō

king rēx, rēgis, *m.*

kingdom rēgnum, –ī, *n.*

know scio ; not to know ignoro
knowledge scientia, -ae, *f.*

labor labor, -oris, *m.*
labyrinth labyrinthum, -i, *n.*
lack deficio ; be lacking desum
land terra, -ae, *f.*
language lingua, -ae, *f.*
last supremus, -a, -um ; extremus,
 -a, -um
late in the day multo die
later, *adv.* post
latter hic, haec, hoc
launch deduco
lay aside depono
lay waste populor
lead conduco, duco ; lead on, influence adduco
leadership principatus, -us, *m.*
learn cognosco, disco
leave relinquo
left sinister, -tra, -trum
legion legio, -onis, *f.*
less minus
letter litterae, -arum, *f. pl.*
lieutenant legatus, -i, *m.*
lift sublevo
light levis, -e ; light-armed levis
 armaturae
likewise, *pron.* idem, eadem, idem ;
 adv. item
line acies, -ei, *f.;* agmen, -inis, *n.*
lion leo, leonis, *m.*
little, a paulum ; by a little paulo
live vivo
load onus, -eris, *n.*
long (time) diu
look on aspicio
loud magnus, -a, -um
love amo
Lower Region Orcus, -i, *m.*

magistrate magistratus, -us, *m.*
make facio, comparo ; make restitution satisfacio ; make trial of
 experior ; make war on bellum
 infero
man homo, -inis, *m.;* vir, -i, *m.;*
 of man humanus, -a, -um
many multus, -a, -um
maritime maritimus, -a, -um
marry in matrimonium duco
master dominus, -i, *m.*
material materia, -ae, *f.*
matter res, rei, *f.*
meanwhile, in the meantime in-
 terea, interim
meet, run to meet occurro
merchant mercator, -oris, *m.*
messenger nuntius, -i, *m.*
middle, midst of medius, -a, -um
midnight media nox
miles milia passuum
military militaris, -e ; military
 science res militaris, *f.*
mind animus, -i, *m.*
more amplius
mountain mons, montis, *m.;* top
 of the mountain summus mons, *m.*
move moveo
multitude multitudo, -inis, *f.*
my meus, -a, -um

narrow angustus, -a, -um
narrow pass angustiae, -arum, *f. pl.*
nature natura, -ae, *f.*
near by propinquus, -a, -um
necessary, be oportet
neglect neglego
neither neuter, -tra, -trum
never numquam
nevertheless tamen
new novus, -a, -um

next proximus, -a, -um
night nox, noctis, *f.*; at night nocturnus, -a, -um
no nūllus, -a, -um
nobility nōbilitās, -tātis, *f.*
noon merīdiēs, -ēī, *m.*
no one nēmō; *gen.* nūllīus; *abl.* nūllō
not nōn; (and) not, nor neque; and that . . . not nēve; is it not? nōnne; not only . . . but also nōn modo . . . sed etiam, nōn sōlum . . . sed etiam
noteworthy īnsignis, -e
nothing nihil
notice animadvertō
not yet nōndum
now nunc
number numerus, -ī, *m.*; multitūdō, -inis, *f.*
nymph nympha, -ae, *f.*

oar rēmus, -ī, *m.*
oath iūs iūrandum
obey pāreō
obtain obtineō, nancīscor; obtain one's request impetrō
occur incidō
offer offerō
old-time prīstinus
on, *prep.* in, *w. abl.*; upon in, *w. acc.*; on account of ob, *w. acc.*
one ūnus, -a, -um; one . . . the other alter . . . alter; one at a time singulī, -ae, -a, singulāris, -e; one from one ship, one from another alius ex aliā nāve
only the, alone *adj.* sōlus, -a, -um
only, *adv.* omnīnō, modo
open, *verb* aperiō
open, *adj.* apertus, -a, -um

opinion sententia, -ae, *f.*
opportune opportūnus, -a, -um
opportunity occāsiō, -ōnis, *f.*; facultās, -tātis, *f.*
opposite adversus, -a, -um
or aut
oracle ōrāculum, -ī, *n.*
order, in order that ut; *neg.* nē
order imperō, iubeō
other alter, -era, -erum; alius, -a, -ud; the others cēterī, -ōrum, *m. pl.*, reliquī, -ōrum, *m. pl.*
otherwise aliter
our, ours noster, -tra, -trum; our men nostrī, -ōrum, *m. pl.*
outside of, *adv., or prep. w. acc.* extrā
overcome opprimō, superō
ox taurus, -ī, *m.*

palace, royal rēgia, -ae, *f.*
part pars, partis, *f.*
pass through pervādō
path via, -ae, *f.*
peace pāx, pācis, *f.*
people populus, -ī, *m.*
perish pereō
permit patior, permittō; it is permitted licet
persuade persuādeō
pick, choose legō
place, arrange, *verb* collocō; place in command praeficiō
place, *noun* locus, -ī, *m.*; *pl.* loca, -ōrum, *n.*; to the same place eōdem
plain plānitiēs, -ēī, *f.*
plan cōnsilium, -ī, *n.*
plead dīcō
please placeō
poplar tree pōpulus, -ī, *f.*
port portus, -ūs, *m.*

power **rēgnum, -ī,** *n.*
praise **laudō**
prayer **prex, precis,** *f.*
prefect **praefectus, -ī,** *m.*
prefer **mālō**
prepare **comparō, parō**
prepared **parātus, -a, -um**
press forward **īnstō**
private **prīvātus, -a, -um**
proceed, enter **ingredior**
produce **ēdō**
prolong **prōdūcō**
promise **polliceor**
propose **prōpōnō**
protection **praesidium, -ī,** *n.;* to the protection **in fidem**
province **prōvincia, -ae,** *f.*
punishment **supplicium, -ī,** *n.;* inflict punishment, punish **supplicium sūmō dē**
purpose **ad** *or* **causā** *w. gerund or gerundive*
pursue **prōsequor**
put on **impōnō, induō**

quaestor **quaestor, -ōris,** *m.*
quarrel **contrōversia, -ae,** *f.*
quarters **pars, partis,** *f.;* from all quarters **undique**
queen **rēgīna, -ae,** *f.*
quite **omnīnō**

race **genus, -eris,** *n.*
rampart **agger, aggeris,** *m.*
rashly **temerē**
rather **magis, potius**
reach **attingō**
receive **excipiō**
recount **commemorō**
recover **recipiō** *w. reflexive*
reduce **redigō**

refinement **hūmānitās, -tātis,** *f.*
region **regiō, -ōnis,** *f.*
relatives **necessāriī, -ōrum,** *m. pl.*
remain **remaneō ;** (be left) **supersum**
remarkable **ēgregius, -a, -um**
repair **reficiō**
report **renūntiō, ēnūntiō, nūntiō**
repulse **repellō**
reputation **opīniō, -ōnis,** *f.*
resist **resistō**
resources **opēs, -um,** *f. pl.*
response **respōnsum, -ī,** *n.*
rest **quiēs, -ētis,** *f.*
rest, the **cēterī, -ae, -a ; reliquus, -a, -um ;** *also used as noun*
restore **restituō**
retard **tardō**
return **redeō, revertor**
reward **praemium, -ī,** *n.*
river **flūmen, -inis,** *n.*
rock **rūpēs, -is,** *f.*
rope **fūnis, -is,** *m.*
rumor **rūmor, -ōris,** *m.*
run **currō ;** run to meet **occurrō**

safe **tūtus, -a, -um**
safety **salūs, -ūtis,** *f.*
sail **solvō nāvem**
sail-yard **antemna, -ae,** *f.*
sake of, for the **causā,** *preceded by the genitive*
same **īdem, eadem, idem**
say **dīcō, inquam** (*parenthetical*) ;
say . . . not, deny **negō**
scarcely **vix**
scatter **dispergō**
scout **explōrātor, -ōris,** *m.*
sea **mare, maris,** *n.*
secretly **clam**
see **videō, cōnspiciō, cōnspicor, perspiciō ;** see to it **cūrō**

seek **quaerō ;** seek out **conquīrō**
seize **rapiō, dētrahō, comprehendō**
select **ēligō**
self-confidence **fīdūcia, –ae,** *f.*
send **mittō ;** send ahead **praemittō**
separate **dīvidō**
servitude **servitūs, –tūtis,** *f.*
set fire to **incendō**
set out **proficīscor,** ~~proficio,~~ **prō-gredior, ēgredior**
several **nōn nūllus, –a, –um ;** com-**plūrēs, –a**
shatter **frangō ;** shattered, *adj.* **frāctus, –a, –um**
she **ea, haec, illa**
shield **scūtum, –ī,** *n.*
ship **nāvis, –is,** *f.;* warship **nāvis longa,** *f.*
shore **lītus, –oris,** *n.*
short **brevis, –e**
show **praebeō, dēmōnstrō, ostendō, praestō**
side **latus, –eris,** *n.*
siege **oppugnātiō, –ōnis,** *f.*
sight **cōnspectus, –ūs,** *m.*
signal **signum, –ī,** *n.*
since **cum,** *w. subjunctive; also abl. abs.*
sister **soror, –ōris,** *f.*
size **magnitūdō, –inis,** *f.*
skilled, skillful **perītus, –a, –um**
slinger **funditor, –ōris,** *m.*
small **exiguus, –a, –um**
so **tam, ita ;** so great **tantus, –a, –um**
soldier **mīles, –itis,** *m.*
some(one) **aliquis ;** *adj.* **aliquī**
son **fīlius, –ī,** *m.*
space **intervāllum, –ī,** *n.*
speed **celeritās, –tātis,** *f.*
stag **cervus, –ī,** *m.*
stand **stō**

state **cīvitās, –tātis** *f.*
stay **maneō**
still, *adv.* **tamen**
stone **lapis, –idis,** *m.*
stop **prohibeō**
storm, *noun* **tempestās, –tātis,** *f.*
storm, *verb* **expugnō**
story **fābula, –ae,** *f.*
strange **ignōtus, –a, –um**
strength **virēs, –ium,** *f. pl.*
stripped **nūdātus, –a, –um**
subdued **pācātus, –a, –um**
succeed **succēdō**
succession, in **continuus, –a, –um**
such **tālis, –e ;** such great **tantus, –a, –um**
suddenly **subitō**
suitable **idōneus, –a, –um ;** oppor-**tūnus, –a, –um**
summer **aestās, –tātis,** *f.*
summon **arcessō**
sun **sōl, sōlis,** *m.*
sunset **sōlis occāsus,** *m.*
supply **cōpia, –ae,** *f.;* **commeātus, –ūs,** *m.*
surpass **antecēdō, praecēdō, praestō**
surrender, *noun* **dēditiō, –ōnis,** *f.*
surrender, *verb* **dēdō ;** *w. reflex.* **prōdō**
surround **circumveniō, circumsistō**
suspect **suspicor**
suspicion **suspīciō, –ōnis,** *f.*
swamp **palūs, –ūdis,** *f.*

table **mēnsa, –ae,** *f.*
talk **loquor ;** talk together (to each other) **inter sē colloquor (loquor)**
task **labor, –ōris,** *m.*
ten **decem**
territory **fīnēs, –ium,** *m. pl.*
terror **terror, –ōris,** *m.*

than **ac, quam**
thanks **grātia, –ae,** *f.*
that, *pron. or adj.* **ille, is** ; that (of
    yours) **iste**
that, *conj.,* *purpose and result* **ut** ;
    that not, *purpose* **nē,** *result* **ut**
    . . . **nōn** ; *after words of doubting*
    quīn ; *after verbs of fearing* **nē**
then **tum**
there, *adv.* **eō**
therefore **itaque**
thing **rēs, reī,** *f.*
think **arbitror**
this **hic, is** ; (thus) **sīc**
three days **trīduum**
through **per** *w. acc.*
throw **prōiciō** ; throw into confusion
    perturbō
time **tempus, –oris,** *n.*
to, *prep.* **in, ad,** *w. acc.*
tooth **dēns, dentis,** *m.*
torture **cruciātus, –ūs,** *m.*
touch **tangō**
toward, *prep.* **ad, in,** *w. acc.*
tower **turris, –is,** *f.*
town **oppidum, –ī,** *n.*
train **īnstituō**
training **disciplīna, –ae,** *f.*
tranquillity **tranquillitās, –tātis,** *f.*
transport, *noun* **nāvis onerāria,** *f.*
treachery **perfidia, –ae,** *f.*
tree **arbor, –oris,** *f.*
tribe **gēns, gentis,** *f.*
tribune **tribūnus, –ī,** *m.*
trumpet **tuba, –ae,** *f.*
try out **explōrō**
tumult **tumultus, –ūs,** *m.*
turn **vertō** ; turn away (from)
    āvertō
two **duo, duae, duo** ; two days
    bīduum, –ī, *n.*

unarmed **inermis, –e**
understand **intellegō**
undertake **suscipiō**
unencumbered **expedītus, –a, –um**
unfavorable **aliēnus, –a, –um** ; in-
    īquus, –a, –um
unfriendly **inimīcus, –a, –um**
unhappy **miser, –era, –erum**
unharmed **incolumis, –e**
unless **nisi**
unlike **absimilis, –e**
until **dum** ; *adv.* **usque**
unwilling **invītus, –a, –um** ; be un-
    willing **nōlō**
upon, *prep.* **in,** *w. acc.*
upper **superus, –a, –um**
urge on **incitō**
use, *noun* **ūsus, ūsūs,** *m.*
use, *verb* **ūtor**
usual **solitus, –a, –um**

valley **vallēs, –is,** *f.*
village **vīcus, –ī,** *m.*
voice **vōx, vōcis,** *f.*
vow **cōnfirmō**

wage **gerō**
wagon **carrus, –ī,** *m.*
wait **exspectō**
wall **pariēs, –etis,** *m.;* **mūrus, –ī,** *m.*
wander **vagor**
war **bellum, –ī,** *n.;* wage war **bel-
    lum gerō**
watch **vigilia, –ae,** *f.*
water **aqua, –ae,** *f.*
way, right of way **iter, itineris,** *n.*
weapon **tēlum, –ī,** *n.*
weary **dēfessus, –a, –um**
weather **tempestās, –tātis,** *f.*
weep **fleō**
weigh (anchor) **tollō**

west solis occāsus, *m.*
whatever quīcumque, quaecumque, quodcumque
when cum, ubi
whence unde
where ubi, in quō locō
while dum
while, a little, *adv.* paulisper
who, which, what, that, *relative pron.* quī, quae, quod
who, which, what, *interrog. pron.* quis, quid ; *interrog. adj.* quī, quae, quod
whole tōtus, –a, –um
why cūr, quam ob rem
width lātitūdō, –inis, *f.*
wife uxor, –ōris, *f.*
wind ventus, –ī, *m.*
wine vīnum, –ī, *n.*
wing āla, –ae, *f.*
winter, *verb* hiemō
wish volō

with, *prep.* cum, *w. abl.*
within, *prep.* intrā, *w. acc.*
without, *prep.* sine, *w. abl.*
witness testis, –is, *m.*
woman mulier, –eris, *f.*
woods silva, –ae, *f.*
work opus, operis, *n.* ; labor, –ōris, *m.* ; opera, –ae, *f.*
world terra, –ae, *f.;* orbis terrārum
worn out cōnfectus, –a, –um ; dēfessus, –a, –um
wretched miser, –era, –erum
wrongdoing maleficium, –ī, *n.*

year annus, –ī, *m.*
yoke, *noun* iugum, –ī, *n.*
yoke, *verb* iungō
you, *sing.* tū ; *pl.* vōs
young man adulēscēns, –entis, *m.*
your *sing.* tuus, –a, –um ; *pl.* vester, –tra, –trum

INDEX

The numbers refer to pages. **Boldface numbers** refer to pages in Syntax for Reference; *italics* to review (Iterātiō) in The Argonauts. Reference to the many notes in the text concerning forms and principles of syntax is given only in special cases.

79

Passive Periphrastic
Gerundive + sum
all tenses I am to be
            I ought to be
            I must be

Independent volitive subj.
used in 1st & 3rd, sentence in pres. tense

Substantive Volitive follows verbs
    (volō) imperō, persuadeō
    quaerō, rogō, petō + pres. & imp.
                      subj.
            ut, nē

On purpose, indirect statement,
substantive volitive, indirect question,
cum causal a reflexive pronoun
or adj. may refer to subject of
main clause.

Subj.

purpose ut or nē - pres. + imp.

Result ut " ut nōn - " " "

Indirect Question Interrogative word -
　　　　　　　　any tense of subj.
　　　　　　according to sequence of

. Cum Circumstantial — Imp. + Plup.　tenses
　"　causal
　"　adverstanal all 4 "
　　　　　pres. "

Imp.　) Imp.) Pres.
Perf.　) or Fut.) or
Plup.　) Pluperf. Fut.perf.) Perf.

_____

purpose
ad + acc. gerund or gerundive
gen. gerund or gerundive + causā
He coming to fight
venit) ut pugnet
　　{ ad pugandum
　　{ pugnandī causā
　　 quī pugnet
He was coming to see the queen
veniēbat ut rēginam vidēret,
　　　　ad " videndam
　　　　rēginae videndae causā

tam ____ ~~modify~~ to modify, adj, adv

idlō

416 - Fall of Rome

1066 - Normans conquered

sis   britain

ita - " " " verbs

In a purpose clause a reflexive
pronoun or adj. may refer to
the subj. of the main verb.
In a result clause a reflexive
refers to a subj. of its own clause.

Pluperfect Subj.

act. Perf. stem + 6 isse's + personal
                                                    endings

Pass Perf. pass. part. + imp.
subj. of sum.

Subj. Vol. - Pres. + Imp.
   "   Result - 4